Redress for Historical I

Redress for Historical Injustices in the United States

On Reparations for Slavery, Jim Crow, and Their Legacies

EDITED BY MICHAEL T. MARTIN
AND MARILYN YAQUINTO

Duke University Press   *Durham & London*   2007

© 2007 Duke University Press
All rights reserved
Printed in the United States of America on acid-free paper ∞
Designed by Erin Kirk New
Typeset in Sabon by Keystone Typesetting, Inc.
Library of Congress Cataloging-in-Publication Data appear
on the last printed page of this book.

Acknowledgments for previously printed material appear
at the end of this book.

To Fannie Lou Hamer — slave descendent, sharecropper, and grassroots organizer;

and Robert S. Browne — economist, Pan-Africanist, and champion of the oppressed everywhere.

Both battled social injustices deep in the past as well as those shackling the future. We honor their memory, as their work reminds us of how collective action begins with the will to resist.

The Negro is a slave who has been allowed to assume the attitude of a master. The white man is a master who has allowed his slaves to eat at his table. — **Frantz Fanon,** *Black Skin, White Masks* (1952)

The issue here is not whether or not we can, or will, win reparations. The issue rather is whether we will fight for reparations, because we have decided for ourselves that they are our due.
—**Randall Robinson,** *Thoughts about Restitution* (2001)

We must face our long history, still not behind us, of slavery, segregation and racism.—**Howard Zinn,** "Lessons of Iraq War Start U.S. History," *The Progressive* (2006)

Contents

Preface xiii

Acknowledgments xix

On Redress for Racial Injustice 1
    Michael T. Martin and Marilyn Yaquinto

Part 1. Racial Inequality and White Privilege

Racial Injustices in U.S. History and Their Legacy 33
    David Lyons

Race Preferences and Race Privileges 55
    Michael K. Brown, Martin Carnoy, Elliott Currie, Troy Duster,
    David B. Oppenheimer, Marjorie M. Shultz, and David Wellman

A Sociology of Wealth and Racial Inequality 91
    Melvin L. Oliver and Thomas M. Shapiro

Part 2. Law, Citizenship, and the State

The Case for Reparations 121
    Robert Fullinwider

Toward a Theory of Racial Reparations 134
    James Bolner

The Constitutionality of Black Reparations 143
    Boris L. Bittker and Roy L. Brooks

The Theory of Restitution: The African American Case   160
    Richard America

Reparations to African Americans?   170
    J. Angelo Corlett

Part 3. Reparations: Formation and Modes of Redress

"A Day of Reckoning": Dreams of Reparations   203
    Robin D. G. Kelley

Forty Acres, or, An Act of Bad Faith   222
    Jeffrey R. Kerr-Ritchie

The Economic Basis for Reparations to Black America   238
    Robert S. Browne

The Political Economy of Ending Racism and the World Conference against Racism: The Economics of Reparations   249
    William Darity Jr. and Dania Frank

The Rise of the Reparations Movement   255
    Martha Biondi

Part 4. Case Studies of Injustice and Intervention

Nineteenth-Century New York City's Complicity with Slavery: Documenting the Case for Reparations   275
    Alan Singer

Railroads, Race, and Reparations   294
    Theodore Kornweibel Jr.

Reparations: A Viable Strategy to Address the Enigma of African American Health   305
    David R. Williams and Chiquita Collins

Residential Segregation and Persistent Urban Poverty   331
    Douglas S. Massey

Part 5. Mobilizing Strategies

The Politics of Racial Reparations   353
    Charles P. Henry

The Case for U.S. Reparations to African Americans   371
    Adrienne D. Davis

The Promises and Pitfalls of Reparations   379
    Yusuf Nuruddin

Repatriation as Reparations for Slavery and Jim Crow   402
    Robert Johnson Jr.

What's Next? Japanese American Redress and African American Reparations   411
    Eric K. Yamamoto

The Reparations Movement: An Assessment of Recent and Current Activism   427
    Sam Anderson, Muntu Matsimela, and Yusuf Nuruddin

Reparations: Strategic Considerations for Black Americans   447
    C. J. Munford

Tulsa Reparations: The Survivors' Story   452
    Charles J. Ogletree Jr.

Race for Power: The Global Balance of Power and Reparations   469
    Gerald Horne

Documents

Section 1. Federal Acts and Resolutions

The Second Confiscation Act (1862)   486

Special Field Orders, No. 15 (1865)   490

Freedmen's Bureau Act (1865)   493

Southern Homestead Act (1866)   495

House Resolution 29 (1867)   498

Civil Liberties Act (1988)   501

House Resolution 356 (2000)   503

House Resolution 40 (2005)   506

Senate Resolution 39 (2005)   513

Senate Resolution 44 (2005)   515

Section 2. State Legislation

Michigan House Bill No. 5562 (2000)   519

California Senate Bill No. 2199 (2000)   520

California Senate Joint Resolution No. 1 (2001)   522

New Jersey African-American Reconciliation Study Commission Act (2003)   524

Texas House Joint Resolution 25 (2003)   530

Maryland House Joint Resolution 4 (2004)   533

Section 3. Municipal Resolutions

City of Detroit (1989)   537

City of Chicago (2000)   539

City of San Francisco (2001)   542

City of New York Resolution 41 (2002)   544

City of New York Resolution 219 (2002)   547

District of Columbia (2003)   549

City of New York Resolution 57 (2004)   552

City of New York Resolution 195 (2004)   554

City of Philadelphia (2004)   556

Section 4. Advocacy and Activism

United Negro Improvement Association (1920)   560
"Declaration of the Rights of the Negro Peoples of the World"

Civil Rights Congress (1951)   567
    "We Charge Genocide"

Malcolm X (1964)   580
    Appeal to African Heads of State

Black Panther Party for Self Defense (1967)   585
    What We Want; What We Believe

Republic of New Africa (1968)   588
    Declaration of Independence

Black Panther Party (1969)   592
    Reparations for Vietnam

National Black Economic Development Conference (1969)   593
    The Black Manifesto

National Black Political Agenda (1972)   600
    The Gary Declaration

Black Panther Party (1973)   606
    Petition to the United Nations

Nation of Islam (1990)   608
    A Case for Reparations

Black Radical Congress (1999)   612
    The Freedom Agenda

Reparations Support Committee (1999/2000)   620
    "To the President of the United States of America"

Randall Robinson, TransAfrica Forum (2000)   621
    Restatement of the Black Manifesto

National Coalition of Blacks for Reparations in America (2000)   625
    The Reparations Campaign

The NDABA Movement (2004)   629
    National Reparations Petition

NAACP (2005)   631
    NAACP Supports Reintroduction of Reparations Study Legislation

American Bar Association Recommendation (2006)   634

Episcopal Church (2006)   635
    Call for the Episcopal Church to Study Responsibility for Reparations

Section 5. Case Studies of Redress

The White House (1997)   638
    Apology for Study Done in Tuskegee

Oklahoma Commission to Study the Tulsa Race Riot of 1921 (2000)   642

Mandate for the Greensboro Truth and Reconciliation Commission (2004)   645

Rosewood Victims v. State of Florida (2004)   649
    Special Master's Final Report

Florida Statute 1004.60 (2004)   657

Florida Statute 1009.55 (2004)   658

Section 6. Lawsuits

Timothy Pigford, et al., Plaintiffs, v. Dan Glickman, Secretary, United States Department of Agriculture, Defendant (1998)   661
    Opinion

Civil Actions Nos. 97–1978, 98–1693 (1999)   665
    Opinion

In re African-American Slave Descendants Litigation (2004)   668
    Opinion

Selected Bibliography   673

Contributors   683

Acknowledgment of Copyrights   687

Index   691

Preface

At the conference "The Moral Legacy of Slavery: Repairing Injustice," held in 2002 at Bowling Green State University, the discussion of reparations to African Americans sparked an intense debate among the participants in attendance. Sponsored by the Department of Philosophy, the conference featured scholars whose interests intersect with black studies, law, history, philosophy, and political activism. The roster was distinguished by Lucius T. Outlaw, Tommy Lott, Charles Mills, Howard McGary, and Gerald Horne, whose paper concludes this book; conference papers by David Lyons and Robert Fullinwider, recently updated, are included in this book as well.

Given the complexity and divisive nature of the conference's concerns, exchanges between participants were often emotional, even at times contentious. No example captures these sentiments better than someone in the audience who walked to the podium after a paper had been presented, checkbook in hand, asking what amount of money would settle the matter. Her provocative gesture shocked, then angered many members in the audience, especially since the subject of the paper by the presenter, McGary, was on forgiveness and reconciliation rather than about monetary or any other type of compensation. The person who brought the challenge explained that her gesture was meant to expose the conference's real aim — indeed, that of the reparations movement itself — to garner cash payments to African Americans for the sins of slavery, which, she pointed out, had ended more than a century ago. Moreover, given history's record of oppressed peoples, and referencing her own Jewish ancestry, she asked on what basis we should determine historical injury, let alone devise an equitable level of compensation for one group at the expense of another, especially in the present day.

Her assertion, indeed allegation, and skepticism aptly capture a major obstacle before what is called the contemporary reparations movement in America. First, it elicits the misconception that welfare and affirmative action are existing forms of reparations, so why pay again? Second, it narrows the focus to cash payments as the primary goal of reparations, whereas monetary compensation is but one strategy in a multipronged approach for redress and reconciliation with the past. It is the combined moral, political, and material investment in the lives of the descendents of slaves—along with other African peoples in the diaspora—that is the desired outcome of the prevailing reparations movement.

While slavery remains the most egregious evidence and testimony of exploitation, its institutional abolishment failed to immediately or completely halt the well-established institutional and social practices of inequality, which continued into the twentieth century and in part remains with us today, as many contributors to this volume of essays contend. The trajectory of racial injustice, first sanctioned in slavery, endures through Reconstruction, Jim Crow, and in the present period of neoconservatism, whose goal is in part to dismantle the social, economic, and political gains of the 1960s civil rights movement. Moreover, the person's challenge not only assumes that American institutions have become color blind, but that past inequities have been largely eliminated through affirmative action and other remedial interventions to the system since slavery was abolished. Such critics of reparations point to the legislative victories, political gains, and passage of time as proof that such "repairs" are unwarranted, even dangerous, reaching beyond restitution to gaining an artificial "advantage" over other population groups who also suffered historical injustices. In this manner, the burden of proof rests on oppressed peoples to settle the matter of recency and degree of severity by setting up a hierarchy of harm, in which history's losers compare and trump each other's experiences to re-earn what is already their due.

The type of one-time, no-strings-attached payment she proposed at the conference also does little to remedy the direct and indirect consequences of such macrohistorical injuries, let alone challenge the system that fostered and continues to maintain racial inequalities. Rather, they deflect attention away from white privilege, accrued from centuries of "affirmative action" that resulted from what W. E. B. Du Bois called "the wages of whiteness."

Finally, her comparative harm argument highlights another area of confusion regarding reparations: that its goal is to secure restitution on behalf of a few individuals, when, actually, it aims at restorative justice for the collective—and aspires to ultimately reach across racial, class, and national divides.

Much like the conference, this book highlights the array of approaches to redress, both specific to historical circumstance and also universal in their appeal to the sanctity of basic human rights; they are as distinctive as they are interrelated. In addition, while we do not specifically endorse or prioritize any one approach to redress, we encourage their mutual address and the discovery of their stark presentation of sobering commonalities.

The very term *redress* in the title of this book suggests a purposeful inclusivity, encompassing a variety of remedies enunciated in the campaigns and movements under study. While this book is devoted to the study of the reparations movement in the United States, it also links its evolution to redress struggles abroad and to anticapitalist formations and social movements for workers' rights and social justice. Essays in the book, in fact, delineate the interdependency between issues, including, for example, connections between economic hardship and political impotency and between educational deprivation and declining health care, to name but two examples. While we acknowledge the differences among approaches, we believe their claims echo one another and collectively evoke a potent condemnation of racial injustices.

In this manner, it is our hope that a vast and diverse readership utilizes this collection, which is at once specific and correlative, national and global, providing readers with an array of historically informed perspectives, case studies, and strategies for redress. It is designed for activists and politicians as well as researchers, scholars, and students in a variety of fields, including Africana studies, American studies, area studies, history, law, public policy, international relations, and diaspora studies. Increasingly, social science courses and law schools are including the study of redress in their curricula. For example, while the University of Detroit Mercy, offers a course on the "moral, philosophical and historical perspectives" of reparations, Duke University emphasizes the "economics of reparations" and Rutgers University links reparations with the concepts of "justice" and "forgiveness."

Beyond the classroom, political think tanks and activist organizations are increasingly focusing on the racial and ethnic aspects of human rights violations. Their reports contribute to the growing corpus of scholarly works, journal essays, and academic conferences devoted to the study of slavery and colonization, and contemporary forms in which subjugation of people of color and racial inequality persist. Indeed, hundreds of scholarly articles and more than a dozen books have been published during the past decade, among the most recent, *The Essence of Reparations* by writer and playwright Amiri Baraka (2003); *Reparations for Slavery: A Reader*, edited by Ronald P. Salzberger and Mary C. Turck (2004); and *Atonement and Forgiveness: A New Model for Black Reparations* by law professor Roy L. Brooks (2004).

Since the new century began, the number of related conferences is on the rise, too, including one held at UCLA in 2001 cosponsored by programs dedicated to the study of African American, American Indian, Asian American, and Chicano experiences. They call for the collective examination of historical injustices as well as the development of broad-based strategies for restitution. That same year, the David A. Clarke Law School at the University of the District of Columbia hosted a panel discussion devoted to "Reparations in the 21st Century," which, similar to other venues, included judges and policymakers, as well as scholars, to examine the legal precedents for lawsuits and case studies involving reparations.

Gatherings elsewhere in the world are also tackling the subject of redress, connecting both local and global perspectives, including a conference in Sarajevo in August 2005, which stressed the "themes of reconciliation" and suggested incorporating global institutions and networks, along with international law, to draft redressive policy measures. Specifically focused on the world's African diaspora, a 2004 Australian conference referenced the "upsurge of national and international exhibitions and conferences on the impact of slavery" and spotlighted UNESCO's Slave Route Project, which centered on the Atlantic World. However, conference organizers also chose to address the enduring forms of slavery that continue today in many parts of the world and that adversely affect some 27 million people as victims of bonded and child labor, prostitution, slavery by descent, and other forms of human rights violations. These occurrences are not *unrelated* to the past, but in many ways are dependent on the continuance of policies and practices that first enabled imperial states to establish a world order, hegemonizing the rest of the planet.

Visual media, too, have contributed to the growing focus on redress, including the 2002 documentary on the "back to Africa" movement, which examines repatriation as one form of reparations that is discussed in several of the essays in this book. A documentary in 2004, a one-hour original production for the U.S. cable television network TV One, focused specifically on reparations and featured writers and educators along with elected officials, including Congressman John Conyers (D-MI), the sponsor of House Resolution 40 (HR 40) that remains the centerpiece of many discussions and political efforts. The latest documentary, which debuted in the spring of 2005, is *New World Reparations*, produced by the Hollywood actor and filmmaker Mario Van Peebles, who points out the incongruity of paying reparations to our enemies "when we win wars," yet denying our own citizens fair compensation for official actions that harmed them.

Any consideration of redress for slavery and colonization (and their shared legacies) is framed by those developments. Yet, we join with this book's contributors, and the loosely aligned community they represent, in insisting that the United States and other imperial nation-states account for historical racial injustices and other pandemic crimes against humanity. However, there are those civil rights supporters who agree in principle with the claim for redress but who warn that the prevailing climate of virulent conservatism renders any discussion of rectification and reparations inopportune and needlessly confrontational. On the contrary, we are convinced that such regressive tendencies actually affirm the need not only to reiterate the advancements and goals of past civil and human rights campaigns (now threatened), but also to serve as a precondition for any further progress.[1]

A failure to address the past—whether in Selma, Soweto, or São Paulo, where the legacies of racial injustices are as disturbingly current as they are painfully tangible—makes it urgently clear that, despite the hostile social environment, the time to act is now. This moment is no less contentious or more opportune than other junctures in American history when African Americans demanded justice denied.

Note

1. See William Julius Wilson's comments on reparations in Tim Lake and Marilyn Yaquinto, *Racial Politics, Globalization, and the Urban Underclass: An Interview with William Julius Wilson*, Working Papers Series on Historical Systems, Peoples, and Cultures, No. 13, Bowling Green State University, Bowling Green, Ohio, 2003.

Acknowledgments

We are indebted to many individuals who contributed to this collection, especially to those who participated in the conference "The Moral Legacy of Slavery: Repairing Injustice" hosted by the Department of Philosophy at Bowling Green State University in 2002. However substantive, the conference made clear the need to expand and extend the conversation on redress for slavery to Jim Crow and their legacies in the contemporary period. Among the participants, we especially extend our thanks to Carolyn Council and David Coop. For financial support, we express our appreciation to Gary Lee, interim chair, and to the Department of Ethnic Studies at Bowling Green State University. To the anonymous reviewers at Duke University Press, we are grateful for their comments and helpful suggestions for the organization of the collection. We thank Charles Mills, Leah Wise, Manning Marable, Lamont Yeakey, Ewart Skinner, Kathryne V. Lindberg, Michael Bragdon, and Michael Yaquinto for their encouragement during the preparation of the manuscript. And no less important, we thank our editor, Reynolds Smith, for his consideration and support of this project and Sharon Parks Torian, senior editorial assistant, for her patience and essential interventions during the review and production stages of this publication. Finally, we express our gratitude to Mark A. Mastromarino, Assistant Managing Editor, the copyeditor Judith Hoover, and the marketing staff of the Press who labored, at this critical production stage, to bring this project to press.

On Redress for Racial Injustice

MICHAEL T. MARTIN AND MARILYN YAQUINTO

> Horror! I call thee yet once more!
> Bear me to that accursed shore,
> Where on the stake the Negro writhes.
> Assume thy sacred terrors then! dispense
> The gales of Pestilence!
> Arouse the opprest; teach them to know their power;
> Lead them to vengeance! and in that dread hour
> When ruin rages wide,
> I will behold and smile by Mercy's side.
> — "To Horror," by Robert Southey, poet and abolitionist, 1791

The increasingly resonant and coordinated demand for redress for racial injustices constitutes a global project of moral necessity and historical importance: in the United States, redress for slavery and Jim Crow, and the enduring and systemic inequalities they spawned; in Africa, the Caribbean, and South America, for slavery, colonization, and regimes of legalized racial discrimination. Proponents of redress contend that "without truth, justice and reparations, victims and their communities will feel that the new order has failed them" and that "real reconciliation requires an honest examination of history to uncover and recognize past crimes."[1] Indeed, one prominent reparationist in the United States asserts, "Reparations are the central issue of race relations in America in the twenty-first century. Until we address it seriously, we will continue to make only modest progress with some of the larger issues."[2]

Embedded in these two purposeful and provocative claims is the moral imperative to recover the long and grievous history of slavery and colonization and to acknowledge their shared legacies in the postcolonial period. These are legacies in which injustices and structural inequalities shaped by centuries of global apartheid continue to adversely affect the development of

Africa and the fate of Africans and African descendants worldwide, among other dispossessed peoples.[3] Also implied is the idea, affirmed by Gayatri Chakravorty Spivak in her meditation on injustice, that human rights "is not only about having or claiming a right or a set of rights; it is also about righting wrongs, about being the dispenser of these rights."[4]

Together these claims accentuate the central theme and title of this book, *Redress for Historical Injustices in the United States: On Reparations for Slavery, Jim Crow, and Their Legacies*. In the aftermath of the cold war, they also reference aggrieved population groups and allude to Western hegemony, as well as to a period in global capitalism distinguished by the renewal of the North–South polarity and ascension of minority rights in world affairs.

While the outcome and efficacy of redress for racial injustices is uncertain, given the current conjuncture of neoliberalism and assertions of empire, redress forms a fertile site for coalition building and activism in a global struggle for justice and human rights.

The Book's Organization

The book comprises five parts containing essays and a section containing documents consisting of primary and secondary source materials, which are referenced by contributors or included by the editors as useful background information for readers to readily consult. Unlike the anthologies, monographs, and plethora of recent essays that do not situate redress campaigns within transnational contexts or larger social movements, this volume of critical essays features the historical expanse and case studies that investigate the modalities of redress and its evolution in the United States from an inchoate formation to the contemporary period's multi-issue organizations and agendas.[5] These writings interrogate the moral, legal, and strategic arguments for and against redress for slavery and Jim Crow. They also explicate the municipal, state, national, and international contexts for redress while inviting larger debates about race, justice, human rights, and American democracy.

We examine in this introductory essay the primary trajectories of reparations, emphasizing an increasingly coordinated and multipronged approach composed of legislation, litigation, and political mobilization strategies. Case studies of injustice—as sites for redress struggles—are examined historically and sectorally, including health care, and residential segregation. The essays that follow assess the movement's strategies, strengths, limitations, and possibilities during the present conjuncture in world affairs; revisit redress schemes of the past, including repatriation; and consider the opportunities for coalition building within the United States and abroad.

We use the term *redress* to suggest a purposeful inclusivity. It aptly encompasses the many and varied descriptors applied to campaigns and movements, however disparate or distinguishable by circumstance, geography, or the passage of time. In spirit, though, they share a common aim at "repairing" historical injustices and atoning for injuries and crimes against victimized population groups. These measures can range from mere apologies, as in the case of the U.S. Senate's recent apology (Senate Resolution 39; see Documents, section 1) for having failed to enact antilynching legislation during the first half of the twentieth century, to official acknowledgments of wrongdoing, to reparations involving monetary compensation, government programs that invest in wronged communities, repatriation, or restitution of lost property and/or rights.[6]

Slavery and the Redress Movement

The foremost historical foundation of the redress movement in the United States is the institution of slavery, which was not marginal to, or an aberration in, the nation's formation, but fundamental to it. During the colonial period, a racialized social order evolved, as did codified slave laws and institutionalized slave practices, at the level of everyday life. Constitutionally inscribed and morally and forcibly sanctioned slavery lasted in the republic until 1865. What followed slavery was a century of segregation, exploitation, and deprivation—the social and economic consequences of which continue to adversely affect the life chances of African Americans.

As our starting point in part 1, David Lyons periodizes the four moments or "racial junctures" that legally codified white supremacy as well as regulated its institutional practices through the Second Reconstruction. Next is an essay by Michael K. Brown et al., who track race-based inequities along a continuum that extends from slavery to the current preference for "color-blind" policies. They conclude that a remedy far more ambitious than simply amending current affirmative action policies is required to alter the relationship of the entrenched white advantage/black disadvantage.[7] Melvin L. Oliver and Thomas M. Shapiro's seminal study of racial inequality in the United States concludes part 1. The authors focus on wealth rather than income, arguing that social policy and institutional discrimination, among other factors, account for disparities between population groups and assert that "materially, whites and blacks constitute two nations." They discuss three essential factors that generate inequality in American society and that mitigate the accumulation of wealth by African Americans, concluding that a "racial reparations movement" is an appropriate means to address racial inequality.

The Black Manifestos

The central claims and organizing principles of the redress movement are enunciated in the *Black Manifesto* (1969) and the *Restatement of the Black Manifesto* (2000; see Documents, section 4). Both are premised on the historical fact that the United States was constitutionally founded on slavery and that the persistence of racial inequality and injustice in American society is derived from slavery.[8]

It may be useful to quote at length several of the essential declarations in the *Restatement of the Black Manifesto* (hereafter, the *Manifesto*):

> Whereas the United States government has never acknowledged or taken responsibility for its role in the enslavement of Africans and the promotion of white supremacy; Whereas the experience of enslavement, segregation, and discrimination continues to limit the life chances and opportunities of African Americans; Whereas all Americans and the United States government have benefited enormously and continue to benefit from the unjust expropriation of uncompensated labor by enslaved Africans, the subordination and segregation of the descendants of the enslaved, as well as from discrimination against African Americans; Whereas the principle that reparations is the appropriate remedy whenever a government unjustly abrogates the rights of a domestic group or foreign people whose rights such government is obligated to protect or uphold has been internationally recognized; let it be hereinafter resolved.
> First . . . It is never too late to seek justice. . . .
> Second, *the government bears responsibility*. . . .
> Third, *the injury survives the death of victims*. . . .
> Therefore, hearings should be held in the Congress of the United States to establish the basis for reparations to African Americans, and to determine the amount of such reparations; where after, a private trust should be established for the benefit of all African Americans.[9]

The *Manifesto* articulates the legal principle for reparations for African Americans. According to Wade Henderson, executive director of the Leadership Conference for Civil Rights (LCCR), this principle affirms that "for every wrong there is a remedy, and that that remedy is not extinguished by time itself, particularly when the manifestations of the problem are current-day and visible to all." The issue, contends Henderson, is "how do you establish that principle beyond a doubt?"[10]

The *Manifesto* (2000) judiciously avoids specifying how to assess damages for reparations, instead calling for congressional hearings to determine the criteria for compensation; it also intentionally does not specify the types of reparations except to call for the establishment of a "private trust," as well as to implicate the U.S. government as a principal benefactor and enforcer of slavery.

In making the global case for reparations, Ali A. Mazrui asks, "How do we assess the damage for reparations? Do we do it on the basis of damage to African people? Or do we do it on the basis of gain to economies which formerly used slave labor? So do you do it by benefit to recipients or do you do it by damage to African people?"[11] While a member of the Group of Eminent Persons, established by the Organization for African Unity in 1992 to address reparations in the larger context of African slavery and colonization, Mazrui delineates three categories of reparations, which, broadly defined, are "capital transfer," "skill transfer," and "power sharing." The first is self-evident, implying financial compensation; the second concerns the acquisition of skills (and presumably knowledge) to compensate for the deprivation and underdevelopment caused by slavery and colonization; and the third calls for greater participation by African nations in institutions such as the World Bank as well as permanent membership on the United Nations Security Council.[12] Within these three categories, reparations can take several forms. For example, they may involve financial compensation for (246 years of) unpaid labor during slavery, the restitution of lost property, or other forms of dispensation for the incalculable loss of slave descendants' "African culture, heritage, family, language[s] and religion[s] . . . self-identity and self-worth . . . destroyed by repression and hatred."[13] Although controversial, Henry Louis Gates advocates that reparations are appropriate for addressing the struggle against pandemic illnesses like HIV/AIDS that have disproportionately affected Africans.[14] However much such a pandemic exacerbates existing global inequalities, as a contemporary phenomenon it lacks the historical basis on which most redress-related injuries are predicated.

In part 2, Robert Fullinwider, James Bolner, Boris L. Bittker and Roy L. Brooks, Richard America, and J. Angelo Corlett theorize and contest the historical and legal claims for redress addressed in the *Manifesto*. Unlike arguments that rest on the primacy of chattel slavery, Fullinwider's de-emphasizes slavery, along with the benefits accrued to whites, for reparations claims. By distinguishing "civil" from "personal" responsibility, he makes the case for reparations on the basis of citizenship and collective responsibility. As such,

African Americans would be obliged to contribute to any reparations settlement as citizens, just as Americans of Japanese ancestry have done for members of their community interned during World War Two.

In anticipation of affirmative action policies in the 1970s and now refuted in recent years, Bolner argues against the criticism that "benign racial treatment" violates the Constitution. He surveys the implicit and overt racial sentiments and concerns in numerous court comments, such as Judge Van Voorhis's charge that using race to promote integration is as wrong as using race to promote segregation. Invoking the *Japanese Exclusion Cases* decided during World War Two and *Brown v. the Board of Education*, he argues that since race was once used to commit the wrong, race should be the basis used to correct it. For Bolner the relevant question is, "What constitutes racial injury and how may persons so injured be afforded benign racial treatment?"

Brooks, who updates Bittker's 1973 essay, argues that remedies created statutorily by Congress may be more successful than a constitutionally based approach to redress. He revisits the "strict scrutiny test" used by judges in evaluating Jim Crow and other "suspicious" legislative enactments and contends that the court finds much restitutive legislation not drawn narrowly enough to meet a "compelling government interest," making the court a poor choice of redress.

In the case of "historic economic injustices" against nations, races, or other social groups, Richard America delineates six conditions for a theory of restitution, among them, to reconstruct historic economic relations and "to specify the 'fair' standards . . . that were violated, usually by force"; to account for the "pattern of transactions"; to determine the difference between "actual" and "fair" standards and estimate the value of the deviation; and to determine specific forms in which financial restitution would be made to the wronged party. For America, the central problem is racism, enabling "the coerced and manipulated diversion of income and wealth from blacks to whites." The solution to the "race problem," he argues, is "a matter of making racism less attractive economically."

Finally, in Corlett's trenchant essay, a reparations argument is made on the basis of "collective moral liability responsibility." First, Corlett makes the important distinction, often unremarked by proponents and critics alike, "of whether or not reparations to African Americans are morally required from the question of which *policies* of reparations would be justified if it turns out that such reparations are required in the first place." Second, he distinguishes between Native American and African American claims for reparations, noting that the former relates to massive land theft and broken treaties. Like other contributors to this volume, Corlett's claim for reparations is against the federal government (the state) for slavery and Jim Crow.

Historical Context

The call for reparations in the United States is not of recent vintage. On his march through Confederate territory in 1865, General William Tecumseh Sherman issued Special Field Order No. 15 on January 16, which reserved land largely in the Sea Islands and on the South Carolina and Georgia coasts for the settlement of freed blacks (see Documents, section 1). That year, nearly forty thousand former slaves settled on four hundred thousand acres in the "Sherman Reservation."[15] Although Sherman (and his contemporaries who advocated land distribution) did not define it in terms of reparations, he ordered that each family of ex-slaves be given "not more than forty acres of tillable land" and "subject to the approval of the President of the United States, a possessory title in writing." However, the terms of the land distribution were unclear, asserts historian John David Smith.[16] Was the federal government leasing or giving title of the land to the ex-slaves?

When the Bureau of Refugees, Freedmen and Abandoned Land (also known as the Freedmen's Bureau; see Documents, section 1) was established in March 1865, Congress authorized it to lease confiscated or abandoned lands to former slaves who would have the option to "purchase the land and receive such titles thereto as the United States can convey."[17] President Johnson, however, undermined the Bureau's efforts by ordering the restoration of property to the former Confederates he had pardoned. In 1866, Congress passed the Southern Homestead Act (see Documents, section 1). Eighty-acre plots were set aside in five southern states for former slaves to purchase. The land, though, was of poor quality, and blacks lacked the capital to purchase farm implements. By 1876, Congress repealed the Southern Homestead Act, and with it, ushered in the demise of Reconstruction federal land distribution policies. For a detailed analysis of the origins and legacy of *Forty Acres and a Mule* and the failure of land distribution following the Civil War, see Jeffrey R. Kerr-Ritchie's essay in part 3. Unlike those who advance moral arguments for reparations, Kerr-Ritchie stresses the fact that a promise, indeed a commitment that should be honored, was abrogated by the federal government because it clashed with the "free market dictates" of northern business interests and Republican politics.

During the civil rights struggle in the 1960s, Martin Luther King Jr., in a speech at the 1963 convocation in Washington, declared Sherman's march "a check which has come back marked insufficient funds." Black nationalists, among them the Nation of Islam, the Malcolm X Society, and the Black Panther Party, demanded a "homeland" in a partitioned United States.[18] For black separatists, the "land question" constituted, in part, a form of reparations in lieu of financial restitution. The "homeland" or "nation" was theorized from a model of race and ethnic relations based on the concept of *internal colonialism*, which posited that black–white relations in the United States were those of colonizer and colonized (see Documents, section 4).[19] While some separatists endeavored to establish self-sustaining black enclaves, as a national project it failed amid the severity and pervasiveness of racial conflict during the 1960s.

The essays by Yusuf Nuruddin and Robert Johnson Jr. (in part 5) further elaborate black nationalist claims. They address the land question and repatriation as forms of compensation for reparations claims. For Nuruddin, "The legitimate demand for reparations in the form of a sovereign nation-state remains more a consciousness-raising tool than a practical formulation." For Johnson, the objective is to obtain funds from Congress to repatriate African descendants in the United States to Africa.

In part 3, Robin D. G. Kelley chronicles the reparations movement from its origins through the period of 1960s black activism to the present. He asserts that the reparations campaign is essentially a social movement that "was never entirely, or even primarily, about money," but rather "about social justice, reconciliation, reconstructing the internal life of black America, and eliminating institutional racism." Kelley's assessment of reparations campaigns within a larger historical project contributes to the study of social movements and links these campaigns to other national and transnational struggles for redress as well as to anticapitalist formations for workers' rights and self-determination.

In a 1971 conference paper by the recently deceased economist Robert S. Browne, the economic motivations for reparations resonate today. Browne's objective: "to provide the black community with the share of the national wealth and income which it would by now have had if it had been treated as other immigrant communities were, rather than enslaved." He lucidly summarizes the basis for the preeminence of the United States as an "industrial power of the twentieth century" accomplished through the deployment of slave labor, and delineates the factors required to calculate a "minimal" reparations claim for "unpaid slave labor prior to 1863," while also considering the "underpayment of black people since 1863." Browne suggests several schemes, among them, "a per capita cash payment to each black

American alive," investing the payment in "income-earning assets" (funds for education, housing, and skills training, perhaps not dissimilar to the private trust called for in the *Manifesto*), "a per capita cash payment accompanied by an internationally negotiated repatriation plan with one or more African nations," and "a territorial grant to the black community supplemented by a payment in cash or kind to assist in the building of an independent black nation in North America."

Taking up where Browne left off thirty-five years earlier, William Darity Jr. and Dania Frank address issues of eligibility, types, and magnitude of reparations, asserting that "economics can provide useful insights in determining" reparations claims. Like Corlett and other contributors to this book, Darity and Frank argue that a case can be made for Jim Crow, since its victims are still living. Describing post-Reconstruction as a period of "terror that allowed whites to take black lives and black-owned property with impunity," they delineate criteria for reparations claims and propose five types of reparations.

Trajectories of Today's Reparations Movement

In the contemporary period, the cause of and movement for reparations increasingly resonates among African Americans of all social classes, notwithstanding opposition from conservatives, the disfavor and antagonism of the majority of white Americans, and the objections of some prominent black intellectuals.

Opposition to Reparations

Opponents' arguments — from left to right — vary. Many dehistoricize slavery and disassociate it from the deprivations and lower social status of slave descendants, dismissing the movement's goals as impractical or invoking the national good against African Americans' demands for racial justice. Specifically, they assert that slavery's transgressions have no bearing on the living descendants of slaves; that it is impossible to calculate the debt owed to them; that the Thirteenth, Fourteenth, and Fifteenth Amendments to the Constitution compensated blacks for the deprivations endured under slavery; and that litigation for reparations would "pour salt in the American wound of the past."[20] Others argue that reparations should be paid only to the survivors, as in the Holocaust reparations settlements, which categorically disqualify the living descendants of slaves from compensation. Another claim is that not all blacks were slaves and that immigrants who arrived in the United States after slavery experienced discrimination as well. Are they liable for reparations, or should they, too, receive compensation? The Pulitzer Prize–winning African American journalist E. R. Shipp is one who has denied federal government responsibility: "But what about those Blacks whose ancestors may have been enslaved not in North Carolina or Georgia, but in Jamaica or Haiti? Why should the American government compensate them for what the British or the Spanish or the French might have done?"[21]

Some critics have invoked economic comparisons between blacks in the United States and those abroad, claiming that "African Americans are the best educated, wealthiest blacks on the planet." Or, when U.S. complicity in the slave trade is acknowledged, they apportion more blame to African complicity. African American economist Walter E. Williams argues, "If the government got the money from the tooth fairy or Santa Claus, that'd be great. But the government has to take the money from citizens, and there are no citizens alive today who were responsible for slavery."[22] John McWhorter asserts that the welfare and affirmative action policies enacted by the federal government in the mid-1960s constitute a form of compensation or reparations for slavery.[23] Similarly, Stuart E. Eizenstat, a former Clinton administration official who negotiated settlements on behalf of Holocaust victims, counsels, "For slavery qua slavery, I think the appropriate remedy is affirmative government action in general, rather than reparations."[24] It seems that the underlying resistance among most whites to reparations, especially direct cash payments, is rooted in the unstated belief that welfare and affirmative action constitute a type of reparation and that, therefore, African Americans are already beneficiaries of the government's largesse. Another, perhaps more cynical view purports that African Americans cannot be trusted to use reparations to improve their circumstances.

Moreover, the prominent African American economist Glenn Loury has concluded that America "needs some reckoning with the racist past, but reparations encourage the wrong kind of reckoning." By analogy, he claims that under South Africa's Truth and Reconciliation Commission (TRC), the pardoning of state officials who confessed to political crimes was far more significant and enduring than a "money settlement" for slavery because it documented the "truth" of what had happened to nonwhites under apartheid. Loury's alternative to reparations pivots on the premise and myth of Americans' capacity to transcend race for the national good. In place of reparations, he has argued for a "reparation" that "would entail constructing and inculcating in our citizens an account of how we have come to be as we are — one that avoids putting the responsibility for the current problems of African Americans wholly on their [whites'] shoulders."[25] While Loury's entreaty to a higher moral order and "national fellowship and comity" may appeal to antireparationists, and seemingly relieve the federal government of direct responsibility, the fact is that the TRC, in its final report, did recommend financial compensation to families of the victims of apartheid.[26]

Support for Reparations

Momentum in support of reparations, however, has developed by mobilizing and broadening the movement's base; by continuing the legal strategy in the courts, especially against corporate entities; and by aligning with other international redress struggles, principally in Africa. Other domestic factors contributing to the movement's renewal in the United States include the successful lobby for reparations to American citizens of Japanese descent interned during World War Two and Florida's 1994 decision to compensate the nine remaining African American survivors of the Rosewood race riot in 1923, which destroyed the town. In the case of the former, each survivor of the internment or his or her heir was awarded, during the Clinton presidency, $20,000 under the Civil Liberties Act of 1988; in the case of the latter, each survivor of the riot, according to several reports, received $150,000 for the assessed value of his or her destroyed property (see Documents, sections 1 and 5).

The public's awareness about slavery, its role in American society, and the evolving debate on reparations has also expanded as a consequence of the proliferation in the 1990s of literary and scholarly works, academic conferences and forums, and media coverage devoted to the study of slavery.[27] However, these activities, though important to the public and specialized literary and academic audiences, have yet to be coordinated into an effective political mobilization (and lobbying) strategy by reparationists.

The movement's revival has also been energized by several recent developments in the international sphere. Germany's compensation to Holocaust survivors and slave laborers during World War Two, the Vatican's apology "for its misdeeds of the past," and Swiss banks' "atonement for appropriating the accounts of Holocaust victims" have established, among other claims, precedents for reparations to survivors (or their living heirs) of genocide and other violations of human rights.[28]

Next we illustrate the various trajectories that the redress movement in the United States has followed in recent years and indicate some of its achievements.

Legislation Strategy

In 1989, Congressman John Conyers Jr. (D-MI) first introduced the Commission to Study Reparations Proposals for African Americans Act. The bill was intended "to investigate differing options to resolve the issue of the effects of slavery." Since 1989, Conyers has campaigned in Congress to establish the commission, reintroducing the bill as House Resolution 40 (HR 40; see Documents, section 1). Although HR 40 has been stalled in Congress since it was first proposed and does not decree reparations or specify a plan or remedy, "it would establish the first federally chartered commission to study the impact of slavery on African Americans and recommend a range of appropriate remedies."[29] The commission's symbolic and practical importance is apparent, as it would formally begin a national dialogue and identify the injustices committed under slavery, as well as within institutions that benefited from it, such as federal and municipal governments that, for example, employed slaves to build public works.[30] It would presumably determine slavery's role in civil society and its impact on race relations and assess its enduring effects and consequences on descendants of slavery, black and white. By implicating Congress in the proposed investigation, a national debate would follow, in which claims for government restitution could be determined and pursued. More important, and essential for reconciliation, it would signify America's capacity to confront and recover its past. House Resolution 40 foregrounds the federal legislative strategy of the redress movement and, as Bittker and Brooks argue in their essay (part 2), holds more promise for reparations than the judicial approach.

At the level of state and municipal governments, at least ten cities (including Chicago, Washington, and Detroit) have passed resolutions in support of Conyers's legislation (see Documents, sections 2 and 3).[31] Organizations and groups such as the NAACP have also passed resolutions in support of HR 40 (see Documents, section 4). Moreover, in 2001, California passed a law requiring state-licensed insurance companies to disclose whether they "ever sold policies insuring slave owners against the loss of their slave property, and if so to whom."[32] The passage of these resolutions, especially the California law, advance the legislative strategy at the state and municipal levels and may have important implications for future claims against corporate entities, facilitating plaintiffs' access to the records of companies liable to litigation (see Documents, section 2).[33]

Litigation Strategy

In 1999, a discrimination suit on behalf of more than twenty thousand black farmers against the U.S. Department of Agriculture was ostensibly settled by the federal government. In the view of Charles J. Ogletree, this "represents the largest civil-rights settlement by the government ever, with a likely payout of about $2 billion" (see Documents, section 6).[34] The actual settlement in the lawsuit, *Pigford v. Glickman*, was $2.3 billion. However, five years later, the Environmental Working Group found that of the $2.3 billion, three-quarters had not been paid, and of every ten claimants, nine had been denied. A new lawsuit was filed in 2004 for $20 billion on behalf of twenty-five thousand black farmers.

In 2001, the Tulsa Race Riot Commission finally published its recommendations on events that had taken place some sixty years earlier (see Documents, section 5). The period 1898 to 1923 was distinguished by major race riots in the United States, with an especially brutal one occurring in Tulsa, Oklahoma, in 1921. It claimed the lives of nearly three hundred black residents of the Greenwood district. White deputies and Oklahoma National Guardsmen were implicated in the rioting, in which victims were shot and lynched; this was followed by arson attacks that destroyed more than a thousand homes in Greenwood. In the aftermath of the riot, city officials promised to compensate the survivors of Greenwood but never did. In 1997, the state of Oklahoma established a commission to look into the riot, and nearly five years later, the Tulsa Race Riot Commission recommended that the state compensate the survivors. However, that same year, the governor of Oklahoma, Frank Keating, denied the state's culpability and claimed that "state law prohibits Oklahoma from making reparations for any past mass crime committed by its officials or on the state's behalf."[35]

Consequently, a local group, the Tulsa Reparations Coalition, formed a committee to explore "the possibility of filing a lawsuit against Tulsa that would challenge the existing law and seek reparations."[36] Having failed for two years to advance their claims against the state of Oklahoma and Tulsa, the Coalition enlisted the support of the Reparations Coordinating Committee, cochaired by Ogletree, a law professor and member of the board of directors of TransAfrica Forum; Randall Robinson, the founder and former president of TransAfrica Forum; and Adjoa A. Aiyetoro, a senior legal consultant for the National Coalition of Blacks for Reparations in America (N'COBRA).

In March 2003, Ogletree and a team of lawyers filed a lawsuit in federal court in the Northern District of Oklahoma on behalf of the survivors of the

1921 Tulsa riot. The lawsuit, *Alexander v. State of Oklahoma*, alleges that the Oklahoma State Legislature and the city of Tulsa "misled or prevented victims of the riot from filing lawsuits in 1921" and failed to compensate the survivors of the riot as the Commission had recommended in 2001.[37]

The significance of the Tulsa lawsuit is twofold. First, as part of a larger reparations strategy, it constitutes a test case undertaken by an organization advocating reparations for slavery. Second, the lawsuit establishes a relationship between reparations for slavery and other "acts" of racial violence in the twentieth century, enhancing the prospects for future legal action over reparations. According to Ogletree, "The Tulsa case will be the linchpin of litigations focused on real acts of racial violence against living people or to their descendants. We'll be able to bring claims and that is just scratching the surface addressing the horrors of the 20th century. . . . Tulsa makes it clear what happened and how horrific it was and how it has been ignored. But the more important point is that the broader reparations struggle will not end. It will just begin."[38]

Although, the 10th Circuit Court of Appeals ruled against the plaintiffs in 2004, arguing that the statute of limitations had expired, and the U.S. Supreme Court declined to hear the case in 2005, the Tulsa lawsuit prominently distinguishes the second evolving trajectory of the reparations movement: litigation. Of particular importance, this strategy targets corporate entities as well as federal, state, and municipal governments. Pursued by the Reparations Coordinating Committee and N'COBRA, it asserts that a historical relationship exists between the slave economy, corporations, and governments in the contemporary period. Premised on the claim that slavery was fundamental to the American economy, both North and South, the legal strategy seeks compensation from governments and companies that once profited from slavery, whether by employing slave labor, insuring slave owners against "property" loss, or investing financially in other aspects of the slave trade.

For Ogletree, "Litigation will show what slavery meant, how it was profitable and how the issue of white privilege is still with us. Litigation is a place to start, because it focuses attention on the issue."[39] Similarly, for Robinson, the legal argument is persuasive: "When government participates in a crime against humanity, and benefits from it, then that government is under the law obliged to make the victims whole. That's recognized as a principle of law."[40]

Litigation is also being pursued against economic entities and other private institutions, as Martha Biondi discusses in her essay in part 3, pointing out how litigation not only advances HR 40, but has implications and relevancy to the UN and other international organizations.

The motivation for pursuing the litigation strategy against commercial and private institutions is explained by Deadria Farmer-Paellmann, the plaintiff in one high-profile lawsuit: "I turned to corporations, after finding how difficult it would be to win a claim against the [federal] government, given sovereign immunity, the statute of limitations, and an opinion by a relatively liberal court rejecting the idea. If you can show a company made immoral gains by profiting from slavery, you can file an action for unjust enrichment."[41] Law professor Robert Sedler, however, argues that even lawsuits against corporations are difficult to pursue. The plaintiff must show that the corporations profited from slavery, overcome the problem of the constitutional legality of slavery, and, with litigation against the federal government, resolve the issue of the statute of limitations unless the plaintiff can demonstrate that the corporations continue to profit from the gains they obtained under slavery.[42]

Despite these obstacles, several corporate entities have been targeted for scrutiny and possible litigation. For example, the New York Life Insurance Company was found to have issued policies for slaves in Maryland and Virginia. As investigations continue, banks — along with insurance, tobacco, and railroad companies — will be identified as targets for class-action lawsuits.

In March 2002, a federal class-action lawsuit in New York was filed against FleetBoston Financial Corporation, the insurance firm Aetna, and the railroad company CSX ("and other to-be-named companies") on behalf of the descendants of African slaves in compensation for profits these corporations earned from the slave trade and slave labor (see Documents, section 6).[43] The Aetna Insurance Company of Hartford insured slaves against injury and death for slave owners; FleetBoston's predecessor, Providence Bank, was implicated in the slave trade, financing slave ships; and CSX's predecessor, Northern Pacific, employed slave labor leased from slave owners during the antebellum period (see Documents, section 6). Appropriately, the essay by Theodore Kornweibel Jr. in part 4 examines the role of slave labor in the building and operation of railroads in southern and border states, noting that railroad building was so dangerous that many slave owners refused to allow their slaves to do such work, while others protected their property with life insurance policies.

Should the lawsuit succeed against FleetBoston, Aetna, and CSX, an economic and educational fund would be created for the "uplifting of African Americans."[44] The establishment of a fund or trust for the benefit of *all* African Americans, as called for in the *Manifesto*, is significant because it would affirm the principle of collective rather than individual compensation for wrongs committed against a population group. The fund would also underscore the specificity and ubiquity of racial exploitation under slavery. The idea of a fund appears to enjoy greater support than individual compensation and reflects a deeper maturation and historical commitment on the part of reparationists. Other lawsuits are likely to follow and private institutions will be investigated. According to Ogletree, "Brown University, Yale University and Harvard Law School . . . have made headlines recently as the beneficiaries of grants and endowments traced back to slavery and are probable targets."[45]

With regard to other potential sites for litigation where the social and economic consequences of slavery and Jim Crow persist, we direct the reader to the case studies in part 4 by Alan Singer, David R. Williams and Chiquita Collins, and Douglas S. Massey. Each essay concerns a particular sector in American society. Singer examines New York City's complicity with slavery during the nineteenth century by deploying slave labor in the construction of buildings and assisting Cuban sugar barons to obtain slaves after the slave trade was made illegal; he also details the collaboration of merchants, financiers, and politicians with the southern cotton trade. Williams and Collins argue that the history of discrimination, racism, and segregation has produced lasting health consequences for African Americans. Massey analyzes how black poverty is sustained by "residential segregation by race" and how racism is "deeply institutionalized at all levels of American society"; he warns that "as long as high levels of racial segregation persist, black poverty will be endemic and racial divisions will grow."

Broadening the Agenda

While the legislation and litigation strategies proceed, a parallel and interrelated formation is emerging that has national as well as international implications for the redress movement. Several largely disparate organizations with common political goals—though not necessarily similar ideological orientations—have begun to coalesce into a broad and multi-issue alliance, in which reparations constitute one among several shared grievances and demands. The organizing agenda of this nascent alliance centers on fundamental political, economic, social, and environmental issues and includes human rights, white supremacy, state terrorism, global capitalism, democracy, women's and workers' rights, global justice, and, in the case of at least several groups, the support of liberation struggles for self-determination.

The alliance's formation and practices reflect this convergence and internationalization of political agendas. For example, TransAfrica Forum's "core principles," under the acronym DARAS, concern "debt relief, AIDS, reparations, agricultural subsidies, and sovereignty."[46] Its objective is to build alliances with labor organizations, community activists, youth, students, and academics to "forge new activism." Similarly, the *Freedom Agenda* of the anticapitalist and working-class-oriented Black Radical Congress (BRC) addresses struggles for human rights, political democracy, the environment, reparations, the right of self-determination for African Americans, and support of liberation struggles throughout the world, especially in the African diaspora (see Documents, section 4).[47]

Along with overlapping and shared political agendas, these organizations support each other's mobilizing activities and often participate in the same forums, conferences, rallies, marches (such as the "Millions for Reparations" march on Washington in August 2002), and national and international coordinating activities. Again, TransAfrica Forum and the BRC illustrate this development. TransAfrica board chairman Danny Glover and then-president Bill Fletcher have both addressed the national congress, "War, Racism and Repression: Confronting the U.S. Empire!" (sponsored by the BRC in June 2003).[48] Hosted by the Center for African American Studies at Seton Hall University, one of the congress's eight objectives was developing "an internationalist perspective on reparations, peace [and] justice."[49] In a subsequent conference held in 2005, "Confronting Empire: The Fight for Global Justice," held at Georgia State University, the BRC sponsored a workshop devoted to "reparations as a political response to slavery and racism."[50]

Other single- or multi-issue organizations in the United States associated with the alliance, or that support reparations, include N'COBRA, which is engaged in various educational activities to mobilize for reparations and lobby Congress to support HR 40; the Reparations Coordinating Committee, which is pursuing the Tulsa case and other lawsuits; and the Reparations Mobilization Coalition, which is focused on developing a reparations primer for "grassroots education and mobilization" (see Documents, section 4). Independently and together, these organizations' activities constitute the political mobilization (coalition-building and educational) strategy of the reparations movement in the United States. In conjunction with the legislative and litigation strategies discussed earlier, a national movement, inclusive of civil rights organizations, is evolving, with growing and coordinated links to redress struggles in Africa and the Caribbean.

A case in point is the UN World Conference against Racism, Racial Discrimination, Xenophobia, and Related Intolerance (WCAR) held in Durban, South Africa, in 2001. Disputes and acrimony arose among delegates and diplomats from the 166 nations in attendance, including disagreements between some African leaders regarding reparations and efforts by U.S. and some European delegations to undermine discussions about both reparations and Israel's continuing hegemony of the occupied territories.[51] Still, the practical and symbolic importance of the WCAR was manifest in its final declaration.[52] Two of its final provisions are of direct importance to the redress movement:

> [13.] We acknowledge that slavery and the slave trade, including the transatlantic slave trade, were appalling tragedies in the history of humanity not only because of their abhorrent barbarism but also in terms of their magnitude, organized nature and especially their negation of the essence of the victims and further acknowledge that slavery and the slave trade are a *crime against humanity* [emphasis added] and should always have been so, especially the transatlantic slave trade, and are among the major sources and manifestations of racism, racial discrimination, xenophobia and related intolerance, and that Africans and people of African descent, Asians and people of Asian descent and indigenous peoples were victims of these acts and continue to be victims of their consequences....
>
> [104.] We also strongly reaffirm as a pressing requirement of justice that victims of human rights violations resulting from racism, racial discrimination, xenophobia and related intolerance, especially in the light of their vulnerable situation socially, culturally and economically, should be assured of having access to justice, including legal assistance where appropriate, and effective and appropriate protection and remedies, including *the right to seek just and adequate reparation or satisfaction for any damage suffered* [emphasis added] as a result of such discrimination, as enshrined in numerous international and regional human rights instruments, in particular the Universal Declaration of Human Rights and the International Convention on the Elimination of All Forms of Racial Discrimination.[53]

Although the final agreement in Durban failed to satisfy delegates of African nations, African American delegates applauded the declaration, affirming that it was a "rendezvous with history."[54] Indeed, Henderson of LCCR concluded, "By recognizing slavery as a crime against humanity, the document sets the stage for legislative and legal action to address historic inequities."[55] Concurring with Henderson, Ogletree further suggested that the declaration's statement on slavery constituted "a legal determination that may enable the reparations movement [in the United States] to extend its reach to international forums."[56]

In the aftermath of the WCAR, reparations organizations were formed in several sites in the African diaspora, such as the Jamaica Reparations Movement in 2002. In addition, an international reparations conference, organized by the African/African Descendants Caucus, was held in Barbados the same year. Lacking resources and representation from countries in the Caribbean and Latin America, and having voted to exclude non-Africans, the conference was mired in controversy and reportedly condemned by reparationists worldwide.[57] This dispute notwithstanding, according to one delegate, Muntu Matsimela, the conference was a "very positive, progressive" meeting where "radical discussions" took place. The Global African Congress, one of several post-Durban formations, was founded in Barbados.[58]

An Expanding Global Network

In the wake of the cold war, global capitalism is distinguished by increasing poverty and inequality on a world scale, proliferating ethnic and religious conflict, and the militarization and environmental degradation of the planet. This is occurring during a period when American imperial ambitions are cynically exercised with indifference to human suffering and in contravention of international covenants and law. In counterpoint to these developments, an international network and alliance for global justice, inchoate though conspicuous, is evolving. Revisiting many of the structural inequalities and issues that characterized the North–South polarity in the 1960s, the multi-issue agenda of the alliance emphasizes political democracy and justice, human rights, debt relief, the restoration and maintenance of a sustainable environment, and reparations, including capital transfers, as discussed by Mazrui earlier. More important, it upholds the principle that economic development is one, albeit essential, factor of social development and progress.

The reparations movement in the United States is an increasingly prominent part of this expanding network, while continuing the struggle begun during the Civil War and by nationalists and civil rights organizations in the 1960s. In both Africa and the United States, the 1990s marked a watershed in revitalized efforts for redress. It is not a coincidence that in the 1990s the resurgence of the redress movement in the United States—and minority rights and North–South issues resuming center stage in world affairs—occurred precisely when the cold war/East–West conflict declined in the wake of the Soviet Union's dissolution.

In consideration of the broad array of political and ideological concerns addressed by the global alliance, part 5 includes mobilization strategies and modalities for redress. In Yusuf Nuruddin's interview with Sam Anderson and Muntu Matsimela, Matsimela contends that reparation is "a civil rights issue and a human rights issue.... There's a direct relationship—an inextricable link—between civil rights and human rights; and reparations encompasses both of them." For Anderson, reparations is "a political movement, and in that context, we see the impending war [against Iraq] in the Middle

East as something that, as reparationists, we're in opposition to." For Nuruddin, reparations has a "proletarian character"; he argues that reparations in the United States is "a working-class agenda and ... the Left in general—White or Black—should support reparations"[59] (see Nuruddin, part 5). In agreement with Nuruddin, the BRC proclaims the reparations movement's working-class orientation as a fundamental principle of its organizing strategy. Through efforts to broaden its agenda and constituencies, as well as mobilize support for reparations, TransAfrica Forum, too, is "partnering with youth and students, labor organizations, academics, community activists, and individuals whose interests converge with TransAfrica's."[60]

C. J. Munford's essay in part 5 targets these larger political concerns, asserting that, while the reparations movement is "an attack on capitalism" and "a race-specific matter," a coalition between a "Black America *united* for reparations, and an antiracist White minority rallying in support of Black reparations can prevail over mass White opposition." By establishing a direct relationship between race and the class character of reparations in the United States (and internationally), several of the contributors address critical issues that remain unresolved. First, it gives greater specificity to the group on whose behalf reparations are championed. Second, reparations are distinguished as a site for black working-class agency. Third, this approach invites progressive groups and organizations to support the reparations movement on the basis of class rather than racial solidarity, in theory avoiding the historical problems associated with identity politics.

Here, Ogletree's admonition is particularly compelling in consideration of the "class" of African Americans who should benefit most from reparations:

> The reparations movement should not, I believe, focus on payments to individuals.[61] The damage has been done to a group—African-American slaves and their descendents—but it has not been done equally within the group. The reparations movement must aim at undoing the damage where that damage has been most severe and where the history of race in America has left its most telling evidence.... The reparations movement must therefore focus on the poorest of the poor—it must finance social recovery from the bottom-stuck, providing an opportunity to address comprehensively the problems of those who have not substantially benefited from integration or affirmative action.[62]

Of the three strategies pursued by reparationists in the United States (and abroad)—legislation, litigation, and political mobilization—litigation is arguably the most effective at this time, but perhaps of limited utility, because, as Matsimela observes, "All litigation is going to wind up in the Supreme Court, if the Supreme Court chooses to hear it. That is to say, it will be taken to the Supreme Court by the plaintiff . . . or by the defendants, whether corporate entities, estates, or state or federal government entities."[63] Nevertheless, the legal strategy is essential for what it will disclose about the duplicity of governments and corporations and other private entities during and after slavery rather than for what it may achieve in terms of actual compensation to the descendants of slaves. The legal strategy may also serve a symbolic as much as a practical function while complementing and enhancing the legislative and political mobilization strategies. In part 5, the essays by Charles P. Henry and Ogletree and the interview with Anderson and Matsimela assess the relative merits of the three strategies. Adrienne Davis examines the deployment of the Thirteenth Amendment to pursue litigation cases for reparations claims, and Eric K. Yamamoto analyzes the Japanese redress campaign to illuminate a strategy for African American reparations claims.

At the federal level, the legislative strategy has been unsuccessful since HR 40 was first introduced in Congress in 1989. However, lobbying efforts at the municipal and state levels have begun to yield results as city and state legislatures adopt resolutions that endorse and support HR 40 (see Documents, sections 2 and 3). The passage of HR 40 or a similar bill would be without precedent, implicating the federal government in a national inquiry and debate about slavery and its continuing legacy. Moreover, it would provide the necessary historical records and federal documents to advance the litigation strategy, including against the federal government itself. The passage of HR 40 remains uncertain and will require a more effective lobbying strategy and campaign in Congress. Indeed, adoption of the bill will largely pivot on the success of the lobbying efforts of N'COBRA, TransAfrica Forum, and civil rights and labor organizations; it also will depend on the mobilization of a broad-based and diverse constituency.

Among the three trajectories of reparations, and the obstacles and resistance to them, political mobilization may yet prove the most effective though problematic strategy in the United States (and Europe). For Matsimela and other reparationist organizers, "political mobilization of the great numbers of our people and allies and supporters in this country [is] the essential ingredient, the essential factor in achieving reparations."[64] Although political mobilization, if not litigation, has, to some extent, been successful at the local level with regard to several lawsuits (e.g., the Tulsa case), at the national level it has been difficult to implement because it necessarily depends on an infrastructure (including a coordinating apparatus) at the community, municipal, state, and regional levels that would require substantial resources to maintain.

A number of organizations that are aware of this dilemma, including N'COBRA, the BRC, and TransAfrica Forum, have stepped up their educational and coalition-building activities and are rethinking strategies for political mobilization. A case in point is the 2002 "Millions for Reparations" rally held in Washington, D.C. The rally was organized by a pre-WCAR formation, the December 12th Movement, and the Chicago-based National Black United Front. But it was poorly attended and some civil rights organizations were not represented. In particular, African American communities, especially in the Washington-Baltimore area, had not been mobilized. According to Anderson, "There was really no formal coalition work in organizing for that rally."[65] In recognition of the problems associated with the rally and the organizational deficiencies within the movement, the Reparations Mobilization Coalition is planning for a National Reparations Congress first slated for 2005. The Congress is intended, notes Anderson, to assemble "all the reparations groups and key individuals . . . to have a united front strategy and tactic around the struggle for reparations."[66]

Political mobilization also involves networking and coalition building at the international level, as noted earlier. In his essay in part 5, Gerald Horne elaborates a strategy to mobilize the movement in the United States into productive alliances with sectors in the international community.[67] Horne counsels that the reparations movement should seek "to take advantage of the emerging contradictions between the burgeoning European Union and the United States," along with Africa and Latin America, where opportunities for coalition building abound. He has identified pressure points between nations that can be leveraged to support reparations. The current rift among member states in the European Union as well as between the United States, France, and Germany over the Iraq war illustrates his point. Whether or not these cleavages can be used on behalf of reparations is, however, unclear.

Similarly, it has been suggested that reparationists should seek alliances with Japanese Latinos who were imprisoned after being deported to the United States by Latin American governments during World War Two.[68] Other potential allies include Mexican *braceros* who worked in the United States during World War Two and who have now filed a class-action lawsuit for reparations. The Middle East is another site for alliances, particularly with regard to the 3 million displaced Palestinian refugees in the occupied territories, Jordan, Lebanon, and Syria, and whose development needs constitute a form of reparations for the losses they suffered since the *Nakba* in 1948. On the domestic front, as Yamamoto suggests, reparationists should also seek alliances with Japanese American communities that have waged an effective and successful reparations campaign for Americans of Japanese ancestry interned during World War Two.[69]

We conclude that strategic alliances among civil rights organizations, anticapitalist formations, and reparationists in the United States strengthen ties with an emerging international movement and represent an important development in the long history of reparations. This is especially significant in the present conjuncture of neoliberalism and U.S. imperial assertions. Reparationists' campaigns, increasingly aligned and coordinated with other counterhegemonic formations worldwide, pose a challenge to global capitalism and First World nations whose ill-gotten gains were pillaged from the countries and peoples under slavery and colonialism. Perhaps the International Court of Justice is the appropriate venue, as Ricardo Rene Laremont suggests, to prosecute reparations claims for slavery, colonization, and other crimes against humanity on behalf of *all* humanity.[70]

As the *Manifesto* enunciated the historical and moral raison d'être for reparations in the United States, so, too, does this compelling statement by Oruno D. Lara, for the world:

> Today, at the dawning of the 21st century, we will not accept to be manipulated, we will not accept words and crowd-pleasing promises which are not kept. We want and we demand reparations. . . . The Committee for Reparations should take into account the disastrous economic, social and political situation inherited by the survivors of slavery in the 19th and 20th centuries. . . . The collective catastrophe is on such a global scale that the conventional notion of indemnity or reparation becomes meaningless. We have reached the "incompensational," the non-reparable. A final and obvious reason to demand reparations is that it is the most appropriate way to brand History and to root the crime at the heart of mankind so it will never be forgotten.[71]

Notes

Parts of this essay appeared in *Race and Class* 45, no. 4 (2004).

1. Alex Boraine and Paul van Zyl, "Moving On Requires Looking Back," *International Herald Tribune*, 1 August 2003.

2. Charles J. Ogletree Jr., as quoted in Adrian Brune, "Tulsa's Shame," *The Nation*, 18 March 2002.

3. By "global apartheid," we use Salih Booker and William Minter's definition: "an international system of minority rule whose attributes include: differential access to basic human rights; wealth and power structured by race and place; structural racism, embedded in global economic processes, political institutions and cultural assumptions; and the international practice of double standards that assume inferior rights to be appropriate for certain 'others,' defined by location, origin, race or gender." See Booker and Minter, "Global Apartheid," *The Nation*, 9 July 2001.

4. Gayatri Chakravorty Spivak, "Righting Wrongs," *South Atlantic Quarterly* 103, nos. 2–3 (2004): 523.

5. For example, see Schuchter, *Reparations*; Feagin, *Racist America*; Lecky and Wright, *Black Manifesto*; Brooks, *When Sorry Isn't Enough*; Winbush, *Should America Pay?*; Robinson, *The Debt*; and Corlett, *Race, Racism, and Reparations*.

6. See Sheryl Gay Stolberg, "Senate Issues Apology over Failure on Lynching Law," *New York Times*, 14 June 2005.

7. Although not included in this collection, the seminal work of Charles Mills is relevant to conceptualizations of race in the contemporary period. In "Racial Exploitation and the Wages of Whiteness," Mills interrogates the analytical limitations of mainstream models of racism and Marxist orthodoxy, revisioning normative political theory to account for racial injustice. He proposes a redeployment of the concept of white supremacy to clarify the strategic distinction between racial and class exploitation. Having been inculcated by theoretical paradigms that privilege whiteness, or which view the experiences of whites as representative of all members of a particular class, scholars and policymakers alike have promoted a misleading picture of the United States, in particular, "as a liberal democracy free of the hierarchical social structures of the Old World." By reframing normative theories of exploitation, Mills foregrounds the structuring role and continuing saliency of race in the contemporary period. His essay appears in M. T. Martin and Yaquinto, *America's Unpaid Debt*.

8. For a brief historical overview of racial preferences, see "A Long History of Affirmative Action—For Whites," in *Race: The Power of an Illusion* (San Francisco: California Newsreel, 2003), available at www.newsreel.org/guides/race/whiteadv.htm (accessed 20 August 2003).

9. For full text, see Randall Robinson's "Restatement of the Black Manifesto" at *HarlemLive*, www.harlemlive.org/community/activist/thedebt/manifesto.html (accessed 5 July 2005).

10. "The Case for Black Reparations"; see transcript of Proceedings, *TransAfrica Forum*, 2000, available at www.transafricaforum.org/reports/reparations_print.shtml (accessed 18 August 2003).

11. Ibid.

12. Ibid.

13. John Conyers, "The Proposed Reparations Study Commission," available at www.house.gov/conyers/news_reparations.htm (accessed 17 July 2003).

14. Gates, "The Future of Slavery's Past."

15. See John David Smith, "The Enduring Myth of 'Forty Acres and a Mule,'" *Chronicle of Higher Education*, 21 February 2003, B11.

16. Ibid.

17. Ibid.

18. See Robert S. Browne, "A Case for Separation," in Robert S. Browne and Bayard Rustin, eds., *Separatism or Integration: Which Way for America?—A Dialogue* (New York: Philip Randolph Educational Fund, 1968), 7–15. Some black nationalists of this period took inspiration from an earlier emigrationist movement led by Marcus Garvey during the 1920s. His Universal Negro Improvement Association endeavored to establish a homeland for African Americans in Liberia. For an analysis of this movement, see Ibrahim Sundiata's recent study, *Brothers and Strangers: Black Zion, Black Slavery, 1914–1940* (Durham, N.C.: Duke University Press, 2004); Robert A. Hill and Barbara Bair, eds., *Marcus Garvey: Life and Lessons* (Berkeley: University of California Press, 1987); and Robert A. Hill, ed., *The Marcus Garvey and Universal Negro Improvement Association Papers*, vol. 9 (Berkeley: University of California Press, 1995).

19. See the seminal texts by Robert Blauner, "Internal Colonialism and Ghetto Revolt," *Social Problems* 15, no. 4 (1969): 393–408, and Stokley Carmichael and Charles V. Hamilton, *Black

Power: The Politics of Liberation in America (New York: Random House, 1967); see also Blauner's recent book, in which he assesses his earlier views and assumptions about race relations in the contemporary period: *Still the Big News: Racial Oppression in America* (Berkeley: University of California Press, 2001).

20. David Horowitz quoted in "Harvard Professor, Reparations Group File Suit," *Harvard Crimson*, 25 February 2003.

21. E. R. Shipp, "Does America Owe Us?," *Essence*, February 2003, 126.

22. Tamar Lewin, "Calls for Slavery Restitution Getting Louder," *New York Times*, 4 June 2001.

23. See John H. McWhorter, "The Reparations Racket: America Has Already Made Amends for Slavery," *City Journal* 14, no. 2 (2004).

24. Ibid.

25. Glenn C. Loury, "It's Futile to Put a Price on Slavery," *New York Times*, 29 May 2000.

26. See Ginger Thompson, "South Africa to Pay $3,900 to Each Family of Apartheid Victims," *New York Times*, 16 April 2003.

27. See Doreen Carvajal, "Slavery's Truths (and Tales) Come Flocking Home," *New York Times*, 28 March 1999.

28. Brent Staples, "America, Too, Should Pay Reparations for Its Past," *International Herald Tribune*, 25 July 2000. Note that in 1953 the German Bundestag approved a "restitution law" to compensate thousands of persons persecuted under Nazi rule, in addition to the West German–Israeli reparations agreement in which Israel received $822 million to resettle Jews in Israel; see "Reparations for War Loss," *International Herald Tribune*, first published 31 July 1953 and reprinted 31 July 2003.

29. Conyers, "The Proposed Reparations Study Commission."

30. A case in point and discussed in the essay by Alan Singer in this volume is New York City's complicity with slavery during the nineteenth century.

31. Michael A. Fletcher, "Calls for Reparations Grow Louder as Blacks Tally Slavery's Toll," *International Herald Tribune*, 27 December 2000.

32. Lewin, "Calls for Slavery Restitution Getting Louder."

33. Damien Jackson, "40 Acres and a Mule Denied," 17 November 2004, *Alternet*, available at www.alternet.org/story/20511/ (accessed 17 November 2004).

34. See Charles J. Ogletree Jr., "Litigating the Legacy of Slavery," op-ed, *New York Times*, 31 March 2002.

35. Adrian Brune, "Tulsa's Shame: Race Riot Victims Still Wait for Promised Reparations," *The Nation*, 18 March 2002, 11–14.

36. Ibid., 12.

37. See Adrian Brune, "A Long Wait for Justice," *Village Voice*, 30 April 2003, 1–2.

38. "Al Brody and Charles Ogletree Discuss the Issue of Slavery Reparations and the Race Riots of 1921 in Oklahoma," *Tavis Smiley Show*, National Public Radio, 26 February 2003.

39. Lewin, "Calls for Slavery Restitution Getting Louder."

40. Ibid.

41. Ibid.

42. Neal Conan, "Corporate Reparations for Slavery." *Talk of the Nation*. National Public Radio, 3 April 2002. Available at http://www.npr.org/templates/story/story.php?storyId=114016.

43. Ogletree, "Litigating the Legacy of Slavery."

44. Conan, "Corporate Reparations for Slavery."

45. Ibid. See also Brent Staples, "Wrestling with the Legacy of Slavery at Yale," editorial, *New York Times*, 14 August 2001; and Kate Zernike, "Slavers in Yale's Past Are Focus of Reparations Debate," *New York Times*, 13 August 2001.

46. See Charles Cobb Jr., "Fight for Global Justice Is TransAfrica's Immense Task, Says Danny Glover," *TransAfrica Forum*, 15 November 2002, available at www.transafricaforum.org/newsletter/news_nov15_02.html (accessed 5 July 2005).

47. For the full text of the *Freedom Agenda*, see "The Freedom Agenda of the Black Radical Congress," Black Radical Congress National Council, April 17, 1999, available at www.blackradicalcongress.org/aboutus/freedomagenda.html (accessed 5 July 2005). Founded in Chicago in 1998, the BRC's stated objective is to unify progressives, including "revolutionary nationalists," "radical Black feminists and womanists," "socialists and communists," radical intellectuals, and black workers.

48. Glover delivered the keynote address on "Peace, Reparations and Justice."

49. See the call for the conference, "War, Racism and Repression: Confronting the U.S. Empire!," available at www.eblackstudies.org/brc/fightback/ (accessed 5 July 2005).

50. See "Confronting Empire: The Fight for Global Justice," 17–29 June 2005, Georgia State University, Atlanta, available at www.blackradicalcongress.org/agenda.html (accessed 6 July 2005).

51. Of the 166 nations represented, the Bush administration sent a midlevel delegation, which withdrew, along with the Israeli delegation, because they objected to statements in the draft declaration condemning Israeli state practices as racist. Several, especially African American critics contend that reparations was the principal motive for the U.S. delegation's withdrawal to undermine the conference. See Steven Inskeep, "UN Conference on Racism and Reparations for Slavery" (transcript), *Talk of the Nation*, 4 September 2001, 3. For an overview of the experiences of the members of a delegation of southern activists from the United States, along with their views about the contentious issues debated at the conference, see *Report on the REJN Delegation to the United Nations World Conference against Racism* (Durham, N.C.: Southeast Regional Economic Justice Network, March 2002).

52. See two reports: Rachel L. Swarns, "Overshadowed, Slavery Debate Boils at Racism Conference," *New York Times*, 6 September 2002; and Justin Podur, "Non-Reformist Reparations for Africa," *Z Magazine*, February 2002.

53. United Nations, *Declaration*, World Conference against Racism, Racial Discrimination, Xenophobia and Related Intolerance, No. 13, 2001, pp. 6, 18, available at www.un.org/WCAR/ (accessed 28 August 2003).

54. Rachel L. Swarns, "After Much Wrangling, an Accord at U.N. Race Meeting," *New York Times*, 9 September 2001. Critics argue that in the drafting process, "First World issues were dominant," and that in the Declaration itself "the problem of racism [is] overwhelmingly from the point of view of marginalized minorities in the developed countries. Third world perspectives, and especially African perspectives, are largely absent." See "Evaluating the WCAR NGO Forum (and preparing for the WSSD)," available at http://www.anc.org.za/ancdocs/pubs/umrabulo/umrabulo131.html.

55. Swarns, "After Much Wrangling."

56. Ogletree, "Litigating the Legacy of Slavery."

57. See two reports about the conference and this issue: Barbara Makeda and Blake Hannah, "Reparations Movement at a Crossroads"; and Sam Anderson and Muntu Matsimela, "The Reparations Movement: An Assessment of Recent and Current Activism," both in *Socialism and Democracy* 17, no. 1 (2003): 270–273.

58. Anderson and Matsimela, "The Reparations Movement," 272.

59. Ibid., 268.

60. "Remarks by Danny Glover before National Press Club," *TransAfrica Forum*, 12 November 2002, 4, available at www.transafricaforum.org/newsletter/news_nov12_02_npc.html (accessed 28 August 2003).

61. Estimates of restitution for lost wages to slaves range from $2 trillion to $4 trillion. A model based on intergenerational transfers of wealth determined that the average compensation to a two-adult black family would be about $35,000. See Dalton Conley, "The Cost of Slavery," *New York Times*, 15 February 2003.

62. Ibid.

63. Anderson and Matsimela, "The Reparations Movement," 264. This is also likely to happen with lawsuits filed in other nations as well.

64. Ibid., 264–265.

65. Ibid., 270; and see Shipp, "Does America Owe Us?," 1–3, for two opposing views of the rally.

66. Anderson and Matsimela, "The Reparations Movement," 261.

67. See Gerald Horne, "Race for Power: The Global Balance of Power and Reparations," in Martin and Yaquinto, 79–90.

68. See Richard L. Vázquez, "Justice for Japanese Latinos," LasCulturas.com, 2001, available at www.lasculturas.com/aa/aa060701a.php (accessed 23 August 2002). Germans and Italians were also deported from Latin America to the United States.

69. See Eric K. Yamamoto's statement in "The Case for Black Reparations," transcript, 7–8, available at TransAfrica Forum, 2000, http://www.transafricaforum.org/reports/reparations_print.shtml.

70. Ricardo Rene Laremont, "Political versus Legal Strategies for the African Slavery Reparations Movement," *African Studies Quarterly*, available at www.web.africa.ufl.edu/asq/v2/v2i4a3.htm (accessed 27 April 2004).

71. Oruno D. Lara, "In Defense of Reparations," *Renaissance Noire* 3, no. 3 (2001): 157.

Part 1

Racial Inequality and White Privilege

Introduction

Essays by David Lyons, Michael K. Brown et al., and Melvin L. Oliver and Thomas M. Shapiro map black inequality and the racialization processes that have sustained white privilege from the colonial period through Jim Crow, the New Deal, and the contemporary period. Lyons derives reparations claims in chattel slavery, first institutionalized by colonial practices and legislation as well as supportive public policies until the Civil War. He argues that many of the race-based inequities that preceded the Civil War were extended well into the twentieth century. Among Lyons's proposals are reparations as a means of redress for the legacies of slavery and Jim Crow.

Brown et al. extend Lyons's critical overview to the current period, challenging the "racial realists" who assert that racism is a thing of the past or a matter of blacks not taking advantage of available opportunities and that the "political failures" of the civil rights movement are the direct consequence of activists doing more harm than good. The authors explicate how conservatives' focus on improved job skills and education for blacks — as a means to end discrimination — ignores how Jim Crow invested in white privilege, enabling whites to accumulate wealth while blacks "disaccumulated" it. Like Lyons, they counter the argument that redress for African Americans for past wrongs is unnecessary and unfair, asserting that whites have been the beneficiaries of "affirmative action" for the past 360 years.

In Oliver and Shapiro's landmark study, three essential factors are examined. The first is rooted in social structure, in which the labor market, schooling, and family life, among other factors, conjoin to perpetuate inequality.

The second, institutional and social policy, concerns differential access to housing markets and mortgage financing, along with the "racial valuation of neighborhoods" that deprives African Americans of assets comparable to whites. The third factor concerns the dramatic disparities in wealth between whites and blacks caused by intergenerational transfers of money, cultural capital, and social mobility. Together, these factors account for the persistence of racial inequality in American society.

Racial Injustices in U.S. History and Their Legacy

DAVID LYONS

Introduction

This essay concerns the creation of racial hierarchy in the United States, its perpetuation, and its persisting consequences. The "racial junctures" are brief periods of U.S. history in which decisions were made that profoundly affected racial stratification.

When Africans first came to the colonies, they did not enter chattel slavery, for there was no such system; it was created by colonial legislatures. After the War for Independence, the slave system was protected by the new Constitution. After the Civil War, slavery was abolished, but the federal government permitted the reestablishment of racial subjugation.

Racial stratification in the United States was not inevitable, at least in any sense that negates moral responsibility. Alternatives were recognized by those who made the relevant decisions. Satisfactory alternatives would have been difficult to achieve, but that is another matter. Consider a recent case. By the time of the 1942 Wannsee Conference, the Nazi leadership had decided to exterminate Jews, Roma, and others. Alternatives were not seriously considered, but they were understood well enough by the conference participants. The Holocaust was not inevitable, at least in any sense that negates moral responsibility.

It is arguable that a fourth racial juncture occurred in the last third of the twentieth century, when America faced its most promising opportunity to eliminate the legacy of slavery and Jim Crow but left the racial hierarchy substantially undisturbed.

The Creation of Chattel Slavery

In 1619, "20 and odd Negroes" were bought from a Dutch ship in Jamestown.[1] This suggests that the Africans were chattels—that they could be bought and sold, were destined for perpetual servitude, and that their children would suffer the same fate. The Virginia colonists had just learned how to survive and perhaps even prosper — by cultivating tobacco as a cash crop for export. That required laborers. Virginia planters initially relied on European indentured servants, who worked for a period of years in return for their passage to America. But the conditions of servitude were typically harsh and the mortality rate was high enough to discourage some potential servants who had a choice in the matter. Inducements were increased, and the costs of importing servants from Britain rose considerably.[2]

When Britain became a major participant in the slave trade, in the last third of the seventeenth century, the purchase of an African slave began to seem economically more attractive to Virginia planters than the price of a temporary servant. Planters began to substitute slave for indentured labor. The same applies to Maryland, where tobacco could likewise be cultivated profitably. Before long, the Carolinas, where conditions favored rice and indigo plantations, likewise imported substantial numbers of African slaves.[3]

But the reference to "slaves" is misleading. We know from case reports as late as the 1670s that some Africans worked as indentured servants and could use colonial courts to enforce their contracts and to secure compensation for service beyond the contractual period.[4] That would not have been possible if the Africans had been chattel slaves.

Unlike Spain and Portugal, Britain had no laws regulating slavery. But the colonists had the power to enact such laws, for the British colonies began as private ventures chartered by the Crown. As royal domains, they were not subject to parliamentary control until the middle of the eighteenth century. They were free to create their own laws, subject only to a Crown veto.[5] And neither the Crown nor, later, Parliament was motivated to interfere with slavery in the colonies, whose economies engaged the British in very profitable activities, including the slave trade itself.

The records of Virginia legislation imply even more clearly that the legal framework of chattel slavery did not exist for most of the colony's first few decades but was constructed during the last third of the seventeenth century. Here are some of the principal measures:

1. The Virginia legislature began the process with its 1662 enactment "that all children borne in this country shalbe held bond or free only according to the condition of the mother."[6] This represents a deliberate departure from the common law.[7] It had been decided that servitude for Africans would be inheritable.
2. As a result of prior contact with Europeans, some Africans had been

baptized, and Christian doctrine made them ineligible for enslavement.[8] There was uncertainty among the Protestant churches as to whether the baptism of someone who was already a slave had the same effect.[9] That helps to explain a Virginia enactment of 1667 "that the conferring of baptisme doth not alter the condition of the person as to his bondage or freedome."[10] This permitted both the continued enslavement of someone after baptism and the enslavement of Africans who became Christians before they arrived in America.

3. For masters, discipline of Africans who were held in servitude without indentures presented a problem. The extension of servitude was a punishment available against indentured servants but not against those who served for life. The Virginia legislature addressed the issue in a 1668 enactment by permitting the most severe corporal punishments for those whose servitude could not be extended: "If any slave resists his master . . . and by the extremity of the correction should chance to die, . . . his death shall not be accompted ffelony, but the master . . . be acquit from molestation, since it cannot be presumed that prepensed malice (which alone makes murther ffelony) should induce any man to destroy his owne estate."[11] This gave masters maximum control over those held in lifetime bondage and adds another constituent of chattel slavery.

4. In 1682, the Virginia legislature addressed the racial dimension of chattel slavery in America by declaring "that all servants . . . imported into this country . . . whether Negroes, Moores, Mollattoes or Indians, who and whose parentage and native country are not christian at the time of their first purchase of such servant by some christian . . . shall be . . . slaves to all intents and purposes, any law, usage or custome to the contrary notwithstanding."[12] Lifetime, inheritable slavery was for people of color, and only them.[13] The Virginia legislature was creating a racially differentiated, two-tier labor system.

Colonial records indicate that, prior to this legislation, economic and social stratification had not been tightly color-coded. Marriages with European Americans were not uncommon. Some African servants, including slaves, secured their own freedom, became independent farmers, and joined communities of free African Americans or were recognized as members of racially mixed communities.[14]

Most of the early African immigrants came from the west coast of Africa, where for a century and a half there had been considerable contact with Europeans, and many had been in other European colonies prior to Virginia. They differed from most who came during the height of the slave trade to North America, who came mainly from the African interior and were unfamiliar with Europeans, their language, or their culture.[15] Many of the early arrivals knew the ways of Europeans, and many had already been converted to Christianity.[16]

There has been some dispute among historians concerning cause-and-effect relations between chattel slavery and white racist attitudes.[17] My point here is that, despite notions of white superiority among some portion of the European American population, it was initially neither assumed nor ordained that people of color should become a rigidly subjugated caste. Those who shaped the direction of the colony *decided* to color-code the social system. I want now to suggest a factor that may have encouraged that decision.

In seventeenth-century Virginia, servants from Europe and Africa cooperated in many settings. They worked together, shared living conditions and grievances, and ran away from bondage together.[18] In 1676, they joined together in Bacon's Rebellion.[19] Many landless whites and blacks hoped to gain land by dispossessing Native Americans. Bacon promised freedom to black slaves, who were especially affected by developments in public policy. Colonial legislation was dampening their hopes for freedom and reducing their conditions generally.[20] The rebels opposed the governing elite, who already possessed considerable land and wanted peaceful relations with the neighboring Indians. The rebels forced the governor to flee Jamestown, which they burned to the ground. British troops crossed the Atlantic to put down the rebellion, which faltered when Bacon fell ill and died.

Bacon's Rebellion was not the first uprising against the colonial elite, but it was undoubtedly the most threatening rebellion prior to the 1770s. The experience may well have contributed to the determination of those who shaped colonial policies to drive a wedge between whites and blacks. By forcing servants of color to the bottom of a race-based social system, they accorded relative privilege, dignity, and opportunity to those with white skins. In 1682, shortly after Bacon's Rebellion, as we have seen, the Virginia legislature consigned people of color to slavery.

5. To cement the system and decrease effective opposition to the colonial elite, it was deemed necessary to do more. In 1691, the Virginia legislature banned interracial marriages and procreation.[21] This measure was not universally approved by the white community and was opposed by some of its propertied members.[22] The same enactment sanctioned the killing of runaway slaves, restricted severely the freeing of slaves, and required that freed slaves be transported out of the colony at the owner's expense. Blacks were to occupy the bottom caste, identified with slavery.

These efforts achieved some measure of success. In subsequent years, as European Americans were acculturated in a system that consigned African Americans to the bottom and penalized fraternization, they were encouraged to believe that the social hierarchy had a valid foundation.

In sum, the system of chattel slavery that developed in Virginia was not inevitable.[23] For several decades, social mobility was possible even for African servants, who might acquire economic independence and respected social status. Faced with this prospect and that of a unified laboring class, the ruling elite imposed a racial caste system.

The Legal Entrenchment of Slavery

Until it was abolished by ratification of the Thirteenth Amendment in 1865, slavery was not expressly mentioned in the Constitution. But several provisions were understood by the framers and later by state and federal officials to refer to slavery. Following are the clearest examples.

The three-fifths clause provided that representation in Congress "shall be apportioned among the several States . . . according to their respective numbers, which shall be determined by adding to the whole number of free persons, including those bound to service for a term of years, and excluding Indians not taxed, three-fifths of all other persons."[24] Indentured servants were expressly included in the category of "free persons" and Native Americans were excluded from the apportionment, so that only those in lifelong, hereditary slavery occupied the category "other persons." While suffrage was denied slaves, their numbers contributed to slave owners' influence within the federal government — not only in Congress but also in the executive branch (as the electoral college reflected congressional representation) and the federal judiciary (selected by the president).[25]

The slave trade provisions prevented Congress for twenty years from banning "the migration or importation of such persons as any of the States now existing shall think proper to admit" and exempted this provision from amendment for the same period.[26]

The fugitive slave clause provided for the return of "person[s] held to service or labour" to those "to whom such service or labour may be due";[27] it was understood to concern runaway slaves. After a fugitive slave act was enacted in 1793, persons accused of trying to escape from slavery or of aiding them were prosecuted in the courts.[28]

The constitutional accommodation of chattel slavery seems to clash with the doctrine of universal human rights that a decade earlier was invoked to justify the colonial rebellion. The contradiction had frequently been noted, especially by friends of the American rebels when the latter complained of being reduced to "slaves" by Crown or Parliament.[29]

In his *Dred Scott* opinion, Chief Justice Roger Taney denied there was any contradiction. According to Taney, the founders never dreamed of including people of African descent within the body politic. Africans "had for more than a century before been regarded as beings of an inferior order, and altogether unfit to associate with the white race, either in social or political relations; and so far inferior, that they had no rights which the white man was bound to respect." Furthermore, "This opinion was at that time fixed and universal in the civilized portion of the white race. It was regarded as an axiom in morals as well as in politics, which no one thought of disputing, or supposed to be open to dispute."[30]

Taney was mistaken. At the very time chattel slavery was being established, in the late seventeenth century, objections to it were being publicly expressed in America. In the eighteenth century, antislavery sentiment was disseminated in print and from the pulpits of various denominations, South as well as North. When the Constitutional Convention was meeting, three northern states had already abolished slavery, three more had enacted gradual emancipation statutes, and three others would follow, as would three of the states that would soon be carved out of the Northwest Territory. This helps to explain why some delegates to the convention from slave states expressed a fear of attacks upon slavery and demanded that slavery be protected.[31]

The Constitution helped to solve that problem. Slavery could be protected by excluding its regulation from the list of enumerated federal powers and ensuring that no power directly implied such an authority. That was done.[32]

The Lower South (Georgia and the Carolinas) had lost many slaves during the war and wanted the slave trade protected. It was worried not only about antislavery agitation but also about Virginia and Maryland, which had a surplus of slaves and opposed their importation. The demand for tobacco had declined, and Chesapeake planters could profit from the internal slave trade if the Constitution protected slavery but permitted the banning of traffic in slaves from abroad.[33] Merely omitting regulation of the slave trade from the list of federal powers would not solve this problem, because northern states wanted the federal government to regulate external commerce, which could include the slave trade. As a compromise, northern delegates accepted the slave trade provision as well as a ban on the taxation of exports (such as the slave states' cash crops).[34]

But no such compromise was involved in the other constitutional accommodations made to slavery. Consider the three-fifths clause. The slave states did not make it a condition for union in the way that delegates from South Carolina insisted upon protections for slavery and the slave trade. Furthermore, the idea of counting slaves for purposes of representation lacked any precedents in Confederation practice[35] or in the slave states themselves, and the three-fifths formula lacked any rationale. The North agreed to it without seeking concessions in return.[36]

The fugitive slave clause was even more readily accepted. It was proposed at the end of the Convention and was subjected to neither bargaining nor debate. Northern delegates would have appreciated that it would rankle both antislavery interests and those who feared federal encroachment upon state autonomy. It, too, was a gift to the South.[37]

Why was the North so accommodating?[38] There is reason to regard the northern delegates as unrepresentative of northern sentiment. The delegates largely represented commercial and plantation interests. Although abolition was becoming official policy of the northern states, their delegates proved uninterested in the issue.[39] Very few delegates were opponents of slavery, and delegates from New England almost always favored concessions to it. When Connecticut's Oliver Ellsworth declined to consider the merits of slavery, he explained, "What enriches a part enriches the whole."[40]

A constitution so supportive of slavery was not inevitable. Consider the following factors:

1. The Chesapeake region was a center of antislavery sentiment. Between 1782 and 1790, the Upper South repealed bans on the private manumission of slaves and permitted freed slaves to remain. Meanwhile, demand for slaves continued to grow in the Lower South, where plantations were expanding. Upper South slave owners could have secured high prices selling their surplus slaves to the Lower South, but many chose instead to free slaves. Their manumission documents express antislavery sentiments explicitly.[41] This means that an abolitionist North had potential allies in the Upper South.
2. The Lower South was not in a good bargaining position. There is reason to discount their threats to abandon the Union if the Convention refused to accommodate slavery. Georgia and South Carolina wanted the protection a strong Union could afford them against powerful Native American nations, and Georgia felt vulnerable to Spanish Florida on its southern border (an escape route for runaway slaves and a staging area for opponents of the slave state). The Lower South might have agreed to much less than they got, such as a constitution that tolerated but did not support slavery.[42]

3. It is unclear whether the Lower South had the strength to succeed on its own as a tiny pro-slavery union. Even if it had been able to form an independent union with the Upper South, its prospects would have been dubious. A northern union would have had a diverse agricultural base, a shipping industry, and a textile industry that could have used domestic wool and imported cotton. By contrast, a southern union, dependent on cash crops and little industry, would have faced greater difficulty.[43]
4. In fact, given the weakness of the Lower South and attitudes within the Upper South, it has been suggested that a more representative convention could have endorsed a national program of abolition.[44] South Carolina's expressed anxieties about slavery tend to confirm that abolition was a threat. If so, abolition was imaginable.

A national abolition program would have included compensation for slave owners. Gouverneur Morris proposed a federal tax for the very purpose.[45] The Northwest Territory was just then being opened for settlement. Half a billion acres was available, and land sales might have generated the revenue. The addition of one dollar to the price of an acre would have raised a considerable portion, if not all, of the estimated $90 million that would have been required for compensated abolition.[46]

In sum, the Constitution that was proposed by the Convention and that was later ratified accommodated slavery. The evidence indicates that it did so excessively, beyond what was required for an agreement between those who represented slave owners' interests and those who were opposed to slavery. Furthermore, despite South Carolina's insistence upon protections for slavery, we can imagine a Union embarked from the start on an antislavery project. There was widespread popular support for such a program at the time, and the new nation possessed the assets to affect it successfully.

The First Reconstruction

Before the Civil War had ended, the abolition of slavery had become a Union objective.[47] Two central issues for national policy were how to deal with the states that had seceded and the fate of 4 million ex-slaves.

Lincoln's successor, Andrew Johnson, was wedded to white supremacy. With his blessing, new governments in the defeated states established Black Codes, which much resembled the former Slave Codes. Freedmen were coerced into labor contracts. Widespread violence enforced the new system.

Dismayed by Johnson's policies, Congress sought to end the most glaring inequities that were inherited from a society built upon chattel slavery and racist ideology. Congress mandated legal equality for blacks, freedom in economic relations, and universal manhood suffrage. It passed the first Civil Rights Act, despite Johnson's veto. Congress renewed the Freedmen's Bureau, again over Johnson's veto (see Documents, section 1). The Bureau had provided emergency relief (to whites as well as blacks) and would help to enforce the new rights and establish new institutions, such as public schools.[48]

Congress laid down requirements for new state constitutions, including universal male suffrage and acceptance of the Fourteenth Amendment. It proposed the Fifteenth Amendment, which prohibited racial exclusion from voting, and passed enforcement legislation. In 1875, Congress mandated equal access to public accommodations.

An electoral crisis following disputed elections in Louisiana and South Carolina was ended by the Hayes-Tilden agreement of 1877, which is thought of as the end of Reconstruction. Federal troops were withdrawn from the capitals of those states, decisive electoral votes were assigned to the Republican candidate, and federal supervision of southern elections was subsequently ended.

Over the next generation, through force, fraud, and various legal devices, blacks were driven from political participation, and the federal government declined to intervene.[49] While some freedmen migrated to cities, most became sharecroppers on land that had been restored to its original owners. The lynching of blacks was widely practiced, reaching a peak in the 1890s, when a lynching occurred every two or three days. Antilynching legislation, frequently proposed, never made it through both houses of Congress.[50] White supremacy was violently reestablished. Racial segregation was imposed and was sanctified by *Plessy v. Ferguson* in 1896.[51]

Long before *Plessy*, however, much Reconstruction law had been undermined by the Supreme Court. The Court would not accept the expansion of federal power that was mandated by the constitutional amendments. The Fourteenth Amendment was limited severely; guarantees of voting rights against private parties' violent interference was nullified; and public accommodations were treated as immune to federal regulation.[52]

The Court's decisions did much to defeat Reconstruction, but more sympathetic judicial action would not have prevented its demise. In the South, wealth and political power were concentrated in the planter class—those who possessed the largest land holdings. So long as they retained so much of the land and blacks were forced to work it for them,[53] the planters would maintain economic and political dominance.

A reconstruction program with a reasonable hope of ensuring blacks and poor whites the opportunity to effectively exercise their nominal rights would have had to end planter control of the South. It would have included land reform: the confiscation of large land holdings and some distribution to the freedmen.[54]

Freedmen wanted control over their own work and the products of their labor. They recognized that their labor had paid for the land, had cleared it, and had earned cash for the crops they raised upon it.[55] Their demands and expectations — forty good acres — appear quite reasonable. They had a just claim to compensation from those to whom they had been enslaved, and the means of compensation were available: the very land they had worked as slaves. Their land reform proposals were supported by some poor whites, who likewise sought land; by some agents of the Freemen's Bureau, who were authorized by law to redistribute some land, and did so when possible; and by some prominent political leaders who endorsed large-scale land reform.[56]

Land was available. A great deal of land in the West and South was owned by the federal government; much acreage was abandoned during the war; and much land was seized for nonpayment of taxes. In addition, a vast amount was potentially subject to confiscation[57] (see Documents, section 1).

Before the war ended, some plantation land came under black control. When the U.S. Navy occupied Port Royal, South Carolina, in 1861, most whites fled and the thousands of slaves who remained raised food crops for their own consumption. For a time it seemed that the land would remain in their possession. In 1862, after the 10,000-acre plantation at Davis Bend, Mississippi, was abandoned by its owner, slaves took it over. The following year General Grant authorized their development of an autonomous community, which became a refuge for displaced freedmen, who there grew cotton profitably on a large scale for several years. In 1865, General Sherman allocated the Sea Islands and coastal land south of Charleston to freedmen, each family to have forty acres and the loan of a mule (see Documents, section 1). Forty thousand blacks soon settled on the 400,000 acres that were available. They were led to believe the land was theirs. The Freedmen's Bureau gained control of more than 850,000 acres of abandoned land. Authorized by federal law to rent abandoned and confiscated land in forty-acre lots for eventual sale at long-term credit, it distributed some land to freedmen. Some southern Reconstruction governments also addressed the issue. The most ambitious program was established by South Carolina, which purchased and resold land on long-term credit, enabling 14,000 black families to acquire homesteads permanently.[58]

In 1865 Thaddeus Stevens proposed a comprehensive program that would have involved seizing 400 million acres that were owned by the wealthiest 10 percent of southern landowners. Forty acres would have been allocated to each adult freedman and the remaining 90 percent of the acreage to be seized would have been sold in lots of no more than 500 acres. The proceeds would have provided pensions for Civil War veterans, compensation to loyal unionists for property losses in the war, and retirement of the national debt. This program would have made possible a genuine reconstruction of the South. It would have broken the planters' oligarchic control and promoted widely diffused wealth and political power. But in 1866 Stevens's proposal was rejected by Congress, which enacted instead the Southern Homestead Act[59] (see Documents, section 1).

Most of the land that seemed to have been transferred to freedmen was auctioned to investors and speculators or returned to its former owners. In 1863 and 1864, most of the land near Port Royal that slaves had been allowed to take over was auctioned off by government agents, and only a couple of thousand freedmen were able to retain land. In 1878, the Davis Bend property was returned to the Davis family. In violation of federal legislation, President Johnson ordered that all land that had been distributed be returned to its previous owners. Blacks appealed, to no avail. When they tried to retain such land, the U.S. Army removed them by force.[60]

Thus Reconstruction established the legal basis of some basic rights for 4 million African Americans who had lacked any such rights at all, and it secured at least some of those rights, if only temporarily. Freedmen were aided in fending off some of the brutal violence to which they were subjected. Blacks, including ex-slaves, voted and held public office.[61] State governments were reformed. Public schools and hospitals were established. When Reconstruction ended, many of these advances were reversed. By the early twentieth century, blacks were once again excluded from political participation and consigned to the lowest social and economic orders. The South was permitted to ignore federal law and to create a new, distinctively brutal form of white supremacy.[62]

During the seventeenth and eighteenth centuries, the colonies created and the new nation resolved to protect the system of racial subjugation and exploitation that we know as chattel slavery. The abolition of that system in the nineteenth century represents a significant shift in U.S. public policy. Reconstruction was an attempt to carry that reformation further. It was, however, aborted. The United States officially committed itself to civil rights for blacks, but it failed to enforce its own laws. As in the eighteenth century, the nation's public policy fell tragically short of its promises and pretensions. The opportunity to address white supremacy was permitted to pass, the freedmen were betrayed, a brutally oppressive regime was permitted to replace chattel slavery, and the need for a Second Reconstruction soon became evident to people of good will.[63]

The Second Reconstruction

Reconstruction did not end all at once. Despite the pressures, fraud, and violence, many freedmen continued to vote, some were elected to public office, and they persisted in their struggle for economic and political autonomy. For a while it appeared that they would create an effective political coalition with poor whites in the People's Party, but the arrangement proved to be unstable. Even so, great effort and brutality were required to exclude African Americans from the public sphere and to minimize their economic independence.[64]

By the turn of the century, white supremacy had acquired a new form, known as Jim Crow. The southern states adopted new constitutions along with various legal devices to ensure the exclusion of blacks from the ballot box and public office: the white primary, the poll tax, the understanding requirement, and others. These devices supplemented terror, of which lynching was the horrific, frequently public representative. Once Jim Crow was firmly established, lynching declined gradually. Political power had been restored to economically powerful whites. Increasing numbers of freedmen migrated to urban areas, but most became locked as sharecroppers in a modified plantation system. The federal government averted its eyes. Its Reconstruction amendments and civil rights legislation were all but dead letters.[65] Although occasionally inconvenienced by legal challenges, the Jim Crow system survived into the second half of the twentieth century.

Following World War Two, however, several developments threatened the racist regime. Black veterans returned to civilian life determined to realize the nation's democratic promises. Wartime propaganda against racism had generated more enlightened attitudes among whites. The newly founded United Nations embraced a Universal Declaration of Human Rights. Colonial liberation movements gave rise to independent nations whose populations of color were appalled at Jim Crow in America, which film and video made more visible than ever. Cold War competition between the United States and the USSR led American statesmen to deplore such unfavorable images of our domestic arrangements, especially the brutal suppression by police and other public servants of peaceful civil rights demonstrations. In this confluence of circumstances, challenges to Jim Crow began to achieve success, despite lethal violence (indeed, sometimes because of lethal violence — when it took the lives of white civil rights workers).[66]

With the *Brown* decision of 1954,[67] the federal judiciary began seriously to contemplate vigorous enforcement of blacks' civil rights. By the mid-1960s, Congress felt obliged to enact significant civil rights legislation, including the Civil Rights Act of 1964, the Voting Rights Act of 1965, the Fair Housing Act of 1968, and the Equal Employment Act of 1972. During the same period, increasing embarrassment and concern about the scandal of widespread poverty within the affluent United States[68] contributed to the creation of public programs such as food stamps, Medicare (for the elderly and disabled), Medicaid (for children and the poor), Supplemental Security Income (serving needy aged, disabled, and blind Americans), the Comprehensive Employment and Training Act (subsidizing low-wage jobs in nonprofit and public settings), and Head Start (a preschool program for poor children). Some existing programs, such as Aid to Families with Dependent Children (or "welfare"),[69] were expanded. Because of African Americans' disproportionate share of economic disadvantages, such programs are of special relevance here.

Like the First Reconstruction, the Second involved significant departures from established public policy. The nation committed itself (once again) to equal rights, antidiscrimination law was enacted and enforced, and southern blacks were enabled to vote and hold public office. Blacks faced new opportunities not only in education but also in skilled trades and the professions. Political rhetoric was reformed: explicitly racist appeals became unacceptable, at least for mainstream candidates, and explicitly racist comments were no longer found in public policy statements. Overt discrimination and antiblack violence were reduced.[70] White supremacy was officially rejected. And, unlike those from the First Reconstruction, these changes have come to seem irreversible.

There are other, less fortunate parallels between the First and the Second Reconstruction. Criticism of government aid to blacks resembled that of the nineteenth century, to the point of regarding such measures as discrimination against whites. By the early 1980s, government policy had reduced interventions on behalf of blacks and government assistance was reduced.[71] But the chief similarity is their failure to undo much of the inequitable legacy of slavery and Jim Crow — the entrenched disadvantages of African Americans.

After slavery, freedmen with minimal resources, facing overt discrimination, were driven into peonage or menial urban occupations, while nutritional, educational, and medical programs that had been created mainly to aid them were eliminated.[72] Generation after generation, the vast majority of African Americans entered working lives without a decent share of the nation's resources and with significantly lower life prospects than their white peers.[73] After Jim Crow, anti-black discrimination was lessened and opportunities for blacks were increased. But nutritional, educational, medical, employment, and housing programs that were developed in the 1960s likewise faced cutbacks, which were severe by the 1980s and are continuing today. For example, the real benefits of Medicare and Medicaid have been reduced.[74] Government continues to resist the development of comprehensive medical insurance, and thus preventive medicine, which is now unavailable for 40-odd million.[75] Federal subsidies for low-income families to rent private housing have decreased.[76] The Comprehensive Employment and Training Act programs have ended.[77] Eligibility for food stamps has been restricted. Aid to Families with Dependent Children has been eliminated; its replacement, Temporary Assistance to Needy Families, sets lifetime limits on receipt of aid, requires more work from mothers of young children, and denies four-year college study as a means to improved employment.[78] Despite such work requirements, the government has made woefully inadequate provision for child day care.[79]

Most important, the social programs of the twentieth century have failed to address the deep, systemic character of Jim Crow's legacy. African Americans entered the Second Reconstruction with wealth, income, and life prospects disproportionately lower than that of their white peers. Despite less overt discrimination and more school and job opportunities, that deficit remains substantial.[80] For example, blacks' life expectancy is substantially less than that of whites; blacks have significantly inferior access to health care; they have substantially higher unemployment rates; and past discrimination has left African Americans with radically lower net worth and financial assets.[81] This *wealth gap* is most significant, for the life prospects of children depend on their parents' assets more than on their income. Between generations, there is less upward mobility for blacks than for whites and more downward mobility.[82]

Consider one of the clearest legacies of Jim Crow: residential segregation. The black ghetto has been a feature of U.S. cities with substantial black populations for as long as anyone who is alive today might remember. But the black ghetto did not exist until the twentieth century; it was a product of Jim Crow. More severe in the North than the South, its creation was occasioned by increasing black migration to the cities and was exacerbated by the lack of housing construction during World War Two.[83]

The black urban ghetto resulted most directly from, or was intensified by, actions of home owners, real estate agents and associations, mortgage and insurance providers, local officials, and federal agencies. The means used began with violence but expanded to restrictive covenants, boycotts of real estate agents who served blacks, realtors' systematic diversion of black clients from white communities, "redlining," "blockbusting," government support for highways serving white suburbs, public housing policies (regarding their location and clientele), and resistance to integration by local officials when the prospect of integration arises.[84]

By 1940, the isolation of blacks within segregated urban communities was greater than had ever been experienced by any other ethnic group in America. European newcomers initially lived in communities of immigrants that were ethnically heterogeneous; most lived outside such enclaves, and the condition was temporary. Not so for African Americans. Following World War Two, as white suburbs expanded, black ghettos increased in size and density, giving rise to what sociologists call "hypersegregation." And, in further contrast with other groups, income does not significantly ameliorate residential segregation for blacks.[85]

Hypersegregation persists, and it deepens Jim Crow's legacy. Public policies can adversely affect the black urban ghetto without hurting a significant number of whites. Diverting public services from the ghetto can seem politically prudent to politicians who rely primarily on the votes of whites, whose communities reap the diverted benefits. Poorly endowed public schools are familiar features of the ghetto, along with less adequate public transportation for those who most need it. As poverty is more concentrated among blacks, it is most concentrated in the black urban ghetto, along with unemployment, the withdrawal of commercial institutions, and the reduced maintenance of real property. Social contacts with whites are minimized, along with job opportunities and business networking.[86]

Public policies have intensified the ghettoization of blacks. Redlining was not invented by federal agencies, but it was institutionalized by the Home Owners Loan Corporation, the Federal Housing Administration, and the Veterans Administration. "Slum clearance" programs destabilized conditions in the ghetto. Many public housing projects, typically high-density, were located within or adjacent to existing ghettos, and as they accommodated fewer ghetto dwellers than slum clearance displaced, more pressure was placed upon housing in the ghetto. The segregation policies of public housing authorities ensured that black isolation would be promoted further. Just when public housing authorities were ordered to stop promoting segregation, funding for public housing was halted.[87]

Federal legislation has addressed housing discrimination: the Fair Housing

Act of 1968, which was strengthened in 1988; the Housing and Community Development Act of 1974; the Home Mortgage Disclosure Act of 1975; and the Community Reinvestment Act of 1977. But with inadequate resources devoted to their weak enforcement provisions, and with resistance by Realtors and local politicians, these measures have had minimal effect.[88]

Blockbusting and white flight can occur only when some communities are maintained as white domains. When housing discrimination was prohibited, real estate agents developed covert measures to divert black renters and home buyers from white communities. Such discriminatory practices can be identified, but private, nonprofit organizations have carried the burden of doing so. Their effective but labor-intensive "audits" were substantially reduced with the end of CETA (Comprehensive Employment and Training Act), which had supported a variety of community-based antipoverty jobs.[89]

Residential segregation and its associated evils are especially important for present purposes, because they have contributed most substantially to the wealth gap, for private housing is the principal financial asset of most families in the United States, white or black. The policies that have promoted or tolerated residential segregation have thus helped entrench the legacy of slavery and Jim Crow.

Now, fifty years after the emergence to the wider public view of the civil rights movement, we find poverty continuing disproportionately among African Americans. We also find a reduction and weakening of those public policies and social programs that might plausibly be regarded as addressing the systematic disadvantages that constitute the legacy of Jim Crow.

Postscript: Addressing the Legacy

Racial subordination in the United States did not end with the abolition of slavery. After Reconstruction was abandoned, racial subordination was preserved under Jim Crow, largely contrary to law. Jim Crow continued well into the second half of the twentieth century.

Slavery and Jim Crow imposed massive material deprivation and left entrenched systems of disadvantage and indignity, which the Second Reconstruction never fully addressed.[90] These conditions are not distant echoes of a slave system that ended a century and a half ago. The system of racial subjugation that began in slavery was continued under Jim Crow until the relatively recent past, and the wrongs of neither slavery nor Jim Crow have been fully undone. Corrective justice is required to eliminate the deeply entrenched, persisting racial hierarchy.

As the history we have reviewed reveals, racial subordination and its consequences were not the result of private decisions but rested crucially on public policy. Whatever else corrective justice may require, it calls for a national rectification project to eliminate the inequities that flow from past public policies. Corrective justice requires a comprehensive set of programs dedicated to that end. Nothing less is conscionable.[91]

Notes

This is a revised and shortened version of "Unfinished Business: Racial Junctures in U.S. History and Their Legacy," in M. T. Martin and M. Yaquinto, *America's Unpaid Debt*, 11–47; also published in Meyer, *Justice in Time*, 271–298. Copyright © David Lyons 2005.

1. I consider only Virginia in this section. Virginia was the first British colony in North America to import Africans for labor and became the leading mainland British colony with a slave-based economy. For the "20 and odd Negroes" at Jamestown, see Kingsbury, *The Records of the Virginia Company of London*, 3: 243.
2. Blackburn, *The Making of New World Slavery*, 230, 256–258; Kolchin, *American Slavery*, 8–10; Nash, *Red, White, and Black*, 51.
3. Berlin, *Many Thousands Gone*, 109–110, 143–144; Blackburn, *The Making of New World Slavery*, 315–322; Kolchin, *American Slavery*, 10–14; Nash, *Red, White, and Black*, 154–158.
4. See *Re Edward Mozingo* (1672) and *Moore v. Light* (1673), in Finkelman, *The Law of Freedom and Bondage*, 13.
5. J. A. Bush, "The British Constitution and the Creation of American Slavery," in Finkelman, *Slavery and the Law*, 379–418. In 1624 the king revoked Virginia's charter and it became a Crown colony, but that made no effective difference to the colony's autonomy.
6. Hening, ed., *The Statutes at large*, 2: 170.
7. Morris, *Southern Slavery and the Law*, 43; Blackburn, *The Making of New World Slavery*, 265–266.
8. This doctrine accompanied Europeans in their colonial adventures. Thus in the fifteenth century Portugal and Spain were authorized by the pope to kill or enslave infidels. "Bull Romanus Pontifex of Pope Nicholas V, January 8, 1455," in Ehler and Morrall, *Church and State throughout the Centuries*, 144–151; "Bull Inter Caetera of Alexander VI, May 3, 1493," in Davenport, *European Treaties*, 60–63. In somewhat similar terms, Henry VII authorized the Cabots' voyage across the Atlantic. "The First Letters Patent Granted to John Cabot and His Sons, 5 March 1496," in Williamson, *The Cabot Voyages*, 204–205.
9. Blackburn, *The Making of New World Slavery*, 231–232, 240, 250; Higginbotham, *In the Matter of Color*, 20–21, 36–37; Kolchin, *American Slavery*, 15.
10. Hening, *The Statutes at Large*, 2: 260.
11. Ibid., 2: 270. Although this enactment identifies "negroes" as those bound to serve for life, other evidence noted here implies that some of the early African servants in the colonies did not serve for life.
12. Ibid., 2: 490–493.
13. This division of humanity became a feature of U.S. law as, for instance, Congress in 1790

limited naturalized citizenship to "white" persons. The restriction remained for nearly two centuries, save for the exception made for persons of African ancestry by the Naturalization and Enforcement Act of 1870.

14. Blackburn, *The Making of New World Slavery*, 228, 240, 266; Berlin, *Many Thousands Gone*, 29–46.

15. Berlin, *Many Thousands Gone*, 102–105; Blackburn, *The Making of New World Slavery*, 255, 258; Kolchin, *American Slavery*, 16–17.

16. Berlin, *Many Thousands Gone*, 29, 44–45.

17. Allen, *The Invention of the White Race*, 2: 3–21.

18. Berlin, *Many Thousands Gone*, 45; Higginbotham, *In the Matter of Color*, 26–30.

19. Berlin, *Many Thousands Gone*, 45; Washburn, *The Governor and the Rebel*, 80.

20. Two related interests might have increased African Americans' willingness to participate. On the one hand, insofar as they could envisage the possibility of achieving freedom, they too wanted land to be available; on the other hand, as legislation was extinguishing those prospects, they had grievances against the elite, who became targets of the rebellion.

21. Finkelman, *The Law of Freedom and Bondage*, 18.

22. Berlin, *Many Thousands Gone*, 44.

23. For contemporaneous alternatives, see Blackburn, *The Making of New World Slavery*, 350–363.

24. Article I, section 2, paragraph 3.

25. Finkelman, "Making a Covenant with Death," in *Slavery and the Founders*, n. 23, 199–200; Finkelman, "The Founders and Slavery," 413.

26. Article I, section 9, paragraph 1, and Article V, respectively.

27. Article IV, section 2, paragraph 3.

28. Cover, *Justice Accused*, 159–191.

29. Litwack, *North of Slavery*, 7–9.

30. Scott v. Sandford, 60 U.S. 393, 407 (1857).

31. Nash, *Red, White, and Black*, 7–20. Although racial stratification was entrenched and racism was widespread, many whites objected to slavery on self-interested or moral grounds.

32. Finkelman, *Slavery and the Founders*, 9; Finkelman, "The Founders and Slavery," 443–444.

33. Finkelman, *Slavery and the Founders*, 26–28; Finkelman, "The Founders and Slavery," 418, 421.

34. Finkelman, *Slavery and the Founders*, 22–34; Finkelman, "The Founders and Slavery," 433–441.

35. Finkelman, *Slavery and the Founders*, 429. The formula had been proposed under the Articles of Confederation as a basis for calculating a direct tax, but not as a basis for representation.

36. Finkelman, *Slavery and the Founders*, 10–20, 22–25; Finkelman, "The Founders and Slavery," 427–430.

37. Finkelman, *Slavery and the Founders*, 30–32; Finkelman, "The Founders and Slavery," 438–439. Northern states used "personal liberty laws" to impede enforcement of the Fugitive Slave Act. Morris, *Free Men All*. These efforts were halted by the Supreme Court in *Prigg v. Pennsylvania*, 41 U.S. 539 (1842).

38. In addition to the provisions mentioned, several others supported slavery, for example, Article I, section 8, paragraph 15, which conferred on Congress the authority to "suppress Insurrections," such as slave revolts. Finkelman, *Slavery and the Founders*, 7–8; Finkelman, "The Founders and Slavery," 439–443.

39. Nash, *Race and Revolution*, 37–42.
40. Finkelman, *Slavery and the Founders*, 26; Finkelman, "The Founders and Slavery," 432, 434. New England merchants profited from the trade in slaves and their products. Finkelman, *Slavery and the Founders*, 23.
41. Nash, *Race and Revolution*, 17–19; but see Finkelman, "The Founders and Slavery," 424–425.
42. Finkelman, "The Founders and Slavery," 425–445.
43. Nash, *Race and Revolution*, 28–29; Finkelman, "The Founders and Slavery," 415–416.
44. In the 1780s and for a few years thereafter—until the cotton gin changed all calculations. Nash, *Race and Revolution*, 36–37, 42–47; but see Ellis, *Founding Brothers*, 104–108.
45. Finkelman, *Slavery and the Founders*, 24; Ellis, *Founding Brothers*, 92. The convention did not pursue the idea, nor did Congress when Elbridge Gerry of Connecticut made such a proposal in 1790. As Ellis notes (86–87, 90, 105), "several emancipation schemes" were proposed from the 1770s on.
46. Nash, *Race and Revolution*, 36–37.
47. The Thirteenth Amendment to the U.S. Constitution, prohibiting slavery, was proposed and ratified in 1865, the same year the war ended.
48. Foner, *Reconstruction*, 68–70, 143–153, 157–170, 243–251.
49. Ibid., 575–601; Franklin, *Reconstruction after the Civil War*, 168–169, 174–175.
50. Dray, *At the Hands of Persons Unknown*; Zangrando, *The NAACP Crusade against Lynching*.
51. Foner, *Reconstruction*, 404–405, 537; Plessy v. Ferguson, 163 U.S. 537.
52. For limitations to the Fourteenth Amendment, see, especially, The Slaughterhouse Cases, 83 U.S. 36 (1973). Nullification of voting rights started with *U.S. v. Reese*, 92 U.S. 214 (1875). For public accommodations, see Civil Rights Cases, 109 U.S. 3 (1883).
53. During Reconstruction, freedmen worked as wage laborers under white drivers; as tenants, for a set rent; or as sharecroppers, for a portion of the crop. Many chose sharecropping because it seemed to afford the most autonomy; most blacks who remained in agricultural labor, as most freedmen did, became sharecroppers. After Reconstruction, however, when planters controlled the accounts and could cheat with impunity, sharecroppers became mired in debt. Foner, *Reconstruction*, 103–109, 171–175, 404–405, 537.
54. Foner (ibid., 109) remarks that effective land reform would also have required access to reasonable credit and to markets.
55. Ibid., 105, 160–164, 374–374.
56. Ibid., 68–69, 302, 309–310, 329.
57. Ibid., 51.
58. Ibid., 58–59, 69–70, 78–79, 158–159, 329.
59. Ibid., 234–236, 246, 308–309.
60. Ibid., 52–53, 159–164. Johnson also vetoed a bill that would have facilitated land reform (51).
61. For a brief account, see Franklin and Moss, *From Slavery to Freedom*, 227–231, 237–244. Until this century, of course, women were excluded from the suffrage.
62. Foner, *Reconstruction*, 587–601.
63. Franklin and Moss, *From Slavery to Freedom*, 211–219; Foner, *Reconstruction*, 582–612.
64. Woodward, *The Strange Career of Jim Crow*, 53, 65; Marable, *Race, Reform, and Rebellion*, 9–11.
65. Woodward, *The Strange Career of Jim Crow*, 82–93; President's Committee on Civil Rights, *To Secure These Rights*, 35–40.

66. V. Harding, R. D. G. Kelley, and E. Lewis, "We Changed the World," in Kelley and Lewis, *To Make Our World Anew*, 452–454, 513–514; Woodward, *The Strange Career of Jim Crow*, 130–134; Marable, *Race, Reform, and Rebellion*, 86–87.

67. Brown v. Board of Education of Topeka Kansas, 347 U.S. 483.

68. See, e.g., Harrington, *The Other America*.

69. Formerly Aid to Dependent Children, established under the Social Security Act of 1935.

70. Marable, *Race, Reform, and Rebellion*, 149–150.

71. Ibid., 152, 207–213, 221.

72. Foner, *Reconstruction*, 587–601.

73. President's Committee on Civil Rights, *To Secure These Rights*, 53–79.

74. Harding et al., "We Changed the World," 599. But note that Medicaid has been expanded for children.

75. Ibid., 130.

76. Massey and Denton, *American Apartheid*, 231.

77. Ibid., 230; Harding et al., "We Changed the World," 599.

78 Harding et al.,"We Changed the World," 599.

79. Ibid.

80. Marable, *Race, Reform, and Rebellion*, 227–230.

81. On life expectancy, see G. E. Sandefur et al., "An Overview of Racial and Ethnic Demographic Trends," in Smelser, Wilson, and Mitchell, *America Becoming*, 1: 40, 82–83. On access to health care, see R. S. Kingston and H. W. Nickens, "Racial and Ethnic Differences in Health: Recent Trends, Current Patterns, Future Prospects," in *America Becoming*, 2: 253, 281. On unemployment, see H. J. Holzer, "Racial Differences in Labor Market Outcomes among Men," in *America Becoming*, 2: 98–110. On financial status, see M. L. Oliver and T. M. Shapiro, "Wealth and Racial Stratification," in *America Becoming*, 2: 222, 228, 231.

82. Oliver and Shapiro, *Black Wealth/White Wealth*, 158.

83. Massey and Denton, *American Apartheid*, 42–49.

84. Ibid. 26–42, 51–52, 55–57. Redlining identifies black neighborhoods, within which loans are denied. In blockbusting, blacks are brought into a neighborhood, leading intolerant whites to leave; more blacks are brought in, leading less intolerant whites to leave; and so on, while blacks gain housing at inflated rents and prices.

85. Ibid., 32f, 74–78, 84–88.

86. Ibid., 153–60; Denton, "The Role of Residential Segregation," 1–13.

87. Massey and Denton, *American Apartheid*, 51–59, 227.

88. Ibid., 230–234.

89. Ibid., 229–230.

90. Oliver and Shapiro, *Black Wealth/White Wealth*, 90, 152–170.

91. For a discussion of reparations and corrective justice, see my "Corrective Justice, Equal Opportunity, and the Legacy of Slavery and Jim Crow," 84 *Boston University Law Review* 1375 (2004).

Bibliography

Allen, Theodore W. *The Invention of the White Race*. New York: Verso, 1994–1997.

Berlin, Ira. *Many Thousands Gone: The First Two Centuries of Slavery in North America*. Cambridge, Mass.: Harvard University Press, 1998.

Blackburn, Robin. *The Making of New World Slavery: From the Baroque to the Modern 1492–1800*. New York: Verso, 1998.

Cover, Robert M. *Justice Accused: Antislavery and the Judicial Process*. New Haven: Yale University Press, 1975.

Davenport, Frances G., ed. *European Treaties Bearing on the History of the United States and Its Dependencies*. Gloucester, Mass.: Peter Smith, 1967.

Denton, Nancy. "The Role of Residential Segregation in Promoting and Maintaining Inequality in Wealth and Property," 34 *Indiana Law Review* 1206 (2001): 1–13.

Dray, Philip. *At the Hands of Persons Unknown: The Lynching of Black America*. New York: Random House, 2002.

Ehler, Sidney Z., and John B. Morrall, trans. and eds. *Church and State through the Centuries: A Collection of Historic Documents with Commentaries*. Westminster, Md.: Newman Press, 1954.

Ellis, Joseph. *Founding Brothers: The Revolutionary Generation*. New York: Vintage, 2002.

Finkelman, Paul. "The Founders and Slavery," 13 *Yale Journal of Law and the Humanities* 413 (2001): 413–49.

———, ed. *The Law of Freedom and Bondage: A Casebook*. New York: Oceana Publications, 1986.

———. *Slavery and the Founders*. 2nd ed. New York: M. E. Sharpe, 2001.

———, ed. *Slavery and the Law: Race and Liberty in the Age of Jefferson*. Madison, Wisc.: Madison House, 1997.

Foner, Eric. *Reconstruction 1863–1877: America's Unfinished Revolution*. New York: Harper and Row, 1988.

Franklin, John Hope. *Reconstruction after the Civil War*. Chicago: University of Chicago Press, 1994.

Franklin, John Hope, and Alfred A. Moss Jr. *From Slavery to Freedom: A History of African Americans*. New York: McGraw-Hill, 1994.

Harrington, Michael. *The Other America: Poverty in the United States*. New York: Macmillan, 1962.

Hening, William Waller, ed. *The Statutes at large, being a collection of all the laws of Virginia, from the first session of the legislature, in the year 1619*. 13 vols. Richmond, Va.: Samuel Pleasants and others, 1809–1823.

Higginbotham, A. Leon, Jr. *In The Matter of Color: Race and the American Legal Process: The Colonial Period*. New York: Oxford University Press, 1978.

Kelley, Robin D. G., and Earl Lewis, eds. *To Make Our World Anew: A History of African Americans*. New York: Oxford University Press, 2000.

Kingsbury, Susan Myra, ed. *The Records of the Virginia Company of London*. 4 vols. Washington, D.C.: U.S. Government Printing Office, 1906–1935.

Kolchin, Peter. *American Slavery 1619–1877*. New York: Hill and Wang, 1995.

Litwack, Leon F. *North of Slavery: The Negro in the Free States, 1790–1860*. Chicago: University of Chicago Press, 1961.

Marable, Manning. *Race, Reform, and Rebellion: The Second Reconstruction in Black America, 1945–1990*. Jackson: University Press of Mississippi, 1991.

Martin, Michael T., and Marilyn Yaquinto, eds. *America's Unpaid Debt: Slavery and Racial Justice*. Bowling Green, Ohio: Department of Ethnic Studies, 2003.

Massey, Douglas S., and Nancy A. Denton. *American Apartheid: Segregation and the Making of the Underclass*. Cambridge, Mass.: Harvard University Press, 1993.

Meyer, Lukas H., ed. *Justice in Time: Responding to Historical Injustice.* Baden-Baden: NOMOS Verlagsgesellschaft, 2004.

Morris, Thomas D. *Free Men All: The Personal Liberty Laws of the North, 1780–1861.* Baltimore: Johns Hopkins University Press, c. 1974.

———. *Southern Slavery and the Law, 1619–1860.* Chapel Hill: University of North Carolina Press, 1996.

Nash, Gary B. *Race and Revolution.* Madison, Wisc.: Madison House, 1990.

———. *Red, White, and Black: The Peoples of Early North America.* Upper Saddle River, N.J.: Prentice-Hall, 2000.

Oliver, Melvin L., and Thomas M. Shapiro. *Black Wealth/White Wealth: A New Perspective on Racial Inequality.* New York: Routledge, 1997.

President's Committee on Civil Rights. *To Secure These Rights: Report of the President's Committee on Civil Rights.* Washington, D.C.: U.S. Government Printing Office, 1947.

Smelser, Neil J., William Julius Wilson, and Faith Mitchell, eds. *America Becoming: Racial Trends and Their Consequences.* 2 vols. Washington, D.C.: National Academy Press, 2001.

Washburn, Wilcomb E. *The Governor and the Rebel: A History of Bacon's Rebellion in Virginia.* New York: Norton, 1972.

Williamson, James Alexander, ed. *The Cabot Voyages and Bristol Discovery under Henry VII.* Cambridge, England: Cambridge University Press, 1962.

Woodward, C. Vann. *The Strange Career of Jim Crow.* New York: Oxford University Press, 1974.

Zangrando, Robert L. *The NAACP Crusade against Lynching, 1909–1950.* Philadelphia: Temple University Press 1980.

Race Preferences and Race Privileges

MICHAEL K. BROWN, MARTIN CARNOY,
ELLIOTT CURRIE, TROY DUSTER, DAVID B. OPPENHEIMER,
MARJORIE M. SHULTZ, AND DAVID WELLMAN

At the beginning of the twentieth century, the African American leader and scholar W. E. B. Du Bois declared that the "problem of the twentieth century" was "the problem of the color line." Today, as a new century begins, race is still a pervasive and troubling fault line running through American life. We are not divided because we fail to "get along," as Rodney King lamented after the Los Angeles riots a decade ago. Nor is it because diehard advocates of affirmative action insist on stirring up racial discord. What divides Americans is profound disagreement over the legacy of the civil rights movement. At the core of our national debate are very different opinions about the meaning of race in contemporary America and the prospects for racial equality in the future.

The crude racial prejudice of the Jim Crow era has been discredited and replaced by a new understanding of race and racial inequality. This new understanding began with a backlash against the Great Society and took hold after the Reagan-Bush revolution in the 1980s. The current set of beliefs about race rests on three tenets held by many white Americans. First, they believe the civil rights revolution was successful, and they wholeheartedly accept the principles enshrined in civil rights laws. They assume civil rights laws ended racial inequality by striking down legal segregation and outlawing discrimination against workers and voters. They think racism has been eradicated even though racist hotheads can still be found throughout America. While potentially dangerous, racial extremists are considered a tiny minority who occupy political space only on the fringes of mainstream white America.

Second, if vestiges of racial inequality persist, they believe that is because blacks have failed to take advantage of opportunities created by the civil rights revolution. In their view, if blacks are less successful than whites, it is not because America is still a racist society. In fact, a substantial majority believe that black Americans do not try hard enough to succeed and "with the connivance of government, they take what they have not earned."[1]

Finally, most white Americans think the United States is rapidly becoming a color-blind society, and they see little need or justification for affirmative action or other color-conscious policies. Inspired by the ideals so eloquently expressed in Martin Luther King Jr.'s "I have a dream" speech, they embrace his vision of a color-blind America and look forward to the day when race will not determine one's fate, when a person is evaluated, in King's words, by the content of one's character rather than the color of one's skin.

Jim Sleeper echoes these sentiments. Author of a caustic critique of white liberals and civil rights leaders, he rejects any suggestion that Du Bois's warning is still relevant to America's racial divide. The nation's future lies in a color-blind society, he believes, and "it is America's destiny to show the world how to eliminate racial differences — culturally, morally, and even physically — as factors in human striving."[2] If Americans remain racially divided, he asserts, it is because we have abandoned "the great achievement of the civil rights era — the hopeful consensus that formed in the 1960s around King's vision of a single, shared community." Tamar Jacoby agrees. The author of a lengthy study of racial conflict in three cities, she attributes the failure to create a color-blind society to a "new" black separatism and the "condescension of well-meaning whites who think that they are advancing race relations by encouraging alienation and identity politics."[3]

On the surface at least, these beliefs about race are compelling. They appeal to widely held principles like fairness and equality of opportunity, diminishing the differences between liberals and conservatives. More important, they also resonate with the experiences of many white Americans. In an era when economic inequality is growing, when many families stand still financially despite earning two and sometimes three incomes, these beliefs provide a convenient explanation for their circumstances. Historically, class inequality has exacerbated racial inequality, and the present is no different. The idea that lazy blacks get government handouts inflames white men whose real wages barely increased during the 1990s economic boom. And for whites turned away from elite colleges and professional schools that accept African Americans, these notions provide an outlet for deep resentment.[4]

The goal of a color-blind America is an old and cherished idea. When segregation was legal and racial classification determined where one sat or drank or worked or lived or went to school, color-blindness meant abolishing the color-coded laws of southern apartheid. Color-blindness was the opposite of Jim Crow. It was liberals who championed the idea of color-blindness in the 1960s, while conservatives were ardent defenders of racial segregation.[5] Thirty-five years ago many Americans, inspired by the civil rights movement's transcendent vision of an inclusive society, passionately searched for solutions to the problem of racial inequality. While nationalists on both ends were often strident, apocalyptic, and pessimistic, the liberal architects of color-blind politics were optimistic and confident that this approach would generate greater equality between the races.

The triumph of the civil rights movement, however, exposed the limits of color-blind social policy: What good were civil rights if one was too poor to use them? As Martin Luther King Jr. told his aide Bayard Rustin after the explosion in Watts, "I worked to get these people the right to eat hamburgers, and now I've got to do something . . . to help them get the money to buy it."[6] And in a posthumously published essay, he wrote about what it would take to achieve a genuinely inclusive society. His vision went beyond color-blind civil rights laws: "Many whites who concede that Negroes should have equal access to public facilities and the untrammeled right to vote cannot understand that we do not intend to remain in the basement of the economic structure; they cannot understand why a porter or housemaid would dare dream of a day when his work will be more useful, more remunerative and a pathway to rising opportunity. This incomprehension is a heavy burden in our efforts to win white allies for the long struggle."[7]

Too many whites in America have failed to heed Martin Luther King Jr.'s warning of what it would take to achieve a genuinely inclusive society. Writing twenty-five years after *Brown v. Board of Education* was decided, Judge Robert L. Carter, who argued the case before the Supreme Court alongside Thurgood Marshall, observed, "It was not until *Brown I* was decided that blacks were able to understand that the fundamental vice was not legally enforced *racial segregation* itself; that this was a mere by-product, a symptom of the greater and more pernicious disease—white supremacy." Unlike those who believe that the dream of integration was subverted by color-conscious policies, Carter pointed out that "white supremacy is no mere regional contamination. It infects us nationwide," he wrote, "and remains in the basic virus that has debilitated blacks' efforts to secure equality in this country."[8]

With the clarity of hindsight, we can now see that it was naïve to believe America could wipe out three hundred years of physical, legal, cultural, spiritual, and political oppression based on race in a mere thirty years. The belief, even the hope, that the nation would glide into color-blindness was foolish. Indeed, there are good reasons to believe the current goal of a color-blind society is at least as naïve as the optimism of the 1960s and conveniently masks color-coded privileges.

The conflict over color-conscious public policies poses a powerful challenge: the issue in the debate goes beyond the future of specific policies to the very meaning of racial equality and inclusion. Advocates of color-blind policies believe that the defenders of color-conscious remedies to achieve racial justice are separatists who practice "identity politics." They oppose race-conscious solutions on the grounds that racial inclusion requires only that individuals be treated similarly under the law — no more, no less.

Those of us who disagree wonder whether it would be fair, even if it were possible and desirable, to now use color-blind and race-neutral criteria when people apply for jobs, adoptions, home loans or second mortgages, and college admissions. Racial equality requires social and political changes that go beyond superficially equal access or treatment.

Today, many white Americans are concerned only with whether they are, individually, guilty of something called racism. Having examined their souls and concluded that they are not personally guilty of any direct act of discrimination, many whites convince themselves that they are not racists and then wash their hands of the problem posed by persistent racial inequality. This predilection to search for personal guilt has been reinforced by a Supreme Court that analogously locates the constitutional problem of racial injustice solely in an individual's intent to discriminate.

But if Americans go no deeper than an inquiry into personal guilt, we will stumble backward into the twenty-first century, having come no closer to solving the problem of the color line. Given America's history, why should anyone be surprised to find white privilege so woven into the unexamined institutional practices, habits of mind, and received truths that Americans can barely see it? After three decades of simply admitting Asian American, Latino American, and African American individuals into institutions that remain static in terms of culture, values, and practices, the inadequacy of that solution should be obvious.

The proponents of color-blind policies and their critics have very different understandings of race and of the causes of racial inequality. People's views on these questions have become polarized, meaningful exchange is rare, and the public policy debate has stalemated. For these reasons we think it is time to get beyond the debate over affirmative action or individual guilt and try to figure out why racial inequality continues to be an intractable American problem. Toward that end, we take a careful look at the emerging public understanding of race and racism in America. By thoroughly scrutinizing this evolving perspective and then comparing it to an alternative view, we want to show what is at stake in the current American debate over racial equality and inclusion.

The Emerging Racial Paradigm

In the past few years a number of books have appeared that elaborate and refine the new popular understanding of race and racial inequality in America. Besides Jim Sleeper's *Liberal Racism* (1997) and Tamar Jacoby's *Someone Else's House* (1998), these include Dinesh D'Souza's *The End of Racism* (1995), Shelby Steele's *A Dream Deferred* (1999), and, most important, Stephen and Abigail Thernstrom's *America in Black and White: One Nation Indivisible* (1997). These books are promoted as reasoned and factually informed discussions of race in America. All of the authors give this emerging understanding of race and racism the appearance of scholarly heft and intellectual legitimacy. And they represent a diverse set of political positions. Sleeper is a self-identified liberal who believes that color-conscious policies dodge the "reality of social class divisions, which are arguably more fundamental than racial divisions in perpetuating social injustice." D'Souza, Jacoby, Steele, and the Thernstroms are conservatives.[9] Yet all might be identified as "racial realists," as Alan Wolfe calls the proponents of this perspective.

Although each of these authors has written a very different book about race, all set out to demolish the claims of color-conscious policy advocates and anyone who suggests that racial discrimination is a persistent American problem. Sleeper chastises liberals, either those who protest police mistreatment of blacks or *New York Times* editorial writers that hold African Americans to lower standards of behavior and accomplishment than whites. Jacoby argues that most of the blame for the failure of integration lies with blacks. And the Thernstroms' book is a not so subtle rejoinder to both the Kerner Commission's national report on race in America, issued in the aftermath of the 1960s urban upheavals, and Andrew Hacker's *Two Nations: Black and White, Separate, Hostile, Unequal* (1992).

The Kerner Commission concluded that "our nation is moving toward two societies, one black, one white—separate and unequal." Hacker updated the Kerner Commission's assessment and provided substantial data documenting the differing conditions and fates of black and white Americans. The Thernstroms wade into the debate accusing critics of the racial status quo like Hacker of polemical posturing. They claim that, by contrast, their analysis complies with standards of neutrality and is committed to factual reporting. *America in Black and White*, the Thernstroms assert, is a treatise that overcomes ideology and addresses the hard truths. Their stated aim is to move beyond dichotomies, to find more complicated options, to construct an analysis that transcends race.

Racial realists make three related claims. First, they say that America has made great progress in rectifying racial injustice in the past thirty-five years. The economic divide between whites and blacks, in their view, is exaggerated, and white Americans have been receptive to demands for racial equality. Thus, racism is a thing of the past. Sleeper accuses liberals of a "fixation on color" and says they do not want "truly to 'get beyond racism.'" As he sees it, liberals consistently ignore evidence of racial harmony, of blacks and whites working together, or of growing intermarriage between blacks and whites. Instead, they favor a portrait of America as irredeemably racist.[10]

One reason race has remained so politically and socially divisive, racial realists often say, is that ill-conceived and unnecessary race-conscious policies such as affirmative action have been adopted. They believe these policies exacerbate white animosities and do more harm than good. One recent study, in fact, claims that merely mentioning affirmative action to otherwise nonprejudiced whites "increases significantly the likelihood that they will perceive blacks as irresponsible and lazy."[11] Many opponents of affirmative action point out that were it not for these distorting and distracting policies whipping up racial consciousness, race would virtually disappear as a marker of social identity. Race remains divisive, in their view, because race-conscious agitators exploit it to demand race-conscious policies.[12]

The racial realists' second claim is that persistent racial inequalities in income, employment, residence, and political representation cannot be explained by white racism, even though a small percentage of whites remain intransigent racists. As they see it, the problem is the lethargic, incorrigible, and often pathological behavior of people who fail to take responsibility for their own lives. In D'Souza's view, persistent and deep black poverty is attributable to the moral and cultural failure of African Americans, not to discrimination.[13]

For racial realists, color-blindness means, among other things, recognizing black failure. Jacoby reports that she has a note above her desk that reads: "'If you can't call a black thug a thug, you're a racist.' It is," she says, "an idea I stand by."[14] Racial realists charge that blacks and their liberal supporters are unwilling to acknowledge the failures of black people. Sleeper calls this the sin of liberal racism. He thinks that white liberals are guilty of holding blacks to a lower standard. They set "the bar so much lower" for blacks, he writes, "that it denies them the satisfactions of equal accomplishment and opportunity."[15] It is also counterproductive. Jacoby argues that the idea that racism still matters just encourages blacks to believe the fallacy that "all responsibility for change lies with whites." Contemporary allegations of racism, the Thernstroms insist, are mainly a cover, an excuse. Blaming whites — arguing that the "white score is always zero" or that "white racism remains a constant" — simply obscures the reality of black failure, self-doubt, and lack of effort. It deflects attention from changing the values and habits of many black people to overcome the "development gap" between blacks and whites, a process Jacoby calls "acculturation."[16]

The racial realists' final assertion is that the civil rights movement's political failures are caused by the manipulative, expedient behavior of black nationalists and the civil rights establishment. Or, as Alan Wolfe puts the matter in a review of Tamar Jacoby's recent book on integration, "Those who claim to speak in the name of African Americans do not always serve the interests of those for whom they supposedly speak."[17] The real problem today is not racists like David Duke who still prey on white fears. Instead, the genuine obstacles are misguided black militants like Al Sharpton who overdramatize white racism and white apologists who have a pathological need to feel guilty. Racial realists feel that since black civil rights leaders and militants benefit from government handouts and affirmative action, they have a vested interest in denying racial progress and fomenting racial divisions. Many black politicians, according to the Thernstroms, particularly those elected to Congress, ignore the real needs of their constituents and pursue instead "the rhetoric of racial empowerment" and separatism.[18]

Although racial realists do not claim that racism has ended completely, they want race to disappear. For them, color-blindness is not simply a legal standard; it is a particular kind of social order, one where racial identity is irrelevant. They believe a color-blind society can uncouple individual behavior from group identification, allowing genuine inclusion of all people. In their view, were this allowed to happen, individuals who refused to follow common moral standards would be stigmatized as individuals, not as members of a particular group.[19]

Ironically, like some multiculturalists, racial realists assume that the real problem facing America is not racial discrimination. Instead, it is a problem of recognition and identity, of how people see themselves. Were it not for racial preferences and black hopelessness-helplessness, the Thernstroms believe, race would virtually disappear as a political and social issue in the United States. Racial realists pay only lip service to the idea that racial discrimination matters; they do not seriously investigate how and why racism persists after the dismantling of Jim Crow laws or what causes racial inequality. They would much prefer to slay the evil dragon of racial separatism. For racial realists, upholding Martin Luther King Jr.'s noble dream to transform "the jangling discords of our nation into a beautiful symphony of brotherhood" requires that the words *race* (and *racism*) must disappear from our political lexicon, and, along with rights, personal responsibility (read black failure) must be acknowledged.[20]

Racial realists did not produce this new assemblage of beliefs about race and racial inequality; they have codified it. And their case against color-conscious public policies has found receptive audiences throughout the country, among both Republicans and Democrats, young and old. But their synthesis of this new set of beliefs was not, as they claim, produced by nonpartisan, neutral observations of race in America. Rather, it is an offshoot of the conservative turn in American politics. Like Dinesh D'Souza and most conservatives, racial realists categorically reject biological explanations for racial inequality while subscribing to the notion that any possibility for reducing racial inequality is undermined by black behavior and values. Like other conservatives, both D'Souza and the Thernstroms believe in a version of racial realism that assumes that government intervention only makes things worse. Racial progress, in this view, is best achieved by letting the free market work its magic. In this instance, conservative ideology, like racial realism, makes a case against color-conscious policies and represents a generation of conservative attacks on liberal social policy.[21] In an important sense, the public's new understanding of race and racism is both a cause and a consequence of the emergence of modern conservatism, which is the context for the rise of racial realism.

It is time to take a cold, hard look at the case for racial realism and the new understanding of racism that it synthesizes. In the following analysis, we assume people bear certain responsibility for the outcomes of their lives. We do not ignore or make excuses when broadly accepted moral and legal standards are violated. Nor do we attribute every problem and failure in communities of color to persistent racism. But we cannot accept the proposition that racial inequality does not matter and that racism has all but disappeared from American life. In our judgment, the new public understanding subscribes to a false dichotomy: either we have racial prejudice or we have black failure. We think this view is deeply flawed. We present an alternative perspective, one that is sustained by empirical evidence and is more consonant with the realities of race in America as the nation enters the twenty-first century.

We use the term *racial realists* to refer to individuals who subscribe to the new belief system. Racial realists do not agree on every tenet of the new understanding of racial inequality, and they span, as we have indicated, the political spectrum. However, many of the writers we consider are conservatives, and they combine racial realism with political conservatism. When we analyze their views, we refer to them as conservatives rather than racial realists.

The Logic of Color-Blind Policies and Free Market Racism

The racial realists claim that segregation was defeated and white prejudice minimized after Congress passed the 1964 Civil Rights Act and the 1965 Voting Rights Act, but that these gains have been derailed by the misguided policies of the civil rights establishment and liberal politicians. They believe that the United States made greater progress in removing racial prejudice and racist behavior in this period than many liberals will acknowledge. The Thernstroms cite big changes in racial attitudes among whites since the 1940s as evidence for this assertion. White prejudice, in their estimation, started to decline much earlier than most people realize. The shift began, the Thernstroms argue, in the early 1950s. And when the civil rights movement abolished Jim Crow, white racism withered away.

Equating attitudes with institutional practices, the Thernstroms boldly assert that racial inequality substantially diminished between 1940 and 1970. This progress, they contend, accompanied economic growth and individual achievements in education, not government programs. This claim radically twists the commonly held assumption that civil rights policies were responsible for the growth of the black middle class. There is no question that since the early 1940s African Americans have made enormous strides in income, occupation, and education. But the Thernstroms claim that the black middle class made its greatest strides prior to affirmative action policies and government programs designed to assist African Americans. The largest income gains and the greatest reductions in poverty rates, they assert, did not come in the 1960s but in the two decades following the Great Depression. According to the Thernstroms, Lyndon Johnson's Great Society played a small role in the creation of a flourishing black middle class and the alleviation of black poverty.

This historical account enables the Thernstroms to make an inference that is vital to the new understanding of race and racism. In this reading of history, African American economic progress—narrowing the racial gaps in wages, occupation, employment, and wealth—depends almost entirely on reducing the deficit in black people's levels of education, job skills, and experience. The idea here is that individuals succeed economically when they acquire the skills and experience valued by employers. The Thernstroms, along with many of the writers and scholars on whom they depend, assume that the most important factors that determine economic achievement for blacks are growth of the economy and the opportunity for employers to rationally choose between skilled and unskilled workers in competitive labor markets, not the elimination of institutional practices that systematically privilege whites. In this view, racial differences in employment, wages, and family income will presumably disappear as blacks acquire more job-related skills and education.[22]

Not every racial realist accepts the Thernstroms' historical account of black people's economic progress. But many people believe that after the 1960s, labor market discrimination was substantially diminished or eliminated and that what matters now is education and job skills. White racism, in their view, has very little to do with black income and wages or persistently high poverty rates in the black community.[23] It clearly makes much more sense, these people think, to look at the counterproductive and antisocial choices of poor blacks—choices that lead young women to have babies out of wedlock, young men to commit crimes, and young men and women to drop out of school.

When the Thernstroms argue that labor market discrimination was relatively unimportant in the 1940s and assert that labor market discrimination is all but gone, they rely on the economic theory of discrimination. This theory assumes that in competitive economic markets, discrimination is short-lived because ruthlessly competitive entrepreneurs will take advantage of the opportunities racial exclusion provides and hire low-wage black workers instead of their high-priced white counterparts. Victims of market discrimination, therefore, will always have an option to work, because some employers will not subordinate their chance to make a profit on cheap black labor to a desire to exclude black workers. In "a world of free access to open markets," the legal scholar Richard Epstein writes, "systematic discrimination, even by a large majority, offers little peril to the isolated minority."[24] Because the theory assumes that competition drives discriminatory employers out of the market, any differences in wages or income must be attributable to differences in education, job skills, or cultural values. In this account, when de jure segregation was demolished by 1960s civil rights legislation, blacks were free to compete on a more or less equal basis with whites. As a result, race-conscious policies that guarantee employment or education are not only unnecessary but are also harmful to the free market.

For the Thernstroms, as well as for the full range of racial realists and conservatives who subscribe to this remarkable revisionist history of racism since the 1960s, the main problem facing America was *state-sponsored* racial discrimination. The difficulty with Jim Crow laws in this view was not that they institutionalized white supremacy and racial domination. The problem with *Plessy v. Ferguson* (1896), which upheld the power of state governments to segregate public facilities and transportation by race, is that it interfered with an unfettered market. According to Epstein, southern politicians were catering to the prejudices of white voters by imposing legally binding segregation throughout the South. But these misguided laws made it impossible for employers to hire blacks and pay equal wages to blacks and whites, and this then short-circuited competition in labor markets. In this vein, he is troubled because the Supreme Court did not strike down these laws on the grounds that they interfered with the "liberty of contract," as it did when it struck down minimum wage and hours laws in the North. Epstein argues that even if segregated labor markets were to emerge in a free, competitive economic market, it would be the result of voluntary choices rather than coercion and therefore "must be sharply distinguished from the system of government-mandated segregation on grounds of race."[25]

Voluntary, individual choice is crucial to the color-blind worldview one finds in racial realism and to the new understanding of racial inequality that it promotes. Although the civil rights movement demolished publicly sanctioned racist laws, racial realists do not believe civil rights laws were intended or designed to promote integration or to eliminate racial differences in economic status. Color-blindness in this view is a formal guarantee of equality before the law; it only means that government may not treat individuals unfairly or discriminate against them. But being blind to color does not mean that racial differences in income, wages, or status will disappear. According to this version of color-blindness, people will rise or fall according to their own efforts and abilities. The onus of responsibility for success is squarely on the individual.

It should not be surprising, therefore, that these proponents of color-blindness strongly believe affirmative action policies in the late 1960s twisted and distorted the goals and statutory achievements of the civil rights movement. Affirmative action, in their view, refers to any race-conscious policy that mandates racial integration in schools, the creation of black or Latino majority legislative districts, or preferences in college admissions, employment, and business contracts. In each case, critics argue that the original, laudable goals of the civil rights movement were perverted by arrogant elites — black civil rights leaders, judges, and white liberals — who insisted on imposing their agenda and subverted the dream of a color-blind society.

The Thernstroms are typical of this sentiment. Their account of school desegregation is a classic attack on race-conscious policies. Desegregation was an entirely appropriate goal in their estimation, and it could have been achieved by abolishing Jim Crow laws and constructing school district boundaries that promoted racial balance. But, unfortunately, self-aggrandizing civil rights leaders and radical white liberals replaced this sensible policy with court-ordered busing, together with other forms of forced integration, and the results were predictably bad. In their view, the same scenario was played out with race-conscious employment policies, college admissions, business set-asides, and legislative redistricting. So far as the Thernstroms are concerned, all color-conscious policies, like much governmental regulation, are wasteful, make things worse, are prone to corruption, and, in this instance, stir up the reservoirs of racial resentment. If that were not serious enough, the Thernstroms add, none of these policies provide jobs for black students or raise their cognitive abilities.

This is racial realism's intellectual framework. It is reflected in and reinforced by contemporary white American public opinion about issues triggered by race. Persistent racial inequality is accepted as normal; African Americans are thought to be "the cultural architects of their own disadvantage." Lawrence Bobo calls this "laissez-faire racism."[26]

The Persistence of Durable Racial Inequality

This snapshot of race in America is out of focus. Racial realists pose the wrong question. The real issue, so far as they are concerned, is whether the United States has made progress in reducing racial inequality. But every serious student of contemporary racial inequality concedes there has been progress. The Thernstroms remind us repeatedly that the good news "regarding the emergence of a strong black middle class has not received the attention it deserves."[27] Good tidings, they assert, are neglected because of a volatile mixture of "black anger" and "white guilt." This is hardly true. Every gain the black middle class has made, every uptick in black employment is trumpeted from the rooftops. There is no gainsaying the progress of the black middle class, but to dwell on this amounts to celebrating economic gains while ignoring the large and persistent gaps in economic and social well-being between blacks and whites.

An abundance of evidence documents persistently large gaps between blacks and whites in family income, wages, and wealth since the economic boom of the post–World War Two years and *after* the civil rights revolution. Black families have clearly gained relative to whites over the past fifty-five years, but the absolute income gap between them has widened. In 2001, the real median income of black families was 62 percent of that of whites, only 10 points higher than it was in 1947, when the ratio was 52 percent. Over the same period, however, the *absolute* real median income gap doubled, rising from $10,386 to $20,469.[28] (If one compares black family income to that of non-Hispanic whites, a more accurate measure, the ratio is 58 percent, a gap that is largely unchanged since the early 1970s.)[29]

Relative to non-Hispanic white men, black men made income gains between 1972 and 2001. Their real median income rose from 60 percent to 67.5 percent of white median income. The absolute gap declined slightly over the same period, falling from $11,624 to $10,325. (Almost all of black males' income gains came during the economic boom of the late 1990s; at the beginning of the decade black male income relative to whites' was lower than it was in 1972.) The picture for black women is very different. Compared to non-Hispanic white women, black women's real median income declined from 92 percent in 1972 to a low point of 79 percent in 1988 and then rose to 94.5 percent by 2001. The absolute gap in annual income between black and white women is much smaller than the one for the men—a reflection of the wage discrimination experienced by all women.[30] Large disparities in income remain even when the comparison is restricted to full-time workers, despite a black unemployment rate that is much higher than the rate for whites.[31]

Just as important is the startling persistence of racial inequality in other areas of American life, despite laws passed to address the disparities. Housing and health care are two matters vital to the well-being of individuals and their families, and both illustrate the limits of the civil rights revolution. The 1968 Civil Rights Act outlawed housing discrimination, yet African Americans continue to be the most residentially segregated group in the United States (see Massey, part 4). They are far more likely to live in segregated neighborhoods than either Asian Americans or Latinos.[32] Blacks are much less likely to own a home, and when they can get a mortgage, they receive far less favorable terms than do comparable whites. For example, between 1993 and 1998, subprime lending—loans with higher interest rates and predatory foreclosure practices—grew by thirty times in Chicago's black neighborhoods, but by only two and one-half times in white residential areas. Race, not social class, explains this difference: in 1998, subprime lenders made 53 percent of the home-equity loans in middle-income black areas but only 12 percent of the loans in middle-income white areas.[33]

Medicare and Medicaid succeeded in expanding access to health care to many people, a clear example of progress. Racial and income differences in the use of health care facilities, including hospital stays as well as visits to doctors' offices, diminished substantially after these two laws were enacted. These laws made a difference; largely because of Medicaid, black infant mortality rates dropped by half between 1960 and 1980. Yet racial differences for many health indicators remained unchanged or in some cases widened. The black infant mortality rate remained twice as high as the white rate, and by 1998 it had actually widened.[34] Moreover, one specialist on race and health care has pointed out that in 1995 "black age-adjusted mortality rates were still 1.61 times that of whites, a disparity essentially unchanged since 1950."[35] In other words, neither the civil rights revolution nor diminishing prejudice have made much difference to racial disparities in mortality, the most fundamental measure of health. Neither income nor poverty status alone can explain these racial differences[36] (see Williams and Collins, part 4).

One reason for these disparities is that blacks and Latinos are still much less likely to have access to primary care physicians than whites. For example, in South Central Los Angeles, where the population is overwhelmingly African American and Latino, the ratio of primary care physicians to the population is 1 to 12,993. By comparison, in wealthy Bel Air, only a few miles away, the ratio is 1 to 214.[37] Limited access to primary care shows up in many basic health statistics. David Smith reports that "the proportion of blacks receiving adequate prenatal care, up-to-date childhood immunizations, flu shots as seniors, and cancer screenings lags significantly behind whites, even though most of the financial barriers to such preventive services have been eliminated."[38] African Americans, Latinos, and members of other minority groups account for 75 percent of active cases of tuberculosis, and the Centers for Disease Control reports that blacks are five times as likely to die of asthma as are whites.[39] Even when blacks have *equal* access to medical care, recent evidence indicates that significant racial disparities in treatment and care remain. For example, among Medicare beneficiaries of similar age, gender, and income, blacks are 25 percent less likely to have mammography screening for breast cancer and 57 percent less likely to have reduction of hip fracture.[40]

Any credible analysis of race in America at the beginning of the twenty-first century must confront and account for these durable and persistent inequalities between blacks and whites. Many proponents of racial realism as well as those Americans who subscribe to the new explanation for racial inequality fail to do this for two reasons. First, they ignore or obscure dramatic and persistent facts of racial inequality. Second, the methodological assumptions that guide their investigation of race in America lead them to ignore alternative explanations that more closely "fit" the evidence they do cite. In the following analysis, we address each of these concerns.

The Minimal Relevance of Individual Choice to Durable Racial Inequality

Today the predominant approach to understanding racial stratification in American life assumes that "social life results chiefly or exclusively from the actions of self-motivated, interest-seeking persons."[41] For those promulgating this view, it is solely the stated intentions and choices of individuals that explain discrimination. It leads writers to focus on individual whites' beliefs about African Americans and civil rights. Throughout *America in Black and White*, for example, the Thernstroms focus on the positive upward spiral of individual whites' attitudes as measured by public opinion data. The positive shift in expressed attitudes is then assumed, prima facie, to be evidence of behavior. If (white) people say they are not discriminating against blacks, the Thernstroms believe them, and infer that discrimination must be diminishing. In a like manner, persistent racial inequality is attributed to blacks' individual choices of lifestyles and attitudes.

The Thernstroms' assessment of residential discrimination is a prime illustration of how individual intentions and choices are used to explain racial inequality. They do not deny that residential segregation remains very high. Instead, the Thernstroms argue that it has declined somewhat and that this is real evidence of racial progress.[42] They go on to argue, however, that housing would be even less segregated but for the choices of blacks. Public opinion surveys prove whites are quite willing to accept blacks as neighbors. The problem, they argue, is that public opinion data show blacks would prefer to live in neighborhoods that are at least 50 percent African American. Thus, they conclude that the preferences of blacks, not white racism, produces segregated housing. In other words, present-day segregation is caused by ethnic group loyalty.[43]

Just as the Thernstroms think housing segregation reflects black preferences, Sally Satel, a psychiatrist, contends that racial differences in health and well-being are due to blacks' bad lifestyle choices. Like other conservatives, Satel thinks declining individual prejudice and the elimination of de jure segregation mean that racism is largely a thing of the past. Angered that "accusations of medical bias still linger" decades after segregation has ended, Satel severely criticizes federal funding of studies on racial and ethnic disparities in health care and any suggestion that there is a relationship between blacks' and Latinos' health and discrimination or powerlessness. Satel accuses the public health establishment of neglecting the vital role of individual choices in health outcomes in its rush to analyze social injustice. "Taking responsibility for one's own health comes to be virtually ignored," she complains.[44]

Satel's criticisms about the documentation of racial disparities evade fundamental questions regarding the institutional structure of health care and racially disparate outcomes. By focusing on the stated intentions and choices of individuals, conservatives like the Thernstroms and Satel ignore the systemic and routine practices of white Americans and the consequences of their behavior. Whether these actions are motivated by group values and interests or operate through private and public institutions, the inescapable results are harmful to African Americans and other people of color.

When social scientists analyze income, employment, or occupational disparities between categorical groups — blacks-whites, men-women — they assume these gaps in material well-being are due mostly to differences in education and job skills that would affect an individual's productivity and thus that person's ability to succeed in competitive labor markets. Studies of wage discrimination, for example, typically proceed by removing the effects of individual characteristics such as education or experience that might explain wage differences between men and women or between racial groups. Any remaining gap in wages is then attributed to discrimination. Yet as Ruth Milkman and Eleanor Townsley explain, "This approach . . . fails to capture the depth with which gender discrimination and the norms associated with it are embedded in the economic order — in fact, they are embedded so deeply that a willful act of discrimination is not really necessary to maintain gender inequality."[45] One problem with this approach is that an individual's job experience and education may have been shaped by deeply embedded patterns of discrimination — a racially biased allocation of public resources to schools, for example — which means that education is not independent of discrimination. By focusing only on individuals and the skills they bring to the labor market, moreover, analysts obscure the relationship between racial groups, a fundamental element in the development of durable racial inequality.

In the following we will show how and why the specific intentions and choices of individuals regarding racial discrimination or exclusion are frequently irrelevant to the emergence and maintenance of social and economic inequalities in the United States. One cannot assume that individuals are the only appropriate unit of analysis. By making this assumption, Satel, the Thernstroms, and other like-minded interpreters of contemporary racial inequality neglect the collective actions of groups, the role of intermediary institutions, and the cumulative effects of durable racial inequality.

Group Hoarding and the Economic Theory of Discrimination

As we indicated earlier, the economic theory of labor market discrimination is a theory of individual choice. This one-dimensional theory, however, is empirically flawed. Because it assumes that economic competition drives out discrimination, the theory cannot explain why racial inequality persists once education, training, and experience are taken into account. Nor can it explain historical patterns of labor market segregation in both the North and the South. And recent attempts to rescue the theory by attributing differences in the economic success of African Americans and immigrants to cultural values have failed miserably.[46]

While individuals can and do discriminate, labor market discrimination is better understood as a group phenomenon. It is an instance of what Charles Tilly calls *opportunity hoarding*. This occurs when members of a group acquire and monopolize access to valuable resources or privileges. Most people know that informal networks of family, extended kinship, friendships, and associates are the typical routes to employment. Employers commonly recruit new workers through informal ties and word-of-mouth suggestions; current employees typically identify job candidates.[47] Because workers tend to be friends and acquaintances of members of the same race and sex, a bias toward re-creating a homogeneous workforce is overwhelming. Discrimination, therefore, can be passive and unobtrusive. One need not be a racist to use one's position to benefit friends and acquaintances, even if it means awarding jobs to whites rather than blacks.[48]

But the process of labor market discrimination is not always so passive. Once members of a group acquire access to resources, they may hoard the resources by denying access to outsiders. Tilly suggests that hoarding can be found in a variety of groups, including immigrants, criminal conspiracies, and even elite military units.[49] Once a group of employees acquire the best jobs and perks, they can make it difficult for employers to hire outsiders. Insiders can harass unwanted workers by disrupting their work and reducing their value to employers, which can eventually exclude outsiders. Intimidation is a way for insiders to discourage outsiders from even applying for a job. Justifying exclusionary practices with beliefs that denigrate the work habits and skills of excluded workers is the final step in this process. For a long time white workers used the "myth of the machine"—the idea that black workers were incapable of working with machines—to exclude African American workers from skilled, higher paying work.[50]

The Thernstroms assume that changing attitudes toward blacks is the key to reducing racial inequalities in wages, income, and employment. It makes more sense, however, to examine racial labor market competition—a prime example of opportunity hoarding—to get a better handle on a critical determinant of racial inequality. Simple models of discrimination that assume that unequal rewards to otherwise identical workers are motivated by prejudice do not capture the complexity and depth of racially divided labor markets in the twentieth century. When white workers compete for jobs, they use their advantages to exclude or subordinate black or Latino workers. Two prominent labor market economists, William Darity Jr. and Samuel Myers Jr., write that discrimination is "endogenously linked to the employment needs of non-black males." Competition between black and white workers intensifies when blacks threaten the status of white workers, either because the blacks have acquired the education and job skills to be competitive or because the job opportunities for whites diminish.[51] Employers' evaluations of the skills and talents of black workers are often based on negative stereotypes of their productivity rather than on independent assessments of their work. These stereotypes are the residue of racial labor market competition and push black workers to the bottom of the employment queue.[52]

Racial labor market competition is obviously affected by the state of the economy. When economic growth is sluggish or depressed, labor markets are slack and competition for jobs unleashes white racism. Robust economic growth produces tight labor markets as demand for workers rises, and typically has a greater impact on black unemployment rates than on white unemployment rates. Similarly, as high-wage manufacturing jobs are eliminated and whites are displaced, competition intensifies between blacks and whites for low- and moderate-wage service jobs. Job competition based on race can be modified by public policies that regulate wages and access to jobs through full employment or affirmative action policies. But unless or until a third party steps in to demand or induce employers to pursue a different recruitment strategy, a homogeneous racial and gendered workforce will almost inevitably be reproduced.

Institutions and the Routine, Ordinary Generation of Inequality

Because the realist analysis of racial inequality assumes that racism is produced exclusively by the intentions and choices of individuals, intermediate institutions that play a crucial part in generating and maintaining racial inequality are rarely analyzed. The routine practices of corporations, law firms, banks, athletic teams, labor unions, the military, and educational institutions tend to be ignored or minimized. These institutions are neither scrutinized nor analyzed unless or until they institute strategies that redress past social grievances. Accordingly, advocates of this approach to racial inequality believe that individual access to previously segregated institutions is all that is necessary to redress past racial injustice. They never discuss the ways these institutions might be transformed to accommodate or better engage the groups they formerly excluded.

Any analysis of racial inequality that routinely neglects organizations and practices that, intentionally or *unintentionally*, generate or maintain racial inequalities over long periods of time is incomplete and misleading. Such an analysis will be unable, for example, to detect the ways real estate and mortgage lending industries routinely sustain segregated housing markets and discriminate against would-be black homeowners. It will also not notice that discrimination in the criminal justice system is produced by a large number of small decisions by the police that single out young black men, the results of which then extend to their treatment in adult courts.

Nowhere is the folly of neglecting institutional practices more apparent than in the case of racial disparities in health care and mortality. Many health care institutions remain partially segregated despite the end of Jim Crow and federal laws that prohibit distribution of federal funds to institutions that discriminate. The private nursing home industry, for example, has continued to be segregated, largely because for-profit nursing homes are reluctant to accept Medicaid patients, particularly elderly blacks, and state governments have little incentive to enforce civil rights laws. Elderly blacks are therefore less likely to use private nursing homes even though they have a greater need for such care. In Pennsylvania the segregation index for nursing homes is almost as high as the indexes for housing in metropolitan areas.[53] Moreover, nonwhites are almost twice as likely as whites to be admitted to a nursing home sanctioned by state officials for serious deficiencies in care and facilities.[54]

Segregated and unequal treatment in health care is an endemic problem, though not one that is attributable to the actions of prejudiced individuals. David Barton Smith concludes his detailed assessment of racial disparities in health care by noting that

> at least some of the reported differences in rates of drug addiction, sexually transmitted diseases, and possibly even infant mortality reflect differences in the screening and reporting practices of the settings in which care is provided to blacks as opposed to those catering to whites. Such screening and reporting is more likely to be a part of the standard operating procedures of the more urban clinic settings where blacks disproportionately receive their care. In effect, these differences in procedures amount to an institutionalized form of racial profiling.[55]

While there are numerous examples of how economic, educational, and governmental organizations unintentionally produce unequal racial outcomes, it is also the case that certain institutions do better than others in reducing racial inequalities. Some universities that use affirmative action policies, for example, do better at graduating black students than universities that admit students strictly on the basis of test scores. Nor do blacks with low test scores always have lower graduation rates, as is typically assumed. It makes sense to focus our attention on institutional practices that mitigate and reduce racial inequalities. These practices will not be discovered, however, when one looks for racism in individual motivations and presumes that people with good intentions will do the right thing if only government gets out of the way.

Cumulative Inequalities

Inequalities are cumulative, a fact adherents of the new public wisdom on race ignore in their rush to celebrate progress. The story told by the Thernstroms in *America in Black and White*, for example, is disturbingly, sometimes even stunningly, ahistorical. This may seem surprising because the book does trace race relations over time, from the early 1940s to the present, and one of the authors is a prize-winning Harvard historian. Yet the book is insensitive to the ways the past shapes the future. By assuming that behavioral changes are produced by changes in attitudes, the Thernstroms implicitly distinguish between past and present discrimination.[56] But if discrimination has declined, this means one cannot look to history to explain the persistence of racial inequalities. As a result, proponents of the new understanding of racial inequality are forced to focus on individual motivations. But this neglects how the past has shaped contemporary patterns of racial inequality, and how it continues to constrain the choices of African Americans and other groups. Thus, conservatives and their realist colleagues ignore how the accumulation of wealth — economic, cultural, social, and political capital — molds economic opportunities for all Americans over time, especially blacks, Latinos, and other racial minorities. Wealth matters. At the conclusion of his book on race, wealth, and social policy in the United States, Dalton Conley writes, "One may conclude that the locus of racial inequality no longer lies in the labor market, but rather in class and property relations that, in turn, affect other outcomes. While young African American men may have the opportunity to obtain the same education, income, and wealth as whites, in actuality, they are on a slippery slope, for the discrimination their parents faced in the housing and credit markets sets the stage for perpetual economic disadvantage."[57]

When the economy falters, privileged members of society are able to help themselves over the difficult bumps and fluctuations of a market economy.

Their net worth, not wages, provides the necessary reserves to ride out cyclical downturns in the economy or other disasters. Although the Thernstroms acknowledge racial differences in wealth, they attribute the black deficit to age and family structure. African American families, they argue, are younger and are more likely to be headed by single parents. Both factors militate against wealth accumulation and both, not coincidentally, are characteristics about which individuals exercise some choice.[58] Differences in the accumulation of wealth between different racial groups, however, are not solely the result of age, family structure, or the inclination to save — blacks and whites save about the same proportions of their income.[59] In fact, African Americans lost much of the wealth they acquired after the Civil War to white thievery and discrimination. A recent study by the Associated Press found that more than four hundred blacks were dispossessed of more than twenty-four thousand acres of farm and timber land in the South, worth millions of dollars today, through fraud, discrimination by lenders, and other illegal means.[60]

Since inequalities accumulate over generations, an analysis of racial inequalities in the distribution of wealth explodes any distinction between past and present racism. Cumulative inequality undermines racial conservatives' efforts to restrict the effects of racism to the past. Today's racial disparities in wealth reflect the legacies of slavery, Jim Crow, and labor market discrimination (see Oliver and Shapiro, part 1).

The Origins of Durable Racial Inequality

Discussions of racial inequality commonly dwell on only one side of the color line. We talk about *black* poverty, *black* unemployment, *black* crime, and public policies for *blacks*. We rarely, however, talk about the gains whites receive from the troubles experienced by blacks. Only when the diverging fates of black and white Americans are considered together — within the same analytic framework — will it be possible to move beyond the current stale debate over how to transform the American color line.

In our view, the persistence of racial inequality stems from the long-term effects of labor market discrimination and institutional practices that have created cumulative inequalities by race. The result is a durable pattern of racial stratification. Whites have gained or *accumulated* opportunities, while African Americans and other racial groups have lost opportunities — they suffer from *disaccumulation* of the accoutrements of economic opportunity.

Rather than investigating racial inequality by focusing on individual intentions and choices, we concentrate on the relationship between white accumulation and black and Latino disaccumulation.

Accumulation versus Disaccumulation

The idea of accumulation is straightforward and can be illustrated with a simple example. Investment counselors routinely explain to their clients the importance of long-term investments. For example, a young couple that set aside just $40 a month beginning in 1970 and simply let it sit in an account paying 5 percent interest would accumulate about $34,000, or more than double the amount invested, by the year 2000. Rolling over modest investments of capital produces an impressive accumulation. Similarly, very small economic and social advantages can have large cumulative effects over many generations.

While accumulation is relatively well understood, there is a parallel and symmetrical idea that is usually ignored. This is the idea of *dis*investment and, over time, what might be called *dis*accumulation. Just as a positive investment of $40 can accumulate over time, so too can a negative investment produce a downward spiral. Consider what happens if one owes the Internal Revenue Service a few hundred dollars but allows that debt to go unpaid for a decade. The amount of that debt can increase dramatically and can lead to a debt of several thousand dollars. The amount owed can increase fivefold. From the point of view of the debtor, this is negative accumulation, or for purposes of this discussion, disaccumulation. Just as economic advantages (for example, access to skilled trades) can accumulate, economic disadvantages (such as exclusion from well-paying jobs) can also be compounded over time.

Home ownership is a good example of how the principle of accumulation and disaccumulation works in a racial context. Today's very large gap in median net worth between whites and African Americans is mostly due to the discrepancy in the value of the equity in their respective homes. Blacks experience more difficulty obtaining mortgage loans, and when they do purchase a house, it is usually worth less than a comparable white-owned home. White flight and residential segregation lower the value of black homes. As blacks move into a neighborhood, whites move out, fearing that property values will decline. As whites leave, the fear becomes a reality and housing prices decline. The refusal of white Americans to live in neighborhoods where blacks make up more than 20 percent of the population means that white-owned housing is implicitly more highly valued than black-owned housing. Redlining completes the circle: banks refuse to underwrite mortgage loans, or they rate them as a higher risk. As a consequence, when black homeowners can get a loan, they pay higher interest rates for less valuable property. This results in disinvestment in black neighborhoods and translates into fewer amenities, more abandoned buildings, and a lower property tax base. Because white communities do not suffer the consequences of residential disaccumulation—indeed, they receive advantages denied to black homeowners—the value of their housing increases and they accumulate wealth. In this way interlocking patterns of racialized accumulation and disaccumulation create durable inequality.[61]

The distribution of economic wealth is central to any account of racial inequality, but it is not the only dimension of racial accumulation and disaccumulation. For example, inadequate access to health care contributes to disaccumulation in communities of color. Health is fundamental to every aspect of life: without health, a student cannot do well in school; a worker cannot hold a job, much less excel at one; a family member cannot be an effective parent or spouse. Health crises and the staggering costs they impose are critical underlying causes of poverty, homelessness, and bankruptcy. Housing, employment, and education are vital, but without health, and the care necessary to maintain it, the quality of life, indeed life itself, is uncertain. The effect is cumulative. Inadequate prenatal care results in low birth-weight babies, which in turn leads to infant mortality and to severe physical and mental disabilities among those who survive.[62] One-fifth to one-third of African American children are anemic, and they account for a disproportionate number of children exposed to lead poisoning. Both problems impair intellectual functions and school performance.[63]

Accumulation also includes cultural and social advantages—meeting "the right people" at Harvard, Yale, and Princeton (who can and often do provide a substantial boost to one's career), for example. As we will subsequently document in more depth, a symmetrical process operates in the criminal justice system, with the opposite consequences: judges frequently incarcerate black juveniles rather than sending them home because the court believes these youngsters have fewer outside resources to help them. However well intentioned, these decisions then become part of the juvenile's record, counting against him or her in future scrapes with the criminal justice system. Diverting black youth to state institutions rather than sending them home is analogous to acquiring a small debt that can be compounded. Similarly, critics of affirmative action are correct when they tell black students who have been denied admission to the University of California at Berkeley that "there is nothing wrong with attending UC Riverside." But that is only half the story. Elite institutions are saturated with an accumulated legacy of power and privilege along lines of race and gender. The advice to attend Riverside ignores that who you meet at Harvard, Yale, or Princeton — or at Berkeley, Ann Arbor, or Madison — is an important aspect of the accumulation of economic and social advantage.

Many Americans, but particularly conservatives, object to the idea that past discrimination matters in the present. Marianne Means, a columnist for the Hearst newspaper chain, harshly condemns growing black demands for reparations. "We should not be a party," she writes, "to whipping up a guilt trip that is a ploy to get handouts for a social evil that officially ended nearly 140 years ago."[64] Racial realists believe that the accumulation of wealth and power by white Americans over the past 360 years is irrelevant to current patterns of racial stratification, and the use of race-conscious remedies to redress past racial injustices is therefore unnecessary and unfair. As they see it, basing current policies on past practices is wallowing in the past. The main impediment to racial equality, they feel, is state-sponsored discrimination, and the civil rights movement put an end to that. Thus, past discrimination should not matter. Ironically, adherents of this point of view ignore a different form of state-sponsored racial inequality: the use of public policy to advantage whites. Racism is not simply a matter of legal segregation; it is also policies that favor whites.

The Strange Career of Race Preferences in U.S. Public Policy and Law

Curiously, the current debate over race-conscious remedies assumes that the sole beneficiaries of these policies are blacks and other racial minorities. If, however, affirmative action is defined as "race and gender preferences codified into law and enforced through public policy and social customs," then it is strange and peculiar, arbitrary and incorrect, to suggest that affirmative action began in the summer of 1963 when President John F. Kennedy issued Executive Order 10925. Given the above definition, routinely cited by opponents of affirmative action, the more accurate beginning date for this legal and public policy is 1641. That is when the fledgling jurisdictions that would later become the first states began to specify in law that rights to property, ownership of goods and services, and the right to vote would be restricted by race and gender. In 1790, Congress formally restricted citizenship via naturalization to "white persons," a restriction that remained in place until 1952.[65]

Understood in this way, affirmative action has been in effect for 360 years, not 39. For the first 330 years, the deck was officially and legally stacked on behalf of whites and males.[66] In *Dred Scott* (1857), Supreme Court Chief Justice Roger Taney posed the matter in remarkably candid terms: "Can a negro, whose ancestors were imported into this country, and sold as slaves, become a member of the political community, formed and brought into existence by the Constitution of the United States, and as such become entitled to all rights, and privileges, and immunities, guaranteed by that instrument to the citizen?"[67] He answered his own question in unequivocal language. " 'We the people,' " wrote Justice Taney, leaving no room for doubt, was never intended to include blacks, slave or free. "Neither Dred Scott nor any other person of African descent," he ruled, "had any citizenship rights which were binding on white American society." The authority cited by Justice Taney in his 1857 Supreme Court ruling was that the Constitution, the courts at every level, the federal government, and the states all routinely denied blacks equal access to rights of citizenship.[68]

Thus, since the inception of the United States, wealth and institutional support have been invested on the white side of the color line, leading to an accumulation of economic and social advantages among European Americans. On the black side, economic and institutional disinvestment has been the practice, resulting in a process of disaccumulation. When President Kennedy issued Executive Order 10925 in the summer of 1963, he was therefore simply trying to open doors that had been sealed shut for more than three centuries. Now, after only four decades of "racial and gender preferences," a vigorous and partially successful attack is being waged against affirmative action programs that were instituted to reverse three hundred years of disinvestment in black communities. Yet when power and wealth were being invested and accumulated on their side of the color line, white Americans registered hardly any opposition to the arrangement.[69]

The Origins of Modern State-Sponsored Racial Inequality

One need not go back three hundred years to find the antecedents of contemporary white advantage. The New Deal is the most recent benchmark for the accumulation of white privilege and the generation of black disadvantage. Franklin D. Roosevelt's policies were instrumental to both the cause of racial equality and the perpetuation of racial inequality. New Deal agricultural policies paved the way for the mechanization of southern agriculture and precipitated black (and white) migration to the North and the entry of blacks into manufacturing jobs. The Wagner Act legalized unions; minimum wage laws put an economic floor under all workers; the Social Security Act gave workers a measure of security; and the Employment Act of 1946 codified the government's responsibility for aggregate employment and price levels. These policies, combined with postwar economic growth, undermined the prewar northern racial order, set in motion changes that would dismantle Jim Crow, and reduced black as well as white poverty.

African Americans benefited from New Deal policies. They gained from the growth of public employment and governmental transfers like social security and welfare. The Great Society went further, reducing racial inequality, ameliorating poverty among the black poor, and helping to build a new black middle class. But if federal social policy promoted racial equality, it also created and sustained racial hierarchies. Welfare states are as much instruments of stratification as they are of equality. The New Deal's class-based, or race-neutral, social policies did not affect blacks and whites in identical ways. Federal social policy contributed disproportionately to the prosperity of the white middle class from the 1940s on. Whites received more from the New Deal than old-age protection and insurance against the business cycle. Housing subsidies paved the way for a white exodus to the suburbs; federal tax breaks secured union-bargained health and pension benefits and lowered the cost to workers; veterans' benefits were an avenue of upward mobility for many white men. To assume that government policies benefited only blacks or were color-blind, as many white Americans commonly believe, is like looking at the world with one eye.

Three laws passed by Congress in the mid-1930s were instrumental in generating the pattern of racial stratification that emerged during the New Deal: the Social Security Act, the Wagner Act, and the Federal Housing Act. These laws contributed to the accumulation of wealth in white households, and they did more than any other combination of factors to sow and nurture the seeds of the future urban ghetto and produce a welfare system in which recipients would be disproportionately black. It is commonly assumed that the New Deal was based on broad and inclusive policies. While there is some truth to the claim that Roosevelt's New Deal was designed, as Jill Quadagno states it, to provide a "floor of protection for the industrial working class," it was riddled with discrimination. Brokered compromises over New Deal labor and social policies also reinforced racial segregation through social welfare programs, labor policy, and housing policy.[70] How and why did this happen?

Although the Social Security Act created a work-related social right to an old-age pension and unemployment compensation, Congress defied the Roosevelt administration and explicitly excluded domestic and agricultural workers from coverage. It also exempted public employees as well as workers in nonprofit, voluntary organizations. Only 53 percent of all workers, about 26 million people, were initially covered by the old-age insurance title of the Social Security Act, and less than half of all workers were covered by unemployment compensation. Congress subsequently excluded these exempt workers from the Wagner Act and the 1938 Fair Labor Standards Act as well.[71]

Congress's rejection of universal coverage was not a race-neutral decision undertaken because, as some people claimed at the time, it was difficult to collect payroll taxes from agricultural and domestic workers. As Charles Houston, dean of the Howard University Law School, told the Senate Finance Committee, "It [the Social Security bill] looks like a sieve with the holes just big enough for the majority of Negroes to fall through." Almost three-fifths of the black labor force was denied coverage. When self-employed black sharecroppers are added to the list of excluded workers, it is likely that three-quarters or more of African Americans were denied benefits and the protection of federal law. Black women, of whom 90 percent were domestic workers, were especially disadvantaged by these occupational exclusions.[72]

Agricultural and domestic workers were excluded largely because southern legislators refused to allow implementation of any national social welfare policies that included black workers. Roosevelt presided over a fragile coalition of northern industrial workers and southern whites bound to an agrarian economic order. Although blacks began to leave the party of Lincoln for the party of Roosevelt, three-quarters of the African American population still lived in the South, where they could not vote. Southerners feared that federal social policies would raise the pay of southern black workers and sharecroppers and that this in turn would undermine their system of racial apartheid. Black criticisms of the legislation were ignored as Roosevelt acquiesced to southern demands, believing he could not defy powerful southern committee chairmen and still pass needed social welfare legislation.

As black workers moved north into industrial jobs, they were eventually included under the Social Security Act, and Congress ultimately extended coverage of old-age insurance to agricultural workers in 1950 and 1954. Although the Social Security Administration made every effort to treat black and white workers equally, black workers were nevertheless severely disadvantaged by the work-related eligibility provisions of the Social Security Act. Both old-age insurance and unemployment compensation rewarded stable, long-term employment and penalized intermittent employment regardless of the reason. In the name of fiscal integrity, the architects of social insurance in the 1930s were adamant that malingerers, those on relief, and those weakly attached to the labor market be excluded from eligibility and their benefits limited. Due to labor market discrimination and the seasonal nature of agricultural labor, many blacks have not had stable, long-term employment records. Thus, they have had only limited eligibility for old-age and unemployment benefits.

The racial consequences of wage-related eligibility provisions were already apparent in the 1930s. Because labor market discrimination lowers the wages of black workers relative to white workers or denies them employment altogether, blacks receive lower benefits than whites from old-age insurance and unemployment compensation or are denied access altogether. By 1939, for example, only 20 percent of white workers who worked in industries covered by social insurance and who paid payroll taxes for old-age insurance were uninsured, but more than twice as many black workers (42 percent) were uninsured.[73] From the outset, social security transferred income from African American workers to white workers. This disparity continues today. Even though most black workers are currently covered by social security, on average they still receive lower benefits than whites and pay a higher proportion of their income in social security taxes.[74] Like old-age insurance, there is little evidence of overt discrimination in unemployment compensation: eligible black workers are almost as likely as white workers are to receive benefits. But because states imposed strict eligibility requirements during the 1940s and 1950s, black workers were disproportionately excluded.[75] Social insurance is neither universal nor race-neutral.

In combination, labor market discrimination and work-related eligibility requirements excluded blacks from work and social insurance programs in the 1930s, forcing many to go on relief and later on welfare and Aid to Dependent Children. In fact, most black women were excluded from the unemployment compensation system until the late 1960s. This is because domestic workers were statutorily excluded from unemployment compensation, and as late as the 1950s more than half of all black women in the civilian labor force still worked as domestics. Unemployed black women typically had nowhere to turn but welfare, and this is exactly what they did. By the 1960s, African Americans accounted for two-fifths of all welfare recipients, a participation rate that did not change much even when the welfare rolls expanded in the 1960s. It is labor market discrimination and New Deal social policies, not welfare, as the conservatives believe, that has harmed black families. The problem cannot be explained by a pathological black family structure.[76]

Social insurance in the United States has operated much like a sieve, just as Charles Houston predicted, and blacks have fallen through the holes. The Wagner Act and the 1937 Housing Act compounded the problem, enlarging the holes in the sieve. Sometimes labeled the Magna Charta of the labor movement, the 1935 Wagner Act was, upon closer inspection, the

Magna Charta of *white* labor. Black leaders tried to add an antidiscrimination amendment to the law, but the American Federation of Labor and the white southerners who controlled key congressional committees fought it. As a result, the final version excluded black workers. The law legalized the closed shop, which, as Roy Wilkins of the NAACP pointed out, would empower "organized labor to exclude from employment in any industry those who do not belong to a union." The law also outlawed strikebreaking, a weapon black workers had used successfully to force their way into northern industries. Preventing blacks from entering into newly protected labor unions meant that black workers were subject to the racist inclinations of white workers.[77] One of the consequences of the Wagner Act's failure to protect black workers was that union rules confined them to low-wage unskilled jobs. When these jobs were eliminated as businesses modernized after World War Two, black unskilled workers were replaced by automated manufacturing technologies.[78] Thus, the current high levels of black unemployment can be traced directly to New Deal legislation that allowed white workers to deny job opportunities to blacks.

State-sponsored racial inequality was also augmented by a third set of New Deal policies: federal housing and urban renewal legislation. These policies sealed the fate of America's cities by establishing "apartheid without walls." Contrary to the commonly held notion that white flight is responsible for creating ghettos and barrios, it was actually the federal government's explicit racial policy that created these enclaves.

Each of these policies, routinely hailed as major progressive government interventions to boost the economy and place a safety net under all citizens, was instrumental in creating long-running patterns of accumulation and disaccumulation based on race. These policies, along with others, institutionalized white advantage over blacks and other people of color.

Racial Equality and the Possessive Investment in Whiteness after the Civil Rights Revolution

In the post–civil rights era, formal equality before the law coexists with de facto white privilege and whites' resentment of race-conscious remedies. Whites' resentment reflects their "possessive investment in whiteness."[79] Historically, white Americans have accumulated advantages in housing, work, education, and security based solely on the color of their skin. Being white, as a consequence, literally has value. Though race may be a cultural and biological fiction, whiteness, like blackness, is a very real social and legal identity.

Both identities are crucial in determining one's social and economic status. This is why, when Professor Andrew Hacker asked his white students how much money they would demand if they were changed from white to black, they felt it was reasonable to ask for $50 million if they were to be black for the rest of their lives, or $1 million a year for each year they were black.[80] That was the financial value they placed on being white. It was, to use W. E. B. Du Bois's phrase, the dollar amount they attached to their "wages of whiteness." The idea of a possessive investment in whiteness helps to explain the structures of durable racial inequality and the color-coded community processes of accumulation and disaccumulation. The formation of racial identity, in turn, connects interests to attitudes toward public issues that have racial consequences and color-conscious remedies.

In one important, and ironic, respect, the combination of legal equality with social and economic racial inequality at the end of the civil rights movement is similar to the relationship between blacks and whites at the end of Reconstruction. *Plessy v. Ferguson*, which marked the end of Reconstruction by upholding the doctrine of "separate but equal," was the culmination of a long debate over the meaning of racial equality that began with the abolitionists' struggle against slavery. At the time, it was commonly understood that the Fourteenth Amendment guaranteed equality before the law and that political rights (such as the right to serve as a juror) presumably could not be abrogated. But few believed that the Thirteenth, Fourteenth, or Fifteenth amendments required social or economic equality between blacks and whites. Not even the defenders of a color-blind Constitution accepted this idea. Indeed, Justice John Marshall Harlan's defense of a color-blind Constitution in his dissenting opinion in *Plessy* explicitly assumed the inferiority of African Americans and distinguished between legal and social equality.[81] The stigma of slavery lingered long after "the peculiar institution" was dismantled. As Tocqueville observed about the antebellum North, "The prejudice rejecting the Negroes seems to increase in proportion to their emancipation, and inequality cuts deep into mores as it is effaced from the laws."[82]

Americans still face the question of what racial inequality means and what the nation is obligated to do about it. The civil rights movement repudiated racial classifications as a means to subordinate racial groups, and for most Americans that is sufficient. The contemporary controversy over the civil rights policies, however, cannot be reduced, no matter how hard racial realists try, to a debate over repealing color-conscious remedies like affirmative action. The larger question facing Americans is whether equality requires a commitment to go beyond formal legal equality and to rectify three hundred years of racial oppression and subordination. Racial realists and conservatives think a color-blind Constitution means that public remedies to end social inequality between racial groups are illegitimate, the equivalent of "racial social engineering." This view sharply distinguishes between public and private spheres of action. Government should be held to a strict standard of racial neutrality, proponents argue; the use of laws (or policies) to rectify racial inequalities is wrong.

We reject this position. If America is to achieve a larger measure of racial equality, we think the government must use public policies to root out enduring racial inequality. This does not mean we think affirmative action plans are the remedy. Arguments over affirmative action do not help us understand the etiology and persistence of white privilege. Nor do they help find ways to achieve genuine racial equality. We think it makes more sense to consider carefully how labor market discrimination, private institutional practices, and public policies have generated the accumulation of economic and social advantages in white communities, and the concomitant disaccumulation of social and economic capital in communities of color. By comparing the assumptions, arguments, and evidence articulated by racial realists to an alternative framework, we think it is possible to see the major differences between these two perspectives and the remedies that follow from a theory that focuses on cumulative inequalities.

Notes

1. Donald R. Kinder and Tali Mendelberg, "Individualism Reconsidered: Principles and Prejudice in Contemporary American Opinion," in David O. Sears, Jim Sidanius, and Lawrence Bobo, eds., *Racialized Politics: The Debate about Racism in America* (Chicago: University of Chicago Press, 2000), 61.

2. Jim Sleeper, *Liberal Racism* (New York: Penguin Books, 1997), 7, 175.

3. Tamar Jacoby, *Someone Else's House: America's Unfinished Struggle for Integration* (New York: The Free Press, 1998), 4–5, 9.

4. Whether opposition to color-conscious policies is motivated by adherence to political principles or reflects a new manifestation of white racism is the subject of many of the essays in Sears, Sidanius, and Bobo, eds., *Racialized Politics: The Debate about Racism in America.* The wages of full-time male workers have risen only 1.3 percent since 1989. Alexander Stille, "Grounded by an Income Gap: Inequality Just Keeps Growing in the U.S.," *New York Times*, December 15, 2001, A15.

5. Southern Democrats and conservative Republicans from the Southwest, including Barry Goldwater and George H. W. Bush, the latter representing a conservative Texas constituency in Congress at the time, voted against the 1964 Civil Rights Act.

6. David Garrow, *Bearing the Cross: Martin Luther King, Jr., and the Southern Christian Leadership Conference* (New York: Vintage Books, 1988), 439.

7. Martin Luther King Jr., "A Testament of Hope," in James M. Washington, ed., *A Testa-*

ment of Hope: The Essential Writings of Martin Luther King, Jr. (New York: Harper and Row, 1986), 316.

8. Robert L. Carter, "A Reassessment of *Brown v. Board*," in Derrick Bell, ed., *Shades of Brown: New Perspectives on School Desegregation* (New York: Teacher's College, Columbia University, 1980), 23–24. *Brown I* declared "separate but equal" unconstitutional in 1954. In *Brown II*, decided in 1955, the Court ruled that local jurisdictions should desegregate with "all deliberate speed."

9. Jim Sleeper, *The Closest of Strangers: Liberalism and the Politics of Race in America* (New York: W. W. Norton, 1990), 160.

10. Sleeper, *Liberal Racism*, 9, 77–78.

11. Paul M. Sniderman and Thomas Piazza, *The Scar of Race* (Cambridge, Mass.: Harvard University Press, 1993), 103.

12. For recent examples, see, among others, Terry Eastland, "Endgame for Affirmative Action," *Wall Street Journal*, March 28, 1996; Todd Gaziano, "The New 'Massive Resistance,'" *Policy Review* 89 (1998): 22–29; John H. McWhorter, *Losing the Race: Self-Sabotage in Black America* (New York: Free Press, 2000).

13. Dinesh D'Souza, *The End of Racism: Principles for a Multiracial Society* (New York: The Free Press, 1995), chapter 12.

14. Jacoby, *Someone Else's House*, 10.

15. Sleeper, *Liberal Racism*, 4.

16. Stephen Thernstrom and Abigail Thernstrom, *America in Black and White: One Nation, Indivisible* (New York: Simon and Schuster, 1997), 495, 498, 505; Jacoby, *Someone Else's House*, 9, 539–40.

17. Alan Wolfe, "Enough Blame to Go Around," *New York Times Book Review*, June 21, 1998, 12.

18. Thernstrom and Thernstrom, *America in Black and White*, 299–300; D'Souza, *End of Racism*, chapter 6.

19. Sleeper, *Liberal Racism*, 178.

20. Dr. Martin Luther King Jr., "I Have a Dream," in James Washington, ed., *A Testament of Hope*, 219; Sleeper, *Liberal Racism*, 178.

21. Conservative writers and think tanks have been in the forefront of the fight against affirmative action and other color-conscious policies. The D'Souza and Thernstrom books in particular are typical of conservative criticism of liberal policies. The research for *America in Black and White* was underwritten by many of the most influential conservative foundations, including the John M. Olin Foundation, the Smith Richardson Foundation, the Earhart Foundation, and the Carthage Foundation. Jacoby's research was sponsored by many of the same foundations. Both Jacoby and Abigail Thernstrom have been affiliated with the Manhattan Institute, an influential conservative think tank in New York City.

22. Thernstrom and Thernstrom, *America in Black and White*, 189–94; see also James Smith and Finis Welch, *Closing the Gap: Forty Years of Economic Progress for Blacks* (Santa Monica, Calif.: Rand Corporation, 1986). The Thernstroms' interpretation of black economic progress assumes that labor market discrimination was not a serious obstacle to good jobs and high wages for black workers after World War II. If this version of history is wrong and labor market discrimination was the cause of low wages and high unemployment, it would make little difference if blacks acquired more education. The Thernstroms' argument is implausible, and there is little evidence to support it. It rests on their assertion that the black unemployment rate was only slightly higher than the white unemployment rate in 1940, but twice as many blacks in the North

were unemployed as in the South. This, the Thernstroms say, is "exactly the opposite of what we would expect if unemployment had been mainly the result of discrimination" since one would expect Mississippi employers to treat blacks less fairly than employers in the North (Thernstrom and Thernstrom, *America in Black and White*, 245). The Thernstroms are wrong to presume that labor market discrimination was unimportant in the North. In the late 1930s, black unemployment rates in northern cities were two to four times higher than white unemployment rates, mainly because of the virulent labor market discrimination unleashed during the Depression when white workers displaced blacks. See Michael K. Brown, *Race, Money, and the American Welfare State* (Ithaca: Cornell University Press, 1999), 68–70; W. A. Sundstrom, "Last Hired, First Fired? Unemployment and Black Workers during the Great Depression," *The Journal of Economic History*, 52 (1991): 415–29. Moreover, unemployment figures for blacks in the South are misleading because seasonal workers (mainly farm workers) were excluded, and many of those reported as employed were unpaid family workers, which is "often little better than a make-shift activity for sons and daughters of farmers [and sharecroppers] when they cannot find other employment." U.S. Bureau of the Census, *Sixteenth Census of the United States: 1940, Population*, vol. 3, *The Labor Force*, part 1: *U.S. Summary* (Washington, D.C.: U. S. Government Printing Office, 1943), 5, 7. There is no reason to presume that the difference in unemployment rates reflects a lack of discrimination in the South.

23. For a clear statement of this argument, see James A. Heckman, "Detecting Discrimination," *Journal of Economic Perspectives* 12 (1998): 101–16; for a critique, see William A. Darity Jr. and Patrick L. Mason, "Evidence on Discrimination in Employment: Codes of Color, Codes of Gender," *Journal of Economic Perspectives* 12 (1998): 63–90.

24. Richard Epstein, *Forbidden Grounds: The Case against Employment Discrimination Laws* (Cambridge, Mass.: Harvard University Press, 1992), 32. It should be noted that in his original statement of the economic theory of discrimination, Gary Becker acknowledged labor market discrimination and set out to explain why it occurred in specific circumstances. See Gary Becker, *The Economics of Discrimination*, 2nd ed. (Chicago: University of Chicago Press, 1971).

25. Epstein, *Forbidden Grounds*, 46. Epstein does not assume that segregation leads to wage differences. Wage discrimination and segregation are separate phenomena.

26. Lawrence D. Bobo and Ryan A. Smith, "From Jim Crow Racism to Laissez-Faire Racism: The Transformation of Racial Attitudes," in Wendy F. Katkin, Ned Landsman, and Andrea Tyree, eds., *Beyond Pluralism: The Conception of Groups and Identities in America* (Urbana: University of Illinois Press, 1998), 212.

27. Thernstrom and Thernstrom, *America in Black and White*, 183.

28. U.S. Bureau of the Census, "Raw and Hispanic Origin of Householder—Families by Median and Mean Income: 1947 to 2001" (Table F-5), *Historical Income Tables—Families*, http://www.census.gov/hhes/income/histinc/f05.html (accessed October 9, 2002).

29. Ibid. See also Sheldon Danziger and Peter Gottschalk, *America Unequal* (New York: Russell Sage Foundation, 1995), 71–73. Using a measure of income that adjusts for family size and unrelated individuals, Danziger and Gottschalk show that in 1991 the real median income of black families was 1.85 times the poverty line, compared to 3.54 times for white families. Not until 1991 did black family income reach a level comparable to 1959 family income for the total population. Among nonelderly, two-parent families the ratio rose from 44 percent to 71 percent in 1991, still a large gap. In 2001, after the economic expansion, black married couples' income was 80 percent of white married couples'. However, this measure is not comparable to Danziger's and Gottschalk's and may overstate the ratio.

30. U.S. Bureau of the Census, "Race and Hispanic Origin of People by Median Income and Sex: 1947 to 2,001" (Table P-2), *Historical Income Tables — People*, http://www.census.gov/hhes/income/histinc/p02.html (accessed October 9, 2002).

31. Council of Economic Advisers, *Changing America* (Washington D.C.: U.S. Government Printing Office, 1998), 28. Many economists point out that it makes no sense to exclude unemployed or part-time black workers from these comparisons. Doing so inflates the relative income gain of black workers because low-income black workers (who have higher unemployment rates) and high-income white workers (who presumably retire early) are excluded from the calculations. This biases estimates of black-white earnings ratios upward. See William Darity Jr. and Samuel Myers Jr., *Persistent Disparity: Race and Economic Inequality in the United States since 1945* (Northampton, Mass.: Edward Elgar Publishing, 1998), 46–47.

32. Douglas Massey and Nancy Demon, *American Apartheid: Segregation and the Making of the Underclass* (Cambridge, Mass.: Harvard University Press, 1993), 77, 87–88.

33. Preliminary studies conducted by the National Fair Housing Alliance reveal how this gap is created. The Alliance found that when creditworthy whites approach subprime lenders, they are systematically referred to prime lenders, who make loans on more favorable terms, with lower interest rates and less predatory foreclosure practices.

34. The ratio of black–white infant mortality rate rose from 1.94 in 1980 to 2.35 in 1998. National Center for Health Statistics, "Infant Mortality Rates, Fetal Mortality Rates, and Perinatal Mortality Rates, according to Race: United States, Selected Years 1950–99" (Table 23), *Centers for Disease Control*, http://www.cdc.gov/nchs/products/pubs/pubd/hus/tables/2001/01hus023.pdf (accessed October 9, 2002).

35. David Barton Smith, *Health Care Divided: Race and Healing a Nation* (Ann Arbor: University of Michigan Press, 1999), 210. Smith notes that the National Center for Health Statistics' 1996–97 report documents that blacks' mortality rates are twice as high as those of whites for years of life lost before the age of seventy-five per 100,000 in population.

36. In 1986, for example, among males under 65, those with the highest educational attainment showed the largest relative racial discrepancies in mortality rates. For adult females, the largest relative racial disparity in mortality rates is found in the highest income category. Gregory Pappas et al., "The Increasing Disparity in Mortality between Socioeconomic Groups in the United States, 1960 and 1986," *New England Journal of Medicine* 329 (1987): 103–9.

37. Testimony of Ed Mendoza, Assistant Director, Special Initiatives and Program Evaluation, Office of Statewide Health Planning and Development, before Joint Hearing of the California Senate Committee on Business and Professions and the California Senate Committee on Health and Human Services, March 31, 1997, Handout #4, 1, 11 (unpublished document on file with authors).

38. Smith, *Health Care Divided*, 201.

39. Elizabeth White, "Special Report: Public Health Racial and Ethnic Disparities," *Health Care Policy Report* 9 (2.001): 315; "40% Rise Reported in Asthma and Asthma Deaths," *New York Times*, January 7, 1995, section 2, 10; "Asthma Toll Is Up Sharply, US Reports," *New York Times*, May 3, 1996, C18.

40. Smith, *Health Care Divided*, 208, table 6.8.

41. Charles Tilly, *Durable Inequality* (Berkeley and Los Angeles: University of California Press, 1998), 17.

42. This is misleading because the small decline in residential segregation occurred largely in cities with very small black populations. See Massey and Denton, *American Apartheid*, 66, 221–23.

43. Thernstrom and Thernstrom, *America in Black and White*, 219–30.

44. Sally Satel, PC, M.D., *How Political Correctness Is Corrupting Medicine* (New York: Basic Books, Inc., 2000), 2, 23.

45. Ruth Milkman and Eleanor Townsend, "Gender and the Economy," in Neil J. Smelser and Richard Swedberg, eds., *Handbook of Economic Sociology* (Princeton: Princeton University Press, 1994), 611; cited in Tilly, *Durable Inequality*, 31.

46. William Darity Jr., "What's Left of the Economic Theory of Discrimination," in Steven Shulman and William Darity Jr., eds., *The Question of Discrimination* (Middletown, Conn.: Wesleyan University Press, 1989), 335–74. Economists have advanced a variety of ingenious explanations for the persistence of racial discrimination; all of these assume (at least implicitly) that discrimination is temporary and all are based on individual-level explanations. See Darity and Mason, "Evidence of Discrimination in Employment," 81–87, for a summary. However, James Heckman points out that a bigoted employer can "indulge that taste so long as income is received from entrepreneurial activity"—so long, that is, as there is a willingness to pay the price. See Heckman, "Detecting Discrimination," 112.

47. Peter V. Marsden, "The Hiring Process: Recruitment Methods," *American Behavioral Scientist* 7 (1994): 979–91; Shazia R. Miller and James E. Rosenbaum, "Hiring in a Hobbesian World," *Work and Occupations* 24 (1997): 498–523.

48. Philip Kasinitz and Jay Rosenberg, "Missing the Connection: Social Isolation and Employment on the Brooklyn Waterfront," *Social Problems* 43 (1996): 180–96; for a description see Thomas Sugrue, *The Origins of the Urban Crisis* (Princeton: Princeton University Press, 1996), chapter 4.

49. Tilly, *Durable Inequality*, 91.

50. Economists have developed a very similar theory to Tilly's idea of opportunity hoarding; see Derek Leslie, *An Investigation of Racial Disadvantage* (Manchester: Manchester University Press, 1998), 33–37.

51. Darity and Myers, *Persistent Disparity*, 58.

52. See Reynolds Parley and Walter Alien, *The Color Line and the Quality of Life in America* (New York: Oxford University Press, 1989), 247; Stanley Lieberson, *A Piece of the Pie: Blacks and White Immigrants since 1880* (Berkeley: University of California Press, 1980), 294–313. Epstein assumes that at least one employer will be motivated by the bottom line and not by negative stereotypes. But this neglects the pressure that white workers may bring to bear on employers to exclude blacks.

53. Pennsylvania nursing homes have a segregation index of .68, which means that 68 percent of nursing home residents would have to move in order to equalize the distribution of blacks and whites across all homes. The 1990 average segregation index for northern cities was .78. Some of the segregation in nursing homes is an artifact of residential segregation, but not all of it—the segregation index for Philadelphia nursing homes is .63. Smith, *Health Care Divided*, 264–65, 267; Massey and Denton, *American Apartheid*, 222.

54. Smith, *Health Care Divided*, 267.

55. Ibid., 319–20.

56. William Julius Wilson, *The Truly Disadvantaged* (Chicago: University of Chicago Press, 1987), 11.

57. Conley, *Being Black, Living in the Red* (Berkeley: University of California Press, 1999), 152.

58. Thernstrom and Thernstrom, *America in Black and White*, 197–98.

59. Blacks save 11 percent of their income; whites save 10 percent. Conley, *Being Black, Living in the Red*, 29.

60. Todd Lewan and Delores Barcaly, "Torn from the Land: AP Documents Land Taken from

Blacks through Trickery, Violence and Murder," *Associated Press*, December 2001, http://wire.ap.org/APpackages/torn/ (accessed January 2, 2002).

61. Conley, *Being Black, Living in the Red*, 38–39; Massey and Denton, *American Apartheid*, 54–55.

62. Black babies are one and one-third times as likely as whites to suffer from low birth weight and more than three times as likely to suffer very low birth weight. See W. Michael Byrd and Linda A. Clayton, *An American Health Dilemma*, vol. 1, *A Medical History of African Americans and the Problem of Race: Beginnings to 1900* (New York: Routledge, 2000), 30.

63. Among black children one to six years of age, 11.5 percent had elevated blood lead levels in 1991–94, compared to 2.6 percent of white children of the same age. U.S. Department of Health and Human Services, *Healthy People 2010: Understanding and Improving Health*, 2nd ed. (Washington, D.C.: U.S. Government Printing Office, 2000), 8–21.

64. Marianne Means, "Refocus Racism Conference Agenda," *San Francisco Chronicle*, August 13, 2001, A17.

65. Ian Haney-Lopez, *White by Law: The Legal Construction of Race* (New York: New York University Press, 1996), 1; see also Mary Francis Berry, *Black Resistance, White Law* (New York: Penguin Books, 1995).

66. See George Fredrickson, *The Arrogance of Race* (Middletown, Conn.: Wesleyan University Press, 1988), and *White Supremacy* (New York: Oxford University Press, 1981); and Leon A. Higginbotham, *In the Matter of Color: Race and the American Legal Process* (New York: Oxford University Press, 1978).

67. *Dred Scott v. Sanford*, 19 How. (60 U.S.) 393 (1857).

68. Vincent Harding, *There Is a River: The Black Struggle for Freedom in America* (New York: Oxford University Press, 1983), 201.

69. Stephen Steinberg, *Turning Back: The Retreat from Racial Justice in American Thought and Policy* (Boston: Beacon Press, 1995).

70. Jill Quadagno, *The Color of Welfare* (New York: Oxford University Press, 1994), 19–14.

71. Brown, *Race, Money, and the American Welfare State*, 71.

72. Ibid, 82; U.S. Congress, Senate, Committee on Finance, *Economic Security Act Hearings on S. 1130*, 74th Congress, 1st Session, 1935, 641.

73. Brown, *Race, Money, and the American Welfare State*, 82.

74. Quadagno, *The Color of Welfare*, 160–61.

75. Robert Lieberman, *Shifting the Color Line: Race and the American Welfare State* (Cambridge, Mass.: Harvard University Press, 1998), 198–99, 210.

76. Brown, *Race, Money, and the American Welfare State*, chapters 2. and 5.

77. Herbert Hill, *Black Labor and the American Legal System* (Madison: University of Wisconsin Press, 1985), 105; Quadagno, *The Color of Welfare*, 23; Brown, *Race, Money, and the American Welfare State*, 68.

78. Irving Bernstein, *Promises Kept: John F. Kennedy's New Frontier* (New York: Oxford University Press, 1991), 165–67.

79. George Lipsitz, *The Possessive Investment in Whiteness: How White People Profit from Identity Politics* (Philadelphia: Temple University Press, 1998).

80. Andrew Hacker, *Two Nations* (New York: Ballantine Books, 1992,), 32.

81. Reva B. Siegel, "The Racial Rhetorics of Color-Blind Constitutionalism: The Case of *Hopwood v. Texas*," in Robert Post and Michael Rogin, eds., *Race and Representation: Affirmative Action* (New York: Zone Books, 1998), 49–50.

82. Alexis de Tocqueville, *Democracy in America* (1835; reprint, New York: Anchor Books, 1969), 344.

A Sociology of Wealth and Racial Inequality

MELVIN L. OLIVER AND THOMAS M. SHAPIRO

Understanding Racial Inequality

African Americans are vastly overrepresented among those Americans whose lives are the most economically and socially distressed. As William Julius Wilson has argued in *The Truly Disadvantaged*, "The most disadvantaged segments of the black urban community" have come to make up the majority of "that heterogeneous grouping of families and individuals who are outside the mainstream of the American occupational system" and who are euphemistically called the underclass.[1] With little or no access to jobs, trapped in poor areas with bad schools and little social and economic opportunity, members of the underclass resort to crime, drugs, and other forms of aberrant behavior to make a living and eke some degree of meaning out of their materially impoverished existence. Douglas Massey and Nancy Denton's *American Apartheid* has reinforced in our minds the crucial significance of racial segregation, which Lawrence Bobo calls the veritable "structural linchpin" of American racial inequality.[2]

These facts should not be in dispute. What is in dispute is our understanding of the source of such resounding levels of racial inequality. What factors were responsible for their creation and what are the sources of their continuation? Sociologists and social scientists have focused on either race or class or on some combination or interaction of the two as the overriding factors responsible for racial inequality.

A focus on race suggests that race has had a unique cultural meaning in American society wherein blacks have been oppressed in such a way as to perpetuate their inferiority and second-class citizenship. Race in this context has a socially constructed meaning that is acted on by whites to purposefully limit and constrain the black population. The foundation of this social construction is the ideology of racism. Racism is a belief in the inherent inferiority of one race in relation to another. Racism both justifies and dictates the actions and institutional decisions that adversely affect the target group.

Class explanations emphasize the relational positioning of blacks and whites in society and the differential access to power that accrues to the status of each group. Those classes with access to resources through the ownership or control of capital (in the Marxian variant) or through the occupational hierarchy (in the Weberian variant) are able to translate these resources into policies and structures through their access to power. In some cases this can be seen in the way in which those who control the economy also control the polity. In other cases it can be observed in the way in which institutional elites control institutions. In any case the class perspective emphasizes the relative positions of blacks and whites with respect to the ownership and control of the means of production and to access to valued occupational niches, both historically and contemporaneously. Because blacks have traditionally had access to few of these types of valued resources, they share an interest with the other have-nots. As Raymond Franklin notes in *Shadows of Race and Class*, "Ownership carries with it domination; its absence leads to subordination."[3] The subordinated and unequal status of African Americans, in the class perspective, grows out of the structured class divisions between blacks and a small minority of resource-rich and powerful whites.[4]

Each of these perspectives has been successfully applied to understanding racial inequality. However, each also has major failings. The emphasis on race creates problems of evidence. Especially in the contemporary period, as William Julius Wilson notes in *The Declining Significance of Race*, it is difficult to trace the enduring existence of racial inequality to an articulated ideology of racism. The trail of historical evidence proudly left in previous periods is made less evident by heightened sensitivity to legal sanctions and racial civility in language. Thus those who still emphasize race in the modern era speak of covert racism and use as evidence racial disparities in income, jobs, and housing. In fact, however, impersonal structural forces whose racial motivation cannot be ascertained are often the cause of the black disadvantage that observers identify. Likewise, class perspectives usually wash away any reference to race. Moreover, the class-based analysis that blacks united with low-income white workers and other disadvantaged groups would be the most likely source of collective opposition to current social economic arrangements has given way to continued estrangement between these groups. The materialist perspective that policy should address broad class groups as opposed to specific racial groups leaves the unique historical legacy of race untouched.

Despite these weaknesses it is imperative that race and class factors be taken into consideration in any attempt to understand contemporary racial inequality. It is clear, however, that a singular focus on one as opposed to another is counterproductive. Take, for example, earnings inequality. As economists assert, earnings are affected today more by class than by racial factors. Human capital attributes (such as education, experience, skills, etc.) that may result from historical disadvantages play an important role in the earnings gap between blacks and whites. But because of the unique position of black Americans, earnings must be viewed in relation to joblessness. If you do not have a job, you have no earnings. Here it is clear that race and class are important. As structural changes in the economy have occurred, blacks have been disproportionately disadvantaged. Such structural changes as the movement of entry-level jobs outside of the central city, the change in the economy from goods to service production, and the shift to higher skill levels have created a jobless black population.[5] Furthermore, increasing numbers of new entrants into the labor market find low-skill jobs below poverty wages that do not support a family. Nevertheless, race is important as well. Evidence from employers shows that negative racial attitudes about black workers are still motivating their hiring practices, particularly in reference to central-city blacks and in the service economy. In service jobs nonblacks are preferred over blacks, particularly black men, a preference that contributes to the low wages blacks earn, to high rates of joblessness, and thus to earnings inequality.

Because of the way in which they reveal the effect of historical factors on contemporary processes, racial differences in wealth provide an important means of combining race and class arguments about racial inequality. We therefore turn to a theoretical discussion of wealth and race that develops aspects of traditional race and class arguments in an attempt to illuminate the processes that have led to wealth disparities between black and white Americans.

Toward a Sociology of Race and Wealth

A sociology of race and wealth must go beyond the traditional analysis of wealth that economists have elaborated. Economists begin with the assumption that wealth is a combination of inheritance, earnings, and savings and is enhanced by prudent consumption and investment patterns over a person's lifetime. Of course, individual variability in any of these factors depends on a whole set of other relationships that are sociologically relevant. Obviously one's inheritance depends on the family into which one is born. If one's family of origin is wealthy, one's chances of accumulating more wealth in a lifetime are greater. Earnings, the economists tell us, are a function of the productivity of our human capital: our education, experience, and skills. Since these are, at least in part, dependent on an investment in training activities, they can be acquired by means of inherited resources. Savings are a function of both our earning power and our consumption patterns. Spendthrifts will have little or no disposable income to save, while those who are frugal can find ways to put money aside. Those with high levels of human capital, who socially interact in the right circles and who have knowledge of investment opportunities, will increase their wealth substantially more during their lifetime than will those who are only thrifty. And since money usually grows over time, the earlier one starts and the longer one's money is invested, the more wealth one will be able to amass. Economists therefore explain differences in wealth accumulation by pointing to the lack of resources that blacks inherit compared to whites, their low investment in human capital, and their extravagant patterns of consumption.

Sociologists do not so much disagree with the economists' emphasis on these three factors and their relationship to human capital in explaining black-white differences in wealth; rather, they are concerned that economists have not properly appreciated the social context in which the processes in question take place. Quite likely, formal models would accurately predict wealth differences. However, in the real world, an emphasis on these factors isolated from the social context misses the underlying reasons why whites and blacks have displayed such strong differences in their ability to generate wealth. The major reason that blacks and whites differ in their ability to accumulate wealth is not only that they come from different class backgrounds or that their consumption patterns are different or that they fail to save at the same rate, but that the structure of investment opportunity that blacks and whites face has been dramatically different. Work and wages play a smaller role in the accumulation of wealth than the prevailing discourse admits.

Blacks and whites have faced an opportunity to create wealth that has been structured by the intersection of class and race. Economists rightly note that blacks' lack of desirable human capital attributes places them at a disadvantage in the wealth accumulation process. However, those human capital deficiencies can be traced, in part, to barriers that denied blacks access to quality education, job training opportunities, jobs, and other work-related factors. Below we develop three concepts—the racialization of the state, the economic detour, and the sedimentation of racial inequality—to help us situate the distinct structures of investment opportunity that blacks and whites have faced in their attempts to generate wealth.

Racialization of the State

The context of one's opportunity to acquire land, build community, and generate wealth has been structured particularly by state policy. Slavery itself, the most constricting of social systems, was a result of state policy that gave blacks severely limited economic rights. Slaves were by law not able to own property or accumulate assets. In contrast, no matter how poor whites were, they had the right — if they were males, that is — if not the ability, to buy land, enter into contracts, own businesses, and develop wealth assets that could build equity and economic self-sufficiency for themselves and their families. Some argue that it was the inability to participate in and develop a habit of savings during slavery that directly accounts for low wealth development among blacks today. Using a cultural argument, they assert that slaves developed a habit of excessive consumerism and not one of savings and thrift.[6] This distorts the historical reality, however. While slaves were legally not able to amass wealth, they did, in large numbers, acquire assets through thrift, intelligence, industry, and their owners' liberal paternalism. These assets were used to buy their own and their loved ones' freedom, however, and thus did not form the core of a material legacy that could be passed from generation to generation. Whites could use their wealth for the future; black slaves' savings could only buy the freedom that whites took for granted.

Slavery was only one of the racialized state policies that have inhibited the acquisition of assets for African Americans. The homestead laws that opened up the East during colonial times and West during the nineteenth century created vastly different opportunities for black and white settlers. One commentator even suggests land grants "allowed three-fourths of America's colonial families to own their own farms."[7] Black settlers in California, the "Golden State," found that their claims for homestead status were not legally enforceable.[8] Thus African Americans were largely barred from taking advantage of the nineteenth-century federal land-grant program.

A centerpiece of New Deal social legislation and a cornerstone of the modern welfare state, the old-age insurance program of the Social Security Act of 1935 virtually excluded African Americans and Latinos, for it exempted agricultural and domestic workers from coverage and marginalized low-wage workers. As Gwendolyn Mink shows in "The Lady and the Tramp," men's benefits were tied to wages, military service, and unionism rather than to need or any notion of equality. Thus blacks were disadvantaged in New Deal legislation because they were historically less well paid, less fully employed, disproportionately ineligible for military service, and less fully unionized than white men.[9] Minority workers were covered by social security and New Deal labor policies if employed in eligible occupations and if they earned the minimum amount required. Because minority wages were so low, minority workers fell disproportionately below the threshold of coverage in comparison to whites. In 1935, for example, 42 percent of black workers in occupations covered by social insurance did not earn enough to qualify for benefits, compared to 22 percent of whites.

Not only were blacks initially disadvantaged in their eligibility for social security, but they have disproportionately paid more into the system and received less. Because social security contributions are made on a flat rate and black workers earn less, as Jill Quadagno explains in *The Color of Welfare*, "Black men were taxed on 100 percent of their income, on average, while white men earned a considerable amount of untaxed income."[10] Black workers also earn lower retirement benefits. And benefits do not extend as long as for whites because their life span is shorter. Furthermore, since more black women are single, divorced, or separated, they cannot look forward to sharing a spouse's benefit. As Quadagno notes, again, the tax contributions of black working women "subsidize the benefits of white housewives."[11] In many ways social security is a model state program that allows families to preserve assets built over a lifetime. For African Americans, however, it is a different kind of model of state bias. Initially built on concessions made to white racial privilege in the South, the social security program today is a system in which blacks pay more to receive less. It is a prime example of how the political process and state policy build opportunities for asset accumulation sharply skewed along racial lines.

We now turn to three other instruments of state policy that we feel have been central to creating structured opportunities for whites to build assets while significantly curtailing access to those same opportunities among blacks. Sometimes the aim was blatantly racial; sometimes the racial intention was not clear. In both instances, however, the results have been explicitly racial. They are the Federal Housing Authority (FHA); the Supplementary Social Security Act, which laid the foundation for our present day Aid to Families with Dependent Children (AFDC); and the U.S. tax code. In each case state policies have created differential opportunities for blacks and whites to develop disposable income and to generate wealth.

Federal Housing Authority

The development of low-interest, long-term mortgages backed by the federal government marked the appearance of a crucial opportunity for the average American family to generate a wealth stake. The purchase of a home has now become the primary mechanism for generating wealth. However, the FHA's conscious decision to channel loans away from the central city and to the suburbs has had a powerful effect on the creation of segregated housing in post–World War Two America. George Lipsitz reports in "The Possessive Investment in Whiteness" that in the Los Angeles area of Boyle Heights, FHA appraisers denied home loans to prospective buyers because the neighborhood was "a melting pot area literally honeycombed with diverse and subversive elements."[12] Official government policy supported the prejudiced attitudes of private finance companies, Realtors, appraisers, and a white public resistant to sharing social space with blacks.

The FHA's official handbook even went so far as to provide a model "restrictive covenant" that would pass court scrutiny to prospective white home buyers. Such policies gave support to white neighborhoods like those in East Detroit in 1940. Concerned that blacks would move in, the Eastern Detroit Realty Association sponsored a luncheon on the "the benefits of an improvement association," where the speaker, a lawyer, lectured on how "to effect legal restrictions against the influx of colored residents into white communities."[13] He went on to present the elements needed to institute a legally enforceable restrictive covenant for "a district of two miles square." Such a task was too much for one man and would require an "organization" that could mobilize and gain the cooperation of "everyone in a subdivision." Imagine the hurdles that are placed in the path of blacks attempts to move into white neighborhoods when communities, Realtors, lawyers, and the federal government are all wholly united behind such restrictions!

Restrictive covenants and other "segregation makers" have been ruled unconstitutional in a number of important court cases. But the legacy of the FHA's contribution to racial residential segregation lives on in the inability of blacks to incorporate themselves into integrated neighborhoods in which the equity and demand for their homes is maintained. This is seen most clearly in the fact that black middle-class homeowners end up with less valuable homes even when their incomes are similar to those of whites. When black middle-class families pursue the American Dream in white neighborhoods adjacent to existing black communities, a familiar process occurs. As one study explains it, "White households will begin to move out and those neighborhoods will tend to undergo complete racial transition or to 'tip.' Typically, when the percentage of blacks in a neighborhood increases to a relatively small amount, 10 to 20 percent, white demand for housing in the neighborhood will fall off and the neighborhood will tip toward segregation."[14]

Even though the neighborhood initially has high market value generated by the black demand for houses, as the segregation process kicks in, housing values rise at a slower rate. By the end of the racial transition housing prices have declined as white homeowners flee. Thus middle-class blacks encounter lower rates of home appreciation than do similar middle-class whites in all-white communities. As Raymond Franklin notes in *Shadows of Race and Class*, this is an example of how race and class considerations are involved in producing black-white wealth differentials. The "shadow" of class creates a situation of race. To quote Franklin:

> In sum, because there is a white fear of being inundated with lower-class black "hordes" who lack market capacities, it becomes necessary to prevent the entry of middle-class black families who have market capacities. In this way, middle-class blacks are discriminated against for purely racial reasons. . . . Given the "uncertainty inherent in racial integration and racial transition," white families—unwilling to risk falling property values—leave the area. This, of course, leads to falling prices, enabling poorer blacks to enter the neighborhood "until segregation becomes complete."[15]

The impact of race and class is also channeled through institutional mechanisms that help to destabilize black communities. Insurance redlining begins to make it difficult and/or expensive for homes and businesses to secure coverage. City services begin to decline, contributing to blight. As the community declines, it becomes the center for antisocial activities: drug dealing, hanging out, and robbery and violence.[16] In this context the initial investment that the middle-class black family makes either stops growing or grows at a rate that is substantially lower than the rate at which a comparable investment made by a similarly well-off, middle-class white in an all-white community would gain in value. Racialized state policy contributed to this pattern, and the pattern continues unabated today.

Aid to Families with Dependent Children

Within the public mind and according to the current political debate, AFDC has become synonymous with "welfare," even though it represents less than 10 percent of all assistance for the poor. The small sums paid to women and their children are designed not to provide families a springboard for their future but to help them survive in a minimal way from day to day.[17] When the initial legislation for AFDC was passed, few of its supporters envisioned a program that would serve large numbers of African American women and their children; the ideal recipient, according to Michael Katz in *In the Shadow of the Poor House*, "was a white widow and her young children." Until the mid-1960s states enforced this perception through the establishment of eligibility requirements that disproportionately excluded black women and their children. Southern states routinely deemed black women and their children "unsuitable" for welfare by way of demeaning home inspections and searches. Northern states likewise created barriers that were directly targeted at black-female-headed families. They participated in "midnight raids" to discover whether a "man was in the house" or recomputed budgets to find clients ineligible and keep them off the rolls. Nonetheless, by the mid-1960s minorities were disproportionately beneficiaries of AFDC, despite intentions to the contrary. In 1988, while blacks and Hispanics made up only 44 percent of all women who headed households, they constituted 55 percent of all AFDC recipients.[18]

In exchange for modest and sometimes niggardly levels of income support, women must go through an "assets test" before they are eligible. Michael Sherraden describes it this way in his *Assets and the Poor*: "The assets test requires that recipients have no more than minimal assets (usually $1,500, with home equity excluded) in order to become or remain eligible for the program. The asset test effectively prohibits recipients from accumulating savings."[19] As a consequence, women enter welfare on the economic edge. They deplete almost all of their savings in order to become eligible for a program that will not provide more than a subsistence living. What little savings remain are usually drawn down to meet routine shortfalls and emergencies. The result is that AFDC has become for many women, especially African American women, a state-sponsored policy to encourage and maintain asset poverty.

To underscore the impact of AFDC's strictures let us draw the distinction between this program and Supplementary Security Income (SSI), a program that provides benefits for children and women whose spouses have died or become disabled after paying into social security. In contrast to AFDC benefits, SSI payments are generous. More important perhaps, eligibility for SSI does not require drawing down a family's assets as part of a "means test." The result, which is built into the structure of American welfare policy, is that "means-tested" programs like AFDC and "non-means-tested" social insurance programs like social security and SSI, in Michael Katz's words, have "preserved class distinctions" and "in no way redistribute income."[20] It is also an example of how the racialization of the state preserves and broadens the already deep wealth divisions between black and white.

The Internal Revenue Code

A substantial portion of state expenditures take the form of tax benefits, or "fiscal welfare." These benefits are hidden in the tax code as taxes individuals do not have to pay because the government has decided to encourage certain types of activity and behavior and not others. In *America: Who Really Pays the Taxes?* Donald Barlett and James Steele write that one of the most cherished privileges of the very rich and powerful resides in their ability to influence the tax code for their own benefit by protecting capital assets. Tax advantages may come in the form of different rates on certain types of income, tax deferral, or deductions, exclusions, and credits. Many are asset-based: if you own certain assets, you receive a tax break. In turn, these tax breaks directly help people accumulate financial and real assets. They benefit not only the wealthy but the broad middle class of homeowners and pension holders as well. More important, since blacks have fewer assets to begin with, the effect of the tax code's "fiscal welfare" is to limit the flow of tax relief to blacks and to redirect it to those who already have assets. The seemingly race-neutral tax code thus generates a racial effect that deepens rather than equalizes the economic gulf between blacks and whites.

Two examples will illustrate how the current functioning of the tax code represents yet another form of the "racialization of state policy." The *lower tax rates on capital gains* and the *deduction for home mortgages and real estate taxes*, we argue, flow differentially to blacks and whites because of the fact that blacks generally have fewer and different types of assets than whites with similar incomes.

For most of our nation's tax history the Internal Revenue Code has encouraged private investment by offering lower tax rates for income gained through "capital assets." This policy exists to encourage investment and further asset accumulation, not to provide more spendable income. In 1994, earned income in the top bracket was taxed at 39.6 percent, for example, while capital gains were taxed at 24 percent, a figure that can go as low as 14 percent. One has to be networked with accountants, tax advisers, investors, partners, and friends knowledgeable about where to channel money to take advantage of these breaks. Capital gains may be derived from the sale of stocks, bonds, commodities, and other assets. In 1989 the IRS reported that $150.2 billion in capital gains income was reported by taxpayers.[21] While this sounds like a lot of capital gains for everyone to divvy up, the lion's share (72 percent) went to individuals and families earning more than $100,000 yearly. These families represented only 1 percent of all tax filers. The remaining $42 billion in capital gains income was reported by only 7.2 million people with incomes of under $100,000 per year. This group represented only 6 percent of tax filers. Thus for more than nine of every ten tax filers (93 percent) no capital gains income was reported. Clearly then, the tax-reduction benefits on capital gains income are highly concentrated among the nation's wealthiest individuals and families. Thus it would follow that blacks, given their lower incomes and fewer assets, would be much less likely than whites to gain the tax advantage associated with capital gains. The black disadvantage becomes most obvious when one compares middle-class and higher-income blacks to whites at a similar level of earnings. Despite comparable incomes, middle-class blacks have fewer of their wealth holdings in capital-producing assets than similarly situated whites. Our data show that among high-earning families ($50,000 a year or more) 17 percent of whites' assets are in stocks, bonds, and mortgages versus 5.4 percent for blacks. Thus while race-neutral in intent, the current tax policy on capital gains provides disproportionate benefits to high-income whites, while limiting a major tax benefit to practically all African Americans.

Accessible to a larger group of Americans are those tax deductions, exclusions, and deferrals that the IRS provides to homeowners. Four IRS-mandated benefits can flow from home ownership: (1) the home mortgage interest deduction; (2) the deduction for local real estate taxes; (3) the avoidance of taxes on the sale of a home when it is "rolled over" into another residence; and (4) the one-time permanent exclusion of up to $125,000 of profit on the sale of a home after the age of fifty-five. Put quite simply, since blacks are less likely to own homes, they are less likely to be able to take advantage of these benefits. Furthermore, since black homes are on average less expensive than white homes, blacks derive less benefit than whites when they do utilize these tax provisions.[22] And finally, since most of the benefits in question here are available only when taxpayers itemize their deductions, there is a great deal of concern that many black taxpayers may not take advantage of the tax breaks they are eligible for because they file the short tax form. The stakes here are very high. The subsidy that goes to homeowners in the form of tax deductions for mortgage interest and property taxes alone comes to $54 billion, about $20 billion of which goes to the top 5 percent of taxpayers.

These examples illustrate how the U.S. tax code channels benefits and encourages property and capital asset accumulation differentially by race. They are but a few of several examples that could have been used. Tax provisions pertaining to inheritance, gift income, alimony payments, pensions and Keogh accounts, and property appreciation, along with the marriage tax and the child care credit on their face are not color-coded, yet they carry with them the potential to channel benefits away from most blacks and toward some whites. State policy has racialized the opportunities for the development of wealth, creating and sustaining the existing patterns of wealth inequality and extending them into the future.

Black Self-Employment: The Economic Detour

In American society one of the most celebrated paths to economic self-sufficiency, both in reality and in myth, has been self-employment. It is a risky undertaking that more often than not fails. But for many Americans the rewards of success associated with self-employment have been the key to economic success and wealth accumulation. Blacks have been portrayed in the sociological literature as the American ethnic group with the lowest rate and degree of success in using self-employment as a means of social mobility. The successful Japanese and Jewish experiences in self-employment, for example, have been used to demonstrate a range of supposed failings in the African American community.[23] This form of invidious comparison projects a whole range of "positive" characteristics onto those who have been successful in self-employment while casting African Americans as socially deficient and constitutionally impaired when it comes to creating flourishing businesses.[24] This same argument has been extended to newly arrived Cubans, Koreans, and Jamaicans. Ethnic comparisons that disadvantage blacks fail to adequately capture the harsh effects of the kind of hostility, unequaled in any other group, that African Americans have had to face in securing a foothold in self-employment. Racist state policy, Jim Crow segregation, discrimination, and violence have punctuated black entrepreneurial efforts of all kinds. Blacks have faced levels of hardship in their pursuit of self-employment that have never been experienced as fully by or applied as consistently to other ethnic groups, even other nonwhite ethnics.[25]

The deficit model of the so-called black failure to successfully create self-employment needs to be amended.[26] The stress placed by this model on the lack of a business tradition, the inexperience and lack of education that black business owners have often had, and the absence of racial solidarity among black consumers must be transcended. Instead, we need to view the black experience in self-employment as one similar to that of other ethnic groups whose members have sometimes been encouraged by societal hostility to follow this path to economic independence. The distinction is that black Americans have taken this path under circumstances inimical to their success.

As Max Weber pointed out in *The Protestant Ethic and the Spirit of Capitalism*, when groups face national oppression, one form of reaction is entrepreneurship. Immigrant groups like the Japanese in California and the Chinese in Mississippi responded to the societal hostility (e.g., discrimination) against them by immersing themselves in small business enterprises. But unlike blacks, as John Butler states in his *Entrepreneurship and Self-Help among Black Americans*, "they were able to enter the open market and compete."[27] They faced few restrictions to commerce. They could penetrate as much of a market as their economic capacity and tolerance for risk could accommodate. They thus carved comfortable economic niches and were able to succeed, albeit on a moderate scale.

Blacks, by contrast, faced a much grimmer opportunity picture. Here is where the concept of the "economic detour" has relevance. With predispositions like those of immigrants to the idea of self-employment, blacks faced an environment where they were by law restricted from participation in business on the open market, especially from the postbellum period to the middle of the twentieth century. Explicit state and local policies restricted the rights and freedoms of blacks as economic agents. Many types of businesses were off-limits to them, and more important, they were restricted to all-black segregated markets. While whites and other ethnic groups could do business with blacks, whites, and whomever else they pleased, black business was prohibited from entering into any but all-black markets. This restriction had a devastating impact on the ability of blacks to build and maintain successful businesses. As Edna Bonacich and John Modell point out in *The Economic Basis of Ethnic Solidarity* with regard to the Japanese, this group's greatest success occurred when they developed customer bases outside the Japanese community.[28] When they were restricted to their own group, their economic success was not nearly as great. The African American experience in entrepreneurship re-creates this duality. As John Butler observes, "It is true throughout history, when Afro-American business enterprises developed a clientele outside of their community, they were more likely to be successful."[29]

Barred from the most lucrative markets and attempting to provide high levels of goods and services under the constraints of segregation and discrimination, blacks remain the only group who have been required to take what Merah Stuart in 1940 first called an "economic detour."

> This [exclusion from the market] is not his preference. Yet it seems to be his only recourse. It is an economic detour which no other racial group in this country is required to travel. Any type of foreigner, Oriental or "what not," can usually attract to his business a surviving degree of patronage of the native American. No matter that he may be fresh from foreign shores with no contribution to the national welfare of his credit; no matter that he sends every dollar of his American-earned profit back to his foreign home . . . yet he can find a welcome place on the economic broadway to America.[30]

The African American, by contrast, despite "centuries of unrequited toil"[31] in service to building this country, "must turn to a detour that leads he knows not where." What he does know is that he must seek his customers or clients "from within his own race," no matter the business. And in doing so, he must compete for those customers with others who simultaneously enjoy access to greater and more lucrative markets.

This policy created conditions in which blacks, again according to Stuart, "were forced into the role of consumer." Self-employment became an important symbol of community empowerment. As Stuart goes on to suggest, "Seeking a way, therefore, to have a chance at the beneficial reaction of his spent dollars in the form of employment created; seeking a way to avoid buying insults and assure himself courtesy when he buys the necessities of life; seeking respect, the American Negro has been driven into an awkward, selfish corner, attempting to operate racial business to rear a stepchild economy."[32]

The inability of blacks to compete in an open market has ensured low levels of black business development and has kept black businesses relatively small.[33] Despite the obstacles they have faced, however, blacks have produced impressive results at various times in American history, even under conditions associated with the "economic detour." Before slavery was abolished, free blacks, in both southern and northern cities, built successful enterprises that required substantial skill and ingenuity. The 1838 document entitled "A Register of Trades of Colored People in the City of Philadelphia and Districts" lists over five hundred persons in fifty-seven different occupations and a host of business owners in industries ranging from sailboat building to lumber, catering, and blacksmithing. Free blacks during Reconstruction, as Abram Harris's classic *The Negro as Capitalist* points out, "had practically no competition" in spheres that whites avoided because of their "servile status."[34] Other cities also had considerable free black business activity. John Butler describes Cincinnati as the "center of enterprise for the free black population of the Middle West."[35] In 1840 half of Cincinnati's black population were freedmen who had begun acquiring property and building businesses. By 1852 they held a half million dollars' worth of property.

Blacks also created their own opportunities for capital formation and business development. The first of these opportunities took the form of mutual aid societies. Initially organized to provide social insurance, they soon started capturing capital for black business development. But rather quickly free blacks also organized a "trade in money" that captured savings and formed the basis of an independent black banking system.[36]

While these developments among free blacks before slavery ended looked promising, there were signs that the detour was about to occur. Investment opportunities were few and far between for blacks with money. In 1852, for example, Maryland passed a law designed explicitly to limit African American investments. In addition, during this period blacks were not allowed access to the stock market. After the Civil War, free blacks' fortunes began to dovetail with those of the freed slaves. As C. Vann Woodward recounts in *The Strange Career of Jim Crow*, discriminatory laws prohibited free blacks and former slave artisans with skills from practicing their trade, and segregation became the law of the land.

Blacks nevertheless continued their pursuit of economic self-sufficiency through self-employment under these opprobrious conditions. As Butler reports, "Between 1867 and 1917 the number of Afro-American enterprises increased from four thousand to fifty thousand."[37] These businesses developed within the confines of the "economic detour": they were segregated enterprises marketing goods and services to an entirely black clientele. Joseph A. Pierce, in his benchmark 1947 study of nearly five thousand black businesses in the North and South entitled *Negro Business and Business Education*, summarizes the effects of the economic detour that blacks faced:

> Restricted patronage does not permit the enterprises owned and operated by Negroes to capitalize on the recognized advantages of normal commercial expansion. It tends to stifle business ingenuity and imagination, because it limits the variety of needs and demands to those of one racial group—a race that is kept in a lower bracket of purchasing power largely because of this limitation. The practice of Negro business in catering almost exclusively to Negroes has contributed to the development of an attitude that the Negro consumer is obligated, as a matter of racial loyalty, to trade with enterprises owned and operated by Negroes.[38]

The overwhelming odds that black business owners faced render all the more resounding the victories that they were able to achieve. In Durham, North Carolina, blacks were able to develop what we would describe today as an "ethnic enclave."[39] Anchored by a major African American corporation, North Carolina Mutual Insurance Company, by 1949 over three hundred African American firms dotted the business section of Durham dubbed "Hayti." Owing to a combination of factors, African Americans in Durham managed to establish thriving businesses that served both the black and white markets: restaurants, tailor shops, groceries, and a hosiery mill. Despite urban renewal in the 1960s, which destroyed over one hundred enterprises and six hundred homes, the enclave character of the "Hayti" district survives today. But this is a unique story. The other extreme is the experience of cities like Wilmington, North Carolina, and Tulsa, Oklahoma. Once home to flourishing black businesses that managed to provide decent livings for their proprietors and their families, these cities today retain no more than fleeting memories of a time long past, a time washed away from historical and contemporary memory by the deadliest obstacle of all to black business: organized violence.

What appear to have been vibrant middle-class business communities that served as the foundation of black life in both Wilmington and Tulsa were destroyed at the hands of white mobs. Black business success in these cities both threatened white business competitors and provoked the racial fears of poor whites. According to Leon Prather's *We Have Taken a City*, in Wilmington, "there was grumbling among the white professional classes" because "black entrepreneurs, located conspicuously downtown, deprived white businessmen of legitimate sources of income to which they thought they were entitled."[40] Marking the nadir of black oppression, the Wilmington Riot of 1898 created an "economic diaspora" in which black businessmen were forced to steal away in the night, seeking refuge in the woods and subsequently dispersing to northern and southeastern cities. Prather evaluates the impact of the riot by noting that, "immediately after the massacres, white businesses moved in and filled the economic gaps left by the flight of the blacks. When the turbulence receded the integrated neighborhoods had disappeared."[41] Prather concludes that this racial coup d'etat was largely forgotten in the annals of America but notes that blacks kept the story alive, combining it with similar incidents in a collective narrative.

A similar "economic diaspora" was promulgated in Tulsa in 1921 (see Documents, part 5). Blacks in Tulsa developed their own business district within the boundaries of the economic detour. John Butler recounts that the Greenwood District encompassed forty-one grocers and meat markets, thirty restaurants, fifteen physicians, five hotels, two theaters, and two newspapers.[42] The black community also included many wealthy blacks who had invested in and profited from oil leases. Some five hundred blacks who owned small parcels of oil land resisted all offers and threats made by whites to sell these lands. "Every increase in the price of oil made the strife more bitter."[43] In early 1921 prominent blacks had been warned to leave Oklahoma or suffer the consequences. Fearing that a local black delivery boy was about to be lynched for allegedly attacking a white woman, the black community took up arms to ensure that the judicial process would be followed. In response to a spiral of rumors, whites organized, looted stores of arms, and invaded the Greenwood District. Blacks fought back, but the violence did not stop with individual assaults. Stores were burned. Churches, schools, and newspapers that had been built by blacks also met the torch. When the destruction was over, eighteen thousand homes and enterprises were left in cinder, over four thousand blacks were left homeless, and three hundred people died (both black and white). As Butler understatedly reports, "What happened in Tulsa was more than a riot. It was also the destruction of the efforts of entrepreneurs and the end of the Greenwood business district."[44]

The Sedimentation of Racial Inequality

The disadvantaged status of contemporary African Americans cannot be divorced from the historical processes that undergird racial inequality. The past has a living effect on the present. We argue that the best indicator of this sedimentation of racial inequality is wealth. Wealth is one indicator of material disparity that captures the historical legacy of low wages, personal and organizational discrimination, and institutionalized racism. The low levels of wealth accumulation evidenced by current generations of black Americans best represent the position of blacks in the stratificational order of American society.

Each generation of blacks generally began life with few material assets and confronted a world that systematically thwarted any attempts to economically better their lives. In addition to the barriers that we have just described in connection with the racialization of state policy and the economic detour, blacks also faced other major obstacles in their quest for economic security. In the South, for example, as W. E. B. Du Bois notes in *Black Reconstruction in America*, blacks were tied to a system of peonage that kept them in debt virtually from cradle to grave. Schooling was segregated and unequally funded.[45] Blacks in the smokestack industries of the North and the South were paid less and assigned to unskilled and dirty jobs.[46] The result was that generation after generation of blacks remained anchored to the lowest economic status in American society. The effect of this "generation after generation" of poverty and economic scarcity for the accumulation of wealth has been to "sediment" this kind of inequality into the social structure.

The sedimentation of inequality occurred because blacks had barriers thrown up against them in their quest for material self-sufficiency. Whites in general, but well-off whites in particular, were able to amass assets and use their secure economic status to pass their wealth from generation to generation. What is often not acknowledged is that the accumulation of wealth for some whites is intimately tied to the poverty of wealth for most blacks. Just as blacks have had "cumulative disadvantages," whites have had "cumulative advantages."[47] Practically every circumstance of bias and discrimination against blacks has produced a circumstance and opportunity of positive gain for whites. When black workers were paid less than white workers, white workers gained a benefit; when black businesses were confined to the segregated black market, white businesses received the benefit of diminished competition; when FHA policies denied loans to blacks, whites were the beneficiaries of the spectacular growth of good housing and housing equity in the suburbs. The cumulative effect of such a process has been to sediment blacks at the bottom of the social hierarchy and to artificially raise the relative position of some whites in society.

To understand the sedimentation of racial inequality, particularly with respect to wealth, is to acknowledge the way in which structural disadvantages have been layered one upon the other to produce black disadvantage and white privilege. Returning again to the Federal Housing Act of 1934, we may recall that the federal government placed its credit behind private loans to home buyers, thus putting home ownership within the reach of millions of citizens for the first time. White homeowners who had taken advantage of FHA financing policies saw the value of their homes increase dramatically, especially during the 1970s, when housing prices tripled.[48] As previously noted, the same FHA policies excluded blacks and segregated them into all-black areas that either were destroyed during urban renewal in the 1960s or benefited only marginally from the inflation of the 1970s. Those who were locked out of the housing market by FHA policies and who later sought to become first-time home buyers faced rising housing costs that curtailed their ability to purchase the kind of home they desired. The postwar generation of whites whose parents gained a foothold in the housing market through the FHA will harvest a bounteous inheritance in the years to come. Thus the process of asset accumulation that began in the 1930s has become layered over and over by social and economic trends that magnify inequality over time and across generations.

Why Racial Wealth Inequality Persists

The contemporary effects of race are vividly depicted in the racial pattern of wealth accumulation that our analysis has exposed. We have compiled a careful, factual account of how contemporary discrimination along demographic, social, and economic lines results in unequal wealth reservoirs for whites and blacks. Our examination has proven insightful in two respects. It shows that unequal background and social conditions result in unequal resources. Whether it be a matter of education, occupation, family status, or other characteristics positively correlated with income and wealth, blacks are most likely to come out on the short end of the stick. This is no surprise.

Our examination of contemporary conditions also found, more surprisingly, that equally positioned whites and blacks have highly unequal amounts of wealth. Matching whites and blacks on key individual factors correlated with asset acquisition demonstrated the gnawing persistence of large magnitudes of wealth difference. Because it allows us to look at several factors at once, regression analysis was then called into play. Even when whites and blacks were matched on all the identifiably important factors, we could still not account for about three-quarters of the racial wealth difference. If white and black households shared all the wealth-associated characteristics we examined, blacks would still confront a $43,000 net worth handicap!

We argue, furthermore, that the racialization of the welfare state and institutional discrimination are fundamental reasons for the persistent wealth disparities we observed. Government policies that have paved the way for whites to amass wealth have simultaneously discriminated against blacks in their quest for economic security. From the era of slavery on through the failure of the freedman to gain land and the Jim Crow laws that restricted black entrepreneurs, opportunity structures for asset accumulation rewarded whites and penalized blacks. Federal Housing Authority policies then thwarted black attempts to get in on the ground floor of home ownership, and segregation limited their ability to take advantage of the massive equity buildup that whites have benefited from in the housing market. As we have also seen, the formal rules of government programs like social security and AFDC have had discriminatory impacts on black Americans. And finally, the U.S. tax code has systematically privileged whites and those with assets over and against asset-poor black Americans.

These policies are not the result of the workings of the free market or the demands of modern industrial society; they are, rather, a function of the political power of elites. The powerful protect and extend their interests by way of discriminatory laws and social policies, while minorities unite to contest them. Black political mobilization has removed barriers to black economic security, but the process is uneven. As blacks take one step forward, new and more intransigent legislative or judicial decisions push them back two steps. Nowhere has this trend been more evident than in the quest for housing. While the Supreme Court barred state courts from enforcing restrictive covenants, they did not prevent property owners from adhering to these covenants voluntarily, thereby denying black homeowners any legal recourse against racist whites.[49] Similarly, while the Fair Housing Act banned discrimination by race in the housing market, it provided compensation only for "individual victims of discrimination," a fact that blunts the act's effectiveness as an antidiscrimination tool.[50] These Pyrrhic victories have in no way put an end to residential segregation, and black fortunes continue to stagnate.

Our empirical investigation of housing and mortgage markets demonstrates the way in which racialized state policies interact with other forms of institutional discrimination to prevent blacks from accumulating wealth in the form of residential equity. At each stage of the process blacks are thwarted. It is harder for blacks to get approved for a mortgage—and thus to buy a home—than for whites, even when applicants are equally qualified. More insidious still, African Americans who do get mortgages pay higher interest rates than whites. Finally, given the persistence of residential segregation, houses located in black communities do not rise in value nearly as much as those in white neighborhoods. The average racial difference in home equity amounts to over $20,000 among those who currently hold mortgages.

The inheritance of accumulated disadvantages over generations has, in many ways, shortchanged African Americans of the rather dramatic mobility gains they have achieved. While blacks have made stunning educational strides, entered middle-class occupations at an impressive rate, and moved into political positions in numbers unheard of a quarter of a century ago, they have been unable to surmount the historical obstacles that inhibit their accumulation of wealth. Still today, they bear the brunt of the sedimentation of racial inequality.

The Substantive Implications of Our Findings

What are the implications of our findings? First, our research underscores the need to include in any analysis of economic well-being not only income but private wealth. In American society, a stable economic foundation must include a command over assets as well as an adequate income flow. Nowhere is this observation better illustrated than by the case of black Americans. Too much of the current celebration of black success is related to the emergence of a professional and middle-class black population that has access to a steady income. Even the most visibly successful numbers of the black community—movie and TV stars, athletes, and other performers—are on salary. But income streams do not necessarily translate into wealth pools. Furthermore, when one is black, one's current status is not easily passed on to the next generation. The presence of assets can pave the way for an extension and consolidation of status for a family over several generations.

This is not, however, an analysis that emphasizes large levels of wealth. The wealth that can make a difference in the lives of families and children need not be in the million-dollar or six-figure range. Nonetheless, it is increasingly clear that a significant amount of assets will be needed in order to provide the requisites for success in our increasingly technologically minded society. Technological change and the new organization of jobs have challenged our traditional conception of how to prepare for a career and what to expect from it. Education in the future will be lifelong, as technological jobs change at a rapid pace. Assets will play an important role in allowing people to take advantage of training and retraining opportunities. In the economy of the twenty-first century children will require a solid educational foundation, and parents will most likely need to develop new skills on a regular basis. The presence or absence of assets will have much to say about the mobility patterns of the future.

Second, our investigation of wealth has revealed deeper, historically rooted economic cleavages between the races than were previously believed to exist. The interaction of race and class in the wealth accumulation process is clear. Historical practices, racist in their essence, have produced class hierarchies that, on the contemporary scene, reproduce wealth inequality. As important, contemporary racial disadvantages deprive those in the black middle class from building on their wealth assets at the same pace as similarly situated white Americans. The shadow of race falls most darkly, however, on the black underclass, whose members find themselves at the bottom of the economic hierarchy. Their inability to accumulate assets is thus grounded primarily in their low-class backgrounds. The wealth deficit of the black middle class, by contrast, is affected more by the racial character of certain policies deriving in part from the fears and anxieties that whites harbor regarding lower-class blacks than by the actual class background of middle-class blacks. As Raymond Franklin suggests in *Shadows of Race and Class*, "The overcrowding of blacks in the lower class . . . casts a shadow on middle-class members of the black population that have credentials but are excluded and discriminated against on racial grounds."

Given the mutually reinforcing and historically accumulated race and class barriers that blacks encounter in attempting to achieve a measure of economic security, we argue that a focus on job opportunity is not sufficient to the task of eradicating racial disadvantage in America. Equal opportunity, even in the best of circumstances, does not lead to equality. This is a double-edged statement. First, we believe that equal opportunity policies and programs, when given a chance, do succeed in lowering some of the more blatant barriers to black advancement. But given the historically sedimented nature of racial wealth disparities, a focus on equal opportunity will only yield partial results. Blacks will make some gains, but so will whites, with initial inequalities persisting at another level. As blacks get better jobs and higher incomes, whites also advance. Thus, as Edwin Dorn points out in *Rules and Racial Equality*:

To say that current inequality is the result of discrimination against blacks is to state only half the problem. The other half—is discrimination in favor of whites. It follows that merely eliminating discrimination is insufficient. The very direction of bias must be reversed, at least temporarily. If we wish to eliminate substantive inequality we waste effort when we debate whether some form of special treatment for the disadvantaged group is necessary. What we must debate is how it can be accomplished.

How do we link the opportunity structure to policies that promote asset formation and begin to close the wealth gap? In our view we must take a three-pronged approach. First, we must directly address the historically generated as well as current institutional disadvantages that limit the ability of blacks, as a group, to accumulate wealth resources. Second, we must resolutely promote asset acquisition among those at the bottom of the social structure who have been locked out of the wealth accumulation process, be they black or white. Third, we must take aim at the massive concentration of wealth that is held by the richest Americans. Without redistributing America's wealth, we will not succeed at creating a more just society. Even as we advance this agenda, policies that safeguard equal opportunity must be defended. In short, we must make racial justice a national priority.

The Racial Reparations Movement

A growing social movement within the black community for racial reparations attempts to address the historical origins of what House Resolution 40 in 1993 called the "lingering negative effects of the institution of slavery and discrimination" in the United States (see Documents, section 1). With a host of community-based organizations agitating and educating with respect to the issue, this movement has taken off since the passage of the legislation approving reparations for Japanese Americans interned during World War Two (see Documents, section 1). For the torment and humiliation suffered at that time each family was awarded $20,000. Since 1989 black Representative John Conyers of Michigan has introduced into the House Judiciary Committee each year a bill to set up a commission to study whether "any form of compensation to the descendants of African slaves is warranted." While the bill has yet to reach the floor of Congress, it has opened up this issue to public debate and discussion.

Given the historical nature of wealth, monetary reparations are, in our view, an appropriate way of addressing the issue of racial inequity. The fruits of their labor and the ability to accumulate wealth was denied African Americans by law and social custom during 250 years of slavery. This initial inequality has been aggravated during each new generation, as the artificial head start accorded to practically all whites has been reinforced by racialized state policy and economic disadvantages to which only blacks have been subject. We can trace the sedimented material inequality that now confronts us directly to this opprobrious past. Reparations would represent both a practical and a moral approach to the issue of racial injustice. As the philosopher Bernard Boxill argues:

> One of the reasons for which blacks claim the right to compensation for slavery is that since the property rights of slaves to "keep what they produce" were violated by the system of slavery to the general advantage of the white population, and, since the slaves would presumably have exercised their libertarian-right to bequeath their property to their descendants, their descendants, the present black population, have rights to that part of the wealth of the present white population derived from violating black property rights during slavery. . . . [Whites] also wronged [the slaves] by depriving them of their inheritance — of what Kunta Kinte would have provided them with, and passed on to them, had he been compensated — a stable home, education, income, and traditions.[51]

While reparations based on similar logic have occurred in both the United States and other societies, it may be a testament to the persistence of antiblack racial attitudes in America that the prospects for such compensation are minimal. The objections are many: Are present-day whites to blame for the past? Who among blacks should receive such reparations? Would reparations of this sort really improve the economic situation of blacks today? We are not sure that racial reparations are the choice — political or economic — that America should make at this historical juncture. They may inflame more racial antagonism than they extinguish. But the reparations debate does open up the issue of how the past affects the present; it can focus attention on the historical structuring of racial inequality and, in particular, wealth. What we fear most is the prospect of reparations becoming a settlement, a payoff for silence, the terms of which go something like this: "Okay. You have been wronged. My family didn't do it, but some amends are in order. Let's pay it. But in return, we will hear no more about racial inequality and racism. Everything is now color-blind and fair. The social programs that were supposed to help you because you were disadvantaged are now over. No more!" Instead, racial reparations should be the first step in a collective journey to racial equality.

Any set of policy recommendations that requires new revenues and implies a redistribution of benefits toward the disadvantaged faces formidable political and ideological obstacles. In an era of stagnant incomes for the working and middle classes, race has become even more of an ideological hot button in the arena of national politics. The conservative cast of American political discourse in the 1990s is in large measure rooted in white opposition to the liberal policies of the 1960s. According to Thomas and Mary Edsall's *Chain Reaction*, a pernicious ideology that joins opposition to opportunities for blacks and a distrust of government has "functioned to force the attention of the public on the costs of federal policies and programs."[52]

We believe that the program we have outlined could be put into place within the fiscal confines of present budget realities. For example, the tax structure reforms we discussed would help defray the expenses associated with asset development accounts and other increased social welfare benefits. But when it comes to race and social policy, ideology tends to reign. Despite the cost effectiveness of our program it is likely that it would be opposed mostly on ideological grounds. As Martin Carnoy in *Faded Dreams* resignedly notes, "The negative intertwining of race with 'tax and spend,' 'welfare state' economic policy remains a potentially highly successful conservative political card. . . . There is absolutely no doubt that the card will be played and played repeatedly."[53]

To move beyond the present impasse we must embark on a national conversation that realistically interprets our present dilemmas as a legacy of the past that if not addressed will forever distort the American Dream.

Notes

1. William J. Wilson, *The Truly Disadvantaged* (Chicago: University of Chicago Press, 1987), 8.

2. Lawrence Bobo, "Keeping the Linchpin in Place: Testing the Multiple Sources of Opposition to Residential Integration," *Revue Internationale de Psychologic Sociale* 2 (1989): 307.

3. Raymond S. Franklin, *Shadows of Race and Class* (Minneapolis: University of Minnesota Press, 1991), xviii.

4. For discussions of class as a factor in racial inequality, see Paul A. Baran and Paul M. Sweezy, *Monopoly Capital* (New York: Monthly Review Press, 1966) and Oliver C. Cox, *Caste, Race, and Class* (New York: Modern Reader Paperback, 1948).

5. See James H. Johnson, and Melvin L. Oliver, "Structural Changes in the U.S. Economy and Black Male Joblessness: A Reassessment," in *Urban Labor Markets and Job Opportunity*, eds. George Peterson and Wayne Vroman (Washington, D.C.: Urban Institute Press, 1992), 113–47; John D. Kasarda, "Jobs, Migration and Emerging Urban Mismatches," in *Urban Change and Poverty*, eds. M. G. H. McGeary and L. E. Lynn, Jr. (Washington, D.C.: National Academy Press, 1988), 148–98; and Wilson, *The Truly Disadvantaged*.

6. John Sibley Butler, *Entrepreneurs hip and Self-Help among Black Americans: A Recon-

struction of Race and Economics (Albany: State University of New York Press, 1991); Ivan Light, *Ethnic Enterprise in America* (Berkeley: University of California Press, 1972); and Gunnar Myrdal, *An American Dilemma* (New York: Harper, 1944).

7. Claud Anderson, *Black Labor, White Wealth: The Search for Power and Economic Justice* (Englewood, Md.: Duncan and Duncan, 1994), 123.

8. Delilah Beasley, *Negro Trail Blazers of California* (Los Angeles: Times Mirror Print and Binding House, 1919).

9. Jill Quadagno, *The Color of Welfare* (New York: Oxford University Press, 1994), 20–24.

10. Ibid, 161.

11. Ibid, 162.

12. George Lipsitz, "The Possessive Investment in Whiteness: The 'White' Problem in American Studies," *American Quarterly* (fall 1995).

13. Richard Walter Thomas, *Life for Us is What We Make It: Building Black Community in Detroit, 1915–1945* (Bloomington: Indiana University Press, 1992), 140.

14. Peter Mieszkowski and Richard F. Syron, "Economic Explanation for Housing Segregation," *New England Economic Review* (November–December 1979): 33–34.

15. Franklin, *Shadows of Race and Class*, 126.

16. Wesley G. Skogan, *Disorder and Decline: Crime and the Spiral of Decay in American Neighborhoods* (New York: Free Press, 1990).

17. Mark R. Rank, *Living on the Edge: The Realities of Welfare in America* (New York: Columbia University Press, 1994); and Carol Stack, *All Our Kin* (New York: Harper, 1974).

18. Michael Sherraden, *Assets and the Poor: A New American Welfare Policy* (New York: Sharpe, 1991), 63.

19. Ibid, 64.

20. Michael Katz, *In the Shadow of the Poor House: A Social History of Welfare in America* (New York: Basic Books, 1986), 247.

21. Donald L. Barlett, and James B. Steele, *America: What Went Wrong?* (Kansas City: Andrews and McMeel, 1992).

22. See Mary R. Jackman and Robert W. Jackman, "Racial Inequalities in Home Ownership," *Social Forces* 58 (1980): 1221–33; Paul Ong and Eugene Grigsby III, "Race and Life Cycle Effects on Home Ownership in Los Angeles, 1970 to 1980," *Urban Affairs Quarterly* 23 (1988): 601–15; and Hayward Derrick Horton and Melvin E. Thomas, "Race, Class, and Family Structure: Differences in Housing Values for Black and White Homeowners," unpublished ms., 1993.

23. Light, *Ethnic Enterprise in America*, and "Asian Enterprise in America: Chinese, Japanese, and Koreans in Small Business," in *Self-Help in Urban America: Patterns of Minority Economic Development*, ed. Scott Cummings (New York: Kennikat, 1980), 33–57.

24. Butler, *Entrepreneurship and Self-Help among Black Americans*, 1–78.

25. The central notion of blacks' unparalleled levels of hardship with respect to self-employment cannot be developed within the confines of this discussion. See Bob Blauner, *Racial Oppression in America* (New York: Harper, 1972); W. E. B. Du Bois, *Black Reconstruction in America* (New York: Harcourt, Brace, 1935); Eric Foner, *Reconstruction: America's Unfinished Revolution* (New York: Harper, 1988); C. Vann Woodward, *The Strange Career of Jim Crow* (New York: Oxford University Press, 1995); Harold M. Baron, "The Demand for Black Labor: Historical Notes on the Political Economy of Racism," *Radical America* 5, no. 2 (1971):1–46; Herman David Bloch, *The Circle of Discrimination: An Economic and Social Study of the Black Man in New York* (New York: New York University Press, 1969); and Edna Bonacich, "Ad-

vanced Capitalism and Black–White Relations in the United States: A Split Labor Market Interpretation," *American Sociological Review* 37 (1976): 547–59.

26. Edward F. Frazier, *Black Bourgeoisie* (Glenco, Ill.: Free Press, 1957); and Light, *Ethnic Enterprise in America*.

27. Butler, *Entrepreneurship and Self-Help among Black Americans*, 71.

28. Edna Bonacich and John Modell, *The Economic Basis of Ethnic Solidarity: Small Business in the Japanese American Community* (Berkeley: University of California Press, 1980).

29. Butler, *Entrepreneurship and Self-Help among Black Americans*, 72.

30. Merah S. Stuart, *An Economic Detour: A History of Insurance in the Lives of American Negroes* (New York: Wendell Malliett, 1940), xxiii.

31. Ibid, xxiii.

32. Ibid, xxxi.

33. Butler, *Entrepreneurship and Self-Help among Black Americans*, 38.

34. Abram L. Harris, *The Negro as Capitalist* (College Park, Md.: McGrath, 1936), 9.

35. Butler, *Entrepreneurship and Self-Help among Black Americans*, 42.

36. Ibid, 41–48.

37. Ibid, 147.

38. Joseph A. Pierce, *Negro Business and Business Education* (New York: Harper, 1947), 31.

39. Butler, *Entrepreneurship and Self-Help among Black Americans*, 180.

40. H. Leon Prather, *We Have Taken a City* (Rutherford, N,J,: Fairleigh Dickinson University Press, 1984), 179.

41. Ibid, 183.

42. Butler, *Entrepreneurship and Self-Help among Black Americans*, 206–21.

43. Ibid, 221.

44. Ibid, 209.

45. Gerald D. Jaynes and Robin Williams, eds., *A Common Destiny: Blacks and American Society* (Washington, D.C.: National Academy Press, 1989); and Stanley Lieberson, *A Piece of the Pie* (Berkeley: University of California Press, 1980).

46. Bloch, *The Circle of Discrimination,* and Bonacich, "Advanced Capitalism and Black–White Relations in the United States."

47. Blauner, *Racial Oppression in America*; Lipsitz, "The Possessive Investment in Whiteness"; and Lester C. Thurow, *Generating Inequality: Mechanisms of Distribution in the U.S. Economy* (New York: Basic Books, 1975).

48. John Adams, "Growth of U.S. Cities and Recent Trends in Urban Real Estate Values," in *Cities and Their Vital Systems*, eds. J. H. Ausubel and R. Herman (Washington, D.C.: National Academy Press, 1988), 108–45.

49. Arlene Zarembka, *The Urban Housing Crisis* (New York: Greenwood Press, 1990), 101–2.

50. Ibid, 106.

51. Bernard Boxill, *Blacks and Social Justice* (Totowa, N.J.: Rowman and Allanheld, 1984).

52. Thomas Byrne Edsall and Mary Edsall, *Chain Reaction* (New York: Norton, 1991), 11.

53. Martin Carnoy, *Faded Dreams: The Politics and Economics of Race in America* (Cambridge: Cambridge University Press, 1994), 225–26.

Part 2

Law, Citizenship, and the State

Introduction

The legal and historical claims for redress, as well as the processes of identifying the culpable parties, are examined in these five essays. Unlike Lyons and Brown in part 1, Robert Fullinwider contends that, while reparations are a necessary "catharsis" and means to mitigate black economic inequality, he advocates de-emphasizing both slavery and the benefits accrued to whites in determining reparations claims; doing so "not only improves the legal case . . . [but] strengthens both the tactical and the moral cases as well by stripping them of diversionary complications." Fullinwider also takes issue with Randall Robinson's assertion in *The Debt* that "nations, individuals, *whites as a racial entity*" (Fullinwider's emphasis) are the debtors because they benefited from slavery and segregation, arguing that this position is neo-racialist. For Fullinwider, citizenship and collective responsibility are central principles in his case for reparations; together, they implicate both white and black citizens for reparations claims.

Writing in 1968, before affirmative action was envisioned, implemented, and later denounced, James Bolner anticipates (and heeds Fullinwider's counsel made three decades later) and emphasizes housing, education, and employment rather than slavery as the key to "racial peace" and restitution. He contends that the Civil Rights Act and Voting Rights Act are the most appropriate and effective means for reparations legislation because they provide workable rationales that build on *Brown v. the Board of Education* to enact laws "guaranteeing integrated neighborhoods" and employment opportunities for African Americans. Bolner concludes, perhaps naïvely, given the current conservative political climate in the United States (and increasingly in its Supreme Court), "The implementation of reparations programs by the executive and legislative branches of the central government would probably not be blocked on constitutional grounds by the judiciary."

Roy L. Brooks updates Boris L. Bittker's 1973 essay, and like Fullinwider and Bolner, rejects reparations claims based on the ancient injustice of slavery. He revisits the "strict scrutiny test" and concludes that statutorily created remedies by Congress may be more successful than a constitutionally based approach. He notes that common to the two approaches, constitutional and statutory, is that they "are group- rather than individual-focused, and, more important, both seek to deal with the residual effects of prior acts of discrimination." Similarly, Richard America, preferring the term "restitution" to "reparations," suggests that the rationale for restitution is "to correct a current, not a past, injustice," rather than to compensate for past wrongs; he recommends affirmative action, set-asides, scholarships, and housing mortgages as appropriate forms of restitution.

In counterpoint to America, J. Angelo Corlett argues that "affirmative action in many forms amounts to programs of preferential treatment the benefits of which are *earned* by recipients, whereas this is not true of reparations." Moreover, contrary to Fullinwider, Bolner, and America, Corlett argues a reparations claim for slavery (and Jim Crow) which rests on "the illicit taking by force and/or fraud of the surplus labor value of the slaves." This leads him to claim that "forced labor power and the extraction of value from it is morally unjust and must be rectified by way of compensation and/or punishment."

The Case for Reparations

ROBERT FULLINWIDER

Because of its visibility, Randall Robinson's new book, *The Debt: What America Owes to Blacks*, may rekindle a broad public debate on reparations. The issue is not new, nor is public debate about it. In 1969, the civil rights leader James Forman presented the *Black Manifesto* to American churches, demanding that they pay blacks $500 million in reparations (see Documents, section 4). The *Manifesto* argued that for three and a half centuries blacks in America had been "exploited and degraded, brutalized, killed and persecuted" by whites. This treatment was part of a persistent institutional pattern of, first, legal slavery and, later, legal discrimination and forced segregation. Through slavery and discrimination, the *Manifesto* went on to contend, whites have extracted enormous wealth from black labor with little return to blacks themselves. These facts constitute grounds for reparations on a massive scale. American churches were but the first institutions asked by Forman to discharge this great debt.

The *Manifesto* achieved immediate notoriety and stimulated debate in newspapers and magazines. Within a short period, however, public excitement died away.

The issue of reparations has always found favor within the African American community itself, taking root not long after the freeing of the slaves during the Civil War. It flourished around World War One with the Marcus Garvey movement and later found voice in Forman's *Black Manifesto* (see Documents, section 4). It has recently regained vitality, given new life by a recent precedent, the Civil Liberties Act of 1988, in which Congress authorized payment of reparations to Japanese American citizens who had been interned during World War Two. In each session of Congress since 1989, Representative John Conyers has introduced a bill to create a commission to study reparations for slavery and segregation (see Documents, section 1). Although the bill has made no legislative headway, the publication now of Randall Robinson's new book reflects the growing sense among many African Americans that the time is right to push reparations back onto the public agenda.

If public debate is to prove fruitful, however, both proponents and opponents of reparations will have to sidestep certain common but toxic confusions. In a long article in *The Washington Post* last December, these confusions were much on display. The article's lead questions — "Should the U.S. pay reparations to the descendants of slaves?" and "Why shouldn't the great grandchildren of those who worked for free and were deprived of education and were kept in bondage be compensated?" — were countered by another: "Why should Americans who never owned slaves pay for the sins of ancestors they don't even know?" The article quoted Congressman Henry Hyde's firm answer to the last question: "The notion of collective guilt for what people did [200-plus] years ago, that this generation should pay a debt for that generation, is an idea whose time has gone. I never owned a slave. I never oppressed anybody. I don't know that I should have to pay for someone who did [own slaves] generations before I was born." His response didn't satisfy at least one African American, whose letter to the editor noted, "Henry Hyde, like many whites, is quick to say, 'I never owned a slave.' . . . Why should I pay . . . for something my ancestors did? . . . Well, because some people are descendants of slave owners and have profited from the labor of blacks who were never paid for their labor."

Personal versus Civil Liability

The demand for reparations to African Americans cannot be casually dismissed. It is grounded in a basic moral norm, a norm presupposed, for example, in the biblical injunction at Exodus 22: "If a man steal an ox, or a sheep, and kill it, or sell it; he shall restore five oxen for an ox, and four sheep for a sheep." *You must make good the wrongs you do.* This principle in one form or another underlies every mature moral and legal system in the world. At the same time, however, Henry Hyde's distaste for collective guilt seems equally well-founded: "The father shall not be put to death for the children, neither shall the children be put to death for the fathers: every man shall be put to death for his own sin" (Deuteronomy 24:16). *We must not penalize one person for another's misdeeds.* Does, then, the demand for reparations pose a conflict between two distinct and equally basic moral principles? Not if the demand is properly understood.

Henry Hyde echoes a common but confused sentiment. If *personal* liability for slavery or past racial oppression were being imputed to him, then the congressman's response would be appropriate. He denies personal responsibility for the wrongs to be made good. But personal responsibility and liability are not at stake. The real issues are *corporate* responsibility, the responsibility of the nation as a whole, and *civic* responsibility, the responsibility of each citizen to do his fair part in honoring the nation's obligations. When Congress passed the Civil Liberties Act of 1988, no one assumed that individual Americans were being held accountable for personal wrongdoing. The interning of Japanese Americans was an act of the U.S. government and its agents. At the time, the government acted for putatively good reasons. Following the Japanese attack on Pearl Harbor, American officials were concerned about the security of the West Coast from similar attack or sabotage. Whether the government actually acted from honorable motives or not, the point remains that with the passage of time thoughtful Americans — and the government itself — have come to view the internment as an unjustified response to the war with Japan, and one that wronged its victims. The Civil Liberties Act, and the token reparations it paid ($20,000 to each interned Japanese American or to his or her surviving spouse or children), represented an official apology and a small step toward making whole the material losses incurred by the internees. The reparations were appropriated out of general revenues. Consequently, Henry Hyde, as taxpayer, contributed a small portion, not because he had any *personal* responsibility for the internment but because as a *citizen* he is required to bear his share of the government's necessary expenditures.

One can make a parallel argument for reparations to African Americans. Although countless individual Americans throughout our history exploited their power or standing to oppress African Americans, that power and standing itself derived from law — first from the latitude of the English Crown, then from the Constitution of 1787 (which accepted slavery in the states where it was established), and finally from the tissue of post–Civil War "Jim Crow" laws, rules, and social conventions that enforced de jure and de facto racial segregation. The chief wrongs done to African Americans, thus, were not simply the sum of many individual oppressions added together but were the corporate acts of a nation that imposed or tolerated regimes of slavery, apartheid, peonage, and disenfranchisement. Just as it was the nation that owed Japanese Americans reparations, so it is the nation that owes reparations to African Americans. And so it is that Americans not as *individuals* but as *citizens* owe support for the nation's debt.

Confusions about Liability

The foregoing seems simple and plain enough. Why then do so many opponents of reparations confuse the matter? We might content ourselves to speculate unflatteringly about their motives, were it not for the fact that the proponents of reparations often fall into the same and worse confusions. A recent spate of articles in law reviews demonstrates that the distinctions among corporate, civic, and personal liability prove elusive. These articles try to make the case for reparations and answer objections to it. To accept the reasonableness of reparations, they contend, we have to abandon the "individualistic" models characteristic of American law and think in terms of group rights and group wrongs. "The guiding paradigm of traditional remedies law," writes Rhonda Magee in the *Virginia Law Review*, "is the one plaintiff, one defendant lawsuit in which the plaintiff seeks the position she would have occupied 'but for' the wrong committed by the defendant." Within this paradigm, the demand by blacks for reparations seems unsustainable, since we can no longer identify individual successors to slave owners or state agents who promulgated legal oppression of blacks, nor separate out the respective harms to the successors of those who lived under slavery and Jim Crow.

However, at least with respect to the matter of liability, it is not the "individualism" of American law that we need to give up but the assumption, implicitly at work here, that all liability is personal. The argument for reparations fits comfortably enough within the traditional paradigm when we make sure the focus is on corporate liability, for the corporate actor in question, the United States, *is* an "individual" under law. Indeed, precisely because it is an "individual" that doesn't die, it can acquire and retain debts over many generations, though individual Americans come and go. That is why Henry Hyde can indeed owe something as a result of his ancestors' actions.

Nevertheless, Magee and others insist on the indispensability of "group" conceptions of victims and wrongdoers. In the words of Mari Matsuda, victims of racial oppression "necessarily think of themselves as a group, because they are treated and survive as a group. [Even] the wealthy Black person still comes up against the color line." The "group damage engendered by past wrongs ties victim group members together, satisfying the horizontal unity sought by the legal mind." Similarly, a "horizontal connection exists as well within the perpetrator group." Members of the latter—whites— continue to benefit from past wrongs and from the contemporary privilege their skin color confers upon them. Finally, a horizontal relation of moral causality obtains between the two groups. . . . The respective entitlements and liabilities *distribute* within each group to its *individual* members, who are all tied to one another by the "victim"/"victimizer" attributes.

Magee, Matsuda, and other defenders of reparations labor to establish that the harms of slavery and discrimination affect *each and every* African American (even the wealthy black runs up against the color line) and the culpability for the harms extends to *each and every* white (every white unjustly benefits from white-skin privilege). This picture, in fact, does not represent some new "group" paradigm at all, but an individualism run rampant, the product of failing to keep distinct personal and civic liability.

The real lines of liability, I contend, run this way: . . . The connection of citizens to the creditor "group" . . . is indirect and vertical, not direct and horizontal. Thus Henry Hyde owes something not because he is white or a member of the perpetrator "group" but because he is a citizen. The various "horizontal" connections among citizens are irrelevant. Indeed, included in the citizen "group" are African Americans themselves. They too will contribute in support of the government's reparations.

This outcome strikes the writers I am discussing here as an anomaly that needs explaining. In fact, it is no anomaly at all once we appreciate that blacks are citizens as well as victims and that their equal citizenship is reflected in their *civic* obligation to support government reparations — whether those reparations are paid to Japanese Americans or even to themselves in their capacity as wronged individuals.

Unfortunately, the ghost of personal responsibility is not so easily exorcised from these legal essays. This is especially true in the case of Vincene Verdun, writing in the *Tulane Law Review*. Although self-consciously rejecting "individualistic" thinking in favor of "group" thinking, she nevertheless edges close to the proper conclusion when she observes that the "wrongdoer" owing reparations is American "society." However, her failure fully to grasp the *corporate* nature of "society" is betrayed by her next move. "Treating society as the wrongdoer," she observes, "necessarily includes the injured parties in the classification of wrongdoer. If society pays, it will do so at least in part with tax dollars, and African Americans pay taxes." Nevertheless, "there is a ring of propriety in having African Americans share in the . . . burdens," observes Verdun. Why? Here we expect Verdun to note that African Americans are citizens like everyone else. Instead, she locates the propriety in their own guilt!

Opponents of reparations are quick to point out that Africans participated in the slave trade and [some] African Americans owned slaves. The truth in these statements cannot be rebutted. Vincent Verdun [the author's father, introduced in a prologue] is an injured party, because he was deprived of his rightful inheritance because his great-great-great grandmother was a slave. On the other hand, his great-great-great grandfather [the offspring of a French plantation owner and his black slave, and who was later emancipated and given land] was a slave owner.

Now, aside from the fact that the situation Verdun describes was fairly rare, what possible connection could exist between Vincent Verdun, who lived his life as a black man, and his slave-owning great-great-great-grandfather that would visit on him the sins of his ancestor? Indeed, what connection between this ancestor and Vincene Verdun herself could lead her to confess, as she later does, that her "heritage," deriving from both "master and slave," makes her not only a victim but one of the "wrongdoers," the group that owes reparations? No connection exists between these two Verduns and their long-ago ancestor except one: blood. Evidently, guilt travels through blood, since neither Vincene nor her father derived any lasting benefit or privilege from their ancestor—indeed, their only significant inheritance was the color of their skin.

The racialist assumption embedded in Verdun's "confession" speaks for itself. What would prompt a level-headed legal scholar to step into such a malodorous swamp? The explanation lies in Verdun's failure, despite her ostensible attachment to "group" thinking over "individualistic" thinking, fully to appreciate the various ontologies of groups and the difference between collective and corporate liability, a failure Magee and Matsuda share with her. She seems to assume that any property that characterizes "society" must characterize each of its members. If "society" is a "wrongdoer," then each member of society must be a wrongdoer. It is easy enough for her to view every white as a "wrongdoer" but she is forced to stretch to include blacks themselves as part of the "wrongdoers" since they, too, are part of "society": they are taxpayers.

When "society" is understood *corporately*, however, the "wrongdoing" of society does not distribute to each of its members. Individual citizens may be blameless for the wrongs of their nation. That the burden of payment for national wrongdoing falls to them simply reflects their *civic* roles and not anything about their *persons*. In making the case for reparations, it is a mistake to go looking for *personal complicity* on the part of those who must pay. And worse yet, it is a mistake to turn the putative personal complicity into guilt-by-blood.

Randall Robinson himself is less than careful in this regard. Sometimes in his book it is "white society" that must pay reparations, sometimes the "whole society." At one place, the debtors are characterized as those—"nations, individuals, *whites as a racial entity*"—who benefited from slavery and segregation. Finally, Robinson, too, appeals to blood: the value of the labor stolen from slaves, he says, has been compounding "through the blood lines" of slave owners. Just how blood transmits and compounds debt he does not say.

The imprecision and neoracialist overtones in *The Debt* evidently caused Robinson some second thoughts. He recently wrote in *The Nation* that "individual Americans need not feel defensive or under attack" as a result of the call for reparations. "No one holds any living person responsible" for slavery or its successor regime of Jim Crow. We must all, "as a nation," address reparations, he writes. That is the right focus.

Making the Case for Reparations

Avoiding the confusion about corporate, civic, and personal liability clears the way to explore more fruitfully the positive case for reparations. How should that case go? The argument mounted by Robinson, Verdun, Magee, and other African Americans bases reparations on the great wrong of slavery as well as the more recent wrongs of legally sanctioned discrimination. Further, the argument stresses the purported benefits that whites over the centuries have extracted from slavery, Jim Crow, and a general social system of white supremacy.

However, basing reparations on slavery and on the great benefits accrued to whites invites complication and controversy. I suggest the case is actually strengthened by dropping both slavery and the benefits reaped by whites as grounds for reparations. Let me explain.

First, although the proposition that whites as a whole have benefited enormously from past racial oppression might seem self-evident, and remains an article of faith among the reparationists, whether slavery and segregation in fact yielded *net* positive economic benefits to this country and to whom those *net* benefits flowed (to all or only some whites) are difficult questions to answer. More important, trying to answer them is diversionary and unnecessary. A sufficient basis for reparations lies in the *wrong* done African Americans by the nation, whether or not anyone really benefited from it. After all, the basis of the Civil Liberties Act of 1988 was not some putative benefit Americans had extracted from the internment of Japanese Americans in 1942–1945. The basis was the *wrong* done to the internees.

What wrong to African Americans, then, should current reparations address? Making slavery the basis for reparations is unwise for two reasons. First, doing so invites the retort that America has already paid for the wrong of slavery, not with money but with the blood shed in the Civil War. The attempt successfully to parry this retort leads to complications, since whether to reckon the blood sacrifice of the Civil War as expiation for the sins of the past and how to weigh that sacrifice against any unpaid debt to the newly liberated slaves are questions that invite calculations prone to sophistical quibbling on either side.

A second reason it is unwise to base reparations on the fact of slavery is that the passage of time since abolition has now itself become a morally significant factor. Whatever condition they find themselves in, people have the responsibility to make the best of their circumstances, to provide for themselves even if they start with the most meager resources. For example, between 1865 and 1965, millions of immigrants came to America penniless and with little to offer but their physical labor. By dint of hard work, they and their successor generations eventually blended into the larger American fabric.

Over time one might have expected a similar process to play itself out for the newly liberated slaves, especially since their numbers would have allowed them to possess considerable political power in several states. Yet this process didn't occur. Why not? Because, after having made the newly freed slaves citizens, the federal government abandoned them. It allowed southern whites, through terror and law, to recapture control of state governments, disenfranchise African Americans, and, through the apparatus of Jim Crow, reduce them to virtual peonage. Indeed, America's highest court put its official stamp on state apartheid in its 1896 ruling, *Plessy v. Ferguson*, a ruling that Justice Harlan, in dissent, accurately predicted would one day be viewed by Americans as no less pernicious than the Court's fateful decision in *Dred Scott*.

In sum, governments — state and federal — made no effort to vindicate the rights to full and equal citizenship the Civil War amendments extended to blacks, a failure that prevented African Americans from successfully following the immigrant model. That failure persisted into recent times. The United States began to expend real effort toward defending the basic rights of blacks only after the 1954 Supreme Court ruling in *Brown v. Board of Education*, an effort far from complete today.

Had the federal government done nothing after 1865 except vigorously protect the civil and voting rights of blacks, the legacy of slavery would have faded considerably if not wholly by now through the industry of blacks themselves. That the legacy still persists owes much, if not all, to the post–Civil War oppression of African Americans, and it is *this* wrong that offers the most direct and salient basis for reparations.

Answering Objections

Some may object that the post–Civil War oppression of African Americans still leaves the case for reparations unpersuasive. They might insist that reparations are not possible or, alternatively, that they are not necessary.

Consider the first, that reparations are not possible because we can't now really identify who should get what. I argued earlier that the individualist legal paradigm creates no real difficulties in dealing with liability for reparations. However, doesn't it generate problems about *entitlement* to reparations? To whom should reparations be paid? Should *every* individual black person receive reparations? Quite obviously, different blacks have fared very differently under past segregation. Most of those affected worst are long dead. How was the legacy of their wrongful deprivations diffused to their descendants down to the present moment? How do we trace the damages?

Most living African Americans have incurred their own indignities and damages under discrimination, but how do we match reparations to losses? Do we pay the same to the child of middle-class blacks who immigrated to the United States from the West Indies twenty years ago that we pay to an elderly retiree who spent half his life as a field hand in Mississippi? Mari Matsuda says that even the wealthy black person comes up against the color line. True enough. But the damage to him has not been the same as the damage to others. A scheme of reparations like the program for Japanese American internees that pays a flat sum to every black, whatever his background and economic condition, does not seem very attractive. So might the opponent of reparations argue.

This objection would carry more force if justice forbade paying reparations unless we could identify the exact victims and the exact degree of their victimization. However, while justice requires that we take special care to identify the proper "wrongdoers" from whom to extract compensation, it is less insistent that we scrupulously avoid compensating "victims" who weren't real victims, especially if such avoidance would mean not compensating anyone at all. Because the effects of a hundred years of racial oppression have been dispersed so widely throughout the African American community, it makes sense to adopt some scheme of reparations that *morally approximates* rather than actually effects the restoration of victims to their "rightful places"—the positions they would have occupied but for the past history of oppression. Congress could follow the precedent of post–World War Two Germany. Apart from paying compensation to some identifiable individual victims of its war crimes, Germany made reparation payments to organizations that represented European and world Jewry, including to the State of Israel, on the reasonable assumption that these organizations in the course of their efforts to resettle displaced Jews would benefit many of the victims of the Nazi regime. Similarly, Congress could fashion a reparations plan to fund specially designated organizations who would act on behalf of the African American community. A reparations program need not involve government indiscriminately writing checks to individual African Americans.

Even if the first objection is not telling, what about the second? Are reparations actually necessary? The opponent of reparations might argue that the country did enough when it passed the civil rights laws of the 1960s. In the words of Jonathan Yardley, these laws "are concrete, purposeful and immensely significant attempts to eliminate the vestiges of slavery, to make the country equally free to all its citizens." Moreover, their "effect has been incalculable." Actually, it might be better to say that their effect is quite calculable. We can easily measure, for example, the growth of the black middle class since the 1960s, the near-parity between black and white high school graduation rates, and the upsurge in black public officials and legislators. We can also count the growth of African Americans on campus over the last forty years, and calculate the narrowed gap in earnings between similarly skilled black and white workers. Surely, then, we can extrapolate from these improvements to even further progress for African Americans in the near future. What would reparations add?

The answer is that reparations would add something quite important. Although the gains from the civil rights laws of the 1960s are undeniable, they should not be overstated. In particular, the narrowing income gap between whites and blacks masks a tremendous *wealth* gap. As Dalton Conley points out in an important new study, "At all income, occupational, and education levels, black families on average have drastically lower levels of wealth than similar white families." Moreover, he argues, it is the wealth rather than income of parents that proves pivotal to a child's ascending the academic and economic ladders to the middle class and beyond.

The black–white wealth gap is large, enduring, and damaging. Moreover, it is for the most part a direct legacy of official and unofficial discrimination lasting into the 1960s. Consequently, reparations at this late date would not be gratuitous; there is real work for them to do. A properly structured reparations program enacted by Congress could funnel substantial resources over three or four decades into organizations specifically designed and monitored to *create wealth* among African Americans — organizations that would assist development of neighborhoods, ownership of homes, creation of businesses, and expansion of human capital. These organizations could direct their energies and investments toward local and small-scale interventions to interrupt the cycle of poverty and hopelessness that traps the black underclass and toward broad-based efforts to secure the growing middle class in its economic purchase on the American dream. Such investments in infrastructure and wealth creation would go some distance toward repairing for African Americans as a whole the damages occasioned by a hundred years of legal oppression.

The Limits of Reparations

The foregoing represents barely the sketch of a case for reparations. But it does suggest the contours of a specific, "lean" strategy: reparations (1) based on the wrongs done African Americans by the legal regime of racial discrimination that lasted until thirty-some years ago, and (2) designed to stimulate creation of wealth, broadly conceived, in the African American community. It is "lean" because it omits elements many African Americans embrace, particularly the argument about slavery and the wealth that was purportedly extracted from it. Thirty years ago, in discussing a proposal put forward by Yale law professor Boris Bittker that the "post–Civil War wrongs are more than sufficient to support" a claim for reparations, the African American legal scholar Derrick Bell conceded that "the legal argument for reparations improves with the exclusion of the slavery period." Nevertheless, such exclusion, he thought, represents a "tactical loss." It "sacrifices much of the emotional component that provides moral leverage for black reparations demands." To the contrary, excluding slavery not only improves the legal case for reparations, it strengthens both the tactical and the moral cases as well by stripping them of diversionary complications.

It is true, however, that excluding slavery may sacrifice for African Americans some of the *emotional* resonance of the reparations argument, and this aspect may turn out, in the eyes of some, to be the most vital part of all. Although Randall Robinson's *The Debt* seems on its face to be addressed to a larger public, its real audience is other African Americans. It is a book less about the details of reparations (they receive little more than a nod in the next-to-last chapter) than about Robinson's unrequited anger at slavery and the "staggering breadth of America's crime" against blacks. The real crime of slavery for Robinson? It has "maliciously shorn" African Americans of their "natural identity" and destroyed their self-esteem, leaving a people riven by self-hatred, self-doubt, and self-rejection. The real and continuing injury has been psychic. (Similarly for Vincene Verdun: "It is emotional injury, stemming from the badge of inferiority and from the stigma attached to race which marks every African American, that composes the most significant injury of slavery.")

Thus, for Robinson the emotional resonance of slavery for African Americans is not some unnecessary complicating factor to be trimmed away from a clean argument for reparations, it is the centerpiece for an aggressive, collective demand for redress. By pressuring "white society" to confess its sin of slavery and by "implacably demand[ing]" their full due, African Americans will "find" their own "voice." Fighting the fight for reparations on the basis of slavery will bring "catharsis." African Americans will rediscover their identity and know themselves to be a worthy people, win or lose.

Robinson's vision starkly poses a crucial question: What do African Americans take to be the real stakes in a reparations argument? Is the goal to succeed (with as many allies as possible) against high odds in achieving a reparations enactment by Congress that will bring some limited but vital wealth creation to African American communities? Or is the goal of reparations to force a debate on their terms, as a vehicle of self-discovery and emotional self-renewal, however socially divisive it becomes and however remote it makes actual enactment of reparations? Readers of *The Debt* will not find a clear rendering of the trade-offs between these goals that Robinson is willing to countenance, but they cannot fail to see his passion for staking out the "sin" of slavery as the field on which to do battle. If this passion is unyielding, however, the debate about reparations may never really engage Americans at large. This would be too bad. A real public debate, stripped of disabling confusions while sharply focused on manageable grounds and practical results, could do every citizen a service.

Sources

Randall Robinson, *The Debt: What America Owes to Blacks* (Dutton, 1999); Randall Robinson, "America's Debt to Blacks," *The Nation* 270 (March 13, 2000); *Black Manifesto* appears as appendix to Boris Bittker, *The Case for Black Reparations* (Random House, 1973); Henry Hyde quoted from Kevin Merida, "Did Freedom Alone Pay a Nation's Debt? Rep. John Conyers Jr. Has a Question. He's Willing to Wait a Long Time for the Answer," *The Washington Post* (November 23, 1999); see also the letter to the editor from Juanita Adams, *The Washington Post* (November 29, 1999); Rhonda V. Magee, "The Master's Tools, from the Bottom Up: Responses to African-American Reparations Theory in Mainstream and Outsider Remedies Discourse," *Virginia Law Review* 79 (May 1993); Mari J. Matsuda, "Looking to the Bottom: Critical Legal Studies and Reparations," *Harvard Civil Rights— Civil Liberties Law Review* 22 (spring 1987); Vincene Verdun, "If the Shoe Fits, Wear It: An Analysis of Reparations to African Americans," *Tulane Law Review* 67 (February 1993). A large literature exists on the question of the economic benefits of slavery; a classic work is Eric Williams, *Capitalism and Slavery* (University of North Carolina Press, 1944). See also Alfred H. Conrad and John R. Meyer, *The Economics of Slavery and Other Studies in Econometric History* (Aldine Publishing Co., 1964); Hugh G. J. Aitken, ed., *Did Slavery Pay? Readings in the Economics of Black Slavery in the United States* (Houghton Mifflin, 1971); Robert W. Fogel and Stanley L. Engerman, *Time on the Cross: The Economics of American Negro Slavery* (Little, Brown, 1974); Herbert G. Gutman, *Slavery and the Numbers Game: A Critique of Time on the Cross* (University of Illinois Press, 1975); Paul A. David et al., *Reckoning with Slavery: A Critical Study in the Quantitative History of American Negro Slavery* (Oxford University Press, 1976); Elizabeth Fox-Genovese and Eugene D. Genovese, *Fruits of Merchant Capital: Slavery and Bourgeois Property in the Rise and Expansion of Capitalism* (Oxford University Press, 1983); James Oakes, *Slavery and Freedom: An Interpretation of the Old South* (Knopf, 1990). Concerning whether the Civil War "paid" for slavery, see, for example, letter to the editor by Joseph Lucas, *The Washington Post* (November 29, 1999); also Robert S. McElvaine, "They Didn't March to Free the Slaves," in Roy L. Brooks, ed., *When Sorry Isn't Enough: The Controversy over Apologies and Reparations for Human Injustice* (New York University Press, 1999), and in that same volume, Thomas Geoghegan, "Lincoln Apologizes," and Mary E. Smith, "Clinton and Conservatives Oppose Slavery Reparations." Jonathan Yardley quoted from "Reparations: It's Too Late," *The Washington Post* (November 29, 1999). Information about black progress and wealth comes from Stephen Thernstrom and Abigail Thernstrom, *America in Black and White: One Nation, Indivisible* (Simon and Schuster, 1997); William Spriggs, ed., *The State of Black America 1999* (National Urban League, 1999); Dalton Conley, *Being Black, Living in the Red: Race, Wealth, and Social Policy in America* (University of California Press, 1999). Derrick Bell quote from "Dissection of a Dream," *Harvard Civil Rights — Civil Liberties Law Review* 9 (January 1974). For an idea of reparations similar to mine, see Robert Westley, "Many Billions Gone: Is It Time to Reconsider the Case for Black Reparations?," *Boston College Law Review* 40 (December 1998), which proposes the establishment of a private trust through which reparations would be paid to "any project or pursuit aimed at the educational and economic empowerment of the trust beneficiaries to be determined on the basis of need."

Toward a Theory of Racial Reparations

JAMES BOLNER

One of the chief concerns of contemporary public law in the United States is also one of the most ancient: the treatment of nonwhite minorities, especially the Negro minority. During the major portion of the postslavery period the "liberal" ideal in treatment of Negroes has been "nondiscrimination."[1] There are few, if any, indications that this policy is proving successful in assimilating Negroes into the social order. The successor to nondiscrimination is benign racial treatment, and it is this policy which this essay explores. Specifically, the essay examines certain aspects of the attempt to render legitimate and orderly the assimilation of Negroes through benign racial treatment of them. A sketch of a theory of racial reparations and the major criticisms of the approach are examined, and, finally, the prospects for racial reparations programs are surveyed.

Two Justifications of Racial Reparations

Reparations in the sense used here denotes benefits extended in various forms to those injured by racial discrimination practiced by, or with the acquiescence of, the government of a representative democracy. Reparations are not to be understood as an indiscriminate bonus for nonwhites, but merely as payment of damages to those nonwhites who have been injured by racial discrimination.[2] Claims advanced by a nonwhite resident of a jurisdiction which has observed a policy of nondiscrimination should be viewed in a different light from claims pressed by a resident, say, of Alabama. It would seem untenable to assume that a nonwhite, regardless of how successful he seems to be in life, has not been injured by discrimination. Neither are we suggesting a sophisticated retaliation against living white persons for the misdeeds of their ancestors.

A quite different approach — one which perhaps is more persuasive — must now be considered: reparations extended to minority groups humiliated or injured in the past is a simple way out of a nasty problem. Justice in this connection is a bonus. The interest in civil order, public tranquility, and public peace is considered so great that it is permissible to single out individuals on the basis of their race where social malaise is demonstrably associated with that group. Assuming that social and economic disorder are chronically associated with a particular racial group, one may argue that the community may employ race as a criterion in breaking the vicious cycle. On this rationale, integration, or the deliberate bringing together of individuals because of their race, is considered good since it contributes to the general welfare in the broadest sense. The use of racial criteria to separate individuals and groups, the argument continues, is sometimes bad and sometimes good, depending on the circumstances. What proportion of the racial mix to prescribe would depend on the circumstances.[3] There will be those, of course, who will recommend benign racial treatment of minority group members precisely because it seems to buy racial peace at the same time that it gives nonwhites their due. A federal district judge approximated this position when he noted, "It is neither just nor sensible to proscribe segregation having its basis in affirmative state action while at the same time failing to provide a remedy for segregation which grows out of discrimination in housing, or other economic or social factors."[4]

A Critique of the Theory

At the outset two objections can be anticipated. The first concerns constitutional colorblindness; if the first Mr. Justice Harlan's felicitous phrase, "Our constitution is color blind,"[5] were taken to bar any and all treatment on the basis of race, then the country would be deftly laced into a constitutional straitjacket and prevented from dealing with a major social problem. The remarks which follow assume that the Constitution permits racial treatment save where such treatment is oppressive. The second objection is that any reparations program is by definition a show of preference to nonwhites. In one sense, benign treatment on racial grounds does not mean adverse treatment for certain individuals (in the present case these are whites) with whom they compete; when persons compete for housing, jobs, or school assignments, there will be winners and losers. But rigging the process so as to make whites the automatic losers can best be explained by saying that whites here are being called upon to assist the community in meeting its obligation. That the disappointed white applicants may never have inflicted racial injury is not a relevant consideration. It is not a case of "an eye for an eye," but a case of doing one's duty in setting aright a community wrong. It is difficult to see how an approach which would treat whites as having been deprived of their rights can provide a satisfactory and realistic point of departure.

Now let us assume that a political regime embarks on a thoroughgoing racial program based on either the reparations or the buying peace foundations. What happens to the keystone principle of the humanitarian credo: treat each individual on his intrinsic merits and not on the basis of the accident of color? While it might be more conducive to the public order, is racial integration less violative of public morality than racial segregation? If barring nonwhites from "private" public places and housing and "private" employment is offensive to good morals because it rests on an accidental factor such as color, and if the essence of the wrong is the refusal to treat them like everyone else, is it permissible to base a decision on the same accidental factor in granting them benefits? It would seem that in discriminating in favor of the individual the individual may be gleeful during the entire operation, but moral injury would be perpetrated just the same. (One may also suggest that benign racial treatment of nonwhites is a substitution of a community paternalism for the paternalism of a former "master"; on this basis benign racial treatment ought to be as offensive as the post-slavery dependency of Negroes upon their former masters, since it implies a judgment of racial inferiority.)

Treatment on the basis of race, as an attempt will be made to show below, is not per se indefensible; the worthiness of the objective is a salient consideration. Nevertheless, it is not a pretty business, for there remains the implication of inherent racial inferiority of the minority group members; nonwhites' "special characteristics and circumstances" (analogous to those of physically handicapped or neurotic persons) are found to be occasioned by racial differences parallel to "physiological, psychological or sociological variances from the norm occasioned by other factors."[6]

A most forceful judicial statement critical of benign racial treatment was set forth by Judge Van Voorhis in his dissenting opinion in a recent New York case upholding the principle. Said the judge: "Where is the line to be drawn between allocating persons by law to schools or other institutions or facilities according to color to promote integration, and doing the same thing in order to promote segregation? Is the underlying principle not the same in either instance? Both depend on racism. If one is legally justifiable, then so is the other."[7]

The argument that benign racial treatment would "force governmental authorities to re-enter the field of racial classification" cannot be lightly dismissed.[8] Today the governmental attitude might be sympathetic only to benign racial laws, but tomorrow the result might well be different. Consider the best known example of a justifiable use of race by government: the *Japanese Exclusion Cases* decided during World War Two.[9] There the Court sanctioned military orders employing race as a criterion for segregating Japanese Americans from allegedly "more loyal" citizens. In attacking the majority's deference to military expediency, Justice Murphy declared that "racial discrimination" in any form and in any degree had no justifiable part whatever in our democratic way of life."[10] In even stronger language Justice Jackson accused the majority of sanctioning "the principle of racial discrimination . . . and of transplanting American citizens." That principle, he argued, "then lies about like a loaded weapon ready for the hand of an urgent need. Every repetition imbeds that principle more deeply in our law and thinking and expands it to new purposes. All who observe the work of courts are familiar with what Judge Cardozo described as the tendency of a principle to expand itself to the limit of its logic."[11]

Even in the 1955 decree in *Brown v. Board of Education* the Supreme Court spoke of "public schools [administered on a racially nondiscriminatory basis]" as the goal toward which it was striving.[12] In the companion case of *Bolling v. Sharpe* in which the *Brown* was applied to the District of Columbia, the Court specifically said, "Classifications based solely upon race must be scrutinized with particular care, since they are contrary to our traditions and hence constitutionally suspect."[13] Indeed, it would seem that the Supreme Court and federal courts generally were unaware that benign racial programs would be needed or forthcoming. In any event, it is clear that it is as easy to extract support for such programs from the school desegregation litigation as it is to find, in the same place, absolute condemnations of the use of race as a criterion by public authority.

It would seem that if an ethnic minority's reparations claims can never be met on the basis of ethnic differences, then the damage would go unrepaired. If the wrong consists in using race as a criterion, it would seem curious to repair the damage with more of the same. Yet, the injured individuals are identifiable solely by their ethnic traits. A way out has been suggested above. In order for the community to make reparations to injured members of a racial minority, it must use factors other than race. The community must be attributed a duty to extend reparations to all injured by governmental action or inaction before reparations for racial injuries may be justified. ("Community" injury to American Indians and the poor, and the victims of crime come to mind.) Proponents of benign racial treatment may contend that their claim deserves high priority because of the gravity of the community's offense. The approach is appealing, since individuals are not being compensated because they are members of a racial minority, but simply because they were injured and the community considers itself responsible. The relevant questions then become: what constitutes racial injury and how may persons so injured be afforded benign racial treatment.

It is only possible here to suggest how such questions may be answered. The definition of *racial injury* could be prescribed by statute, or left to emerge from the body of rules created by the adjudicating agency, subject, of course, to modification by statute. Very probably a case-by-case approach would be necessary. The form benign racial treatment would take would pose certain problems. Where simple racial discrimination is involved it is possible to redress grievances by declaring discriminatory acts amenable to the judicial process; where racial identification is to be followed by treatment on a racial basis, the problem is different.[14] Once minority group members can no longer claim that they are being denied access to education, public accommodation, employment, the political process, and housing because of their race their claims become blurred. It cannot be argued, at least not convincingly, that nonwhites should be given a handicap in the courtroom by barring witnesses from appearing for their adversaries, or that nonwhites should be given two votes while majority group members have only one. Indeed, if direct cash payments or tax benefits are ruled out, the areas in which compensation for racial injury are plausible are limited to those in which such programs are physically practicable. The chief areas are housing, education, and employment; these are the very areas which seem to loom large in the mind of the policy planner as he searches for racial peace.

The Future of Racial Reparations

The prospects for full-fledged racial reparations programs brighten with the increase in the incidence of racial disturbances and with the increase of the political strength of nonwhites. To proponents of such programs, the passage of the 1964 Civil Rights Act and the 1965 Voting Rights Act seems a logical step to the enactment of reparations programs.[15] The thrust of the 1964 and 1965 legislation, however, was largely directed against the values of Southern whites; the support of the non-Southern public for the housing provisions of the proposed Civil Rights Act of 1966 was less than overwhelming.[16] If the federal executive and legislative branches decide on a policy of racial reparations, however, there are indications that the judiciary would erect no obstacles in their path.[17]

The national commerce power seems to be an inexhaustible source of federal authority. The federal government has effectively preempted regulation of labor relations. Where dwellings are constructed with materials and by persons obviously involved in activities affecting interstate commerce, can there be any doubt that legislation barring the creation of nonwhite concentrations would be upheld?[18] The constitutional rationale for reparations legislation has already been suggested by the Supreme Court in its 1964 opinions in the *Civil Rights Cases*.[19]

Moreover, it is significant that the Supreme Court has sanctioned the use of race in administering public programs so long as the use was for a "good" purpose. While the Court has relied on its 1954 *Brown v. Board* precedent in overturning racial segregation in a variety of public endeavors, in 1961 the Court let stand (by denying certiorari) a lower federal court ruling compelling local authorities to take corrective steps to balance the schools' nonwhite and white populations.[20] In 1964 the Court let stand another ruling asserting that no one has a constitutional right to attend a racially balanced school.[21] Apparently the Justices were satisfied that Gary, Indiana, public schools were operated on a "neighborhood school plan, honestly and conscientiously constructed and with no intention or purpose to segregate the races."[22] Later in 1964 the Court refused to review a New York state court decision upholding the authority of state officials to take steps to correct racial imbalance by rearranging school attendance zones.[23] In March 1965, the *Gary* principle was reaffirmed as the Court concurred in a lower federal court's approval of "honest" neighborhood schools in Kansas City, Kansas, despite the resulting racial imbalance.[24] At the opening of its 1965 term the Court once again endorsed New York's deliberate use of race as a factor in administering its schools; the Court declined to review a state court ruling that state officials were not acting "arbitrarily or illegally" in taking steps to correct racial imbalance in public schools.[25] In none of these cases has the Supreme Court written an opinion, but the constitutional rule seems to be as follows: while members of racial minorities have no constitutional right to attend racially balanced (or even integrated) schools, state authorities may use race as a criterion in administering the educational system (presumably to achieve racial balance or integration, but not to achieve segregation).

If public authority may use race as a criterion in providing quality, integrated education, it would seem that parallel steps in the housing and employment areas would be permissible. Laws guaranteeing integrated neighborhoods by limiting nonwhite concentrations to certain quotas and providing incentives to attract whites into nonwhite neighborhoods would seem beyond constitutional reproach. To require employers to hire a certain percentage of nonwhites (say, corresponding to the local or national nonwhite percentage of the labor force) would seem equally defensible.

Summary and Conclusions

Members of racial minorities have a justifiable claim to reparations from the community which has either participated, directly or indirectly, or acquiesced in racial discrimination. If one accepts the principle that individuals should be treated on their merits and not on the basis of color, then racial treatment, whether benign or adverse, is inconsistent with this principle. However, the community may proceed to extend reparations in the form of special treatment, in such areas as housing, employment, and education to individuals injured by racial discrimination. The implementation of reparations programs by the executive and legislative branches of the central government would probably not be blocked on constitutional grounds by the judiciary.

Notes

1. In support of this proposition, see Vern Countryman, ed., *Discrimination and the Law* (Chicago, 1965) and Robert J. Harris, *The Quest for Equality* (Baton Rouge, 1960).

2. One may consider the government extending reparations to be upholding the conditions of the "social compact" by compensating parties whose terms of agreement have been violated. For an elaboration of this aspect of social compact theory, see Joseph Tussman, *Obligation and the Body Politic* (New York, 1960), especially chap. 1.

3. See Owen M. Fiss, "Racial Imbalance in the Public Schools: The Constitutional Concepts," *Harvard Law Review* 78 (January 1965): 571; Robert F. Drinan, "Racially Balanced Schools: Psychological and Legal Aspects," *Catholic Lawyer* 2 (winter 1965): 16; Robert L. Carter, "De Facto School Segregation: An Examination of the Legal and Constitutional Questions Presented," *Western Reserve Law Review* 16 (May 1965): 502; and *Morean v. Board of Education*, 210 A. 2d 97 (1964).

4. *Barksdale v. Springfield School Committee*, 237 F. Supp. 543, 546 (1965).

5. *Plessy v. Ferguson*, 163 U. S. 537, 559 (1896).

6. See *Springfield School Committee v. Barksdale*, 348 F. 2d 261, 266 (1965).

7. *Allen v. Hummel*, 258 N. Y. S. 2d 77, 82 (1965). Continued Van Voorhis:

> There is an important difference between obliterating the color line by admitting a boy or girl or man or woman to school, to employment, to a residential location or to a place of public accommodation without regard to color, and allocating people to locations, employments or facilities because of their color. . . . It is one thing to insist that a person should not be excluded by law from a vocation, school, theatre, hotel, restaurant or public conveyance because of race; it is quite another matter and, as it seems to me, doing the reverse, to allocate these advantages according to racial quotas or on some other proportional basis.

8. John Kaplan, "Segregation Litigation and the Schools. Part II: The General Northern Problem," *Northwestern University Law Review* 53 (May–June 1963): 188. See also the dissenting opinion by Moore, Circuit Judge, in *Taylor v. Board of Education*, 294 F. 2d 36, 40.

9. *Hirabayshi v. United States*, 320 U. S. 81 (1943) and *Korematsu v. United States*, 323 U. S. 214 (1944). See Eugene V. Rostow, "The Japanese-American Cases: A Disaster," *Yale Law Journal* 54 (June 1945): 489.

10. *Korematsu v. United States*, 323 U. S. 214, 242 (1944).

11. Ibid., 246, citing Benjamin Cardozo, *The Nature of the Judicial Process* (New Haven, 1921), 51.

12. 349 U. S. 294, 301 (1955).

13. 347 U. S. 497, 499 (1954). The Court cited as authority the *Korematsu and Hirabayshi* cases (see note 9 above).

14. This is the course followed in Titles II and VII of the Civil Rights Act of 1964, 78 Stat., 241, and in Title IV (Housing) of the proposed Civil Rights Act of 1966 (see HR 14765 and S. 3296, 89th Cong. 2nd Sess). The technique of the 1965 Voting Rights Act, 79 Stat. 437, whereby Negroes disfranchised arbitrarily in the past may be summarily placed on the voting rolls, is somewhat different.

15. 78 Stat. 247; 79 Stat. 437.

16. See HR 14766 and S. 3296, 89th Cong. 2d sess.

17. For some insights as to why state and local antidiscrimination laws are ineffective, see Duane Lockard, "The Politics of Antidiscrimination Legislation," *Harvard Journal on Legislation* 3 (December 1965): 3; Michael I. Sovern, *Legal Restraints on Racial Discrimination in Employment* (New York, 1966), chap. 2; and Herbert Hill, "Racial Inequality in Employment: The Patterns of Discrimination." *The Annals* 1957 (January 1965): 30. Testifying before the House Judiciary Committee in support of HR 14765, the attorney general of the United States noted that "some seventeen states, the District of Columbia, Puerto Rico, the Virgin Islands, and a large number of municipalities" had enacted fair housing laws. The work of volunteer groups, judicial and executive action, and the "patchwork of state and local laws" were found inadequate. Department of Justice, "Statement by Attorney General Nicholas de B. Katzenbach," May 4, 1966.

18. For an enlightening treatment of this point, see Boris I. Bittker, "The Case of the Checker-Board Ordinance: An Experiment in Race Relations," *Yale Law Journal* 71 (July 1962): 1387. *Mulkey v. Reitman*, 50 Cal. Rptr. 881, 413 P. 2d 825 (1966) gives a summary of the open housing controversy in California; for a survey of the open housing controversy in Michigan, see Normal C. Thomas, *Rule 9: Politics, Administration, and Civil Rights* (New York, 1966).

19. *Heart of Atlanta Motel v. United States*, 397 U. S. 241 (1964); *Katzenbach v. McClung*, 397 U. S. 274 (1964).

20. *Brown v. Board of Education*, 347 U.S. 483 (1954). *Baltimore v. Dawson*, 220 F. 2d 386, aff'd, 350 U. S. 877 (1955), (public beaches and bathhouses); *Holmes v. Atlanta*, 233 F. 2d 93 aff'd, 350 U. S. 879 (1955) (golf course): *Gayle v. Browder*, 142 F. Supp. 707, aff'd, 352 U. S. 903 (1956) (city buses); *New Orleans Park Improvement Assn. v. Detiege*, 252 F. 2d 122, aff'd, 358 U. S. 54 (1958) (public park facilities). See also the cases cited by J. Clark in *Goss v. Board of Education*, 373 U. S. 683, 687–688 (1963). *Taylor v. Board of Education*, 191 F. Supp. 181, aff'd. 294 F, 2d 36, cert. denied, 368 U. S. 940 (1961).

21. *Bell v. School City of Gary*, 213 F. Supp. 819, aff'd, 324 F. 2d 209 (1963), cert. denied, 377 U. S. 924 (1964). See John Kaplan, "Segregation Litigation and the Schools — Part II: The Gary Litigation," *Northwestern University Law Review* 59 (May–June 1964): 121.

22. 313 F. Supp. 819, 823 (1963).

23. *Balabin v. Rubin*, 248 N. Y. S. 2d 574, *aff'd*, 250 N. Y. S. 2d 281, 199 N. E. 2d 375, *cert.* denied, 379 U. S. 881 (1964).

24. *Downs v. Board of Education*, 336 F. 2d 988 (1964). Justice Douglas was of the opinion that certiorari should have been granted.

25. *Vetere v. Mitchell*, 251 N. Y. S. 2d 480 (1965), *aff'd* in *Allen v. Hummel*, 258 N. Y. S. 2d 77 (1965), *cert.* denied in *Vetere v. Allen*, 86 S. Ct. 60 (1965); *Addabbo v. Donovan*, 256 N. Y. S. 2d 178, *cert.* denied, 86 S. Ct. 241 (1965).

The Constitutionality of Black Reparations

BORIS I. BITTKER AND ROY L. BROOKS

In 1973, Boris Bittker discussed the constitutionality of black reparations in a chapter of his book, The Case for Black Reparations.[1] *In the following essay, Roy L. Brooks updates that discussion with Bittker's permission.*

Does the Constitution permit the federal government to establish and finance a program of reparations whose benefits would go to black citizens exclusively? It is, of course, common practice for governmental benefits to be distributed to a limited class of persons. Thus, we take it for granted that poor people but not rich ones get welfare payments, that veterans but not nonveterans qualify for benefits under the G.I. Bill of Rights, that homeowners but not tenants qualify for home-mortgage guarantees, and that farmers but not city people qualify for farm price supports and agricultural extension services. Moreover, in an earlier age the lines of demarcation drawn by Congress or the state legislature in the distribution of benefits were virtually immune to judicial review; echoing the popular maxim that beggars can't be choosers, it was said that no one has a constitutional right to public "largesse." This curt response is no longer in vogue, and the courts are now more willing to review the qualifications laid down in legislation on the complaint of an aggrieved person to see if his or her exclusion is so unreasonable as to violate the Fifth Amendment's guarantee of "due process of law" or the Fourteenth Amendment's guarantee of "equal protection of the laws."[2] In these judicial forays, however, the courts acknowledge that legislative bodies have an exceedingly wide range for the exercise of discretion, and the legislative judgment is rarely overturned.

Against this background, black reparations might be regarded as simply a routine legislative action to meet the claims of one defined group of citizens by establishing a program from which others (viz., whites) are excluded. Asked to enlarge the program to include whites (for example, on the ground that many whites have also suffered from governmental neglect or misconduct), or to enjoin its operation entirely, the Supreme Court might repeat what it said when an Oklahoma optician argued that he was denied the equal protection of the laws by a state law that regulated his business but exempted the sellers of ready-to-wear eyeglasses with which his products competed:

> The problem of legislative classification is a perennial one, admitting of no doctrinaire definition. Evils in the same field may be of different dimensions and proportions, requiring different remedies. Or so the legislature may think. Or the reform may take one step at a time, addressing itself to the phase of the problem which seems most acute to the legislative mind. The legislature may select one phase of one field and apply a remedy there, neglecting the others. The prohibition of the Equal Protection Clause goes no further than the invidious discrimination.[3]

In a similar vein, the Supreme Court upheld the conviction of a Maryland storekeeper for selling a loose-leaf binder and a can of floor wax in violation of the state's Sunday closing laws, despite the fact that the laws exempted the sale of cigarettes, gasoline, candy, and a bewildering array of other products. Rejecting the defendant's argument that these statutory distinctions were so arbitrary and capricious as to deny him the equal protection of the laws, the Court said:

> Although no precise formula has been developed, the Court has held that [the equal protection clause of] the Fourteenth Amendment permits the States a wide scope of discretion in enacting laws which affect some groups of citizens differently than others. The constitutional safeguard is offended only if the classification rests on grounds wholly irrelevant to the achievement of the State's objective. State legislatures are presumed to have acted within their constitutional power despite the fact that, in practice, their laws result in some inequality. A statutory discrimination will not be set aside if any state of facts reasonably may be conceived to justify it.[4]

Although expressed in cases involving the constitutionality of state action under the equal protection clause of the Fourteenth Amendment, judicial deference to the legislature's judgment is an equally common response when federal action is attacked under the due process clause of the Fifth Amendment.[5]

This reluctance to interfere with legislative solutions, however, does not extend to laws embodying distinctions based on race, color, or religion. They encounter a more skeptical reception, epitomized in the Supreme Court's statement that "distinctions between citizens solely because of their ancestry are by their very nature odious to a free people whose institutions are founded upon the doctrine of equality."[6] More succinctly, Justice John Marshall Harlan said in 1896 that the "Constitution is color-blind." He made this remark in his dissenting opinion in *Plessy v. Ferguson*, where the majority upheld a state segregation statute, but it is often said that his view was vindicated and endorsed by *Brown v. Board of Education* in 1954, when the Supreme Court rejected the *Plessy* precedent.[7]

Years later, Justice Antonin Scalia, quoting one of Boris I. Bittker's colleagues, would articulate a similar view of the Constitution:

> The difficulty of overcoming the effects of past discrimination is as nothing compared with the difficulty of eradicating from our society the source of those effects, which is the tendency — fatal to a Nation such as ours — to classify and judge men and women on the basis of their country of origin or the color of their skin. A solution to the first problem that aggravates the second is no solution at all. I share the view expressed by Alexander Bickel that "[t]he lesson of the great decisions of the Supreme Court and the lesson of contemporary history have been the same for at least a generation: discrimination on the basis of race is illegal, immoral, unconstitutional, inherently wrong, and destructive of democratic society."[8]

Can these generalizations, founded on the equal protection clause of the Fourteenth Amendment and also on a more basic theory of democracy, be squared with racial distinctions having a compensatory purpose? Or do they confine governmental actions to the elimination of racial disparities for the future, requiring us to let bygones be bygones?

It is interesting to discover that Section 5 of the Fourteenth Amendment, authorizing Congress to enact appropriate legislation to enforce the amendment's prohibitions, was once described by the Supreme Court as having an exclusively racial purpose. "We doubt very much," said the Court in 1872, "whether any action of a State not directed by way of discrimination against the negroes as a class, or on account of their race, will ever be held to come within the purview of this provision."[9] This prophecy was not borne out, however, and, as we shall see, the Supreme Court in recent years has often asserted that legislation for the exclusive benefit of one racial group would ordinarily violate the Fourteenth Amendment and, by extension, the Fifth Amendment, even if animated by a benign purpose.[10]

Three decades ago, Bittker struggled with these issues in an article entitled "The Case of the Checker-Board Ordinance: An Experiment in Race Relations."[11] His arena was an imaginary lawsuit brought by a black who had been denied the right to buy a house designated for "white occupancy only" in New Harmony, Illinois, a utopian community in which every dwelling was assigned to either black or white occupancy in a checkerboard pattern. In this fable the ordinance was enacted to achieve integration by legal compulsion, following testimony by students of American race relations that private discrimination and prejudice are heightened by segregated housing patterns but lowered by integrated patterns; that a community with a stable pattern of integrated housing would enrich the lives of all its citizens by enlarging their relations with persons of the other race; and that whites either would not move to New Harmony or would tend to leave if they thought they would be greatly outnumbered by Negroes. The central issue in this hypothetical lawsuit was whether the equal protection clause of the Fourteenth Amendment permits citizens to be classified by race in the administration of a "benign" governmental program.

Because Bittker found the question troublesome and resistant to a clear solution, he cast the discussion in the form of separate opinions by three appellate judges. The first judge wrote the briefest opinion, concluding that the Constitution prohibits the use of race or color as a criterion of state action, at least in regulating the ownership and occupancy of land. He relied primarily on two Supreme Court decisions. One, decided in 1917, held that a municipal ordinance forbidding blacks to move into or occupy houses in residential blocks that were predominantly occupied by whites (and imposing reciprocal restrictions on whites) violated the due process clause of the Fourteenth Amendment.[12] The other, announced in 1948, cited the equal protection clause in holding that state courts could not enforce restrictive covenants voluntarily adopted by private landowners to preserve the racial character of their neighborhoods, even though the state courts stood ready to enforce such covenants against potential white occupants as well as against blacks: "The rights established [by the Fourteenth Amendment] are personal rights.... Equal protection of the laws is not achieved through indiscriminate imposition of inequalities."[13] The hypothetical judge's conclusion that New Harmony's checkerboard ordinance was inconsistent with these cases was reinforced, in his opinion, by the Supreme Court's 1954 condemnation of public school segregation in *Brown v. Board of Education*. Not unlike proponents of California's Proposition 209,[14] the judge read *Brown* as a vindication of Justice Harlan's color-blind principle.

For Bittker's second hypothetical judge, this conclusion was an unacceptable interpretation of the Constitution. He accused his colleague of mechanically applying constitutional provisions designed to prevent discrimination against the newly emancipated slaves to a very different area, namely, remedial or compensatory legislation:

> The Fourteenth Amendment is almost one hundred years old, and its life has been replete with irony: railroads, utility companies, banks, employers of child labor, chain stores, money lenders, aliens, and a host of other groups and institutions have all found nurture in the due process and equal protection clauses, leaving so little room for the Negro that he seemed to be the fourteenth amendment's forgot-

ten man. This despite the Supreme Court's early recognition that "the one pervading purpose" of the thirteenth, fourteenth, and fifteenth amendments was to insure "the freedom of the slave race, the security and firm establishment of that freedom, and the protection of the newly-made freeman and citizen from the oppressions of those who had formerly exercised unlimited dominion over him." . . . The kaleidoscope of life often refuses to reflect our confident predictions, but seldom has a forecast been so completely lost to sight. Even so, the crowning irony comes today, when the racial zoning, restrictive covenant and school segregation cases, which had begun to restore the fourteenth amendment to the Negro, are used as weapons to destroy the first local legislation to ameliorate the condition of the Negro that has passed in review before this court.[15]

In harmony with this approach, the second judge distinguished the cases on which the first judge had relied, arguing that racial classifications are not unconstitutional per se, but only if they impute inferiority to one of the groups: "Any legislation that treats individuals (minors, women, men of draft age, veterans, lawyers, Indians, etc.) as members of a class necessarily distinguishes them from others; but the legislation does not 'discriminate' (in an invidious sense) if the classification is validated by some appropriate purpose or effect."[16] To illustrate this principle (now commonly called the "nonsubordination principle"),[17] the second judge pointed out that race has often been used by the courts as a factor in passing on the constitutionality of criminal convictions:

> In reviewing criminal cases in which violations of the due process clause have been alleged (e.g., denial of counsel, involuntary confessions, unreasonable delays in arraignment, etc.) the federal courts have often referred to the defendant's race or color. Without suggesting that race or color were crucial in all of these cases, or indeed in any, I cannot believe that they were merely neutral circumstances, like the defendant's social security number. Race, to the contrary, has been treated as a relevant circumstance, like the defendant's youth, poverty, illiteracy, or friendlessness, in judging whether he received due process of law. Rigorous proof of racial prejudice has not been demanded, however, and it would not be unreasonable to describe these cases as exercises of benevolent vigilance thought necessary to protect Negroes as a class from improper practices by the police and trial courts.[18]

Other racial classifications that are permitted because of their "remedial" character, according to the second judge, are the restricted rights of certain American Indians to dispose of their property until the secretary of the interior certified them as competent to handle their own affairs, and cases permitting a black defendant in a criminal case to get a new trial if blacks were systematically excluded from his jury.[19] He went on to conclude that the checkerboard ordinance, though it restricted the freedom of the black plaintiff to live where he wished, was a similarly reasonable effort to correct a social evil, and that it was consistent with the constitutional guarantees of due process and equal protection.

Recent scholarship finds additional support for the nonsubordination principle in several other Supreme Court opinions. Three of the most unlikely sources are *Plessy*, *Brown*, and *Bolling v. Sharpe*:

> *Plessy* upheld a statute that separated African American passengers from white passengers in railway cars. The Supreme Court accepted the argument that the statute's racial distinction "has no tendency to destroy the legal equality of the races, or reestablish a state of involuntary servitude." This view of the statute gave birth to the Court's "separate but equal" doctrine. What is so revealing about this opinion is that the Court addressed the contention of the plaintiff that the statute stamped African Americans with a "badge of inferiority." The Court responded that such a suggestion of inferiority did not arise from the statute itself but from its interpretation by African Americans. It is of some moment that the Court felt it necessary to rebut the charges of racial subordination. If the 14th Amendment vindicated only the colorblind principle, there would be no need to discuss the issue of racial subordination. Because the Court did not find racial subordination in *Plessy*, it concluded that the statute was constitutional.[20]

Proponents of the colorblind principle invariably cite *Brown* as support for the principle. But the opinion does not even so much as mention the word "colorblind" or cite to Justice Harlan's dissent in *Plessy* wherein the term is actually used. The Supreme Court in *Brown* ruled that "separate educational facilities are inherently unequal." At the time of *Brown*, that was certainly true, not only in Topeka, Kansas, but in most other Jim Crow school districts across the country. "The policy of separating the races is usually interpreted as denoting the inferiority of the Negro group," the Court noted. Thus, a close reading of *Brown* seems to indicate that the Court intended to invalidate only those racial classifications that subordinate or stigmatize a racial group. The same must be said of *Bolling v. Sharpe*, in which the Court, on the same day that it decided *Brown*, overturned a school segregation law in Washington, D.C. School segregation in the nation's capital was unconstitutional, the Court said, because it was not "reasonably related to any proper governmental objective, and thus it imposes on Negroes a burden." Arguably, neither *Brown* nor *Bolling* stand for the colorblind principle; both vindicate the nonsubordination principle.[21]

The nonsubordination principle and the colorblind principle cannot easily coexist, if at all. Colorblindness is less concerned with social equality (what is sometimes called "measurable equality"); nonsubordination is less concerned with legal equality (what is sometimes called "formal equal opportunity"). This tension is highlighted, yet often overlooked, in Justice Harlan's dissent in *Plessy*, in which he believed that colorblindness would *not* lead to a restructuring of the social order. Instead, he believed that whites would retain their social dominance under a color-blind Constitution. The very paragraph that sets forth the colorblind principle begins as follows: "The white race deems itself to be the dominant race in this country. And so it is, in prestige, in achievements, in education, in wealth and in power. So, I doubt not, it will continue to be for all time, if it remains true to its great heritage and holds fast to the principles of constitutional liberty."[22] Proponents of the nonsubordination principle might ask: What good is legal equality without social equality?

This is not to say that the nonsubordination principle rejects a fundamental tenet of our liberal democratic society—namely, the belief that the state should remain neutral as to race. The nonsubordination principle accepts this command, but asserts that the lingering effects of slavery and Jim Crow implicate the state in a continuing regime of racial subordination that, at times, can only be brought to an end through a benign use of race.[23]

The third judge in the checkerboard fable argued that the distinction between benign and malevolent uses of racial classifications threatened to undermine the constitutional objective of equality. If a checkerboard pattern of individual houses is permissible, why not a checkerboard of city blocks or wards, or a local white-black ratio corresponding to the state or national ratio or to a sociologist's recipe for a "good mix" of racial groups? If housing is a permissible area for experimentation, why not proportional racial representations in schools, employment, or voting? If these quotas, limitations, and privileges are permissible ways to compensate for past injustices toward blacks, why not similar devices for other minorities, distinguished by religion, national origin, or economic status?

At a more fundamental level, the third judge, similar to today's proponents of California's Proposition 209,[24] rejected his colleague's theory that benign racial legislation can be distinguished from legislation that imputes inferiority to one of the groups:

> Even the most well-intended legislation may be felt as humiliating by its objects, and especially so in a country that professes that "all men are created equal." . . . Viewed in this light, [New Harmony's] ordinance carries with it the offensive implication that is the unfortunate but seemingly inevitable concomitant of official charity or paternalism. Beyond that, it rests on, or is tantamount to, an official

finding that whites will not live side-by-side with Negroes except under legal compulsion. Perhaps this will be regarded by some as an official condemnation of the attitude of whites, in no sense reflecting adversely on Negroes; but just as many Negroes could not write off racial segregation in the public schools as merely a monument to white inhumanity, so I doubt if the implications of New Harmony's ordinance will leave them unscathed. Rather, many Negroes may ask themselves, as victims of private prejudice often do, what they have done to instill such distaste in others; and this inward search—made more acute by the fact that similar legal measures are not deemed necessary for other minority groups—may be equally destructive of self-esteem whether the finding that integrated housing cannot be achieved without legal compulsion is correct or not.[25]

As to the Indian cases cited by his colleague to establish that the Constitution permits racial classifications of a remedial character, the third judge argued that they should serve instead "to warn us that the role of the Great White Father may be bitterly resented by those in his tutelage and that a guardian ordinarily prefers to postpone rather than to advance the day when his wards must face the rigors of freedom." He went on to say that even if the criminal cases involving black defendants, on which his colleague relied, display a rule of "benevolent vigilance" for the rights of blacks, this does not "lead to the conclusion that legislatures may exercise in other areas of life whatever benevolent supervision they may believe is required by the social problems they perceive."[26]

The hypothetical third judge anticipated the views held by conservative black Americans in the 1990s. For example, Justice Clarence Thomas argued in *Adarand Constructors, Inc. v. Peña* that

there is [no] "paternalism exception to the principle of equal protection . . ." and that "there can be no doubt that racial paternalism and its unintended consequences can be as poisonous and pernicious as any other form of discrimination." So-called "benign" discrimination teaches many that because of chronic and apparently immutable handicaps, minorities cannot compete with them without their patronizing indulgence. . . . Such programs . . . stamp minorities with a badge of inferiority and may cause them to develop dependencies or to adopt an attitude that they are "entitled" to preferences.[27]

Likewise, another prominent black American, the author and academician Shelby Steele, has argued that the use of benign race-conscious programs in higher education has caused blacks to suffer "inferiority anxiety"—that is, self-doubt and a fear of competing with white Americans.[28]

In 1962, when Bittker argued all three sides in this inconclusive debate, the constitutionality of a "remedial" racial classification was only a cloud on the horizon. It was perceived as a problem by a few public housing agencies that were covertly applying a "benign" quota on black occupancy to prevent it from reaching the "tipping point" at which whites were expected to move out. Since then, however, the cloud has moved directly overhead, blown by the winds of change let loose by *Brown v. Board of Education*.

When *Brown* was decided, it was widely thought that compliance with its mandate "to admit [schoolchildren] to public schools on a racially non-discriminatory basis" could be achieved by the repeal of all school segregation laws and the assignment of pupils to schools on the basis of school districts with "neutral" boundaries (e.g., highways, rivers, railroad tracks, and political subdivisions).[29] Thus, the plaintiffs in *Brown* framed the basic question in the case as whether the State of Kansas had the power to enforce the state statute by which racially segregated public elementary schools were maintained.[30] This suggested that the existence of predominantly or wholly black or white schools would not violate the Constitution, provided the new school-attendance zones followed "neutral" boundaries and were not gerrymandered to perpetuate a division along racial lines. The goal of *Brown*, proponents of this limited mode of compliance argued, was not integration but the elimination of compulsory segregation. Indeed, some argued that the deliberate selection of boundaries to achieve a "desirable" racial mix would be improper, based on the theory of a color-blind Constitution.

In the ensuing years, the Supreme Court has revisited this issue on numerous occasions. The tension between integration and color-blindness, two morally defensible perspectives on civil rights, came before the Court in a variety of contexts (primarily education, employment, and voting) under the rubric of affirmative action.[31] Beginning in 1978 with *Regents of the University of California v. Bakke* and ending in 1995 with *Adarand Constructors, Inc. v. Peña*,[32] these cases, all of which deal with constitutional challenges to the use of racial preferences or quotas in the public sphere, provide the legal framework for assessing the constitutionality of black reparations. This framework begins with an understanding of the "strict scrutiny test," as explained by Brooks on another occasion:

> The strict scrutiny test is nowhere to be found in the Constitution or in its legislative history. It is a legal doctrine made up entirely by judges. Developed as a means to facilitate close judicial review of Jim Crow and other "suspicious" legislative enactments, the strict scrutiny test applies to lawsuits brought under the equal protection clause of the Fourteenth Amendment or the equal protection component of the Fifth Amendment's due process clause. The former constitutional provision protects against state actions and the latter against federal actions.[33]

Now a fixture in constitutional law, the strict scrutiny test is the legal system's primary means of implementing . . . [the color-blind principle]. It commands the omission of race in the government's formulation of laws and public policies. More importantly, it operates to strike down, as a denial of equal protection of the laws, any governmental activity or legislation that is either predicated upon an explicit racial or other "suspect classification" or violative of a "fundamental personal interest."[34] The act under scrutiny is saved from judicial strangulation only if the government can meet a two-fold burden. First, the classification must be justified by a "compelling governmental interest." Second, the means chosen to achieve that purpose must be the least restrictive, narrowly tailored means available.[35]

As applied by the Supreme Court, the strict scrutiny test sets up a standard of judicial review so rigorous as to be fatal to most applicable legislative acts. The first burden is particularly difficult to meet. Protecting national security and remedying past institutional or individual discrimination are among the few (if not the only) times the government has been able to demonstrate a compelling governmental interest to the Supreme Court's satisfaction.[36]

The Court, however, has attempted to balance the interventionist proclivity of the strict scrutiny test with a more deferential form of judicial review. Legislative acts not predicated on a suspect classification or violative of a fundamental personal interest—which is where the great majority of legislative acts fall—do not offend constitutional equal protection if they can be rationally related to a legitimate governmental purpose. The "rational basis test" provides the widest degree of judicial comity to even speculative legislative judgments.[37]

Explicit gender-based classifications are not suspect classifications and, hence, are not subject to strict scrutiny. Neither are they reviewed under the rational basis test. Rather, the Supreme Court employs a "middle-tier" or an "intermediate level" of scrutiny. Under this standard, the classification in question must serve important governmental objectives and must be substantially related to the achievement of those objectives.[38]

> The strict scrutiny test and the rational basis test are so predictably applied that the judicial outcome is virtually determined by the type of legislation under review. Legislation involving a suspect classification or a fundamental personal interest most likely will not survive constitutional scrutiny; whereas legislation involving economic classifications probably will be sustained. The Supreme Court's analysis for equal protection claims is in this sense outcome-determinative.[39]

Prior to *Adarand Constructors, Inc. v. Peña*, the Supreme Court seemed to suggest that the strict scrutiny test did not apply to race-based affirmative action plans created by Congress. Indeed in *City of Richmond v. Croson Co.*, the first case in which a majority of justices held that the strict scrutiny test governed the benign use of race by state or local government, Chief Justice William Rehnquist and Justices Sandra Day O'Connor and Byron White ruled that Congress, as a coequal branch of government, is entitled to greater deference than cities and states.[40] Agreeing with *Croson*'s dicta, a majority of the justices in a subsequent case, *Metro Broadcasting, Inc. v. FCC*, applied the intermediate standard of review in upholding the constitutionality of a congressional affirmative action plan favoring racial minorities. Speaking for the Court, Justice William Brennan wrote, "We hold that benign race-conscious measures mandated by Congress—even if those measures are not 'remedial' in the sense of being designed to compensate victims of past governmental or societal discrimination—are constitutionally permissible to the extent that they serve important governmental objectives within the power of Congress and are substantially related to the achievement of those objectives."[41] The decision in this case was split by the narrowest of margins, five to four.

Demonstrating a fair amount of indecision, the Supreme Court just five years later, and by another five-four margin, reversed *Metro Broadcasting*. The *Adarand* majority accused the *Metro Broadcasting* majority of taking a "surprising turn" in treating benign racial classifications by the federal government "less skeptically than others." Not unlike the first and third hypothetical judges in Bittker's checkerboard fable presented some thirty-six years ago, the *Adarand* majority believed that the color-blind principle should be vindicated. As a matter of basic democratic theory, the Court wrote:

> The Fifth and Fourteenth Amendments to the Constitution protect persons, not groups. It follows from that principle that all governmental action based on race—a group classification long recognized as "in most circumstances irrelevant and therefore prohibited"—should be subjected to detailed judicial inquiry to ensure that the personal right to equal protection of the laws has not been infringed. These ideas have long been central to this Court's understanding of equal protection, and holding "benign" state and federal racial classifications to different standards does not square with them.[42]

Adarand would seem to sound the death knell for black reparations, unless they can be tendered as compensation for the government's racial discrimination against blacks. A recent circuit court opinion, *Jacobs v. Barr*,[43] makes this clear.

Jacobs dealt with the constitutionality of the Civil Liberties Act of 1988.[44] In this unprecedented legislation, Congress, on behalf of the federal government, apologized and provided atonement money of $20,000 each to citizens and permanent resident aliens of Japanese ancestry who were forcibly relocated and placed in internment camps during World War Two. The Act also apologized and provided reparations awards of $12,000 each to the Aleuts who were forcibly relocated from their homelands to Alaska during that time. No other groups are entitled to compensation under the Act. In *Jacobs*, the plaintiff, a German American who was detained with his German father during the war, challenged this feature of the Act on grounds that it denied him equal protection of the laws. The court found ample evidence in the legislative history of the Act that Japanese American and Aleutian internees were the victims of racial prejudice at the hands of the federal government, whereas German American internees were not. For example, no mass exclusion or detention of German or Italian Americans was ordered, and those detained, including the plaintiff and his father, were first given due process hearings to establish their threat to national security. The circuit court therefore ruled that the Act passed constitutional muster under both the intermediate scrutiny test, which was the controlling standard of review at the time the case was brought, and the strict scrutiny test. "Congress . . . had clear and sufficient reason to compensate interns of Japanese but not German descent; and the compensation is substantially related (as well as narrowly tailored) to Congress's compelling interest in redressing a shameful example of national discrimination."[45]

Slavery and Jim Crow are undeniably shameful episodes of "national discrimination" (discrimination as official federal policy, not mere societal discrimination) against black Americans. Congress can certainly find ample evidence of this in the historical record should it decide to enact legislation for blacks similar to the Civil Liberties Act of 1988.[46] Legislation may be the only realistic way to proceed given the reluctance of courts to fashion their own monetary remedies. Indeed, it was in large part the failure of Japanese Americans to obtain monetary reparations through the courts that led to the pursuit of legislation resulting in the Civil Liberties Act.

But will the beneficiaries of black reparations, like those of the Civil Liberties Act, have to be actual victims of federal discrimination? As we move farther away from the Jim Crow era (circa 1865–1968), establishing privity between the wrongdoer and the victim will become as problematic as it is for slavery-based claims. For this reason, proponents of reparations have argued for "new connections between victims and perpetrators," including the recognition that today's blacks belong to the same victim class as prior generations of blacks, that many black families can trace their genealogy to identifiable victims of slavery or Jim Crow, and that the U.S. government, even though it no longer officially discriminates, assumes the liabilities of past administrations and congresses.[47] These arguments are based on public policy considerations and not on legal doctrine. Indeed, they assume the absence of legal support for paying reparations to nonvictims, which may not be the case entirely.

Arguably, legal support for atonement money going to nonvictims can be based on two grounds—one constitutionally based, the other statutorily created. As to the first, we have already seen that the Supreme Court's affirmative action case law upholds race-conscious remedies designed to redress the perpetrator's past discrimination. Because such discrimination can occur years, even decades, prior to the crafting of the remedy, the beneficiary and the victim need not be, and often are not, the same person. Victim-beneficiary alienation seems to be built into the controlling constitutional law.[48]

Second, Congress has enacted legislation that provides relief to certain nonvictims of employment discrimination. Section 706(g) of Title VII of the 1964 Civil Rights Act, the nation's primary employment discrimination law, empowers a court to order, upon a finding of unlawful discrimination, specific forms of relief "or any other equitable relief as the court deems appropriate."[49] This provision was intended, Congress said, "to give the courts wide discretion in exercising their equitable powers to fashion the most complete relief possible."[50] The Supreme Court has held that the last sentence of section 706(g), which prohibits a court from ordering a Title VII defendant to hire, reinstate, promote, or provide payback to an individual for any reason "other than" discrimination in violation of Title VII, does not prohibit a court from awarding (or an employer from granting through a consent decree) preferential, race-conscious remedies that benefit nonvictims.[51] On its face, the Court said, the last sentence does not "state that all prospective remedial orders must be limited so that they only benefit the specific victims of the employer's or union's past discriminatory acts."[52] While it is true that the nonvictims in these cases were incidental beneficiaries of nonmonetary relief, and that nonvictim black Americans would be targeted beneficiaries of monetary relief under most reparations plans, the Supreme Court's reasoning could easily extend beyond the specific facts of the cases. The purpose of such relief, the Court has reasoned, is "not to make identified victims whole," but to dismantle the lingering effects of prior discrimination and to prevent discrimination in the future.[53]

Using section 706(g) and the Civil Liberties Act as models, Congress might be able to enact a statute that made a legislative finding of past governmental discrimination against blacks as a group and then proceeded to award atonement money or other forms of reparations (e.g., affirmative action) to contemporary blacks. The purpose of the award would be atonement for past sins and not compensation to actual victims. This reasoning provides a logical basis for benefiting nonvictims. To borrow from the Supreme Court, "Such relief is provided to the class as a whole rather than to individual members; no individual is entitled to relief, and beneficiaries need not show that they were themselves victims of discrimination."[54]

The remarkable regularity and balance between the constitutional and statutory standards should not go unnoticed. Both are group- rather than individual-focused, and, more important, both seek to deal with the residual effects of prior acts of discrimination. The latter purpose would seem to provide the necessary legal grounds for deciding the privity issue. But in the end, a judicial resolution of that and other legal questions surrounding black reparations might well turn on public policy considerations, as is usually the case.

Notes

1. Boris I. Bittker, *The Case for Black Reparations* (New York: Vintage Books, 1973), chap. 11. For reviews of Bittker's book, see Ira B. Shepard, "Book Review," *Georgia Law Review* 7 (1973): 587; Derrick A. Bell Jr., "Dissection of a Dream," *Harvard Civil Rights–Civil Liberties Law Review* 9 (1974): 156; Mark Tushnet, "The Utopian Technician," *Yale Law Journal* 93 (1983): 208. For other discussion of the constitutionality of black reparations, see, e.g., Mari J. Matsuda, "Looking to the Bottom: Critical Legal Studies and Reparations," *Harvard Civil Rights–Civil Liberties Law Review* 22 (1987): 323; Rhonda V. Magee, "The Master's Tools, from the Bottom Up: Responses to American Reparations Theory in Mainstream and Outsider Remedies Discourse," *Virginia Law Review* 79 (1993): 863, 897–904.

2. See, e.g., *Adarand Constructors, Inc. v. Peña*, 518 U.S. 200 (1995) (race); *United States v. Virginia*, 518 U.S. 515 (1996) (gender); *City of Cleburne v. Cleburne Living Center, Inc.*, 473 U.S. 432 (1985) (discussing various standards of judicial review). See, generally, Erwin Chemerinsky, *Constitutional Law: Principles and Policies* (New York: Aspen Law and Business, 1997), 638–746; Van Alstyne, "The Demise of the Right-Privilege Distinction in Constitutional Law," *Harvard Law Review* 81 (1968): 1439.

3. *Williamson v. Lee Optical Co.*, 348 U.S. 483, 489 (1955).

4. *McGowan v. Maryland*, 366 U.S. 420, 425–426 (1961).

5. See, e.g., *Adarand Constructors, Inc. v. Peña*, 515 U.S. 200 (1995); *Bolling v. Sharpe*, 347 U.S. 497 (1954).

6. *Hirabayashi v. United States*, 320 U.S. 81, 100 (1943).

7. *Plessy v. Ferguson*, 163 U.S. 537, 559 (1896); *Brown v. Board of Education*, 347 U.S. 483 (1954). There is disagreement over how to read *Brown*. *Brown* is commonly understood as overturning *Plessy* and the "separate but equal" doctrine. Some scholars, however, argue that the *Brown* Court attempted to distinguish *Plessy* instead of overruling it. See, e.g., Lino Graglia, *Disaster by Decree: The Supreme Court Decisions on Race and the Schools* (Ithaca, N.Y.:

Cornell University Press, 1976), 26–30. Note that the *Brown* Court found it necessary to mention that *Plessy* "involv[ed] not education but transportation" (347 U.S. at 491). For a detailed discussion and scholarly analysis of *Brown*, see, generally, Leon Friedman, ed., *Argument: The Oral Argument before the Supreme Court in Brown v. Board of Education of Topeka, 1952–55* (New York: Chelsea House Publishers, 1969); "Symposium: *Brown v. Board of Education*," *Southern Illinois University Law Journal* 20 (1995): 1.

8. *City of Richmond v. J. A. Croson Co.*, 488 U.S. 469, 520–521 (1989) (Scalia, J., concurring in the judgment) (quoting Alexander Bickel, *The Morality of Consent* [New Haven: Yale University Press, 1975], 133).

9. *Slaughter-House Cases*, 83 U.S. 36, 81 (1872).

10. See, e.g., *Adarand Constructors, Inc. v. Peña*, 515 U.S. 200 (1995); *City of Richmond v. Croson*, 488 U.S. 469 (1989).

11. Boris I. Bittker, "The Case of the Checker-Board Ordinance: An Experiment in Race Relations," *Yale Law Journal* 71 (1962): 1387.

12. *Buchanan v. Warley*, 245 U.S. 60 (1917).

13. *Shelley v. Kraemer*, 334 U.S. 1, 22 (1948).

14. Proposition 209 (or the "California Civil Rights Initiative") amended the California Constitution in 1996. Section 31(a) of the California Constitution now reads: "The State shall not discriminate against or grant preferential treatment to any individual or group on the basis of race, sex, color, ethnicity, or national origin in the operation of public employment, public education, or public contracting" (California Constitution, Article 1, Section 31(a)). Put simply, Proposition 209 ends most governmental affirmative action in California. The subsequent constitutional challenge to Proposition 209 was unsuccessful. See *Coalition for Economic Equity v. Wilson*, 110 F.3d 1431 (1997) (vacating the preliminary injunction and finding no unequal "political structure" that obstructs minorities from receiving protection against unequal treatment). For a more detailed analysis of Proposition 209, see Eugene Volokh, "The California Civil Rights Initiative: An Interpretive Guide," *University of California Los Angeles Law Review* 44 (1997): 1335. For a criticism of Proposition 209, see Derrick A. Bell, "California's Proposition 209: A Temporary Diversion on the Road to Racial Disaster," *Loyola Law Review* 30 (1997): 1447.

15. Bittker, "The Case of the Checker-Board Ordinance," 1393.

16. Ibid., 1394. For a more detailed discussion, see, e.g., Roy L. Brooks, *Integration or Separation?* (Cambridge, Mass.: Harvard University Press, 1996), 199–213.

17. Brooks, *Integration or Separation?*, 208.

18. Bittker, "The Case of the Checker-Board Ordinance," 1407.

19. For the first type of case, see *Squire v. Capoeman*, 351 U.S. 1 (1956); for the second type, see *Batson v. Kentucky*, 476 U.S. 79 (1986). See also *Powers v. Ohio*, 499 U.S. 400 (1991) (civil cases).

20. *Bolling v. Sharpe*, 347 U.S. 497 (1954).

21. Brooks, *Integration or Separation?*, 208, 210–211 (citations omitted).

22. *Plessy v. Ferguson*, 163 U.S. at 558 (Harlan, J., dissenting).

23. For a more detailed discussion, see Roy L. Brooks, *Critical Procedure* (Durham, N.C.: Carolina Academic Press, 1998), 5–7.

24. See the discussion of Proposition 209 above.

25. Bittker, "The Case of the Checker-Board Ordinance," 1419–1420.

26. Ibid., 1422, 1423.

27. *Adarand Constructors, Inc. v. Peña*, 515 U.S. 200, 240–241 (1995).

28. See Shelby Steele, *The Content of Our Character: A New Vision of Race in America* (New York: St. Martin's Press, 1990), 47, 55, 62–63, 68–70, 108–109, 113–125, 156–157.

29. *Brown v. Board of Education*, 349 U.S. 294, 301 (1955) (*Brown II*).

30. See Friedman, ed., *Argument*, 15.

31. For a discussion of these cases, see, e.g., Roy L. Brooks, Gilbert P. Carrasco, and Gordon A. Martin, *Civil Rights Litigation: Cases and Perspectives* (Durham, N.C.: Carolina Academic Press, 1995), chap. 10; Jed Rubenfeld, "Affirmative Action," *Yale Law Journal* 107 (1997): 427.

32. *Regents of the University of California v. Bakke*, 438 U.S. 265 (1978); *Adarand Constructors, Inc. v. Peña*, 515 U.S. 200 (1995). In *Bakke*, a divided Supreme Court ruled 5 to 4 that state educational institutions could not set aside a specific number of slots for which only racial minorities could compete. Although important as a starting point for any discussion of benign racial classification, *Bakke*'s precedential value is rather questionable. *Bakke* is a poor case from which to draw conclusions about the application of the equal protection clause in general and the controlling standard of judicial review for black reparations as well as other forms of race-based affirmative action. Only Justice Lewis Powell invalidated the racial quota on equal protection grounds. He was also the only justice to use the strict scrutiny test as the constitutional standard of review for race-based affirmative action. Significantly, the four justices who would not scrutinize benign quotas strictly — William Brennan, Thurgood Marshall, Harry Blackmun, and (possibly) Byron White — have not won the day in subsequent benign quota or preference cases. Since *Bakke*, a majority of Supreme Court justices have taken the position that all explicit racial classifications — whether racially exclusive or inclusive — are subject to strict scrutiny, and that only national security or the defendant's past or current intentional discrimination, not societal discrimination, will justify the use of such a classification. See, e.g., *City of Richmond v. Croson*, 488 U.S. 469 (1989); *Adarand Constructors, Inc. v. Peña*, 515 U.S. 200 (1995).

33. For state actions, see, e.g., *United States v. Paradise*, 480 U.S. 149, 166 (1987) (cases cited therein). See also *Brown v. Board of Education*, 347 U.S. 483 (1954); *City of Richmond v. Croson*, 488 U.S. 46 (1989). For federal actions, see, e.g., *Local 28 of Sheet Metal Workers v. EEOC*, 478 U.S. 421, 479–480 (1986) (cases cited therein). See also *Bolling v. Sharpe*, 347 U.S. 497 (1954).

34. See, e.g., *McDonald v. Board of Election Commissioners of Chicago*, 394 U.S. 802, 807 (1969). See, generally, Polyvios G. Polyviou, *The Equal Protection of the Laws* (London: Duckworth, 1980); Note, "Developments in the Law — Equal Protection," *Harvard Law Review* 82 (1969): 1065. See also *Reynolds v. Sims*, 377 U.S. 533, 561–562 (1964). Fundamental personal interest includes the right to procreate, *Skinner v. Oklahoma*, 316 U.S. 535 (1942); the right to vote, *Reynolds*, 377 U.S. 533; and the right to interstate travel, *Shapiro v. Thompson*, 394 U.S. 618 (1969).

35. See, e.g., *Wygant v. Jackson Board of Education*, 476 U.S. 267, 273–274 (1986) (Powell, J., concurring); *Palmore v. Sidoti*, 466 U.S. 429, 432 (1984); *Loving v. Virginia*, 388 U.S. 1, 11 (1967). See also *McLaughlin v. Florida*, 397 U.S. 184 (1964); *Shelley v. Kraemer*, 334 U.S. 1 (1948).

36. See *Korematsu v. United States*, 323 U.S. 214 (1944). See *Paradise*, 480 U.S. at 166 (cases cited therein).

37. See, e.g., *McDonald v. Board of Election Commissioners of Chicago*, 394 U.S. 802, 809 (1969). "Legislatures are presumed to have acted constitutionally." Ibid. Roy L. Brooks, *Rethinking the American Race Problem* (Berkeley: University of California Press, 1990), 51–52 (internal citations renumbered).

38. See, e.g., *United States v. Virginia*, 518 U.S. 515 (1996); *Craig v. Boren*, 429 U.S. 191

(1976). See also Gerald Gunther, *Constitutional Law*, 11th ed. (Mineola, N.Y.: Foundation Press, 1985), 642–664; Craig C. Ducat and Harold W. Chase, *Constitutional Interpretations*, 3d ed. (St. Paul, Minn.: West, 1983), 692, 861–871.

39. Craig C. Ducat and Harold W. Chase, *Constitutional Interpretations*, 3rd ed. (St. Paul, Minn.: West, 1983).

40. *City of Richmond v. Croson*, 488 U.S. 469, 486–494 (1989) (Part II of Justice O'Connor's opinion in which Chief Justice Rehnquist and Justice White joined).

41. *Metro Broadcasting, Inc. v. FCC*, 497 U.S. 547, 564–565 (1990).

42. *Adarand Constructors, Inc. v. Peña*, 515 U.S. at 227.

43. *Jacobs v. Barr*, 959 F.2d 313 (D.C. Cir. 1992), *cert. denied* 506 U.S. 831 (1992).

44. 50 App. U.S.C., Sections 1989(a)–1989(d).

45. *Jacobs v. Barr*, 959 F.2d at 322.

46. See, e.g., Brooks, Carrasco, and Martin, *Civil Rights Litigation*, 5–8; Bittker, *The Case for Black Reparations*, 8–26.

47. See, e.g., Matsuda, "Looking to the Bottom," 374–385.

48. See, e.g., *Fullilove v. Klutznick*, 448 U.S. 448, 478 (1980) (Congress had "evidence of a long history of marked disparity in the percentage of public contracts awarded to minority business enterprises").

49. 42 U.S.C., Sections 2000(e)–2005(g).

50. *Congressional Record* 118 (1972): 7168.

51. *Local 28, Sheet Metal Workers' International Association v. Equal Employment Opportunity Commission*, 478 U.S. 421, 424, 446–447 (1986); *Local Number 93, International Association of Firefighters v. City of Cleveland*, 478 U.S. 501, 516 (1986).

52. *Sheet Metal Workers,'* 478 U.S. at 474 n.46.

53. See ibid., p. 474.

54. Ibid.

The Theory of Restitution

The African American Case

RICHARD AMERICA

Summary and Recommendations

Whenever there are chronic grievances — between nations, races, or other large social groups — a fundamental issue is invariably the sense that one party has perpetrated unremedied historic economic injustices. The theory of restitution is based on the intuition that it is possible:

To reconstruct historic economic relations
To specify "fair" standards — prices, wages, terms of trade, interest rates, return on investment — that were violated, usually by force
To audit the historic pattern of transactions between the groups, and compare the actual with the "fair" standard
To then estimate the deviation from "fairness"
To designate that result as unjust enrichment, and estimate its present value and distribution
To then draw policy implications that will usually be in the form of lump sum or other redistributive income and wealth transfers, in-kind subsidies, or investments in real and human capital.

For over 370 years, income and wealth have been coercively diverted from Africans and African Americans to the benefit of Europeans and European Americans. This was primarily done through slavery and then discrimination in education, housing, and labor and capital markets.

It is possible now to reconstruct that history in some detail. And it is possible to develop theory and method to measure the magnitude of the income and wealth transfers, and to estimate their present value and distribution.

These unjust enrichments were not dissipated. They were transferred intergenerationally, and are currently enjoyed by whites in the top 30 percent of the income and wealth distribution (see Oliver and Shapiro, part 1).

Since the processes that produced the benefits are now widely regarded as wrong, illegal and illegitimate — violating current standards of fairness — the benefits that have been produced are unjust. They should, therefore, be returned to those who were harmed or to their descendants collectively.

So there is a case for restitution. And the debt — which amounts, by some estimates, to $5 trillion to $10 trillion — can be paid through adjustments in tax and budget policies over the next forty years. The debt should be paid primarily through investments in human capital, housing, and business formation.

The Problem

Several contributors to this volume have reviewed the economics of poverty. And they have chronicled the disparities by race in economic life. The inequalities are well known. And the basic reasons for continuing chronic economic distress, among a large minority of African Americans, have been thoroughly analyzed. But the descriptions and analyses have not produced behavior changes or innovative policies sufficient to eliminate the phenomenon of gross disparities in income and wealth by race. It is possible that the real problem is still not properly specified.

The race problem can be accurately defined this way: It is, for all practical purposes, the coerced and manipulated diversion of income and wealth from blacks to whites. That is the problem in a nutshell. Racism is a social mechanism that justifies and helps make possible a wide range of decisions. These occur in education, housing, finance, and employment and training. And they make possible and reinforce the wrongful accumulation of wealth by the beneficiaries of racism as a class. So racism, whatever else it might also be, is an instrument for creating and maintaining economic dominance and unjust economic relationships. It has persisted because, among other reasons, it is beneficial to many people.

Solving the primary American social problem — the race problem — is, therefore, a matter of making racism less attractive economically. Part of the solution is to retrieve some or all of the wrongful benefits that racism has produced for the white majority, and to intervene in markets and educational processes so they do not generate further benefits.

But the focus should be keenly on the benefit side — the benefits accruing to white Americans from continuing racial discrimination against blacks. For too long, we have focused simply on the costs of racism. And that way of looking at the problem is one reason relatively little progress has been made against intransigent, chronic economic underperformance and persistent poverty.

Discussion

For generations the idea has persisted that whites owe blacks money. It has never been a mainstream idea. It has never had strong adherents in high places. It has never had strong theoretical or practical support among economists and policy analysts. Nonetheless, the idea has enough intuitive power that it never completely went away.

The idea that forty acres and a mule had somehow been promised after emancipation — rather than simply proposed — has endured. And that notion has kept alive the feeling that there really is something to the idea that even such a vast amorphous injustice as racial exclusion, exploitation, and discrimination in many forms, and in many markets, can lead to a kind of debt. This obligation has also been felt but not articulated by many whites. And it seems to underlie many acts of altruism, "compassion," and charity. Some whites have gone further and said they acknowledge some kind of moral debt. But few have gone all the way to this idea: that the past produced tangible benefits to the white majority; these were accumulated, compounded, and bequeathed, and today there is a measurable, unjust enrichment that should be surrendered and transferred back in some orderly, democratically agreed-upon way.

But that is the most obvious policy implication of the concept of restitution. The word used here is restitution rather than reparations. Reparations has inflammatory connotations. And it's associated commonly with the aftermath and consequence of military victory and defeat. Losers in war pay reparations, under duress. That's not what we have in mind. Instead, the concept is that justice and morality are operating broadly. And these are not compatible with holding in perpetuity benefits derived from past immoral and wrongful systemic transactions and processes. So, at the end of the twentieth century, Americans have the opportunity to look at their history collectively. They can acknowledge that much wealth has been built by methods that cannot stand scrutiny by today's standards. They may have been acceptable at the time. But moral people cannot accept the fruits of wrongful actions that were committed in their behalf — as posterity — by their collective if not direct biological ancestors.

Boris Bittker's 1972 book, *The Case for Black Reparations* (Random

House) examined these questions thoroughly and successfully. He dealt with all the common objections: that raising these issues now so late in the game is ex post facto, and that we don't mete out justice that way under our system. On the contrary, he said, there is ample precedent for finding retroactive guilt, and correcting it, if practicable.

Guilt, incidentally, in the emotional sense, is not the point. That's another common objection. "Why try to play on guilt?" No. The point is that a careful examination leads to a finding of guilt. But it doesn't matter whether culprits feel emotional guilt or not. They are guilty in any event. So restitution, when all is said and done, depends on a large majority of Americans concluding that the distribution of income and wealth, by race, cannot be justified. It's based on wrongful acts. It implies an obligation to make restitution. And the key is to find ways that are politically feasible and practical in the actual circumstances.

Background and History

Slavery produced benefits for over two hundred years. Agricultural slavery was primary. But many Americans only think of slavery in terms of agricultural commodity production. In fact, slavery generated great benefits in other ways as well. Slaves were used in manufacturing, services, and in activities that today would be called municipal or state government, running transportation, utility, and emergency services. Also vitally important, slaves cleared land and built infrastructure: roads, dams, levees, canals, railroads, and bridges.

Without this labor, it can be argued, the nation would not have expanded West as it did. Indeed, it is possible, and perhaps probable, that the United States would never have become a continental nation. It likely would not have been able to complete the Louisiana Purchase, nor gain the territories that became the Southwest and West Coast states so vital to twentieth-century growth. The United States could well have ended, territorially, at about the Mississippi River, and never emerged as a world power. The point is not to speculate on counterfactual history. But the crucial role of slave labor in creating the basis for expansion and total continental development is worth underlining.

Slave-produced goods and services benefited most whites indirectly and passively. This happened through the process of human capital formation. Slaves made it possible for many whites to go into more rewarding occupations, gain increased skills, and generate greater lifetime earnings for themselves and their descendants. In these indirect and passive ways, slavery produced enormous benefits beyond those usually considered that flowed directly from production.

Discrimination

Similarly, after slavery, exclusion and discrimination allowed millions of Americans and immigrants to enter occupations with greater prospects. In these ways, racism generated income and wealth that flows to present-day recipients. That is an important reality. It should not be minimized.

Theodore Hershberg, at the University of Pennsylvania, has studied immigration. He found that successful, accomplished black tradespeople and skilled operators were displaced by immigrants. So it is not simply a matter of black entrance being blocked. Black earnings were established, and then forcibly discontinued by private practice, and by conscious, active, wrongful interventionist public policy.

Discrimination continued through the mid-twentieth century. And in the past one hundred years it produced far greater benefits than those piled up during the preceding 270 years because of the far greater population and size of the economy. So the most significant sources of unjust enrichments have fairly recent origins, notwithstanding the dramatic effects of compound interest on the earlier, longer stream of coercively, interracially diverted income.

Processes

Exploitation, exclusion, and discrimination were mechanisms that produced unjust enrichment. Exploitation is a loaded term. It carries great emotional baggage with the general public even when used in a technical sense. Here it simply refers to super benefits over and above "normal" returns on investment, or above a unit of labor's marginal productivity.

Exclusion refers to what is usually known as occupational discrimination, in which whites occupied jobs that otherwise, in a freely competitive market, would have been occupied by blacks of equal ability and training, exerting equal effort.

Discrimination refers to three other phenomena in addition to occupational discrimination:

First, employment discrimination is commonly seen in the last hired, first fired practice. Blacks and whites of equal endowments experience different lengths of employment in similar economic cycles.

Second, wage discrimination refers to whites and blacks, equally endowed, receiving different wages for the same occupational and skill contribution.

Third, there are other forms of discrimination, as outlined by Lester Thurow in *Generating Inequality* (Basic Books, 1975). These include capital, housing, medical/health, and other subtle twentieth-century practices.

Result

All these differential practices produce a diversion of benefits by race. All of them made whites better off relative to blacks, in the aggregate, than they otherwise would have been in a society, and in markets, using free and openly competitive selection processes.

The total consequence of all these direct and indirect, active and passive methods of diverting income and wealth interracially resulted in a massive unjust enrichment that can be measured, and that is enjoyed even to the present. The important objective is to refine the theory, locate and organize data, and create an econometric technique that can shed light on the processes' quantitative impact.

Measurement

There have been estimates; they have been preliminary and illustrative, not final and conclusive. In *The Wealth of Races* (edited by R. F. America, Greenwood, 1990), Marketti, Neal, Chachere, and Udinsky, and Swinton applied contrasting methods over differing time periods. There is room for much more work of this kind. The National Association for the Advancement of Colored People, the National Urban League, the Joint Center for Political and Economic Studies, and other civil rights groups should systematically engage in this task. And government organizations like the Bureau of Labor Statistics, Federal Reserve Board, Congressional Budget Office, Office of Management and Budget, General Accounting Office, House Ways and Means Committee, House and Senate Budget Committees, and Joint Economic Committee should as well.

Finally, the National Bureau of Economic Research, Brookings Institution, American Enterprise Institute, Progressive Policy Institute, Upjohn Institute,

Urban Institute, Center for Budget and Policy Priorities, Economic Policy Institute, Committee on Economic Development, and other think tanks and research centers should also make it a priority to track this issue. They should produce measurements of the unjust enrichment over the entire period, 1619 to 1992, and they should track the annual consequences of discrimination, both costs and benefits.

Indeed, someone should create and produce an annual discrimination index. This would give readings on the economic consequences of discrimination much the same as readings on prices, corporate securities, employment, interest rates, output, and other important aggregate and sectoral activities. This quantification of harmful behavior would help reduce it. That is, the announcement of monthly, quarterly, and annual results would tend to shed light on discrimination as never before. The victims have always known, intuitively, that they've been hurt. But they've not had any idea by how much.

The beneficiaries don't seem to realize that they are beneficiaries. The information will be salutary for all concerned, although it might produce grumbling among technicians who will quibble over technique and method. But that will be healthy. It will sharpen the analyses. And it will focus policy discussion on constructive alternatives.

Policy Implications

That leads to the "So what?" question: What difference will this information make? What practical value will restitution theory have?

Reasonable minds may differ. One school of thought says, "There is this debt, and civil rights groups and their friends should militantly demand that it be paid." How do they want it paid? Some say, lump-sum cash — so much per individual. Others say, in government programs — invest in a Domestic Marshall Plan of some kind.

A second school of thought says, "Demanding payment will be counterproductive." In reply, I argue that the United States is suffering prolonged economic stagnation for complex reasons. And one major reason is there is this historic imbalance caused by past injustices. If we look carefully, we see that economic underperformance is caused in part by the alienation of millions of people who believe they are victims of injustice, and so they withhold their best efforts in response.

The argument goes on that getting the entire country back on the healthy track requires that all lagging sectors receive overdue attention. They should be targets of investment, especially in human capital. This argument says,

"Demands will not work, but logic will." If there is restitution to be paid, most voters will come to accept, acknowledge, and respond if they see paying it as in their best interests collectively.

So it is fundamentally a moral issue. But it's also a practical matter. Restitution probably only stands a chance of gaining wide practical acceptance if it's presented in the context of the overall management of the economy and its long-term health. Thus, it may, in fact, gain broad support if it's understood as a matter of general social importance. Here are ways it can be paid.

Affirmative Action

Restitution should be approached as a matter of broad income and wealth redistribution from Haves to Have Nots, and especially, though not only, from white Haves to black Have Nots. Affirmative action is essentially about income and wealth redistribution. But it hasn't been discussed that way. It has not been debated explicitly as a means of changing income and wealth distributions. It has been muddled. Discussion is based on the mistaken concept that restitution is intended to help "make up for past discrimination." That's the wrong formulation. And that's a major reason the concept is so confused in the public mind.

The correct rationale is: we want to correct a current, not a past, injustice. The current injustice is that the top 30 percent of the income distribution, overwhelmingly white, enjoys this $5 trillion to $10 trillion unjust enrichment at the expense of blacks. And the remedy includes affirmative action which will shift occupation, wage, and employment distributions from whites in favor of blacks.

Putting it bluntly, this way will not produce an immediate, enthusiastic embrace. But it will put the matter properly on the table. Then the discussion can be rational and focused on the real problem and its solutions. No more evasion, euphemism, half-truths, and half-measures. Affirmative action should be pursued because it is a good way to pay restitution. But it should also have a sunset. It should end in a limited time, say, two generations. That way it is recognized as not an open-ended process. It will be expected to even the playing field, and then it should no longer be needed.

Set-asides

Business programs that provide entry to previously exclusionary markets are frequently attacked as unfair to white businesses. Those who make that argument generally, though not always, know better. They are dissembling.

168   Theory of Restitution

TABLE 7.1   Current Income Distribution in the United States, by Quintile

Quintile	Percentage of Total Income Received
Top 20	44
Next 20	28
Third 20	14
Fourth 20	9
Fifth 20	5

But the feelings among many disappointed white businesses are real and have political force. The programs should be explicitly seen and presented as paying restitution. That will produce angry reactions, too, at the outset. But when passions subside, there will be a clean reason to redistribute opportunities interracially, which is what set-asides should do. They, too, should have a sunset provision. Two generations should be long enough to produce a large group of competitive African American businesses able to compete in most sectors at small, medium, and large scales.

Other Preferences

Other kinds of preference programs should also be clearly labeled as justified as ways to pay restitution. Housing mortgages, employment and training, scholarships, and so on all are justified as make-whole remedies. They are, or should be, intended to put African Americans, collectively, in their Rightful Place. That means they will be helped to raise their income and wealth to levels they would have achieved but for the wrongful interference of discriminatory practices that favored and benefited whites. This concept of Rightful Place should be asserted confidently, because that is essentially what is being sought. Let it be clear.

Income and Wealth Redistribution

The quintiles now receive earned income roughly in the proportions shown in Table 7.1.

In a fair world they would probably receive shares more or less as shown in Table 7.2.

This would still provide ample incentives to the Haves to produce and take risks. But the effects of past injustice and gross exclusion, exploitation, and domination would be greatly reduced. This kind of distribution is one objective of a program of restitution. The poor would still be poor, but the dis-

TABLE 7.2   Income Distribution in the United States If Income Were More Fairly Shared, by Quintile

Quintile	Percentage of Total Income Received
Top 20	30
Next 20	25
Third 20	20
Fourth 20	15
Fifth 20	10

parities would not be nearly so overwhelming, formidable, and wrongful. Restitution thus helps create incentives for full participation by 20 to 40 percent of the population now underused, underrepresented, and underappreciated, and who unjustly enrich those at the top.

Conclusion: The Theory of Restitution

This entire discussion can be incorporated into a concept statement: Systemic economic arrangements often are imposed by dominant social groups on less powerful ones. Invariably, these patterns of transactions produce costs for the latter and benefits for the former.

Economic injustices, sustained over time, produce cumulative benefits. These can be measured. When they are, the results can then be introduced into public policy discussion for the purpose of acknowledging the transgressions, admitting the consequences, and accepting the fact that remedies are proper, feasible, and just.

So restitution theory offers a basis for correcting the lopsided results of distortions in markets characterized by coercion, exclusion, and discrimination. And it raises the prospect that the simple fact of illuminating economic relationships this way will, in and of itself, tend to reduce the offending behavior. That is because a major reason the injustices were perpetrated in the first place, and then perpetuated, was that a veil of ignorance rested over the phenomena. Restitution theory lifts that veil, and that in itself will make it harder in the future for economic injustices to become systemic. That is because they rely on the fact that their magnitude is not understood. Once that is discovered, in most cases, political and social forces will be mobilized to stop the practices and to retrieve the unjust enrichments that have been produced.

Reparations to African Americans?

J. ANGELO CORLETT

On 26 April 2002, three federal lawsuits were filed in New York seeking reparations to the approximately 35 million African Americans for the enslavement of Africans in the United States. Over sixty companies are targeted by the suits, including Aetna Insurance Company, FleetBoston Financial Services, and the railroad company CSX. Aetna's own company documents reveal that about 33 percent of its initial one thousand policies were written on the lives of slaves, while slave labor was used to build portions of the rail lines for companies like CSX that currently use them. The settlements sought by the suits do not include cash for African Americans. Rather, they include a variety of social programs that would benefit African Americans. The suits are built on a rationale that the consequences of slavery are still having a negative impact on several millions of such persons today, long after slavery.[1] Is there any merit whatsoever to such claims? If so, how much merit is there? Regardless of the legal merit of such claims, what are the *moral* implications of such historic injustices that might be used to ground legal claims for reparations to African Americans today?[2]

Prior to engaging this problem, it is important to explore some preliminary matters of significance, including some ways in which the problem of reparations to African Americans differs from the problem of Native American reparations. It is crucial to separate the question of whether or not reparations to African Americans are morally required from the question of which *policies* of reparations would be justified if it turns out that such reparations are required in the first place. The reason why this is an important distinction is that there are certain objections to reparations to African Americans that seem to conflate the two questions, unwarrantedly assuming, for instance, given the problem of *how* to exact reparative justice, that it somehow follows that reparations to African Americans are unnecessary. Such an inference would follow, it might be assumed, from " 'ought' implies 'can.' " But even if it were the case that no proposed reparations policy to date is plausible for whatever reasons, it would not follow logically that African Americans are not owed reparations of a *just* nature. To think otherwise would be to fallaciously infer that our supposed inability to work through the problem of how to award reparations logically implies something about what African Americans deserve, in this case, as a matter of corrective justice through compensation. For this reason, we must not confuse the question of the moral requirement of reparations to African Americans with the question of how, if such reparations are indeed morally required, they ought to be awarded. The former is a question of deserved compensation based on injustices experienced by African Americans and their forebears; the latter is a question of how such reparations, assuming they are deserved, are to be awarded to African Americans. The same conceptual point holds just as well in the case of reparations to Native Americans. With this point in mind, I now turn to the matter of how some issues of reparations to African Americans differ from some issues of reparations to Native Americans.

One obvious difference between the experiences of Native and African Americans is that while Native Americans experienced both gross human rights violations and massive land theft at the hands of both the U.S. government and several of its citizens, African Americans for the most part experienced the former (but not the latter) by way of the slave trade. In fact, there is a real sense in which the human rights violations of African American slavery were somewhat less severe than those suffered by Native Americans. Not only were several Native Americans enslaved, as were (by definition, all) African Americans' ancestors, and not only were both groups the victims of brutal forms of acculturation (for the former it took the form of Indian boarding schools, for instance; for the latter it took the form of infesting African slaves with various forms of insidious "Christian" religion, however well-intentioned, in the guise of missionary work with "savages"),[3] but as a general rule African slaves were not the subjects of massive killings or of a genocide, as were Native Americans. Instead, they were treated, however inhumanely, as the valuable "property" they were deemed by southern slave masters. So there is a sense in which reparations to Native Americans, if based on a principle of proportionality of reparations to harms and wrongs inflicted, ought to be greater than reparations paid to African Americans. For not only did Native Americans as a set of nations suffer the loss of an entire continent of land and natural minerals and other resources to the United States (as well as to Canada, Mexico, Brazil, Colombia, Guatemala, Peru, and other countries), but the loss of lives and other forms of human sufferings experienced by them are not even rivaled by the horrendous evils of U.S. slavery of Africans. With this understanding, it is nonetheless helpful to investigate philosophically the plausibility of claims to African American reparations for slavery of Africans in the United States. For it is quite clear that the evils experienced by Native and African Americans stand in a class by themselves relative to harms and wrongdoings experienced by other groups at the hands of the U.S. government.[4]

Another difference between the cases of Native and African American oppression is that the Native American experiences often, but not always, involved treaties and their being broken by the U.S. government, while U.S. enslavement of Africans involved no such treaties with the slaves themselves. This is explained by the fact that treaties are made between governing bodies, and African slaves in the United States did not constitute a governing body. Nor were they considered by most U.S. citizens and the U.S. government as sufficiently human to merit treaty negotiations. Perhaps this is one reason why African Americans posed less of a perceived threat to manifest destiny than did Native Americans.

The Argument for Reparations to African Americans

There are a variety of ways in which one might argue in favor of reparations to African Americans, whether or not such claims involve cash settlements, social programs, or some combination thereof. First, such reparations might be sought from *private parties* (e.g., individuals, corporations, and companies) for the unjust enrichments, harms, and/or wrongdoings resulting from the institution of *slavery*. Second, reparations might be sought from *private parties* for the unjust enrichments, harms, and/or wrongdoings resulting from *Jim Crow*. Third, reparations might be sought from *private parties* for the unjust enrichments, harms, and/or wrongdoings resulting from *both slavery and Jim Crow*. Fourth, reparations might be sought from the *U.S. government (and its citizens)* for the unjust enrichments, harms, and/or wrongdoings resulting from *slavery*. Fifth, they might be sought from the *U.S. government* for the unjust enrichments, harms, and/or wrongdoings resulting from *Jim Crow*. Sixth, reparations might be sought from the *U.S. government* due to the unjust enrichments, harms, and/or wrongdoings of *slavery and Jim Crow*. Even more ambitiously, reparations might be sought from *both private parties and the U.S. government* for unjust enrichments, harms, and/or wrongdoings resultant from *slavery*. Moreover, reparations might be sought from *both private parties and the U.S. government* for unjust enrichments, harms, and/or wrongdoings resultant from *Jim Crow*. Finally, and perhaps most ambitiously, reparations might be sought from *both private parties and the U.S. government* for the unjust enrichments, harms, and/or wrongdoings resultant from *both slavery and Jim Crow*. Although plausible cases might be able to be made along each of these lines (perhaps with varying degrees of success), I shall concentrate my attention on the case for the sixth option: the case for reparations to African Americans against the U.S. government for the unjust enrichments, harms, and/or wrongdoings of both slavery and Jim Crow. I construe my arguments for this option to be supportive of the most ambitious one, namely, the case for reparations to African Americans from both private parties and the U.S. government because of the unjust enrichments, harms, and/or wrongdoings of both slavery and Jim Crow.

Recall the reparations argument on behalf of Native Americans, herein modified for the case of African Americans:

1. As much as is humanly possible, instances of clear and substantial historic rights violations ought to be rectified by way of reparations.
2. The U.S. government has committed substantial historic rights violations against millions of African Americans.[5]
3. Therefore, the historic rights violations of the U.S. government against African Americans ought to be rectified by way of reparations, as much as humanly possible.

As with the argument for reparations focusing on Native Americans, there are challenges that might be raised to the move from (2) to (3) in the above argument. I shall consider the following such objections: the objection from historical complexity; the objection to collective responsibility; the objection from historical and normative progress; the affirmative action objection; the objection from social utility; the supersession of historic injustice objection; the anti-private-property-rights objection; and the counterfactual objection. It is important to note that in the case for reparations to African Americans, the objection from internation conquests, the no Native American concept of moral rights objection, the objection from the indeterminacy of Native American identity, the historical reparations objection, the religious freedom objection, and the acquired rights trumping original land rights objection (each discussed in terms of reparations to Native Americans) are either irrelevant, or are answerable quite transparently when taken from the Native American experience and applied to the African American experience.

It is interesting to note that the relevant set of objections, unlike the objections to Native American reparations, does *not* include objections involving land claims by African Americans. Nor does it involve claims to national sovereignty (see exceptions in Documents, section 4). Thus there is a sense in which the reparations argument pertaining to the African American experience is simpler (not simple, but simp*ler*) than the case of Native American reparations. For in the case of Native American reparations, it would seem that any reparations settlement that did not involve a substantial return of land to them is grossly unjust, especially in light of the plausibility of the principle of morally just acquisitions and transfers and the importance of land to Native Americans' philosophies and religions. Yet in the case of African Americans, reparations might well be made in the form of cash settlements much akin to (though in far more substantial financial terms than) the case of Japanese Americans for the harms and wrongs done to them by the U.S. government during World War Two (see Documents, section 1). African American reparations might well take the form of social programs, though this might depend on whether or not sufficient amounts of cash settlements accrue. But one must be ever mindful to not conflate reparations with social programs such as those of the affirmative action variety. On the other hand, if they are required on moral grounds, reparations must be proportional to the harms dealt to the enslaved ancestors of African Americans. And it is dubious that social programs, though helpful, would even approach the doorstep of adequacy as rectification for slavery and Jim Crow.

Moreover, given the genealogical conception of ethnic identity, there seems to be no need to take seriously any objection regarding the determinacy of African American identity (except, of course, where the actual setting of percentage of genealogical tie to an ethnic group is concerned). And since there is (to my knowledge) no record of reparations to African Americans by the U.S. government, the historical reparations objection is irrelevant (see Documents, section 1). Thus I will consider the plausibility of those objections to reparations to African Americans concerning matters of historical complexity, collective responsibility, historical and normative progress, affirmative action, social utility, supersession of historic injustice, private property rights, and counterfactual problems.[6]

An important similarity between Native and African American reparations cases (should reparations be owed) is that each group would appear to have a case not only against the U.S. government, but also against other colonial governments and powers such as Portugal, Spain, England, the Netherlands, France, the Roman Catholic Church, various Southern Baptist churches, and a number of other extant countries and organizations that played substantial roles in the transatlantic slave trade and/or the colonization of the Americas, and/or the founding and sustaining of Jim Crow. So if the respective cases for Native and African American reparations go through as they target the United States, then they might well also succeed if they target those other conspirators to and/or perpetrators of racist evils. With the recent founding of the International Criminal Court (ICC), perhaps arguments can be brought to it that might force the United States to eventually come to terms with its unquestionably evil foundations. Given the fact that reparations to African and Native Americans in any adequate sense have simply been refused or denied generation after generation, perhaps the final court of appeal is the ICC. But the effectiveness of the ICC will in the end rest on its ability to carry out its sanctions.

The main question before us in this essay is whether or not the United States in particular owes reparations to African Americans for the brutality of slavery in the United States. However, it is not only the physical and psychological brutality of slavery that is at issue, but the wrongful gain by way of forced labor power and the surplus labor value that it brings illicitly to slaveholders in particular, and to an entire U.S. economy more generally, and the incessant refusal over generations of the U.S. government to rectify its injustices against African Americans by way of slavery. I refer to this argument as a Marxist one in that it is based primarily, though not exclusively, on the illicit (because forced) labor power of Africans and the illicit (because forced) extraction of labor value from their labor power,[7] which then illicitly (because forced from the slaves) enriched not only slaveholders, but the southern and U.S. economies more generally. But as I shall argue, this Marxist argument hardly depends on whether or not anyone—slaveholder or not—actually benefited from the forced labor power of U.S.-enslaved Africans.

It is important, moreover, to point out that it is not only the injustice of African American slavery (e.g., slavery of Africans in the United States) that is at issue, but also Jim Crow and all of the significant ramifications of segregation throughout the entire United States for generations subsequent to slavery.

The Objections from Intergenerational Justice and to Collective Responsibility

I concur with Bernard Boxill and Howard McGary that what is relevant to the case for African American reparations by the U.S. government is a plausible case for collective moral liability responsibility, along with the historical fact of human rights violations. But each of these points must lead to the conclusion that, say, the current U.S. government owes reparations to contemporary African Americans for the said atrocities of the distant and more recent past.

The conditions necessary and sufficient for collective moral responsibility have been articulated and defended.[8] Elsewhere, I have provided an analysis of the conditions under which collective moral liability responsibility accrues. Besides, fault and guilt, conditions of collective intentionality (construed as acting according to one's own beliefs and wants), knowledge, and voluntariness must also be satisfied to some meaningful extent, and the degree to which a collective is morally liable for a harm and wrongdoing is the extent to which it ought to be punished or forced to compensate the victim(s). As we shall see below, fault and guilt accrue to the U.S. government in its complicity or contribution to U.S. slavery and Jim Crow. And that the U.S. government acted according to its wants and desires, with virtually unfettered voluntariness and with knowledge of the foreseeable consequences of its actions and policies is hardly questionable. So there is little doubt that the U.S. government bears the brunt of liability for the harms and wrongdoings of past generations of slavery and Jim Crow. That current U.S. citizens would end up paying for such reparations (should they be morally required) is congruent with the point that both collectives and individuals can sometimes be held liable for wrongdoings — even though they are not at fault or responsible for the harms that eventuate from them.

However, even assuming the plausibility of the notion of collective moral responsibility, it simply will not suffice to show that there were indeed evils that were perpetrated against African Americans, even by the U.S. government, without also linking the normative case for reparations to the present day.

So even if it is true, as Boxill argues of African American slavery, that

> the slaves had an indisputable moral right to the product of their labor; these products were stolen from them by the slave masters who ultimately passed them on to their descendants; the slaves presumably have conferred their rights of ownership to their descendants; thus, the descendants of slave masters are in possession of wealth to which the descendants of slaves have rights; hence, the descendants of slave masters must return this wealth to the descendants of slaves with a concession that they were not rightfully in possession of it.[9]

McGary is correct in claiming of Boxill's argument that "it fails to show how whites who are not the descendants of slave masters owe a debt of justice to black Americans. In order to argue that the total white community owes the total black community reparations, we must present an argument that shows how all whites, even recent immigrants benefited from slavery and how all blacks felt its damaging effects."[10]

Although I find the cumulative effect of both Boxill's and McGary's arguments convincing, their implied "unjust enrichment argument," though it is quite helpful in establishing a case for collective moral liability responsibility to provide reparations to African Americans, is not necessary for establishing the case for African American reparations. For even if no slave master (or a descendant of one) ever benefited from the enslavement of Africans or the racist treatment of their descendants in the United States, reparations might nonetheless be owed to African Americans today. But how might this be the case? And precisely by whom or what ought the reparations to be paid, and to whom, and what kind of and how much reparation ought to be awarded?

Prior to examining in depth the aforementioned objections to African American reparations, it is important to gain a perspective on the implications of a certain line of reasoning regarding the matter. Consider the "objection from intergenerational justice," which states that justice between generations is problematic because those who pay reparations at time t_{n+1} for significant injustices at time t_n must be the ones directly guilty and at fault for the harms and wrongs done to the group for which reparations are requested. Intergenerational (reparative) justice is problematic because it violates precisely this rule, making allegedly innocent parties pay for what other guilty parties did in harming and wronging others. It is clear how this objection underlies a concern about collective moral liability responsibility. Indeed, the objection from intergenerational justice seems to be the foundation of the objection to collective moral responsibility.

It is important to understand, however, that if the objection from intergenerational justice counts against reparations to African Americans, then by parity of reasoning it also counts to a significant degree against reparations to Israel by Germany prior to the genocide of Jewish persons by the Nazi regime during the World War Two era. Not only does it count in some significant measure against the case for reparations to Israel by Germany, but it also counts against the case for reparations to certain Japanese Americans by the United States for the internment of many Japanese Americans during the same era. The reason that the objection from intergenerational justice counts in some significant measure against these historic acts of reparations is that — even though many German and U.S. citizens who bore the fiscal brunt of such reparations were actually alive as adults during the oppression of Jewish persons during the Nazi attempt to extinguish them and during the U.S. internment of Japanese Americans — millions of "innocent" German and U.S.

citizens ended up paying the reparations in each case, citizens who themselves were children or not even born at the time of the atrocities in question. Thus there is a violation of the principle that forms the bedrock of the objection from intergenerational justice, namely, *that those who are innocent must not suffer harm or be forced to compensate for harms they did not cause.* There is indeed a regress argument at work here, one that attempts to render problematic any attempt to justify reparations to Israel and Japanese Americans in that some allegedly innocent (German and U.S.) parties ended up paying the fiscal brunt of the reparations payments, persons who in some cases could not have had anything whatsoever to do with the evil events in question.

Moreover, it might be argued that political liberalism's claim that individual persons, *and only individual persons*, qualify as moral agents who are morally liable to praise or blame for what they do voluntarily, intentionally, and epistemically poses a challenge to any view of reparations that holds that such reparations are based on intergenerational justice and collective moral liability responsibility. Thus what is needed is a defense of the conception of collective moral liability responsibility that would in turn ground reparative justice claims against the U.S. government and its citizens who would end up bearing the burden of such reparations, intergenerationally speaking.

With these points made, is it true that "we must present an argument that shows how all whites, even recent immigrants benefited from slavery and how all blacks felt its damaging effects"? Although I shall argue that such an argument is not necessary, I believe that the strongest case for reparations owed to African Americans lies precisely along the lines that McGary suggests. Thus even though it is, as I shall argue, unnecessary to show that anyone was unjustly enriched by slavery or Jim Crow in order to prove the case for African American reparations, doing so is surely sufficient to make the case. And the sufficiency of the case seems to depend on the strength of the argument for collective moral responsibility, intergenerationally speaking.

Against the claim that the unjust enrichment argument is needed to prove the case for African American reparations, it should be understood that it is entirely possible that there are significant numbers of people who benefited *accidentally* from the enslavement of Africans in the United States. Yet if someone benefited in such a manner—even from an evil such as race-based slavery—it is unclear whether or not the persons enriched by it are guilty or even at fault and ought therefore to pay reparations for slavery. Would it not be more sensible, morally speaking, to hold accountable only those who, according to the general line of the unjust enrichment argument, benefit *non*accidentally from the evil? I believe that this is what McGary has in mind with his words, however, so I do not see that this point refutes, but rather attempts to significantly clarify and support, his general line of argument.

There is another reason why the unjust enrichment argument is problematic, however well-intentioned. It is that persons might owe reparations to a group even if the persons did not benefit from a particular injustice that forms the basis of the group's receiving reparations. An example of this sort of case would be, say, a European American slave master whose "empire" ended up, largely due to slavery, ruining him forever. Perhaps the forcing of others to do labor for his family and such was far outweighed by his mismanagement of his slaves, social and political pressures against slavery at the time of his having slaves, and other factors. Yet simply because this slave master, perhaps owing to his own incompetence as a master of slaves, did not benefit from his having slaves hardly means that he is not morally responsible for his having slaves. Or, consider the example of an individual act of civil disobedience to U.S. slavery by one who not only refuses to support with her taxes the United States (or even state or local governments) but who also lives a holistic lifestyle of protest against the "peculiar institution." This citizen hardly benefits from U.S. slavery of Africans, but is rather in protest opting out of whatever significant ways she might benefit. Thus we need not demonstrate that those responsible for providing reparations to African Americans were those who benefited from the harms and wrongs against African Americans that would justify such reparations. For an incompetent slave master's not benefiting from slavery hardly exempts him from what he owes based on Boxill's argument that he has deprived slaves of the value of their labor, unforced, and one who protests incessantly and holistically U.S. slavery of Africans benefits, it seems, in no interesting way from it. Otherwise, the unjust enrichment argument would seem to imply that those who benefited most from U.S. slavery ought to be held most accountable for paying their fair share of reparations, for instance, more of the reparations amount than those who benefited significantly less than they. Moreover, when all is said and done, the amount of reparations owed according to this scheme would only be as much as the amount of fiscal benefit to those guilty and at fault for slavery. Yet this amount might not reflect the amount of reparations owed based on the amount of labor value stolen from the slaves. In turn, this scheme of reparations would make African American reparations contingent on the successes and failures of the market of slave holdings, rather than on the value of the labor stolen from the slaves. Since it seems more intuitively plausible to award reparations on the basis of labor value stolen forcibly from slaves, the amount of reparations ought to reflect *this* fact. Yet this would seem to imply that, though establishing the plausibility of claims to unjust enrichment from slavery and Jim Crow is indeed helpful in making the case for reparations to African Americans, we *need not* demonstrate the plausibility of the unjust enrichment argument.

But what precisely would establish, on moral grounds, the plausibility of the reparations argument concerning African Americans? I argue that it is, as Boxill implies, the illicit taking by force and/or fraud of the surplus labor value of the slaves. It is at this point of argument that the principle of morally just acquisitions and transfers plays a fundamental role in the reparations argument for African Americans as it does in the case of Native American reparations. For *whatever is acquired or transferred by morally just means is itself morally just, and whatever is acquired or transferred by morally unjust means is itself morally unjust.* (This is the principle of morally just acquisitions and transfers.) Forced labor power and the extraction of value from it is morally unjust and must be rectified by way of compensation and/or punishment. Since the U.S. government supported the institution of slavery of Africans by permitting slavery to go virtually unchecked for generations, it is responsible for the harmful effects of slavery and liable to pay reparations to descendants of the slaves should such descendants exist or have trusts in their names. Further harms to African Americans accrued as the federal and various state governments institutionalized racism (by way of Jim Crow) against generations of African Americans. This much can serve as the locus of agreement, however, between supporters of African American reparations and their detractors. For detractors might concur that the stealing of the labor power and hence surplus labor value from the slaves entitles reparations to slaves, but to no one else. Thus an argument is needed that establishes on moral grounds reparations to contemporary African Americans, not simply to their forebears who were enslaved or who were victims of Jim Crow.

Boxill provides the basis of such an argument when he states that "the slaves presumably have conferred their rights of ownership to the products of their labor to their descendants." Yet it is precisely at this point where objections to the reparations argument might be challenged as it pertains to African Americans. It might be argued that the very idea of inheritance is morally arbitrary and has no basis in a morally sound system of social living (perhaps because, it might be argued, it violates strict notions of moral desert and responsibility). Be this as it may, it seems that Boxill's point is made in light of the way the legal system works in the United States: *given that inheritance is recognized by U.S. law*, it would seem to follow that the stolen value of the slaves' labor ought to be recognized, naturally, as inherited by the heirs of slaves, who would by (my) definition be African Americans. I too share

Boxill's assumption and shall not here take on the task of challenging the morality of inheritance systems under U.S. law. Yet it is important to recognize that should such systems in the end fail on moral grounds, Boxill's argument runs aground on such problems (as does my own argument here). But then so would the legal practice of inheritance more generally, wreaking significant havoc in U.S. society.

However, my argument for reparations to African Americans does not simply depend for its overall plausibility on matters of inheriting certain rights to compensation to one's descendants. The primary focus of my argument is that to the extent that U.S. slavery and Jim Crow led to widespread injustices to African slaves in the United States and African Americans (their descendants), reparations are owed African Americans by the U.S. government on moral grounds because it is the same governmental system that harmed African slaves as that which either permitted or enacted and enforced Jim Crow, and that exists today as that which has yet to pay reparations even though formal and informal democratic demands for reparations have been made since Reconstruction. Reparations to African Americans, not unlike those to Native Americans, are debts unpaid by an *existing perpetrator*, namely, the U.S. government.[11]

It is at this juncture where the argument for collective moral responsibility (of the U.S. government) must be provided in order for the case for reparations to African Americans to be most plausible. And there are various ways in which the case for collective moral liability responsibility for reparations to African Americans accrues in that the same U.S. government that perpetrated the evils of the past on African (and Native) Americans exists *today*. Thus the continuity through time of the U.S. government defeats the idea that collective moral liability responsibility fails to accrue to the current U.S. government. First, at the level of the most fundamental principles of law, U.S. constitutional law, it might be argued that from generation to generation the U.S. Supreme Court has upheld the fundamental values of the U.S. Constitution and Bill of Rights such that, as Ronald Dworkin has argued, the Supreme Court justices engage in a constant, albeit Herculean, task of interpreting the Constitution as a near "seamless web" in light of interpretive extralegal principles.[12] Indeed, the highest level of U.S. government never seems to challenge the basic principles embedded in the Constitution, but instead uses such principles to guide decision making on a variety of problems in U.S. society.

Second, not only does the U.S. government support and not challenge the fundamental legitimacy of the principles and values embedded in the Constitution, but by far the majority of U.S. citizens do the same. And this is true intergenerationally speaking! Indeed, the typical response to anti-U.S. terrorism is that "we must protect our way of life," meaning that the "freedoms" explicit and implicit in the Constitution and Bill of Rights are to be protected, even by way of retaliatory violence and war. And fortunately, the actions and stated attitudes of so many U.S. officials and citizens speak strongly to this effect. Scarcely would more than a small minority of U.S. citizens in U.S. history serve as counterexamples along these lines. *From generation to generation, then, there is collective support and implementation of the various values deemed important in the documents the contents of which form the very basis of life in U.S. society.* This is intended to support the claim that contemporary collective moral liability responsibility obtains concerning the U.S. government and its citizens to the extent that conditions of collective intentionality, knowledge, and voluntariness are satisfied intergenerationally, though collective fault and guilt need not. For various collective decision-making processes in U.S. society not only preserve from past to current generations of U.S. society the fundamental norms, values, and folkways based on foundationally defining documents of the putative democracy, but this in turn preserves the essential identity of the country as a political unit over time. If this is true, and I can scarcely imagine anyone who would deny that the *United States as a political unit has survived over time*, then why would it not be thought—except by some politically liberal individualist superstition that only individual persons can be moral agents—that U.S. society as a whole inherits, not only the benefits, but the *debts* of its past?

Although it is certainly true that few, if any, U.S. citizens would support the enslavement of Africans in the United States or even Jim Crow and their horrendous results, few U.S. citizens and leaders did much at all to recognize the injustice sufficient to even take seriously the possibility of reparations to African Americans, or to newly freed slaves. This points to a kind of complicity in the continual refusal in the face of constant demands throughout history to award some meaningful justice to those who were harmed severely by the U.S. government and U.S. society.

Additionally, the unjust enrichment argument serves to emphasize the fact that most, if not all, U.S. citizens have been in some significant measure unjustly enriched by slavery and Jim Crow. For example, Aetna Insurance Company and various and sundry tobacco companies, textile companies, and real estate companies engaged in racist and oppressive practices that supported not only slavery, but other forms of anti–African American oppression that unjustly enriched shareholders, employees, managers, and others. Moreover, millions of U.S. citizens were provided rights and privileges that few, if any, African Americans were accorded until recent years. And these rights were systematically denied to African Americans for *generations*, taking the U.S. government until the Civil Rights Act of 1964 to *begin* to correct. To think that millions upon millions of non–African Americans have not been unjustly enriched at the expense of African Americans from 1775 until most recently is to make a mockery of the facts of U.S. history. There was undoubtedly collective or societal support of U.S. slavery and Jim Crow to the extent that without such support those institutions would not have "succeeded" in the ways that they did (at least for whom they did succeed). Until the 1960s, few non–African Americans stood against such racism. One must recall that bad Samaritanism can serve as a form of moral negligence supportive of intentionally harmful wrongdoing.

Thus it is clear how the argument for collective moral responsibility supports the unjust enrichment argument for reparations to African Americans. At various levels of U.S. society, there was in fact governmental and societal support for the enslavement of Africans and Jim Crow. Such injustices should be rectified by way of reparations, rectified by the same government and society that intergenerationally oppressed African slaves and their ancestors. For as Joel Feinberg has so persuasively argued, *the folkways of a society can sometimes reflect the fault of a group's wrongdoing*. Quoting Dwight Macdonald, Feinberg points out that

> the constant and widespread acts of violence "against Negroes through the South, culminating in lynchings, may be considered real 'people's actions,' for which the Southern whites bear collective responsibility [because] the brutality . . . is participated in, actively or with passive sympathy, by the entire white community." The postbellum Southern social system, now beginning to crumble, was contrived outside of political institutions and only winked at by the law. Its brutalities were "instrumentalities for keeping the Negro in his place and maintaining the supraordinate position of the white caste." Does it follow from this charge, that "Southern whites [*all* Southern whites] bear collective responsibility?" I assume that ninety-nine percent of them, having been shaped by the prevailing mores, wholeheartedly approved of these brutalities. But what of the remaining tiny fraction? If they are to be held responsible, they must be so vicariously, on the ground of their strong (and hardly avoidable) solidarity with the majority. But suppose a few hated their Southern tradition, despised their neighbors, and did not think of themselves as Southerners at all? Then perhaps Macdonald's point can be saved by excluding these totally alienated souls altogether from the white Southern community to which Macdonald ascribes collective responsibility. But total alienation is not likely to be widely found in a community that leaves its exit doors open; and, in a community with as powerful social enforcement of mores as the traditional Southern one, the

alienated resident would be in no happier position than the Negro. Collective responsibility, therefore, might be ascribed to all those whites who were not outcasts, taking respectability and material comfort as evidence that a given person did not qualify for the exemption.[13]

To those who might argue that Feinberg's words, if plausible, only apply to European American southerners who supported and were unjustly enriched by slavery and Jim Crow, it might be pointed out that the U.S. government and citizens who were not southerners continually played the role of bad Samaritans in refusing *for generations* to outlaw and enforce the prohibition of such evils. This implicated morally the entire United States for slavery and Jim Crow. Moreover, it must be remembered that segregationism was alive and well throughout the entire U.S. society for generations. From housing to voting rights, to opportunities for education and hiring practices, it was clear and evident that African Americans and even former slaves were not accorded the dignity that was promised all persons under the Constitution and Bill of Rights. It appears, then, that the principle of morally just acquisitions and transfers applies to the case of African American reparations, yet in a somewhat different way than it does to the case of Native American reparations. Unjust enrichment was experienced by most every U.S. citizen in every generation of U.S. history, as the cumulative effects of superior advantages in U.S. society placed European Americans far ahead of African Americans insofar as basic human rights and equal opportunities for life, liberty, and the pursuit of happiness are concerned.

It simply will not do, morally speaking, for one to argue that reparations are not owed because today's U.S. citizenry is "innocent" of any act of slavery or oppression against African Americans. For this line of argument ends up as a "might-makes-right" mentality, as it assumes without argument that a government that for generations ignored and denied demands for justice has rightful cause for not paying what it owes to those against whom it has committed atrocities such as slavery and Jim Crow. Ever since Reconstruction there have been demands for justice to African Americans, often in the form of reparations arguments. So the same governments that harmed African slaves and their descendants via Jim Crow stand to pay what they owe to African Americans. Here I mean by such governments those of the southern states, and even the U.S. government to the extent that it aided and abetted in the oppression of slaves and/or African Americans.[14]

If the foregoing is correct, then it seems that reparations to African Americans are grounded in the historical fact that reparations for slavery were requested but never granted during and subsequent to Reconstruction, and that Jim Crow was not only oppressive of African Americans living (especially) in the southern states, but that such oppression was aided and abetted by the U.S. government in significant ways. One among many specific ways in which the U.S. government aided and abetted the enslavement of Africans in the United States was by way of its enacting and enforcing the Fugitive Slave Laws, whereby a southern slave master could recapture and reenslave his fugitive "property" by way of the federal court system.[15] The U.S. government was a bad Samaritan in that it was grossly negligent as it for generations stood by and permitted southern states to flourish not only under slavery, but under Jim Crow. Recall also that it took the federal government *over a century* subsequent to U.S. slavery to pass (and eventually enforce!) civil rights legislation, primarily to combat Jim Crow and other forms of racist segregation throughout the United States. That the U.S. government was a bad Samaritan along these lines is important, as such bad Samaritanism serves as part of the moral basis for the claim of reparations owed by the same government responsible, in one way or another, for both the evils of slavery and of Jim Crow, and how much reparations are owed. Assumed here, of course, are the ideas that governments have duties to respect and protect the basic human rights of their respective citizens, and that individuals and governments have duties to assist those in need insofar as such assistance does not pose a serious threat to their own well-being. Concerning the case at hand, it is implausible to think that the U.S. government was not a bad Samaritan,[16] as it very well could have acted in various ways to provide adequate justice to slaves and former slaves, and to African Americans for the effects of Jim Crow, and to hold accountable states that failed to comply with civil rights legislation that should have been enacted and enforced immediately subsequent to slavery in the United States. After all, the U.S. government has the military might to ensure its results anywhere within "its own territory." No coalition of southern states could begin to challenge the U.S. military, especially after the devastating loss (by the South) of the Civil War. This placed the federal government in a particularly powerful position vis-à-vis the South. It is clear that there were reasons why it took so long to pass and enforce civil rights legislation. That such reasons are adequate, morally speaking, is quite unclear. Assumed here is the plausibility of the claim that massive and significant human rights violations ought to be handled adequately and as soon as humanly possible, implying that the federal government's handling of human rights violations against African slaves and African Americans was nothing less than morally inept.

Yet with all of this said and done, there is a rather nagging curiosity concerning the issue of why reparations to African Americans is so greatly resisted in the United States.[17] For even if it were conceded, contrary to the previous line of argumentation, that the enslavement of Africans on U.S. soil did not justify reparations to the descendants of such slaves today, there remains a series of queries that tend to suggest the fundamental racism that U.S. citizens have toward African Americans. For might it not be much more plausible on moral grounds to base reparations to African Americans on the depths and almost permanent racist effects of generations of segregation throughout the United States? And is it not true that many millions of African Americans who have experienced the bitter hand (fist?) of Jim Crow's oppression are still alive? And would it not also be true that what Japanese Americans experienced at the hands of the U.S. government was not nearly as harmful as what African Americans experience(d), both in terms of the very kinds of racist oppression and in terms of duration? And would not such facts suggest that, just as the United States willingly apologized[18] and provided reparations to certain Japanese Americans, so too ought the United States to do so to African Americans? Moreover, should not the amount of reparations to African Americans be substantially larger than that which has been provided to certain Japanese Americans? This would follow from both the kinds of anti–African American racist oppression and the duration of it.

One concern here is that my argument fails to consider that U.S. reparations to *certain* Japanese Americans were just that: reparations to only those Japanese Americans who actually suffered in the internment camps during World War Two as opposed to all Japanese Americans as a collective. However, my argument for African American reparations can easily accommodate this concern. For what might be done is that the U.S. government award reparations to only those African Americans who have suffered significant harm under Jim Crow. Even today, this amounts to a substantial number of those who were forced to live under conditions of a much larger, much more brutal and lasting "concentration camp": U.S. segregationist society (north, south, east, and west).

Perhaps it is this final point that makes most U.S. citizens recoil at the very idea of reparations to African Americans. But this simply exposes what is really at work in U.S. society, especially in light of the arguments, the facts underlying them, and how a lesser case of racist harm against some Japanese Americans was handled compared to the incessant refusal of U.S. society to even take seriously reparations to even some African Americans. The inference to the best explanation here seems to emerge as insidious racism, a racism which seeks to cloak itself in the guise of sophisticated philosophical argumentation, argumentation that is not, by the way, applied to the Jewish

(Israeli) and Japanese American cases by parity of reasoning. It is obvious that U.S. citizens do not believe that African Americans deserve reparations, and for at least the reason that amounts to the objection from intergenerational justice. Holding to the plausibility of this objection is not in itself constitutive of racism against African Americans. However, holding this view as a reason against providing reparations to African Americans for the harms of Jim Crow while simultaneously supporting reparations to many Japanese Americans for much lesser oppressive harms seems to demand an explanation as to why such a view is not racist toward African Americans. Sociologically speaking, perhaps it is a case of a society's supporting, however begrudgingly, the injustice they can *afford* to compensate, rather than supporting the full range of what is owed due to their government's evil actions. But it also seems to be a blatant instance of simply expressing significant respect to those whom most citizens feel respect, while denying significant respect to those whom most citizens believe are not worthy of it.[19]

However, yet another concern might be raised about the argument for collective moral responsibility as it is used to bolster the unjust enrichment argument for reparations to African Americans. It challenges the points that have been made above, regarding the generational support (or lack of non-support) of most U.S. citizens of slavery and Jim Crow. The most that can be said in favor of reparations to African Americans, the objection might aver, is that *some* of today's U.S. citizens, namely, those who actually contributed to the harms and wrongdoings in question (Jim Crow, as no U.S. slaveholders are alive today), are morally liable for reparations and ought to be forced to pay them. However, this hardly shows that the *United States* owes reparations to African Americans. Again, today's U.S. citizen, it is argued, is hardly responsible for what happened to African slaves and African Americans in the distant past, as the objection from intergenerational justice states. For the U.S. government is *not* the same government as it was when those atrocities were perpetrated. Different persons compose the government, and the citizenry is *not* the same. Moreover, this is evidenced by the fact that almost everyone in U.S. society recognizes a significant moral progress that has accrued along the lines of its now condemning such evils as totally unjust.

In reply to this version of the objection from intergenerational justice, it is important to consider that whether or not a society owing reparations to a group it has harmed and wronged *recognizes its role in harming and wronging the group* is not a necessary condition of that society's owing reparations to the group. For in the case of the United States paying reparations to certain Japanese Americans, it was surely not the case that the United States as a whole recognized that it owed reparations to certain Japanese Americans.

The anti-Japanese fervor in the United States at that time was rampant, and millions of U.S. citizens despised Japanese ("American" or not) for the events at Pearl Harbor in 1941. The point here is that a society can be incorrect, because it is not infallible in its moral judgments, about whether or not it owes reparations to a group it has harmed. This is especially true of evil societies. Indeed, this is in part what makes some societies evil! No matter how "civilized" a society appears (or proclaims itself) to be, it cannot be genuinely civilized, what John Rawls would deem a "decent" or "reasonably just" society, if it fails to rectify its past evils, no matter how far in the past it perpetrated them. Otherwise, *it is incumbent on the critic of this point to devise a non-self-serving and non-question-begging argument that would establish a moral statute of limitations on historic injustice*. The burden of proof is on those who support a moral statute of limitations on injustice to provide non-question-begging and non-self-serving arguments that would explain its soundness. Otherwise, such a notion is not to be accepted by the epistemically responsible person. Attempts at that feat are sorely lacking in plausibility.

Second, as Feinberg so astutely points out, though moral guilt and fault do not transfer from one generation to the next, liability does (in some cases). In general, collective liability accrues in cases where the conditions of collective solidarity, prior notice, and opportunity for control are satisfied to some meaningful extent. However, he argues,

> an exception . . . is suggested by the case where an institutional group persists through changes of membership and faultless members must answer for harms caused, or commitments made, by an earlier generation of members. Commitments made in the name of an organized group may persist even after the composition of the group and its "will" change. When, nevertheless, the group reneges on a promise, the fault may be that of no individual members, yet the liability for breach of contract, falling on the group as a whole, will distribute burdens quite unavoidably on faultless members.[20]

Now to this line of argument of Feinberg's it might be objected that only individual persons count as moral agents who are liable to blame or praise for what they do, fail to do, or attempt to do. And it is this politically liberal point that haunts the argument for collective moral responsibility, and which undergirds the objection to collective responsibility.

But it is precisely this objection to collective responsibility that must be challenged, and for at least two reasons. First, political liberalism's insistence on the claim that individual persons, *and only individual persons*, are moral agents is highly contestable. For if we assume that only individual moral agents are those who have rights and can be held liable to blame or praise, then it would imply that groups do not have rights to compensation for harms experienced. It would also imply that there can be no collective responsibility for wrongdoing. For there is only individual wrongdoing, and only individuals who are harmed deserve compensation for their harms experienced. That individual persons are moral agents is accepted by liberals and their critics alike. Yet since the liberal adds the highly controversial claim that *only* individual persons are moral agents, he or she owes a plausible argument for the claim that only individual persons are those who can either harm and wrong others or be the victim of harm and wrongdoing and be owed compensation. It is difficult to surmise precisely what an argument for such a claim would amount to, that is, if the argument is not self-serving or question-begging. This ought to make one rather wary of the liberal doctrine of individualism, that is, unless and until such a view can be substantiated by plausible argument. Epistemically speaking, the claim that only individual persons are moral agents is *not* basic, self-evident, or self-justifying external to the politically liberal framework.

However, not only is there no plausible argument in favor of the politically liberal claim that only individual persons count as moral agents, but Feinberg has provided at least a prima facie case for collective personhood. Although Feinberg states that his analysis is intended to be a legal one, there is reason to think that it is morally grounded (e.g., justified by the balance of reason, on his view). Applying Feinberg's words (quoted above) to the case of African Americans and reparations, it might be argued that the U.S. government and society have persisted throughout time, from one generation to the next, from its inception to the present day. At no time whatsoever have more than a "tiny fraction" of U.S. citizens *not* been significantly enriched unjustly as the result of the enslavement of Africans in the United States and Jim Crow, as already explained, however briefly. Given the truth of the principle of morally just acquisitions and transfers, and given the *im*plausibility of a moral statute of limitations on historical injustice, it would appear that there is indeed a plausible case in favor of the moral liability of U.S. citizens and their government for what their forebears and their government did to Africans and African Americans throughout the generations.[21] Thus, contrary to the objection to collective responsibility, there is doubt about the plausibility of the liberal claim about exclusive individual moral agency, as well as some significant reason, especially in light of the doubt about liberal individualism, to think that in some cases collective moral liability accrues even in the absence of collective fault. For there is a real sense in which U.S. citizens, in a plethora of ways, act, neglect to act, or attempt to act (and have throughout U.S. history) such that their cumulative lives, together and separately, amount to a context in which sociality leads to collective responsibility.[22]

The Objection from Historical Complexity

The previous line of reasoning addresses straightforwardly the objection from intergenerational justice, which underlies the objection to collective responsibility. But in answer to the objection from historical complexity, it might be replied that, though U.S. history is complex as regards the enslavement of Africans and Jim Crow oppression of African Americans, there is nonetheless extraordinary historical evidence of the *fact* of U.S. oppression of both groups, along with continual pleas for reparative justice ever since the "Forty Acres and a Mule" suggestion was made and declined during Reconstruction. That every detail of every case of African and African American oppression is unavailable to us because of lost records and the complexities of U.S. history is hardly a good reason for the U.S. government to deny reparations to African Americans. The libraries of volumes of critical U.S. history serve as a resounding reminder of the *fact* of U.S. oppression of these groups. So the objection from historical complexity, not unlike the objection to collective responsibility, is as implausible in the case of reparations to African Americans as it is in the case of reparations to Native Americans.

The Objections from Historical and Normative Progress

Ought African Americans to simply abandon any concern for reparations and instead become "successful" citizens, thereby making such reparations unnecessary as the objections from historical and normative progress aver? Is not U.S. history replete with examples of tremendous successes of African Americans in various areas of life? The insensitivity of this line of reasoning belies a sort of ignorance of what justice entails. First, it blindly assumes that all African Americans have (or should have) a desire to remain "successful" within the society that has systematically oppressed it over several generations. Second, it unwarrantedly assumes that justice ought to pertain at all to the economic or social status of victims of oppression or other forms of wrongdoing. *To the extent that reparations are to accrue to African Americans, they accrue to them regardless of their respective economic or social statuses.*

The Affirmative Action Objection

But what of the affirmative action objection? To think that affirmative action is an instance of reparations is a category mistake, especially if what one means by "affirmative action" is preferential treatment of African Americans in employment hiring. For in such cases, recipients of affirmative action programs *earn* their wages, whereas reparations are a group's *un*earned compensation for being harmed and wronged. This consideration undercuts the plausibility of the affirmative action objection to the reparations argument concerning African Americans.

The Supersession of Historical Injustice Objection

Furthermore, Waldron's incredible supersession of historic injustice objection fails in the case of African American reparations for the same reason that it fails in the case of Native American reparations. For its fundamental plausibility is contingent on the moral justification of a moral statute of limitations on injustice. Yet Waldron provides no argument whatsoever in defense of a moral statute of limitations on historic injustice, making his underlying assumption, along with his objection, unwarranted.[23] Unless and until plausible arguments are provided in favor of a moral statute of limitations on injustice, then there is no good reason to accept such a claim, especially since, contrary to Thomas Reid, beliefs are not innocent until proven guilty.[24]

The Objection from Social Utility

How might the objection from social utility, the anti-private-property-rights objection, and the counterfactual objection regarding the reparations argument for African Americans fare? The objection from social utility avers that if the U.S. government pays adequate reparations to African Americans, then the sheer cost of the reparations would bankrupt the United States, as in the case of reparations to Native Americans. This in turn would send millions of U.S. citizens into abject poverty. Why should the majority of U.S. citizens who are neither African nor Native Americans have to be inconvenienced and plunged into the abyss of poverty and despair by paying reparations to a minority number of citizens? It is, on utilitarian grounds, immoral to provide reparations to any group when the payment of adequate reparations would spell the demise of the majority of people in society.

In reply to this line of utilitarian argument, it is helpful to remind ourselves of how poorly such an argument fared in the case of reparations to Native Americans. Basically, the objection from social utility insists that the disutility experienced by the majority of U.S. citizens as the result of their paying reparations to African Americans (those who lived under Jim Crow) and their forebears (under U.S. slavery) outweighs the harms and wrongdoings done to African slaves and African Americans under Jim Crow. But the magnitude of the respective harms between contemporary U.S. citizens who are not African Americans and African Americans is incomparable, even in light of the fact that there are far fewer African Americans than others in the United States. So on basic grounds of social utility alone, it is unclear that the paying of reparations to African Americans would eventuate in a society that is worse off than it would be otherwise, all things considered. The objection from social utility self-servingly assumes that the "poverty" of several millions of U.S. citizens is clearly greater than the poverty and enslavement (and all that was involved in slavery) of millions of African slaves in the United States. And since reparations to African Americans would eventuate in the former scenario of poverty of millions of U.S. citizens who are not African Americans, then reparations are to be denied on grounds of social utility maximization.

But surely it is questionable to think that "poverty" by today's U.S. standards is anything remotely akin to the horrendous evils of that "peculiar institution"! And if this is plausible, then on what grounds can the objection from social utility warrant nonpayment of reparations to the harms incurred by African Americans and their forebears? Furthermore, even if it is assumed for the sake of argument that social utility is *not* maximized (for all U.S. citizens) economically by way of paying reparations to African Americans, it hardly follows that social utility is not maximized by payment of reparations, *all things considered*. For if *unrectified evil is evil still*, and if the United States refuses to pay adequate reparations to African Americans for its evil treatment of them, then the evil that accompanied the founding and sustaining of the United States in the forms of slavery and Jim Crow stand to condemn the United States as evil. Such moral evil is of a magnitude so significant that it is difficult, if not impossible, to imagine how any amount of economic welfare of U.S. citizens could outweigh the nonpayment of reparations to victims of U.S. oppression. So if the objection from social utility is to be marshaled against the reparations argument as it pertains to African Americans, then it must be marshaled nonselectively concerning what counts as social utility, including, of course, considerations of moral guilt and responsibility for evil. And it is far from obvious that the economic hardships likely to accrue to other U.S. citizens from their paying adequate reparations to African Americans outweigh the historic evils experienced by millions of African Americans and their forebears. Thus the objection from social utility is neutralized, if not defeated, by certain utilitarian considerations themselves.

The Anti-Private-Property-Rights Objection and Counterfactuals

The anti-private-property-rights objection to African American reparations states that the very notion of private property rights is something Africans lacked until they were captured, sold, traded, enslaved, and acculturated into U.S. society. Insofar as reparations are matters of private property rights (e.g., to stolen surplus labor value), they are morally unjustified because they do not represent anything indigenous Africans would have cherished had they not been acculturated to accept the idea in the first place. Note how the anti-private-property-rights objection is fused with Waldron's counterfactual objection, which states that reparations to African Americans are unjustified because it is impossible to calculate in what condition African Americans *would* have been had such historic evils *not* occurred.

In reply to this rather strange line of argument proffered against reparations to African Americans, it must be clarified that *normative ethics* does *not* require that such a standard be satisfied in order for reasonably approximate damages to be awarded to a deserving party. In the case of African Americans, as we have already seen, it is reasonable to think that a fairly accurate calculation can be made of the wages stolen (forcibly withheld) from African slaves by slave masters, along with the kinds of punitive damages for all kinds of basic human rights violations that were inflicted on African slaves in the United States, and on their descendants in the United States. The calculation, when inflation, compounded interest, punitive damages, and penalties for nonpayment are taken into account, might well range into the trillions of dollars (see America, part 1). Yet all of this can be done without having to solve some counterfactual problem. For whether the counterfactual problem is a real problem, it is certainly *not* a difficulty for normative ethics in determining reparations to African Americans, except on the unreasonable assumption that complete and absolutely perfect rectification of African Americans is required in order to justify the said reparations. However, if approximate justice is what such reparations seek to effect, then the counterfactual objection (as well as the anti-private-property-rights objection) seems to be a red herring. For we need not resolve matters of perfect justice in every possible world in order to mete out approximate justice in *this* world. This is important for my line of reasoning in that it is normative, yet aimed at a reasonably just legal system for its enforcement.[25]

Some Possible Reparations Policies

Having argued in favor of reparations to African Americans by the U.S. government, and having defeated or neutralized various leading objections that might be made to the reparations argument concerning African Americans, it is helpful to explore some ways in which such reparations might accrue. First, it is noteworthy that many have argued in favor of affirmative action or preferential treatment as a legitimate form of reparations to African Americans.[26] Indeed, this essay started with a summary of a legal suit that seeks precisely this kind of "reparations" to African Americans. However, to construe affirmative action or preferential treatment as a form of reparations is a category mistake since affirmative action in many forms amounts to programs of preferential treatment the benefits of which are *earned* by recipients, whereas this is not true of reparations. Furthermore, it is a grand confusion to suppose, as most do, that descendants of U.S. slavery who deserve reparations for their ancestors' human rights being violated (in millions of instances, for the duration of their entire lives!) are to be adequately compensated by *earning* their salaries by way of positions awarded them by way of preferential treatment.[27] For it violates principles of what a victim of harm and wrongdoing *deserves* in *proportion* to damages suffered by the victim.

Unlike possible policies of reparations to Native Americans that ought to consider ways in which substantial acres of land as well as monetary damages be awarded to Native Americans, reparations to African Americans ought not involve U.S. territory since the moral entitlement to such territory belongs by and large to Native Americans. So in this regard, reparations to African Americans are relatively simple as they involve some amount of monetary compensation, as in the cases of Germany's reparations to Israel and the reparations to certain Japanese Americans made by the United States.

To argue, as some do, that programs of social welfare or such might be considered as reparations to African Americans not only runs the risk of the category mistake just mentioned, but it also presumes that African Americans ought to or must integrate into the very society the government of which has served as their most ardent oppressor since its very inception. Surely justice cannot require — or even presume — that victims of racist evils ought even to desire to coexist alongside those whose government has oppressed them so badly, without compensation after centuries of brutal human rights violations! This being the case, reparations to African Americans ought not to assume an integrationist posture (see Browne, part 1; Nuruddin and Johnson essays, part 5; and Documents, section 3). And given that the amount of reparations owed to African Americans would be the amount owed for the estimated costs of labor power and value stolen by coercion from the millions of African slaves in the United States and all human rights violations at the hands of the U.S. government and various state governments, it is plausible to assume that African Americans would have sufficient funds to successfully segregate themselves from their U.S. oppressors once and for all. There is no question that thousands, perhaps millions, would desire precisely that.[28]

Strict justice might well require that the U.S. government pay to African Americans as a group (by way, say, of an African American elected congressional body) all of the monies owed African Americans for the evils of slavery and of Jim Crow. Since "ought" implies "can," such payments could not be made in a lump sum any time in the foreseeable future. So some sort of annual "tax" would need to be assessed against those who are not predominantly Native or African Americans. The overall amount of reparations owed would be calculated and then paid over, say, fifty to one hundred years,[29] including compounded interest, penalties for previous nonpayment, inflationary factors, and perhaps even punitive damages. Admittedly, as in the case of Native American reparations, no amount of reparations will truly suffice for the evils wrought on oppressed peoples. But this is hardly a good reason for not making an honest effort to do the right thing in paying some substantial amount to the descendants of slaves and those who were victimized by Jim Crow. Concerns about the possible corruption of African Americans actually distributing the reparations monies need not concern us any more than, say, German citizens have a legitimate concern about how Israel ought to distribute reparations payments received from Germany. Moreover, any suggestion that significant parcels of land be set aside for African Americans as part of a reparations agreement would run afoul of legitimate Native American moral rights to the land.

There is no question that the United States could no longer survive as it now does should it finally own up to what it owes in reparations to African Americans (and to Native Americans). But as we saw, the objection from social utility does not negate the reparations argument in the Native American case nor in the African American case. Whatever suffering accrues to the United States as the result of its paying fair amounts of reparations to Native and African Americans might be seen rightly as the moral cost of constructing a putatively civil society while murdering and otherwise oppressing untold millions of Native and African Americans. If such suffering due to the cost of paying reparations spells the demise of the United States as we know it, then perhaps the costs would serve as a reminder to the rest of the world as to how *not* to build a society. It must be borne in mind that the United States as a perpetrator of severe evils on these groups is not in a moral position to complain about whatever harms it is now forced to endure as the result of its paying adequate reparations to Native and African Americans. Indeed, reparations seem to be the moral cost of the United States to attempt to redeem itself from the dredges of immorality in which it alone has placed itself, generation after generation, by simply refusing to pay what it owes to those whom it has murdered, enslaved, and otherwise oppressed.

In this essay, I have articulated the reparations argument for African Americans. Then I considered an array of objections to the argument, many of which were applied from the case of reparations to Native Americans. Along the way, some similarities and differences between the cases for reparations to African and Native Americans were noted. In the end, it was concluded that not only are reparations owed to Native Americans, but to African Americans also.

As Raimond Gaita writes, "Communities take pleasure and pride in the fact that injustices have been acknowledged and overcome, and that reparation has been made when it is possible. Such pleasure in justice is necessary if people are lucidly to love their community, country, or nation."[30] Perhaps motivated by some complex array of self-serving biases that in turn lead U.S. citizens and their government to repeatedly deny reparations for some of the most horrendous evils in the history of the world, reparations have not been paid to African Americans. This is somewhat surprising, given that so many U.S. citizens and governmental leaders declare loudly that the United States is the best country in the world. But once again, if *unrectified evil is evil still*, and if the United States is responsible for the oppression of African Americans and their forebears, then the United States owes it to African Americans to adequately rectify the evils, however approximately and tardily. Time may heal all wounds, but it hardly erases unrectified evil and severe injustice! And the United States cannot by any stretch of the imagination continue to rightly claim to be a morally legitimate country unless and until it rectifies adequately its past evils. For *the evils of the past do not wither with the mere passing of time*. Rather, they cling to one's being with incessant fury until that moment when the attempted flight from one's evil deeds has ended with evil catching up with one, at times only to terrorize the evildoer with unimaginable vengeance.

Notes

1. Larry Neumeister, "Three Federal Lawsuits Filed in New York Seek Reparations for Slavery," Associated Press, 26 April 2002.
2. By "African Americans," I mean those of African descent whose ancestors were enslaved in the United States, though an extended use of the category might include all such persons whose African ancestors were enslaved throughout the Americas: North, Central, and South.
3. Robert Berkhoffer Jr., *Salvation and the Savage* (New York: Atheneum, 1965).
4. This is not to suggest that Native and African Americans are the only groups worthy of consideration for reparations from the U.S. government. Rather, it is to suggest that a fairminded reading of U.S. history seems to place these two groups in a category apart from all others relative to evils experienced by the U.S. government on what is deemed by most as being U.S. territory.
5. These acts amount to a series of intentional actions that were crimes, torts, and/or contract violations.
6. I mean by this term collective retrospective moral liability responsibility.
7. Those familiar with Karl Marx's criticism of capitalism recognize this point as derivative of his claim that capitalism illicitly extracts labor value from the forced labor power of workers. For discussion of Marx's critique of the exploitation of labor in the capitalist system, see G. A. Cohen, *History, Labour, and Freedom* (Oxford: Oxford University Press, 1988), part 3.
8. For an analysis of the general conditions of collective moral liability responsibility, see J. Angelo Corlett, *Responsibility and Punishment* (Dordrecht: Kluwer Academic, 2001), chapter 7. For an analysis of collective moral liability responsibility as it pertains particularly to reparations to African Americans, see Howard McGary, *Race and Social Justice* (London: Blackwell, 1999), chapter 5. Other discussions of collective responsibility are found in Larry May and Stacey Hoffman, eds., *Collective Responsibility* (Savage, Md.: Rowman and Littlefield, 1991).
9. Bernard Boxill, "The Morality of Reparations," *Social Theory and Practice* 2 (1972): 117.
10. Howard McGary, "Justice and Reparations," *Philosophical Forum* 9 (1977–78): 253.
11. This is not meant to imply that there are not private parties that or who also owe reparations to African Americans based on the extent of their contributory fault or liability for African slavery in the United States and/or for Jim Crow.
12. Ronald Dworkin, *Law's Empire* (Cambridge, Mass.: Harvard University Press, 1986). For critical discussions of Dworkin's theory of legal interpretation, see Andrew Altman, "Legal Realism, Critical Legal Studies, and Dworkin," in *Philosophy of Law*, ed. Joel Feinberg and Hyman Gross, 5th ed. (Belmont, Mass.: Wadsworth, 1995), 176–191; J. Angelo Corlett, "Dworkin's *Empire* Strikes Back!," *Statute Law Review* 21 (2000): 43–56; Timothy Endicott, "Are There Any Rules?," *Journal of Ethics* 5 (2001): 199–220; J. L. Mackie, "The Third Theory of Law," in *Philosophy of Law*, ed. Feinberg and Gross, 162–168.
13. Joel Feinberg, *Doing and Deserving* (Princeton, N.J.: Princeton University Press, 1970), 247–248.
14. This is not meant to imply that northern or western state governments were innocent in the oppression of African Americans, as each had its own way of enforcing racist policies and/or practices of housing, education, and employment discrimination against them.
15. For a discussion of how the federal courts decided such cases, see Robert Cover, *Justice Accused* (New Haven: Yale University Press, 1975); Ronald Dworkin, "Review of Robert Cover, *Justice Accused*," *Times Literary Supplement*, 5 December 1975.
16. For discussions of Bad Samaritanism, see Joel Feinberg, "The Moral and Legal Respon-

sibility of the Bad Samaritan," in *Freedom and Fulfillment* (Princeton, N.J.: Princeton University Press, 1992), 175–196; and John Kleinig, "Good Samaritanism," in *Philosophy of Law*, ed. Feinberg and Gross, 529–532.

17. For a discussion of this particular issue, see Rodney C. Roberts, "Why Have the Injustices Perpetrated against Blacks in America Not Been Rectified?," *Journal of Social Philosophy* 32 (2001): 357–373; Laurence Thomas, "Morality, Consistency, and the Self: A Lesson from Rectification," *Journal of Social Philosophy* 32 (2001): 374–381; Bernard Boxill, "Power and Persuasion," *Journal of Social Philosophy* 32 (2001): 382–385.

18. For philosophical analyses of the nature of an apology, see J. Angelo Corlett, *Responsibility and Punishment* (Dordrecht: Kluwer Academic, 2001), chapter 6; Jeffrie G. Murphy, *Character, Liberty, and the Law* (Dordrecht: Kluwer Academic, 1998).

19. I borrow this point from Bernard Boxill.

20. Feinberg, *Doing and Deserving*, 249.

21. It becomes increasingly astounding, on moral grounds, how it is that so many millions of U.S. citizens and government officials take such pride in their own political forebears and how the United States was founded as a putative democracy, yet when a link from such citizens and leaders to the evil pasts of slavery and Jim Crow are concerned, such citizens and leaders suddenly disavow any link to such historic evils.

22. For an analysis of collective responsibility in terms of collective guilt, see Margaret Gilbert, "Group Wrongs and Guilt Feelings," *Journal of Ethics* 1 (1997): 65–84; Margaret Gilbert, *Sociality and Responsibility* (Lanham, Md.: Rowman and Littlefield, 2000); Margaret Gilbert, "Collective Guilt and Collective Guilt Feelings," *Journal of Ethics* 6 (2002): 115–143.

23. For a critical assessment of philosophical arguments given for a moral statute of limitations on injustice, see Rodney C. Roberts, "The Morality of a Moral Statute of Limitations on Injustice," *Journal of Ethics* 7 (2003): 115–138.

24. J. Angelo Corlett, *Analyzing Social Knowledge* (Totowa, N.J.: Rowman and Littlefield, 1996), chapter 5.

25. The same can be said plausibly concerning Native Americans.

26. One recent example is found in Howard McGary, *Race and Social Justice* (London: Blackwell, 1999), 100–104.

27. Of particular importance, McGary does *not* make such an assumption.

28. This general line of argument can also be applied to the Native American case for reparations.

29. In perpetuity payments of reparations to Native and African Americans run the danger of such ethnic groups being diluted over time (relative to whatever percentage of ethnicity is required for public policy purposes) such that members of the oppressed groups in question receive lesser percentages of reparations payments. I suggest, then, that an adequate amount of reparations be paid to each group within a century so that more of those who experienced some of the historic evils can benefit from reparations. On the other hand, if reparations payments end up being inadequate in sum, then it would seem fair to make such payments accrue in perpetuity.

30. Raimond Gaita, *A Common Humanity* (London: Routledge, 1998), 85.

Part 3

Reparations

Formation and Modes of Redress

Introduction

The five essays in this part address the evolution and the different modalities of redress in the United States, including its changing frame of reference and political trajectory. Robin D. G. Kelley declares that reparations campaigns of the past and present constitute a social movement, which is linked to other national and transnational anticapitalist formations and struggles for social justice. Like Fullinwider and Bolner, as well as William Darity Jr. and Dania Frank, Kelley also contends that one does not have to reach back to slavery to make the case for reparations; one can find the justification for reparations in Jim Crow. Concerned with the period in the immediate aftermath of the Civil War and during Reconstruction, Jeffrey R. Kerr-Ritchie dispenses with the moral arguments for reparations (and the failure of black leaders to address land rights) and stresses the federal government's capitulation to the "free market dictates" of northern business interests and Republican politics, which abrogated the government's promise of land redistribution to freed blacks. For Kerr-Ritchie, the sanctity of private property and economic imperatives accounts for the failure to make good on the promise of "Forty Acres and a Mule."

Robert S. Browne's essay is especially useful for determining financial and territorial dispensations for reparations. In his schemata for a "minimal" reparations claim for unpaid slave labor and "underpayment" of black people since emancipation, he includes compensation for the denial of opportunities for black people "to acquire a share of America's land and natural resources when they were widely available to white settlers." Like Corlett,

Browne distinguishes between the merits of the claim for reparations and the "implementation of a reparations payment." He suggests several possibilities, two of which invoke the schemes of repatriation: one derived from the "back-to-Africa" movements of the late nineteenth century and early twentieth, the other rooted in the Black Nation project articulated in the 1960s by nationalist groups in the United States (see also the essays by Nuruddin and Johnson in part 5). William Darity Jr. and Dania Frank, too, argue the case for reparations for Jim Crow and elaborate on Browne's schemata for reparations claims. They assert that "black wealth" and "prosperous black communities" were annihilated during Jim Crow and that there are living victims for reparations claims. Emphasizing an economic approach, they propose two criteria for eligibility and five types of reparations programs: lump-sum payments, creation of a trust fund (as suggested in the *Manifesto*), vouchers for "asset building," in-kind compensation (to guarantee educational opportunities and medical insurances), and funds to create "new institutions" that enhance black communities.

Martha Biondi, like Kelley, maps the historical evolution of reparations and underscores their current incarnation in the United States, especially in relation to "global anticapitalist and anti-imperialist" formations. She highlights corporate litigation as a means to reparations, among other modes of redress, while also remaining cognizant of its limitations. Similarly, like Kelley, she raises the often ignored historical importance of sexual slavery and the "undertheorized and underdiscussed" concern with black women's exploitation, even within movements aimed at black empowerment.

"A Day of Reckoning"

Dreams of Reparations

ROBIN D. G. KELLEY

> I'm not bitter, neither am I cruel
> But ain't nobody paid for slavery yet
> I may be crazy, but I ain't no fool.
> About my forty acres and my mule. . . .
>
> One hundred years of debt at ten percent
> Per year, per forty acres and per mule
> Now add that up.
> — Oscar Brown Jr., "Forty Acres and a Mule," 1964
>
> You hear these white people talk about they've pulled themselves up by their own bootstraps. Well they took our boots, no less our straps, and then after they made us a citizen, honey, what did they turn around and do? They passed black codes in order to take from us all the benefits of citizenship. — "Queen Mother" Audley Moore, 1978

The Civil War had barely been settled when Colonel P. H. Anderson of Big Spring, Tennessee, dispatched a letter to his former slave, Jourdon, inviting him to return to the Anderson plantation as a paid laborer. Despite promises of freedom, good treatment, and fair wages, Jourdon was more than a little suspicious of the offer. With the help of Lydia Maria Child, a prolific writer, abolitionist, and schoolteacher, he dictated a very powerful letter to his old master. He began by expressing concern that he and his wife, Mandy, were

> afraid to go back without proof that you were disposed to treat us justly and kindly; and we have concluded to test your sincerity by asking you to send us our wages for the time we served you. This will make us forget and forgive old scores, and rely on your justice and friendship in the future. I served you faithfully for thirty-two years, and Mandy twenty years. At twenty-five dollars a month for me, and two dollars a week for Mandy, our earnings would amount to eleven thousand

six hundred and eighty dollars. Add to this the interest for the time our wages have been kept back, and deduct what you paid for our clothing, and three doctor's visits to me, and pulling a tooth for Mandy, and the balance will show what we are in justice entitled to. Please send the money by Adam's Express, in care of V. Winters, Esq., Dayton, Ohio. If you fail to pay us for faithful labors in the past, we can have little faith in your promises in the future. We trust the good Maker has opened your eyes to the wrongs which you and your fathers have done to me and my fathers, in making us toil for you for generations without recompense. Here I draw my wages every Saturday night; but in Tennessee there was never any payday for the Negroes any more than for the horses and cows. Surely there will be a day of reckoning for those who defraud the laborer of his hire.

In answering this letter, please state if there would be any safety for my Milly and Jane, who are now grown up, and both good-looking girls. You know how it was with poor Matilda and Catherine. I would rather stay here and starve — and die, if it come to that — than have my girls brought to shame by the violence and wickedness of their young masters....

Say howdy to George Carter, and thank him for taking the pistol from you when you were shooting at me.

By even the most elementary principles of liberal capitalism, Jourdon Anderson presents a sound, reasonable case for receiving compensation for years of unpaid labor. He was the colonel's property, to be sure, but the fact that he could write such a letter and make such a brilliant case distinguishes him from "the horses and cows" that also served the needs of the plantation without pay. Indeed, by today's standards Jourdon is being charitable by asking only for back wages and interest. He does not make a case for damages despite the physical and psychological abuse visited upon his whole family — the rape, the violence, the horrible living conditions, the mere fact of bondage.

My guess is that most of you laughed out loud after reading Jourdon's letter and some might have found it incredible. The colonel probably laughed, too, dismissing his former slave's request as absurd. One hundred and thirty-seven years have passed since the enactment of the Thirteenth Amendment ending slavery in the United States, and most of America is still dismissing demands for reparations, claiming that the very idea violates the basic principles of U.S. democracy and laissez-faire capitalism. As I wrote these words, the U.S. delegation to the historic World Conference against Racism in Durban, South Africa, walked out, in part because the conference refused even to discuss the question of reparations. Slavery is behind us, we are told, and any payments to black people would be divisive or an act of discrimination *against white people*. Others argue that black people have already received billions of dollars of aid through welfare and poverty programs and therefore if there was a debt owed us, it has been paid many times over. Right-wing critics like Dinesh D'Souza go one step further, arguing that the only people deserving of reparations are the slave masters, and presumably their descendants, since the government "freed" their property without compensation! Besides denying the basic humanity of the enslaved and not accounting for the tremendous wealth the master class acquired by exploiting unpaid labor, D'Souza's twisted logic conveniently ignores the fact that the vast majority of slaveholders committed treason against the United States and were never punished. Jourdon's letter exposes this irony as well: "I thought the Yankees would have hung you long before this, for harboring Rebs they found at your house. I suppose they never heard about your going to Colonel Martin's to kill the Union soldier that was left by his company in their stable."

For African Americans in search of freedom, the question of reparations was never a laughing matter. And as Jourdon Anderson's letter makes clear, it is a very old issue. Indeed, as early as 1854, a convention of black emigrationists called on the federal government to provide a "national indemnity" as a "redress of our grievances for the unparalleled wrongs . . . which we suffered at the hands of this American people." Immediately after the war, Sojourner Truth organized a petition seeking free public land for former slaves. "America owes to my people some of the dividends," she argued. "I shall make them understand that there is a debt to the Negro people which they can never repay. At least, then, they must make amends." Bishop Henry McNeil Turner calculated the debt at some $40 billion. For the next century and a half, there have been numerous movements intent on making "amends."

Today there are countless proposals for reparations as partial compensation for slavery and/or postslavery racial discrimination. The growing support for reparations is partly linked to the passage of the Civil Liberties Act of 1988 authorizing reparations payments to Japanese Americans interned during World War Two, and to Congressman John Conyers's bill, which has been in committee since it was first introduced in 1989, to create a commission to study the issue of reparations for black people. And, of course, there are many precedents. Besides interned Japanese and Jewish Holocaust victims, the latter having received payments both from the German state and private corporations, we can point to the Alaska Claims Settlement of 1971, in which the United States awarded indigenous Alaskans $1 billion and more than 44 million acres. An even more immediate and perhaps more relevant example is the Rosewood, Florida, settlement. In 1995, nine former residents of Rosewood, once an all-black town, were awarded $150,000 each as restitution for property destroyed by white mobs during the 1923 pogrom (see Documents, section 4). Given the overwhelming destruction and loss of life, these sums were hardly adequate. Nevertheless, the settlement set a precedent for all victims of racist violence and exploitation, especially when they were indirectly sanctioned by the state through legalized segregation or, in other instances, legalized slavery.

Partly as a result of these precedents and the organizing efforts of various movements, we have seen a proliferation of books, articles, and public debates on the issue of reparations based on all manner of economic calculations, legal loopholes, and a wide range of political and moral arguments. My purpose is not to weigh the pros and cons of one proposal against another, or to come up with my own calculations of what slavery and racial discrimination cost us. Much outstanding work along these lines has been done by writers such as Robert Allen, Kimberle Crenshaw, William Darity Jr., David Swinton, Robert K. Fullinwider, Clarence Munford, Melvin Oliver and Thomas Shapiro, Randall Robinson, and a battery of law professors too numerous to list here. (See essays by Dairty, Fullinwider, Munford, and Oliver and Shapiro.) While I do make a case for reparations, I'm more interested in the historical vision and imagination that has animated the movement since the days of slavery. Except for among groups like the National Coalition of Blacks for Reparations in America (N'COBRA) and the Black Radical Congress, such a vision of the future is sorely lacking in most contemporary arguments for reparations (see Documents, section 4). By looking at the reparations campaign in the United States as a social movement, we discover that it was never entirely, or even primarily, about money. The demand for reparations was about social justice, reconciliation, reconstructing the internal life of black America, and eliminating institutional racism. This is why reparations proposals from black radical movements focus less on individual payments than on securing funds to build autonomous black institutions, improving community life, and in some cases establishing a homeland that will enable African Americans to develop a political economy geared more toward collective needs than toward accumulation.

"Forty Acres and a Mule"

African American troops who survived the Civil War had it right: they were the liberators, their ex-masters the rebels. They believed that the rebels' land should be divided up among the folks who toiled for so many generations without pay. And some of the ex-slaves did just that, parceling out their former masters' property, staking claims to abandoned plantation lands, preparing to inherit the earth they had turned into wealth for idle white people. There were a few precedents for their expectations. In January 1865, Union General William T. Sherman had issued Special Field Order 15, designating land along the South Carolina coast and on the Sea Islands to be distributed among freed people (see Documents, section 1). Each family was to receive forty acres, and General Sherman made some army mules and confiscated animals available for cultivation. The idea, of course, was to make the ex-slaves self-sufficient. Altogether, Sherman was able to settle some 40,000 freed people on seized lands. Congress followed up two months later with the first Freedmen's Bureau Bill, which promised to provide "every male citizen, whether refugee or freedman," with "not more than forty acres of land" (see Documents, section 1). President Andrew Johnson wasn't having it: he promptly vetoed Congress's bill and reversed General Sherman's order. In 1867, radical Republican leader Thaddeus Stevens tried again, introducing a resolution in Congress calling for the enforcement of the Confiscation Act of 1861 to seize some four hundred million acres of land from the ex-Confederate states (see Documents, section 1). One million families of former slaves would have received forty-acre plots and $50 in cash as start-up money. Stevens believed that the South should pay an indemnity for the war, and the seizure of land was part of that payment. It would have also broken the back of the plantation economy, because the power and wealth of the planter class depended on the availability of cheap black labor. But Congress did not support land seizure. Eventually, under President Johnson, nearly all the land confiscated from the Confederate plantation owners was restored in exchange for oaths of loyalty. Although the Freedmen's Bureau was created to administer to the needs of black people, it legally controlled only 0.2 percent of the land in the South, and not all of it was arable.

African Americans began the period of Reconstruction landless and frustrated, though many remained hopeful that the federal government would fulfill its promise of land. At mass meetings, in churches, in the privacy of their own homes, they spoke of their anticipated forty acres not as some kind of gift or handout but as back payment for slavery. A few radical Republicans continued to press for a redistribution of land that could make southern black people self-sufficient and neutralize the power of the landlord class. Meanwhile, pro-planter forces pressured the federal government to compensate the former slave owners for their losses. Believe it or not, they succeeded in Washington, D.C. In 1862, Congress passed laws compensating slave owners for freeing their slaves. The payments were rendered through the Board of Commissioners for the Emancipation in the District of Columbia.

Nine years later, Congress established the Southern Claims Commission so that southerners loyal to the Union during the war might be compensated for their own loss of property.

In the late nineteenth century, the movement to secure some kind of restitution for black people was given new life when William R. Vaughan, a white Democrat from Alabama, launched a national movement to grant pensions to ex-slaves. Vaughan believed that such a pension plan not only was just but could also relieve southern taxpayers from the burden of supporting this rapidly aging black population. (Of course, under Jim Crow southern blacks were hardly a tax burden; in many cases, the African American taxpaying and laboring population carried more than its share of the burden, to the point of subsidizing public services for white people.) Vaughan proposed that ex-slaves age seventy and older receive an initial payment of $500 and then $15 a month. Those between sixty and seventy years old would receive $300 and $12 a month, and ex-slaves fifty to sixty years old would receive $100 and $8 a month. Any freed people younger than fifty would not receive an initial payment, but a monthly pension of $4. Between 1890 and 1903, Vaughan succeeded in getting nine bills to this effect introduced into the Congress, but none became law—indeed, none of these bills got past committee.

Vaughan tried to drum up grassroots support for the pension campaign, publishing a newspaper and launching chapters of Vaughan's Ex-Slave Pension Club throughout the country. As historian Walter B. Hill points out, by 1897 several other organizations came on the scene, challenging Vaughan's hegemony over the ex-slave pension movement. A few of these groups proved to be frauds, intent on stealing from unsuspecting black people. Individuals would falsely represent themselves as club organizers or as officers of the U.S. government, and collect fees and issue certificates that the newly recruited members were told they needed in order to verify their former status as slaves. The black people who bought into these phony clubs mailed their bogus certificates to the Pension Bureau for payment only to be told that the certificates were worthless. Although Vaughan himself was never indicted for fraud, it is worth noting that by the time his movement collapsed around 1903, he had earned over $100,000 from fees collected.

One of the organizations challenging Vaughan's clubs was the Ex-Slave Mutual Relief, Bounty and Pension Association, founded in 1897 by two African Americans, Reverend Isaiah H. Dickerson and Mrs. Callie D. House. Their purpose was to petition Congress to pass the Mason Bill—the legislation introduced by Nebraska Congressman W. J. Connell at Vaughan's behest—and build a broad movement that could provide mutual assistance to its members. Indeed, it seems as though some of the clubs functioned like mutual benefit associations, reinforcing strong community bonds and a deep sense of mission. The association chartered several chapters throughout the South, holding annual conventions and mobilizing community support for the pension bill. The federal government launched an investigation of Dickerson and House almost as soon as they started recruiting members. In March 1901 Dickerson was imprisoned for "obtaining money under false pretense," and thirteen years later Callie D. House, who now headed the association, was indicted on mail fraud charges. She ended up pleading guilty, claiming that she thought the pensions bill had passed and had been sincerely working to help ex-slaves file claims. House's defense is entirely plausible, especially considering the fact that neither she nor Dickerson made any money. Nevertheless, by 1917 the Ex-Slave Mutual Relief, Bounty and Pension Association, the last organization fighting for pension legislation, and the only one led by black people, had been thoroughly destroyed.

Free the Land, Reparations Now!

During the first half of the twentieth century, few African American movements took up the demand for reparations, though by then "forty acres and a mule" had become shorthand for broken promises. The Garvey movement condemned Europe's seizure of Africa and its wealth, including its people, as an act of theft, all of which the UNIA vowed to "reclaim," but it made no direct request for reparations (see Documents, section 4). However, explicit demands for some kind of indemnity picked up steam after World War Two, inspired in part by the creation of the state of Israel and Germany's reparations to Holocaust victims, which began in earnest in 1952. All told, Germany paid more than $58 billion. Not surprisingly, territory once again became a critical issue for some radical black nationalist groups. Organizations such as the Forty-ninth State Movement and the African Nationalist (Alajo) Independence-Partition Party of North America advocated reparations in the form of land on which to create a black state. The Alajo Party's "Declaration of Self-Determination of the African-American Captive Nation," issued in January 1963, argued for restitution based on the fact that the United States "was built with the unrequited slave labor of our African ancestors." As restitution, the declaration demanded that "all land south of the Mason Dixon line where our people constitute the majority, be partitioned to establish a territory for Self-Government for the African Nation in the United States."

One of the pioneers of the post–World War Two black reparations movement was "Queen Mother" Audley Moore. A major figure in the history of black radicalism, she started out as a devoted member of the Garvey movement before joining the CPUSA in the 1930s, although she had never abandoned black nationalism. In 1950 she left the CP and founded, among other things, the Universal Association of Ethiopian Women, which focused attention on welfare, prisoners rights, antilynching, and anti-interracial rape. She also launched the African-American Party of National Liberation in 1963 and played a major role mentoring young activists in RAM (Revolutionary Action Movement). By her recollections, she came to the issue of reparations of 1962 after discovering a clause in the *Methodist Encyclopedia* that "considers an enslaved people satisfied with their condition if the people do not demand recompense before 100 years have passed." As it was the centennial of the Emancipation Proclamation, she promptly formed the Reparations Committee of Descendants of U.S. Slaves, Inc., and issued a demand for federal reparations as partial compensation for slavery and Jim Crow. Her organization came up with a figure of $500 trillion to be spread over the next four generations, and it made an effort to present its case to President Kennedy — though Moore got only as far as his secretary.

The crucial point that Moore emphasized in making the demand was that a thoroughly democratic structure needed to be in place so that ordinary people could decide what to do with the money. The money was not to be controlled by a "little clique," nor was it intended to line the pockets of individuals. It had to be both substantial and community-controlled to enable African Americans "to put up some steel mills, some industry with the reparation, to benefit the whole people." She also wanted to accommodate those who "wanted to take their reparation and go to Africa." What she did not want, however, was a "poverty program." She insisted that had the government focused on reparations rather than on a War on Poverty, black people would have been much better off. Besides being a pittance of what was owed black people, she complained that the War on Poverty gave the government and a handful of black elites control over our destiny. And the very idea that black people were damaged goods in need of help had dire psychological consequences: "We don't realize how detrimental it is for us to be under a poverty program. We, who gave the world civilization, we the wealthiest people on earth who have been robbed of all of our birthright, our inheritance."

By the mid- to late 1960s, most black radical movements had either adopted some form of reparations claim or at least debated the issue (see Documents, section 4). The Nation of Islam added a demand to its plan for a separate state that "our former slave masters"—in the form of the U.S. government—provide "fertile and minerally rich" land and fund the territory for the first twenty to twenty-five years, or until the residents were self-sufficient. The Black Panther Party for Self-Defense, founded in 1966, included a demand for reparations in its platform. Point 3 stated, "We believe that this racist government has robbed us and now we are demanding the overdue debt of forty acres and two mules. Forty acres and two mules were promised 100 years ago as restitution for slave labor and mass murder of black people. We will accept payment in currency which will be distributed to our many communities." It went on to argue that German reparations for the Holocaust set a precedent, especially since the "American racist has taken part in the slaughter of over fifty million Black people." The Panthers never came up with a figure or a plan, just the principle that black people deserved reparations.

The *Black Manifesto*, issued in spring 1969, was the first systematic, fully elaborated plan for reparations to emerge from the black freedom movement. The document came about when James Forman, a leader and radical voice in SNCC, was asked to speak at the national Black Economic Development Conference (BEDC) in Detroit organized by the Interreligious Foundation for Community Organization (IFCO). Forman and activists he had met in the Detroit-based League of Revolutionary Black Workers, notably Mike Hamlin, Ken Cockrel, and John Watson, decided to take over what would have been a liberal community development conference. They succeeded, positioning six League members on the BEDC steering committee and creating what was essentially a black socialist agenda. The key document, however, was the *Black Manifesto*, which demanded $500 million in reparations to be paid by *white Christian churches* (later they included Jewish synagogues) (see Documents, section 4). That IFCO was a major Protestant institution only partly explains why Forman targeted churches. His primary reason was that white religious institutions participated in and benefited from racist and capitalist exploitation of black people.

Half a billion dollars is a paltry sum (by their estimate, it amounted to $15 a head), but Forman and fellow drafters of the *Black Manifesto* considered their request seed money to build a new revolutionary movement and to strengthen black political and economic institutions. Topping the list was the need for land. Given the long history of African Americans' struggle for land, it is not surprising that $200 million was set aside for a Southern Land Bank (a poignant demand today given the recent $1 billion settlement for black farmers discriminated against by the U.S. Department of Agriculture) (see

Documents, section 6). Because of the explicit anticapitalist vision of the drafters of the *Manifesto*, the land bank was intended especially for "people who want to establish cooperative farms but who have no funds."

Some of the other demands turned out to be even more imaginative. To protect black workers and their families "fighting racist working conditions" at work as well as within their unions, the *Manifesto* designated $20 million for a National Black Labor Strike Fund. And to help welfare recipients organize more effectively, the BEDC planned to give the National Welfare Rights Organization a subsidy of $10 million. The *Manifesto* also recognized the racist war being waged on black people's image, here and abroad. Forman and other BEDC drafters of the document wanted black people to exercise more control over the media. They insisted that the media and the educational system brainwashed black youth, in particular, teaching "us to believe in the U.S.A. and salute the flag and go off to Santo Domingo, the Congo, or Vietnam fighting for this white 'Christian' nation." And so they earmarked $40 million to launch publishing houses in Detroit, Atlanta, Los Angeles, and New York; another $40 million was to be used to establish four television networks. They wanted $30 million to build a research skills center to facilitate the study of "the problems of black people," and designated $10 million for a skills training center to teach community organization, photography, movie making, television and radio manufacturing and repair, and other communications-related skills. Another $20 million would be used to support a United Black Appeal responsible for raising money for the BEDC. Besides funding "a Black Anti-Defamation League which will protect our African image," the appeal would promote the development of cooperatives in African countries and provide material support to African liberation movements. The remaining $130 million were to be used to establish a black university in the South, acknowledging that the majority of historically black colleges and universities in the region at the time were largely funded and administered by liberal whites.

It was a tall order, to be sure, but still monetarily less than what most reparations movements were asking for. In order to realize the demands of the *Black Manifesto*, BEDC proposed massive civil disobedience directed at churches. The planned sit-ins and mass disruptions were not simply tactics to win reparations but deliberate attacks on the institutionalized Church itself. Forman, in particular, felt that Christianity had been a source of oppression; by teaching passivity and acceptance of the dominant order, he argued, Christianity had kept black people from embracing revolution. Nevertheless, despite Forman's unrelenting frontal attack on white churches, a few religious leaders were moved enough by the *Manifesto*'s arguments to contribute money. Altogether, the movement raised about $1 million, though most of it went to IFCO, which eventually withdrew its support for the *Black Manifesto*. The BEDC received only about $300,000, and most of that was parceled out to other movements. The little bit it did keep was used to launch Black Star Publications, a publishing house for radical black writers.

For Forman and the radical leadership of the BEDC, the *Black Manifesto* was not an end in itself. They wanted to revolutionize society and they knew that even if their campaign succeeded, money alone would not lead to the kind of society they hoped to build. As Forman explained:

> Reparations did not represent any kind of long-range goal in our minds, but an intermediate step on the path to liberation. We saw it as a politically correct step, for the concept of reparation reflected the need to adjust past wrongs — to compensate for the enslavement of black people by Christians and their subsequent exploitation by Christians and Jews in the United States. Our demands . . . would not merely involve money but would be a call for revolutionary action, a Manifesto that spoke of the human misery of black people under capitalism and imperialism, and pointed the way to ending those conditions.

In 1971, Forman and his comrades in the BEDC founded the Black Workers Congress (BWC) in an effort to realize their radical anticapitalist vision. The BWC advocated workers' control of industry, the economy, and the state, to be brought about through cooperatives, united front groups, neighborhood centers, student organizations, and ultimately a revolutionary party. Within three years, the BWC transformed itself into a multiracial Marxist-Leninist party, purging Forman in the process.

If bringing the issue of reparations to a national audience was one of the goals of the *Black Manifesto*, it proved to be a stunning success. During the early 1970s, articles and books on reparations were everywhere. The *Review of Black Political Economy* ran several substantive articles using regression analysis and a variety of databases to calculate the cost of slavery and Jim Crow. In 1973, a white law professor named Boris Bittker published *The Case for Black Reparations*, which argued for redress not for slavery but for segregation, arguing that Jim Crow violated the equal protection clause of the Fourteenth Amendment (see Bittker and Brooks, part 2). He found language in what was basically an anti-Klan statute passed during Reconstruction that provided for redress to any injured party deprived of constitutional rights. While the flurry of publications and debates advanced the economic and juridical case for reparations, they were less concerned with the larger question of how to reconstruct society.

In contrast to the professors, other social movements picked up where the

Black Manifesto left off. The Republic of New Africa (RNA), another organization with roots in Detroit, advocated reparations but with the intention of building an independent black nation in the continental United States (see Documents, section 4). Founded in 1968 by brothers Gaidi and Imari Obadele (Milton and Richard Henry), the RNA reformulated the old black belt thesis, arguing that the states of South Carolina, Georgia, Alabama, Mississippi, and Louisiana constituted "subjugated territory" with the right to self-determination. They demanded that the U.S. government hand over the territory to African Americans and establish the RNA as a government in exile. In addition to the transfer of land, the RNA initially called for reparations from the U.S. government in the amount of $400 billion to sustain the new nation during its first few years.

The plan, authored by Imari Obadele in 1972, was called the "Anti-Depression Program of the Republic of New Africa." In it he portrayed the new nation as a beautiful, free space for black people, somewhat reminiscent of the way black people have imagined Africa. It stood in stark contrast to the overcrowded, rat-infested ghettos many urban African Americans knew as home. But the promise of a Republic of New Africa also meant transforming the ghettos of North America. "We shall bring about a new dimension in breathing and growing space for those who remain where they are; We shall immensely relieve pressure on the crowded northern and western ghettoes and spatially and materially restructure and abolish the growing black slums of the South." The new nation would not follow in the path of American capitalism. Rather, its economy would be based on Tanzania's model of African socialism, *Ujamaa*—roughly translated, "cooperative economics." Like Forman and the BEDC, the RNA concluded that New Africans need a system "for need, not for profit." "The means of production in New Africa," Obadele declared, "will be in the trust of the state to best accomplish this end, and the further ends of rapidly ending want and creating surpluses."

Many critics, even those sympathetic to territorial nationalist organizations, are quick to dismiss the land question as impractical or even impossible. But if we treat the land issue literally in terms of controlling territory with national borders and moving people back and forth across those borders, then we miss key elements of the RNA's vision and its implications for a broader black radical conception of freedom. First, land is wealth, pure and simple. Historically, it has been fundamental for economic independence and sustainability, not to mention a central source of heritable wealth in the United States. Indeed, even if we limited our scope to homeownership, the miracle of the postwar (white) middle class can be explained by rising property values. The return on their investment enabled suburban white homeowners to pass on wealth as well as educational opportunities to their children. Fewer African Americans owned property, in part because they started out with no capital, were paid less for the same work, tended to have higher rates of unemployment, and confronted a system of Jim Crow that denied them access to much of the housing market. And those who did own homes suffered from discriminatory policies and practices from lending institutions, real estate firms, and the Federal Housing Administration. As a result, substantially lower black home values not only reduce gross equity but make it difficult for African Americans to use their residence as collateral for obtaining loans for other investments, such as college or business (see essays by Brown et al. and Oliver and Shapiro, both in part 1).

Second, and perhaps more important, land is space, territory on which people can begin to reconstruct their lives. The dream, after all, is to create a new society free of the overseer's watchful eye. How can any group of people govern itself without land? How can the RNA establish communal villages on the Tanzanian model without territory on which to do so? When MOVE, a black nationalist group in Philadelphia, tried to create an alternative society in the middle of the city, confrontations with neighbors and the police ultimately led to its violent destruction: 11 MOVE members died and 250 people were left homeless as a result of a military campaign against them. Besides, proponents of a new state or repatriation to another place are really just looking for a new beginning, a place where they can be free and develop their own culture without interference. The impulse for territory, then, is not just a matter of land; it is a matter of finding free space. And this desire for free space cannot be suppressed or dismissed (see Johnson, part 5).

So, if new land is not available, is it possible to persuade the people of the "old land" to support the same things the movement wants? Can groups like the RNA win over the multiracial masses to their program and turn the United States into the kind of society they imagine for the Republic of New Africa? On the surface, the question may seem absurd, but when we examine the RNA's broad aims its general commitment to the liberation of humanity is crystal clear. Despite its nationalist rubric, the aims of the "Anti-Depression Program" are deeply internationalist and humanist in that they call for the overthrow of all forms of oppression around the globe and propose to make new subjects who are self-reliant, intelligent, self-possessed, and committed to social change. The RNA made it perfectly clear, in the "Anti-Depression Program" and in other statements and actions, that these larger goals cannot be accomplished by simply receiving land and money from the state:

Ours is a revolution against oppression—our own oppression and that of all people in the world. And it is a revolution for a better life, a better station for mankind, a surer harmony with the forces of life in the universe. We therefore see these as the aims of our revolution:
— *to assure all people in the New Society maximum opportunity and equal access to that maximum;*
— *to promote industriousness, responsibility, scholarship, and service;*
— *to protect and promote the personal dignity and integrity of the individual and his natural rights;*
— *to encourage and reward the individual for hard work and initiative and insight and devotion to the Revolution.*

The RNA experienced more than its share of state repression during the late 1960s and the 1970s; several of its members, including Imari Obadele, were jailed on charges ranging from assault to conspiracy and sedition. But the RNA survived, reconstituted itself as the New Afrikan Movement, and continued to press for reparations through N'COBRA. Imari Obadele, founder of N'COBRA, drafted a plan for reparations that went far beyond the RNA's "Anti-Depression Program." Presented to the U.S. Congress in 1987, the document was called "An Act to Stimulate Economic Growth in the United States and Compensate, in Part, for the Grievous Wrongs of Slavery and the Unjust Enrichment Which Accrued to the United States Therefrom." In this plan, Congress would be obliged to pay out not less than $3 billion annually to African Americans. One-third of this sum was to be paid directly to families; another one-third would go to the duly elected government of the Republic of New Afrika. (Elections would be monitored by the UN or some comparable international body.) The remaining one-third would support a National Congress of Organizations composed of churches, black civic organizations, and community-based movements committed to ending "the scourge of drugs and crime in New Afrikan communities and [advancing] the social, economic, educational, or cultural progress and enrichment of New Afrikan people." Participating groups would have had to be in operation for a minimum of two years before the passage of legislation.

Knowing that the United States would not simply hand over the southern states, Obadele proposed a plebiscite to determine the will of the black community for a separate state. Employing carefully worded, legalistic language, the plan required that at least 10 percent of the black population older than sixteen years sign petitions before such a plebiscite could be held. The petition process would be overseen by judges appointed by the president of the United States, the UN, and the RNA. The sovereign status of each state in question, then, would be determined by a majority of voters. If the majority of voters elected to become part of the Republic of New Afrika, residents of these states could leave and maintain U.S. citizenship, stay and become citizens of the RNA, or enjoy dual citizenship irrespective of where they lived. What is not clear from the document, however, is whether or not white people can choose New Afrikan citizenship or residency in the South. Judging from the carefully worded and extremely democratic tone of the document, it seems quite possible that nonblack people fully committed to black liberation and a "New Afrikan" way of life could join the republic, though it is not encouraged.

On May 19, 1999 (Malcolm X's birthday), N'COBRA did hold a plebiscite on reparations, though the purpose was to raise community awareness and mobilize African Americans to elect "economic development commissioners" (EDCs) who would serve as local organizers for the reparations campaign. Preparation for the plebiscite gave N'COBRA an opportunity to circulate its latest "main and immediate demands." These included $25,000 in cash for black families and individuals; the immediate release of all political prisoners as well as nonviolent black prisoners with cash reparations and, for those who needed it, "medical care/substance abuse treatment"; "10 billion dollars to create 10 schools" to retrain African (American) youth, the unemployed, and recently released prisoners; and $1 billion to create an economic development fund that would be run by the EDCs. The "Act" also registered N'COBRA's support of black farmers' $1 billion lawsuit against the federal government, and reiterated its commitment to self-determination and the right to form an independent black state.

In short, N'COBRA continues to uphold a radical concept of reparations as more than a paycheck and an apology. It regards the campaign as part of a many-pronged attack on race and class oppression, an analysis of the root cause of inequality, and a means to mobilize African Americans to struggle for social change, self-transformation, and self-reliance. Indeed, self-reliance is a key phrase: N'COBRA and the New Afrikan Movement consistently advocate educational programs with the intention of reducing crime, drug addiction, and self-hatred and promoting communal values, self-worth, and a commitment to community. Grassroots community involvement in the campaign not only builds support but also has the potential to transform participants through study groups, forums, and relationships forged in the context of a social movement—perhaps not unlike the black ex-slave pension movement at the beginning of the twentieth century. Finally, like so many other reparations campaigns coming out of black radical movements, N'COBRA continues to view the struggle in global terms. Among other things, it maintains links to the Africa Reparations Movement (ARM). An outgrowth of the

First Pan-African Conference on Reparations in Abuja, Nigeria, held in 1993, ARM focuses on issues relating to the continent, notably the cancellation of African nations' debt, the return of stolen art objects, and recognition of the Atlantic slave trade as a crime against humanity.

A Case for Reparations . . . and Transformation

If we think of reparations as part of a broad strategy to radically transform society — redistributing wealth, creating a democratic and caring public culture, exposing the ways capitalism and slavery produced massive inequality — then the ongoing struggle for reparations holds enormous promise for revitalizing movements for social justice. Consider the context: for at least the last quarter century we have witnessed a general backlash against the black community. As I argued in *Yo' Mama's Disfunktional!* (1997), Republican and Democratic administrations dismantled most state protections for poor people of color, expanded the urban police state, virtually eliminated affirmative action and welfare as we knew it, and significantly weakened institutions and laws created to protect civil rights. All these cutbacks were justified by a discourse that blamed black behavior for contemporary urban poverty and turned what were once called "rights" (i.e., welfare) into "privileges." The argument for reparations recasts these measures not only as rights but as payback. It shows how more than two centuries of U.S policy facilitated accumulation among white property owners while further impoverishing African Americans. Thus federal assistance to black people in any form is not a gift but a down payment for centuries of unpaid labor, violence, and exploitation.

We need not go all the way back to slavery to make the case. We can point to more than a century of discrimination to explain the myriad ways U.S. policies have enriched upper- and middle-class whites at the expense of black people and other people of color. Let us take just one example: education. During Reconstruction, African Americans led the fight for free universal public education in the United States, not just for themselves but for everyone. After being barred from reading and writing while in bondage, newly freed people regarded education as one of the most basic rights and privileges of citizenship. Education was so important, in fact, that they were willing to pay for public schools or start their own. In South Carolina, for example, freed people contributed nearly $13,000 to keep twenty-three schools running, schools that had been established by the Freedmen's Bureau. Indeed, between 1866 and 1870, newly freed people contributed more than three-quarters of a million dollars in cash to sustain their own schools. Once African Americans won the franchise, they made it possible for universal compulsory education to be written into state constitutions throughout the South. They also elected black legislators who succeeded in establishing boards of education and requiring compulsory education with "no distinction to be made in favor of any class of persons." In South Carolina in 1868, black and progressive white legislators made sure textbooks were provided free of charge, and within two years close to sixteen thousand black children and eleven thousand white children attended public schools.

As soon as the federal government withdrew its support for Reconstruction and the southern planter class and New South industrialists imposed formal segregation, black students were relegated to inferior schools and denied full attendance. Rural schools for blacks, for example, often operated only a few weeks out of the year. And yet black wage earners continued to pay taxes to support public education. In the Jim Crow South it was not unusual for African Americans to contribute 40 percent of the school budget but attend schools that received 10 percent of the expenditures. One study conducted by researchers at Atlanta University in 1901 concluded that black taxpayers were actually subsidizing white schools. More recently, two years after the Supreme Court ordered desegregation of schools in 1954, the state of Virginia introduced publicly funded school vouchers to help white families send their children to private schools rather than endure integration. The vouchers were eventually deemed unconstitutional, but during that short period of time African American taxes were being used to help pay for white children's private school tuition. In light of how our separate and unequal education has benefited whites and cost African Americans, claims that affirmative action is "reverse discrimination" or a "special privilege" ring hollow at best.

The reparations movement exposes the history of white privilege and helps us all understand how wealth and poverty are made under capitalism—particularly a capitalism shaped immeasurably by slavery and racism. It stresses the fact that labor—not CEOs, not scientists and technicians, not the magic of the so-called free market—creates wealth. The reparations movement provides an analysis of our situation that challenges victim-blaming explanations, explaining that exploitation and regressive policies create poverty, not bad behavior. It ought to compel us to pay attention to the centrality of racism in the U.S. political economy, because one of the consequences of racial differentials in income and economic opportunity is downward pressure on wages for *all* working people, irrespective of color. It should also make us look at gender, because men and women did not experience exploitation in the same manner. We need to consider things like women's unpaid labor, reproduction, sexual abuse, and ways to make restitution for these distinctive forms of exploitation. At the very least, the reparations movement ought to clarify issues like what constitutes a "family" if payments are to be made to such units, or how we might imagine remaking relationships between men and women, boys and girls, adults and children. If radical transformation of society is one of the goals of the reparations movement, then these questions cannot be ignored. Unfortunately, most arguments in support of reparations scarcely mention gender.

In the end, a successful reparations campaign has the potential to benefit the entire nation, not just the black community. Since most plans emphasize investments in institutions rather than individual payments, the result would bring a massive infusion of capital for infrastructure, housing, schools, and related institutions in communities with large black populations. Monies would also be made available to support civic organizations and help establish a strong civil society among people of African descent, which in turn would strengthen civil society as a whole. Presumably, social ills such as crime, drug use, and violence would be reduced considerably and thus alter the world's image of black people. Furthermore, the historically black ghetto communities to which substantial investments would be made also house other poor people of color: Latinos, Afro-Caribbeans, Native Americans, Asian Americans (namely, Filipinos, Samoans, South Asians, Koreans, etc.). They, too, would benefit from improved schools, homes, public life, and a politically strengthened black community. Given the relationship of slavery and racism to the global economy, this outcome makes perfect sense. Many of these poor immigrant groups are themselves products of centuries of imperialism — slavery's handmaiden, if you will — or descendants of slaves, as in the case of many Caribbean and Latin American immigrants. Finally, it should be stressed that reparations for one group will not harm working-class whites. As Robert Westley argued in a recent *Boston College Law Review* article on reparations:

> Racist exploitation has contributed to the persistence of poverty among blacks and the unjust privilege of whites. Redressing these harms through black reparations would help to alleviate part of the problem of persistent poverty. To the extent that poverty remains a problem among nonblacks and blacks alike, it is both just and consistent with the equality principle to demand adequate social welfare, equal educational opportunity and access to jobs. Other national goals, like space exploration or defense, may need to be downsized in order to fulfill the moral obligation of social justice.

Of course, we do not yet live in a society where social justice takes precedence over national defense. This is why the reparations campaign, despite its potential contribution to eliminating racism and remaking the world, can never be an end in itself. Movement leaders have known this all along. The hard work of changing our values and reorganizing social life requires political engagement, community involvement, education, debate and discussion, and dreaming. Money and resources are always important, but a new vision and new values cannot be bought. And without at least a rudimentary critique of the capitalist culture that consumes us, even reparations can have disastrous consequences. Imagine if reparations were treated as start-up capital for black entrepreneurs who merely want to mirror the dominant society. What would really change?

Again, we have to return to Detroit, this time to veteran radical Grace Lee Boggs. For decades she has been making this very point, insisting that we stop begging for inclusion in a corrupt system, take responsibility for transforming our culture, and remake ourselves as human beings. I hope that all of us who believe freedom is worth pursuing will heed her words and recognize the power we already possess:

> What we need to do . . . is encourage groups of all kinds and all ages to participate in creating a vision of the future that will enlarge the humanity of all of us and then, in devising concrete programs on which they can work together, if only in a small way, to move toward their vision. In this unique interim time between historical epochs, this is how we can elicit the hope that is essential to the building of a movement and unleash the energies that in the absence of hope are turned against other people or even against oneself. . . . When people come together voluntarily to create their own vision, they begin wishing it to come into being with such passion that they begin creating an active path leading to it from the present. The spirit and the way to make the spirit live coalesce. Instead of seeing ourselves only as victims, we begin to see ourselves as part of a continuing struggle of human beings, not only to survive but to evolve into more human human beings.

Forty Acres, or, An Act of Bad Faith

JEFFREY R. KERR-RITCHIE

> When we got freed we was going to get forty acres and a mule. Stead of that we didn't get nothing. — Sally Dixon, 1938, in George P. Rawick, ed., *The American Slave: A Composite Autobiography* (Westport, Conn., 1972), 629

The Promise

Most Americans have heard of "forty acres and a mule," but few can explain it. The debate over reparations for slavery has also revealed limited understanding. Opponents think it an insignificant footnote to the past; supporters use it without historical context. This essay offers a succinct account of the origins, nature, and legacy of Forty Acres and a Mule. An earlier talk and this publication aim to intellectually empower supporters, activists, and politicians committed to the reparations movement and broader struggles for social justice by people of African descent.

Scholars have long argued over Forty Acres and a Mule. Some maintain it was a foolish and impractical belief held by former slaves, encouraged by the misguided actions of the federal government. Others insist its origins cannot be established because of a confusing mix of hearsay, wartime expediency, and freedmen's wishes. Some historians of Reconstruction simply use the term without explanation.[1]

Most recent scholarship, however, supports the view that Forty Acres and a Mule emerged sometime during the critical year of 1865, as a consequence of Union military actions and congressional government policies. The two critical factors were General William T. Sherman's Special Field Order, together with the creation of the Freedmen's Bureau by Congress. Let us review each one briefly.

In early January 1865, General Sherman convened a special meeting with former slaves at his Headquarters Military Division of the Mississippi in the Field, at Savannah, Georgia. One of the freedpeople's leaders, the Reverend Garrison Frazier, a sixty-seven-year-old former slave and Baptist elder, provided an eloquent explanation of the difference between property-based and labor-based relations to the assembled Union officers and federal politicians: "Slavery is, receiving by *irresistible power* the work of another man, and not by his *consent*. The freedom, as I understand it, promised by the proclamation [Lincoln's Emancipation Proclamation], is taking us from under the yoke of bondage, and placing us where we could reap the fruit of our own labor, take care of ourselves and assist the Government in maintaining our freedom."[2]

In response, General Sherman issued Special Field Order No. 15 on 16 January 1865 (see Documents, section 1). A coastal strip "thirty miles back from the sea" from Charleston, South Carolina, down to St. John's River, Florida, was "set apart for the settlement of the Negroes now made free by the acts of war and the proclamation of the President of the United States." Furthermore, no white person except Union military personnel was allowed to reside on the islands, where "the sole and exclusive management of affairs will be left to the freedpeoples themselves, subject only to the United States military authority, and the acts of Congress." In addition, "young and able-bodied Negroes" were encouraged to enlist as Union soldiers, their bounties to be used for purchasing "agricultural implements, seeds, tools, boots, clothing and other articles." Once "heads of families" had chosen their land, they were required to subdivide it, "so that each family shall have a plot of not more than forty acres of tillable ground." The military authorities agreed to protect the possessors of these forty-acre homesteads "until such time as they can protect themselves or until Congress shall regulate their title." The "possessory title" of these settlements would be furnished to "each head of family" by a general officer under the auspices of the federal government. General Sherman later authorized the army to loan these freed families mules to help them work their lands. By June 1865, some forty thousand freedpeople had settled on four hundred thousand acres of "Sherman land" along coastal South Carolina and Georgia.[3] Under the exigencies of war, the federal government had committed itself to a policy of emancipation, the civil rights of black soldiers, and the redistribution of land to freed families.

The other major factor behind Forty Acres and a Mule was the creation of the Freedmen's Bureau (see Documents, section 1). On 3 March 1865, Congress funded the creation of the Bureau of Refugees, Freedmen, and Abandoned Lands (Freedmen's Bureau) under the auspices of the War Department. Its mandate was to provide rations for the destitute, to facilitate the transition of slaves into freedmen, and to redistribute land. At the time the federal government held some eight to nine hundred thousand acres consisting of "such tracts of land within the insurrectionary states as shall have been abandoned, or to which the United States shall have acquired title by confiscation or sale, or otherwise." From these lands, forty acres were to be assigned to every male citizen, whether refugee or freedman, for a three-year rental and eventual purchase with "such title as it could convey." Although limited—eight hundred thousand acres would only amount to twenty thousand freedpeople working forty-acre plots—this legislation pointed to the government's clear commitment to the establishment of a small peasantry in the postwar American South. As Professor Wanda Cox pointed out forty-five years ago, this congressional legislation "made in effect a promise of land ownership to the freed slave."[4] Additional military and political commitments to the distribution and redistribution of land were made after Appomattox. Thomas Conway, the Freedmen's Bureau assistant commissioner for Louisiana, leased over sixty thousand acres to freedpeople. General Rufus Saxton, the Freedmen's Bureau commissioner for South Carolina, Georgia, and Florida, announced his intention to provide freedmen with forty-acre homesteads along the lines suggested by General Sherman's Special Order. On 28 July 1865, General O. O. Howard, the Freedmen's Bureau commissioner, issued Circular Order No. 13 from his Washington, D.C., headquarters. Citing congressional legislation, General Howard ordered his assistant commissioners throughout the American South to "select and set apart such confiscated and abandoned lands and property as may be deemed necessary for the immediate use of Refugees and Freedmen, the specific division of which into lots, and rental or sale thereof according to the law establishing the Bureau."[5]

General Howard's order was rescinded in September 1865, but demands for confiscation and land redistribution to the freedmen continued. At Pennsylvania's Republican Convention—held at Lancaster, Pennsylvania, in the same month—Thaddeus Stevens, radical Republican congressman and chair of the powerful House Ways and Means Committee, called for government confiscation of 394 million acres owned by 70,000 white Southerners. Forty million acres would be broken into forty-acres lots and redistributed to freedmen heads of household much like "Sherman's land." The rest of the confiscated land would be divided into farms and sold to the highest bidder. "How can Republican institutions, free schools, free churches, free social intercourse," asked Stevens, "exist in a mingled community of nabobs and serfs?" "If the South is ever to be made a safe republic," the congressman decreed, "let her lands be cultivated by the toil of owners."[6]

Other radical Republicans, including George W. Julian, Benjamin F. Butler, and Charles Sumner, repeatedly stressed the necessity for government confiscation and land redistribution. The prominent abolitionist activist Wendell Phillips called for the allocation of forty to eighty acres and a furnished cottage for each freed family. Apparently, this call became known as a "Wendell Phillips." Indeed, the advent of Congressional Reconstruction encouraged freedpeople in their belief that their northern friends were fighting for their interests, including well-deserved property rights. This belief was strengthened by the circulation of Congressman Steven's bill of 19 March 1867, which proposed the confiscation of 150 million southern acres with each freed household obtaining forty acres (see Documents, section 1). For one decade, this land would be inalienable, followed by the bestowal of absolute title.[7]

Thus, Forty Acres and a Mule emerged during 1865 as a key governmental policy concerned with land redistribution in order to facilitate the transition from slavery to freedom in the American South. The Union military and the Republican Congress set aside confiscated and abandoned lands, where the freedmen's settlements would be legally guaranteed. Some Republican politicians were even more adamant in demanding a fundamental agrarian revolution in land titles to punish the treasonable South, to break up its land-owning monopoly, and to remake the region in the image of a more egalitarian national republic. Knowledge of Forty Acres was disseminated to the freedpeople through radical Republican speeches in pamphlet form, Freedmen's Bureau regulations and laws, homestead and confiscation acts, bureau agents, and northern missionaries and teachers. The rumor mill also played its part.[8]

Although we can precisely date Forty Acres and a Mule, the *concept* was of an earlier provenance. This is crucial, because it supports the view that the freedpeople's belief in the government's commitment to the confiscation and redistribution of land was realistically rooted in wartime practice and policies. In other words, the idea was neither impractical nor wishful thinking, but grounded in material reality.

Much of this practice can be explained by the federal government's desperation to win a war against powerful southern interests. On 6 August 1861 and 17 July 1862, the passage of Congressional Confiscation Acts made Confederate property liable to confiscation (see Documents, section 1). The Direct Tax Act of June 1862 provided for governmental land confiscation where taxes were delinquent.

The rest was seized as "abandoned" or "captured" lands. In the process, northern armies seized everything. Freedpeople heard about this federal policy from angry white southerners, some of the letters dubbing it the work of

Lincoln's thieves. Other freedmen saw Union troops engaged in confiscation activities and were easily persuaded that the property of rebel southerners would soon be redistributed.[9]

This legislative confiscation had real meaning when Union troops occupied parts of the rebellious southern states. The citizens in the parish of Terre Bonne, Louisiana, petitioned Major General Banks on 14 January 1862 concerning their "deplorable conditions." The cause was that "many of the Negroes led astray by designing persons, believe that the plantations and everything on them belong to them, the Negroes." After Union troops visited Jackson, Mississippi, in early 1863, the slaves "measured off land with a plow line making a fair apportionment among themselves, and also divided the cotton and farm implements." Although Confederate authorities subsequently called a halt to land redistribution, one local newspaper reported with alarm, "This is only one instance of the wholesome effects of Abolitionism. . . . Let the country be thus subjugated, and Lincoln's robbers will occupy ever farm in the South." This concern was echoed elsewhere. The "more insolent Negroes actually passed over their former masters' lands, measuring with old ropes and pegs to mark the favorite tracts they designed taking possession of as soon as the word was given."[10]

In March 1863, thousands of acres along the South Carolina, Georgia, and Florida coast and Sea Islands were confiscated and sold at auction. Land was divided into lots ranging from twenty to forty acres. Land once worth $40 to $60 per acre in 1860 sold for $1.25 per acre three years later. As local whites fled the occupying Union army, freedpeople came into possession of land. Eventually, some fifteen hundred acres were sold to freedpeople.[11]

The creation of "Freedmen's Home Colonies" as government-run settlements further supported freedmen's belief in official land distribution. The estates of the former governor of Alabama and a prominent judge in Louisiana were parceled out among the freedpeople.[12] Similar schemes were pursued in Mississippi. General Ulysses S. Grant's successful Mississippi River campaign in the summer of 1863 resulted in the capture of six plantations owned by Jefferson and Joseph Davis about twenty-five miles south of Vicksburg in a fertile peninsula called Davis Bend. In 1864, seventy-five freedpeople working plots of five to one hundred acres showed profits of $500 to $1,000 at season's end. By 1865, freed families were raising an assortment of vegetables, including 12,000 bushels of corn, as well as 1,736 bales of cotton — altogether worth $397,700. Minus disbursements, these freed families showed a profit of $159,200. The Davis Bend experiment, it should be emphasized, was guarded by a regiment of the United States Colored Troops (USCT).[13]

Early 1863 saw the creation of the Bureau of Negro Affairs in the War Department, with C. B. Wilder as superintendent for Hampton in southeastern Virginia. The proposal to settle freedpeople on abandoned farms was attractive to both the federal body and the freedpeople: for the government, it pointed to independent support rather than wasteful welfare; for former slaves, it offered socioeconomic autonomy. The former slaves were also persuaded that they would be able to keep the land once the war had been won. Settlements were established at "Newtown" in York County, "Slabtown" in Elizabeth City County, and on scattered farms in Warwick County and around Norfolk. The land was divided into small plots of eight to ten acres, with each freed family farming independently. In other parts of the Virginia peninsula, former slaves squatted on abandoned lands and tried to eke out their newly found freedom.[14]

In other words, the policy the federal government pursued for settling former slaves on abandoned lands during the Civil War legitimized the idea of Forty Acres and a Mule. There was a familiarity to this policy, which, I would argue, explains both the subsequent military and congressional policy as well as the tenacity with which freedpeople held on to the idea of land distribution and redistribution as part of the government's obligations during Reconstruction.

The freedpeople's determination to obtain forty acres was especially evident in their defense of the right to the land. In June 1865, President Andrew Johnson issued his pardon and amnesty policy to the former Confederates, one consequence being the restoration of former property rights. Dispossessed landowners now demanded the return of their lands. Some freedpeople voiced opposition to their removal from land upon which they had recently settled. Freedman Bayley Wyat protested the injustice of Union eviction from land near Yorktown, Virginia:

> We has a right to the land where we are located. For why? I tell you. Our wives, our children, our husbands, has been sold over and over again to purchase the lands we now locates upon; for that reason we have a divine right to the land.... And den didn't we clear the land, and raise de crops ob corn, ob cotton, ob tobacco, ob rice, ob sugar, ob everything. And den didn't dem large cities in de North grow up on de cotton and de sugars and de rice dat we made?... I say dey has grown rich, and my people is poor.[15]

Wyat's protest amounted to a remarkable mixture of divine right based upon biblical reading together with a labor theory of surplus value similar to Reverend Frazier's explanation to General Sherman. These are the roots of the reparations movement.

Other freedpeople pursued more collective means of protest. In the South Carolina coastlands, freedpeople refused to vacate the land and instead armed themselves. Their actions were supported by the Freedmen's Bureau. Secretary Edwin Stanton and Freedmen's Bureau chief General Howard asserted freedmen "had been led to expect permanent possession of the lands, and to dispossess them would be an act of bad faith." Nevertheless, General Howard visited the region in October 1865, in an effort to persuade the freedpeople of the need to vacate the lands, as mandated by presidential policy. A compromise was struck whereby those who held possessory titles to twenty to forty acres from 1863 to 1865 could keep their land. But few freedpeople had legal title. This was partly because of the federal tax commission's refusal to recognize freedmen's land claims.[16] Similar armed resistance by the freedpeople occurred in Georgia's low country. At the end of 1865, Aaron A. Bradley, a militant local black leader, led efforts by the region's freedpeople to resist President Johnson's order for land restoration. In December 1866, Bradley led armed resistance to land restoration on some Savannah River plantations, while in September 1867, he held a "confiscation-homestead" meeting in Savannah, Georgia.[17]

We should conclude this first section with the power of the gun. The government's promise of land was often tied directly to the mobilization of black men for service in the Union army. This policy was evident in General Sherman's military order, the protection of Davis Bend, and the presence of black Union soldiers in southeast Virginia. In local land disputes in Virginia, South Carolina, and Georgia, the role of USCT veterans was vital. It should come as no surprise, therefore, that reneging on this promise was preceded by the demobilization of black troops. In the fall of 1865, the War Department decided to disband all black regiments raised in the North. A year later, there were only 13,000 black troops left in the South, down from a total mobilization of nearly 85,000, or one-third of the entire occupation army.[18] The removal of this armed force did not end the struggle for land redistribution, but it did terminate a powerful potential force for its implementation at the grass-roots level.

There was nothing mystical, confusing, or bewildering to the freedpeople about land and mules for making freedom work under the sponsorship of the federal government. Rather, land redistribution was a very *real* part of the landscape of Union victory, government policy, and freedpeople's expectations from past labors and present services. Freedpeople believed the federal government was committed to land redistribution, for it had done a great deal to demonstrate this through legislative acts of confiscation, military acts of resettlement, and postwar policies of reconstructing the American South.

Indeed, one is left wondering how a war for the Union and Emancipation could *not* have entailed Forty Acres and a Mule?

The Failure

There are numerous reasons to explain why land redistribution failed to occur in the aftermath of the American Civil War. One traditional argument is that the Republican Party's belief in the sanctity of private property made any attack on property rights unacceptable to Congress.[19] Without denying the U.S. republic's long-standing ideological commitment to life, liberty, and the pursuit of property, this explanation ignores the abolition of slavery as an attack on property rights. Two-thirds of the average slave owner's wealth was held in slaves, while nearly half of southern capital stock was invested in slavery.[20] Lincoln's Emancipation Proclamation and the Thirteenth Amendment to the U.S. Constitution rank as the largest confiscation acts in American history. Moreover, the context of political confrontation after a bloody civil war waged against secessionist traitors made agrarian reform and redistribution of property rights seem not so far-fetched after all. Similar property confiscation and redistribution had occurred during both the French and the Haitian revolutions.[21] Property rights were less sanctified than they might otherwise have been within the context of social revolution.

Another explanation for the failure of land redistribution was the absence of a clearly committed class leadership. According to one older account of Reconstruction, "The Negroes did not yet have a class among them capable of independently leading the agrarian revolution through to its end." More recently, one scholar expressed surprise that no "[black] convention debated the democratization of land proprietorship." In a well-researched study of black political leadership in Reconstruction South Carolina, another historian emphasized the opposition from some black legislators to land reform in spite of its popular demand by constituents. Thus, the absence of class leadership explains the failure of land redistribution among freedpeople.[22]

While it is true that these black conventions were dominated by questions of civil and political rights, much of this agenda had to do with the limitations of coalition politics and issues of feasibility. Delegates to the Georgia State Convention equivocated on key issues of suffrage and land distribution because of their ties to northern allies. The redistribution of land was not on the agenda of many northern and southern Unionist legislators working with freedmen legislators. Even some radical Republicans insisted upon the secondary significance of land distribution. "If I were a black man, with the chains just stricken from my limbs," said Congressman James M. Ashley, "and you should offer me the ballot, or a cabin and forty acres of cotton land, I would take the ballot."[23]

Moreover, we should not ignore those clear examples of class leadership on the land question. In a statement made to the U.S. Congress from the Colored People's Convention of South Carolina in November 1865, the "colored people" of the state requested "that a fair and impartial instruction be given to the pledges of the government to us concerning the land question."[24] In the first State Convention of Georgia, which freedpeople held in Augusta in January 1866, the delegates resolved for the disposition of government lands to the freedpeople at affordable rates rather than for free.[25] According to the Address of the Colored Convention to the People of Alabama in May 1867, one of the major reasons that nine-tenths of the state's colored people would vote the Republican ticket was because the Republican Party "passed new homestead laws, enabling the poor to obtain land." At the 1867 State Constitutional Convention held in Richmond, Virginia, Buckingham County Representative Francis Moss was so insistent upon land redistribution that the Richmond press caricatured him as "Francis Forty-Acres-of-Land-and-a-Mule Moss." His constituents ignored these derogatory labels, electing Moss for terms in the Senate (1869–1871) and the House of Delegates (1874–1875).[26] Although many of these convention records no longer survive, future research in the local press, planter papers, and legal proceedings will likely reveal numerous other calls and struggles for the "democratization of land." Indeed, it would be surprising if this was not the case, given the preponderance of black political representatives from rural districts. Forty Acres was of central concern to their constituents. We have already seen the vigor with which freedpeople defended their newly won rights to the land at the local level.[27]

If the sanctity of property rights and the lack of class leadership do not explain why land confiscation failed, why was it that freedpeople did not receive their duly promised Forty Acres and a Mule? This historian is persuaded by three major reasons.

First, the meaning of freedom for the freedpeople clashed with the free market dictates of northern businessmen and Republican politicians. The primary interest of northern business—whether mercantile, financial, or manufacturing—"was the restoration and expansion of cotton culture." This would give northeastern manufacturers a share in the national and foreign markets in India and China. The United States could also recapture control of the world market for raw cotton production, which had been expanded by British imperial interests in Egypt and India as a result of the cotton embargo imposed during the Civil War. The resumption of cotton exports would help to increase foreign exchange, which would pay the huge public debt accrued as the price for winning the war. The free cotton economy would restore and extend the market for northern products in the American South, creating a revitalized home market.[28]

One major obstacle to restoring the cotton economy was the freedpeople. They had a different understanding of freedom, which did not embrace cotton production because of its association with slavery. During the Civil War, Union-occupied areas such as South Carolina had revealed the contrasting ways that the former slaves understood their freedom. In an article on black farmers on government-controlled lands in South Carolina and on the Georgia Sea Islands, the Boston lawyer Edward Pierce reported, "They were beginning to plant cotton in their patches, but were disinclined to plant cotton, regarding it as a badge of servitude." The Boston reformer Edward Philbrick passed along the sentiments of the freedpeople on the Sea Islands in testimony to Congress in 1865: "Cotton is no good for nigger. Corn good for nigger; ground nuts good for nigger; cotton good for massa; if massa want cotton he may make it himself, cotton do nigger no good; cotton make nigger perish."[29]

Moreover, the former slaves' distaste for cash crop production was already a familiar feature of other postemancipation societies such as independent Haiti and British Jamaica in which freedpeople had sought subsistence over cash crop economies. In those areas, it was noted, former slaves had accumulated land, thus becoming small peasant farmers.[30]

Hence, to redistribute land would not only jeopardize cash crop production in the South, but would deal a devastating blow to the Atlantic cotton economy. More broadly speaking, interest in the political economy of cotton profits in a global economy predominated over the moral economy of freedmen pursuing freedom. Freedpeople could not receive land because past experience suggested they were not interested in fulfilling the productive potential of that land with the production of cash crops. As Professor Cox succinctly put it, "There is no evidence of the direct influence of northern business leaders in the final formulation of the Freedmen's Bureau Act, but the desire for abundant cheap cotton helps to explain why Congress did not make a *gift* of land to the freedmen."[31] Underlying this notion of productive resources from land and labor lurks the key to understanding the bloody history of colonial slavery, the expropriation of lands away from Native Americans, and the imposition of bourgeois freedoms upon former slaves in postslave societies. By the 1860s, the failure of Forty Acres was the latest act in a global drama of imperial domination.

The second explanation for the failure of land redistribution was the desire of northern financiers to maximize the value of the lands in which they were investing. The system of slave labor had made southern land valuable because of its massive human capital investment. Emancipation freed labor from the land, thus significantly reducing land prices. The value of Virginia real estate, for instance, fell by more than 25 percent during the 1860s. In the major slave tobacco regions of the Virginia Southside, real estate prices fell from less than $13 per acre to less than $8 per acre during the decade. The depreciation in land values in the "cotton" South ranged from a 55 percent decline in Georgia to a 70 percent drop in Louisiana.[32]

Many white southerners welcomed northern investments after the Confederacy's surrender at Appomattox. Northerners purchased land, leased plantations, and formed partnerships with southern planters. Some businessmen, along with many former soldiers, invested their savings in the South as a quick way to make a buck from the lucrative cotton. These "carpetbaggers" brought with them a belief in the superiority of free over slave labor. Needless to say, this included their management of the "Negroes." More important, the existence of speculative capital played a crucial role in maintaining the plantation system. Land values increased from this northern investment as land titles did not change hands and cash crop production soon recommenced. Keeping the freedpeople propertyless further increased the value of these lands. Land redistribution would have kept property values down and scared away outside investment. As Professor Lawrence N. Powell neatly summarizes, "At the very moment when Republicans in Congress were deliberating measures that would limit the power of the ex-slaveholders, northern investors were helping to rescue a land system that would limit the freedoms of the ex-slaves."[33]

The third major reason for the failure of land redistribution to freedpeople was the predominance of speculation and accumulation by northern monopoly interests. In May 1862, the Thirty-seventh Congress, dominated by Republicans, passed the Homestead Act. It stipulated quarter sections of 160 acres of "unoccupied" land to homesteaders for a nominal fee after five years of residence. By June 1864, farmers had settled on over 1.2 million acres. To the poor, this act gave the illusion of land distribution. In actuality, between 1864 and 1869, speculators acquired nearly 50 million acres, much of it formerly inhabited by Native Americans.[34]

Immigrants and citizens were eligible but not people of African descent, presumably because, according to the 1857 *Dred Scott* decision, they were not considered citizens. Inclusion of freedmen in homestead legislation came in 1866 through the passage of Indiana Congressman George W. Julian's Southern Homestead Act, which opened settlement of public lands in the

South to freedmen and loyal whites (see Documents, section 1). This did not lead to major land reform because the best land was owned by planters, while public lands were swampy and timbered and had no link to transport hubs. Also, freedmen lacked capital, while federal land offices were sparse. Only four thousand freed families were registered by 1869: of these, three thousand lived in thinly populated Florida. Most public land went to lumber companies.[35] Indeed, northern capitalists and Republican leaders were much more concerned with pursuing land speculations in the American West and South for railroad and mining companies than with distributing land to former slaves. One scholar estimates that the federal government provided more than 158 million acres to western railroad promoters, of which 115 million acres were certified and patented. In this sense, American Reconstruction was not a revolution in land redistribution but a consolidation of bourgeois capital interests in the favorable climate of victorious northern states.[36]

The Memory

Having explained the origin, concept, and failure of Forty Acres and a Mule, let us conclude with the issue of its legacy. Most obviously, there was not an agrarian revolution in the postemancipation American South. The dictates of the cotton economy, northern investors, and alternative speculations precluded the distribution and redistribution of land to the freedpeople. Despite the wartime policies of the federal government, together with the passage of important laws in the aftermath of Union victory, these promises of freedom went unfulfilled.

The failure of land redistribution after the Civil War, however, should not blind us to the fact that some freedpeople did obtain their forty acres. In Virginia, the amount of land owned by people of African descent increased tenfold, that is, from one hundred thousand acres in the early 1870s to more than 1 million acres by 1900. In the Sea Islands adjacent to the South Carolina and Georgia coastline, former slaves enjoyed possessory title to the land for generations after the promise of "Sherman's land." It has recently been estimated that 15 percent of black households in Mississippi owned land in 1910.[37] It should be emphasized that this land accumulation had nothing to do with the federal government's failed promise of Forty Acres and a Mule. Freedpeople's landholdings—usually of less acreage than forty acres and of poor quality at that—resulted from a complex series of factors. These included an older generation's persistence to own the land; prolonged agricultural depression from 1873 through 1896, making land cheaper, less productive, and more available; and cash remittances from younger to older generations.[38]

Moreover, freedpeople never forgot their Forty Acres. Black voters supported some Reconstruction politicians because they promised forty acres. Swindlers preyed on the desires of former slaves through various duplicitous moneymaking schemes, including costly attorney's fees and bogus slave pensions. Some peddlers sold freedpeople wooden pegs, told them to stake out their land, and never returned. In 1871, the congressional joint committee on the Ku Klux Klan reported, "The Negroes heard and were inclined to believe [those reports] by their own sense of justice, which suggested that as their labor had produced the greater part of the property, they should have a portion. Hence, the idea was widespread and common among them that each head of a family would have 'forty acres and a mule.'" In researching his article on "forty acres and a mule" published in 1906, Professor Walter Fleming was "assured by old Negroes that a general topic of conversation in some Negro 'quarters' was the intention of the federals to confiscate the lands and divide them among the Blacks." He reported that some blacks still believed a "homestead and the mule will be given over to them."[39] Meanwhile, General Sherman's memoirs, composed and published in the reactionary climate of the 1890s, falsely claimed that forty-acre homesteads had only been a temporary measure.[40]

During the 1930s, the federally funded Works Progress Administration conducted a series of interviews with surviving former slaves. Some of their oral testimony suggests powerful memories of emancipation's failure — a failure no doubt enhanced by the decade's depressed conditions. Former slave Gabe Butler recalled, "Sum of the de slaves sed when dey wud be sot free dey wud git forty acres uf land fum Mr. Lincoln an' sum sed dey wud git plenty uf good things to eat an' sum sed dey wudnt have to work any more, kaze Mr. Lincoln wud give dem everything." Turner Jacobs, another slave, observed that Lincoln "promise every nigger forty acres and a mule. We never did get dat mule or dose forty acres either, ceptin by hard work." Sally Dixon recalled being "told when we got freed we was going to get forty acres and a mule. Stead of that we didn't get nothing."[41] By the 1930s, "forty acres" had become a collective memory among older generations of former slaves, an indication of the failure of the federal government to fulfill its promise to make emancipation mean something tangible, material, and long-lasting.

Most recently, opponents of the reparations movement have challenged its premises: modern moralities are being imposed upon a very different past. In contrast, this essay argues that Forty Acres had less to do with morals than with war and postwar realities. Forty Acres was all about the federal government's failure to deliver on its promises and meet the reasonable expectations of the freedpeople. The redistribution of land concerned neither welfare relief nor handouts; rather, it was rooted in centuries of uncompensated enslaved labor. Former slaves were not given their freedom; they died helping the Union to win its war against the secessionist South, and in the process secured their own freedom. (A fruitful analogy can be made with the national liberation struggle in Zimbabwe, the government's failure to redistribute land, and the present political fallout.) In the Union-occupied New Orleans of 1862, a pamphlet was found on the street signed by an anonymous "colored man": "We heave been in it [the country] Slaves over two hundred And fifty years we have made the contry and So far Saved the union."[42] No more eloquent case could be made for America's historical act of bad faith.

Notes

1. William A. Dunning, *Reconstruction, Political and Economic, 1865–1877* (1907; New York: Harper, 1962), 46–47; Vernon Lane Wharton, *The Negro in Mississippi, 1865–1890* (1947; New York: Harper, 1965), 59; John Hope Franklin, *Reconstruction after the Civil War* (Chicago: University of Chicago Press, 1961), 114.

2. Ira Berlin et al., *Freedom's Soldiers: The Black Military Experience in the Civil War* (Cambridge, England: Cambridge University Press, 1998), 149.

3. Eric Foner, *Reconstruction: America's Unfinished Revolution, 1863–1877* (New York: Harper and Row, 1988), 70; Kenneth Stampp, *The Era of Reconstruction, 1865–1877* (New York: Vintage, 1965), 125; Special Field Orders No. 15, from William T. Sherman, *Memoirs*, vol. 2, 250, reproduced in James S. Allen, *Reconstruction: The Battle for Democracy, 1865–1876* (New York: International Publishers, 1937), 225–27.

4. Foner, *Reconstruction*, 69–70; David Herbert Donald et al., *The Civil War and Reconstruction* (New York: Norton, 2001), 504–5; William S. McFeeley, *Yankee Stepfather: General O. O. Howard and the Freedmen* (New York: Norton, 1968), 104–5; Wanda Cox, "The Promise of Land for the Freedmen," *Mississippi Valley Historical Review* 1005 (June 1958–March 1959): 413, 418.

5. McFeeley, *Yankee Stepfather*, 104–5.

6. W. E. B. Du Bois, *Black Reconstruction in America, 1860–1880* (1935; New York: Atheneum, 1992), 198, 368.

7. Ibid.; Foner, *Reconstruction*, 236; Walter L. Fleming, "Forty Acres and a Mule," *North American Review* 182 (1906): 731–33; C. L. R. James, *American Civilization* (Oxford: Blackwell, 1993), 96.

8. Fleming, "Forty Acres," 730; Steven Hahn, "'Extravagant Expectations' of Freedom: Rumor, Political Struggle, and the Christmas Insurrection Scare of 1865 in the American South," *Past and Present* 157 (November 1997): 122–58.

9. Fleming, "Forty Acres," 721–22; Ira Berlin et al., *Slaves No More: 3 Essays on Emancipation and the Civil War* (Cambridge, England: Cambridge University Press, 1992), 124.

10. Ira Berlin, Thavolia Glymph, Steven F. Miller, Joseph P. Reidy, Leslie S. Rowland, and Julie Saville, eds., *The Wartime Genesis of Free Labor: The Lower South. Freedom: A Documentary History of Emancipation*, series 1, vol. 3 (New York: Cambridge University Press, 1990), 408–9.

11. Fleming, "Forty Acres," 724.

12. Ibid.

13. Wharton, *Negro in Mississippi*, 38–41; Stampp, *Era of Reconstruction*, 125–26; Fleming, "Forty Acres," 724.

14. Robert F. Engs, *Freedom's First Generation: Black Hampton, Virginia, 1861–1890* (Philadelphia: University of Pennsylvania Press, 1979), 36–41; Allen, *Reconstruction*, 44; Fleming, "Forty Acres," 724; Berlin et al., *Slaves No More*, 109.

15. Foner, *Reconstruction*, 105.

16. Fleming, "Forty Acres," 726–28; Cox, "Promise," 428.

17. Eric Foner, *Freedom's Lawmakers: A Directory of Black Officeholders During Reconstruction* (Baton Rouge: Louisiana State University Press, 1993), 24; Joseph P. Reidy, "Aaron A. Bradley: Voice of Black Labor in the Georgia Low Country," in *Southern Black Leaders of the Reconstruction Era*, ed., Howard N. Rabinowitz (Urbana: University of Illinois Press, 1982), 281–308.

18. Hahn, "'Extravagant Expectations,'" 131, 154, n.58.

19. Wharton, *Negro in Mississippi*, 41; Stampp, *Era of Reconstruction*, 130.

20. Gavin Wright, *Old South, New South: Revolutions in the Southern Economy Since the Civil War* (New York: Basic Books, 1986), 19; Roger L. Ransom and Richard Sutch, *One Kind of Freedom: The Economic Consequences of Emancipation* (Cambridge, England: Cambridge University Press, 1977), 52.

21. Allen, *Reconstruction*, 45; Alex Dupuy, *Haiti in the World Economy: Class, Race, and Underdevelopment Since 1700* (Boulder, Colo.: Westview Press, 1989), chap. 4.

22. Allen, *Reconstruction*, 68; Leon F. Litwack, *Been in the Storm So Long: The Aftermath of Slavery* (New York: Vintage, 1979), 521; Thomas Holt, *Black over White: Negro Political Leadership in South Carolina during Reconstruction* (Urbana: University of Illinois Press, 1977), 17–18, 131.

23. Joseph P. Reidy, *From Slavery to Agrarian Capitalism in the Cotton Plantation South, Central Georgia, 1800–1880* (Chapel Hill: University of North Carolina Press, 1992), 180; Foner, *Reconstruction*, 236.

24. Quoted in Allen, *Reconstruction*, 228.

25. Reidy, *Agrarian Capitalism*, 179–80.

26. Jeffrey R. Kerr-Ritchie, *Freedpeople in the Tobacco South, Virginia, 1860–1900* (Chapel Hill: University of North Carolina Press, 1999), 79.

27. See notes 14–16, above.

28. Cox, "Promise," 435–37; Gerald D. Jaynes, *Branches without Roots: Genesis of the Black Working Class in the American South, 1862–1882* (New York: Oxford University Press, 1986), 12–15.

29. Jaynes, *Branches without Roots*, 13; Du Bois, *Black Reconstruction*, 368–69; Berlin et al., *Slaves No More*, 98–100.

30. Kerr-Ritchie, *Freedpeople*, 100–101; Dupuy, *Haiti*, 51–66.

31. Cox, "Promise," 437. My argument, of course, is that it was not a gift.

32. Kerr-Ritchie, *Freedpeople*, 94; Ransom and Sutch, *One Kind of Freedom*, 51.

33. Jaynes, *Branches without Roots*, 23; Lawrence N. Powell, *New Masters: Northern Planters During the Civil War and Reconstruction* (New Haven: Yale University Press, 1980), 36, 49, 54.

34. Donald et al., *Civil War*, 285; Foner, *Reconstruction*, 21.
35. Foner, *Reconstruction*, 246.
36. Allen, *Reconstruction*, 70–71.
37. Kerr-Ritchie, *Freedpeople*, 211–12; Eric Foner, *Nothing but Freedom: Emancipation and Its Consequences* (Baton Rouge: Louisiana State University Press, 1983) chap. 3; Ted Ownby, *American Dreams in Mississippi: Consumers, Poverty, and Culture, 1830–1998* (Chapel Hill: University of North Carolina Press, 1999), 77.
38. Kerr-Ritchie, *Freedpeople*, chap. 7.
39. Fleming, "Forty Acres," 720, 723, 730, 734–37.
40. Cox, "Promise," 429.
41. George P. Rawick, ed. *The American Slave: A Composite Autobiography* (Westport, Conn.: Greenwood, 1972), series 1, vol. 6, no. 1, 323–24 (Gabe Butler); vol. 8, no. 3, 1119 (Turner Jacobs); vol. 7, no. 2, 629 (Sally Dixon).
42. Ira Berlin et al., *Freedom's Soldiers: The Black Military Experience in the Civil War* (New York: Cambridge University Press, 1998), 110–11.

The Economic Basis for Reparations to Black America

ROBERT S. BROWNE

Introduction

Whether called a domestic Marshall Plan, as the late Whitney Young envisioned it, an overdue promissory note, as Dr. Martin Luther King referred to it, or the accusing word itself, "reparations," as James Forman called it when he hurled his *Black Manifesto* at the altars of America's churches, the demand for a massive capital transfer from the overall American community to its black subset is becoming ever more strident. It is a cry of anguish from the mouths of some, a plea for justice from the mouths of others, and an ominous threat on the lips of yet others. Thus, it raises questions of welfare, equity, and efficiency. For those focusing on ameliorating economic conditions in the black community, some form of major capital transfer is emerging as the sine qua non for genuine development, irrespective of whether it is labeled "reparations" or is called by another name.

Despite the title given to this essay, it is doubtful if one can meaningfully discuss the reparations concept solely within an economic context and in isolation from the associated moral and political considerations which are inseparable from a reparations demand. Conceivably, one could develop a promising cost-benefit analysis or a demonstration of the Pareto optimality of a capital transfer of a specified size to the black community, perhaps by demonstrating that failure to make such a transfer might result in economic wastage of even larger magnitude. But to label such a capital transfer "reparations" and to justify it solely on the basis of economic efficiency while ignoring the myriad equity considerations which the term implies would be so sterile and mechanistic that it would constitute a near insult to the black community's humanity.

For most economists, such a behavioral observation is probably tantamount to disciplinary heresy and may well constitute for some others a delightful confirmation of a secret belief that blacks are not yet ready for the detached type of analysis which characterizes modern economics. Perhaps, indeed, "soul" and Samuelson do not mix. A particularly revealing, if morbid, example of this black humanism is illustrated by the experience of the few antebellum slave markets where slaves were permitted to buy their own freedom. Records suggest that a slave was consistently willing to pay more for his freedom than the market value placed on him by the slave owner.[1] From a strict market point of view, this was clearly a pathetically irrational act on the part of the slave. It apparently derived, as one writer wryly put it, from the slave's excessively sentimental attachment to his own body. Economists abhor gaps in their theoretical framework, however, even when perpetrated by black slaves. So perhaps our current theorists will accommodate these hopelessly sentimental biases of the slave mentality by incorporating into their slave market model an allowance for "internal economies."

Fortified with this appreciation of the discipline's flexibility, one can examine more closely the entire reparational concept as it might apply to American blacks. The first question which arises is, inevitably, What do blacks want the reparations payments to accomplish? There are a number of possibilities to choose from. The objective could be any or all of the following:

1. To punish (or expiate) the white community for the sins of slavery committed by its ancestors and oblige it to render retribution to the descendants of the slaves
2. To provide the black population with restitution for the unpaid labor of its slave ancestors
3. To redirect to blacks that portion of the national income which has been diverted from blacks to whites as a result of slavery and post-Emancipation racial discrimination
4. To provide the black community with the share of the national wealth and income which it would by now have had if it had been treated as other immigrant communities were, rather than enslaved.

This list is illustrative rather than exhaustive, and there is overlap among some of the suggested objectives. The first objective is based more on the psychological needs of portions of the white community than on considerations either of equity or of economics. Compensation for the horrors of slavery cannot be computed in monetary terms, so these objectives need no further elaboration. Since the fourth objective is the most comprehensive, it will be the basis for discussion. An examination of this objective will be arrived at in stages designed to permit examination of the implications of the lesser objectives. This essay is in three sections; the first will indicate the basis for a black restitutional claim; the second will explore means for computing the magnitude of the reparations payment; and the third will suggest the implications which a meaningful effort to extinguish this debt might have for the American economy.

The Basis for a Black Claim to Reparations

Webster's New International Dictionary identifies "reparations" as the "act of making amends or giving satisfaction or compensation for a wrong, injury, etc.; also, the thing done or given; amends, satisfaction; compensation." A second definition describes it as "compensation paid by a defeated nation to cover damages sustained by a victorious nation in time of warfare."

Although modern history offers examples of war reparations of the type described above, the aftermath of World War Two witnessed a reversal of this traditional type of retributional justice. The victorious United States dispensed to, rather than extracted from, its defeated antagonists substantial sums of goods and services. Perhaps the disastrous effects of the heavy reparational demands visited upon Germany following World War One contributed to this 180-degree reversal in what was felt to be the proper treatment of defeated economies.

Indeed, the principal usage of the term "reparations" in the wake of World War Two centered around the claims which were made on the Federal Republic of Germany by the State of Israel. The operative agreement reads in part as follows:

> Whereas unspeakable criminal acts were perpetrated against the Jewish people during the National Socialist regime of terror. And whereas by a declaration in the Bundestag on 27th of September 1951, the Government of the Federal Republic of Germany made known their determination to make good the material damage. And whereas the State of Israel has assumed the heavy burden of resettling so great a number of uprooted and destitute Jewish refugees from Germany and from territories formerly under German rule and has on this basis advanced a claim against the Federal Republic of Germany for global recompense for the cost of the integration of these refugees.[2]

The indemnification agreed to was in the vicinity of $821 million, together with provisions for certain specified commodities and services to be made available by Germany to Israel.

Perhaps the most relevant incident in modern American history is the passage of a federal statute setting up an Indian Claims Commission with jurisdiction to hear and resolve claims arising from the seizure of Indian property and breaches by the United States of its treaties with the Indian nations and tribes.[3] Since passage of that statute, and especially during the past three or four years, there has been a belated surge of interest, within and without government, to consider possible restitution or indemnification for a portion of the land taken from the Indians.

Prior to Emancipation, the black slave "had no rights which the white man was bound to respect."[4] Furthermore, no action was taken at the time of Emancipation to provide a basis for any retroactive claims by the freedmen. Rather, in what many regard as one of the most callous and ill-planned acts of American history, some 4 million illiterate, highly visible, totally unorganized ex-slaves were precipitously severed from their moorings and set adrift in a war-ravaged and economically battered region. In addition, it was an area already engulfed in waves of hostility, and one in which it was inevitable that they would be heavily dependent for their very survival on the same repressive forces which had previously held them in bondage. No effort was made at restitution to the ex-slaves for the crimes which American society had perpetrated upon them or for the labor which they had provided, nor was an effort extended to make the minimal capital investment in this tremendous human resource which could have enabled it to win an equitable place in the overall society. As Gunnar Myrdal cogently observed, "An economic reconstruction of the South which would have succeeded in opening the road to economic independence for the ex-slaves would have had to include, besides Emancipation, suffrage, and full civil liberties: rapid education of the freedmen, abandonment of discrimination, land reform."[5]

During the first century following Emancipation, little effort was made to rectify these failures. The 1963 centennial anniversary of the Emancipation Proclamation found the economic status of the American black man, although dramatically improved from its near-zero base of a century earlier, nevertheless lagging so seriously behind that of white America as to constitute an ominous and growing threat to the security of the society. The 1960s witnessed the first sustained effort to address the issues of black suffrage and civil liberties, of black education, and of racial discrimination. However, the land reform which Myrdal referred to and which today can be most appropriately interpreted as a proxy for redistribution of wealth, has not yet been seriously confronted in America with respect to the ex-slaves and their descendants. It is this deficiency, above all, which the reparations concept must redress.

Although the claims which the American Indian is making on American society are unique, there is also a powerful "specialness" to the black man's claim for reparations. It derives from the distinctiveness of the black man's role in American society. Alone of all the myriad immigrants who came to North America, the African came involuntarily. All other immigrant populations swarmed to America seeking to improve their life situation. The African has provided historians only with indication that he viewed the trip with abhorrence. This fact, indeed, continues to have the most profound implications for the vision which black people have of their sojourn in and their relationship to North America.[6]

But if enslavement in America was a living hell for the African, it was a boon to the American economy, without which it seems hardly probable that the United States would have emerged as the preeminent industrial power of the twentieth century. Throughout the greater portion of the nineteenth century, labor was the vital factor of production in the United States. The scarcity of labor in early America impeded American economic development. The slave labor force not only relieved this scarcity but also made possible the development of the industry which was to spur America's spectacular economic growth. Although cotton is generally credited with providing the basis for the South's economy, in a broader sense it was a major contributor to the North's industrial growth as well; for the South's cotton, largely exported in the early years of the century, emerged increasingly as the vital element in the industrialization of New England. By 1860, cotton manufactures ranked in first place among all manufactures in terms of value added and in second place for total employment provided. For much of the nineteenth century, cotton sustained the American economy and African slave labor was the sine qua non of the cotton culture. Black labor, then, provided an integral—perhaps the integral—input into America's first major industrial mainstay and thus indirectly made possible the transformation of an agricultural economy into an industrial one.

Although particularly hardy in performing the grueling toil of the cotton fields, the African slaves also proved to be very useful in the full range of manual skills to which they were exposed. Their role in the arduous task of railroad building was substantial. The great Southern Pacific railroad, for example, was very largely constructed with slave labor. Indeed, by the 1850s, the growing pressure for a reopening of the African slave trade stemmed directly from the South's wish to industrialize itself using slave labor for the routine tasks. Starobin has meticulously documented the broad usage of slave labor in southern industry and in the construction of the South's infrastructure, as well as by state and federal agencies.[7] Any effort to assess the importance of the contribution of black slaves to the American economy must necessarily reach the conclusion that America's emergence as a major industrial nation was possible only because of the massive input provided by slave labor at a time when labor was the scarce factor in the American production function.

Computation of the Reparation Claim

There has been a growing interest in the economic aspects of the slavery experience. To the earlier interest in whether or not slavery was profitable (either to the slave owner or to the South generally) has more recently been added an interest in measuring the impact of slavery on the total economy and in the effects of slavery on the economic position of the slave himself, and of his descendants.[8]

One of the most explicit of these exercises has been developed by Jim Marketti.[9] Using the tools of capital theory and historical data on the slave population and slave prices, he has derived an estimate of the value of what he terms the "unpaid black equity" in the slave industry. What he has done, in essence, is to compute the income stream which the slaves produced for their owners and compound interest on this income down to the present at alternative rates of interest. He uses slave prices as proxies for "the present value of the exploited net income stream" returned on slave capital at several points in time during the 1790–1860 period. From this data he can derive an implicit net income flow, upon which he compounds interest. By refining the crude decennial census figures to allow for variable income-generating capacities within the slave population, he is able to develop an estimate of the current, compounded value of the labor exploited from black slaves during the 1790–1860 period. His estimates fall within a range of $448 to $995 billion, a range which, coincidentally, would encompass the indemnification being demanded by the black nationalist Republic of New Africa, a prominent black separatist group.[10]

The lower figure for Marketti's range was based on compounding interest at a 5 percent pre-Emancipation rate of return and a 3 percent post-Emancipation rate, whereas the higher figure used a 6 percent rate for the pre-Emancipation period and a 3 percent post-Emancipation rate. The 3 percent rate was chosen because it approximates the rate of growth of America's GNP between 1869 and 1967. A case could, of course, be made for using instead the prime rate of interest, which averaged about 4 percent over this period and which would have yielded a social indebtedness figure substantially higher than Marketti's figure.

Another alternative to the Marketti method which readily suggests itself would be to estimate the income flow due the slaves based on the pre-Emancipation wage rates for labor engaged in work comparable to the slaves' work, and after making a deduction for maintenance costs, to accumulate this adjusted unpaid wage bill down to the present at an appropriate compound rate of interest. A computation of the unpaid wage bill by this second method should provide an interesting comparison with the figure derived by the Marketti method. It might prove to be considerably smaller than Marketti's.

Conrad and Meyer have demonstrated that the value of the slave system to the slave owners of the Old South depended both on the returns derived from the breeding of slaves as well as from the direct labor output of the slaves.[11] Marketti's method would capture these values by its use of slave prices, whereas the latter procedure would include no specific allowance for an income from the breeding process. Clearly, there is a subtlety here which may defy resolution for, as noted in the introduction, slaves exhibited a sentimental attachment to their own bodies which fit poorly into the market calculations of that era. Although slave breeding was purely an economic activity in the perspective of the slave owners, it was probably viewed with a different perspective by the participating slaves themselves. On the other hand, had Marketti used the prices which slaves were willing to pay for their freedom instead of market prices for slaves, his figure would certainly have been much higher.

Implicit in the restitutional concept is not only the unpaid wage bill carried over from slavery but also the need for a calculation of the magnitude of the *underpayment* of freedmen and their descendants during the period since Emancipation. This calculation is likely to be more complicated than that of the unpaid wage bill, for at least three different types of practices contributed to the lower income of the black worker:

1. Lower pay to blacks for identical work performed
2. Exclusion of blacks from jobs for which they were qualified
3. Exclusion of blacks from jobs because they lacked the qualifications.

Possibly the simplest technique for arriving at a crude estimate of the cost to black people of these decades of post-Emancipation discriminatory treatment would be to compile the annual per capita earned income differential between the black and white communities over the period 1863 to 1971 and accumulate each year's differential down to the present time at an appropriate rate of compound interest. Such a procedure, by not distinguishing among the several causes for the lower black worker income, would raise the obvious objection that the former slaves had lower productivity than the general population, were more poorly educated, were concentrated in low-wage areas and occupations, and for various other reasons could not logically be expected to deserve pay scales comparable to whites. The objection may have merit for the first generation of freed slaves, but it rapidly loses its force thereafter. If the ex-slaves had, in fact, been provided the facilities to bring themselves into competitive equality with the white population, one can only assume that they would have done so. Isolated black individuals who had the good fortune to find a sympathetic white sponsor and who went on to acquire education, property, and status are irrefutable proof of what could have been accomplished.

On closer examination, disqualifying even the first generation of freedmen from entitlement to income parity with whites appears to be of dubious validity. The works of Becker, Schultz, and others have demonstrated the generous returns which can accrue from investment in human capital.[12] It might smack of double counting to demand both reimbursement for unpaid slave wages up to the date of Emancipation and then to assume instant equality with the free population the day following Emancipation, thereby ignoring the need for a period of waiting for the investment in human capital to ripen to maturity. But in reality, investment in human capital in pre–Civil War America was largely of the informal variety, requiring little outlay of funds. Slaves were generally prohibited by law from learning to read, so the constraint on their literacy was not a monetary but a legislative one. Thus, the charge of double counting would be inappropriate and a compensatory payment to equalize black and white incomes retroactive to Emancipation would appear to be an equitable means to counteract the handicap placed on the freedmen by:

1. America's refusal to permit them to make a (virtually costless) investment in themselves
2. America's refusal to provide the necessary resources to remedy this deficiency following Emancipation
3. America's discriminatory treatment of black workers even when their productivity was not inferior to that of whites.

Another major handicap borne by blacks because of their heritage of slavery and which the foregoing reparational allowances do not include arose from the slaves' legal exclusion from participating in the acquisition of the millions of acres of North America which were made available at low prices to white settlers and which provided the basis for much of the nonwage income of white America. The frontier was virtually closed by the time of Emancipation; in the ensuing decades myriad real and intangible values have been capitalized into real estate prices, so that the black man's opportunity to share equitably in the ownership of the natural resources of the continent he helped to develop has been lost to him. Only extremely high cash payments or radical land reform programs could undo this inequity—an inequity which reflects itself not only in the well-known income differential between the races but also in the extremely small percentage of America's assets which are owned by blacks.

The development of a minimal reparational formula, then, must encompass at least three elements:

1. A payment for unpaid slave labor prior to 1863
2. A payment for underpayment of black people since 1863
3. A payment to compensate for the black man's being denied the opportunity to acquire a share of America's land and natural resources when they were widely available to white settlers. A method for calculating this payment is not considered in this paper.

The first and second elements and the compound interest thereon will compensate the black community for the chronic nonpayment and underpayment for its labor and for the stock of income-earning capital which it would have accumulated over the years had its labor been compensated at market prices and had opportunities been provided for investment in the human resources of the black community comparable to the opportunities available for whites. The third element will compensate for one specific advantage which was available to early immigrants to America (and blacks were among the earliest) but from which they were deliberately excluded. It should be pointed out again that the reparations concept under examination here has focused exclusively on the compensation necessary to cover the costs bequeathed by slavery to persons now alive. The objective is to restore the black community to the economic position it would have had had it not been subjected to slavery and discrimination. No effort is being made to compensate it for the historical costs borne by its now-deceased slave ancestors in the form of reduced consumption, loss of freedom, brutality, and so on. Such costs approach infinity and are not calculable in monetary terms.

Implementation of a Reparations Payment

Space does not permit a detailed analysis of the implications of the payment of a reparations debt to the black community. A decision to honor such a claim raises immediately a host of intriguing considerations with regard to how the black community would wish the payment to be made. Some idea of the rich range of possibilities is reflected in the brief list which follows:

1. A per capita cash payment to each black American alive on a designated date based on a pro-rata share of the agreed upon reparations debt
2. Investment of the reparations payment in income-earning assets, with the income being allocated annually on a per capita basis to the surviving black American community, in perpetuity
3. Utilization of the reparations payment as funding for a massive government-sponsored program designed to raise educational and skill levels, to provide housing, and generally to improve the economic status of blacks
4. A per capita cash payment accompanied by an internationally negotiated repatriation plan with one or more African nations
5. A collective reparations payment to the black community to be used by it to create the conditions necessary for "takeoff" in the Rostovian sense
6. A territorial grant to the black community supplemented by a payment in cash or kind to assist in the building of an independent black nation in North America. (Proposals 5 and 6 would require that the black community identify a body of representatives which could act in its behalf.)

The foregoing list is obviously not exhaustive. Opportunities exist for a number of variations on these six proposals as well as for totally different conceptualizations. Some of the foregoing suggestions have already been institutionalized; others have been articulated in one form or another by various black groups. Proposal 3, for example, is suggestive of the poverty program as well as of the Freedom Budget proposed by civil rights leaders several years ago, although the sums of money were considerably below even the most modest reparations figure.

Proposal 4 was introduced into the 91st Congress on March 13, 1969, by Congressman Robert N. Nix as HR 8965, a Bill to Authorize Repatriation of Americans of African Descent. Alternative 6 constitutes the operative mechanism for implementation of the proposals to solve America's racial problems by partitioning the United States into two nations, a proposal which has attracted increasing interest in the black community in recent years and which has even been the object of one crude attempt at implementation.

The great variation in the nature of these proposals precludes detailed analysis here of them or their potential impact on either the larger society or the black subset thereof. Repatriation, proposal 4, involving a vast exodus of land, labor, and capital, would clearly have dramatic effects on the American economy. The internal capital transfers involved in proposals 1, 2, 3, and 4 would presumably have less perceptible effects for they would involve no loss of resources to the economy but merely a redistribution within the economy, a redistribution away from the heretofore favored white community and toward the black community. To the extent that it is felt necessary to disguise the redistribution effects which the repatriations payment entails, the reparations are likely to have an inflationary effect on the entire economy. To the extent that America feels able to face the redistributional need openly, via taxation, land reform, or some type of expropriation, the multibillion-dollar internal capital transfer need not seriously affect the state of the economy. Indeed, to the extent that there are macroeconomic effects, they may well be salubrious ones.

Notes

Based on a paper prepared for presentation at the American Economic Association, New Orleans, Louisiana, 28 December 1971.

1. J. Moes, "The Economics of Slavery in the Ante Bellum South: Another Comment." *Journal of Political Economy* 68 (April 1960): 183–187.

2. *State of Israel Documents* relating to the agreement between the government of Israel and the government of the Federal Republic of Germany, signed on 10 September 1952 at Luxembourg. Published by the Government Printer, for the Ministry of Foreign Affairs, Hakirya, Israel, 1953.

3. Act of August 13, 1946, Ch. 959, Sec. 1, 60 Stat. 1049.

4. Quoted from Justice Taney's opinion in the *Dred Scott* case (6 March 1857).

5. Myrdal, *An American Dilemma*.

6. Richard F. America, "A New Rationale for Income Distribution," *Review of Black Political Economy* 2, no. 2 (1972): 3–21; Daisy Collins, "The United States Owes Reparations to Its Black Citizens," *Howard Law Journal* 16 (fall 1970): 82–114; and Graham Hughes, "Reparations for Blacks?," *New York University Law Review* 43 (December 1968): 1063–1074.

7. Robert S. Starobin, *Industrial Slavery in the Old South* (New York: Oxford University Press, 1970).

8. Brian Main, "Toward the Measurement of Historic Debts," *Review of Black Political Economy* 2, no. 2 (1972): 22–42.

9. Jim Marketti, "Black Equity in the Slave Industry," *Review of Black Political Economy*, 2, no. 2 (1972): 43–66.

10. The Republic of New Africa has formulated a demand for $400 billion and five southern states — Louisiana, Mississippi, Alabama, Georgia, and South Carolina — whose capital value Marketti puts at $350 billion. It is not known exactly how the RNA arrived at the figures which it used in its demands.

11. Alfred H. Conrad and John R. Meyer, "The Economics of Slavery in the Ante Bellum South," *Journal of Political Economy* 66 (April 1958): 95–130.

12. Gary S. Becker, "Investments in Human Capital: A Theoretical Analysis," *Journal of Political Economy* Supplement 70 (October 1962): 9–49; Theodore W. Schultz, "Investment in Human Capital," *American Economic Review* 51 (March 1961): 1–17.

The Political Economy of Ending Racism and the World Conference against Racism

The Economics of Reparations

WILLIAM DARITY JR. AND DANIA FRANK

Reparations and Slavery

The U.S. government's posture at the 2001 World Conference against Racism (WCAR), where the transatlantic slave trade was declared a crime against humanity, evaded a warranted claim by African Americans for compensation for the enslavement of their ancestors. This evasive posture is anomalous in light of U.S. government support for and administration of reparations for other groups subjected to recent or historic grievous wrongs.

Indeed, the U.S. government has undertaken numerous reparations payments to Native American tribes for atrocities and treaty violations. Two examples include the 1971 grant of $1 billion and 44 million acres of land to Alaskan natives, and the 1986 grant of $32 million to the Ottawa tribe of Michigan (Benton-Lewis, 1978 [chart]). In addition, in 1990, the U.S. government issued a formal apology to Japanese Americans subjected to internment during World War Two and made a $20,000 payment to each of 60,000 identified victims (Benton-Lewis, 1978, 1).

In a non-U.S. precedent the 1952 German Wiedergatmachung established group-based indemnification for Jewish people worldwide in the aftermath of Nazi persecution. Compensation included payment of more than $800 million to "the State of Israel, on behalf of the half million victims of the Nazis who had found refuge in its borders, and the Conference on Jewish Material Claims Against Germany, on behalf of the victims of Nazi persecution who had immigrated to countries other than Israel" (Westley, 2003, 120). Thus, German reparations payments went to institutional entities (Israel and the Claims Conference), to survivors of the Holocaust who could reasonably establish specific harms or losses (e.g., property lost through confiscation), and to relatives of those killed in the concentration camps. Similar principles governed the much later payment of $25 million by the Austrian government in 1990 to Jewish claimants.

Close to 250 years of the domestic practice of enslavement of African people and their descendants has not elicited a similar response from the U.S. government. The paradox has not been lost on Westley (2003, 122):

> Blacks have never received any group compensation for the crime of slavery imposed upon them by the people and government of the United States. As in the case of the Japanese, Jews received not only material compensation for their losses, but their victimization was also publicly memorialized in Germany, Israel, and the United States (even though there was no legitimate claim of oppression or genocide that Jewish survivors of the Holocaust might assert against the United States). The only "memorial" dedicated to the suffering of Black slaves and the survivors of slavery in the United States is contained in a series of legislative enactments passed after the Civil War. The history of Black Reconstruction shows how these enactments were successively perverted by the courts, and by Congress itself.

Jim Crow Overlooked?

The WCAR's nearly exclusive focus on slavery and the slave trade neglects another compelling pillar of the case for reparations for African Americans, the practice of nearly a century of state-sanctioned apartheid in the United States. The harms of Jim Crow practices are extensive; moreover, unlike U.S. slavery, there still are living direct victims.

Particularly in the U.S. South, the post-Reconstruction period gave way to a climate of terror that allowed whites to take black lives and black-owned property with impunity. An Associated Press report documented 406 cases of black landowners who had 24,000 acres of farms and timberland stolen from them in the first three decades of the twentieth century (Lewan and Barclay, 2001).

Raymond Winbush (2003, 48) has referred to "'whitecapping' as denoting the habit of night riders who confiscated land from vulnerable Blacks during the era of Jim Crow." James Grossman (1997) reports that 239 cases were recorded in Mississippi alone between 1890 and 1910. Furthermore, perpetrators of black property theft "often colluded with local, state and even the federal government to defraud African-Americans of property.... Wholesale burning of courthouses, Black churches, and homes were common ways of destroying evidence of Black land ownership illegally obtained by white terrorists."

The process of white destruction of black wealth reached its apex in the literal annihilation of prosperous black communities in Wilmington, North Carolina, in 1898; in Tulsa, Oklahoma, in 1921; and in Rosewood, Florida, in 1923 (see Documents, section 5). Moreover, lynchings often may have conjoined the murder of blacks with property theft. Winbush speculates that the lynching trail was a trail of stolen black land, contending that lynching victims frequently were black landowners (Barclay, 2001, A3).

Today, while the black–white per capita income ratio is in the 50 percent range, the black–white wealth disparity is far wider. The highest estimates of the racial wealth ratio run in the 15 to 25 percent range (Chitegi, 1999). Since the major source of wealth for most persons today is inheritance (Blau and Graham, 1990), the reduction of black wealth during the Jim Crow era has to have played a key role in producing contemporary racial wealth differentials.

American apartheid also subjected three successive generations of African Americans to separate schools with inferior facilities and resources. Patterns of systematic residential segregation in both North and South restricted black access to neighborhood amenities, quality housing, and hospital services. Differential sentencing and punishment of blacks extending from slavery times to the present have imposed immense costs on individual blacks and on communities of black persons (Betsey, 2001).

Employment discrimination further has constrained the opportunity of blacks to transform their skills and credentials into incomes comparable with whites with similar levels of attainment. Moreover, a recent study using IPUMS (Integrated Public Use Microdata Series) Census data (Darity, Dietrich, and Guilkey, 2001) showed that both labor market discrimination and imposed schooling deficits faced by blacks in the interval 1880 to 1910 significantly weigh down the occupational attainment of their descendants in 1980 and 1990, a century later. Furthermore, current labor market discrimination continues to penalize black earners (Darity et al., 2001), affording a further justification for reparations.

Economics and Reparations

Given the suitability of reparations to compensate blacks for having been subjected to slavery, Jim Crow practices, and ongoing discrimination, economics can provide useful insights in determining (1) eligibility for reparations, (2) types of reparations programs, (3) the long-term effects of reparations, (4) methods of financing reparations, and (5) the magnitude of reparations.

The moral-hazard principle alerts us to potential problems in establishing criteria for eligibility for receipt of African American reparations. Reparations would create a premium for being black in America that previously did not exist. Thus, individuals who had not previously self-identified as black suddenly will have an incentive to declare their African ancestry. To mitigate this problem, we propose two criteria for eligibility: (1) individuals would have to provide reasonable documentation that they had at least one ancestor who was enslaved in the United States, and (2) individuals would have to demonstrate that at least ten years prior to the onset of the reparations program they self-identified as black, African American, colored, or Negro on a legal document.

Economics also leads us to contemplate a reparations program taking a number of forms, none mutually exclusive. One approach would be lump-sum payments to eligible individual African Americans. A second approach would be establishment of a trust fund to which eligible blacks could apply for grants for various asset-building projects, including homeownership, additional education, or start-up funds for self-employment. A third option would be the provision of vouchers that could be used for asset-building purposes, including the purchase of financial assets. Thus, reparations could function as an avenue to undertake a racial redistribution of wealth akin to the mechanism used in Malaysia to build corporate ownership among the native Malays. A fourth approach would be reparations in kind (e.g., guaranteed schooling beyond the high school level or medical insurance). A fifth approach would be use of reparations to build entirely new institutions to promote collective well-being in the black community.

The venerable transfer problem (Keynes, 1929; Johnson, 1955) in international trade theory provides a warning that reparations payments to blacks need not have the long-term effect of closing the racial income or wealth gap. In an extended theoretical inquiry (Darity and Frank, 2002), we examine how different methods of reparations payments to African Americans will affect the black and nonblack populations in the United States. We find that reparations payments that either mandate or provide incentives for blacks to spend on goods and services produced by nonblacks will raise the relative incomes of nonblacks. Without significant productive capacity in place prior to reparations, a lump-sum payment actually could result in an absolute decline in black income. Thus, the structure of a reparations program is critical if it is to close the black–white economic gap in the United States.

How are reparations to be financed? Public finance theory suggests that nonblacks could finance the transfer by paying additional taxes, borrowing (dissaving), or lowering their spending. Alternatively, the United States could borrow by issuing government bonds to finance the reparations program. In general, African Americans should not bear the tax burden of financing their own reparations payments. Blacks paid local, state, and federal taxes for more than eighty years while being disenfranchised in the U.S. South, a paradigmatic case of "taxation without representation." If, however, taxes are levied universally to finance reparations, guarantees must be put in place that the reparations payment net of the tax is substantial for black taxpayers. Furthermore, reparations income should be tax-free.

Finally, economic analysis can be mobilized to establish the magnitude of the reparations payment. Contributors to Richard America's (1990) *Wealth of Races* used a variety of procedures to calculate the debt owed to blacks for slavery. Roger Ransom and Richard Sutch computed the difference between the market value of slaves net of food, shelter, and other consumption over the last fifty years of slavery, which led them to an estimate of $3.4 billion by 1860. Larry Neal used a similar measure of unpaid wages to slaves between 1620 and 1840 compounded at 3 percent to 1983 dollars to reach a figure of $1.4 trillion. James Marketti's estimate of Africans' income forgone via slavery came to a present value estimate by 1983 of $3 to $5 trillion. Richard Vedder et al. sought to estimate the accumulated gains in wealth to white southerners from ownership of enslaved blacks to arrive at a bill of $3.2 million as of 1859. In current dollars these procedures generally lend themselves to present-value estimates in the range of $5 to $10 trillion for the debt for slavery.

These numbers do not take into account the costs of Jim Crow or the costs of present discrimination. Estimates by David Swinton and by Gerald Chachere and Bernadette Chachere of the costs of labor market discrimination during the forty-year period 1929 to 1969 alone run between $500 billion and $1.6 trillion in 1983 dollars. Suffice it to say, the damages to the collective well-being of black people have been enormous, and correspondingly, so is the appropriate bill.

References

America, Richard F. *The Wealth of Races: The Present Value of Benefits from Past Injustices.* Westport, Conn.: Greenwood Press, 1990.

Barclay, Dolores. "Torn from the Land: The Lynching Trail." *Sunday Herald-Sun* (Durham, N.C.), 2 December 2001, A1, A3.

Benton-Lewis, Dorothy. *Black Reparations NOW!* Rockville, Md.: Black Reparations Press, 1978.

Betsey, Charles. "Income and Wealth Transfer Effects of Discrimination in Sentencing." Paper presented at the National Economic Association meeting, New Orleans, January 2001.

Blau, Francine, and John Graham. "Black–White Differences in Wealth and Asset Composition." *Quarterly Journal of Economics* 105, no. 2 (May 1990): 321–339.

Chachere, Gerald, and Bernadette Chachere. "An Illustrative Estimate: The Present Value of the Benefits from Racial Discrimination, 1929–1969." In Richard America, ed., *The Wealth of Races: The Present Value of Benefits from Past Injustices*. Westport, Conn.: Greenwood Press, 1990.

Chiteji, Ngina. "Wealth Holding and Financial Marketplace Participation in Black America." *African-American Research Perspectives* 5, no. 1 (fall 1999): 16–24.

Darity, William, Jr., Jason Dietrich, and David Guilkey. "Persistent Advantage or Disadvantage: Evidence in Support of the Intergenerational Drag Hypothesis." *American Journal of Economics and Sociology* 60, no, 2 (April 2001): 435–470.

Darity, William, Jr., and Dania Frank. "Reparations for African Americans as a Transfer Problem." Unpublished manuscript, Duke University, August 2002.

Grossman, James. *A Chance to Make Good: African-Americans, 1900–1929*. New York: Oxford University Press, 1997.

Johnson, Harry G. "The Transfer Problem: A Note on the Criteria for Changes in the Terms of Trade." *Economica* 22, no. 86 (May 1955): 113–121.

Keynes, J. M. "The German Transfer Problem." *Economic Journal* 39, no. 153 (March 1929): 1–7.

Lewan, Todd, and Dolores Barclay. "Inquiry: Black Landowners Cheated." *Sunday Herald-Sun* (Durham, N.C.), 9 December 2001, A3.

Marketti, James. "Estimated Present Value of Income Diverted During Slavery." In Richard F. America, ed., *The Wealth of Races: The Present Value of Benefits from Past Injustices*. Westport, Conn.: Greenwood Press, 1990.

Neal, Larry. "A Calculation and Comparison of the Current Benefits of Slavery and an Analysis of Who Benefits." In Richard F. America, ed., *The Wealth of Races: The Present Value of Benefits from Past Injustices*. Westport, Conn.: Greenwood Press, 1990.

Ransom, Roger, and Richard Sutch. "Who Pays for Slavery?" In Richard F. America, ed., *The Wealth of Races: The Present Value of Benefits from Past Injustices*. Westport, Conn.: Greenwood Press, 1990.

Swinton, David. "Racial Inequality and Reparations." In Richard F. America, ed., *The Wealth of Races: The Present Value of Benefits from Past Injustices*. Westport, Conn.: Greenwood Press, 1990.

Vedder, Richard, Lowell Gallaway, and David Klingaman. "Black Exploitation and White Benefits: The Civil War Income Revolution." In Richard F. America, ed., *The Wealth of Races: The Present Value of Benefits from Past Injustices*. Westport, Conn.: Greenwood Press, 1990.

Westley, Robert. "Many Billions Gone: Is It Time to Reconsider the Case for Reparations?" In Raymond Winbush, ed., *Should America Pay? Slavery and the Raging Debate over Reparations*. New York: Harper Collins, 2003.

Winbush, Raymond. "The Earth Moved: Stealing Black Land in the United States." In Raymond Winbush, ed., *Should America Pay? Slavery and the Raging Debate over Reparations*. New York: Harper Collins, 2003.

The Rise of the Reparations Movement

MARTHA BIONDI

Reparations — for the transatlantic slave trade, slavery, sexual slavery, genocide, colonialism, apartheid, disfranchisement, and the multiple other forms of racial discrimination and exploitation — has surged to the forefront of antiracist advocacy in the black world, particularly in the United States. It offers an innovative and compelling way to move beyond inadequate and besieged civil rights discourses, to revive black-led global anticapitalist and anti-imperialist projects, and to radically intervene in the discourse of globalization. Indeed, in light of the expansion of international juridical forums and precedents, the recent rise of reparations is inseparable from the rise of globalization. The philosophical and tactical brilliance of reparations lies in its synthesis of moral principles and political economy. If the crimes and depredations inflicted on African nations and African descendants over centuries have relied on strategies of dehumanization in the service of power, profit, and conquest, then the efforts to identify, halt, and redress them must insist on explicit acknowledgment and repudiation of such strategies, alongside comprehensive material efforts to indemnify them. Rather than a retreat into narrow nationalism, as many have cast(igated) it, reparations represents the culmination of a long African American human rights struggle.

The biggest achievement in the rapidly growing reparations movement was the 2001 (finalized in 2002) declaration of the United Nations World Conference against Racism, Racial Discrimination, Xenophobia, and Related Intolerance that "slavery and the transatlantic slave trade are a crime against humanity." This document vindicates the long labors of Ida B. Wells, W. E. B. Du Bois, Monroe Trotter, Marcus Garvey, Paul Robeson, Mary McLeod Bethune, William Patterson, Audley Moore, Malcolm X, Huey Newton, and Imari Obadele to use international bodies and the collective power of African and Asian nations to force the West to confront its own history. In the United States, the World Conference against Racism has drawn heightened attention to reparations initiatives already under way. The Reparations Coordinating

Committee (RCC) and the National Coalition of Blacks for Reparations in America (N'COBRA), working on behalf of 35 million American descendants of enslaved Africans, are preparing to file class action lawsuits against agencies of the federal and state governments. Reparations litigation against private corporations alleged to have profited from slavery has already begun. On March 25, 2002, in a U.S. district court in Brooklyn, Deadria Farmer-Paellmann and other plaintiffs filed suit against Aetna Life Insurance Corporation, FleetBoston Financial Services, and CSX Incorporated, a railroad giant, on the grounds that they "knowingly benefited from a system that enslaved, tortured, starved and exploited human beings."[1]

Still, reparations are not a new demand in African American advocacy. In the nineteenth century, many former slaves expressed the view that the slave system constituted a theft of labor, life, and liberty that demanded an accounting. After the Civil War, landownership constituted a major goal of the former slaves who strongly supported the confiscation, division, and redistribution of large plantations. There were several federal attempts to do this, the most famous being General Sherman's Field Order No. 15, which divided plantations along the Atlantic Coast into forty-acre parcels to be distributed to 40,000 emancipated workers. However, these efforts to construct a foundation for a free labor system in the South — which were not necessarily motivated by a desire to compensate the former slaves for expropriated labor — were later reversed or defeated. In contrast, many slaveholders received compensation for the loss of their slave "property." The U.S. government compensated slave owners on the abolition of slavery in the District of Columbia, and Haiti was forced to pay $150 million in compensation to the French after it achieved independence.

The federal government's betrayal of a promise to transfer land to the former slaves became a foundational story in the oral history of Reconstruction passed down in black families and communities into the twentieth century. Deadria Farmer-Paellmann — the lead plaintiff in the class action lawsuit against Aetna and the researcher who discovered that the company had written life insurance policies on human property — said, "My grandfather always talked about the forty acres and a mule which we were never given." In his 1960s song "Forty Acres and a Mule," Oscar Brown Jr. reminded his listeners that "ain't nobody paid for slavery yet, we had a promise that was taken back."[2]

With northern migration and urbanization, land receded as a primary demand, but the belief that the United States owed a debt to the descendants of enslaved Africans animated twentieth-century black protest and was a much more visible theme in the civil rights/black liberation movement than historical accounts generally acknowledge (see Documents, section 4). In 1955, Audley Moore, a Harlem activist originally from Louisiana, founded the Reparations Committee of Descendants of United States Slaves. "Queen Mother" Moore pioneered grass-roots education on reparations and for the next three decades dedicated herself to spreading the message among black activists and intellectuals. She planted the seed in a young Charles Ogletree Jr. when he was seated next to her on a flight to Tanzania. Currently a professor at Harvard Law School, Ogletree co-chairs the RCC with Adjoa Aiyetoro and Randall Robinson. In his 1963 book, *Why We Can't Wait*, Martin Luther King Jr. argued that the United States owed social and economic compensation to black America for the wrongs of slavery and segregation and vowed to make this the next goal of the black freedom struggle. The A. Philip Randolph Institute lobbied Congress for what it called a Freedom Budget, and the National Urban League advocated a "Marshall Plan for Black America," remedies that embodied the spirit of reparations by insisting on the government's obligation to financially repair the group harm caused by institutionalized racism. The 1969 *Black Manifesto* by James Forman, a leader of the Student Nonviolent Coordinating Committee, demanded reparations in the form of a southern land bank, publishing houses, television networks, universities, and skills training centers. Forman envisioned reparations as an opportunity to reverse the consequences of racial capitalism and promote thoroughgoing social and economic development in black America.[3]

Reparations has long been a goal for a range of U.S. black nationalist groups, usually in concert with the quest for territory and political self-determination. In the late nineteenth century, Henry McNeal Turner, a prominent AME Bishop, critic of U.S. imperialism, and advocate of African American emigration to Africa, called for $40 billion in reparations for slavery. Beginning in the 1940s, the Nation of Islam urged reparations for slavery and called on the federal government to cede several southern states to become the territory of an African American nation. In 1968, the Republic of New Africa called for reparations in tandem with its insistence that neither the former slaves nor their descendants had ever been given the option of imagining themselves as an independent nation. The Black Panther Party shared this view and put its own call for reparations alongside a demand for a UN-sponsored plebiscite in which black people could express a position on their national aspirations. Personifying the links between past and present reparations advocacy, Imari Obadele, one of the founders of the Republic of New Africa, also cofounded N'COBRA in 1988, currently the largest grassroots reparations organization in the United States.[4]

The contemporary reparations struggle also builds on two hallmarks of the black radical tradition: an economic analysis of white supremacy and the use of global solidarity networks and international forums to define national racisms as a violation of international human rights protocols. Black farmers, who filed a class action lawsuit in 1999 against the U.S. Department of Agriculture for discriminatory lending that caused the loss of their land, call their struggle "economic human rights," a phrase that captures the essence of the reparations struggle as well. In the last few years of his life, King came to emphasize what W. E. B. Du Bois had underscored earlier, namely, that legal and political rights would not bring racial equality unless they were accompanied by a confrontation with the economic dimension of white supremacy past and present. Each argued that the fruits of slave labor and subsequent black labor exploitation nurtured American capitalism, which remained hostile to black economic development. Like some other African American antiracist activists who started out as integrationists, they each came to argue that the U.S. political economy needed a fundamental transformation in order to value black humanity and create the conditions for black economic empowerment.

Similarly, reparations builds on a long tradition of black internationalism and pan-Africanist organizing. After World War One, W. E. B. Du Bois organized a pan-African congress in Paris to exert influence on the Paris peace talks. Since World War Two, several African American rights groups have filed petitions seeking UN intervention in the United States to halt the systematic violation of the human rights of black people (see Documents, section 4). Malcolm X's preference for "human rights" over "civil rights" reflected his efforts to politically connect black Americans to a global history of slavery and slave trading and guided his attempts to gain the solidarity of African nations for a petition to the United Nations. Reparations, in short, is neither foreign nor marginal to African American political advocacy. It has been championed most visibly and consistently by black nationalists, yet liberals and leftists, too, have supported remedies and analyses that embody the spirit of reparations.

Still, the reparations movement has never enjoyed greater popularity among African Americans or mainstream black leadership than now, 138 years after the official end of slavery. A variety of developments accounts for its growing appeal. An important context for the rise of the reparations movement is the growing number of national and international settlements in which governments or corporations have been made to atone for and/or compensate a group they knowingly victimized, murdered, deprived of liberty or property, or otherwise wronged. In 1988, Congress granted an apology and compensation to the survivors and relatives of Japanese Americans imprisoned in concentration camps during the Second World War. This had a significant impact on African American organizing, sparking the formation of N'COBRA. A year after the Japanese American settlement, John Conyers, a U.S. representative from Michigan, introduced HR 40, a bill calling for the federal government to study the impact of slavery and make recommendations for reparations to the 35 million American descendants (see Documents, section 1). In 1994, the state of Florida agreed to pay reparations to the survivors of the 1923 Rosewood massacre, and in 1993, Congress formally apologized for the U.S. conquest of Hawaii and the deprivation of sovereignty (see Documents, section 5). These cases indicate the government's willingness to financially repair past injustices motivated by racial hatred, although the Rosewood and Japanese internment cases differ from the slavery case because they grant compensation to individual victims with a demonstrated link to the injustice.[5]

Internationally, many precedents for reparations exist. The German government and private corporations have paid $65.2 billion to survivors of the death camps and forced laborers during the Holocaust. Germany has also paid reparations to the state of Israel, a redress that resembles the African American case somewhat, since the reparation is not made to actual victims of the Holocaust but to Jews collectively through the state of Israel. More recent cases against corporations for using slave laborers in wartime Germany won large settlements and have inspired similar litigation in the United States. In recent years, several countries, including Argentina and South Africa, have established commissions to investigate the injury and harms inflicted during apartheid or periods of military dictatorship. In contrast, the United States has never authorized an examination of this nation's participation in the enslavement of Africans and the segregation and labor exploitation of their descendants. There is neither a national slavery museum nor a memorial to the millions who perished in the transatlantic slave trade.[6]

A second major reason for the rise of the reparations movement is the growing African American conviction that until the United States confronts the full scope of harms inflicted on enslaved Africans and their descendants, genuine healing and racial justice will remain impossible. The assault on the gains of the civil rights era, combined with a growing sense that these very gains are insufficient tools to unmask and defeat white privilege, has sparked a reassessment of the goals and strategies of the racial justice movement. The backlash has been overwhelming, and undertaken by all branches of government. The right, joined in some instances by liberals in the Democratic Party, has targeted affirmative action, voting rights, defendant's rights, civil liberties, welfare, public housing, and public education. While the rise of the reparations movement is connected to this backlash, it is revisionary rather than defensive. It forges new ground — both in theory and practice — to address the legacy of slavery in the United States. Reparations changes the discursive image of African Americans from victims to creditors and revises the dominant narrative of American social, political, and economic history in order to emphasize the debt owed to African Americans. While the civil rights era called for moral change, overcoming personal prejudice, and making official practices consistent with "the American creed," reparation makes us rethink what drove racial domination in the United States. It underscores that white supremacy did not arise from ignorance or personal antipathies, but from the pursuit of wealth, power, land, tobacco, sugar, cotton, silver, railroads, and cheap labor. This shifts the paradigm of antiracist struggle away from African Americans as supplicants "asking for concessions" toward seeking what is properly due to the descendants of slaves. It also builds the basis for more fundamental transformations not only in black socioeconomic status but in how Americans understand class formation in the past and present. One reason that reparations elicits such emotional opposition from many Euro-Americans is that it poses an ideological challenge to the dominant American mythology that has served them so well: it questions the Horatio Alger narrative of upward mobility that American culture promotes in order to rationalize social inequality.

Moreover, political activism against the criminal (in)justice system has shone light on the fact that fifty years after the Voting Rights Act, 13 percent of adult black men have permanently lost the right to vote due to felony convictions, and the numbers are increasing. The roots of this phenomenon actually go back to the political repression following Reconstruction. In Florida, a law disfranchising felons was one way the state circumvented the Fifteenth Amendment and took the ballot away from former slaves and their descendants. In sum, the civil rights movement did not address the untold loss of life, liberty, personhood, culture, language, labor, and wages during slavery. Its goal of ending de jure segregation simply constituted a beginning. A reparations commission could uncover and publicize the historical and structural roots of racial disparities in order to illustrate that resources and opportunities were intentionally and systematically denied to black Americans for generations. Such a process can help point the way toward a remedy and underscore the justness of it.

According to the legal scholar Adrienne D. Davis, innovative reparations litigation can propel the process of moving beyond exhausted and defeated civil rights strategies (see Davis, part 5). The Thirteenth Amendment, she argues, offers unexplored pathways to an emancipatory jurisprudence. A case that relies on the Thirteenth Amendment's prohibition of slavery and its vestiges can get around the color-blind jurisprudence that has captured Fourteenth Amendment litigation. The Thirteenth Amendment, with its very specific connection to enslaved Africans and their descendants, is expressly authorized to focus on racial harms. Moreover, it can authorize federal redress of economic harms, which up to now have been excluded from federal remedy by Fourteenth Amendment case law. Finally, the Thirteenth Amendment does not prohibit a dual attack on private and public acts of discrimination and thus can overcome the Fourteenth Amendment's failure to protect African descendants from private acts of racial harm.[7]

The success of reparations seems dependent on the ability of its advocates to change public consciousness about slavery and segregation. As a retired teacher in Washington, D.C., observed, "At one time I thought that slavery should be forgotten. But I've changed my mind. Our families worked and got nothing."[8] The movement is propelled by the belief that public support will grow as more and more research and data come into public view. Indeed, the rise of the movement is inspiring a range of new scholarship and investigative journalism. Last year, a graduate student study of Yale University disclosed that its origins — including its first endowed scholarship, first endowed professorship, and first endowed library fund — were financed with moneys earned from the slave trade. Moreover, nine of the ten men for whom the prestigious residential colleges at Yale are named owned slaves. *USA Today* and the Associated Press have each conducted pathbreaking investigations into corporate ties to slavery and the theft of black-owned land in the Jim Crow South. Likewise, the *Hartford Courant* devoted an entire issue of its Sunday magazine and an interactive Web site to a comprehensive study of slavery in Connecticut, which educators across the state have begun using.[9]

The reparations push parallels shifts in the nature of scholarship on racial inequality, which emphasizes that Euro-American wealth has come at the expense of African Americans and reveals the culpability of the state. Works on the New Deal state emphasize the exclusions of African Americans from many social programs. When the federal government began to subsidize homeownership, laying the basis for the huge expansion of the middle class, it used a practice called redlining which explicitly labeled black or mixed neighborhoods as bad risks and made them ineligible for loans. Banks also adopted this practice, creating a powerful obstacle to black access to homeownership. Similarly, the pension system created in the Depression intentionally deprived African Americans of benefits that whites received. Social security initially excluded the occupations of agricultural workers and domestic service, precisely because these were the occupations that most African Americans held. Until as recently as 1997, the U.S. Department of Agriculture had a close to zero approval rate for loans to black farmers. Racial preferences in government programs gave whites a big head start in accumulating and passing down assets to their children[10] (see Brown et al. and Oliver and Shapiro, both in part 1).

The fight for reparations is being waged in domestic and international arenas, and with multiple weapons: legislative, legal, and grassroots education. Many advocates think that like the Japanese American internment claim, the claim for reparations to African Americans will ultimately be heard and settled in Congress. The number of congressional supporters of HR 40, first introduced in 1989, has grown, but the bill has never made it out of the Judiciary Committee. Polls show that African Americans strongly support HR 40, and all the major civil rights organizations have endorsed it, including the NAACP, the Southern Christian Leadership Conference, the Rainbow PUSH Coalition, and the Leadership Conference for Civil Rights. In addition, two major international human rights organizations, Africa Action and Human Rights Watch, have also endorsed the call for reparations. In an effort to increase popular support and build pressure on members of Congress, a grassroots reparations movement has developed to urge passage of city and state resolutions calling for congressional action. Chicago passed such a resolution two years ago, as have Baltimore; Dallas; Nashville; Cleveland; Detroit; Evanston, Illinois; and the state of California (see Documents, section 3). During the mobilization in Evanston, the area's congressional representative Jan Schakowsy announced her support for HR 40, exemplifying what the municipal resolution strategy aims to achieve.

Given the Republican Party's success over the last two decades in pushing the federal bench to the right, there is much uncertainty about the fate of reparations litigation. Moreover, competing theories exist on the most appropriate legal arguments and strategy as well as the best ways to achieve standing, overcome the sovereign immunity of the U.S. statute of limitations and the legality of slavery, and other issues. A federal judge's dismissal of a reparations suit against the federal government in 1995 on the grounds that the United States cannot be sued in tort for slavery prompted Deadria Farmer-Paellmann to focus on corporate defendants. Her highly publicized discovery of an Aetna insurance policy issued on the life of a slave has sparked broader investigation of the role that profits from slavery played in laying the foundation for modern American corporate wealth. It also propelled a new round of state and local legislative initiatives. In 2001, California passed a law requiring insurance companies doing business in the state to report information on slaveholder policies (see Documents, section 2). In

August 2002, the Chicago city council passed an ordinance requiring all enterprises conducting business with the city to disclose any profits they might have made from slavery. It will be interesting to assess the reaction of railway giant CSX, which is currently a defendant in a reparations lawsuit and has a major contract with the city of Chicago. The historian Theodore Kornweibel is at work on a study of the use of enslaved labor by antebellum railroads, and he has thus far identified thirty-six lines owned by CSX built by enslaved workers (see Kornweibel, part 4).

The litigation filed in March 2002 against Aetna, Fleet, and CSX has been consolidated with litigation filed in California, Louisiana, Illinois, Texas, and New Jersey and assigned to federal judge Charles Ronald Norgle in Chicago, a Reagan appointee. In Louisiana, over 3,000 named plaintiffs filed a class action lawsuit in September against Brown Brothers Harriman, Aetna, Lloyd's of London, Liggett Group, Brown and Williamson, R. J. Reynolds, the Loews Corporation, and four railroads: CSX, Canadian National, Norfolk Southern, and Union Pacific. In San Francisco, a complaint was filed in a state court in September against Fleet, Aetna, Lloyd's of London, New York Life Insurance. R. J. Reynolds, Brown and Williamson, Loews, and the Canadian National Railway Company. Just as in many of the cases against corporations using slave labor during the Nazi era, lawyers and advocates hope that the litigation, or threat of it, will induce these corporations to make settlements and offer apologies. Reparations advocates also view this litigation as a means to advance HR 40. The media exposure and educational campaigns stimulated by the litigation have raised national awareness of the reparations claim, and activists hope this will gradually build pressure on Congress to step in and make a comprehensive reparations settlement.

There is also litigation not explicitly about "reparations" but closely related to the reparations movement. As a result of a class action lawsuit, *Thompson v. Metropolitan Life Insurance Co.*, Met Life recently agreed to a settlement with its African American policyholders, or their descendants, who were paid lower premiums based on race. This settlement will likely spur more cases. In general, as our knowledge of the extent of thefts and appropriation during the slavery and Jim Crow eras grows, racial justice efforts will increasingly shift toward economic redress.

Despite the publicity and new research generated by the corporate litigation, many reparations activists believe the heart of this struggle must be a confrontation with the U.S. government, whose offices and officials actively encouraged, abetted, and condoned the institution of slavery. Two major groups are preparing litigation against state and federal governments, N'COBRA and the RCC; N'COBRA will file a series of federal lawsuits—the first will focus on the criminal justice system — while the RCC is evidently ready to file its cases soon. These cases, however, will remain steeped in secrecy until they are filed.

Like every single previous movement for racial justice in the United States, reparation has legions of critics. Many skeptics zero in on the question of a remedy — imagining it as impractical due the scope of the injury, or as a political minefield whose implications and price tag are destined to inflame whites. But these objections simply describe the enormity of the task rather than delegitimize it. Reparations advocates and attorneys argue, logically, that the remedy will flow from the nature of the injury, which powerfully underlines the importance of collecting as much documentation, history, and data as possible. In this respect, historians and other scholars have never proven so valuable to a social movement. Nevertheless, a variety of creative proposals have been suggested. Some activists have proposed that a reparations settlement be administered through a trust in order to ensure economic and educational development. Some leaders have called for free education or health care, debt relief, tax relief, or other in-kind transfers. To be sure, the outcome and remedy will indicate the sincerity of the process.

The United Nations has emerged as an extraordinary stage for the reparations movement. Over a decade of advocacy and organizing at the UN Human Rights Commission by (among other African American groups) the December 12th Movement led the United Nations to convene the World Conference against Racism, Racial Discrimination, Xenophobia, and Related Intolerance in Durban, South Africa, in September 2001. There had been other UN world conferences, including one on human rights in Vienna in 1993 and on the status of women in Beijing in 1996. In 1997, the lobbying of several African, Asian, Latin American, and Caribbean nations secured a commitment by the UN for a world conference against racism. In planning meetings, the African Descendants Caucus brought together reparations activists from across the diaspora, including representatives from many U.S. groups: the December 12th Movement, N'COBRA, All for Reparations and Emancipation — a group associated with the Lost/Found Nation of Islam — the Black Radical Congress, and the National Black United Front (NBUF). They formulated an agenda for Durban that stressed three goals: to characterize the institution of slavery and the transatlantic slave trade as crimes against humanity (crimes against humanity have no statute of limitations in international law); to assert the economic motive of white supremacy; and to call for reparations. From the earliest preparatory stages, the United States and the European Union worked aggressively to contain the political reach of the World Conference against Racism — indeed, the words "xenophobia and related intolerance" were added as a concession to the West; the conference was originally intended to have an exclusive focus on Africa and African descendants.

The December 12th Movement and NBUF helped to organize the African American NGOs contingent to the World Conference against Racism, which became known as the Durban 400. Fully cognizant of U.S. and E.U. opposition to their agenda, the Durban 400 aggressively lobbied African, Asian, and Latin American nations to support it. When it became clear that getting a call for reparations into the document was unlikely, the Durban 400 focused on having slavery and the transatlantic slave trade declared crimes against humanity. Gaining the support of the forty-five African nations present proved decisive. Some nations, like Senegal and Zimbabwe, were very supportive from the beginning, but Nigeria and South Africa proved harder to persuade, although they ultimately endorsed it. Evidently, South Africa, whose economic development strategy relies heavily on Western investment, feared alienating the United States.

Representatives of the U.S. government opposed the designation of transatlantic slavery as "a crime against humanity" as well as the effort to include a call for reparations in the final document. The United States threatened to boycott Durban and ultimately only sent lower-level officials, who subsequently engaged in a highly publicized walkout. The United States and Israel had also protested efforts by Middle Eastern nations to characterize the Israeli treatment of Palestinians as akin to colonial conquest and occupation. The mainstream media coverage of the U.S. walkout tended to characterize it as a principled pro-Israeli act, rather than as a cowardly retreat from confronting the history and legacy of slavery.

In the end, the Durban Declaration and Programme of Action signed by 168 nations declared that slavery and the transatlantic slave trade "are crimes against humanity," a determination that reparations advocates hope will make the United States more vulnerable in legal action. One caveat is that the document modifies this assertion with the clause "and should always have been so, especially the transatlantic slave trade." This constitutes an apparent concession to those who argue that slavery was widespread and "lawful" in many parts of the world and is seen as a crime against humanity only in retrospect. Even though the Programme of Action failed to include advocacy of reparations, activists still view it as an extremely important achievement. Despite the U.S. walkout, and the country's failure to sign the document, the World Conference against Racism pushed the issue of reparations irrevocably into international political and media discourse. Moreover, reparations remains a hot-button issue for the body created by the United Nations to implement the results of the conference: the Working Group of Experts on People of African Descent Living in the Diaspora. This working group, whose stature and seriousness remain unclear, is charged with considering the means to eliminate racial discrimination.

Reparations advocates hope to develop and institutionalize the transnational organizing and solidarity that proved so effective at the World Conference against Racism. Toward this end, the African and African Descendant NGO Follow-Up Conference convened in October 2002 in Bridgetown, Barbados, drawing six hundred people. The conference began on a note of controversy when a delegation from the United Kingdom offered a resolution to expel the twenty or so non-African descendants in attendance — reportedly a diverse group which included a Euro- and Asian American couple making a documentary on reparations, a Lebanese activist who came to offer solidarity from the Palestinian struggle, and several white Barbadians working as official translators. After a long debate, conferees passed the resolution, but a few delegations walked out in protest, including the one from Cuba. The varying perspectives on the expulsion shed light on the strains that can arise in a movement that includes a variety of ideological tendencies. Some activists expressed concern that the expulsion would stigmatize the reparations movement as "hypernationalist." They emphasized the urgency of repairing the rifts, particularly with the Cubans, who have a long record of support for African American and African liberation struggles. Yet others have argued that the attention to this issue has been excessive and have defended the expulsion on the grounds that only Africans and African descendants had been invited. The conference generated the Bridgetown Protocols and the creation of a new organization, the Global Afrikan Congress, whose mission is to implement them.[11]

The movement for reparations in other nations has also grown in recent years, although not quite as quickly or as broadly as it has in the United States. A major turning point in the development of support for reparations by African nations was the 1993 Abuja Proclamation sponsored by the Organization of African Unity's Reparations Commission. Many activists in Africa identify debt cancellation as an essential first step in reparations. The U.S. human rights organization Africa Action has condemned the "illegitimate, immoral and crippling foreign debt that African countries owe to the wealthy white countries and the international institutions that represent their economic interests." Every year, forty-eight countries in sub-Saharan Africa pay $13.5 billion to "rich foreign creditors for past loans of questionable legitimacy."[12]

As in the United States, activists in other nations are using litigation against both corporations and nation-states to redress colonialism, slavery, and the slave trade. In Jamaica, attorneys have begun filing what will be a series of lawsuits against European nations in order to recover wealth acquired through the slave trade. They recently filed a case against the British monarchy and served a writ on the queen of England when she visited Jamaica this past year. Litigation will follow against France, Germany, and Belgium, and later against Spain and Portugal. In Namibia, the Herrero ethnic group filed a lawsuit against three German corporations for genocide committed against their ancestors during German colonial rule. The Democratic Republic of Congo has charged Belgium with genocide for the slaughter of millions during a ruthless colonial regime as well as for the assassination of independence leader Patrice Lumumba.[13]

The strategy of corporate litigation has taken off in South Africa, much to the concern of the government, which worries about alienating Western investors. Ed Fagan, an attorney who won a settlement from Swiss banks for victims of the Jewish Holocaust, has filed suit against a variety of corporations on behalf of victims of apartheid. Additionally, in November 2002, two activist groups in South Africa filed suit in a U.S. federal court against twenty global corporations for allegedly encouraging human rights abuses by doing business in apartheid South Africa. The companies ignored a boycott of Pretoria called by the United Nations and supplied the apartheid regime with loans and markets. The litigation, which seeks billions from oil companies, automakers, and banks, reflects, in part, the slowness of the Truth and Reconciliation Commission in awarding their extremely small pledges of reparations. Reflecting the clash between post-apartheid social justice aspirations and the triumph of a market-oriented regime, the South African justice minister Penuell Maduna said, "We are not supporting the claims for individual reparations. We are talking to those very same companies named in the lawsuits about investing in post-apartheid South Africa." The government, however, is not taking a formal position on the litigation.[14]

As the reparations movement stands poised to intensify with the imminent federal litigation, some progressives have raised concerns about the movement's progress toward achieving its post-Durban aim of creating a "critical mass demand for reparations" and expanding the movement's base to reach all sectors of the African American community. The high-profile participation of attorneys new to the reparations movement has alienated some veteran activists. One journalist quipped that the Millions for Reparations Rally in Washington, D.C., in August 2002 constituted an effort by nationalists to recapture leadership of the movement.[15] Perhaps, inevitably, some ideological strains have accompanied the expansion of the movement. Unity and coordination, however, will prove urgent for organizing successful mass demonstrations or other grassroots mobilizations. Finally, the particular exploitation of black women has remained undertheorized and underdiscussed in the movement, although this can be overcome. Will, for example, the pending litigation address sexual slavery or the abuses of the reproductive liberty of African American women since emancipation? According to reparations activists, the primary challenge for the movement lies less in finding the foolproof legal argument or locating the best jurisdiction than in building grassroots support for reparations, both in the United States and around the world.

Notes

1. Corey Dade, "Fleet, 2 Other Firms Sued over Slavery," *Boston Globe Online*, 27 March 2002, www.boston.com/globe.

2. Herb Boyd, "Three Major Corporations Hit with Class Action Lawsuit," *Black World Today*, 31 March 2002, www.tbwt.com.

3. Charles Ogletree Jr., speech to the National Reparations Convention, 23 March 2002, DePaul University, Chicago; Martin Luther King Jr., *Why We Can't Wait* (New York: Penguin Putnam, 2000); Dona C. Hamilton and Charles V. Hamilton, *The Dual Agenda: Race and Social-Welfare Policies of Civil Rights Organizations* (New York: Columbia University Press, 1997); James Forman, *The Making of Black Revolutionaries* (Washington, D.C.: Open Hand, 1985).

4. Robert C. Smith, "Imari Obadele: The Father of the Modern Reparations Movement," www.africana.com.

5. Charles J. Ogletree Jr., "Litigating the Legacy of Slavery," *New York Times*, 31 March 2002.

6. For an examination of national and international precedents, see Robert Westley, "Many Billions Gone: Is It Time to Reconsider the Case for Black Reparations," *Boston College Law Review* 429 (1998): 40.

7. Adrienne D. Davis, "The Case for United States Reparations to African Americans," *Human Rights Brief*, 2000, www.wcl.american.edu/hrbrief/07/3reparation.cfm.

8. Barbara Dodson Walker, quoted in Tamara Audi, "Payback for Slavery: Growing Push for Reparations Tries to Fulfill Broken Promise," 18 September 2000, www.freep.com/news/nw/repay18_20000918.htm.

9. See Anthony Dugdale, J. J. Fueser, and J. Celso de Castro Alves, *Yale, Slavery, and Abolition* (New Haven: Amistad Committee, 2001); *USA Today*, 21 February 2002; "Complicity: How Connecticut Chained Itself to Slavery," *Northeast: The Sunday Magazine of the Hartford Courant*, 29 September 2002; and www.ctnow.com/slavery.

10. See, e.g., Massey and Denton, *American Aparthied*.

11. Information on the World Conference against Racism, the Durban 400, and various lawsuits is based, in part, on phone interviews with Adjoa Aiyetoro, Roger Wareham, and Stan Willis in the fall of 2002.

12. Africa Action, "Position on the World Conference against Racism, Racial Discrimination, Xenophobia, and Related Intolerance," 22 August 2001, www.africapolicy.org.

13. Bert Wilkinson, "Africans Join Hands to Seek Compensation," www.dawn.com/2002/10/08/int10.htm.

14. Ed Stoddard, "S. African Groups File Apartheid Suit against Firms," 12 November 2002, www.reuters.com; and Rory Carroll, "S. Africa Shuns Apartheid lawsuits," *Guardian*, 27 November 2002, www.guardian.co.uk.

15. Off-the-record conversation with a Chicago journalist.

Part 4

Case Studies of Injustice and Intervention

Introduction

Four distinct case studies of redress struggles are examined in this part. Alan Singer challenges historians to reconsider how slavery is remembered and taught and investigates New York City's complicity with slavery. Paradoxically, while slave labor was used to construct buildings, New York City was also a base for abolitionists as well as a stop on the Underground Railroad. The role of slave labor in the building of railroads in southern and border states is the subject of Theodore Kornweibel Jr.'s essay. He notes that some railroad companies purchased slaves outright, while others hired slaves through labor contracts negotiated with their owners. Kornweibel contends that, unlike the banking, textile, and tobacco industries, evidence of antebellum railroads' complicity with slavery is extensive, suggesting that it substantiates a strong case for litigation such as the 2002 federal class-action lawsuit against csx (along with Aetna and FleetBoston Financial Corporation).

David R. Williams and Chiquita Collins direct their concerns to the racial disparities in health between blacks and whites. Their central argument rests on the denial of access to adequate health care for blacks, which stems from segregation, discrimination, and racism. They point out that these racial disparities in health and access to health care demonstrate another legacy of racial inequality with the "potential for reparations." Douglas S. Massey's essay focuses on residential segregation, which he contends contributes to black poverty. He also delineates the factors that keep African Americans in a state of "hypersegregation" in major cities: prejudice, discrimination, and public policy, reflected in the federal government's program of mortgage redlining, state and local government policies, and banking and real estate practices. Massey calls for public policies and interventions by HUD and the Department of Justice to enforce fair housing standards.

Nineteenth-Century New York City's Complicity with Slavery

Documenting the Case for Reparations

ALAN SINGER

Introduction

The New York State Human Rights curriculum is supposed to include guidelines and material for teaching about the European Holocaust, the Great Irish Famine, and Slavery and the Atlantic Slave Trade. An award winning 1,000-page interdisciplinary fourth- through twelfth-grade curriculum on the Great Irish Famine was completed and distributed by the state in 2001 (New York State Education Department, 2001). A number of Holocaust curricula developed by museums, local school districts, and nonprofit agencies (e.g., *Facing History and Ourselves*) are already in use. However, a curriculum for teaching about slavery and the Atlantic slave trade remains trapped in a web of racial politics. This battle has been going on since the early 1990s, when conservative forces in the state launched a "discourse of derision" in an effort to undermine multiculturalism through caricature and ridicule (Cornbeth and Waugh, 1995, 131).

The State Department of Education envisioned the Slavery and the Atlantic Slave Trade curriculum as a celebration of "New York's Freedom Trail," its role in the underground railroad and as a base of operations for abolitionists. Many historians, especially those from the African American community, want students to take a much more critical look at the state's role in promoting and profiting from human bondage. In an effort to support the creation of a curriculum guide, the New York State Council for the Social Studies published a theme issue of *Social Science Docket* (a magazine for social studies teachers cosponsored by the New Jersey Council for the Social Studies) on "Slavery and the North: Complicity and Resistance." This essay weaves together many of the themes and documents developed for that issue. Its principal conclusion is that while many prominent individuals from New York State were important abolitionists and the state did offer safe haven to some escaped slaves, of greater historical importance is the state's often overlooked economic and political complicity with the southern and Caribbean "slavocracy" and the continuing involvement of its merchant and banking elite with the illegal Atlantic slave trade up until the Civil War. The goal of any curriculum should be to help students understand that slavery and the Atlantic slave trade, rather than just being a southern institution, were integral parts of the national and global economy in the eighteenth and nineteenth centuries and produced much of the capital that financed the industrial revolution in Europe and the United States.

Roots of New York City's Complicity

New York City's complicity with slavery has deep roots and involved prominent names. The October 2, 1738, issue of *The New York Weekly Journal* included an advertisement calling for the recapture of a runaway fleeing from his Dutchess County "master." He was described as "a copper colored Negro fellow named Jack, aged about 30 years, speaks nothing but English and reads English." A reward of "forty shillings and all reasonable charges" was to be given to whoever "takes up said run away and secures him to his master" or gives notice of him to John Peter Zenger (Hodges and Brown, 1994, 30). Zenger, who the history textbooks honor as an early champion of freedom of the press, financed this "freedom" through complicity with slavery (D. Kennedy, Cohen, and Bailey, 2002, 101).

On August 13, 1750, the *New York Gazette* ran an advertisement for the recapture of a "Negro wench named Phoebe aged about 45 years, middle sized, and formerly belonged to Dr. Cornelius Van Wyck at Great Neck" (Hodges and Brown, 1994, 84). One of Van Wyck's descendants became the first mayor of a consolidated New York City in 1898. A well-known highway in Queens now bears the family name.

Long before Rudolph Giuliani was "America's mayor," before Ed Koch stopped passers-by to ask "How am I doing?," and before Fiorello LaGuardia read the Sunday comics to Depression-era children on the radio, Fernando Wood was New York City's "model mayor." In the 1850s and 1860s, Wood, who was elected mayor three times, was also a congressional representative from the city. In 1861, as the nation approached civil war, he proposed that New York declare itself a free city so it could continue to trade with and profit from the slave South. Later, as a congressman, Wood opposed the Thirteenth Amendment to the Constitution that ended slavery in the United States as a violation of private property rights (Mushkat, 1990).

In recent years, opinion essays in the *New York Times* by Brent Staples (2000) and Eric Foner (2000) have challenged historians and teachers to rethink the way we think about and teach about slavery in the United States, especially slavery and the northern states. According to Foner, "(o)n the eve of the Civil War, the economic value of slaves in the United States was $3 billion in 1860 currency, more than the combined value of all the factories, railroads and banks in the country. Much of the North's economic prosperity derived from what Abraham Lincoln, in his second inaugural address, called 'the bondman's two hundred and fifty years of unrequited toil'" (Singer, 2001, 16).

In his essay "History Lessons from the Slaves of New York," Staples (2000) described how the Dutch, who built New Amsterdam, "recruited settlers with an advertisement that promised to provide them with slaves who 'would accomplish more work for their masters, at less expense than [white] farm servants, who must be bribed to go thither by a great deal of money and promises.'"

Enslaved Africans helped build Trinity Church, the streets of the early city, and a wooden fortification located where Wall Street is today. This essay by Staples (2000) reported the findings of biological anthropologists from Howard University who studied "the skeletal remains of more than 400 African slaves whose graves were accidentally uncovered during the construction of a federal office tower in lower Manhattan nine years ago."

When it was closed in 1794, the Negro Burial Ground, which was outside that era's city limits, probably contained between 10,000 and 20,000 bodies. Staples believes the research team's work shows that

> colonial New York was just as dependent on slavery as many Southern cities, and in some cases even more so. In addition, the brutality etched on these skeletons easily matches the worst of what we know of slavery in the South. . . . Of the 400 skeletons taken to Howard, about 40 percent are of children under the age of 15, and the most common cause of death was malnutrition. . . . The adult skeletons show that many of these people died of unrelenting hard labor. Strain on the muscles and ligaments was so extreme that muscle attachments were commonly ripped away from the skeleton—taking chunks of bone with them—leaving the body in perpetual pain. (Staples, 2000)

In "Slavery's Fellow Travelers," E. Foner (2000) argued that

> (a)ccounts of the city's rise to commercial prominence in the 19th century rightly point to the Erie Canal's role in opening access to produce from the West, but they don't talk about the equal importance to the city's prosperity of its control

over the South's cotton trade. Because of this connection, New York merchants and bankers were consistently pro-slavery, pressing during the 1840's and 1850's for one concession to the South after another in order to maintain their lucrative access to cotton.

In response to this forgotten history, Foner proposed that "when New York's history is taught in public schools, the city's intimate link with slavery should receive full attention." In addition, "the city should have a permanent exhibition — perhaps even an independent museum — depicting the history of slavery and New York's connection with it."

Foner's position has received powerful documentation through the research efforts of the historian William Katz. In his 1995 book *Eyewitness: A Living Documentary of the African American Contribution to American History*, Katz includes an excerpt from the reminiscences of the New York abolitionist Samuel J. May where he describes an incident at a meeting of the American Antislavery Society in May 1835. According to May's account:

> I was sitting upon the platform of the Houston Street Presbyterian Church in New York, when I was surprised to see a gentleman enter and take his seat who, I knew, was a partner in one of the most prominent mercantile houses in the city. He had not been seated long before he beckoned me to meet him at the door. I did so. "Please walk out with me, sir" said he, "I have something of great importance to communicate." When we had reached the sidewalk he said, with considerable emotion and emphasis, "Mr. May, we are not such fools as not to know that slavery is a great evil, a great wrong. But it was consented to by the founders of our Republic. It was provided for in the Constitution of our Union. A great portion of the property of the Southerners is invested under its sanction; and the business of the North, as well as the South, has become adjusted to it. There are millions upon millions of dollars due from Southerners to the merchants and mechanics of this city alone, the payment of which would be jeopardized by any rupture between the North and the South. We cannot afford, sir, to let you and your associates succeed in your endeavor to overthrow slavery. It is not a matter of principle with us. It is a matter of business necessity. We cannot afford to let you succeed. And I have called you out to let you know, and to let your fellow-laborers know, that we do not mean to allow you to succeed. We mean, sir," said he, with increased emphasis — "we mean, sir, to put you Abolitionists down — by fair means if we can, by foul means if we must." (Katz, 1995, 172)

The accounts of slavery in New York and the North presented by Staples, Katz, and Foner echo the famous front-page editorial by William Lloyd Garrison in the introductory issue of the abolitionist newspaper *The Liberator* (Garrison, 1831, 1). In the editorial, Garrison explained that on a "tour for the purpose of exciting the minds of the people by a series of discourses on the subject of slavery, every place that I visited gave fresh evidence of the fact, that a greater revolution in public sentiment was to be effected in the free states . . . than at the south."

He also related that in the North, he "found contempt more bitter, opposition more active, detraction more relentless, prejudice more stubborn, and apathy more frozen, than among slave owners themselves."

In response to this reception, Garrison "determined, at every hazard, to lift up the standard of emancipation in the eyes of the nation, within sight of Bunker Hill and in the birth place of liberty."

He warned readers that he would not be silenced "till every chain be broken, and every bondman set free" and declared, "Let southern oppressors tremble — let their secret abettors tremble — let their northern apologists tremble — let all the enemies of the persecuted blacks tremble."

In Brooklyn, New York, Reverend Henry Ward Beecher of Plymouth Church espoused similar sentiments. In a sermon delivered in January 1861, in the midst of the nation's secession crisis, Beecher declared that "we who dwell in the North are not without responsibility for this sin. . . . When our Constitution was adopted . . . all the institutions were prepared for liberty, and all the public men were on the side of liberty."

However, because of the "delinquency of the North," the nation's commitment to liberty was "sacrificed." He called the North's failure to preserve liberty "an astounding sin! It is an unparalleled guilt!" ("Think Tank," 2000, B11).

New Yorkers Opposed to Slavery

Soon after the Revolutionary War, some New Yorkers played significant roles in promoting abolition. The New York Manumission Society, under the leadership of John Jay and Alexander Hamilton, helped purchase freedom for enslaved Africans and in 1787 established an African Free School to provide instruction in reading, writing, and arithmetic. The Society also organized boycotts of merchants and newspapers that supported slavery and won a series of unlawful enslavement cases, defending the freedom of black New Yorkers who were threatened with being sent to the South as slaves (New York State Freedom Trail Commission, 2001, 22).

Aaron Burr, a leading Jeffersonian Republican in New York, was a resolute opponent of slavery who argued that whites and blacks were created equal and that women and men should have the same political rights. In 1785, Burr introduced an unsuccessful bill in the state legislature to immediately end slavery in New York. Despite this failure, he campaigned for the next fourteen years against New York's slave-owning landlords and farmers, and artisans who feared job competition from freed blacks. Ultimately, Burr was a major antislavery ally of Governor Jay when the New York legislature agreed to gradual emancipation in 1799 (Brady, 2001; R. Kennedy, 2000).

From 1830 through the Civil War, a number of prominent New Yorkers, both black and white, were leaders in the campaign to end slavery. In the 1830s, Lewis Tappan, a New York City merchant and a white man, was a founder and officer of the American Anti-Slavery Society. At his urging, New York City's leading abolitionists formed a committee to aid in the defense of the Africans on the *Amistad*. During their trial in Connecticut, Lewis Tappan wrote reports published in the *New York Journal of Commerce* (*Social Science Docket*, 2001, 24). Tappan was largely responsible for their sympathetic portrayal in the New York City press as dignified human beings. In one letter he wrote, "Cinquez is about 5 feet 8 inches high, of fine proportions, with a noble air. Indeed, the whole company, although thin in flesh, and generally of slight forms, and limbs especially, are as good looking and intelligent a body of men as we usually meet with. All are young, and several are quite striplings. The Mandingos are described in books as being a very gentle race, cheerful in their dispositions, inquisitive, credulous, simple hearted, and much given to trading propensities."

William Cullen Bryant, a white man, was a poet, editor of the *New York Evening Post*, and a founder of the Republican Party. He was a staunch defender of the free speech rights of abolitionists and his poem "The African Chief" attacked the inhumanity of slavery and the slave trade. Bryant's primary concern in the era before the Civil War was preservation of the Union. He opposed both the expansion of slavery in the West and Garrison's and John Brown's radical calls for the abolition of slavery. However, once war was declared, Bryant argued that while it was "not a war directly aimed at the release of the slave," saving the Union required that Lincoln emancipate enslaved Africans (*Social Science Docket*, 2001, 47).

One of the more important local abolitionists was Reverend Henry Highland Garnet, an African American who was himself a former slave. In an 1843 speech at an abolitionist conference in Buffalo, New York, Garnet called upon slaves in the South to rise up in revolt: "Brethren, arise, arise! Strike for your lives and liberties. Now is the day and the hour. Let every slave throughout the land do this, and the days of slavery are numbered. You cannot be more oppressed than you have been, you cannot suffer greater cruelties than you have already. Rather die freemen than live to be slaves. Remember that you are four millions!" (*Social Science Docket*, 2001, 45).

Reverend Henry Ward Beecher, a white man, was a leading opponent of slavery in the 1850s and the brother of Harriet Beecher Stowe. In 1848, 1856, and 1859, Beecher raised money in his Brooklyn church to purchase the freedom of slaves in symbolic protests against the institution (*Social Science Docket*, 2001, 46). Horace Greeley, a white man, was the founder and an editor of the *New York Tribune*. Greeley took a strong moral tone in his newspaper and campaigned against alcohol and tobacco use, gambling, prostitution, and capital punishment. However, his main concern was the abolition of slavery. In 1860, Greeley supported the presidential campaign of Abraham Lincoln, but was unhappy with Lincoln's hesitant attitude toward emancipation. In an open letter to the president on August 19, 1862, Greeley complained about the Union army's unwillingness to free slaves in captured territory and criticized Lincoln for failing to make slavery the dominant issue of the war, compromising moral principles for political motives (*Social Science Docket*, 2001, 25).

Because of its busy ports and large free black population, the New York City area was an attractive destination for runaways from the border states, including Frederick Washington Bailey (later known as Frederick Douglass). In 1838, a free African American named James Week purchased land in Brooklyn where he established a settlement that would become known as Weeksville. This town was a safe haven for escapees from bondage in the slave states and from racial violence in nearby Manhattan (New York State Freedom Trail Commission, 2001, 22). The New York area was also home to a number of underground railroad stations, especially in Brooklyn. These included the African Wesleyan Methodist Episcopal Church on Bridge Street, where a hidden subcellar provided safety from slave catchers; the Plymouth Church of the Pilgrims in Brooklyn Heights, where Henry Ward Beecher preached from 1847 to 1887; and the Lafayette Avenue Presbyterian Church in Fort Greene, Brooklyn, where fugitives often hid in the basement and heating tunnels (Peterson and Pesato, 2001).

Documenting New York City's Complicity

While some New Yorkers played important roles in combating slavery, the city's merchant and political elite were inextricably tied into the international system of exploitation for profit (P. Foner, 1941/1968, 318). Some indirectly profited from the agricultural commodities produced by an enslaved workforce. Others profited directly by financing and participating in the illegal Atlantic slave trade. They were generally able to avoid arrest and prosecution under laws defining slave trading as piracy (punishable by death) through a legal technicality that limited the jurisdiction of American courts to U.S. citizens.

New York Times editorials from November 10, 1854, and November 24, 1854, explained the workings of the illegal slave trade and the extent of involvement by the city's merchants and bankers:

> In the United States Circuit Court sitting in this City, one Captain James Smith has been convicted of having been engaged in the *Slave-Trade* between the Coast of Africa and the Island of Cuba. . . . The facts which were proved in this case were substantially these: In January last Capt. Smith went to Boston, where he purchased the brig *Julia Moulton*, cleared her in ballast for Newport, and on the 2nd of February brought her to this port. Here he engaged one James Wills as mate, telling him that he was going on a Slave-trading voyage, agreeing to pay him $40 a month on the outward voyage, and from $1,200 to $2,000 for the passage back. A crew was shipped of about fifteen persons, mostly young men, and a large quantity of provisions, water, &c., with lumber, was taken on board. On the 11th of February the brig cleared from this port. And on leaving the dock, Capt. Smith pointed out to the mate a Portuguese named Lemos as the real owner of the vessel, and told him that the Secretary of the Portuguese Consul at this port had accompanied him to Boston and aided him in the purchase of the vessel. The ship was cleared by Capt. Smith and had regular papers for the cape of Good Hope. After she had been out about forty days, the timber on board was used to make a temporary dock or floor in the hold of the vessel, and all the other preparations necessary to receive a cargo of slaves were made. At the end of sixty days, they made land on the coast of Africa at a place called Cobra, where they were boarded by a boat which brought instructions, in accordance with which they cruised at sea for ten days longer, and then put in a port further South called *Ambrozzetta*, well known as a dépôt for the Slave-trade. Here in the course of two or three hours, *six hundred and sixty-four negroes, including forty women, were brought on board and stowed away as cargo in the hold of the brig.* They were placed on their sides, one lying in the lap of another — were taken out occasionally to be fed and aired, and after a voyage of sixty-five days were landed on the South coast of Cuba. They were sent on shore in lighters, under the orders of a person who said he was a consignee, and the *American Consul* at that port. The furniture of the ship was then taken on shore and the ship herself was burned. Wills the mate came to this city in the brig *Mercellus*, where he again met Captain Smith, who refused to pay Wills the balance due him on the contract, amounting to about $440, whereupon Wills imparted the nature of the voyage to a Mr. Donahue, by whom it was laid before the authorities. The result was the arrest, trial and conviction of Captain Smith.
>
> We believe this is the *first* time in which a conviction of being engaged in the African Slave Trade has ever been had in this City — and this is due entirely to a disagreement between the captain and his mate about the payment of a trifling sum

of money. Yet, as we have repeatedly stated in the *Times, scarcely a month passes in which there are not one or more vessels cleared at this port, which embark at once in the Slave-trade and land their cargoes on the coast of Cuba*. The facts given in evidence on this trial show how easily this is done, and with what impunity, so long as all the parties engaged in it are satisfactorily paid for keeping silent. In order to obtain a conviction, the vessel concerned must be, at the time, owned either in whole or in part by an American citizen, or else the party accused must himself be a citizen. The first provision is usually evaded by a sham sale: — the last by procuring a foreigner, usually a Portuguese, as a commander. The only defence (sic) attempted in this case turned upon this point. It was claimed that Mr. Smith was an unnaturalized German, and it was also asserted and partly proved that the ship was *paid for by the Secretary of the Portuguese Consul at this port.*

We have not the slightest doubt that *there are hundreds of Portuguese — merchants and others in this City, who are constantly and largely engaged in this traffic*; who carry it on as their regular business, who grow rich by it, and live in splendid style and claim and hold high rank in the rich circles of our metropolis by virtue of the wealth thus acquired. We believe this fact is very generally known, and that not a month passes in which vessels are not cleared at the Customs House, of whose destination and employment in the Slave-trade, the houses who ship crew for them, and even the officials who prepare and sign their papers are morally certain. This City and Baltimore are now, and have been for years, the great head-quarters of the African Slave-trade. In the face of all our laws, — in defiance of our treaty stipulations and in contempt of armed cruisers and men-of-war, that piratical traffic is largely carried on by ships fitted out in American ports, and under the protection of the American flag. ("The Slave-Trade," 1854, 4)

Slave trading was a capital offense in the United States after 1820. Between 1837 and 1860, seventy-four cases were tried but there were few convictions and punishment tended to be minimal. In 1856, a New York City deputy marshal declared that the business of outfitting slavers had never been pursued "with greater energy than at the present. . . . It is seldom that one or more vessels cannot be designated at the wharves, respecting which there is evidence that she is either in or has been concerned in the traffic [to Cuba]." The men who smuggled enslaved Africans referred to themselves as "blackbirders" and their illegal human cargo as "black ivory."

The British consul claimed that out of 170 known slave trading expeditions for the Cuba slave market between 1859 and 1862, 74 were believed to have sailed from New York City. In the summer of 1859, the bark *Emily* set off from New York stocked as a slaver with a cargo of lumber, fresh water, barrels of rice, codfish, pork and bread, boxes of herring, dozens of pails, and two cases of medicines. It was returned to port under naval guard, but the case against its captain and owners was dismissed. In 1862, Nathaniel Gordon, of the slave ship *Erie*, was the only North American ever executed for slave trading (Thomas, 1997, 770–774). Federal officials in New York were so ineffective in prosecuting slave trading cases that in 1861, a *New York Times* editorial (1861, 4) urged President Lincoln to replace the marshal and district attorney assigned to these cases.

In memoirs published in 1864, Captain James Smith (discussed above) claimed that in 1859, 85 ships capable of carrying a total of 30,000 to 60,000 enslaved Africans were outfitted in the port of New York to serve the slave markets of Cuba (Katz, 1995, 30–31). Smith described New York as "the chief port in the world for the Slave Trade. It is the greatest place in the universe for it. Neither in Cuba, not in the Brazils is it carried on so extensively. Ships that convey Slaves to the West Indies and South America are fitted out in New York. Now and then one sails from Boston and Philadelphia; but New York is our headquarters. . . . I can go down to South Street, and go into a number of houses that help fit out ships for the business." The trade was so profitable that on one voyage, a ship that "cost $13,000 to fit her out completely" delivered a human cargo worth "$220,000" to Cuba.

One of the successful slave ships that operated out of New York City was a ninety-five-foot-long yacht known as the *Wanderer*, whose skipper and part-owner was a member of the New York Yacht Club. The ship, which was built in 1857 in Setauket, New York, was refurbished for the slave trade at Port Jefferson, New York. In 1858, it was used to smuggle between 400 and 600 kidnaped Africans from the Congo area into the Georgia South Sea Islands.

As late as June 1860, as the nation moved toward civil war, *Harper's Weekly* (1860) reported the seizure off the coast of Cuba of the "bark Wildfire, lately owned in the city of New York." The ship, which had left the Congo area thirty-six days before its capture, had on board a human cargo of "five hundred and ten native Africans." According to the article, "About fifty of them were full-grown young men, and about four hundred were boys aged from ten to sixteen years. . . . Ninety and upward had died on the voyage."

However, the more subtle complicity, and the real profits, were in financing commerce in slave-produced commodities, especially Cuban sugar and southern cotton. A front page article in the *New York Times* on November 15, 1852, explained the workings of the Cuban sugar industry, which paid investors two and a half times the normal interest rate on loans and which found it more profitable to smuggle in newly enslaved Africans than to allow for the internal reproduction of its workforce:

> The policy of the (Spanish) Government has been extremely liberal to the producers of sugar, with the purpose of building up and fostering that interest as the

most productive of revenue to the crown. Great privileges have been secured to the sugar planter, such as exemption from all direct taxes except tithes, and immunity from the sale of their estates by any process to satisfy the claims of creditors. Very many of the planters are large borrowers of money, and I have been informed by capitalists that, owing to the last provision, the current rate of interest on their loans is not less than fifteen per cent, at the same time that the notes of merchants and retailers are readily discounted at six per cent. There is no limit to the rate of interest established by law. A very large capital is required to "make a sugar estate." But when the requisite money is at hand, the prices of land are so low that to begin from the foundation is the preferable way for a planter to establish himself. This accounts for the exorbitant usury they are willing to pay. But the more usual way of getting possession of estates is to purchase them in full operation by paying five or ten per cent down, and paying a certain sum, frequently as low as two and a half per cent per annum till the whole be paid. An estate, such as is sold in this way, consists of land, negroes, horses, mules, cattle, hogs, machinery and everything appertaining to a complete establishment. I have heard of sales where the first crop would reimburse the first payment, and each successive crop provide for the current payment, and leave the purchaser from two to four times as much more for regular income. Thus an estate was sold for $450,000 — $50,000 being paid down, and in ninety days the maturing crop produced $50,000, and the remaining $400,000 of the purchase money was payable in annual installments of $10,000, without interest, and the annual product continues not less than $50,000. Cane is seldom planted oftener than once in five years, and on a majority of estates not oftener than once in ten years. When estates are sold, they are sold entire, as above described. The negroes (*sic*) and other stock are not valued separately unless they are separately sold. The rule as to treatment of negroes is said to be "plenty of feed and plenty of work."

The slaves are driven to the field at dawn, after breakfasting before it is light enough to work; have rest and dinner at noon, work till dark, and then supper and locked up to sleep. Marriage is unknown among them — most of the planters pay no regard to breeding slaves, it is cheaper to buy "green" ones from Africa than to raise them, and intercourse between the sexes, when permitted at all, is promiscuous. The African trade is now flourishing, after a nearly total interruption under Concha, who refused the usual bribes, and exerted himself to prevent the importation of slaves with so much success that their value increased about fifty per cent. ("Cuban Affairs," 1852)

During the 1850s, the *New York Times* regularly published updates on the Cuban sugar market for New York City merchants and bankers in reports issued by a special correspondent that were delivered by steamship. A front-page article on July 30, 1860, announced that "business is quite active for this season of the year, and the sugar market firm. . . . Shipments of the week near 30,000 boxes. Sales large and some on speculation. Money somewhat easy to aid transactions. The stock of sugar is 270,000 boxes against 260,000 boxes last year at same date" ("From Havana," 1860).

The financing and operation of the southern cotton trade and its ties with New York City merchants was detailed in a 1852 report to Congress (Albion, 1961, 97):

> Cotton employs upwards of 120,000 tons of steam tonnage.... Cotton affords employment and profit to the southern commission merchant or factor, and to the many and various laborers engaged in carting, storing it, &c., in the southern port; and a second tribute is paid to the underwriter for insurance against fire whilst in store. The "compressing" and relading it for shipment coastwise to eastern Atlantic cities, or to foreign ports, and insurance against the danger of the seas, give additional employment and cause additional charges. The transportation of that portion of the crop is sent along the gulf coast to the principal gulf ports, or coastwise to eastern cities, employs upwards of 1,100,000 tons of *American* shipping in the gulf and Atlantic coasting trade, and upwards of 55,000 American seamen engaged in such trade. As no foreign vessel can participate in the trade, the freights are highly profitable. They ordinarily average from the gulf ports to New York not less than five-eighths of a cent per pound of freight.
>
> In the eastern Atlantic cities, the wharfinger, those who unlade the vessel, the drayman, the storekeeper, the commission merchant, the cotton-broker, the weigher, the packers who compress the bales by steam power or otherwise, the laborers, and those who charge for "mendage," "cordage," &c. &c., the fire insurer, and the shipper, the stevedore, and numerous other persons in those ports, find profitable avocations arising from cotton, whether destined for a home or for a foreign market....
>
> More than 800,000 tons of the navigation of the United States engaged in the foreign trade are employed in carrying American cotton to Europe and elsewhere, and upwards of 40,000 American seamen are given employment in such vessels. It is estimated that the foreign tonnage and seamen employed in carrying American cotton to Europe and elsewhere to foreign countries amount to about one-sixth of that of the United States so employed.

According to the first annual report of the Chamber of Commerce of the State of New York in 1859, even when the Europe-bound cotton trade was not shipped through the port of New York, New York City merchants and bankers often financed the exchange.

> This mode of conducting the more speculative portion of the cotton trade only began to be commonly resorted to four or five years ago, and has been constantly on the increase ever since. There has always been a class of adventurers who wished to have the option of terminating their operations by a sale in New York. A few years ago, this class — a very important one in moving the cotton crop — ordered

the cotton to be shipped to New York; but this necessarily involved double freights, insurances, and expenses on the cotton with only the small advantage of selling for home consumption. Now, however, the plan is to ship the cotton direct to Liverpool, from the Southern port, and to send the samples and bills of lading to New York, where it can be sold, if the adventurer is unwilling to take the risk of the Liverpool market. (Albion, 1961, 116)

Commercial ties between the North and South also provided New York City merchants with a secondary economic benefit. Southern merchants and their families made annual pilgrimages to the city, ordering imported and domestic luxury goods and patronizing hotels, restaurants, and resorts (Albion, 1961, 120). As a result of their financing of the cotton trade, northern merchants and bankers were owed an estimated $200 million by southern planters at the outbreak of the Civil War.

The leading booster of New York City's economic ties with the slaveholding South was probably the congressman and mayor Fernando Wood. As a congressman in the 1840s, Wood was a strong supporter of slavery and the South and he continued his support when he became mayor of New York City in the 1850s. On January 8, 1861, the *New York Times* published the transcript of Mayor Wood's annual report to the city's Common Council. In this message, Wood spoke about the city's options as the United States federal union appeared to be dissolving. He called on the city to declare its own independence to better facilitate continued trade with the slave South.

> We are entering upon the public duties of the year under circumstances as unprecedented as they are gloomy and painful to contemplate. The great trading and producing interests of not only the City of New York, but of the entire country are prostrated by a momentary crisis.... It would seem that a dissolution of the Federal Union is inevitable. Having been formed originally upon a basis of general and mutual protection, but separate local independence—each State reserving the entire and absolute control of its own domestic affairs, it is evidently impossible to keep them together longer than they deem themselves fairly treated by each other, or longer than the interests, honor and fraternity of the people of the several States are satisfied.... It cannot be preserved by coercion or held together by force. A resort to this last dreadful alternative would of itself destroy not only the Government, but the lives and property of the people.
>
> With our aggrieved brethren of the Slave States we have friendly relations and a common sympathy. We have not participated in the warfare upon their constitutional rights or their domestic institutions. While other portions of our State have unfortunately been imbued with the fanatical spirit which actuates a portion of the people of New England, the City of New York has unfalteringly preserved the integrity of its principles in adherence to the compromises of the Constitution and

the equal rights of the people of all the States. Our ships have penetrated to every clime, and so have New York capital, energy and enterprise found their way to every State.... New York has a right to expect and should endeavor to preserve a continuance of uninterrupted intercourse with every section....

I claim for the City the distinction of a municipal corporation, self-existing and sustained by its own inherent and proper vigor.... As a free City, with but a nominal duty on imports, her local government could be supported without taxation upon her people. Thus we could live free from taxes, and have cheap goods nearly duty free. In this she would have the whole and united support of the Southern States as well as of all other States to whose interests and rights under the Constitution she has always been true.... If the Confederacy is broken up the Government is dissolved, and it behooves every distinct community as well as every individual to take care of themselves. ("Message from the Mayor," 1861, 2)

Toward the end of the war, Wood returned to Congress, where he continued to champion the southern cause and opposed the "anti-Slavery Amendment," the Thirteenth Amendment to the U.S. Constitution, as a violation of private property rights. According to a June 15, 1864, article in the *New York Times*:

Mr. Fernando Wood, of New York, said that this was no time for a change of the organic law. We were in the midst of civil war. The din of the conflict and the groans of the dying and wounded are sad evidences of the destruction around us. The entire people are involved directly or indirectly in the dreadful conflict. There was too much excitement in the public mind to admit of calm and cautious investigation. If such a change could be made in the Constitution, this was not the time for it. The effect of such an amendment would produce a revulsion widespread and radical in character, and add to the existing sectional hostility, and, if possible, make the conflict more intense. Among his reasons for opposing the resolution, he said it proposed to make social institutions subject to the Government, and this was an antagonism to the principles which underlie our republican system. It was unjust. It was the breach of good faith, and not reconcilable even with expediency. It struck at property, and involved the extermination of the whites of the Southern States and the forfeiture of their property, and lands to be given to the black race, who may drive the former out of existence.... Mr. Wood argued that the Constitution was a compact and a covenant and that the control of the domestic institutions of the States was never delegated to the general Government, and could not be delegated excepting by the consent of all the States. ("The Anti-Slavery Constitutional Amendment," 1864, 5)

Connecting New York City's history of complicity with slavery to particular individuals or businesses is difficult to establish given that conviction as a slave trader carried a death sentence and because few besides Fernando Wood were so blatant and outspoken about their prejudices and desire for profit and power at whatever the social and moral cost. I believe the following case study illustrates just how deep complicity with slavery ran, even in the most respected circles.

On May 25, 1882, the *New York Times* reported the death of Moses Taylor, "a well-known banker," at age seventy-six. Taylor died of natural causes, leaving behind an estate valued at between $40 and $50 million, an incredible sum for that era. The obituary does not mention race; clearly it was assumed that readers would know that Taylor was a white man ("An Old Merchant's Death," 1882, 10).

Moses Taylor had been born into a relatively prominent New York City family. His father, a cabinetmaker by trade, was also an alderman, state prison inspector, and real estate agent for John Jacob Astor. Moses married as a young man and he and his wife of fifty years had six children. Although raised as a Presbyterian, he later became a benefactor of St. George's Episcopal Church at East 16th Street in Manhattan (Hodas, 1976; Burrows and Wallace, 1999, 657).

During his long career, Moses Taylor was a sugar merchant with offices on South Street at the East River seaport, a finance capitalist and an industrialist, as well as a banker. He was a member of the New York City Chamber of Commerce and a major stockholder, board member, or officer in firms that later merged with or developed into Citibank, Con Edison, Bethlehem Steel, and AT&T. During the Civil War, Taylor worked with Secretary of the Treasury Chase and New York City's leading bankers to finance the northern war effort.

Clearly, Moses Taylor was much more than just "an old merchant." But what exactly was his role in New York City and U.S. history? the *New York Times* obituary ("An Old Merchant's Death," 1882) gives us some other clues: "It was the sugar trade with Cuba that first gave him his reputation as a merchant, and it was this trade that principally accumulated for him, his great fortune.... Upon this he concentrated his remarkable powers and to this he devoted his energies, until he became known throughout the world as one of the most prominent and successful of merchants."

As a result of his success in the sugar trade, Taylor became a member of the board of the City Bank in 1837, and served as its president from 1855 until his death. In the nineteenth century, City Bank, a predecessor of today's Citibank, primarily issued short-term credits to locally based merchants to facilitate the import-export trade. Taylor's personal resources and role as business agent for the leading exporter of Cuban sugar to the United States proved invaluable to the bank, helping it survive financial panics in 1837 and 1857 that bankrupted many of its competitors.

Taylor generally earned a 5 percent commission for brokering the sale of Cuban sugar in the port of New York, as well as additional fees for exchanging currency and negotiating the New York City Customs House. He supervised the investment of profits by the sugar planters in U.S. banks, gas companies, railroads, and real estate; purchased and shipped supplies and machinery to Cuba; operated six of his own boats and numerous chartered vessels in the Cuban trade; repaired and equipped other boats with goods and provisions; provided sugar planters with financing to arrange for land purchases and the acquisition of a labor force; and even supervised the planters' children when they came to New York City as students or to serve as apprentices for mercantile firms.

On the face of it, these appear to be ordinary business ventures, except for one significant issue. The labor force that Taylor and City Bank were helping the Cuban planters acquire was slave labor, often smuggled illegally from Africa on boats outfitted in the port of New York, in violation of the international ban on the Atlantic slave trade. Taylor and City Bank's financing of the Cuban sugar trade between 1830 and 1860 aided and abetted illegal slave trading.

Taylor knew exactly what he was doing. Even after southern states began to vote for secession, Taylor wanted to preserve the Union at any cost to maintain profitable trade relations between northern merchants and slave-owning planters.

Conclusions

Except for their involvement in financing the illegal Cuban slave trade and defending the right of southern planters to own slaves, Moses Taylor and his fellow New York City merchants and bankers were probably good men. They took care of their families, supported their churches, and built vast business empires that shaped this city and country. But it is time that we recognize that just as with laundered drug money today, their money remained dirty and carried with it the blood of its victims.

As a first step in addressing historical wrongs, it is past time that New York City publicly acknowledge its long and prosperous complicity with slavery and the slave trade. Moses Taylor's first office was at 55 South Street, making the South Street Seaport an appropriate site for a monument to the victims of slavery and the eternal struggle for human freedom. In addition, the state and city departments of education must immediately commit the resources needed to finally develop an appropriate Slavery and the Atlantic Slave Trade curriculum guide.

According to the *New York Times* obituary ("An Old Merchant's Death," 1882), "Taylor's death occasioned earnest expressions of regret in downtown business circles" and in "Wall-street and vicinity many flags were flown at half-mast." The companies that he helped found, the businesses that he helped grow, the firms that mourned his passing, should all recognize their direct responsibility for slavery and the slave trade and finance the construction of this monument and the development of the curriculum guide.

But this is only a beginning. Citibank, Con Edison, AT&T, and numerous other North American and European companies built great fortunes at the expense of Africa and Africans and they will need to pay much more. Henry Louis Gates Jr. has proposed that since "many Western nations reaped large and lasting benefits from African slavery, while African nations did not," the industrialized West bears a collective responsibility for the condition of Africa today. He calls for massive investment to stop the spread of AIDS in Africa and to economically develop the continent. I wholeheartedly endorse this proposal but would recommend similar investment in rebuilding American cities, targeting funds to address the continuing racial inequality in American society and the development of the Caribbean islands, home to millions of displaced Africans. The year 2003 marks the hundredth anniversary of the publication of W. E. B. Du Bois's *The Souls of Black Folk* (1903/1994), yet the "color line" remains in American society. The year 2004 is the fiftieth anniversary of the U.S. Supreme Court's landmark *Brown v. The Topeka, Kansas Board of Education* decision, yet American schools remain fundamentally unequal. A more equal society requires ending the savage racial inequities in health care, educational opportunity, employment, wages, and legal rights.

As a *New York Times* editorial noted in 1854, "If the authorities plead that they cannot stop this, they simply confess their own imbecility. If they will not do it, the moral guilt they incur is scarcely less than that of the Slave-traders themselves" ("Editorial," 1854, 4).

References

Albion, R. *The Rise of New York Port (1815–1860)*. Hamden, Conn.: Archon Books, 1961.
"Anti-Slavery Constitutional Amendment, The." *New York Times*, 15 June 1864.
Brady, K. "Abolitionists among New York's Founding Fathers." *Social Science Docket* 1, no. 2 (summer–fall 2001): 23.
Burrows, E., and M. Wallace. *Gotham, A History of New York City to 1898*. New York: Oxford University Press, 1999.
Cardwell, D. "Seeking Out a Just Way to Make Amends for Slavery." *New York Times*, 12 August 2000.

Cornbeth, C., and D. Waugh. *The Great Speckled Bird: Multicultural Politics and Education Policymaking*. New York: St. Martin's Press, 1995.

"Cuban Affairs." *New York Times*, 15 November 1852.

Du Bois, W. E. B. *The Souls of Black Folk*, Library of Freedom SeriesNew York: Gramercy, 1994. (Originally published 1903.)

Editorial. *New York Times*, 24 November 1854.

Editorial. *New York Times*, 18 March 1861.

Finn, R. "Public Lives: Pressing the Cause of the Forgotten Slaves." *New York Times*, 8 August 2000.

Foner, E. "Slavery's Fellow Travelers." *New York Times*, 13 July 2000.

Foner, P. *Business and Slavery: The New York Merchants and the Irrepressible Conflict*. New York: Russell and Russell, 1968. (Originally published 1941.)

"From Havana." the *New York Times*, 30 July 1860.

Garrison, W. *The Liberator*, 1 January 1831. Available at www.pbs.org/wgbh/aia/part4/4h2928t.html.

Gates, H., Jr. "The Future of Slavery's Past." *New York Times*, 29 July 2001, 4, 15.

Haberman, C. "NYC: Carving Out a Corner for Everyone." *New York Times*, 2 February 2002, B1.

Harper's Weekly. 3 June 1860. Available at www.blackhistory.harpweek.com/SlaveryHome.htm.

Hodas, D. *The Business Career of Moses Taylor, Merchant, Finance Capitalist, and Industrialist*. New York: New York University Press, 1976.

Hodges, G., and A. Brown, eds. *"Pretends to Be Free": Runaway Slave Advertisements from Colonial and Revolutionary New York and New Jersey*. New York: Garland, 1994.

Katz, W. *Eyewitness: A Living Documentary of the African American Contribution to American History*. New York: Simon and Schuster, 1995.

Kennedy, D., L. Cohen, and T. Bailey. *The American Pageant*. 12th ed. Boston: Houghton Mifflin, 2002.

Kennedy, R. *Burr, Hamilton, and Jefferson: A Study in Character*. New York: Oxford University Press, 2000.

"Message from the Mayor." *New York Times*, 8 January 1861.

Mushkat, J. *Fernando Wood: A Political Biography*. Kent, Ohio: Kent State University Press, 1990.

New York State Education Department. *New York State Great Irish Famine Curriculum Guide*. Albany: New York State Education Department, 2001.

New York State Freedom Trail Commission. "The Freedom Quest in New York State." *Social Science Docket* 1, no. 2 (summer–fall 2001): 19–22.

Niebuhr, G. "Religion Journal: Church to Repent Its Ties to Slavery." *New York Times*, 26 June 1999.

"An Old Merchant's Death." Obituary. *New York Times*, 25 May 1882.

Peterson, L., and J. Pesato. "Underground Railroad Site in New Jersey and New York." *Social Science Docket* 1, no. 2 (summer–fall 2001): 32–33.

Singer, A. "Slavery and the Northern States: Complicity and Resistance." *Social Science Docket* 1, no. 2 (summer–fall 2001): 16–18.

"The Slave-Trade: An Important Trial." *New York Times*, 10 November 1854.

Social Science Docket. Special Theme Issue: Slavery and the Northern States, 1, no. 2 (summer–fall 2001).

Staples, B. "History Lessons from the Slaves of New York." *New York Times*, 9 January 2000, section 4, 18.
"Think Tank: Sermons on the Climb to the Mountaintop. Message of the Mayor." *New York Times*, 15 January 2000.
Thomas, H. *The Slave Trade, 1440–1870*. New York: Simon and Schuster, 1997.
Zielbauer, P. "A Newspaper Apologizes for Slave-Era Ads." *New York Times*, 6 July 2000.

Railroads, Race, and Reparations

THEODORE KORNWEIBEL JR.

In the thirty-five years before the Civil War and the end of slavery, railroads in every southern and border state with the possible exception of Delaware routinely used slave labor. This practice took two forms. First, slaves along with modest numbers of white workers *constructed* most if not all southern railroads (although white labor predominated in the border states). Second, probably all southern railroads (and some in the border states) were *operated and maintained* by a mixed labor force of whites, enslaved African Americans, and small numbers of free blacks. Despite an incomplete historical record, documents verify the use of slaves on 77 percent of southern railroads (ninety-three lines) built by the end of the Civil War.[1] In short, the use of enslaved labor was well-nigh universal on antebellum southern railroads.[2]

Slave labor was essential to southern railroading and therefore to the economy of the South as a whole. Most southern whites were indifferent to unskilled industrial work, intent instead on becoming independent landowning farmers, and the South was unable to attract large numbers of immigrant laborers for railroad or other manual labor because slavery tended to depress the wages of free workers. Railroad construction projects demanded hundreds of laborers at a time, and the elasticity of slavery provided the necessary hands. Slave owners who had a surplus of bonded labor leased slaves to construction companies, railroads, and other industries. Whether for construction, maintenance, or operations, southern railroads literally could not do without black labor. This reliance on blacks continued after emancipation, as former slaves often continued to perform the same essential roles on the railways.

Antebellum southern railroads clearly profited from the use of enslaved African Americans, who could be obtained more cheaply and worked more rigorously than free white workers. Nearly all the rail lines built before the end of slavery are today owned and operated by four of the five largest railroad corporations in the country. For these reasons, these corporations (and one smaller line) were named as defendants in the various slavery reparations lawsuits filed in 2002 and 2003.

Documenting Railroad Slavery

What is the evidence of the use of slaves by southern railroads? Unfortunately, few antebellum corporate records have survived. More numerous, although widely scattered, are the railroads' published annual reports. Many provide evidence of either the ownership or hiring of slaves, and sometimes both. Another important source is contemporary articles in the *American Railroad Journal*.[3] Finally, numerous antebellum southern newspapers carried advertisements for railroads seeking to hire or purchase slave labor.

Clearly, in the years just before the Civil War, railroads used the labor of more than ten thousand slaves per year. In January 1860, for example, thirty-seven railroads used one hundred or more slaves, including twelve hundred laboring to build the Atlantic and Gulf in southern Georgia, five hundred building the Vicksburg, Shreveport and Texas, and four hundred or more slaves employed on seven other lines. (To put this into context, no single plantation housed twelve hundred slaves, and only a tiny number used even four hundred at a time.) All told, data show that, in 1860, fifty-five southern railroads used about 10,800 slaves. These fifty-five railroads operated nearly three-quarters of the completed railroad mileage in the southern states. The estimated number of slaves used on the remaining trackage is about 3,800, for an estimated total of about 14,600 slaves used on southern railroads at the beginning of 1860.

How representative is this figure? Between 1852 and 1861, a tremendous amount of railway construction took place, resulting in a nearly 300 percent growth in mileage. By 1857, at least ten thousand slaves were used yearly. Construction sometimes proceeded on a massive scale, with contractors employing one thousand slaves at a time, and the onset of the Civil War did not diminish reliance on their muscle. On the contrary, a shortage of white labor, coupled with the destruction of trackage and bridges by armies on both sides, made slave labor all the more valuable (and costly), with some lines having to supplement their own employees and leased slaves with the impressment of slaves as ordered by the Confederate army. Thus, railroads were among the largest industrial employers of slave labor in the South: only commercial fishing, lumbering, and tobacco processing used more slaves. But if slaves used by railroad construction contractors are added to those employed by the railroads themselves, the number of enslaved workers engaged in all aspects of railroading may represent the nation's largest single concentration of industrial slaves in the antebellum years.[4] Distinguishing slaves in railroad construction from those engaged in ongoing railroad operations and maintenance permits a clear understanding of the differing hardships and dangers each group encountered, as well as the diverse contributions of enslaved African American males and females to the South's most widespread and highly capitalized antebellum industry.

Railroad Construction: Toil, Illness, and Death

Railroad construction was extremely arduous. Unlike those who built the transcontinental railroads after the Civil War, antebellum laborers did not have dynamite or, with a handful of exceptions, steam shovels and pile drivers. Instead, most digging was done by hand or with plows and scrapers drawn by animals. Tunneling was also done largely by hand, with only the use of black powder for hard-rock blasting. Construction proceeded in three phases. First, the workforce cleared brush and chopped down trees. This was followed by a process called grubbing, the backbreaking work of digging out boulders and stumps and excavating cuts. Finally, grading involved leveling and filling the uneven ground in preparation for laying crossties and rails.[5] Slaves predominated in all three phases.

The large majority of slaves engaged in railroad building were not owned by contractors or the railroads themselves, but rather were leased from slave owners who had surplus laborers. Railroad building was so dangerous, however, that some owners outright refused to allow even these surplus slaves to do such work, while others sought to protect their investments with life insurance policies.[6]

The most detailed picture of enslaved African Americans' experiences in railroad construction is revealed in the papers of a Mississippi slave owner named Samuel Smith Downey. In 1836, Downey hired twenty-seven of his slaves to a contractor building the Mississippi and Pearl River Railroad from Natchez to Jackson. Among that number were eleven women, several accompanied by their children. One woman labored while pregnant and bore a child in the construction camp. At least two slaves were elderly. In an unusual arrangement, the slaves were accompanied by Downey's agent, physician Joseph T. Hicks, and it is in his letters to Downey that we perceive the hardships of life for slaves engaged in railroad construction.

Nearly all of Downey's slaves became sick at one time or another. Early on, Hicks lamented that "it takes all my time to attend to them — we have been fortunate in not losing any of them." At one time, one-third of the slaves were ill from malaria, dysentery, and whooping cough. Heat also took its toll: Hicks reported that the weather was "too warm for our hands to work all day without killing them." They lived in crude shanties where mosquitoes tormented them at night, he wrote, and the construction contractor fed them spoiled meat. Despite Hicks's ministrations, two children and an adult male died that year, while other contractors' hands died in larger numbers.[7] Summing up the season, Hicks stated that Downey's sick slaves would not have survived without "my unwearied attention."[8]

But Downey apparently felt the risks to his slaves' health were justified, for he leased them again in 1837; once more, Hicks accompanied them. In 1838, however, Downey leased his slaves — including five married couples and their children — directly to Hicks, who had obtained a contract to grade roadbed. During that year, three slaves died and two mothers remained sickly for months after giving birth. Despite these losses, Hicks exulted, "I am doing a very fine business and making money faster than I ever expected to make."

Exactly what labor the enslaved women performed is not revealed in Hicks's reports. Two or three probably functioned as cooks for the group, and a similar number may have worked as laundresses and seamstresses (Downey purchased ready-made garments for the men, but only bolts of cloth for the women). Although the record is not explicit, it is likely that at least some of the women helped grade the railroad alongside the men, at least part time.

Although, as stated earlier, most new lines were built by contractors using hired slaves, some railroads purchased slaves, including a few women, to build their lines. When construction stalled on the Montgomery and West Point Railroad in 1844, for example, the Alabama legislature loaned the beleaguered company $116,783, part of which it used to purchase eighty-four slaves in far-off Virginia. Although several ran away, the company's president declared six years later that the railroad possessed "a valuable force of 53 men, 7 women, and 11 children."[9] After the line was completed, the slaves were employed mostly in track repairs, and the women worked as cooks.

Similar practices were followed on the Mobile and Great Northern Railroad. In 1861, it owned seventy men, eleven women, and four boys. These eighty-five slaves constructed several miles of line entirely through swamps, largely on earthen embankments. In one night, flood waters washed away the results of weeks of labor. So the slaves cut timber and built 1,500 feet of temporary trestles, which were later filled in with dirt. Railroad officials crowed that "it was fortunate that we had a Company force [the railroad's own slaves] to use upon this section, as no contractor would have willingly encountered the difficulties presented in executing the work." Once the line was graded, the company's slaves laid track at the rate of ten miles per month.[10] Bookkeeping records verify that slave ownership was profitable for the Mobile and Great Northern: including time lost for illness, each slave hand, as they were called, averaged $336 worth of labor. Even considering that the railroad paid an average of $1,360 to purchase each slave, it recouped one-fourth of that investment in just one year's work.[11]

In summary, antebellum southern railroads were built largely by slaves. Most new construction was undertaken by contractors, not the railroads themselves, and these contractors typically employed hundreds of slaves at a time. Most contractors did not own their slaves, however, but instead hired (leased) them on a yearly basis from slave owners who had a surplus of laborers. When railroads constructed their own lines, they used either slaves they hired or slaves they owned — and sometimes they used both.

Operating and Maintaining Rail Lines

As soon as southern railroads were completed, they established racial employment patterns that lasted long after slavery. Conductors, also called train captains, were invariably white, as were engineers. (Although some railroad executives suggested that slave engineers would cost less, I have found no evidence of their actual use.) Firemen could be black or white; whites worked as firemen because this was essential training for promotion to engineer. Firing a locomotive was hard physical labor, and far below the status of engineer or conductor. Not only did firemen stoke the locomotive's boiler with cordwood, they also restocked its tender with fuel and water. Some engines had an assistant fireman, known as a wood-passer. Black firemen also helped load and unload baggage on passenger trains and performed other tasks as ordered by the conductor.[12] Derailments and boiler explosions were the occupational hazards to engineers and firemen; injuries and fatalities were not uncommon.

Even more apt to be injured or killed were brakemen (also known as train hands), who held the lowest, least-skilled jobs on a train. Many railroads used slave brakemen, although whites also filled this position. A brakeman's main tasks were to help stop the train and couple cars, that is, attach them together. (Air brakes were not introduced until after the Civil War.) On passenger trains, they stood on open-end platforms, ready to apply the hand brake. On freight trains, brakemen jumped from the top of one car to another, again manually turning brake wheels. They often lost their lives falling off swaying cars, especially at night or in bad weather. The other great danger occurred during so-called link-and-pin couplings, which required the brakeman to stand between two cars, ready to drop a heavy pin through a cast iron link while avoiding being crushed as the cars came together. Switchmen, who were also often slaves, performed the same coupling and uncoupling functions as brakemen, but were stationed in yards.

Slaves filled several other jobs on rail lines. Some men worked as station hands at large depots and freight houses, loading and unloading baggage and freight cars. Those familiar with the variety of skilled tasks performed by plantation slave craftsmen will not be surprised to discover enslaved blacksmiths, finish carpenters, and boilermakers working in antebellum railroad shops, although a majority of black shop workers were unskilled laborers (also called helpers). Enslaved women worked as cooks for track maintenance gangs, while a few were station matrons (essentially janitresses) at the largest terminals. And at least one railroad, the Richmond and Danville, assigned maids to the ladies' cars on their express trains.[13]

Once the construction phase was past, the largest number of slaves employed by railroads worked on maintenance-of-way (MOW) gangs. Railroads divided their lines into sections that ranged in length from five to twelve miles. Each had a white section master and a section gang—comprised of slaves—responsible for keeping their assigned tracks in good repair. Borrowing plantation nomenclature, section masters were usually called overseers, and their qualifications were the same: they had to be able to "handle slaves."

Southern railroads assembled their section crews during the traditional slave hiring season in January. Hiring bonds (contracts) were negotiated with individual owners, specifying the monthly or yearly hire. This figure fluctuated from $100 to $125 per year in 1850 to as much as $200 in 1860. Hiring bonds usually specified that the railroad was responsible for food, clothing, and medical care, but the owner bore the cost of time lost if a slave ran away. Although a number of southern railroad executives believed it would be more profitable to purchase slave labor, and crassly anticipated the growth of their investments as babies were born to female slaves, most railroads were cash-poor and thus hired slaves for MOW rather than purchasing them.

Whether owned or hired, MOW crews endured a hard life and were exposed to the same types of punishments suffered by plantation slaves. According to the 1858 operating rules of the Pensacola and Georgia and the Tallahassee railroads, for example, "Where a negro requires correction, his hands must be tied by the overseer and he will whip him with an ordinary switch or strap not to exceed 39 lashes at one time nor more than 60 for one offense in one day, unless ordered to do so by the supervisor and in his presence."[14] Skilled slaves, such as a blacksmith or cook, were supervised less and allowed more autonomy. So long as a station matron was properly deferential and performed her assigned duties, she, too, likely did not live in daily fear of punishment. The same would be true for slave firemen, brakemen, and station hands as long as they did not appear to be malingering.

After construction was completed, southern railroads relied almost exclusively on enslaved workers to perform the heaviest and hardest labor—track maintenance—while also employing many other slaves to run trains, handle freight, and perform repairs. So essential (and profitable) were blacks to southern railroading that, after emancipation, many freedmen continued to fill the same jobs that had previously been done by slaves.

Origins of the Convict Lease

As difficult as life must have been for hired or purchased slaves, especially those performing hard outdoor manual labor on construction gangs and section crews, others suffered even worse: enslaved and free black convicts in Virginia. Throughout the South, slaves accused of serious crimes were sometimes tried in court, although blacks could not testify against whites. If found guilty, they were sentenced either to death, imprisonment, or sale outside of the state. But in 1858, Virginia's General Assembly authorized a new punishment: the lease of male and female criminals to contractors building railroads and canals. After the Civil War, the other southern states also adopted what was called the convict lease.

Contracts for the yearlong lease of prisoners were negotiated directly with Virginia's governor. During 1860, 111 male and sixteen female convicts labored to build the Covington and Ohio Railroad across the Appalachians into western Virginia. The following year, one contractor secured sixty-four convicts. The men were all adults, but among the females were girls aged ten, fourteen, fifteen, and seventeen at the time of their sentencing. Two women gave birth while on the work site (it is unlikely this was the result of courtship and marriage). Another construction firm building another portion of the same line likewise secured forty black convicts, including girls aged fifteen and sixteen at the time of sentencing.[15]

Since contractors bore the expense of feeding, clothing, supervising, and guarding the convicts, they had ample incentive to extract the maximum labor from them.[16] It is doubtful that they expended anything beyond the bare minimum. In fact, they had invested relatively little in their laborers compared to actual slave owners. And if a convict died during the year, the hire was prorated accordingly. It is likely that the female convicts worked as long and hard as the males, performing most if not all of the same tasks while also having to fend off the sexual depredations of men of both races.

Wreaking Havoc: The Impact on Black Families

Having charted the ways in which slaves labored for antebellum southern railroads, it remains to assess the railroads' impact on the personal lives and welfare of enslaved African Americans. Perhaps the greatest toll was on the black family. Domestic life was largely nonexistent for slaves who constructed railroads or labored on section gangs. Although the overwhelming majority of black railroad workers were male, some enslaved females also labored on construction projects and track gangs. Most contractors employed only males, or mostly males and a handful of females. The same was true for the railroads themselves. Assuming that many enslaved men were married, their wives were left for most of the year to keep families together and endure the hardships of bondage without the presence of their partners. In other words, many enslaved women were, figuratively speaking, railroad widows for most of the year. Others were literally widows, having lost spouses to railroad accidents.

Still other family ties were severed by the railroads' participation in the domestic slave trade. As noted above, when the Montgomery and West Point sought to purchase slaves to help complete construction of its Alabama lines in 1844, it bought eighty-four of them several states away in Virginia. Although some of them may not have been married at the time of their purchase, it is likely that many suffered the common fate of never seeing spouses, parents, or children again. Given the speculative nature of both railroading and slave ownership, a considerable number of railroad-owned slaves must have been permanently separated from their kinfolk. And although some hired slaves worked in proximity to their families and visited them on weekends, others only saw them during the Christmas holidays. In short, railroads wreaked considerable havoc on slave families.

Black women railroaders undoubtedly had a harder life than their sisters on plantations, where more regular family life and emotional and spiritual support derived from strong female networks cushioned the hardships of bondage. Most enslaved women railroaders lived and worked in an overwhelmingly male environment. This imbalance not only contributed to social and emotional isolation, but also to situations in which they were sexually defenseless and exploited.

Reverberations Today

None of the railroad companies operating in 1861 or 1865 exist today as a corporate entity. Beginning soon after the Civil War, all of the lines eventually merged with or were absorbed by others. Railroading today is dominated by five huge systems which are the products of many mergers and acquisitions: Norfolk Southern Corporation (NS); CSX Corporation; Union Pacific Corporation (UP); Canadian National Railway Company (CN); and the Burlington Northern Santa Fe Railway (BNSF). All but BNSF currently operate railroad lines which were initially built and/or maintained by slave labor. One smaller road, the Kansas City Southern Railway (KCS), also operates trackage initially built and/or maintained by bonded workers. I have documented the use of slaves on thirty-five lines now owned by NS; thirty-eight lines now owned by CSX; twelve lines now owned by UP; four lines now owned by CN; and four lines now owned by KCS.[17] (It is possible that a few of these ninety-three antebellum lines have been recently sold to short-line railroad operators, so the precise number of antebellum roads now owned by the large railroads may be slightly less than given here.) What remains clear, however, is that the use of slaves was virtually universal on antebellum southern railroads.

Slavery reparations lawsuits have been filed against several of today's large banking, insurance, textile, and tobacco corporations which had antebellum predecessors that benefited from slavery. Evidence for the number of slaves involved, and the profit derived from these slave-related businesses is, however, scattered, impressionistic, and incomplete. In contrast, there is a great amount of well-documented evidence concerning the use of slaves by antebellum railroads. Of all the corporate defendants named in the slavery reparations lawsuits, the case against the railroads is undoubtedly the strongest.

Notes

1. According to Robert C. Black III, *The Railroads of the Confederacy* (Chapel Hill: University of North Carolina Press, 1952), 113 railroads were built or under construction in the eleven states of the Confederacy as of mid-1861. I have been able to document the use of slaves on 84 of these lines. I also have evidence for 5 more lines not listed by Black, plus 4 more under

construction during the Civil War, for a total of 121 southern railroads operating or being constructed up to 1865.

2. And what of the other 23 percent of southern railroads (eighteen rail lines)? An examination of scattered annual reports for about one-third of them revealed nothing about the type of labor utilized; in other words, neither the use nor nonuse of slaves can yet be proven from available sources. I was not able to locate any annual reports for the remaining lines. But, considering the high degree of political and social acceptance of slavery by antebellum southern whites, the willingness of many slave owners to lease surplus slaves to railroads, and the widespread southern belief that black manual laborers were preferable to white (even Irish) workers, it is highly likely that most if not all of these remaining lines also employed slaves in some capacity. Thus, a strong case can be made for the universality of enslaved African Americans in construction and/or maintenance of antebellum southern railroads.

3. There are few detailed secondary sources for slavery on southern railroads. The two most useful works for this study are Allen W. Trelease, *The North Carolina Railroad, 1849–1871, and the Modernization of North Carolina* (Chapel Hill: University of North Carolina Press, 1991); and James H. Brewer, *The Confederate Negro: Virginia Craftsmen and Military Laborers, 1861–1865* (Durham, N.C.: Duke University Press, 1969).

4. Slaves were commonly used in the following industries: textile mills; iron foundries; tobacco, hemp, and shoe factories; tanneries; bakeries; brick works; sugar refineries; rice and grist mills; blacksmith, carpentry, cabinetry, and wheelwright shops; cotton gins and presses; coal, iron, lead, salt, and gold mines; the lumber industry; turpentine extraction and distillation; commercial fishing; turnpike and canal construction; draying; steamboating; and municipal, state, and federal government use of slaves to construct roads, levees, and military fortifications. See Robert S. Starobin, *Industrial Slavery in the Old South* (New York: Oxford University Press, 1970), chapter 1.

5. Trelease, *North Carolina Railroad*, 34; David E. Paterson, *A Frontier Link with the World: Upson County's Railroad* (Macon, Ga.: Mercer University Press, 1998), 42.

6. Stephen G. Collins, "Progress and Slavery on the South's Railroads," *Railroad History* (autumn 1999): 20; "List of Negroes to be hired out by W. C. Pittman, 1855," Craven County, Slaves and Free Negroes, bonds-petitions, no date, 1775–1861 (broken series), North Carolina State Archives. For an example of the danger of constructing bridges over large or rapid rivers, see *Report of the President of the Charleston and Savannah Rail-Road Company, to the Stockholders* (Charleston, 1861), 21. Only a few corporate reports acknowledged the hazards of mid-nineteenth-century railroading. In addition to the injuries to operating personnel, maintenance-of-way workers (laborers on track gangs) were injured or killed by being run over by trains or hand-cars.

7. Joseph Hicks to Downey, 30 June, 14 July, 25 August 1836, Samuel Smith Downey papers, Duke University. Intestinal and respiratory disorders as well as parasitic and skin diseases were more common at temporary worksites than on plantations and farms or in urban industries. Todd Savitt, *Medicine and Slavery: The Diseases and Health Care of Blacks in Antebellum Virginia* (Urbana: University of Illinois Press, 1978), 81–82.

8 Joseph Hicks to John Hicks, 8 September 1836, Joseph Hicks to Downey, 14 July, 25 August, 8 September, 29 October 1836, Downey Papers.

9. *Annual Report to the Stockholders of the Montgomery and West Point Rail Road Company, for the year ending First March, 1850* (Montgomery, 1850), 6–7.

10. Grading the roadbed required the most arduous labor, using primitive and labor-intensive technology. "Workers used shovels and wheelbarrows to build up or break down the earth so

that it could 'make the grade' and to form a flat foundation for the crossties.... To clear away rocks, slaves dug small holes with picks, packed the holes with gunpowder, and blasted the rock into pieces before digging with picks and shovels." Scott Reynolds Nelson, *Iron Confederacies: Southern Railways, Klan Violence, and Reconstruction* (Chapel Hill: University of North Carolina Press, 1999), 17. Crossties were hand-hewn from both softwood and hardwood logs, but were not as big as modern ties; early solid iron rails weighed around fifty pounds per yard, compared to today's mainline rails weighing 155 pounds per yard. It is unknown whether the proverbial "nine-pound hammer" used to drive spikes in the late nineteenth century was in use in the antebellum period. In any case, early track laying was backbreaking work.

11. *Report of the President and Directors to the Second Annual Meeting of the Stockholders of the Mobile and Gt. Northern R. R. Co.* (Mobile, 1861), 10, 14–15, 17–18, 20–22.

12. Trelease, *North Carolina Railroad*, 61; Ulrich B. Phillips, *A History of Transportation of the Eastern Cotton Belt to 1860* (New York: Octagon Books, 1968), 157; Richard E. Prince, *The Seaboard Air Line Railway: Steam Boats, Locomotives, and History* (Green River, Wyo.: R. E. Prince, 1969), 72.

13. Trelease, *North Carolina Railroad*, 61; Brewer, *Confederate Negro*, 86. Small numbers of enslaved women—perhaps wives of company-owned males—may also have been seamstresses: most hiring contracts specified that railroads were to clothe the slaves, and some companies purchased cloth rather than ready-made garments.

14. Quoted in Prince, *Seaboard Air Line*, 71–72.

15. Contract with Virginia Gov. John Letcher for hire of free Negro and slave convicts, signed by Thomas Roper: [Dec. 1861], Executive Papers, Gov. Letcher, letters received, December 1860, Library of Virginia.

16. Philip J. Schwarz, *Slave Laws in Virginia* (Athens: University of Georgia Press, 1996), 114–115.

17. For a more comprehensive discussion of railroad slavery, see the author's "Railroads and Slavery, *Railroad History*, no. 189 (fall–winter 2003): 34–59.

Reparations

A Viable Strategy to Address the Enigma of African American Health

DAVID R. WILLIAMS AND CHIQUITA COLLINS

This essay argues that improving the socioeconomic conditions of African American (or black) families and communities is a prerequisite to improving the health of African Americans and reducing the black–white gap in health. It begins with an overview of the magnitude of racial differences in health. It next describes the central role of socioeconomic status (SES) in producing these disparities, followed by a discussion of the role of racial residential segregation in creating racial inequality and the multiple mechanisms by which segregation affects health. The essay concludes that reparations are essential to eliminate the negative effects of segregation and are very likely to dramatically reduce racial differences in health.

We use the term *reparations* in the technical sense of its singular form, *reparation*, that emphasizes restitution and compensation to the victim because of the unjust behavior of the aggressor (Osabu-Kle, 2000). Allen (1998) indicated that very early on consideration was given to paying reparations to former slaves. The first call for blacks in the United States to receive reparations to redress "the unparalleled wrongs" and "unmitigated oppression" of slavery came in 1854. In 1865, the Freedmen's Bureau Act passed by the U.S. Congress recognized the justice of reparations and allocated forty acres of land at nominal rent to every former male slave. After this was vetoed by President Andrew Johnson, an alternative proposal in 1867 to provide forty acres and $50 to all former slaves was also rejected by Congress. However, reparations were never paid to the former slaves, and discrimination supported by law and/or custom has prevented their descendants from closing the black–white SES gap in the past 140 years. This long-term economic inequality, rooted in residential segregation, is the central determinant of the current African American health disadvantage. Accordingly, this essay argues that reparations in the form of compensatory social and economic development programs are a needed intervention for eliminating racial differences in economic status and health. These financial reparations would not be paid to individuals but would be targeted at enhancing human capital and building the economic base of disadvantaged communities (Robinson, 2000).

Racial Differences in Health

For almost two hundred years, research has documented that blacks report poorer health than whites for a broad range of indicators of health status (Krieger, 1987). In 1999, the life expectancy at birth of seventy-seven years for whites was six years longer than that of African Americans (National Center for Health Statistics [NCHS], 2002). Contributing to this life expectancy difference is an elevated rate of illness and death for African Americans compared to whites for almost every indicator of physical health. Higher mortality rates for blacks than whites are especially marked for heart disease, cancer, stroke, diabetes, kidney disease, homicide, hypertension, and AIDS (NCHS, 2002).

During the past fifty years, there have been many major initiatives in the United States to improve the health and economic circumstances of vulnerable social groups. The Hill-Burton program sought to increase access to medical care by increasing the number of hospital beds in underserved areas. Medicare and Medicaid provided increased access to medical care for the aging population and the poor. Federal spending on medical care and medical research has skyrocketed, and the U.S. population has reaped benefits from important advances in medical knowledge and technology. In addition, the civil rights movement and the war on poverty sought to open doors of economic opportunity to racial minorities, women, and the poor.

In concert with these changes, the health of both blacks and whites has improved over time. Overall death rates for whites were about 40 percent lower in 2000 than in 1950 (NCHS, 2002). For African Americans, the decline was almost 34 percent. At the same time, there has been no progress in reducing the relative difference in health between blacks and whites in the past fifty years. The age-adjusted overall death rate for African Americans was 22 percent higher than that of whites in 1950 but 33 percent higher in 2000 (NCHS, 2002). Moreover, the black–white ratios of mortality from coronary heart disease, cancer, diabetes, and cirrhosis of the liver were larger in 2000 than in 1950 (NCHS, 2002). The death rate of infants prior to their first birthday provides another vivid illustration of the persisting racial disparities in health. Although the infant mortality rate has declined for both racial groups over time, a black baby born in the United States was 1.6 times more likely to die before his or her first birthday than his or her white

TABLE 17.1 Number of Combat Deaths in America's Major Wars

War	Deaths
Revolutionary War	4,435
War of 1812	2,260
Mexican War	1,733
Civil War	184,594
Spanish-American War	385
World War I	53,513
World War II	292,131
Korean War	33,651
Vietnam War	47,369
Gulf War	148
Excess Deaths for Blacks (annually)	65,960

Source: United States Civil War Center (2002).

counterpart in 1950 but is 2.5 times more likely in 2000 (NCHS, 2002). Such large and persistent racial disparities in health are striking.

These racial differences in health are not just dry statistics. They reflect dramatic loss of life during the most economically productive years. National data on survival for 1999 provide a glimpse of the magnitude of these differences (Anderson and DeTurk, 2002). For every 100,000 black and white females born, some 97,000 white females survive to see their forty-fifth birthday compared to 94,000 black females. Similarly, 87,000 white women survive to age sixty-five compared to 78,000 black women. The differences are even more dramatic for males. Of every 100,000 black and white males born in the United States, 5,400 fewer black males survive to age forty-five and 16,000 fewer black males live to see their sixty-fifth birthday. A 1985 government report estimated that these racial differences in health translated into almost 60,000 "excess deaths" for the black population each year (U.S. Department of Health and Human Services, 1985). That is, 60,000 African Americans die each year that would not die if the black population had mortality rates that were similar to those of the white population. An update of that report using 1991 data found that the number of excess deaths had increased to 66,000 per year (NCHS, 1994).

To place this annual level of premature deaths in the African American population into perspective, Table 17.1 lists the number of combat deaths in the major wars fought by the United States throughout its history. Only the total casualties for the Civil War and World War Two exceed the annual number of excess deaths among blacks. A more recent national tragedy is the terrorist attacks of September 11, 2001. The scope and significance of these events cannot be calculated only in terms of casualties. Nonetheless, they provide a dramatic, contemporary, though imperfect benchmark. The total loss of life for the September 11 attacks is estimated at 2,819 deaths. Thus, the elevated death rates for African Americans can be viewed as a major national tragedy that begs for a comprehensive national response to prevent the loss of so many American lives each year. However, effective intervention is contingent on identifying and addressing the fundamental causes of these disparities.

Centrality of Socioeconomic Status

Existing racial categories do not capture biological distinctiveness, and genetic differences at best make a small contribution to racial disparities in health (Goodman, 2000). For example, sickle cell disease accounts for three-tenths of 1 percent of the black–white differences in mortality (Cooper, 1984). Research has identified socioeconomic status as one of the strongest determinants of variations in health in general (Link and Phelan, 1995; Williams and Collins, 1995) and the major contributor to racial differences in health, in particular (Williams, 1997). Socioeconomic status accounts for much of the racial differences in health, and it is frequently found that SES differences within each racial group are substantially larger than overall racial ones (Williams, 1999).

The key role that SES plays in racial differences in health can be illustrated with self-rated health—a global indicator of health status that is a valid and reliable indicator of overall health status (Idler and Benyamini, 1997). In 1995, national data revealed that 15.4 percent of African Americans reported to be in fair or poor health compared to 8.7 percent of whites (NCHS, 1998). Table 17.2 presents national data on self-assessed health. Two points are noteworthy. First, for both men and women and blacks and whites, income is a strong predictor of variation in health. Poor individuals (below the federal poverty level) have rates of ill health that are 4 to 7 times greater than their high-income peers (household income greater than $50,000). Instructively, the differences by income within each racial group are larger than the overall racial difference. Second, at every level of income, blacks report poorer health status than whites, suggesting that although much of the racial difference in health is accounted for by income, race has an effect on health that is independent of its association with SES. A similar pattern exists for other health outcomes, such as coronary heart disease mortality and life expectancy (NCHS, 1998).

TABLE 17.2 Percentage of Men and Women Reporting Fair or Poor Health, by Race and Income, 1995

	Men		Women	
Household Income	White	Black	White	Black
Poor (below federal poverty level)	30.5	37.4	30.2	38.2
Near Poor (less than twice federal poverty level)	21.3	22.6	17.9	26.1
Middle Income (more than twice federal poverty level but less than $50,000)	9.3	13.1	9.2	14.6
High Income ($50,000 or more)	4.2	5.0	5.8	9.2

Source: National Center for Health Statistics (2002).

The residual effect of race after SES is controlled could reflect the nonequivalence of SES indicators across race, the long-term consequences of exposure to adversity in childhood, and the effect of other aspects of racism (Williams and Collins, 1995). Two studies have reported that experiences of discrimination make an incremental contribution to explaining racial differences in self-rated health after SES is accounted for (Ren, Amick, and Williams, 1999; Williams, Yu, Jackson, and Anderson, 1997). Other aspects of racism may also contribute to these disparities. A recent Institute of Medicine report documented that African Americans and other minorities receive less intensive and poorer medical care than whites in virtually every area of medicine (Smedley, Stith, and Nelson, 2003). The report concluded that discrimination based on health care providers' negative stereotypes of blacks is a likely contributor to these disparities.

In the United States, large and persistent black–white differences in health co-occur with large and persistent black–white differences in SES. There has been little change in the economic gap between blacks and whites in the last quarter of the twentieth century (*Economic Report of the President*, 1998). For example, in 1978, black households had earned 59 cents for every dollar earned by whites and had a poverty rate that was 3.5 times higher and an unemployment rate that was 1.9 times higher. In 1996, compared to whites, African Americans had a poverty rate that was 2.5 times higher, an unemployment rate that was twice as high, and median household earnings that were still 59 cents for every dollar earned by whites.

Analysis of economic and health data during the past fifty years reveals that the narrowing and widening of the black–white gap in economic status has been associated with a parallel narrowing or widening of the black–white gap in health (Williams, 2001). The expansion of the black middle class and the narrowing of the black–white gap in income were greatest in the 1960s, and the economic progress of blacks relative to whites halted in the mid-1970s (*Economic Report of the President*, 1998). Between 1968 and 1978, the period of narrowing racial economic inequality, black men and women experienced a larger decline for multiple causes of death both on a percentage and an absolute basis than their white counterparts (Cooper, Steinhauer, Schatzkin, and Miller, 1981). Life expectancy data during this period showed larger gains for blacks than whites on both a relative and an absolute basis.

In contrast, during the 1980s, in the wake of substantial changes in national social and economic policies, the median income of black households relative to white households fell from the levels of the late 1970s (*Economic Report of the President*, 1998). Throughout the 1980s, blacks' median household income remained below the 59 cents level (for every dollar earned by whites) that it was in 1978. It fell as low as 55 cents in 1982 and did not return to at least 59 cents until the early 1990s. During the early 1980s, the health status of economically vulnerable populations worsened in several states (Lurie, Ward, Shapiro, and Brook, 1984; Mandinger, 1985). Similarly, the black–white gap in health status widened between 1980 and 1991 for multiple health outcomes, including life expectancy, excess deaths, and infant mortality (NCHS, 1994; Williams and Collins, 1995). These patterns reflected not only the relative but also the absolute deterioration in the health status of the black population. For five consecutive years after 1984, there was a progressive decline in the life expectancy at birth for blacks from the 1984 level. Life expectancy for African Americans began to increase in 1990 and by 1992 was slightly higher than in 1984 (NCHS, 1995). In contrast, the life expectancy of whites progressively increased during this period so that the black–white gap in 1992 was wider than in 1984. Thus, effective efforts to reduce racial disparities in health status should seriously grapple with reducing racial disparities in socioeconomic circumstances.

Segregation: Key Determinant of Racial Differences in Socioeconomic Status

Racial residential segregation is the foundation on which black–white disparities in SES have been built in the United States (see Oliver and Shapiro, part 1, and Massey, part 4). Segregation is a fundamental cause of differences in health status between African Americans and whites because it shapes socioeconomic conditions for blacks at the level of the individual, household, and community. The available evidence suggests that segregation is a key determinant of racial differences in socioeconomic mobility and also creates poor health-damaging conditions in the social and physical environment.

There has been a long history of interest in the central role that segregation has played in truncating socioeconomic opportunities for African Americans. In the early 1940s, Myrdal (1944) indicated that although its influence was indirect and impersonal, housing segregation was "basic" to understanding racial inequality in America. Two decades later, sociologist Kenneth Clark (1965) indicated that the "invisible walls" and distinctive "economic colonies" created by residential segregation were a key to understanding racial inequality. Similarly, after the urban riots of the 1960s, the Kerner Commission identified residential segregation as the "linchpin" of American race relations and the source of the large and growing racial inequality in SES (U.S. National Advisory Commission on Civil Disorders, 1988). Historian John Cell (1982) indicated that residential segregation was "one of the most successful political ideologies" of the last century and is "the dominant system of racial regulation and control" in the United States. In the most comprehensive recent treatise on segregation, Massey and Denton (1993, 9) showed that segregation is "the key structural factor for the perpetuation of Black poverty in the U.S." and the "missing link" in efforts to understand urban poverty.

Historical Background

Segregation refers to the physical separation of the races by enforced residence in restricted areas. Cell (1982) showed that the ideology of segregation was developed and advocated by white moderates more than one hundred years ago as a very conscious and deliberate strategy to combat some of the perceived populist and democratizing tendencies of urbanization and industrialization. It was imposed by legislation, supported by major economic institutions, enshrined in the housing policies of the federal government, enforced by the judicial system, and legitimized by the ideology of white supremacy that was advocated by the church and other cultural institutions (Cell, 1982; Jaynes and Williams, 1989). These institutional policies combined with the efforts of vigilant neighborhood organizations, discrimination on the part of real estate agents and home sellers, and restrictive covenants to limit the housing options of blacks to the least desirable residential areas. Segregation was designed to be a "complex, interlocking system of control that regulated the lives" of blacks (Cell, 1982). Prior to the Civil War, segregation was not a feature of life in the South (Cell, 1982; Lieberson, 1980; Massey and Denton, 1993). In the late nineteenth century and the early twentieth, segregation emerged most aggressively in the developing industrial urban centers of the South, and as blacks migrated to the North, segregation ensured that whites were protected from residential proximity to blacks. Accordingly, in both northern and southern cities, levels of black–white segregation increased dramatically between 1860 and 1940 and have remained strikingly stable since then (Massey and Denton, 1993).

The segregation of African Americans in the United States is distinctive. First, although most immigrant groups have experienced some residential segregation in the United States, no immigrant group has ever lived under the high levels of segregation that currently characterize the African American population (Massey and Denton, 1993). Second, early in the twentieth century, segregation increased for blacks at the same time that it was declining for immigrants. For example, in the late nineteenth century and up through 1910, blacks were less segregated than several European immigrant groups (Lieberson, 1980). However, in the post-1910 period, segregation for these European groups and blacks moved in opposite directions, with average segregation declining for European immigrants such that the second generation was less segregated than the first. At the same time, the segregation of blacks became more pronounced. Third, the nature of segregation in immigrant enclaves did not compare to the very high levels of segregation for the black population. Immigrant enclaves were never homogeneous to one immigrant group and always contained persons from multiple nationalities. In most immigrant ghettos, the ethnic immigrant group after which the enclave was named typically did not even constitute a majority of the population of that area. In addition, unlike the pattern for blacks, most members of European ethnic groups did not live in an immigrant enclave (Lieberson, 1980; Massey and Denton, 1993). Thus, ethnic enclaves were temporary in the process of assimilation in contrast to the permanence of hypersegregation for blacks.

Persistence of Segregation in the United States

The Civil Rights Act of 1968 made discrimination in the sale or rental of housing units illegal in the United States, but studies reveal that explicit discrimination in housing persists (W. A. V. Clark, 1992; Fix and Struyk, 1993). Moreover, in more subtle ways, blacks are still discouraged from residing in white residential areas, and whites continue to move out of communities when the black population increases (Shihadeh and Flynn, 1996; Turner, 1993). Thus, although African Americans express the highest support for residence in integrated neighborhoods (Bobo and Zubrinsky, 1996), their residential exclusion remains high and distinctive.

A recent analysis of the 2000 census data documented that levels of segregation remain very high in the United States (Glaeser and Vigdor, 2001). Although this report claims that the level of segregation "declined dramatically" between 1990 and 2000 and is now at its lowest point since about 1920, closer inspection of the data indicates the persistence of extremely high levels of segregation in the United States. On the one hand, the report indicated that segregation declined in 272 of the 317 metropolitan statistical areas (MSAs) between 1990 and 2000 while it increased in 19 MSAs. On the other hand, the magnitude of this decline was small, with the average decline being 5.5 percentage points. Nationally, the index of dissimilarity for the United States declined from .70 in 1990 to .66 in 2000. An index of .66 means that 66 percent of black U.S. residents would have to move to achieve a perfect representation of their group. Generally, a dissimilarity index value above .60 is thought to represent extremely high segregation (Massey and Denton, 1989). In the 2000 census, there were more than seventy-four MSAs with dissimilarity scores greater than .60. Instructively, these metropolitan areas contain the majority of the black population.

The report revealed that the decline in segregation was due to the movement of blacks into formerly all-white census tracts rather than the integration of overwhelmingly black (80 percent or more) census tracts. In fact, between 1990 and 2000, the number of census tracts where more than 80 percent of the population was African American remained constant (Glaeser and Vigdor, 2001). Accordingly, the decline in segregation is due to the reduction of all-white census tracts and has had no impact on very high percentage African American census tracts, the residential isolation of most African Americans, or the concentration of urban poverty (Glaeser and Vigdor, 2001). The report also indicated that segregation had declined the most in small growing cities, especially those of the Southwest and West, and had remained relatively stable in the large metropolitan areas of the Northeast and Midwest. Moreover, there was an inverse relationship between the black percentage of the population in an entire MSA and the decline in segregation. Segregation declined 2.8 percent in MSAs that were more than 25 percent black in 1990. Thus, most of the reduction in segregation has come from the MSAs where the percentage of blacks in the population is very small.

Segregation and Socioeconomic Status

By determining access to education and employment opportunities for African Americans, residential segregation has truncated socioeconomic mobility for blacks and been a central mechanism by which racial inequality has been created and reinforced in the United States (Jaynes and Williams, 1989;

Massey and Denton, 1993). First, residential segregation has led to highly segregated elementary and high schools and is a fundamental cause of racial differences in the quality of education. Because of residential segregation, despite an almost fifty-year-old unanimous Supreme Court decision in *Brown v. Board of Education* that intentional segregation in schools was inherently unequal and unconstitutional, elementary and high school education in the United States remains highly segregated and decidedly unequal (Orfield and Eaton, 1996). Residence determines which public school students can attend, and the funding of public education is under the control of local government. Thus, community resources are important in determining the quality of the neighborhood school.

There is a very strong relationship between residential segregation and the concentration of poverty. Nationally, the correlation between minority (black and Hispanic) percentage and poverty is .66; in metropolitan Chicago, the correlation is .90 for elementary schools (Orfield, 1996). Although there are millions of poor whites in the United States, poor white families tend to be dispersed throughout the community, with many residing in desirable residential areas (Wilson, 1987). Accordingly, in 96 percent of predominantly white schools, the majority of students come from middle-class backgrounds (Orfield, 1996). In contrast, public schools with a high proportion of blacks and Hispanics are dominated by poor children.

The concentration of poverty and not racial composition per se is the basic cause of the problems that plague segregated schools. The catalogue of challenges include lower test scores, fewer students in advanced placement courses, more limited curricula, less qualified teachers, little serious academic counseling, fewer connections with colleges and employers, more deteriorated buildings, higher levels of teen pregnancy, and higher dropout rates (Orfield and Eaton, 1996). These conditions often give rise to peer pressure against academic achievement and in support of crime and substance use. Moreover, levels of segregation for black and Latino students are on the increase (Orfield, 1996). The end result is that these minority students are concentrated in urban schools that have different and inferior courses and lower levels of achievement than the schools attended by white students in adjacent suburban school districts (Orfield and Eaton, 1996). One recent study found that as a growing number of minority families moved to the suburbs between 1987 and 1995, the presence of residential segregation there has led to increased levels of segregation in suburban schools (Reardon and Yun, 2001). Even in integrated schools, black students are disproportionately allocated or tracked into low-ability and non-college-preparatory classes that are characterized by a less demanding curriculum and lower teacher expectations (Jaynes and Williams, 1989). Thus, the high school dropout and graduation rates, the competencies and knowledge of a high school graduate, and the probability of enrollment in college varies by race.

Research also reveals that segregation is a critical determinant of employment opportunities and thus income levels for African Americans. Audit studies (in which trained black and white job applicants with identical qualifications apply for employment) have found that discrimination occurred that favored white over black applicants in one in every five audits (Fix and Struyk, 1993). Such data highlight the role of employment discrimination at the individual level in adversely affecting employment opportunities for blacks. Equally important, institutional discrimination, based on residential segregation, severely restricts access to jobs for blacks. In the past several decades there has been a mass movement of low-skilled, high-pay jobs from many of the urban areas where blacks are concentrated to the suburbs (Kassarda, 1989; Wilson, 1987, 1996). This has created a spatial mismatch in which African Americans reside in areas different from those that have access to high-paying entry-level jobs. It has also led to a skills mismatch in which the available jobs in the urban areas where African Americans live require a level of skill and training that many do not have. Some corporations explicitly use the racial composition of areas in their decision-making process regarding the placement of new plants and the relocation of existing ones (Cole and Deskins, 1988). Negative racial stereotypes of African Americans and the areas where they are concentrated play an important role in these decisions (Kirschenman and Neckerman, 1991; Neckerman and Kirschenman, 1991). Thus, during routine "nonracial" restructuring, relocation, and downsizing, employment facilities are systematically moved to suburban and rural areas, where the proportion of blacks in the labor force is low. A *Wall Street Journal* analysis of more than 35,000 U.S. companies found that blacks were the only racial group that experienced a net job loss during the economic downturn of 1990-1991 (Sharpe, 1993). African Americans had a net job loss of 59,000 jobs, whereas there was a net gain of 71,100 for whites, 55,100 for Asians, and 60,000 for Latinos.

Residential segregation also affects employment opportunities by isolating blacks in segregated communities from both role models of stable employment and social networks that could provide leads about potential jobs (Wilson, 1987). The social isolation created by these structural conditions in segregated residential environments can then induce cultural responses that weaken the commitment to norms and values that may be critical for economic mobility. For example, long-term exposure to conditions of concentrated poverty can undermine a strong work ethic, devalue academic success, and remove the social stigma of imprisonment and educational and economic failure (Shihadeh and Flynn, 1996).

The Consequences of Segregation: Racial Differences in Socioeconomic Status

By determining access to educational and employment opportunity, segregation has been a central force in producing large racial differences in SES. An empirical analysis of the effects of segregation on young African Americans making the transition from school to work documented that getting rid of residential segregation would lead to the elimination of black–white differences in earnings, high school graduation rates, and idleness and would reduce racial differences in single motherhood by two thirds (Cutler, Glaeser, and Vigdor, 1997).

Table 17.3 presents selected socioeconomic characteristics for blacks and whites in the United States. It shows that the median family income for white households in 1996 ($38,787) was almost 1.7 times higher than that of African Americans ($23,482). Compared to whites, blacks are 3 times more likely to be poor. If we combine persons in poverty with persons who are near poor (incomes above poverty but less than twice the poverty level), then one-quarter of white households but more than half of African American households are in this economically vulnerable category. Rates of poverty are especially high among children. In 1996, 40 percent of black children younger than eighteen, compared to 11 percent of their white peers, were growing up poor. Moreover, almost one-third of white children and more than two-thirds of black ones were either poor or near poor. The average level of education was relatively high in the United States in 1996, but racial differences in educational attainment were also evident. Among persons aged twenty-five to sixty-four, nine out of ten whites and eight out of ten African Americans had a high school diploma or more. Whites are also twice as likely as blacks to have graduated from college (29 percent vs. 15 percent).

The unemployment rate for blacks is more than twice that of whites. Racial differences in educational attainment account for part of this disparity. However, large racial differences in unemployment persist even at equivalent levels of education (Council of Economic Advisors, 1998). There is also an overrepresentation of African American workers in the lowest paying sectors of the economy, which accounts in part for the racial differences in income. White-collar occupations (executive, professional, managerial, administrative, technical, clerical, and sales) have higher average compensation than blue-collar and service jobs. Among male civilian workers in the United

TABLE 17.3 Selected Socioeconomic Indicators for Blacks and Whites in the United States, 1996

Indicator	White	Black
Income		
Median Income	$38,787	$23,482
Poverty		
Percentage Poor	8.6	28.4
Percentage Poor and Near Poor	25.6	55.1
Percentage Children Younger Than 18 Poor	11.1	39.9
Percentage Children Younger Than 18 Poor and Near Poor	30.8	68.0
Educational Attainment, Age 25 to 64		
Percentage High School Graduate or Higher	90.5	79.8
Percentage College Graduate or Higher	28.8	14.8
Unemployment[a]		
Percentage Unemployed	4.7	10.5
High School Graduate	4.6	10.8
College Graduate	2.1	3.3
Current Occupation, Age 25 to 64		
Percentage White Collar, Males	52.6	33.5
Percentage Blue Collar/Service, Males	44.1	64.5
Percentage White Collar, Females	77.6	59.3
Percentage Blue Collar/Service, Females	21.3	40.5
Individual Income, by Education, Age 18 and Older[a]		
Median Income, High School Graduate, Male	$28,591	$22,267
Median Income, College Graduate, Male	$48,014	$35,558
Median Income, High School Graduate, Female	$16,270	$15,379
Median Income, College Graduate, Female	$28,667	$29,311
Household Income by Education, Age 25 and Older		
Median Income, High School Graduate, Male	$41,200	$36,020
Median Income, College Graduate, Male	$67,952	$54,500
Median Income, High School Graduate, Female	$37,000	$23,556
Median Income, College Graduate, Female	$64,007	$47,100
Wealth (data for 1995)[b]		
Median Net Worth	$49,030	$7,073
Lowest Income Quartile	$9,720	$1,500
Highest Income Quartile	$123,781	$40,866

Sources: National Center for Health Statistics (1998); [a]U.S. Bureau of the Census (1998); [b]Davern and Fisher (2001).

States, whites are 1.6 times more likely than African Americans to be employed in white-collar positions. Blacks are also 1.5 times more likely to hold blue-collar and service jobs. Similarly, compared to white women, African American women are 1.3 times less likely to be white-collar workers but about twice as likely to be employed in service and blue-collar occupations.

However, many socioeconomic indicators are not equivalent across race (Kaufman, Cooper, and McGee, 1997; Williams and Collins, 1995). As noted earlier, a given level of education may not reflect the same degree of educational preparation and skills across race. There are also racial differences in the income returns for a given level of education, with blacks earning less income than whites at comparable levels of education. These racial differences are more marked for men than for women. In addition, American women of all racial groups earn less than their similarly educated male counterparts. This gender difference in earnings combined with racial differences in household structure (black households are more likely than white ones to be headed by a female) means that racial differences in individual earnings at equivalent levels of education understate racial differences in household income. Table 17.3 shows that in 1996, black households with a college-educated male earned 80 cents ($54,500) for every dollar ($67,952) earned by a comparable white household. Such racial differences in the returns to education are evident at all levels of educational preparation but are more marked for women than for men. For every dollar earned by a household with a similarly educated white woman, households with black women who completed high school earned 64 cents and those with a college degree earned 74 cents.

The largest racial difference evident in Table 17.3 is for wealth. The median net worth of whites is almost 7 times that of blacks. This underscores the extent to which racial differences in income understate racial differences in economic status and resources. At every level of income, blacks have considerably less wealth than whites (Davern and Fisher, 2001). For example, the net worth at the lowest quintile of income is $9,720 for white households compared to $1,500 for African American households. At the highest quintile of income, white households have a net worth of $123,781 compared to $40,866 for black households. Racial differences in wealth also link the current situation of blacks to historic discrimination. For most American families, housing equity is a major source of wealth. Thus, today's black–white differences in wealth are to a considerable degree a direct result of the institutional discrimination in housing practiced in the past (Oliver and Shapiro, 1997; see Oliver and Shapiro, part 1).

Segregation and the Effects of Place

Table 17.4 presents sociodemographic data for the seven cities ranked highest on segregation (dissimilarity index) in the 2000 census and seven of the lowest ranked cities. These data illustrate that a high level of residential segregation and a high percentage of the population being black do not necessarily co-occur. Chicago ranked highest on segregation but was only 37 percent black. Several points are noteworthy about the two groups of cities. In both high- and low-segregation cities, whites have higher levels of educational attainment than blacks. With one exception, Newark, the education levels of blacks tend to exceed that of whites. Unemployment and poverty rates for both racial groups tend to be higher in high- versus low-segregation cities. In general, white households also have a higher median income in all cities, with whites earning more than twice the income of blacks in some cities. Home equity is a major source of wealth for most Americans, and the median value of owner-occupied houses is higher for whites than for blacks, with the greatest gap observed in highly segregated cities. In our nation's capital, for example, black home owners owned houses with a median value of $125,000, whereas white homeowners' median home value was $380,000. Most important, for multiple SES indicators (education, income, and home value), the black–white gap is markedly smaller in low-segregation cities compared to those high on segregation. The poorer profile on some SES indicators for whites in highly segregated cities raises the question of whether this reflects an adverse effect of some of the structural characteristics of highly segregated cities or a selection effect in which more vulnerable whites (in terms of SES, age, and health) opted not to migrate out of highly segregated cities.

Racial residential segregation has also led to unequal access for most blacks to a broad range of services provided by municipal authorities. Compared to more affluent areas, political leaders have been more likely to cut spending and services in poor neighborhoods in general and African American neighborhoods in particular (Shihadeh and Flynn, 1996; Wallace, 1990, 1991). Because poor and minority persons are less active politically, elected officials are less likely to encounter vigorous opposition when services are reduced in these areas. This disinvestment of economic resources in these neighborhoods has led to a decline in the quality of life in those communities (Alba and Logan, 1993). The selective out-migration of many whites and some middle-class blacks from cities to the suburbs has also reduced the urban tax base and the ability of some cities to provide a broad range of supportive social services

TABLE 17.4 Demographic Profile of Seven Cities with High Scores on the Dissimilarity Index (D) and Seven Low Segregation Cities, 2000

City	D	Population Size (000)	Black (%)	Black High School Graduate+ (%)	White High School Graduate+ (%)	Black Jobless Rate (%)	White Jobless Rate (%)	Black Poverty Rate (%)	White Poverty Rate (%)	Black Median Household Income (000)	White Median Household Income (000)	Black Median Home Value (000)	White Median Home Value (000)
High Segregation													
Chicago	88	2,896	36.8	70.7	85.2	18	5	29	8	29	49	92	165
Atlanta	86	416	61.4	66.8	94.2	17	10	33	8	23	62	78	324
New York	85	8,008	26.6	70.4	84.7	14	5	26	12	31	51	178	240
Ft. Lauderdale	85	152	28.9	50.3	90.5	12	4	35	9	23	45	77	194
Washington, D.C.	84	572	60.0	70.4	97.5	15	7	25	8	30	67	125	380
Newark	82	274	53.5	65.1	51.1	19	10	32	16	25	34	111	140
Philadelphia	82	1,518	43.2	68.4	77.1	15	7	29	13	26	37	45	73
Low Segregation													
Moreno Valley, Calif.	32	142	19.9	85.0	87.2	11	7	20	8	42	55	127	124
Clarksville, Tenn.	40	103	23.2	82.4	86.4	10	6	19	7	31	40	80	86
Aurora, Colo.	42	276	13.4	87.5	92.8	7	3	13	5	39	51	148	145
Garland, Tex.	43	216	11.9	84.5	89.4	7	3	13	4	41	55	87	89
Lansing, Mich.	46	119	21.9	80.7	85.7	12	4	27	12	30	36	78	73
Virginia Beach, Va.	48	425	19.0	85.9	92.1	8	3	12	5	39	51	98	130
Las Vegas, Nev.	48	478	10.4	76.1	87.6	14	5	24	7	30	49	122	143

Sources: U.S. Bureau of the Census (2000); Logan (2002).

to economically deprived residential areas. Segregation also leads to racial differences in the purchasing power of income. Many commercial enterprises withdraw from segregated urban areas. There are often fewer services in highly segregated black areas, and the available ones tend to be poorer in quality but higher in price. On average, blacks pay higher costs than whites for housing, food, groceries, insurance, and other services (Williams and Collins, 1995). Research also indicates that residential segregation leads to smaller returns on the investment in real estate for African Americans compared to whites. That is, the growth in housing equity over time, a major source of wealth for most American families, is smaller for blacks in highly segregated areas than for comparable homes in other areas (Oliver and Shapiro, 1997). All of the aforementioned factors combine to reduce the neighborhood and housing quality of highly segregated residential areas.

Some evidence suggests that it is difficult even for middle-class blacks to escape some of the negative neighborhood conditions associated with segregation. There is increasing segregation in some suburban areas (Reardon and Yun, 2001), and middle-class blacks are less able than their white counterparts to translate their higher economic status into desirable residential conditions. Research reveals that middle-class suburban African Americans reside in neighborhoods that are less segregated than those of poor central-city blacks (Alba, Logan, and Stults, 2000). However, compared to white counterparts, middle-class blacks live in poorer quality neighborhoods with white neighbors who are less affluent than they are. A recent analysis of 1990 census data revealed that suburban residence does not buy better housing conditions for blacks (Harris, 1999). The suburban locations where African Americans reside tend to be equivalent or inferior to those of central cities. One recent national study found that whereas residence in the suburbs was associated with lower mortality rates for whites, it predicted markedly elevated mortality rates for blacks, especially for black men (House et al., 2000).

High levels of segregation create distinctive ecological environments on multiple dimensions for African Americans. Sampson and Wilson (1995) reported that in the 171 largest cities in the United States, there was not even one where whites lived in comparable ecological conditions to blacks in terms of poverty rates or rates of single-parent households. These researchers came to the striking conclusion that "the worst urban context in which whites reside is considerably better than the average context of Black communities" (Sampson and Wilson, 1995, 41). This highlights the almost insurmountable challenge of introducing statistical controls for an area effect in black–white contrasts.

Direct Effects of Segregation on Health

Research reveals that residential segregation is related to elevated risk of adult and infant mortality and tuberculosis (Williams and Collins, 2001). There are multiple mechanisms by which the concentrated poverty created by segregation could adversely affect health (Schulz, Williams, Israel, and Lempert, 2002; Williams and Collins, 2001). First, the conditions created by poverty and segregation make it more difficult for residents of those areas to practice desirable health behaviors. The higher cost and poorer quality of grocery items in economically disadvantaged neighborhoods can lead to poorer nutrition. Both the tobacco and alcohol industries heavily bombard poor minority communities with advertising for their products. The lack of recreation for families and concerns about personal safety can also discourage leisure-time physical exercise.

Second, access to high-quality medical care is often a challenge in many segregated neighborhoods. Health care facilities are more likely to close in poor and minority communities than in other areas (Whiteis, 1992), and pharmacies in minority neighborhoods may be less likely to be adequately stocked with medication (Morrison, Wallenstein, Natale, Senzel, and Huang, 2000). Third, given the strong association between SES and the distribution of stress, the concentration of poverty leads to exposure to higher levels of economic hardship as well as other types of chronic and acute stress at the individual, household, and neighborhood levels. For example, African Americans are much more likely than whites to be victims of all types of crime (Council of Economic Advisors, 1998). The weakened community and neighborhood infrastructure in segregated areas can also adversely affect interpersonal relationships and trust among neighbors (Schulz et al., 2002). These resources can potentially reduce at least some of the negative effects of stress on health. Fourth, poor, segregated communities are often victims of institutional neglect and disinvestment. The resulting decline in the urban infrastructure and physical environment results in disproportionate exposure to environmental toxins and poor-quality housing (Bullard, 1994).

Black–white differences in mortality are largest for homicide. Research reveals that residential segregation is at the core of a complex set of mechanisms driving this disparity (Sampson, 1987). The poor educational and employment opportunities in segregated communities result in a small pool of employable or stably employed males. High rates of male unemployment and underemployment in turn generate the high rates of out-of-wedlock births, female-headed households, the "feminization of poverty," and the extreme concentration of poverty in many black communities (Testa, Astone,

Krogh, and Neckerman, 1993; Wilson and Neckerman, 1986). For both blacks and whites, male employment and earnings are positively related to entry into marriage, and economic instability is positively related to marital dissolution (Bishop, 1980; Mare and Winship, 1991; Wilson, 1987). In turn, single-parent households lead to lower levels of social control and guardianship. Sampson (1987) found a strong association between family structure and violent crime that was similar for both blacks and whites. Thus, the high rates of violent crime and homicide for African Americans are determined by their greater exposure to poverty and lack of jobs created by segregation and to the resultant family structures and processes that are induced by these economic conditions.

Reparations and the Reduction of Black–White Inequalities in Health

The evidence reviewed documents the persistence of racial inequalities in health. Although more than half of the African American and white public are unaware of the existence of these disparities in health (Lillie-Blanton, Brodie, Rowland, Altman, and McIntosh, 2000), the U.S. government has recently made a commitment to eliminating them. On February 21, 1996, President Clinton devoted his Saturday morning radio address to the nation to the problem of racial differences in health. He declared that "racial and ethnic disparities in health are unacceptable in a country that values equality and equal opportunity for all. And that is why we must act now." In response, Healthy People 2010, a major planning initiative of the federal government, made the elimination of racial disparities in health in six target areas by the year 2010 a national priority for the Department of Health and Human Services. This initiative has focused on community-based demonstration projects addressing prevention and treatment, educational outreach, and increased research and training.

The success of Healthy People 2010 and related current and future efforts to eliminate racial disparities in health is contingent on identifying and effectively addressing the fundamental causes of these disparities. Efforts to eliminate racial disparities in health that focus only on intermediate causal factors such as increased access to health care, enhanced levels of health information, and behavior change are unlikely to improve the health of the black population and eliminate racial disparities in health (Link and Phelan, 1995; Smedley and Syme, 2000; Williams, 1997). Comprehensive efforts that address the underlying social conditions that give rise to health problems are needed.

This essay has considered the central role of residential segregation and other aspects of racism in shaping the social and economic circumstances and thus the health of the African American population. Racial disparities in health illustrate how the long arm of America's racial past continues to affect the constitutionally guaranteed pursuit of life, liberty, and happiness by the historically disadvantaged. Black–white disparities in health indicate that the achievement of racial parity in SES and health requires more than merely the reduction of negative racial attitudes and values in the United States. What is also needed is a systematic dismantling of racist structures such as residential segregation.

The persistence of high levels of residential segregation for most African Americans also reflects the failure of prior policies to reduce racial economic inequality in the United States. As noted, there has been no narrowing of the racial gap in economic status in the past twenty-five years (*Economic Report of the President*, 1998). Other evidence suggests that the increasing racial and ethnic diversity of the U.S. population is unlikely to reduce the entrenched patterns of segregation for African Americans. Data from Los Angeles indicate that Hispanics were as hostile as whites to having blacks as neighbors and Asians were more hostile than whites (Bobo and Zubrinsky, 1996).

There is nothing inherently negative about living in close proximity to persons of one's own race. Rather, the problems attendant to segregation are linked to the concentration of poverty and the absence of an infrastructure that promotes social and economic opportunity (Massey and Denton, 1993; Sampson and Wilson, 1995; Wilson, 1996). Thus, the elimination of the negative SES and health effects of segregation will require a major infusion of economic capital to rebuild the physical and economic infrastructure of disadvantaged black communities. Monetary reparations are a viable approach to accomplish this (Oliver and Shapiro, 1997).

Opponents of reparations argue that reparations are unnecessary for multiple reasons (Kaminer, 2000; McWhorter, 2001; Reed, 2000; Zinsmeister, 2001). These include the fact that America has already paid its debt to African Americans because (a) there was a large loss of life during the Civil War, (b) the U.S. government has already invested trillions of dollars to improve the social circumstances of blacks (through various welfare programs), and (c) affirmative action and other opportunities have brought economic success to many blacks in recent decades. Moreover, it is argued that there are too many logistical difficulties attendant to making financial payments to the descendants of slaves. Compelling responses have been made to these objections (Allen, 1998; Cha-Jua, 2001; Robinson, 2000). The payment of reparations is based on established legal principles, and there are precedents both in the United States and internationally (Allen, 1998). Moreover, given that the injuries caused by legal segregation persist and there has been systematic decapitalization of African American areas, reparation provides one strategy to infuse capital and create economic opportunities in black areas. Targeting reparations to "investment in education and training, housing, health and business development" (America, 1999) avoids most of the feared logistical difficulties in identifying specific descendants of slaves for monetary payments (see America, part 2).

Neglected in this debate is the potential for reparations to address the nationally recognized problem of racial disparities in health. This essay emphasizes that the concentration of poverty and the social and physical deterioration of segregated neighborhoods are the result of the successful implementation of public policies, including those of the federal government (Massey and Denton, 1993; Massey and Kanaiaupuni, 1993; Wallace and Wallace, 1997). Reparations can trigger a new set of countervailing processes to effectively negate the forces that maintain racial inequality. It should also be noted that it is in the interest of the entire society to reduce the racial gap in SES and health. The forces that affect the health of the African American population are the same factors on a less intensive scale that determine the health of the rest of the population (Cooper et al., 1981). Moreover, health problems that are initially confined to segregated areas often spread to more affluent areas (Wallace and Wallace, 1997). Thus, investments to improve the social conditions of African Americans can have long-term positive consequences for non-blacks as well.

Conclusion

A large gap in health exists between blacks and whites, and it is inextricably linked to the history of race and racism in the United States. Racial differences in SES and health are the predictable results of the successful implementation of residential segregation, a policy that was deliberately set up to create separate and unequal living conditions for blacks. It and other aspects of racism remain central determinants of racial differences in health. Thus, the legacy of slavery and legal discrimination still matters for African Americans in the twenty-first century. According to government estimates, conditions linked to race were responsible for the premature deaths of more than 1 million African Americans in the past two decades. Reparations can break the cycle of racial economic inequality for the health of the African American population. A Marshall Plan type of economic investment funded by a reparations initiative or some similar mechanism is indispensable for any effective effort that would markedly improve the economic well-being and the health of the African American population.

Preparation of this article was supported by Grant MH59575 from the National Institute of Mental Health and Grant R24HD42849 from the National Institute of Child Health and Human Development. The authors wish to thank Scott Wyatt, Nari Kim, and Trisha Matelski for research assistance and Car Nosel for preparing the manuscript.

References

Alba, R. D., and J. R. Logan. "Minority Proximity to Whites in Suburbs: An Individual-level Analysis of Segregation." *American Journal of Sociology* 98 (1993): 1388–1427.
Alba, R. D., J. R. Logan, and B. J. Stults. "How Segregated Are Middle-class African Americans?" *Social Problems* 47 (2000): 543–558.
Allen, R. L. "Past Due: The African American Quest for Reparations." *The Black Scholar* 28, no. 2 (1998): 2–17.
America, R. F. "Reparations and Public Policy." *Review of Black Political Economy* 26, no. 3 (1999): 77–83.
Anderson, R. N., and P. B. DeTurk. *United States Life Tables, 1999* (National Vital Statistics Reports, vol. 50, no. 6). Hyattsville, Md.: National Center for Health Statistics, 2002.
Bishop, J. H. "Jobs, Cash Transfers, and Marital Instability. A Review of the Evidence." *Journal of Human Resources* 15 (1980): 301–334.
Bobo, L., and C. L. Zubrinsky. "Attitudes on Residential Integration: Perceived Status Differences, Mere In-group Preference, or Racial Prejudice?" *Social Forces* 74 (1996): 883–909.
Bullard, R. D. "Urban Infrastructure: Social, Environmental, and Health Risks to African Americans." In L. Livingston, ed., *Handbook of Black American Health: The Mosaic Conditions, Issues, Policies, and Prospects*, 315–330. Westport, Conn.: Greenwood, 1994.
Cell, J. *The Highest Stage of White Supremacy: The Origin of Segregation in South Africa and the American South*. New York: Cambridge University Press, 1982.
Cha-Jua, S. K. "Slavery, Racist Violence, American Apartheid: The Case for Reparations." *New Politics* 8, no. 31 (2001): 46–64.
Clark, K. B. *Dark Ghetto: Dilemmas of Social Power*. New York: Harper and Row, 1965.
Clark, W. A. V. "Residential Preferences and Residential Choices in a Multiethnic Context." *Demography* 29 (1992): 451–466.
Cole, R. E., and D. R. Deskins Jr. "Racial Factors in Site Location and Employment Patterns of Japanese Auto Firms in America." *California Management Review* 31, no. 1 (1988): 9–22.
Cooper, R. S. "A Note on the Biologic Concept of Race and Its Application in Epidemiologic Research." *American Heart Journal* 108 (1984): 715–723.
Cooper, R. S., M. Steinhauer, A. Schatzkin, and W. Miller. "Improved Mortality among U.S. Blacks, 1968–1978: The Role of Antiracist Struggle." *International Journal of Health Service* 11 (1981): 511–522.
Council of Economic Advisers for the President's Initiative on Race. *Changing America: Indicators of Social and Economic Well-being by Race and Hispanic Origin*. Washington, D.C.: Government Printing Office, 1998.

Cutler, D. M., E. L. Glaeser, and J. L. Vigdor. "Are Ghettos Good or Bad?" *Quarterly Journal of Economics* 112 (1997): 827–872.

Davern, M. E., and P. J. Fisher. *U.S. Census Bureau, Current Population Reports, Household Economic Studies Series. Household Net Worth and Asset Ownership: 1995.* Washington, D.C.: Government Printing Office, 2001.

Economic Report of the President. Washington, D.C.: Government Printing Office, 1998.

Fix, M., and R. J. Struyk. *Clear and Convincing Evidence: Measurement of Discrimination in America.* Washington, D.C.: Urban Institute Press, 1993.

Glaeser, E. L., and J. L. Vigdor. *Racial Segregation in the 2000 Census: Promising News.* Washington, D.C.: Brookings Institution, 2001.

Goodman, A. H. "Why Genes Don't Count (for Racial Differences in Health)." *American Journal of Public Health* 90 (2000): 1699–1702.

Harris, D. R. *All Suburbs Are Not Created Equal: A New Look at Racial Differences in Suburban Locations* (Research Report No. 99–440). Ann Arbor: Population Studies Center, University of Michigan, 1999.

House, J. S., J. M. Lepkowski, D. R. Williams, R. P. Mero, P. M. Lantz, S. A. Robert, et al. "Excess Mortality among Urban Residents: How Much, for Whom, and Why." *American Journal of Public Health* 90 (2000): 1898–1904.

Idler, E. L., and Y. Benyamini. "Self-rated Health and Mortality: A Review of Twenty-seven Community Studies." *Journal of Health and Social Behavior* 38 (1997): 21–37.

Jaynes, G. D., and R. M. Williams. *A Common Destiny: Blacks and American Society.* Washington, D.C.: National Academy Press, 1989.

Kaminer, W. "Up from Reparations." *American Prospect* 11, no. 13 (2000): 38–39.

Kassarda, J. D. "Urban Industrial Transition and the Underclass." *Annals of the American Academy of Political and Social Science* 501 (1989): 26–47.

Kaufman, J. S., R. S. Cooper, and D. L. McGee. "Socioeconomic Status and Health in Blacks and Whites: The Problem of Residual Confounding and the Resiliency of Race." *Epidemiology* 8 (1997): 621–628.

Kirschenman, J., and K. M. Neckerman. "'We'd Love to Hire Them, but . . .': The Meaning of Race for Employers." In C. Jencks and P. E. Peterson. eds., *The Urban Underclass*, 203–232. Washington, D.C.: Brookings Institution, 1991.

Krieger, N. "Shades of Difference: Theoretical Underpinnings of the Medical Controversy on Black/White Differences in the United States, 1830–1870." *International Journal of Health Services* 17 (1987): 259–278.

Lieberson, S. *A Piece of the Pie: Black and White Immigrants since 1880.* Berkeley: University of California Press, 1980.

Lillie-Blanton, M., M. Brodie, D. Rowland, D. Altman, M. McIntosh. "Race, Ethnicity, and the Health Care System: Public Perceptions and Experiences." *Medical Care Research and Review* 57 (2000): 218–235.

Link, B. G., and J. Phelan. "Social Conditions as Fundamental Causes of Disease." *Journal of Health and Social Behavior*, extra issue (1995): 80–94.

Logan, J. R. *Separate and Unequal: The Neighborhood Gap for Blacks and Hispanics in Metropolitan America.* Albany, N.Y.: Lewis Mumford Center for Comparative Urban and Regional Research, University of Albany, 2002.

Lurie, N., N. B. Ward, M. F. Shapiro, and R. H. Brook. "Termination from Medi-Cal: Does It Affect Health?" *New England Journal of Medicine* 311 (1984): 480–484.

Mandinger, M. "Health Service Funding Cuts and the Declining Health of the Poor." *New England Journal of Medicine* 313 (1985): 44–47.

Mare, R. D., and C. Winship. "Socioeconomic Change and the Decline of Marriage for Blacks and Whites." In C. Jencks and P. E. Peterson, eds., *The Urban Underclass*, 175–202. Washington, D.C.: Brookings Institution, 1991.

Massey, D. S., and N. A. Denton. "Hypersegregation in U.S. Metropolitan Areas: Black and Hispanic Segregation along Five Dimensions." *Demography* 26 (1989): 373–392.

———. *American Apartheid: Segregation and the Making of the Underclass*. Cambridge, Mass.: Harvard University Press, 1993.

Massey, D. S., and S. M. Kanaiaupuni. "Public Housing and the Concentration of Poverty." *Social Science Quarterly* 74 (1993): 109–122.

McWhorter, J. "Blood Money." *American Enterprise* 12, no. 5 (2001): 18–22.

Morrison, R. S., S. Wallenstein, D. K. Natale, R. S. Senzel, and L.-L. Huang. "'We Don't Carry That': Failure of Pharmacies in Predominantly Non-White Neighborhoods to Stock Opioid Analgesics." *New England Journal of Medicine* 342 (2000): 1023–1026.

Myrdal, G. *An American Dilemma: The Negro Problem and Modern Democracy*. New York: Harper and Brothers Publishers, 1944.

National Center for Health Statistics. *Excess Deaths and Other Mortality Measures for the Black Population: 1979–81 and 1991*. Hyattsville, Md.: Public Health Service, 1994.

———. *Health, United States, 1994* (PHS 95–1232). Hyattsville, Md.: Public Health Service, 1995.

———. *Health, United States, 1998 with Socioeconomic Status and Health Chartbook*. Hyattsville, Md.: U.S. Department of Health and Human Services, 1998.

———. *Health, United States, 2000 with Adolescent Health Chartbook*. Hyattsville, Md.: U.S. Department of Health and Human Services, 2000.

———. *Health, United States, 2002, with Chartbook on Trends in the Health of Americans*. Hyattsville, Md.: U.S. Department of Health and Human Services, 2002.

Neckerman, K. M., and J. Kirschenman. "Hiring Strategies, Racial Bias, and Inner-city Workers." *Social Problems* 38 (1991): 433–447.

Oliver, M. L., and T. M. Shapiro. *Black Wealth/White Wealth: A New Perspective on Racial Inequality*. New York: Routledge, 1997.

Orfield, G. "The Growth of Segregation: African Americans, Latinos, and Unequal Education." In G. Orfield and S. Eaton, eds., *Dismantling Desegregation: The Quiet Reversal of Brown v. Board of Education*, 53–71. New York: New Press, 1996.

Orfield, G., and S. E. Eaton, eds. *Dismantling Desegregation: The Quiet Reversal of Brown v. Board of Education*. New York: New Press, 1996.

Osabu-Kle, D. T. "The African Reparation Cry: Rationale, Estimate, Prospects, and Strategies." *Journal of Black Studies* 30 (2000): 331–350.

Reardon, S. F., and J. T. Yun. "Suburban Racial Change and Suburban School Segregation, 1987–95." *Sociology of Education* 74 (2001): 79–101.

Reed, A., Jr. "The Case against Reparations." *Progressive* 63, no. 12 (2000): 15–17.

Ren, X. S., B. Amick, and D. R. Williams. "Racial/Ethnic Disparities in Health: The Interplay between Discrimination and Socioeconomic Status." *Ethnicity and Disease* 9 (1999): 151–165.

Robinson, R. *The Debt: What America Owes to Blacks*. New York: Dutton, 2000.

Sampson, R. J. "Urban Black Violence: The Effect of Male Joblessness and Family Disruption." *American Journal of Sociology* 93 (1987): 348–382.

Sampson, R. J., and W. J. Wilson. "Toward a Theory of Race, Crime, and Urban Inequality." In J. Hagan and R. D. Peterson, eds., *Crime and Inequality*, 37–54. Stanford: Stanford University Press, 1995.

Schulz, A. J., D. R. Williams, B. A. Israel, and L. B. Lempert. "Racial and Spatial Relations as Fundamental Determinants of Health in Detroit." *Milbank Quarterly* 80 (2002): 677–707.

Sharpe, R. "Losing Ground: In Latest Recession, Only Blacks Suffered Net Employment Loss." *Wall Street Journal*, 14 September 1993, A1.

Shihadeh, E. S., and N. Flynn. "Segregation and Crime: The Effect of Black Social Isolation on the Rates of Black Urban Violence." *Social Forces* 74 (1996): 1325–1352.

Smedley, B. D., A. Y. Stith, and A. R. Nelson. *Unequal Treatment: Confronting Racial and Ethnic Disparities in Health Care.* Washington, D.C.: National Academy Press, 2003.

Smedley, B. D., and S. L. Syme. *Promoting Health: Intervention Strategies from Social and Behavioral Research.* Washington, D.C.: National Academy Press, 2000.

Testa, M., N. M. Astone, M. Krogh, and K. M. Neckerman. "Employment and Marriage among Inner-city Fathers." In W. J. Wilson, ed., *The Ghetto Underclass*, 96–108. Newbury Park, Calif.: Sage, 1993.

Turner, M. A. "Limits on Neighborhood Choice: Evidence of Racial and Ethnic Steering in Urban Housing Markets." In M. Fix and R. J. Struyk, eds., *Clear and Convincing Evidence: Measurement of Discrimination in America*, 117–152. Washington, D.C.: Urban Institute, 1993.

U.S. Bureau of the Census. *Statistical Abstract of the United States: 1998.* Washington, D.C.: Government Printing Office, 1998.

———. *Census of Housing and Population. Summary File 3.* Washington, D.C.: Government Printing Office, 2000.

U.S. Department of Health and Human Services. *Report of the Secretary on Black and Minority Health.* Washington, D.C.: Author, 1985.

United States Civil War Center. *Statistical Summary: America's Major Wars.* 2002. Retrieved 12 December 2002 from www.cwc.lsu.edu/cwc/other/stats/warcost.htm.

U.S. National Advisory Commission on Civil Disorders. *The Kerner Report.* New York: Pantheon, 1988.

Wallace, R. "Urban Desertification, Public Health and Public Order: 'Planned Shrinkage,' Violent Death, Substance Abuse, and AIDS in the Bronx." *Social Science and Medicine* 31 (1990): 801–813.

———. "Expanding Coupled Shock Fronts of Urban Decay and Criminal Behavior: How U.S. Cities Are Becoming 'Hollowed Out.'" *Journal of Quantitative Criminology* 7 (1991): 333–356.

Wallace, R., and D. Wallace. "Socioeconomic Determinants of Health: Community Marginalisation and the Diffusion of Disease and Disorder in the United States." *British Medical Journal* 314 (1997): 1341–1345.

Whiteis, D. G. "Hospital and Community Characteristics in Closures of Urban Hospitals, 1980–87." *Public Health Reports* 107 (1992): 409–416.

Williams, D. R. "Race and Health: Basic Questions, Emerging Directions." *Annals of Epidemiology* 7 (1997): 322–333.

———. "Race, SES, and Health: The Added Effects of Racism and Discrimination." *Annals of the New York Academy of Sciences* 896 (1999): 173–188.

———. "Race and Health: Trends and Policy Implications." In J. A. Auerbach and B. K. Krimgold, eds., *Income, Socioeconomic Status, and Health: Exploring the Relationships*, 67–85. Washington, D.C.: National Policy Association, Academy for Health Services Research and Health Policy, 2001.

Williams, D. R., and C. Collins. "U.S. Socioeconomic and Racial Differences in Health." *Annual Review of Sociology* 21 (1995): 349–386.

———. "Racial Residential Segregation: A Fundamental Cause of Racial Disparities in Health." *Public Health Reports* 116 (2001): 404–415.

Williams, D. R., Y. Yu, J. Jackson, and N. Anderson. "Racial Differences in Physical and Mental Health: Socioeconomic Status, Stress, and Discrimination." *Journal of Health Psychology* 2 (1997): 335–351.

Wilson, W. J. *The Truly Disadvantaged*. Chicago: University of Chicago Press, 1987.

———. *When Work Disappears: The World of the New Urban Poor*. New York: Knopf, 1996.

Wilson, W., and K. M. Neckerman. "Poverty and Family Structure: The Widening Gap between Evidence and Public Policy Issues." In S. H. Danziger and D. H. Weinberg, eds., *Fighting Poverty*, 232–259. Cambridge, Mass.: Harvard University Press, 1986.

Zinsmeister, K. "Has the Debt Been Paid?" *American Enterprise* 12, no. 5 (2001): 4–6.

Residential Segregation and Persistent Urban Poverty

DOUGLAS S. MASSEY

Although the Kerner Commission of 1968 singled out the ghetto as a fundamental structural factor promoting black poverty in the United States, residential segregation has been overlooked in recent academic debates and policy discussions on the urban underclass. Even though a large share of African Americans continues to be segregated involuntarily on the basis of race, thinking within the policy establishment has drifted toward the view that race is declining in significance and that black poverty is largely a class-based phenomenon.

Given this emphasis, research into the causes of urban black poverty has focused largely on race-neutral factors such as economic restructuring, family dissolution, education, culture, and welfare. Although researchers often use the terms "ghetto," "ghetto poor," and "ghetto poverty," few see the ghetto itself as something problematic and few have called for dismantling it as part of a broader attack on urban poverty. Despite its absence from policy discussions, however, residential segregation is not a thing of the past or some neutral fact that can be safely ignored. A large share of black America remains involuntarily segregated, and because life chances are so decisively influenced by where one lives, segregation is deeply implicated in the perpetuation of black poverty.

As a result of their residential segregation, African Americans endure a harsh and extremely disadvantaged environment where poverty, crime, single parenthood, welfare dependency, and educational failure are not only common but also all too frequently the norm. Because of the persistence of white prejudice against black neighbors and the continuation of pervasive discrimination in the real estate and banking industries, a series of barriers exist in the path of black social and geographic mobility. The federal government has not only tolerated this state of affairs but, at key junctures over the past several decades, has intervened actively to sustain it. Residential segregation by race is an embedded feature of life in the United States that is deeply institutionalized at all levels of American society, and as long as high levels of racial segregation persist, black poverty will be endemic and racial divisions will grow.

Trends in Black–White Segregation

In the years following the civil rights movement of the 1960s, urban blacks came to experience one of two basic conditions. Those in metropolitan areas with large black populations experienced extremely high levels of segregation that showed little tendency to decline over time.[1] Suburbanization of blacks lagged well behind the levels of other groups, and the African Americans who did manage to achieve suburban residence remained racially isolated. In sixteen metropolitan areas, blacks were so highly segregated across so many dimensions simultaneously that Nancy Denton and I coined the term "hypersegregation" to describe their situation. Together these metropolitan areas—which include Baltimore, Chicago, Cleveland, Detroit, Los Angeles, Newark, Philadelphia, St. Louis, and Washington, D.C.—contained more than one-third of all African Americans in the United States.[2]

In urban areas where blacks constituted a relatively small share of the population, however, such as Tucson, Phoenix, and Seattle, levels of black–white segregation *declined* after 1970, at times quite rapidly.[3] In these urban areas, African Americans were dispersed widely throughout the metropolitan environment, and in contrast to the situation of large urban black communities, suburbanization brought significant integration and interracial contact. Unfortunately, relatively few African Americans experienced these benign conditions.

The dividing line between these contrasting trends is a metropolitan black fraction of 5 percent. Below this level, desegregation occurred; above it there was little change. Andrew Gross and I developed an index of the degree of segregation required to keep the probability of white–black contact at 5 percent or less.[4] The difference between this index and the level of segregation actually observed in 1970 closely predicted the decline over the ensuing decade. During the 1970s, in other words, urban areas in the United States were moving toward precisely the level of segregation needed to keep the likelihood of white–black contact at 5 percent or less. In areas with small black populations, this pattern implied rapid desegregation; in areas with large black communities, it meant continued segregation and racial isolation.

Preliminary work on the 1990 Census suggests that this split in the urban black experience has continued.[5] Urban areas with large black populations remain highly segregated and have shown little tendency to decline; areas with small black populations continue their move toward integration. Declines were especially rapid in urban areas of the South and West that contained sizable Hispanic populations and large military bases, in addition to small black populations. Although black access to suburbs increased, in areas with large African American populations settlement was restricted to a small number of suburban communities whose racial segregation was increasing; the small number of blacks entering suburbs was not sufficient to affect the overall pattern of high racial segregation within the urban area as a whole. As a result, metropolitan areas that were hypersegregated in 1980 generally remained so in 1990, and some new areas were added to the list.[6]

The high degree of black residential segregation is unprecedented and unique. No other group in the history of the United States has ever experienced such high levels of segregation sustained over such a long period of time. Despite recent declines, the average level of black segregation is still 50 percent greater than that observed among Asians or Hispanics, and the lowest levels of black segregation generally correspond to the highest levels observed for Hispanics and Asians.

The Causes of Racial Residential Segregation

This distinctive pattern of high black segregation cannot be attributed to socioeconomic factors—at least as of 1980, when the last study was carried out.[7] As of that year, black families earning more than $50,000 were just as segregated as those earning under $2,500, and in metropolitan areas with large Hispanic as well as black populations, the poorest Hispanic families were *less* segregated than the most affluent blacks. Similar patterns are observed when data are broken down by education and occupation. Controlling for social class makes little difference in considering the level of black segregation: blacks in large cities are segregated no matter how much they earn, learn, or achieve.

High levels of black segregation are attributable not to a lack of income but to three other factors: prejudice, discrimination, and public policy. White racial prejudice yields a weak demand for housing in integrated neighborhoods and fuels a process of neighborhood racial transition. Pervasive discrimination in the real estate and banking industries keeps blacks out of most neighborhoods, providing prejudiced whites with an avenue of escape when faced with the prospect of black settlement in their neighborhoods. Finally, the federal government itself institutionalized the practice of mortgage redlining and supported state and local governments in their use of urban renewal and public housing programs as part of a deliberate attempt to segregate urban blacks.

Although whites now accept open housing in principle, survey data show that they are reluctant to accept it in practice. Whereas almost 90 percent of white respondents to national surveys agree that "black people have a right to live wherever they can afford to," only 40 percent would be willing to vote for a law stating that a homeowner cannot refuse to sell to someone because of his or her race or skin color.[8]

Moreover, when questions are posed about specific neighborhood compositions, it becomes clear that white tolerance for racial mixing is quite limited. One-third of whites responding to a 1992 Detroit survey said they would feel uncomfortable in a neighborhood where 20 percent of the residents were black, and about the same percentage would be unwilling to enter such an area.[9] When the black share rises to one-third, 59 percent of all whites said they would be unwilling to enter, 44 percent would feel uncomfortable, and 29 percent would seek to leave. At a 50–50 racial mixture, neighborhoods become unacceptable to all but a small minority of whites: 73 percent said they would not want to enter, 53 percent would try to leave, and 65 percent would feel uncomfortable.

In contrast, in both principle and practice African Americans express strong support for integration. Blacks are unanimous in agreeing that "black people have a right to live wherever they can afford to," and 71 percent would vote for a community-wide law to enforce that right.[10] When asked about specific neighborhood racial compositions, they consistently select racially mixed areas as most desirable. Although the most popular choice is a neighborhood that is half-black and half-white, 87 percent of African Americans would be willing to live in a neighborhood that is only 20 percent black.[11]

Although black respondents do express a reluctance to enter all-white neighborhoods, this apprehension does not indicate a rejection of integration per se, but stems from a well-founded fear of hostility and violence. Among black respondents to a 1976 Detroit survey who said they would be reluctant to move into an all-white area, 34 percent believed that white neighbors would be unfriendly and make them feel unwelcome, 37 percent believed they would be made to feel uncomfortable, and 17 percent expressed a fear of violence; 80 percent rejected the view that moving into a white neighborhood would be deserting the black community.[12]

If it were up to them, then, blacks would live in racially mixed neighborhoods. But it is not solely up to them, because their preferences interact with the preferences of whites to produce the neighborhoods we actually observe.

Whereas most blacks pick a 50–50 racial mixture as most desirable, the vast majority of whites are unwilling to enter such a neighborhood, and most would try to leave. This fundamental disparity has been confirmed by surveys conducted in Milwaukee, Omaha, Cincinnati, Kansas City, and Los Angeles, all of which show that blacks strongly prefer a 50–50 mixture and that whites have little tolerance for racial mixtures beyond 20 percent black.[13]

These contrasting attitudes imply a disparity in the demand for housing in integrated neighborhoods. Given the violence, intimidation, and harassment that historically have followed their entry into white areas, blacks are reluctant to be first across the color line. After one or two black families have entered a neighborhood, however, black demand grows rapidly, given the high value placed on integrated housing. This demand escalates as the percentage of blacks rises toward 50 percent, the most preferred neighborhood configuration; beyond this point, it stabilizes and falls off as the black percentage rises toward 100 percent.

The pattern of white demand for housing in racially mixed areas follows precisely the opposite trajectory. Demand is strong for homes in all-white areas, but once one or two black families have entered, white demand begins to falter as some white families leave and others refuse to move in. The acceleration in residential turnover coincides with the expansion of black demand, making it likely that outgoing white households are replaced by black families. As the percentage of blacks rises, white demand drops more steeply and black demand rises at an increasing rate. By the time black demand peaks at the 50 percent mark, almost no whites are willing to enter and the large majority are trying to leave. Thus, racial segregation is fomented by a process of racial turnover fueled by antiblack prejudice on the part of whites.

Although prejudice is a necessary condition for segregation of blacks, however, it alone is not sufficient to maintain the residential color line. Active discrimination against black home-seekers must also occur: some neighborhoods must be kept nonblack if whites are to have an avenue of retreat following black entry elsewhere. Racial discrimination was institutionalized in the real estate industry during the 1920s and well established in private practice by the 1940s.[14] Discriminatory behavior was open and widespread among Realtors at least until 1968, when the Fair Housing Act was passed. After that year, outright refusals to rent or sell to blacks became rare, given that overt discrimination could lead to prosecution under the law.

Black home-seekers now face a more subtle process of exclusion. Rather than encountering "white only" signs, they encounter a series of covert barriers surreptitiously placed in their way. Although each individual act of discrimination may be small and subtle, together they have a powerful and cumulative effect in lowering the probability of blacks entering white neighborhoods. Moreover, because the discrimination is latent it is not noticeable, and the only way to confirm whether or not discrimination has occurred is to compare the treatment of black clients and white clients with similar social and economic characteristics.

Differences in the treatment of white and black home-seekers are measured by means of a housing audit.[15] Teams of white and black auditors are paired and sent to randomly selected Realtors to pose as clients seeking a home or apartment. The auditors are trained to present comparable housing needs and family characteristics and to express similar tastes; they are assigned equivalent social and economic traits by the investigator. After each encounter, the auditors fill out a report of their experiences and the results are tabulated and compared to determine the nature and level of discrimination.

In 1987, George Galster wrote to more than two hundred local fair housing organizations and obtained written reports of seventy-one different audit studies carried out during the 1980s: twenty-one in the home sales market and fifty in the rental market.[16] Despite differences in measures and methods, he concluded that "racial discrimination continues to be a dominant feature of metropolitan housing markets in the 1980s." Using a conservative measure of racial bias, Galster found that blacks averaged a 20 percent chance of experiencing discrimination in the sales market and a 50 percent chance in the rental market.

He also studied six real estate firms located in Cincinnati and Memphis and found that racial steering occurred in roughly 50 percent of the transactions sampled during the mid-1980s.[17] Racial steering occurs when white and black clients are guided to neighborhoods that differ systematically with respect to social and economic characteristics, especially racial composition. Homes shown to blacks tended to be in racially mixed areas and were more likely to be adjacent to neighborhoods with a high percentage of black residents. Whites were rarely shown homes in integrated neighborhoods unless they specifically requested them, and even then they were guided primarily to homes in white areas. Sales agents made numerous positive comments about white neighborhoods to white clients but said little to black home buyers. In a review of thirty-six different audit studies, Galster discovered that selective comments by agents is probably more common than overt steering.[18]

In 1988 the U.S. Department of Housing and Urban Development (HUD) carried out a nationwide audit survey.[19] Twenty audit sites were randomly selected from among metropolitan areas having a central city population exceeding 100,000 and a black population of more than 12 percent. Real estate ads in major metropolitan newspapers were randomly sampled and Realtors were approached by auditors who inquired about the availability of the advertised unit; they also asked about other units that might be on the market. The Housing Discrimination Study (HDS) covered both the rental and sales markets, and the auditors were given incomes and family characteristics appropriate to the housing unit advertised.

The HDS provides little evidence that discrimination against blacks has declined. Indeed, previous studies appear to have understated both the incidence and the severity of housing discrimination in American cities. According to HDS data, housing was made systematically more available to whites in 45 percent of the transactions in the rental market and in 34 percent of those in the sales market. Whites received more favorable credit assistance in 46 percent of sales encounters and were offered more favorable terms in 17 percent of rental transactions. When housing availability and financial assistance were considered together, the likelihood of experiencing racial discrimination was 53 percent in both the rental and the sales markets.

In addition to measuring the incidence of discrimination (that is, the percentage of encounters where discrimination occurs), the HDS study also measured its severity (the number of units made available to whites but not blacks). In stark terms, the severity of housing discrimination is such that blacks are systematically shown, recommended, and invited to inspect far fewer homes than comparably qualified whites. As a result, their access to urban housing is substantially reduced.

Among advertised rental units, the likelihood that an additional unit was shown to whites but not to blacks was 65 percent, and the probability that an additional unit was recommended to whites but not to blacks was 91 percent.[20] The HDS auditors encountered equally severe bias in the marketing of unadvertised units: the likelihood that an additional unit was inspected by blacks was only 62 percent, whereas the probability that whites alone were invited to see another unit was 90 percent.[21] Comparable results were found in urban sales markets, where the severity of discrimination varied from 66 percent to 89 percent. Thus, no matter what index one considers, most of the housing units made available to whites were not brought to the attention of blacks.[22]

Although these audit results are compelling, they do not directly link discrimination with segregation. Using data from an earlier HUD audit study, however, George Galster related cross-metropolitan variation in housing discrimination to the degree of racial segregation in different urban areas.[23] He not only confirmed an empirical link between discrimination and segregation, but also discovered that segregation had important feedback effects on socioeconomic status. Discrimination not only leads to segregation, but segregation, by restricting economic opportunities for blacks, produces interracial economic disparities that incite further discrimination and more segregation.

Galster has also shown that white prejudice and discrimination are connected to patterns of racial change within neighborhoods.[24] In a detailed study of census tracts in the Cleveland area, he found that neighborhoods that were all-white or racially changing evinced much higher rates of discrimination than areas that were stably integrated or predominantly black. Moreover, the pace of racial change was strongly predicted by the percentage of whites who agreed that white people have a right to keep blacks out of their neighborhoods.

The final factor responsible for black residential segregation is government policy. During the 1940s and 1950s the Federal Housing Administration (FHA) invented the practice of redlining and effectively established it as standard practice within the banking industry.[25] As a condition for underwriting a mortgage, the FHA required a neighborhood assessment; neighborhoods that contained black residents, were adjacent to black areas, or were thought to be at risk of attracting blacks at some point in the future were colored red on the agency's residential security maps and systematically denied access to FHA-backed loans. Private lenders originating non-FHA loans took their cue from the government, and the practice of redlining became institutionalized throughout the lending industry.

Black and mixed-race areas were thus denied access to capital, guaranteeing that housing prices would stagnate, dwellings would steadily deteriorate, and whites would be unable to purchase homes in integrated areas. As a result of federal policy, therefore, racial turnover and physical deterioration became inevitable following black entry into a neighborhood. During the early 1970s, lawsuits and pressure from the civil rights community finally forced the FHA to open up its lending program to black participation. Since then, however, whites have deserted the FHA lending program in favor of conventional loans.

Studies show that blacks are still rejected for conventional loans at rates far higher than whites of comparable economic background.[26] Moreover, because of redlining, black and racially mixed areas do not receive the amount of mortgage capital that they would otherwise qualify for on economic criteria alone.[27] Paradoxically, the recent opening up of FHA lending to blacks has only fueled neighborhood racial transition, with FHA loans being used by blacks to buy homes in racially mixed areas from whites, who then flee to all-white neighborhoods using conventional loans that are denied to blacks.

During the period 1950 to 1970 the federal government also promoted segregation through urban renewal and public housing programs administered by HUD. As black in-migration and white suburbanization brought rapid racial turnover to U.S. cities, local elites became alarmed by the threat that expanding ghettos posed to white institutions and business districts. With federal support, they used renewal programs to clear black neighborhoods that were encroaching on white districts and employed public housing as a means of containing the families displaced by "renewal." White city councils blocked the construction of minority housing projects outside the ghetto, however, so most were built on cleared land in black areas, thereby driving up the degree of racial and class isolation.[28]

Racial Segregation and Socioeconomic Mobility

If segregation is imposed on African Americans involuntarily through an interlocking set of individual actions, institutional practices, and government actions that are prejudicial in their intent and discriminatory in their effect, then significant barriers are placed in the path of black social mobility. Because where one lives is such an important determinant of one's life chances, barriers to residential mobility inevitably end up being barriers to social mobility. If one group of people is denied full access to urban housing markets because of skin color, then that group is systematically denied access to the full range of benefits in urban society.

Housing markets are especially important because they distribute much more than a place to live; they also distribute any good or resource that is *correlated* with where one lives. Housing markets do not just distribute houses. They also distribute education, employment, safety, insurance rates, services, and wealth in the form of home equity, and they also determine the level of exposure to crime and drugs and the peer groups that children experience. Research consistently shows that, dollar for dollar of income, year for year of schooling, and unit for unit of occupational status, blacks achieve much less in the way of residential benefits than other racial and ethnic groups.[29]

Because of persistent segregation, blacks are far more likely than whites with the same income to experience inferior schools, isolation from jobs, crime and violence, excessive insurance rates, sagging home values, and peer environments where expectations run to gang membership and teenage pregnancy rather than college attendance. As a result, black families who have improved their lot are much less able than the upwardly mobile of other groups to consolidate their gains, move ahead further, and pass their achievements on to their children.

Segregation and the Concentration of Poverty

Segregation not only harms the interests of individual people and families who experience barriers to residential mobility; it also undermines the community as a whole by concentrating poverty at extraordinary levels. Concentrated poverty occurs because segregation confines any general increase in black poverty to a small number of spatially distinct neighborhoods. Rather than being spread uniformly throughout a metropolitan environment, poor families created by an economic downturn are restricted to a small number of densely settled, tightly packed, and geographically isolated areas. Given a high level of residential segregation, any increase in the poverty rate *must* produce a spatial concentration of poverty; no other result is possible.[30]

Because rates of poverty and levels of segregation differ so much between whites, blacks, and Hispanics, individual members of these groups are structurally constrained to experience markedly different levels of neighborhood poverty. The geographic concentration of poverty is built into the experience of blacks but is alien to the experience of whites, even if the whites themselves are quite poor. Moreover, the basic effect of segregation in concentrating poverty is significantly exacerbated by public housing, which was used during the period 1950 to 1970 in a racially discriminatory manner to confine and isolate urban blacks. Neighborhoods that contain public housing projects have concentrations of poverty that are at least double what they would otherwise be.[31]

In concentrating poverty, segregation acts simultaneously to concentrate anything that is correlated with poverty: crime, drug abuse, welfare dependency, single parenthood, and educational difficulties. To the extent that individual socioeconomic failings follow from prolonged exposure to concentrated poverty and its correlates, therefore, these disadvantages are ultimately produced by the structural organization of metropolitan areas in the United States. The mere fact that blacks are both highly segregated and poor means that individual African Americans are more likely to suffer joblessness and to experience single parenthood than either Hispanics or whites, quite apart from any disadvantages they may suffer with respect to personal or family characteristics.

A growing body of research has linked individual socioeconomic difficulties to the geographic concentration of socioeconomic disadvantage that people experience in their neighborhoods.[32] One study directly linked the socioeconomic disadvantages suffered by individual minority members to the degree of segregation their group experiences in urban society. Using individual, community, and metropolitan data from the fifty largest U.S. metropolitan areas in 1980, Andrew Gross, Mitchell Eggers, and I show that segregation and poverty interact to concentrate poverty geographically within neighborhoods and that exposure to neighborhood poverty subsequently increases the probability of male joblessness and single motherhood among individuals.[33] In this fashion, the structural condition of segregation is linked to individual behaviors that are widely associated with the underclass through the intervening factor of neighborhood poverty.

According to their estimates, increasing the black poverty rate from 10 percent to 40 percent under conditions of no segregation has a relatively modest effect on the neighborhood environment that blacks experience, raising it modestly from about 8 percent to 17 percent. Although the probabilities of male joblessness and single motherhood are sensitive to the rate of poverty that people experience in their neighborhood, this modest change in neighborhood poverty is not enough to affect individual outcomes much. The probability of male joblessness rises only from 36 percent to 40 percent as a result of increased poverty concentration, and the likelihood of single motherhood increases from 23 percent to 28 percent.

In a highly segregated urban area, by contrast, increasing the overall rate of black poverty causes a marked increase in the concentration of poverty with black neighborhoods. As the overall rate of poverty increases from 10 percent to 40 percent, the neighborhood poverty rate likewise goes from 10 percent to 41 percent. This sharp increase in neighborhood poverty has a profound effect on the well-being of individual blacks, even those who have not been pushed into poverty themselves, because segregation forces them to live in neighborhoods with many families who are poor. As a result of the increase in neighborhood poverty to which they are exposed, the probability of joblessness among young black males rises from 40 percent to 53 percent and the likelihood of single motherhood increases from 28 percent to 41 percent.

Thus, increasing the rate of poverty of a segregated group causes its neighborhood environment to deteriorate, which in turn causes individual probabilities of socioeconomic failure to rise. The same rise in poverty without segregation would hardly affect group members at all because it would have marginal effects on the neighborhoods in which they live. In other words, segregation is directly responsible for the creation of a uniquely harsh and disadvantaged black residential environment, making it likely that individual blacks themselves will fail no matter what their socioeconomic characteristics or family background. Racial segregation is the institutional nexus that enables the transmission of poverty from person to person and generation to generation, and it is therefore a primary structural factor behind the perpetuation of the urban underclass.

Public Policy Needs

In the United States today, public policy discussions regarding the urban underclass frequently devolve into debates on the importance of race versus class. By presenting the case for segregation's role as a central cause of urban poverty, I seek to end this specious opposition. The issue is not whether race *or* class perpetuates the urban underclass, but how race *and* class *interact* to undermine the social and economic well-being of black Americans. I argue that race operates powerfully through urban housing markets and that racial segregation interacts with black class structure to produce a uniquely disadvantaged neighborhood environment for many African Americans, an environment that builds a variety of self-perpetuating processes of deprivation into black lives.

Public policies must therefore address both race and class issues if they are to be successful. Race-conscious steps need to be taken to dismantle the institutional apparatus of segregation, and class-specific policies must be implemented to improve the socioeconomic status of African Americans. By themselves, programs targeted to low-income blacks will fail because they will be swamped by powerful environmental influences arising from the disastrous neighborhood conditions that blacks experience because of segregation. Likewise, efforts to reduce segregation will falter unless African Americans acquire the socioeconomic resources that enable them to take full advantage of urban housing markets and the benefits they distribute.

The elimination of residential segregation will require the direct involvement of the federal government to an unprecedented degree, and two departments—Housing and Urban Development and Justice—must throw their institutional weight behind fair-housing enforcement if residential desegregation is to occur. If the ghetto is to be dismantled, HUD in particular must intervene forcefully in eight ways.

First, HUD must increase its financial assistance to local fair-housing organizations in order to enhance their ability to investigate and prosecute individual complaints of housing discrimination. Grants made to local agencies dedicated to fair-housing enforcement will enable them to expand their efforts by hiring more legal staff, implementing more extensive testing programs, and making their services more widely available.

Second, HUD should establish a permanent testing program that is capable of identifying Realtors who engage in a pattern and practice of discrimination. A special unit dedicated to the regular administration of housing audits should be created in HUD under the assistant secretary for fair housing and equal opportunity. Audits of randomly selected Realtors should be conducted annually within metropolitan areas that have large black communities, and when evidence of systematic discrimination is uncovered, the department should compile additional evidence and turn it over to the attorney general for vigorous prosecution. Initially these audits should be targeted to hypersegregated cities.

Third, a staff should be created at HUD under the assistant secretary for fair housing and equal opportunity to scrutinize lending data for unusually high rates of rejection among minority applicants and black neighborhoods. When the rejection rates cannot be explained statistically by social, demographic, economic, credit histories, or other background factors, a systematic case study of the bank's lending practices should be initiated. If clear evidence of discrimination is uncovered, the case should be referred to the attorney general for prosecution; if no discrimination, an equal opportunity lending plan should be negotiated, implemented, and monitored.

Fourth, funding for housing certificate programs authorized under Section 8 of the 1974 Housing and Community Development Act should be expanded, and programs modeled on the Gautreaux Demonstration Project should be more widely implemented. Black public housing residents in Chicago who moved into integrated suburban settings through this demonstration project have been shown to experience greater success in education and employment than a comparable group who remained behind in the ghetto.[34]

Fifth, given the overriding importance of residential mobility to individual well-being, hate crimes directed against blacks moving into white neighborhoods must be considered more severe than ordinary acts of vandalism or assault. Rather than being left only to local authorities, they should be prosecuted at the federal level as violations of the victims' civil rights. Stiff financial penalties and jail terms should be imposed, not in recognition of the severity of the vandalism or violence itself but in acknowledgment of the serious damage that segregation does to the well-being of the nation.

Sixth, HUD should work to strengthen the Voluntary Affirmative Marketing Agreement, a pact reached between HUD and the National Association of

Realtors during the Ford administration. The agreement originally established a network of housing resource boards to enforce the Fair Housing Act with support from HUD, but during the Reagan administration, funds were cut and the agreement was modified to relieve Realtors of responsibility for fair-housing enforcement; new regulations also prohibited the use of testers by local resource boards and made secret the list of real estate boards that had signed the agreement. In strengthening this agreement, this list should once again be made public, the use of testers should be encouraged, and the responsibilities of Realtors to enforce the Fair Housing Act should be spelled out explicitly.

Seventh, HUD should establish new programs and expand existing programs to train Realtors in fair-housing marketing procedures, especially those serving black neighborhoods. Agents catering primarily to white clients should be instructed about advertising and marketing methods to ensure that blacks in segregated communities gain access to information about housing opportunities outside the ghetto, whereas those serving the black share of the market should be trained to market homes throughout the metropolitan area and be instructed especially in how to use the multiple-listing service (MLS). HUD officials and local fair-housing groups should carefully monitor whether Realtors serving blacks are given access to the MLS.

Eighth and finally, the assistant secretary for fair housing and equal opportunity at HUD must take a more active role in overseeing real estate advertising and marketing practices, two areas that have received insufficient federal attention in the past. Realtors in selected metropolitan areas should be sampled and their advertising and marketing practices regularly examined for conformity with federal fair-housing regulations. The Department of Housing and Urban Development should play a larger role in ensuring that black home-seekers are not being systematically and deliberately overlooked by prevailing marketing practices.

For the most part, these policies do not require major changes in legislation. What they require is political will. When there is the will to end segregation, the necessary funds and legislative measures will follow. For America, the failure to end segregation will perpetuate a bitter dilemma that has long divided the nation. If segregation is permitted to continue, poverty inevitably will deepen and become more persistent within a large share of the black community, crime and drugs will become more firmly rooted, and social institutions will fragment further under the weight of deteriorating conditions. As racial inequality sharpens, the fears of whites will grow, racial prejudices will be reinforced, and hostility toward blacks will increase, making the problems of racial justice and equal opportunity even more insoluble.

Until we decide to end the long reign of American apartheid, we cannot hope to move forward as a people and a nation.

Notes

This was the seventeenth annual *Social Service Review* lecture delivered at the School of Social Service Administration, the University of Chicago, April 28, 1994.

1. Douglas S. Massey and Nancy A. Denton, *American Apartheid: Segregation and the Making of the Underclass* (Cambridge, Mass.: Harvard University Press, 1993), chap. 3.
2. Douglas S. Massey and Nancy A. Denton, "Hypersegregation in U.S. Metropolitan Areas: Black and Hispanic Segregation along Five Dimensions," *Demography* 26, no. 3 (August 1989): 373–93.
3. Douglas S. Massey and Nancy A. Denton, "Trends in the Residential Segregation of Blacks, Hispanics, and Asians," *American Sociological Review* 52, no. 6 (December 1987): 802–25.
4. Douglas S. Massey and Andrew B. Gross, "Explaining Trends in Residential Segregation, 1970–1980," *Urban Affairs Quarterly* 27, no. 1 (September 1991): 13–35.
5. Reynolds Farley and William H. Frey, "Changes in the Segregation of Whites from Blacks during the 1980s: Small Steps toward a More Integrated Society," *American Sociological Review* 59, no. 1 (February 1994): 23–45; Mark Schneider and Thomas Phelan, "Black Suburbanization in the 1980's," *Demography* 30, no. 2 (May 1993): 269–80.
6. Nancy A. Denton, "Are African Americans Still Hypersegregated in 1990?" in *Residential Apartheid: The American Legacy*, ed. Robert Bullard (Newbury Park, Calif.: Sage, in press).
7. Nancy A. Denton and Douglas S. Massey, "Residential Segregation of Blacks, Hispanics, and Asians by Socioeconomic Status and Generation," *Social Science Quarterly* 69, no. 4 (December 1988): 797–817.
8. Howard Schuman, Charlotte Steeh, and Lawrence Bobo, *Racial Attitudes in America: Trends and Interpretations* (Cambridge, Mass.: Harvard University Press, 1985); Howard Schuman and Lawrence Bobo, "Survey-based Experiments on White Racial Attitudes toward Residential Integration," *American Journal of Sociology* 94, no. 2 (September 1988): 273–99.
9. Reynolds Farley, Charlotte Steeh, Tara Jackson, Maria Krysan, and Keith Reeves, "The Causes of Continued Racial Residential Segregation: Chocolate City, Vanilla Suburbs Revisited," *Journal of Housing Research* 4, no. 1 (1993): 1–38.
10. Lawrence Bobo, Howard Schuman, and Charlotte Steeh, "Changing Racial Attitudes toward Residential Integration," in *Housing Desegregation and Federal Policy*, ed. John M. Goering (Chapel Hill: University of North Carolina Press, 1986), 152–69.
11. Farley et al., "The Causes of Continued Racial Residential Segregation," 1–38.
12. Reynolds Farley, Suzanne Bianchi, and Diane Colasanto, "Barriers to the Racial Integration of Neighborhoods: The Detroit Case," *Annals of the American Academy of Political and Social Science* 441 (January 1979): 97–113.
13. William A. V. Clark, "Residential Preferences and Neighborhood Racial Segregation: A Test of the Schelling Segregation Model," *Demography* 28, no. 1 (February 1991): 1–19.
14. Massey and Denton, *American Apartheid* (n. 1 above), chap. 2.
15. John Yinger, "Measuring Racial Discrimination with Fair Housing Audits: Caught in the Act," *American Economic Review* 76, no. 5 (December 1986): 991–93.
16. George C. Galster, "Racial Discrimination in Housing Markets during the 1980s: A

Review of the Audit Evidence," *Journal of Planning Education and Research* 9, no. 3 (March 1990): 165–75.

17. George C. Galster, "Racial Steering by Real Estate Agents: Mechanisms and Motives," *Review of Black Political Economy* 19, no. 1 (Summer 1990): 39–63.

18. George C. Galster, "Racial Steering in Urban Housing Markets: A Review of the Audit Evidence," *Review of Black Political Economy* 18, no. 3 (Winter 1990): 105–29.

19. John Yinger, *Housing Discrimination Study: Incidence of Discrimination and Variations in Discriminatory Behavior* (Washington, D.C.: U.S. Department of Housing and Urban Development, Office of Policy Development and Research, 1991), and *Housing Discrimination Study: Incidence and Seventy of Unfavorable Treatment* (Washington, D.C.: U.S. Department of Housing and Urban Development, Office of Policy Development and Research, 1991).

20. Yinger, *Housing Discrimination Study: Incidence of Discrimination and Variations in Discriminatory Behavior*, table 42.

21. Ibid.

22. Ibid., table 44.

23. George C. Galster, "More than Skin Deep: The Effect of Housing Discrimination on the Extent and Pattern of Racial Residential Segregation in the United States," in Goering, ed. *Housing Desegregation and Federal Policy*, 119–38; George C. Galster and W. Mark Keeney, "Race, Residence, Discrimination, and Economic Opportunity: Modeling the Nexus of Urban Racial Phenomena," *Urban Affairs Quarterly* 24, no. 1 (September 1988): 87–117.

24. George C. Galster, "The Ecology of Racial Discrimination in Housing: An Exploratory Model," *Urban Affairs Quarterly* 23, no. 1 (September 1987): 84–107, "White Flight from Racially Integrated Neighbourhoods in the 1970s: The Cleveland Experience," *Urban Studies* 27, no. 3 (March 1990): 385–99, and "Neighborhood Racial Change, Segregationist Sentiments, and Affirmative Marketing Policies," *Journal of Urban Economics* 27, no. 3 (March 1990): 344–61.

25. Kenneth T. Jackson, *Crabgrass Frontier: The Suburbanization of the United States* (New York: Oxford University Press, 1985), chap. 11.

26. Harold A. Black and Robert L. Schweitzer, "A Canonical Analysis of Mortgage Lending Terms: Testing for Lending Discrimination at a Commercial Bank," *Urban Studies* 22, no. 1 (January 1985): 13–20.

27. Louis G. Pol, Rebecca F. Guy, and Andrew J. Bush, "Discrimination in the Home Lending Market: A Macro Perspective," *Social Science Quarterly* 63, no. 4 (December 1982): 716–28; Gregory D. Squires, William Velez, and Karl E. Taueber, "Insurance Redlining, Agency Location, and the Process of Urban Disinvestment," *Urban Affairs Quarterly* 26, no. 4 (June 1991): 567–88; Harriet Tee Taggart and Kevin W. Smith, "Redlining: An Assessment of the Evidence of Disinvestment in Metropolitan Boston," *Urban Affairs Quarterly* 17, no. 1 (September 1981): 91–107.

28. Arnold R. Hirsch, *Making the Second Ghetto: Race and Housing in Chicago, 1940–1960* (Cambridge: Cambridge University Press, 1983); John F. Bauman, *Public Housing, Race, and Renewal: Urban Planning in Philadelphia, 1920–1974* (Philadelphia: Temple University Press, 1987); Ira Goldstein and William L. Yancey, "Public Housing Projects, Blacks, and Public Policy: The Historical Ecology of Public Housing in Philadelphia," in Goering, ed., *Housing Desegregation and Federal Policy*; Douglas S. Massey and Shawn M. Kanaiaupuni, "Public Housing and the Concentration of Poverty," *Social Science Quarterly* 74, no. 1 (March 1993): 109–22.

29. Richard D. Alba and John R. Logan, "Variations on Two Themes: Racial and Ethnic

Patterns in the Attainment of Suburban Residence," *Demography* 28, no. 3 (August 1991): 431–53; Douglas S. Massey and Nancy A. Denton, "Spatial Assimilation as a Socioeconomic Process," *American Sociological Review* 50, no. 1 (February 1985): 94–105; Douglas S. Massey and Eric Fong, "Segregation and Neighborhood Quality: Blacks, Hispanics, and Asians in the San Francisco Metropolitan Area," *Social Forces* 69, no. 1 (September 1990): 15–32; Douglas S. Massey, Gretchen A. Condran, and Nancy A. Denton, "The Effect of Residential Segregation on Black Social and Economic Well-being," *Social Forces* 66, no. 1 (September 1987): 29–57.

30. Douglas S. Massey, "American Apartheid: Segregation and the Making of the Underclass," *American Journal of Sociology* 96, no. 2 (September 1990): 329–58; Massey and Denton, *American Apartheid*, chap. 5.

31. Massey and Kanaiaupuni, "Public Housing and the Concentration of Poverty."

32. Christopher Jencks and Susan E. Mayer, "The Social Consequences of Growing Up in a Poor Neighborhood," in *Inner City Poverty in the United States*, eds. Laurence E. Lynn Jr., and Michael G. H. McGeary (Washington, D.C.: National Academy Press, 1990), 111–86; Dennis P. Hogan and Evelyn M. Kitagawa, "The Impact of Social Status, Family Structure, and Neighborhood on the Fertility of Black Adolescents," *American Journal of Sociology* 90, no. 4 (January 1985); 825–55; Frank F. Furstenburg Jr., S. Philip Morgan, Kristin A. Moore, and James Peterson, "Race Differences in the Timing of Adolescent Intercourse," *American Sociological Review* 52, no. 4 (August 1987): 511–18; Jonathan Crane, "The Epidemic Theory of Ghettos and Neighborhood Effects on Dropping Out and Teenage Childbearing," *American Journal of Sociology* 96, no. 5 (March 1991): 1226–59.

33. Douglas S. Massey, Andrew B. Gross, and Mitchell L. Eggers, "Segregation, the Concentration of Poverty, and the Life Chances of Individuals," *Social Science Research* 20, no. 4 (December 1991): 397–420.

34. James E. Rosenbaum and Susan J. Popkin, "Employment and Earnings of Low-Income Blacks Who Move to Middle Class Suburbs," in *The Urban Underclass*, eds. Christopher Jencks and Paul E. Peterson (Washington, D.C.: Brookings Institution, 1991), 342–56; James E. Rosenbaum, "Black Pioneers—Do Their Moves to the Suburbs Increase Economic Opportunity for Mothers and Children?" *Housing Policy Debate* 2, no. 4 (1991): 1179–1214.

Part 5

Mobilizing Strategies

Introduction

This concluding section addresses the three strategies for redress—litigation, legislation, and mobilization—and further elaborates their modalities. The essay by Charles P. Henry and interview with reparationists Sam Anderson and Muntu Matsimela assess the relative merits of each strategy and the movement's linkages to redress and anticapitalist formations abroad. Henry identifies the political obstacles to reparations during the current era of neoconservatism and outlines a broad and transnational strategy that includes an apology for slavery, collective compensation ("rehabilitati[on] of devastated communities" and "creative antitrust action"), and mobilization against "the entire history of racism in the United States and its exercise abroad." C. J. Munford's project, like that of Anderson and Matsimela's, is no less a critique of Western capitalism and "white supremacy." His proposed strategy pivots on black leadership of multiracial coalitions that call for a "Black America *united* for reparations and an antiracist White minority rallying in support of Black reparations."

Less expansive and transformational than Henry's or Anderson and Matsimela's projects, the essay by Charles J. Ogletree Jr. emphasizes reparations litigation and multiracial coalition politics. Although in a different way than Munford, Ogletree also advocates an "interest convergence," especially between reparationists and the majority (read: white) population. Adrienne Davis, too, emphasizes litigation and the utility of the Thirteenth Amendment to pursue reparations claims. Like other contributors to this book, she argues that modern forms of racial discrimination are derived from slavery and account for racial and economic injustice in the contemporary period. Eric K. Yamamoto also addresses the litigation approach but applies the lessons of the Japanese American redress campaign. He identifies areas that presently mitigate reparations claims, including ideological barriers that hinder empathy with slaves' ancestors as victims, along with problems in clearly identifying perpetrators among contemporary plaintiffs. Yamamoto counsels a "dual strategy" for African Americans' reparations that limits claims and claimants and, concomitantly, pursues a "path" through the courts to educate and publicize larger reparations issues.

Both Yusuf Nuruddin and Robert Johnson Jr., like Browne (see part 3), address two acutely problematical forms of reparations. While Johnson views repatriation as potentially a "viable and effective form of reparations," Nuruddin considers a separate nation-state to be an effective organizing principle rather than a practical remedy.

Given developments in world affairs and the unpopularity of the redress movement in the United States, Gerald Horne, in the book's concluding essay, counsels a strategy that engages the international community — rhetorically, litigiously, and politically. Along the lines suggested by Matsimela and Anderson, as well as the editors in their introductory essay, Horne argues that from slavery's abolition to Jim Crow's erosion in the 1950s, progressive social reforms were driven in no small measure by pressure from international critics and advocates. While emphasizing other forms of mobilization (including lawsuits), Horne suggests areas where rifts among nation-states may be exploited and alliances made possible, which in tandem would strengthen the efforts of reparationists in the United States.

The Politics of Racial Reparations

CHARLES P. HENRY

When Congressman Tony Hall of Ohio introduced a resolution providing a simple apology for slavery in 1997, he said he received more hate mail than at any other time in his long political career. On a well-publicized official visit to several African nations, President Clinton offered an apology to Africans for the slave trade but pointedly did not apologize to African Americans (Brooks, 1999). This refusal came in the context of a virtual flood of apologies. Nationally, President Clinton apologized to indigenous Hawaiians for the illegal U.S.-aided overthrow of their sovereign nation and near decimation of Hawaiian life that followed; the Methodist Church apologized to Native Americans in Wyoming for their 1865 post-treaty slaughter at the hands of the U.S. Cavalry led by a Methodist minister; the federal government agreed to apologize and provide limited reparations for Japanese Latin Americans kidnapped from Latin American countries and placed in U.S. internment camps as hostages during the Second World War; and the Southern Baptist Convention apologized to African Americans for their support of the institution of slavery (Yamamoto, 1998). Why was the U.S. government unwilling to apologize to African Americans as it had to other groups or as church groups had done?

One answer is that the refusal to apologize for the institution of slavery and declare it a crime against humanity is an implicit acknowledgment that slavery was not a deviation—it was the norm. No national political leader urged the abolition of slavery at the founding, just as no national political leader today has urged an apology. To recognize the role of slavery and its consequences undermines the concept of American exceptionalism. It exposes the economic exploitation at the heart of white supremacy that now must be viewed as a part of the American creed. Thus, the vociferous and negative response to an apology/reparation is to erase slavery from the national conscience.

Few social observers would argue that we are currently in an era of relative racial progress. What, then, accounts for the current black interest in reparations, an issue that has failed to win mainstream support in the best of times? We suggest two factors are key to this resurgence.

Beginning in 1989, the Supreme Court attacked a number of affirmative action programs in its decision in *J. A. Croson v. City of Richmond* (1989), *Wards Cove Packing Co., Inc. v. Antonio* (1989), and *Aderand Contractors v. Pena* (1995). This court action, following eight years of active hostility to black civil rights on the part of the Reagan administration, created a crisis environment in which the gains of the civil rights movement were put in jeopardy. Popularly, the black counterpublic saw those years as the end of the second Reconstruction.

The 1980s were reminiscent — symbolically and substantively — of the rollback of black progress that followed the first Reconstruction. The decade began with presidential candidate Ronald Reagan speaking to thousands of cheering whites at the Neshoba County Fair in Mississippi. The county fairgrounds are just outside Philadelphia, Mississippi, the infamous site of the murder of three civil rights workers in 1964. After warming up the crowd with attacks on Washington bureaucrats, big government, and welfare, Reagan then shouted, "I believe in states' rights. I believe that we've distorted the balance of our government by giving powers that were never intended in the Constitution to the federal establishment" (as cited in Hutchinson, 1996, 176).

Symbolically, the decade closed with George Bush vetoing the 1990 civil rights bill. Bush's election as president was widely attributed to his use of the escape of convicted black murderer William (Willie) Horton as a wedge issue in his attack on Massachusetts governor Michael Dukakis, his Democratic opponent. Several years after the election, when voters were asked what they remembered about the 1988 campaign, they provided three names: Dukakis, Bush, and Horton (Mendelberg, 2001).

Substantially, an overwhelming amount of evidence exists of a growing disparity between blacks and whites on basic socioeconomic indicators. Moreover, the evidence also demonstrates a growing disparity between the black middle class and the black poor. These post–civil rights movement trends continued from the Reagan-Bush administrations through the Clinton administration.

Andrew Hacker's (1993) classic *Two Nations* was one of the first works to draw attention to these trends. More recent works are highlighted by the following figures:

In general, southern GEO metropolitan areas appeared to be converging to a
  level of black–white segregation in the range of 65 to 70, about 10 points

below their northern counterparts, which range from 75 to 80 percent segregated (Massey and Denton, 1993).

Forty percent of all urban schools are intensely segregated (90 percent students of color; Applied Research Center 2000).

The ratio of black incomes to white incomes increased from 53 percent in 1967 to 58 percent in 1992, but in absolute terms the discrepancy in income rose from $4,700 to $6,700 (Hochschild, 1995).

The ratio of black to white poverty has remained at 3:1, and there are now about 4 million fewer poor whites than thirty years ago, but 686,000 more poor blacks (Hochschild, 1995).

The poorest one-fifth of African Americans lost almost as large a share of their income as the richest one-fifth gained of theirs (Hochschild, 1995).

A smaller fraction of African Americans owned houses in 1990 than did whites in 1920, and the value of black-owned homes is barely more than one half of the value of houses owned by whites (Hochschild, 1995).

The median net worth of white households is more than eight times that of black households (Feagin, 2000).

For blacks and whites, the number of well-off Americans who are the victims of violence is steadily decreasing, whereas the number of poor Americans who are victimized by violence is steadily increasing (Hochschild, 1995).

From 1969 to 1999, federal funding for education decreased from 1.35 percent to 1.03 percent of the federal budget, whereas prison spending has risen from 0.42 percent to 1.52 percent of the federal budget (Applied Research Center, 2000).

African Americans are 12 percent of the U.S. population and 12 percent of U.S. drug users, yet they are 38 percent of those arrested for drug-related offenses (Weich and Angulo, 2000).

Of all black men in Alabama and Florida, 31 percent are permanently disenfranchised as a result of felony convictions. Nationally, 1.4 million black men have lost the right to vote due to felony convictions (Weich and Angulo, 2000).

Black male life expectancy is actually declining. In 1993, only 66 percent of African American men reached age 60, compared to 84 percent of white men ("Evaluating Reparations," 2001).

Even the black middle class—which is now roughly one-third of black families—has limited mobility. Blacks hold less than 4 percent of the 26,000 jobs in magazine and newspaper journalism, are less than 2 percent of the lawyers working in the 250 largest law firms, and are less than 1 percent of the partners. Only thirty-seven of the 20,000 partners in major accounting firms are black, whereas black professionals and managers are almost twice as likely to be unemployed as whites in similar job categories. Even economic success does not lead out of the ghetto because a black earning more than $50,000 per year is as likely to live in a segregated neighborhood as someone black making $2,500 a year (Lipsitz, 1998).

Current prospects for reversing these trends seem remote. President George W. Bush assumed office after a contested election process in which black voters in Florida were disproportionately disenfranchised ("Black Election," 2001). More recently, former and future Senate Majority Leader Trent Lott, in a tribute to Senator Strom Thurmond, said, "I want to say this about my state: When Strom Thurmond ran for president, we voted for him. We're proud of it. And if the rest of the country had followed our lead, we wouldn't have had all these problems over all these years" (as cited in Edsall, 2002, A13). In 1948, Thurmond split from the Democratic Party to form the Dixiecrat Party, dedicated to the preservation of racial segregation. Lott did not specify what "all these problems" were.

The second catalytic agent was provided by the passage of the Civil Liberties Act of 1988 (50 U.S.C. app 1989). Successful action on the part of Japanese Americans in gaining reparations for their internment during the Second World War provided a model for a badly demoralized community of black political activists. Their case proved inspiring because Japanese Americans represented a small, apparently prosperous fraction of the American population (three-tenths of 1 percent) concentrated in a few West Coast states that had been relatively inactive as a political community. Moreover, they succeeded in an environment of near-record federal deficits with a president elected for his conservatism. They succeeded for several reasons.[1]

First, Japanese Americans had a well-documented grievance. As early as 1941, an internal report prepared by the State Department had determined that Japanese Americans possessed an exceptional degree of loyalty to the United States and that they were no threat to America's security. Similar reports by the FBI and Naval Intelligence confirmed these findings yet were not made public until after the war. Congress created a study commission of well-respected figures to examine the facts and make recommendations in 1980. The commission's fact-finding report was issued well in advance of its recommendations, allowing it to serve as a public education tool and not get lost in a debate over compensation.

Second, there was little formal opposition. Japanese American activists feared a negative reaction from veterans' groups arguing that everyone had sacrificed during the Second World War. Yet, these groups were largely neutral, with two even passing general resolutions of support in national meetings. These veterans' groups were heavily influenced by the war record of

Japanese Americans fighting in the 100th Battalion (from Hawaii), called the 442nd Regimental Combat Team. This unit was the most decorated group of its size in the Second World War. A small organization called the Americans for Historical Accuracy led by Lillian Baker did oppose the legislation in congressional hearings. Baker's opposition, however, was largely seen as racist retribution for the loss of her husband in fighting in the Pacific during the war. Congress had already passed three pieces of legislation dealing with Japanese American claims prior to 1988 and starting in 1948. Given the lack of strong opposition, legislators could view their vote on this issue as a throwaway vote.

Third, the Japanese American Citizens League (JACL) first began addressing the issue of redress in 1970. Although factions such as the National Council for Japanese American Redress (NCJAR) developed and pursued a class-action lawsuit, the JACL was able to maintain its credibility as the oldest and largest Japanese American civic organization. The 1982 report of the study commission (Hatamiya, 1993) created by Congress served as a catalyst within the Japanese American community. In fact, the study commission hearings opened an emotional floodgate of pent-up feelings among older Japanese Americans that generated a new energy and commitment on the issue. Consequently, both major parties endorsed redress for Japanese Americans in their 1984 presidential platforms.

Fourth, internal changes in Congress following the 1986 elections put more favorable legislators in key positions. Among them was Representative Barney Frank (D-MA), replacing Representative Glickman (R-KS) as chair of the subcommittee in which the legislation rested. A group of four well-respected, senior Japanese American legislators then pushed hard for the bill's passage. In the Senate, Daniel Inouye (D-HI) took the early lead, with Spark Matsunaga (D-HI) doing the later lobbying. Norm Mineta (D-CA) and Robert Matsui (D-CA) led the fight in the House. To gain the support of Senator Stevens (R-AK), redress for Aleutian Islanders was attached to the legislation.

Fifth, the redress issue was framed as a constitutional issue rather than a racial issue. The internment of Japanese Americans was presented as governmental discrimination violating the rights of private citizens and denying them equal opportunity. Framed in this way, Republicans such as Newt Gingrich, Alan Simpson, Jack Kemp, and Henry Hyde were able to support it.

Finally, a variety of external factors may have assisted passage of the bill. Legal battles in the *coram nobis* cases of *Korematsu v. United States* (1944), *Hirabayashi v. United States* (1987), and *Hohri v. United States* (1984), as well as the class-action suit of NCJAR, made arguments in support of legislative redress more compelling. Media also gave generally favorable coverage to the Japanese American efforts. Passage of the Civil Liberties Act of 1988 authorized a national apology, an education fund, and individual payments of $20,000 to each surviving internee[2] (see Documents, section 1).

The success of the Civil Liberties Act of 1988 sparked a spate of race apologies and served as a catalyst for renewed interest in African American reparations. Representative John Conyers (D-MI) submitted HR 40 (originally HR 3745; symbolically recalling 40 acres, number is requested by the representative), the Commission to Study Reparations Proposals for African Americans Act (1989) the following year. Modeled after the Japanese American study commission bill that preceded the Civil Liberties Act of 1988, Conyers's legislation would:

Acknowledge the fundamental injustice and inhumanity of slavery
Establish a commission to study slavery and its subsequent racial and economic discrimination against freed slaves
Study the effect of those forces on today's living African Americans
Make recommendations to Congress on appropriate remedies to redress the harm inflicted on living African Americans. (Brooks, 1999)

The National Coalition of Blacks for Reparations (N'COBRA) was also formed in the late 1980s to develop a grassroots reparations movement. Black activist Ron Daniels made reparations a central issue in his independent bid for the presidency in 1992.

Internationally, Nigerian President Ibrahim Babangia took the lead in establishing a reparations movement during his tenure as head of the Organization of African Unity (OAU; established in 1963). After the first meeting of the International Conference on Reparations in Lagos, Nigeria, in the winter of 1990, the OAU set up the Group of Eminent Persons. In 1992, the OAU formally embraced and endorsed reparations as "the last stage in the decolonization process." This summit of African heads of state meeting in Dakar, Senegal, formally created an international committee called the Group of Eminent Persons (established in 1990) and charged it with determining the scope of damages and a strategy for achieving reparations. Jamaican diplomat Dr. Dudley Thompson was chosen to chair the group (Obadele, 1996). After a second conference in 1993, the OAU issued the Abuja Proclamation that articulated a grievance against the United States and western European nations linking slavery and colonialism:

Emphasizing that an admission of guilt is a necessary step to reverse this situation (damage to African peoples);
Emphatically convinced that what matters is not the guilt but the responsibility of those states whose economic evolution once depended on slave labour and colonialism and whose forebears participated either in selling and buying Africans, or in owning them, or in colonizing them;
Convinced that the pursuit of reparations by the African peoples on the continent and in the Diaspora will be a learning experience in self-discovery and in uniting political and psychological experiences;
Calls upon the international community to recognize that there is a unique and unprecedented moral debt of compensation to the Africans as the most humiliated and exploited people of the last four centuries of modern history. (as cited in R. Robinson, 2000, 220)

Since 1994, numerous reparations claims have been filed against the U.S. government in federal court, none of which have been successful.

In 1994, the Internal Revenue Service reported receiving about 20,000 bogus tax-reparation claims. Capitalizing on the publicity around federal payments to Japanese Americans, con artists falsely informed blacks that the federal government had passed similar legislation for African Americans and offered to file their claims for a fee. In 2001, the Social Security Administration issued a special alert to senior citizens involving a reparations scam. An investigation by the agency found that the Slave Reparation Act duped more than 29,000 people (Mayer, 2001; Singletory, 2001). The agency received nearly 80,000 returns claiming more than $2.7 billion in false reparation refunds (Internal Revenue Service, 2002). Throughout the 1990s, a number of individual cities and states have taken some action on reparations. Cities like Tulsa, Oklahoma, and Elaine, Arkansas, have considered payments to survivors of racist violence. Other cities, such as Dallas, Atlanta, Nashville, Cleveland, Chicago, and Detroit, have passed bills that provide symbolic support for reparations. In New York and California, the state legislatures have passed bills dealing with some aspect of reparations (Austin, 2001; see Documents, sections 2 and 3).

Despite some success at the state and local levels, the Conyers bill, which generated grassroots organizations and has led to the passage of resolutions of support in several major cities, has remained buried in subcommittee at the national level. At this point, it might be instructive to compare the African American case for reparations to the successful Japanese American example. Legal scholar Roy L. Brooks (1999) set forth a theory of redress informed by a number of reparations claims from various groups. Brooks established four conditions for successful redress: (a) the demands or claims for redress must be placed in the hands of legislators rather than judges; (b) public and private political pressure must be exerted on the legislators; (c) strong internal (group) support is required; and (d) the claim must be meritorious (Brooks, 1999).

On the first condition, Conyers's bill squarely places redress for slavery on the congressional agenda, as does Rep. Tony Hall's resolution calling for an apology. As was the case with Japanese American claims, activists pursued political and legal strategies. Deadria Farmer-Paellmann and Edward Fagan filed a class-action reparation suit against private corporations (FleetBoston, Aetna, and CSX Railroad) with antebellum roots. The suit was filed in federal district court and seeks up to $1.4 trillion ("Slave Descendents Seek," 2002). Harvard law professor Charles Ogletree, on behalf of the Reparations Coordinating Committee, filed a federal class-action lawsuit in March 2002 seeking reparations on behalf of all African American descendants of slaves. The lawsuit is limited to Aetna, CSX Railroad, FleetBoston, and other companies to be named later; however, the Committee is also planning additional reparations lawsuits including suits against the government (Ogletree, 2002). As we saw in the Japanese American case, these parallel legal and legislative tracks may actually complement rather than detract from one another. It is also interesting to note that N'COBRA—the grassroots reparations organization with some twenty-six local chapters—has devoted at least as much attention to the legal arena as to political activity.

Although Conyers has had as many as forty cosponsors for his bill, current Republican control of the Congress makes the prospect of getting the bill out of committee and onto the floor for a vote remote at best. During the Clinton administration, Vice President Al Gore was asked for his views on reparations. He said, "I think that it is a question that needs to be dealt with respectfully and with great sensitivity to those who are interested in the idea, not really for the money it represents but rather for the symbolic atonement they associate with it. At the end of the day, most agree that it's not a politically feasible idea" ("Why Reparations," 2002, 6). When asked specifically about the Conyers bill calling for a study commission, Gore added, "I'm for handling it sensitively without conveying a sense that it's ever likely to occur, because it's not" ("Why Reparations," 2002, 6). Senator Patrick Leahy (D-VT) opined, "I suspect there are a lot of things we could have reparations on. Is it a debate that benefits anyone—black or white? I don't know the answer to that question" ("Why Reparations," 2002, 6). Senator Rick Santorum (R-PA) said, "I have never been a fan of reparations for anything, there have always been bad things that have happened to people. Slavery was awful. But I don't think there is anything to be gained by going backward to try to come up with some way to pay for something that you can't put a monetary price tag on" ("Why Reparations," 2002, 6). Sen. Olympia Snowe (R-ME) stated, "It's something I certainly would consider... Has anybody held hearings on this issue?" ("Why Reparations," 2002, 6). The Democratic Party adopted a plank endorsing the idea of establishing a federal commission to study the lingering effects of slavery in the summer of 2000 (Fletcher, 2000).

Congressional views largely reflect public opinion on reparations. A March 28–29, 2001, Fox News-Opinion Dynamics Poll of registered voters reported that 81 percent were opposed to reparations, whereas 11 percent supported it ("Slave Reparations Debate Heating Up," 2001). A national ABC News poll revealed that 67 percent of whites believe black people are discriminated against, yet in liberal New York City 62 percent of New Yorkers do not think blacks are even owed an apology (Iuce, 2002). In the same city, 62 percent of blacks support reparations, but only 22 percent of whites agree (Iuce, 2002). In more conservative Chicago, a *Chicago Tribune* poll was running three to one against reparations until U.S. Rep. Bobby Rush urged blacks to respond to the poll (Race Relations, 2002). A CNN/*USA Today*/Gallup Poll found 90 percent of white respondents were opposed to cash reparations, whereas 55 percent of blacks supported cash payments ("Suit Seeks Billions in Slave Reparations," 2002).

Even with the stimulus of the Reagan-Bush retrenchment and the example of the Civil Liberties Act of 1988, blacks needed a core community of believers or network of activists to mainstream reparations as an issue. Black nationalist activists who were better organized and focused than disillusioned black liberals during this period provided this. Black nationalism has always enjoyed increased popularity in the African American community when the larger society has cut off or narrowed access to the mainstream (Dawson, 2001; Bracey, Meier, and Rudwick, 1970). Another key to mobilizing resources was a shift in the attitudes of the black middle class. Newly affluent blacks have become more frustrated and alienated over racial progress than have lower-class blacks. Members of the black middle class such as Randall Robinson bring increased credibility and clout to an issue that had been marginalized during the twentieth century.

Supporters of reparations outside the black nationalist community have probably never heard of Queen Mother Moore. Yet, for most of the 1950s and 1960s, she was the best-known advocate of African American reparations. Operating out of Harlem and her organization, the Universal Association of Ethiopian Women, Moore actively promoted reparations from 1950 until her death in 1996. Moore, who had been a Garveyite (a member of Garvey's organization, the Universal Negro Improvement Association) and then a communist, spent much of her time pressing for reparations through the United Nations (Lanker, 1989).

A 1987 conference on the U.S. Constitution sponsored by the National Conference of Black Lawyers produced the N'COBRA. Kalonji T. Olusegun and Adjou Aiyetoro led the new organization, and it is the largest national organization devoted solely to reparations. Although supporting the Conyers bill, it has also engaged in education campaigns designed to pressure state and local legislators to support reparations. Given its origins, it is not surprising that N'COBRA has been involved in legal action on reparations (Hakim, 1994). However, as historian Clarence Munford (2001, 386) stated, "The organization must break with nationalist sectarianism" if it is to develop a true mass base (see Munford, part 5). Another group working in coalition with N'COBRA is the Black Reparations Commission, established in 1978 and headed by Dorothy Lewis. Silis Muhammad of the Lost Found Nation of Islam formed a more recent group, the National Commission for Reparations, in 1991. Like Queen Mother Moore, this group addresses much of its attention to the UN, seeking to apply international laws within the framework of the international system. Yussef Naim Kly, head of the International Human Rights Association for American Minorities — in applying international law to the reparations debate — has aided these groups (Hakim, 1994).

In its 1974 Black Agenda, the National Black Political Assembly (NBPA) endorsed the concept of African American reparations. Activists from the NBPA are currently active in the reparations movement. Ron Daniels, for example, has recently formed an Institute of the Black World with reparations serving as a major theme for their work (Herb Boyd, personal communication, April 16, 2001; Ron Daniels, personal communication, April 16, 2001). Older nationalist organizations (such as the Black United Front, led by Conrad Worrill, and the Republic of New Africa, led by Imari Obadele) have been active supporters of the reparations movement. The African National Reparations Organization linked to the African People's Socialist Party has conducted yearly tribunals on U.S. racism since 1982 and demanded $4.1 trillion in reparations for stolen labor (Hakim, 1994).

Although many of the meetings, conferences, and tribunals sponsored by these groups open with the pouring of traditional African libations and African drumming, black nationalists are now not alone in their demands. Perhaps no one typifies the newfound respectability of the reparations movement more than Randall Robinson. Robinson, a graduate of Harvard Law School, was the founder and (until recently) president of TransAfrica, a U.S.

lobby for Africa and the Caribbean. Brother of the late network news anchor Max Robinson, R. Robinson is very much a member of the black leadership class. His best-selling book, *The Debt: What America Owes to Blacks*, was the first exposure many Americans of all races had to the reparations debate. In the introduction to that book, he expressed frustration with such diversionary programs as affirmative action that ignore the black poor and offer no solutions to black problems. Moreover, the book reproduces a pointed critique of the Clinton administration by political scientist Ronald Walters and puzzles over black affection for the former president:

> In his first term, Clinton's policies followed a distinct slant toward a more conservative and Republican course on social issues. He sponsored the most punitive crime bill in history, which passed in 1993; after suffering the defeat of his "economic stimulus package," which contained funds for urban development, he never put it back on the table. He signed the most punitive welfare reform bill in history, effecting a revolution in New Deal policy toward government support for the poor; and thousands of people silently have been sifted out of federal government employment through the "reinventing government program." . . . When one examines the impact of the crime bill on the sharply increased criminalization of black youth in particular, the exposure of the poorest blacks to the labor market without sufficient training or family support, and the lack of investment in urban schools or communities, Clinton's positive initiatives may be viewed as largely symbolic. (R. Robinson, 2000, 100)

Robinson (2000, 247) concluded that if black claims are to have any chance of success here, "We must make it clear to America that we will not allow ourselves to be ignored."

Robinson's frustration and anger reflect a widespread feeling among the black middle class. Political scientist Jennifer Hochschild (1995, 26) stated, "Not only has the idea of universal participation been denied to most Americans, but also the very fact of its denial has itself been denied in our national self-image." The result of this denial is that whites believe race discrimination is declining whereas blacks believe the opposite. More precisely, poor African Americans now have more faith in the American dream than middle-class blacks. Hochschild reported that although both classes of African Americans were more optimistic for their race in the 1960s than in the 1980s, the optimism of affluent blacks has plummeted when compared to that of poor blacks. Affluent blacks more closely identify with their racial status than their class status, more so than any other racial/class group. Perhaps this explains why unlike the upwardly mobile immigrants of all other groups, the new black middle-class commitment to the American dream is declining, not rising.[3]

Michael Dawson's (2001, 309) findings also reflect declining support for liberalism among blacks: "Liberalism has become a weak force in shaping the politics of the black community, even though a large percentage of blacks support the radical egalitarian program." By 2000, 71 percent of African Americans believed racial progress would not be achieved in their lifetimes or not at all (Dawson, 2001). Dawson also recognized that there are multiple liberal traditions within the black community just as in the larger society. Overall, however, he believed that black liberals' concern with the egalitarian aspects of liberalism leads them to seek a much stronger state than other American liberals. Historically, for example, public opinion polling in the 1960s and 1970s revealed that blacks ranked equality at the top and liberty toward the bottom of their value scales, whereas whites did the opposite. What shifts over time, moving blacks from hope to despair, says Dawson (2001, 275), "are the evaluation of white willingness to 'accept' black equality, the evaluation of the nature of American society, and the assessment of prospects for gaining full democratic citizenship."

Not all black citizens are nationalists or liberals. The rise of the new black middle class also produced a new black neoconservatism. Linguist John McWhorter (2001), for example, wrote an opinion piece for the *Los Angeles Times* titled "Why I Don't Want Reparations for Slavery." McWhorter stated, "If all Black Americans living below the poverty line were given a subsidy to move to the suburbs, free tuition for college and/or a small business loan, all indications are that, for most, in the long run it would make no difference in the overall condition of their lives" (M5). Journalist Juan Williams (2002), not generally considered a conservative, has opposed reparations, fearing it will spark white backlash and result in a further segregation of the black poor. He also feared that it will mean an end to the moral responsibility that Americans bear for racial oppression. Unlike Robinson, Williams preferred support for affirmative action and welfare. In fact, he accused affluent blacks like Robinson of wanting to "take control of the massive budgets dedicated to social-welfare policy" (A26). Despite their prominence in the media, black conservatives enjoy less support in the black community than adherents of any black ideology with virtually no mass support (Dawson, 2001).[4]

When compared to Japanese American support for reparations, the African American community can look unfocused and fragmented. Yet, reparations have a much longer history in the black community, with organizations devoted to that single issue alone. The success of the Japanese American struggle helped to mainstream the issue in the African American community. With such mainstream organizations as the NAACP and the Urban League joining the reparations movement, the issue gained new respectability (see

Documents, section 4). Academics and professionals joined in sponsoring recent conferences at Columbia University, Fisk, University of California at Los Angeles, the University of California at Berkeley Law School, and the National Bar Association. In addition, as we have seen, many of the leaders of reparations organizations are lawyers or academics. Democratic politicians heavily dependent on black voters could not summarily dismiss the issue as in the past. Neither could they endorse it given the strong white opposition to reparations. Can reparations be framed in a way that attracts broad political support, as did the Japanese American claim?

At some levels, the case for Japanese American reparations was framed in ways that would be difficult to apply to the African American claim. The obvious difference with the Japanese American case is the lack of identifiable victims as a distinct group. Opponents point to the absence of ex-slaves and the success of many current African Americans. In the case of the black underclass, they argue that the problems of the black poor are not causally connected to a past injustice.[5] Another obvious difference is the scope of the settlement. The payments issued under the Civil Liberties Act of 1988 totaled less than $2 billion. Despite arguments that the cost of slavery cannot be measured, a number of scholars have quantified the material costs (America, 1993; see America, part 2). The most conservative figures total approximately $1.5 trillion. In fact, one argument against reparations is not that the claim is not meritorious but that it is simply too large to be paid, although this argument ignores the issue of an apology.

Beyond these obvious differences lie more subtle issues. Hatamiya (1993) gave credit to the American civil rights movement for changing the climate to permit such claims as those of Japanese Americans to be heard. Yet, she labeled civil rights as special interest legislation and argued that Japanese American redress had to be presented as a constitutional issue rather than a racial issue. Politically this may be true, but it ignores the fact that Japanese Americans (as a group) were interned because of their race, unlike German Americans and Italian Americans who were treated on an individual basis. Moreover, it assumes that a constitutional issue cannot be a racial issue; however, a strong argument can be made that race was central to both the writing of and implementation of the Constitution (Mills, 1997; D. Robinson, 1979).

According to Eric Yamamoto (1998), framing the Japanese American claim in terms of the "super patriot/model minority" served several interests (see Yamamato, part 5). It aided the Japanese American internees, but it also served the government's practical and policy interests. "Practically, it enabled the government to award reparations to a relatively small number of highly deserving Japanese Americans," said Yamamoto, "without opening the floodgates to reparations for other racial groups" (57).[6] Policywise, the United States could proclaim its commitment to democracy and human rights in the face of a Soviet empire that was beginning to crumble. Reparation claims could be acknowledged in the absence of a cold war. See, for example, the renewed U.S. support for Jewish Holocaust claims against the Swiss government.

Black Americans are often portrayed, as McWhorter (2001) demonstrated, as the opposite of the model minority. Despite the differences, the success of the Japanese American claim did assist African Americans because the federal government recognized a group claim. If the focus can be kept on group harm then the solution can be framed as an effort to repair the damage. The solution does not rest in individual payment but in a restructuring of the institutions and relationships that produce gross disparities in wealth and well-being. Racial attitudes will not change without such a restructuring. Although Dwight Eisenhower was often fond of saying law could not change men's hearts, his own armed forces are the most successful example of affirmative action in American society. To ignore the African American claim for reparations is ███████████████████████████████ 7), lack of legal or legisla████████████████████████████████rious than the acts thems████████████████████████████████ood of its victims.

Ultimately t████████████████████████████████ll be determined by facto████████████████████████████████lement. As it stands, blac████████████████████████████████ons to the forefront of the████████████████████████████████y is due to several factors.████████████████████████████████y means of government as████████████████████████████████ment. Historically, such ████████████████████████████████y to black nationalist con████████████████████████████████occupying the leading role████████████████████████████████ for some of these group████████████████████████████████ than the international a████████████████████████████████ck middle class has force████████████████████████████████ainstream political discou████████████████████████████████ Ogletree, and the organizers of academic reparations conferences bring increased legitimacy to the cause, they have pursued the primarily elite strategy of legal action. Similarly, such organizations as the NAACP and Urban League—although vocally supporting the call for reparations—see it as one of a host of organizational concerns with no special priority. Third, reparations has enabled its advocates to assume the moral high ground lost after the civil rights movement. To a large extent, white opposition to an apology for slavery is a refusal to concede the high ground. David Gresson argued, "The racial liberation movement and its companion liberation movements represented losses for white men as moral heroes; the emotional and symbolic aspects of this loss, moreover, were greater than any material loss the American dominant majority sustained" (as cited in McPhail, 2002, 189). "Increasingly," says Gresson, "whites experienced themselves as oppressed victims of an uncaring authority and cited efforts on behalf of blacks, Hispanics, Native Americans and other ethnics as 'reverse racism'—the birth cry of modern white racial recovery rhetoric" (189–190). In short, the current reparations movement has achieved a rhetorical unity that has put its opponents on the defensive.

To succeed politically—substantively or symbolically—the movement must agree on some specific goals and some specific targets. One obvious goal and target would be an apology from Congress, the president, or both for slavery and its consequences. Some reparations advocates opposed an apology because they fear it forecloses further concessions. Yet, it is difficult to imagine governmental agreement for substantive compensation without first acknowledging some moral guilt. In fact, the term *reparation* implies atonement, whereas responses lacking such expressions are properly called *settlements*. The recent South African Truth Commission followed a process of recognition, responsibility, reconstruction, and then reparation (Brooks, 1999).

Another goal and target on which consensus seems to be building is for group or collective compensation from the federal government. Although there are still advocates for individual payments, it seems clear that the individual harm suffered by African Americans varies greatly. It is morally and politically more compelling to argue that development banks and educational trust funds should be set up for those most economically and educationally disadvantaged. Such an approach avoids the issue of compensating affluent blacks who will nonetheless be paying taxes that support the program. Although the issue of who will control the funds and who will qualify to apply are not insignificant, they are surmountable and should be addressed after agreement on a general program. Such programs can and should be seen as rehabilitative of devastated communities.

Some reparations advocates have endorsed governmental action to redistribute wealth in the private sphere. Creative antitrust action could, for example, be used to spread the wealth to African Americans and other minorities in overconcentrated industries much as the AT&T breakup assisted white entrepreneurs. Major corporations might be required to sell off units to minorities to complete mergers (America, 1993). These types of programs, however, are likely to be seen as benefiting already affluent blacks and thus garner less black support and more white hostility. Actions affecting the private sphere may best be left to the legal arena, where several cases are pending and where consumer pressure might force some settlements.

Finally, the reparations movement needs to make clear that its concern is not with slavery alone but with the entire history of racism in the United States and its exercise abroad. It is true that there are no living former slaves, but every African American has directly or indirectly experienced racial discrimination or is indirectly influenced by it. The failure to treat reparations as a legitimate issue acknowledges that America is far from a color-blind society. The frustrated and prophetic voice of Martin Luther King Jr. recognized this nearly forty years ago when he said:

> A true revolution of values will soon cause us to question the fairness and justice of many of our past and present policies. On the one hand we are called to play the Good Samaritan on life's roadside, but that will be only an initial act. One day we must come to see that the whole Jericho Road must be transformed so that men and women will not be constantly beaten and robbed as they make their journey on life's highway. True compassion is more than flinging a coin to a beggar. It comes to see that an edifice which produces beggars needs restructuring. (as cited in Carson, 1998, 340)

Notes

1. This section is drawn largely from Leslie T. Hatamiya (1993).
2. Hatamiya (1993) reported that Reagan and then Bush proposed budgets containing no redress funds for 1989 and only $20 million for 1990. Senator Inouye, as the number-two ranking Democrat on the Appropriations Committee, was able to pry loose the needed funding as an entitlement program over three years that included a $400 million increase over the original appropriation.
3. Hochschild noted that much of what makes affluent black women feel deprived compared with others has more to do with gender than with race.
4. Dawson stated that black feminists face the most obstacles in disseminating their views, and the black Marxism and the radical tradition lost much of their mass character in the 1990s.
5. Orlando Patterson (1998) argued the opposite.
6. Hatamiya (1993) noted that Reagan's approval was influenced by his participation in a 1945 ceremony awarding a Distinguished Service Cross to the family of Kazuo Masuda of the 442nd who had died in combat but was not allowed to be buried in the local cemetery in Santa Ana, California.

References

Aderand Contractors v. Pena, 903–1841, slip opinion (1995).
America, R. F. *Paying the Social Debt: What White America Owes Black America*. Westport, Conn.: Praeger, 1993.
Applied Research Center. *Still Separate, Still Unequal*. Oakland, Calif.: Author, May 2000.
Austin, A. "Activists Discuss Slave Reparations." Associated Press, 7 March 2001.
"Black Election: 2000." *The Black Scholar* 31, no. 2 (summer 2001).
Bracey, J. H., Jr., A. Meier, and E. P. Rudwick, eds. *Black Nationalism in America*. Indianapolis: Bobbs-Merrill, 1970.
Brooks, R. L. *When Sorry Isn't Enough: The Controversy over Apologies and Reparations for Human Injustice*. New York: New York University Press, 1999.
Carson, C., ed. *The Autobiography of Martin Luther King, Jr*. New York: Warner Books, 1998.
Dawson, M. C. *Black Visions: The Roots of Contemporary African American Political Ideologies*. Chicago: University of Chicago Press, 2001.
Edsall, T. B. " 'Poor Choice of Words,' Lott Says." *Washington Post*. 10 December 2002, A13.
"Evaluating Reparations." *Washington Post*. 10 April 2001, A18.
Feagin, J. R. *Racist America: Roots, Current Realities, and Future Reparations*. New York: Routledge, 2000.
Fletcher, M. A. "Putting a Price on Slavery's Legacy." *Washington Post*. 26 December 2000.
Hacker, A. *Two Nations: Black and White, Separate, Hostile, Unequal*. New York: Ballantine, 1993.
Hakim, I. *Reparations, the Cure for America's Race Problem*. Hampton, Va.: U. B. and U.S. Communications Systems, 1994.
Hatamiya, L. T. *Righting a Wrong: Japanese Americans and the Passage of the Civil Liberties Act of 1988*. Stanford: Stanford University Press, 1993.
Hirabayashi v. United States, 828 F. 2d 591 (1987).
Hochschild, J. L. *Facing Up to the American Dream: Race, Class and the Soul of America*. Princeton: Princeton University Press, 1995.
Hohri v. United States, 586 F. Supp. 769 (D.D.C. 1984).
Hutchinson, E. O. *Betrayed: A History of Presidential Failure to Protect Black Lives*. Boulder, Colo.: Westview, 1996.
Iuce, A. "Getting Back on the Bus." *Village Voice*. 14–20 August 2002.
Internal Revenue Service. *Slavery Reparation Scams Surge, IRS Urges Taxpayers Not to File False Claims*. Online bulletin from the IRS, 24 January 2002.
J. A. Croson v. City of Richmond, 488 U.S. 469 (1989).
Korematsu v. United States, 323 U.S. 214 (1944).
Lanker, B. *I Dream a World: Portraits of Black Women Who Changed America*. New York: Tabori and Chang, 1989.
Lipsitz, G. *The Possessive Investment in Whiteness: How White People Profit from Identity Politics*. Philadelphia: Temple University Press, 1998.
Massey, D. S., and N. A. Denton. *American Apartheid: Segregation and the Making of the Underclass*. Cambridge, Mass.: Harvard University Press, 1993.
Matsuda, M. J. "Looking to the Bottom: Critical Legal Studies and Reparations." *Harvard Civil Rights–Civil Liberties Law Review* 22, no. 3 (spring 1987): 323–400.
Mayer, C. "Flier Offering Slave Reparations Solicits Personal Information." *Washington Post*. 9 July 2001, A2.

McPhail, M. L. *The Rhetoric of Racism Revisited: Reparations or Separation?* Lanham, Md.: Rowman and Littlefield, 2002.

McWhorter, J. W. "Why I Don't Want Reparations." *Los Angeles Times.* 15 July 2001, M5.

Mendelberg, T. *The Race Card: Campaign Strategy, Implicit Messages, and the Norm of Equality.* Princeton: Princeton University Press, 2001.

Mills, C. W. *The Racial Contract.* Ithaca, N.Y.: Cornell University Press, 1997.

Munford, Clarence J. Race and Civilization: Rebirth of Black Centrality. Trenton, N.J.: Africa World Press, 2001.

Obadele, I. A. *The New International Law Regime and United States Foreign Policy.* Baton Rouge, La.: Malcom Generation, 1996.

Ogletree, C. J. "Litigating the Legacy of Slavery." *New York Times.* 31 March 2002.

Patterson, O. *Rituals of Blood: Consequences of Slavery in Two American Centuries.* New York: Basic Books, 1998.

Race Relations. *40 Acres and a Luxury Sedan.* Retrieved 19 June 2002, from www.about racerelations.com.

Robinson, D. *Slavery in the Structure of American Politics.* New York: Norton, 1979.

Robinson, R. *The Debt: What America Owes to Blacks.* New York: E. P. Dutton, 2000.

Singletory, M. "The Color of Money." *Washington Post.* 4 March 2001, H1.

"Slave Descendants Seek $1.4 Trillion in Reparations from Fleet Boston, Other." *Andrews Insurance Litigation Report.* 24 January 2002.

"Slave Reparations Debate Heating Up." *Arizona Republic.* 25 July 2001.

"Suit Seeks Billions in Slave Reparations." Retrieved 28 March 2002, from www.CNN.com/Law Center.

Wards Cove Packing Co., Inc. v. Antonio, 109 S. Ct. 2115 (1989).

Weich, R. H., and C. T. Angulo. *Justice on Trial.* Washington, D.C.: Leadership Conference on Civil Rights, 2000.

"Why Reparations?" *The Afrocentric Experience,* 22 October 2002.

Williams, J. "Slavery Isn't the Issue." *Wall Street Journal.* 9 April 2002, A26.

Yamamoto, E. K. "Racial Reparations: Japanese American Redress and African American Claims." *Boston College Law Review* 40 (December 1998): 477.

The Case for U.S. Reparations to African Americans

ADRIENNE D. DAVIS

> Rep.a.ra.tions: Payment of a debt owed; the act of repairing a wrong or injury; to atone for wrongdoings; to make amends; to make one whole again; the payment of damages; to repair a nation; compensation in money, land, or materials for damages. — National Coalition of Blacks for Reparations in America

The political and juridical viability of reparations for descendants of enslaved black people is emerging as a highly contested concept in U.S. debates about justice and law. For decades, reparations have been an essential part of the international discourses of war and human rights. Even the United States has paid some reparations awards to Native nations. Today, Korean women seek reparations from the Japanese government as recompense for what amounted to sexual enslavement during World War Two. And in addition to ongoing suits against the German state, Holocaust survivors seek damages awards from corporations who enslaved them, banks who appropriated their funds, and insurance companies that refused to pay the life insurance claims of those murdered. Among the political mainstream in the United States, there is support for all of these reparations efforts. From newspaper op-eds to legislation, Americans have expressed their outrage about these immoral practices. California State Senator Tom Hayden wrote a law giving the state jurisdiction over claims stemming from World War Two slave labor issues and extending the statute of limitations for filing such claims until 2010. Also, California, the sixth largest economy in the world, bars insurance companies who refused to pay or work to settle claims from doing business in the state. Within U.S. legal culture the language of economic rights and justice is persuasive and remedies seem natural.

Yet the U.S. government has refused to consider the need for domestic reparations to be paid for the labor and sexual slavery enforced in the United States for over two centuries. In contrast to Hayden's legislation, U.S. Representative John Conyers's bill, HR 40, Commission to Study Reparation Proposals for African Americans Act, introduced in 1993 to study the economic effects of slavery on black Americans, has not made it out of the House of Representatives Subcommittee on Civil and Constitutional Rights. At its initial vote, the bill received twenty-eight cosponsors out of 435 members in the House of Representatives. Only ten of those cosponsors were not black. Even as the United States demands other nations make moral and economic recompense for their actions, it declines to consider even the possibility of repairing its own history.

Since 1995, I have been involved in the black reparations effort, now well over a century old. I am a member of the three-year-old Reparations Litigation Committee convened by the National Coalition of Blacks for Reparations in America. The chair of that committee, Adjoa Aiyetoro, and I have cotaught courses on litigating reparations at the Washington College of Law (WCL), and supervised students in independent research efforts. To the best of my knowledge, WCL is the only law school in the United States to offer such a course. What has emerged from our work is the conclusion that reparations for black Americans are warranted, justifiable, feasible, and fair.

The Case for Reparations

But what are reparations? What support do they find in law? How are they different from ordinary civil lawsuits and other civil rights remedies? Who awards them and who gets them? The framework of reparations is the duty to repair injury imposed on another. Unlike tort law, which addresses individual injury, in their conceptualization, reparations suits frame harm as group-based, even when the plaintiffs are individuals. Unlike criminal law, the harm is explicitly conceived of as against the group, not the state. Therefore, unlike criminal cases, the decision for bringing and shaping reparations lawsuits should lie with the victims, not with the state. In this sense, these suits should be organized at the grass-roots level and should be designed to recompense the harm as understood by communities, not decided by lawyers.

Another distinction is that the explicit function of reparations would be national atonement for the moral wrong and financial injuries of enslavement to black Americans. The primacy of atonement and morality differentiates such suits from ordinary civil suits that do not rest on these principles.

Finally, such suits emphasize the economic damage of enslavement to black Americans as serious and in need of national recognition and compensation. In this sense, they depart from other civil rights remedies that address post-slavery racial harms or rest on political or criminal remedies. Affirmative action, for instance, was a remedy to combat existing racism against blacks and the ongoing effects of postslavery racial apartheid. It did not compensate black people for slave labor, nor did it seek to. The point of reparations is not to "make blacks equal" or to ensure racial opportunities, like affirmative action. These are necessary and important goals, but other causes of action and frameworks of analysis address them better. Instead, the theory of domestic reparations is to identify and atone for economic injuries and harms that blacks as a group suffered under enslavement.

We have identified two distinct but related judicial legal principles that justify and support reparations for black Americans: the equitable remedy of restitution for unjust enrichment and the Thirteenth Amendment prohibition against badges and incidents of slavery. I will sketch the contours of the latter, as the former is not innovative in its inherent conception, although it is in its application.

Those who know American history are typically familiar with the political assaults and human rights depredations that enslaved people suffered. Enslaved people and many free blacks could not vote, serve on juries, or testify against whites in a court of law. In addition, the state authorized slaveholders to inflict with impunity horrific violence, including beatings that scarred and maimed, as well as rapes and other sexual coercion. In some instances, what would be criminal homicide if committed against a white went unpunished when done against an enslaved black. Literacy was denied in most states, and the slaveholding states employed a variety of mechanisms of varying brutality to suppress cultural as well as political self-determination. These denials of bodily autonomy, citizenship, and dignity were the most visible deprivations.

But American enslavement also suppressed what I have called economic personality. Enslavement denied blacks the economic fruits of their two hundred years of backbreaking labor. They could not make and enforce contracts. Property rights of use, ownership, or management did not follow from their market participation in the labor force, but were systematically denied by the state. The slaveholding states did not confer legal status on black families; through inheritance, the family is one of the primary institutions of wealth transfer, but black slaves were excluded from intergenerational wealth transfer, one of the centerpieces of Anglo-American culture. From the public sphere of market work to the intimate sphere of the family, black economic relationships were systematically and often brutally suppressed. For the first 250 years of American economic history, the law excluded blacks from the market in a society in which market participation was emerging as vital to personal, political, and social well-being.

Furthermore, political and economic personality are closely intertwined. For blacks as for many other groups, the denial of full citizenship rights, such as voting and jury service, was also accompanied by circumscribed market rights: property, contract, inheritance, and labor. Denial of economic rights marked lesser citizenship, as did refusal at the ballot box. Reparations seek to remedy the suppression of over two centuries of black economic personality.

The Case Theory

Our primary theory of the case rests on the Thirteenth Amendment of the U.S. Constitution, the first in the trilogy of post–Civil War (1865–1870) amendments. Its better known sisters are the Fourteenth and Fifteenth Amendments; each of these spawned a compelling and contested twentieth-century jurisprudence, on equal protection of law and voting rights, respectively. The Thirteenth Amendment, passed in 1865, prohibits slavery and involuntary servitude. It has two sections: "Section 1. Neither slavery nor involuntary servitude, except as a punishment for crime whereof the party shall have been duly convicted, shall exist within the United States, or any place subject to their jurisdiction. Section 2. Congress shall have power to enforce this article by appropriate legislation." The amendment was followed the next year by the Civil Rights Act of 1866, which overruled the U.S. Supreme Court's denial of black citizenship in *Dred Scott v. Sandford* in 1857. Significantly, the Civil Rights Act also authorized basic economic rights of property and contract in addition to access to courts. Each of the three amendments represented some effort to grant meaningful citizenship to blacks and to prevent southern states from reenslaving the race in new forms. But they have generated quite different jurisprudences. Although the Fourteenth Amendment is the best known, it is the Thirteenth Amendment that would best support a reparations cause of action.

All three amendments were fairly buried in the racial retrenchment following the Reconstruction period after the Civil War. Despite congressional intent to ensure meaningful black citizenship, it was not until the mid-twentieth century that the U.S. Supreme Court began that effort in earnest. During the years in which Chief Justice Warren presided over the Supreme Court (1953–1969), the Fourteenth Amendment emerged as the original engine for combating racial supremacy. The Fourteenth Amendment provides for equal protection to all people before the law. The possibility of a fully racially liberatory interpretation was almost immediately limited, however, as the Court concluded that state action and discriminatory intent were required to trigger Fourteenth Amendment violations. Under this interpretation, the Fourteenth Amendment did not reach purely "private" acts—

a jurisprudential category invented to contrast with the doctrine of state action—and mere racial inequity or racially biased acts did not constitute violations of the Fourteenth Amendment if invidious intent could not be proven. In its post-Warren incarnations, the U.S. Supreme Court interpreted the Fourteenth Amendment to be a guarantee of color-blindness rather than racial equality. Under this conceptualization, white Americans as much as black Americans suffer the harms of race, although blacks were enslaved and systematically denied all meaningful rights, while whites held them in bondage.

The Thirteenth Amendment has promise both as a cause of action for reparations and as an intervention into the jurisprudence of color-blindness. The critical twentieth-century case law that gave antidiscrimination content to the Thirteenth Amendment was *Jones v. Alfred H. Mayer, Co.*, decided in 1968. In that case, the U.S. Supreme Court resurrected the validity of the 1866 Civil Rights Act and the Thirteenth Amendment to conclude that a private actor's refusal to sell property to blacks violated federal civil rights law. The *Jones* decision focused on Section 2 of the amendment, noting that it specifically gave Congress power to end what the Court named the badges and vestiges of slavery. As legal scholar Douglas Colbert summarizes it in a *Harvard Civil Rights–Civil Liberties Law Review* article, the Court refused to limit its interpretation of the amendment to eliminating only the formal "auction block," while allowing black slavery to continue unimpeded in new forms.

Although the *Jones* decision focused on Section 2 of the Amendment, many legal scholars and judges have urged a restoration of the meaning of the first section, which is arguably the more significant one. Not only can Congress pass legislation to eliminate enslavement under Section 2, but there is a state imperative to actively eliminate enslavement and its badges and incidents, as required in Section 1 of the amendment. Constitutional theorists have argued about the applicability of this theory in contexts ranging from labor, to forced prostitution, to children's rights, to abortion. Despite these creative and promising scholarly treatments, the Thirteenth Amendment remains an underlitigated doctrine and its ban on slavery an undertheorized concept in the struggle for racial justice.

A Jurisprudence of the Thirteenth Amendment

Developing Section 1 of the Thirteenth Amendment is potentially valuable to a reparations movement for several reasons. The theory of reparations is economic recompense from public and private actors for the ongoing effects of black enslavement. Starting with the last point, unlike the Fourteenth Amendment, the Thirteenth offers a direct framework to connect contemporary economic depredations to blacks to the economic violence of slavery. This is important because people working at the grass-roots elements of the campaign conceptualize reparations as repairing slavery. Casting reparations as less than this, a remedy for an abstracted racism, for instance, would most likely lose political support from the black community and sympathetic non-blacks. A crucial part of what reparations remedies repair is the psychic damage done by state-inflicted or -sanctioned injuries. This implicates the essential core of the U.S. legal system: wrongs done for which injury can be shown warrant recompense absent a compelling reason justifying the harm. Reparations are more than an economic payment; they are a deeply philosophical recognition of the humanity and worth of one wronged. A cause of action for reparations that does not explicitly incorporate slavery will almost certainly fail as a political and moral as well as a legal matter. And because it exists as an antislavery imperative, the Thirteenth Amendment does not exclude considerations of the ongoing racial effects of enslavement. Slavery explicitly was a racial institution. In every state but Delaware, blacks were presumed by law to be slaves; proving one was legally white constituted a defense to slavery. The badges and incidents of slavery the Thirteenth Amendment opposes will overwhelmingly manifest in racial forms. The amendment does not prohibit, and even invites, analyses of racial harm.

The Thirteenth Amendment also diverges from the Fourteenth Amendment in the intent requirement. Unlike the Fourteenth, the Thirteenth Amendment has not been interpreted to require state action and intent to discriminate. Because its emphasis is on eliminating slavery and its relics, its jurisprudence recognizes that actors, private and public, can often unwittingly permit and perpetuate the customs and norms of slavery. Finally, the legislative history of the Thirteenth Amendment shows it was meant to protect economic rights as well as political rights. Douglas Colbert shows how the legislative debates explicitly were about, not just the end of servitude, but the extent of affirmative black rights. He concludes: "By linking present racial discrimination to this nation's history of slavery and apartheid, a Thirteenth Amendment analysis uniquely addresses existing racial and economic injustice as modern relics and badges of slavery." It thereby offers the perfect theory for awarding black reparations.

In summary, the Thirteenth Amendment did not end slavery with the understanding that racial economic castes would replace formal black slavery. To prevent this, the amendment calls for policies and state efforts to end the economic manifestations of black slavery, whether perpetuated by the state or a private individual, with or without invidious intent. The goal of the Thirteenth Amendment is to end the badges and incidents of slavery, not to engender color-blindness.

Preparation for Litigation

Certain legal procedural obstacles are to be anticipated, such as statute of limitations, laches, standing, and sovereign immunity. Some can be avoided with expert technical lawyering. Others will require more substantive strategies. But rather than being viewed as diversions, surmounting some of those barriers may enhance the political and judicial viability of the suit. For instance, the statute of limitations on bringing suit may appear daunting. Reparations are based on a harm stemming from slavery; the statute has run on practically every cause of action we have conceived. However, under the doctrine of continuing violation of rights, a statute of limitations may be tolled. Reparations lawyers must therefore identify deprivations of black economic personality under slavery that continued postslavery, into this century.

While there are several potential causes of action, one of the primary ones involves denial of federal benefits. Not only were enslaved blacks unable to enforce property rights, but much of the massive homestead distributions of land in the American West during the nineteenth century excluded blacks, either directly or de facto. In addition, black veterans returning from World War Two found patterns of earlier wars repeated when they received lesser benefits than did their white compatriots. In programs initiated for returning soldiers in the Servicemen's Readjustment Act of 1944, commonly known as "the G.I. Bill," mortgage and school tuition benefits extended to black soldiers were devalued due to state-endorsed and -enforced segregation. There were far fewer places they could attend school or purchase housing. The schools they were able to attend and houses they were able to buy were less valuable because they were black institutions and neighborhoods, respectively, in an economy that valued whiteness. Finally, in the mid-twentieth century, the federal government took several steps to subsidize the construction of suburbs as racially segregated spaces, which simultaneously devalued black property in urban areas. Independent, private banks followed these federal guidelines, and blacks found themselves doubly squeezed into emerging ghettoes and out of suburbs being invented as white. Like the homestead acts, the G.I. bills for soldiers and the federal housing programs were moments of massive government subsidization that supported an emerging middle class. Blacks were excluded from this process and denied economic personality in ways that reflected the badges of slavery.

Another obstacle may be resolved by distinguishing legislative and judicial reparations awards. Standing is frequently raised as a procedural obstacle to judicial reparations; unlike comfort women and internment victims, American slaves and their direct heirs are no longer alive. Moreover, part of the invidiousness of slavery is that the system ripped apart black families, denying them the possibility of keeping records and genealogies. The fact that few blacks can trace their ancestry to specific enslaved persons is part of the injury of enslavement. One could approach this obstacle in two ways. One could utilize equitable principles to argue that one who actively destroys records cannot then invoke that absence to recuse its own legal liability. Another approach is to craft a series of causes of action, stemming from different continuing violations, similar to the strategy for statute of limitations. Because these actions will have to conform to the statute of limitations and the harms extend into this century, blacks today should be more able to identify and prove legal relationships with those affected. In the case of World War Two veterans, many will still be alive today.

Conclusion

Putting racism into economic language is important. A significant effect of racism is its dissociation of blacks from markets and economics. Part of the reason so many Americans are skeptical of awarding reparations is the absence of a compelling discourse of black economic personality and desert of wealth. Reparations are recognition of the severe economic harm inflicted on blacks. Developing a reparations cause of action will yield several positive results. In defining the contours of a Thirteenth Amendment–based racial jurisprudence, it will turn the nation's attention toward what black slavery entailed, connect current acts, including private ones, to customs, norms, and history stemming from slavery and segregation, and comprehend slavery's ongoing economic effects. When confronted with this history, then perhaps we can come to a national consensus on what the antislavery imperative of the Thirteenth Amendment means.

The Promises and Pitfalls of Reparations

YUSUF NURUDDIN

The demand for reparations is the *international human rights* agenda for the twenty-first century, one that attempts to redress "the problem of the twentieth century," as stated by Du Bois, "the problem of the color line,—the relations of the darker to the lighter races men in Asia and Africa, in America and the islands of the sea."[1] Elsewhere in this volume are essays which address the international dimensions of reparations—in particular the debt owed to Africa by Western powers for the holocaust of slavery and colonialism. (I don't use the word "holocaust" lightly: over 10 million Africans were killed in the Congo alone during the Belgian occupation under King Leopold's rule).[2] Not only is redress for this crime against humanity an international issue, there is also *international solidarity* of African peoples, continental and Diasporan, in this reparations movement. The worldwide issues are complex, involving the case-by-case specifics of former colonial relationships, the adjudication of international law, and the restructuring of international debt and loan agreements. For the sake of clarity, I will restrict my focus to the issue of reparations owed to African Americans for their enslavement in the United States.

The demand for reparations, once dismissed by reactionaries as the futile cry of a "fringe group of angry black militants," is now indisputably the *mainstream* civil rights agenda for the opening decade of the twenty-first century. Organizations such as N'COBRA—the National Coalition of Blacks for Reparations in America—have struggled to lay the groundwork for this reparations movement for over a decade, and Congressman John Conyers (D-MI) has introduced legislation (HR 40) annually since 1989 which calls for a commission to study the legacy of slavery and the feasibility of reparations. Those efforts notwithstanding, the mainstreaming of the reparations agenda is due, in no small measure, to the endeavors of Randall Robinson, the former director of TransAfrica. His book *The Debt: What America Owes to Blacks*,[3] published in the millennial year 2000, was a clarion call for reparations, which reached the ears of all African Americans regardless of class or political ideology. Robinson was also responsible for enlisting the aid of Harvard Law School professor Charles J. Ogletree Jr. to assemble a legal team and pursue avenues of reparations litigation.

Of course, human agency can only be effective in the ripe historical moment. Marcus Garvey, known for his visionary Pan-Africanism rather than any materialist conception of history, once stated with Marxist clarity, "When all else fails to organize our people, conditions will."[4] The material conditions in Blackamerica were ripe for a reparations movement. In the public discourse generated by this movement, some reactionary whites have argued that the movement by African Americans to obtain reparations for slavery would divide the American people. The American people are *already* divided — by stark economic inequalities. These structural inequalities are the material conditions which have mobilized the African American populace — across class lines — in support of a reparations agenda. A study of households conducted in the mid-1980s showed that while income gaps between blacks and whites were closing, the median white American family owned eleven times as much wealth (real estate, investments, savings, etc.) as the median black American family.[5] During the 1990s and into the twenty-first century this racial wealth divide has been widening. Wealth is often accumulated through inheritance; thus the origins of this widening divide may be traced back many generations. The civil rights movement dismantled American apartheid (de jure segregation — but certainly not de facto segregation, as a tour through any of America's inner cities and suburbs will reveal), qualitatively transforming the landscape of civil liberties, access, and opportunities for African Americans. Yet the dismantling of the social and political aspects of American apartheid has not led to African American community empowerment or development, just as the dismantling of the social and political aspects of Zimbabwean and South African apartheid has not led to national reconstruction in those societies — because in all three societies, the economic resources (including the land and the mineral wealth, all ill-gotten gains) remained concentrated in the hands of whites.

Unyielding structural inequalities have betrayed the civil rights movement in the United States, just as they have betrayed the revolution in southern Africa. The Rev. Dr. Martin Luther King Jr.'s dream lies dormant because there was never a full integration of African Americans into the economy — because there is still black poverty in the midst of white affluence. Many political analysts of the current "post–civil rights" era have observed that if King were alive today, his focus would be on achieving economic parity and economic justice.

Now that the demand for reparations has been embraced by the black establishment, and thereby made reputable and legitimate in the eyes of the black bourgeoisie as well as in the eyes of the nonadvanced sector of the masses who rely upon the imprimatur of "bona fide" black leaders, a groundswell has been achieved. With the exception of literally a *handful* of black conservatives who view reparations as but another entitlement program which fosters a sense of dependency and victimization that is detrimental to black progress, there is near unanimity in the African American community on this issue. The black managerial and professional class, the black working class, and the black lumpen all want reparations; blacks regardless of their ideology—integrationist-assimilationist, nationalist-separatist, Marxist-Leninist, feminist, or Afrocentrist—all want reparations. There is a surety of victory in the air, a sense of invincibility that emerges from the heady combination of moral authority (we *must* be compensated for this crime against humanity!) and unflinching solidarity. Yet it is certain that class contradictions will emerge as the movement becomes more focused on the logistics of implementing reparations. How the resulting struggle is conducted will have great bearing on the state of Blackamerica for decades to come. In fact, we would be remiss if we did not recognize that the fashioning of the class character of reparations policy will be one of the monumentally decisive moments in the entire course of African American history.

That conflicting class interests—those of the working class, upper middle class, and underclass—would emerge in the struggle for reparations should not be surprising. Struggles for national liberation always have internal class conflicts. The principle of unity and struggle defines the working-class strategy in national liberation struggles. In other words, the black working class must unite with the black bourgeoisie in the struggle to gain reparations from white America, but black workers must struggle against the bourgeoisie for control of the specific reparations agenda. In the face of white supremacy, the unity of African people is an absolute necessity. But emotional calls for black unity often becloud the conflictual class interests that exists within Blackamerica. Because the transfer of wealth involved in a just reparations settlement would not be trivial, it is important that the black working class move in a Lukacsian sense from being "a class in itself" to "a class *for* itself," in short, that it become conscious of its particular interests and organize around a reparations agenda which represents these interests. Reparations settlements could involve individual cash payments, investments in community development projects, the transfer of land, tax exemptions, tuition exemptions, or any combination of these factors. The way reparations settlements are structured could be more advantageous to one class than another. It is often argued that class divisions among African Americans are largely fictional, that there is no real black bourgeoisie—that at best Afroamerica has a class of petty bourgeoisie or even *lumpenbourgeoisie*, that is, tenuous struggling sub-bourgeoisie, who are "one paycheck away from being homeless"; that is, if laid off or fired they would not be able to make their mortgage payments. I argue that there are substantial class differences among African Americans and that the internal struggle for the shape of reparations will sharpen these real differences. We cannot mask ideological differences either; some demands for reparations have a more revolutionary character to them than others. Some formulations of reparations are consumer-oriented palliatives while others challenge the very legitimacy of the existing nation-state (perhaps prematurely). In launching a reparations movement it is necessary that we be very conscious of the class issues and the ideological issues that shape the various types of reparations demands.

Some historical background would be instructive in this regard. The demand for reparations has been long-standing in radical black activist circles — reaching back *at least* to the Black Power movement of the 1960s, which was where and when I first came into political consciousness. For those of us who are seasoned black activists, the concept of reparations has been in our political vocabulary since our nascent days of activism in high schools or as undergraduates. I was a college freshman in 1969, the year when James Forman, acting as a spokesperson for a Black Economic Development Conference, interrupted the worship service at Manhattan's Riverside Church and read from the pulpit a *Black Manifesto* demanding that "white Christian churches and Jewish synagogues, which are part and parcel of the system of capitalism . . . begin to pay reparations to black people in this country"[6] (see Documents, section 4). Forman demanded a total of a half billion dollars to be allocated in detailed amounts for establishment of the following black-owned and -operated projects: a southern land bank for evicted black farmers; major publishing and printing industries in Detroit, Atlanta, Los Angeles, and New York; state-of-the-art television networks in Detroit, Chicago, Cleveland, and Washington, D.C.; a social research center; a training center for developing both community organizing skills and media technology skills; subsidy for the existing National Welfare Rights Organization; a National Black Labor Strike and Defense Fund; an International Black Appeal which would develop cooperative business in the United States and in Africa, fund liberation movements in Africa, and fund a Black Antidefamation League to protect the African image; and a black university in the South. Given a population of over 30 million black people, he calculated that the $500 million demand amounted to merely "15 dollars for every black brother and sister in the United States." Needless to say the white religious establishment balked at these demands.

The *Black Manifesto* was not the first demand by African Americans for reparations. The Nation of Islam demanded reparations as early as the 1950s. This demand was disseminated widely beginning around 1960 with the publication of *Muhammad Speaks*. This official news organ of the Nation of Islam under Elijah Muhammad's leadership soon became one of the most popularly read weekly newspapers in the black community. It carried a ten-point platform on the back page of each edition entitled "What the Muslims Want." Besides the call for democratic rights — freedom, justice, equality of social opportunity and employment opportunity, equal education, and an end to police brutality and racial violence — the ten-point program also included demands for reparations: the establishment of a separate state or territory for the descendents of slaves; the release of all black death-row prisoners; and until equal justice is established, tax exemption for all black people.[7] The Black Panther Party's ten-point platform, developed in 1966, had many similarities. It called for democratic rights: freedom, justice, full employment, relevant education, decent housing, trial by a jury of peers, and an end to police brutality and murder. In addition the platform called for reparations (special compensatory measures to repair the damage exacted by slavery, segregation, and continued oppression); freedom for all black prisoners; the exemption of all black men from military service; and the right to a United Nations–supervised plebiscite to determine "the will of the black people as to their national identity." Point 3 of the Black Panther Party's platform was the most explicit:

> *We want an end to the robbery by the white man of our Black Community*. We believe this racist government has robbed us and now we are demanding the overdue debt of forty acres and two mules. Forty acres and two mules was promised 100 years ago as restitution for slave labor and the mass murder of black people. We will accept the payment in currency which will be distributed to our many communities. The Germans are now aiding Jews in Israel for the genocide of the Jewish people. The Germans murdered ten million Jews. The American racist has taken part in the slaughter of over fifty million black people; therefore we feel that this is a modest demand that we make.[8]

This is not an attempt to give a summary history of the demand for reparations by African Americans because in one form or another the demand has always been a part of our history, as the following examples illustrate. In 1951, William Patterson and Paul Robeson led delegations of African Americans to United Nations offices in Paris and New York to submit petitions —

with compiled documented evidence of lynchings and racial violence — charging the U.S. government with genocide and seeking redress (but not monetary compensation)[9] (see Documents, section 4). In 1955, the venerable black American activist and Pan-Africanist Queen Mother (Audley) Moore authored a pamphlet on reparations; in 1962, she met with President Kennedy to discuss the issue.[10] In 1963 she formed an organization — the Reparations Committee for the Descendants of American Slaves — which sought $500 million as partial compensation for historic injustice and which filed at least one lawsuit for reparations in a California court. The National Movement for a 49th State preceded Queen Mother Moore's reparation activity by two decades.[11] In 1934, this organization, headquartered in Chicago, posed to America the challenge of creating a new state of the federal union exclusively populated and governed by blacks. The creation of a forty-ninth state would be "an opportunity for the nation to reduce its debt to the Negro for past exploitation." In 1913, over twenty years before the 49th State movement, a black state was proposed in a book entitled *Prophetic Liberation of the Colored Race of the United States of America: Command to His People* by Arthur Anderson.[12] Turning to the nineteenth century for examples, in the 1860s — during and after the Civil War — there was a mass demand for land on the part of freedmen.[13] Earlier, from 1810 through the 1820s, compensation for slavery meant securing funds from white America for repatriation to the Motherland. Free black men such as shipbuilder Paul Cuffe and Bishop Daniel Coker worked in concert with the American Colonization Society (in spite of the Society's racist motives) to resettle ex-slaves in Sierra Leone and Liberia.[14]

As this survey of past demands for reparations demonstrates, individual payments or disbursements to the victims or descendants of victims — such as the $20,000 issued as compensation to each Japanese American who was interred in detention camps during World War Two — was not always the form of reparations, though the idea of payment to an individual seems to dominate the popular imagination and the heated popular discourse between blacks and whites.

Historically, one of the most frequently articulated demands for reparations has been for land — repatriation to sovereign land on the African continent or ownership of land in the Black Belt South via either sovereignty, federal statehood, or simply title and deed (see Johnson, part 5, and Documents, section 4). During the Civil War, African Americans did receive such reparations. In January 1865, shortly after Union General William Tecumseh Sherman victoriously marched through Georgia, he issued Special Field Order Number 15. Quoting the historians Hine, Hine, and Harrold:

This military directive set aside a thirty-mile wide tract of land along the Atlantic coast from Charleston, South Carolina, 245 miles south to Jacksonville, Florida. White owners had abandoned the land, and Sherman reserved it for black families. The head of each family would receive "possessory title" to forty acres of land. Sherman also gave the freed men the use of army mules, thus giving rise to the slogan, "Forty areas and a mule."

Within six months 40,000 freed people were working 400,000 acres in South Carolina and Georgia low country and on the Sea Islands. . . .

Meanwhile, hundreds of former slaves had been cultivating land for three years. In late 1861, Union military forces carved out an enclave around Beaufort and Port Royal, South Carolina, that remained under federal authority for the rest of the war. White planters fled to the interior leaving their slaves behind. Under the supervision of U.S. treasury officials northern reformers and missionaries began to work the land in what came to be known as the "Port Royal Experiment." When Treasury agents auctioned off portions of the land for non-payment of taxes, freedman purchased some of it.[15]

In July 1865, a few months after the end of war, General Oliver Howard, the director of the Bureau of Refugees, Freedmen and Abandoned Lands (commonly called the Freedmen's Bureau) issued Circular 13 setting aside forty-acre plots for freedmen. "But," say Hine, Hine, and Harrold, "the allocation had hardly begun when the order was revoked [by President Andrew Johnson] and it was announced that land already distributed under General Sherman's Special Field Order #15 was to be returned to its previous white owners."[16]

The most radical of the contemporary formulations of reparations is for the return of these "forty acres" in the context of a sovereign nation-state composed of land in Black Belt South — land now occupied by the contiguous states of Mississippi, Louisiana, Alabama, Georgia, and South Carolina. The African Blood Brotherhood, a left nationalist formation cotemporaneous with the Garvey movement, first advanced this Black Belt thesis and in 1928 the thesis was adopted by the CPUSA — although repudiated several years later.[17] The Nation of Islam repeated the call for a separate state on "this continent or elsewhere" with the further stipulations that the land be "fertile and minerally rich" and that the former slave master supply the needs for this new state for twenty to twenty-five years until it becomes productive and self-sufficient.[18] In the contemporary struggle for reparations, the Black Belt independence is advanced by the New African Liberation Front (NALF), which is composed of the December 12th Movement, the Republic of New Africa (RNA), the New African People's Organization (NAPO) which is an RNA splinter group, and the Malcolm X Grassroots Coalition which is a youth affiliate of NAPO. Both RNA and NAPO have close organizational ties with the National Coalition of Blacks for Reparations in America (N'COBRA); the founding members of N'COBRA were members of RNA and NAPO. However, N'COBRA functions as a united front, embracing any person or organization that endorses the movement, regardless of its formulation.

However, in the absence of a widespread and well-coordinated violent insurrection, a secessionist demand by nationalists-separatists would not be entertained by the U.S. federal government. (Even with the threat of armed struggle, it is unlikely that the United States would negotiate such a demand. The more likely scenario is that it would mobilize its war machine to crush such an insurgence. This scenario might include the mass incarceration and genocidal extermination of black people in detention camps, as depicted in John A. Williams's famed novel, *The Man Who Cried I Am* and poet-songwriter Gil Scott-Heron's recording "The King Alfred Plan," and which formed the essence of the political education "tours" at the Black People's Topographical Research Centers of the 1970s.)[19] Hence the legitimate demand for reparations in the form of a sovereign nation-state remains more a consciousness-raising tool than a practical formulation. Freedom, especially in the form of national self-determination, is never given — it has to be taken. And the price for freedom — as Malcolm cautioned for those who think that it can be taken easily — is death.

Land as a form of reparation need not, however, be structured as a sovereign independent state — nor does it need to be allocated only within the confines of the Black Belt South. There are probably a number of creative ways in which large tracts of urban or rural land can be deeded to black communities and function as semi-autonomous enclaves. I will not attempt in this essay to suggest what those arrangements would look like, but there certainly are precedents in the recent settlements of land claims made by Native Americans. (As an aside, many African Americans legitimately can establish their Native American ancestry and entitlement to Native American rights and benefits. There are even "tribes" that are mixed with African ancestry. Some of the most hostile white reactions to Native American land claims have been directed toward these tribes.)

I am not suggesting that we create a semi-autonomous Afroamerica which is a federation of far-flung Bantustans dotted with casinos, selling tax-free cigarettes and economically dependent upon tourism, but I am saying that land — whether as individual real estate holdings or as publicly owned commons — should be a real item of discussion in any reparations settlement. One has only to glimpse at the quality of life in any low-income housing project in any inner city to realize that overcrowding — the violation of basic human territorial instincts—contributes to social pathology. We certainly can attest to the fact that the mainstream society's fear of *social explosions* (uprisings, insurrections, "riots") has led to socially engineered policies of containment. (Containment of what? Containment of violence and aggression. According to the famous *frustration-aggression hypothesis* formulated by a team of Yale social psychologists, frustration, i.e., the blocking of aspirations, leads to aggression.[20] Aggression in turn must find an outlet. The normal targets for the aggression would be the source of frustration; if that target is not available a secondary target would be innocent bystanders; the third target, if the first two are unavailable, is one's own self, i.e., literal self-destruction, or internalized aggression. In real-world terms, if the oppressive white power structure which blocks black aspirations is not an available target for inner-city black aggression, then black-on-black crime rates will rise, as will self-destructive alcoholism and drug addiction. Every death by drug overdose is listed in the coroner's office as a suicide.) The socially engineered policy of containment—the dumping of drugs and weapons in the black ghettos—has resulted in *social implosions*: violent inward collapsing and destruction of community life via domestic violence, via narcoterrorism (i.e., turf wars for the control of the drug trade), and the host of other pathological behaviors that abound on the tiny patches of land that apartheid has allocated to us.

In summing up the importance of land reparations I will deviate, for just a moment, from a basic Marxist conception—the transition from a feudal stage of production to a capitalist stage of production—long enough to quote from the nineteenth-century American political economist and social reformer Henry George:

> The widespread social evils which everywhere oppress men amid an advancing civilization, spring from a great primary wrong—the appropriation, as the exclusive property of some men, of the land on which and from which we must all live. From this fundamental injustice flow all the injustices which distort and endanger modern development, which condemn the producer of wealth to poverty and pamper the non-producer in luxury, which rear the tenement house with the palace, plant the brothel behind the church, and compel us to build prisons as we open new schools.[21]

In this capitalist stage of production, however, there is a strong argument for the kinds of reparations formulations which James Forman advocated—placing the ownership and control of industry in the hands of the black community. And in this late stage of capitalism, this age of globalization, where the control of mass communication is crucial for counterhegemonic discourse, the formation of class consciousness, and mobilization and organization of the working class and the oppressed, Forman was prescient in demanding black ownership and control of media outlets: publishing houses and TV stations (radio stations should be added to his demand as well).

We should remain cognizant of the facts that slave labor in cotton and tobacco fields in the antebellum South produced a wealthy class of agrarian capitalists—*and that slave trading by New England merchants produced profits which financed the development of the textile industry.*[22] The use of water-mill-powered machinery for the large-scale manufacture of textiles marked the beginning of the industrial revolution in the United States. The new class of industrial capitalists reinvested money from the textile industries into other burgeoning industries; hence the profits generated by the trading in African slaves propelled the United States into the age of industrial capitalism.

It is fitting, then, that reparation—which is essentially a socialist project, in the sense that it would involve a massive redistribution of wealth—encompass not only the transfer of land or real estate, but the financing of industry in the African American community. Redistribution of wealth is not a matter of charity; it is a matter of economic justice—as the development, or rather overdevelopment of the U.S. capitalist economy was directly contingent upon the institution of slavery: the superexploitation of the human resources of Africa, that is, the underdeveloping of the black community. I would argue that the economic development of the black community should involve the financing of not only high-tech industries such as computer factories, or the mass communication industries which Forman advocated, but also low-tech manufacturing plants. There is no reason why the people of Harlem or Bedford-Stuyvesant cannot own and operate their own bicycle factory or manufacture strollers, baby carriages, or metal furniture—kitchen tables and chairs—which are competitive on the market. The creation of industrial factories would only be one dimension of a reparations economic development model; an infrastructure of creatively structured financial institutions such as savings and loan associations, credit associations, and consumer cooperatives have to be developed as well.

The ownership and control of industry by a community corporation is, of course, an experiment in socialism or at least veering toward socialism. I am not an economist, but I suppose that worker-owned-and-operated industries would represent some kind of transitional economy and perhaps the proper term for such industries would be cooperatives. Furthermore, I assume that there might be difficulties with such cooperatives but hopefully not insurmountable problems such as C. J. Munford, a Marxist-trained historian, seems to indicate (see Munford, part 5). At a recent Reparations Conference, Munford argued that two different economic systems, a small black cooperative or socialist system of production and a larger white capitalism or private ownership of production, would not be able to coexist in the same society.[23] The capitalist system would eventually overwhelm the smaller socialist system.

Nevertheless, any valid plan for reparations must include an intensive investment in community development. In the past I have used freely the analogy of the Marshall Plan to indicate the necessary levels of capital infusion into the economic infrastructures of the black ghettos, but I have been put on notice that the European Recovery Program was merely one of America's instruments for dominating the global economy. For lack of a better analogy, I will continue to use this one, but guardedly. There is an appropriate analogy of more recent vintage. In the post-9/11 climate there has been much talk about re-erecting the Twin Towers and rebuilding New York City. As many astute black people have pointed out, long before the destruction of the World Trade Center, there was a Ground Zero which existed in the ghettos of black America. Reparations should repair and rebuild the Ground Zero Ghetto.

A Marshall Plan or Ground Zero Plan would not simply involve the economic development; the reconstruction and development of inner-city housing, schools, health care delivery systems, day care centers, and other public institutions which directly impact upon the quality of life in the inner city would all be a part of the reparations agenda.

Malcolm X eloquently stated that the main difference between the black community and other ethnic enclaves in America, for example, Little Italy or Chinatown, is that the black community is controlled politically and economically by outsiders, by people who do not live in the community. The black ghetto is a colony—complete with colonial administrators such as judges, social workers, and teachers; an occupying army, the police; and colonial exploiters, the nonblack (white, Arab, Korean, etc.) merchants who do a thriving business in the black community (although the late controversial Khalid Muhammad probably exaggerated when he stated that everyday outsider merchants "take tractor-trailer truckloads of cash out of Harlem"). In his 1964 speech "The Ballot or the Bullet" Malcolm articulated its ideology as "the political, economic, and social philosophy of black nationalism." He defined his economic philosophy of black nationalism:

> The economic philosophy of black nationalism is pure and simple. It only means that we should control the economy of our community. Why should white people be running all the stores in our community? Why should white people be running the banks of our community? Why should the economy of our community be in the hands of the white man? Why? If a black man can't move his store into a white community, you tell me why a white man should move his store into a black community. The philosophy of black nationalism involves a re-education program in the black community in regards to economics. Our people have to be made to see that any time you take your dollar out of your community and spend it in a community where you don't live, the community where you live will get poorer and poorer, and the community where you spend your money will get richer and richer. Then you wonder why where you live is always a ghetto or a slum area. And where you and I are concerned, not only do we lose it when we spend it out of the community, but the white man has got all our stores in the community tied up; so that though we spend it in the community, at sundown the man who runs the store takes it over across town somewhere. He's got us in a vise.
>
> So the economic philosophy of black nationalism means in every church, in every civic organization, in every fraternal order, it's time now for our people to become conscious of the importance of controlling the economy of our community. If we own the stores, if we operate the businesses, if we try and establish some industry in our own community, then we're developing to the position where we are creating employment for our own kind. Once you gain control of the economy of your own community, then you don't have to picket and boycott and beg some cracker downtown for a job in his business.[24]

If C. J. Munford is correct in his assessment that black cooperatives or collectively owned and operated industries could not thrive in a capitalist economy, then funds for community business development would have to be allocated to private black businessmen. A reparations program structured in this manner would only serve the class interests of the black bourgeoisie and petty bourgeoisie. Malcolm did not have a vision of bourgeois nationalism where a neocolonial elite or national bourgeoisie gained control over the economy of the black community. Robert Allen in his classic text *Black Awakening in Capitalist America* described the co-optation of the 1960s Black Power movement by corporate America:

> Led by corporations such as the Ford Foundation, the Urban Coalition and the National Alliance of Businessmen, the corporatists are attempting with considerable success to co-opt the black power movement. Their strategy is to equate black power with black capitalism.
>
> In this task the white corporate elite has found an ally in the black bourgeoisie, the new, militant black middle class.... The members of this class consist of black

professionals, technicians, professors, government workers, etc. . . . They were made militant by the civil rights movement; yet many of them oppose integration because they have seen its failures. Like the black masses, they denounced the old black elite of Tomming preachers, teachers and businessmen-politicians. This new elite seeks to overthrow and take the place of the old elite. To do this it has formed an informal alliance with the corporate forces which run white (and black) America.[25]

Allen summarizes the attitude of the new black elite toward the white corporatists: "Give us a piece of the action and we will run the black communities and keep them quiet for you."[26] Another part of this new black elite were the so-called poverty pimps—the class who grew rich through administrating antipoverty programs in the 1960s during President Lyndon Baines Johnson's attempt to build a "Great Society" via a "War on Poverty." Frequently the administrators grew rich as a result of mismanagement, nepotism, fraud, and misappropriations of funds. History repeats itself. Allen's book is not merely an analysis of the 1960s, it is a cautionary tale of what can happen again. What Allen alerts us to is one of the potential pitfalls of the reparations movement. Reparations could result in the continued empowerment and economic advancement of the new black elite at the expense of the masses of working-class and poor peoples. This pitfall can be termed the embourgeoisement or bourgeoisification of reparations.

Another equally disastrous potential pitfall of reparations is lumpenization of reparations. The use of terms such as "lumpen" or "underclass" is distasteful and analytically incorrect for many Marxists who see the masses of the poor or chronically unemployed as a reserve army of labor. Furthermore, as the social philosopher Bill Lawson notes, important questions about the term "underclass" remain unanswered. For example: Are the poor and the underclass synonymous or distinct groups? And if they are distinct, then what is the characteristic which distinguishes them from one another? Is it geographical concentration, length of time one remains in poverty, attitudes, or behavior? Do the two groups overlap? Or is one group a subset of the other? If so, which is the larger group and which the subset?[27] The feminization of poverty and the criminalization of black male youths introduce even more troubling questions. The term "lumpenproletariat" has the connotation of a class which subsists through criminal behavior.[28] Are impoverished female-headed households "lumpen"? Are even the teenagers who are racially profiled, stopped, and frisked without probable cause, and arrested for possession of tiny amounts of marijuana lumpen? What about the victims of the police policy of "zero tolerance," who are arrested for minor offenses such as drinking beer in public. When these young men are sent through the central booking, are they lumpen? The answer to all of these questions, of course is, no. They are not "lumpen" in this classical Marxist sense of lumpenproletariat. Yet to deny that the existence of a underclass culture—in which people valorize "gangsterism" or "thug life," view time spent in jail as a badge of honor, indulge in the most blatant forms of verbal misogyny, don't have a husband or a wife but have "my baby father" and "my baby mother," eat five chicken wings with ketchup and hot sauce and a side order of pork fried rice with duck sauce for dinner every night and hurl anti-Asian epithets at the people who sell and prepare that dinner, gamble away their rent money shooting "see-low" on the corner, and show off their cell phones on the bus by having loud conversations with their homies—would be unscientific in the face of obvious social behavior. Sociologists or urban anthropologists would have to take notice of the social norms and values of this underclass or lumpen culture. Still, I utilize the term "lumpen," realizing that there is a precedent for it in the language of the Black Panther Party.[29]

Having introduced this notion of "lumpen culture" for the purpose of analyzing reparations, I will not expend much time engaging in the debate about reasons for the existence of poverty or the underclass. I will simply state that I am neither a "behavioralist/culturalist" nor a "structuralist." Posing the question as cultural values/cultural behavior versus structural inequality is to me patently false—and a false question necessarily yields a false answer. Rather than view the causal factor as an "either/or" choice, I view causation as a "both/and" situation—a confluence of dual causal factors. Poverty is perpetuated by both structural inequality and cultural values/cultural behavior. The process is dialectical. Certainly structural inequality, the economic infrastructure, is at the base of the problem, but the superstructure of ideology, beliefs, and values interacts with the base in a very Gramscian way. There is an economic crisis shaping the quality of life of the underclass, but there is also a cultural crisis exerting a strong negative influence as well. This does not mean that I am an advocate of assimilation or Anglo conformity. No, the underclass should not adopt white middle-class values. There are alternative cultural systems—countercultural rather than subcultural—offering the option of *resistance* to cultural hegemony and oppression rather than the option of acquiescence as assimilation or Anglo conformity offers, or the "option" of *participation* in one's own oppression as the lumpen or underclass subculture offers.

Maulana Karenga, a professor of black studies and political science and the creator of the black cultural celebration Kwanzaa and the alternative cultural nationalist system of Kawaida (which he describes "an on-going synthesis of the best of nationalist, Pan Africanist and socialist thought and practice"), states, "The key crisis in black life is the cultural crisis, i.e., the crisis in views and values. The vision crisis is defined by a deficient and ineffective grasp of self, society and the world, and the value crisis by incorrect and self-limiting categories of commitment, and priorities which in turn limit our human possibilities." He goes on to state that at the heart of this cultural crisis is the fact that black people have a *popular culture* rather than a *national culture*. The negative views and values which constitute this popular culture are (1) a high level of reactiveness rather than pro-activeness, (2) a high level of lumpenism, (3) a high level of simple survival orientation, (4) a high level of present-time orientation, (5) an overemphasis on fun and games, and (6) a high-level of myth orientation and grandiose dreams.[30] This "popular culture" of course sounds very much like "culture of poverty." Karenga elucidates on each of the above views/values. In his amplification on "lumpenism" he states in part that "hustler values permeate Black popular culture, i.e., emphasis on quick money at any cost . . . conning, gettin' over."

The psychologist Na'im Akbar adds to Karenga's litany of negative cultural values when he states that black people possess a set of pathological attitudes that are a legacy of slavery. Included among the eight attitudes which Akbar lists are negative attitudes toward work and property and a propensity for playing the clown role. One of the attitudes toward property is *conspicuous consumption*.[31]

Note that both Karenga and Akbar attribute these values to the black community in general, not to any specific underclass. Herein lies the gist of the problem. The ghetto is a product of American apartheid. It is racially homogeneous but heterogeneous in its class configuration. In this transclass community, the poor and/or underclass live side by side with the working class — and with a small minority of the black bourgeoisie (frequently buppies but also some older professionals such as doctors or lawyers who live near their clientele). The values of lumpen culture and the values of the working-class culture often vie for hegemony in the ghetto. In this sense, lumpen underclass values permeate the culture of the ghetto; that is, many — though not all — lumpen values and behaviors are transmitted to members of the working class, especially the working poor, and especially the youth who socialize in school or in voluntary peer group associations. What starts out as lumpen culture then becomes mainstream black ghetto culture or "black popular culture" which is described by Karenga.

Given the pervasiveness of this popular culture, the culture of poverty, underclass culture, or lumpen culture — with its emphasis on present-time orientation (immediate rather than delayed gratification), "getting paid," fun and games, and conspicuous consumption — a blanket cash payment of reparations would not be in the best interests of community development or community uplift. I may be roundly criticized for this assertion as a "bourgeois social scientist" who is insensitive to the needs of the poor. Furthermore, given the feminization of poverty and the number of female-headed households that are impoverished, my remarks could be misconstrued as an attack on the plight of black women. So let me clarify that I am not anti–cash payment. In fact, I would emphatically state that if reparations are structured in part as cash payments, the poor and underclass is the segment of the black community which is most in need and most deserving of a receiving such a reparations check in the mail. I am arguing, however, that such checks should be designated for specific purchases, that payments be made in small increments over a period of years rather than in one lump sum, and that prior to the receipt of such payments the designated recipients enroll in a mandatory six-month seminar in money management and consumer education.[32]

Imagine for a moment if none of the above stipulations were applied. In the worst-case scenario, a lump sum payment of reparations, in lumpen culture, would be considered the "mother of all mother days" ("mother's day" is ghetto slang for the first of the month, the date when welfare checks — or aid to mothers with dependent children — arrive in the mail). Sales of liquor and illicit drugs would reach an all-time high, as would sales of designer clothes. If reparation checks arrived on a Friday, half of the recipients would be broke by Monday morning — with nothing to show for it except fancy new clothes, gold-plated jewelry, a collection of the latest CDs and videos, a 53-inch high-definition widescreen projection TV, and memories of a great weekend. Of course I exaggerate in order to make a point, but as a community of consumers rather than producers — and conspicuous consumers at that — the African American poor would not enjoy long-term benefits from sudden wealth. C. J. Munford pointed out in his Reparations Conference paper that cash transfers are at best short-term redistributions of wealth because in a capitalist system the money is ultimately recirculated to the ruling class. All one has to do is read about the number of million-dollar lottery winners who soon found themselves in economic difficulty in order to realize that massive social problems caused by centuries of oppression and institutional racism cannot be solved or repaired by putting a check in the mail.[33]

Yet there are some ways in which cash payments can be productive. Checks can be issued which are specifically designated for educational purposes, allowing the recipient to utilize the money for tuition — at a trade school, liberal arts college, graduate or professional school — or as a "voucher" for private education at the elementary or secondary level.[34] Checks could also be issued which are designated for mortgage payments or home improvements, or the purchase of major household appliances. Or perhaps monies could be earmarked for small entrepreneurial ventures, such as vending inventory. (Though this would be handled better by encouraging entrepreneurs to apply for small business grants from a reparations-funded community development corporation.)

In the final analysis, however, cash payments should not represent more than, say, 10 to 25 percent of the total reparations payments. The other 75 to 90 percent should be utilized to dismantle the worst aspects of apartheid: joblessness and the substandard conditions of public housing, education, health care delivery systems, day care facilities, parks and recreational facilities, and so on. (I would include the upgrading of prison conditions since they warehouse such a high percentage of African American men and women.) Reparations in my vision should ultimately be a community empowerment program, with billions of dollars being allocated in increments over the next several decades for the reconstruction and redevelopment of the cities, towns, and hamlets of the Black Belt South and the northern inner cities where the overwhelming population of African Americans reside. A one-time lump-sum payment of reparations even for this type of reconstruction and redevelopment would be inadvisable on two counts. First, it would probably "bankrupt" America to pay the amount that is due African Americans—an amount which is in the multibillions or trillions, not the paltry $500 million sum cited by well-meaning activists in the 1960s (of course, the sum grows because of inflation and interest, but even in 1960s dollars, their figure was probably grossly underestimated). More important, however, reparations is a national endowment to black people which does not solely belong to the living generations of African Americans, but to several future generations as well. We were enslaved for over three hundred years and payments of reparations for that oppression cannot and should not be made in one lump sum. Reparations should be paid in annual installments or in larger installments every five to ten years for the next seventy-five to one hundred years. America would love to get off the hook for its centuries of racism by making a lump-sum cash payment to miseducated consumers or even a lump-sum investment in building (but not maintaining) new community projects. We forget that the payment of reparations absolves the nation of any past injustices; if that money were misspent or if investments in community projects were poorly allocated and black Americans remained in the same conditions of impoverishment, then . . . well it would just be too bad. "We paid you, you had your chance, sorry fella." We could never charge racism or discrimination again. This is why I stated in the beginning of this essay that the way we structure reparations will be one of the most momentous decisions in the history of the African American people.

A lot of energy has been expended on (1) how we should get reparations, for example, via litigation or legislation, and (2) who should pay, private corporations or governments.[35] (Some diligent researchers have even traced the network of companies, banks, and insurance companies which profited from the slave trade.)[36] All of this is good and necessary work. Now we must get to the job of deciding what a reparations program must look like. Maulana Karenga in his wisdom stated that we must initiate a national black and white dialogue on the issue of reparations, and that that national conversation must not merely focus on the calculation of monetary compensation, but also on the moral and ethical issues of the holocaust of slavery which was a monstrous crime against humanity. For Karenga, reparations must have four components: (1) admission of the moral wrong, (2) apology, (3) recognition in the form of national monuments/memorials, (3) compensation, and (4) measures to prevent future racism.[37] No one could argue with this, but I would add that as we initiate this national interracial dialogue in public forums such as this book, as an act of self-determination (*kujichagalia*) African Americans must also initiate national dialogues among ourselves. This internal dialogue must result in the shaping of our own policy about what the package of compensation should look like. Those of us who are not well-grounded in the community empowerment/community control struggles of the 1960s would do well to prepare for such an internal dialogue by reviewing the literature of community control.[38] To this end of initiating this internal dialogue and creating a body of grass-roots brothers and sisters who can formulate the policy for, and oversee the implementation of, a national reparations compensation program, Amiri Baraka has called for a national representative assembly, a democratically elected congress or parliament representative of the masses of African American working-class people.[39] The people who would be elected would not be the typical slate of sleazy and corrupt politicians who have misrepresented our interests over and over again in the past. This slate would come from the tried and true community activists and organizers and neighborhood leaders who have demonstrated commitment and dedication to the struggle of African people, the people who are our statesmen. Frantz Fanon states, "Every generation, out of relative obscurity, must discover its mission and either fulfill it or betray it." Our mission is to secure the resources to build a self-sufficient and independent community. Reparations and self-governance must go hand in hand. This is how we will ensure and protect our collective interests, for ourselves and for our future generations, so that, as Maulana Karenga so often says, "We can once again step back on the stage of human history as a free, proud and productive people."

Marcus Garvey told us, "Up You Mighty Race, you can accomplish what you will."[40]

With the proper administration, the proper management, the proper governance of the reparations resources, we can.

Reparations: It's not about getting paid. It's about Nation Time.

Notes

1. William Edward Burghardt DuBois, *The Souls of Black Folk*, 1903.
2. Adam Hochschild, *King Leopold's Ghost: A Story of Greed, Terror and Heroism in Colonial Africa* (Boston: Houghton Mifflin, 1998).
3. Robinson, *The Debt*. The book is largely anecdotal and a good portion of it addresses the issue of "psychic damage" caused to African Americans by Eurocentric distortions, falsifications, and omissions of black history. For Robinson, reparations must include not only monetary compensation but multiculturalism, that is, an acknowledgment by white America of the African and African American contributions to American and world civilization.
4. Shawna Maglangbayan, *The Black Handbook: Selected Quotations from Garvey, Lumnumba and Malcolm* (Chicago: Third World Press, 1973), pamphlet.
5. The 11:1 white–black ratio of median wealth was reported as a front-page story in the *New York Times* in the mid-1980s. This index may be as high as 12.5:1, according to another study. In a review of Oliver and Shapiro's *Black Wealth/White Wealth*, Robert A. Margo writing in the *Independent Review* 1, no. 3 (1997), states: "Drawing on SIPP (Survey of Income and Program Participation) data for the late 1980s, chapter 4 presents some basic evidence of wealth inequality in contemporary America, including the unsettling finding (p. 86) that the black–white ratio of median wealth is only 0.08 percent [i.e., white–black ratio of median wealth 12.5:1 percent] while the black–white ratio of median household income is 0.62."
6. For a discussion of Forman's *Black Manifesto*, see C. Eric Lincoln, *The Black Church Since Frazier* in the dual book E. Franklin Frazier, *The Negro Church in America*/C. Eric Lincoln, *The Black Church Since Frazier* (New York: Schocken Books, 1974), 130–134. The full text of the *Black Manifesto* is in Documents, Section 4.
7. Ibid. See "What the Muslims Want," in James L. Golden and Richard D. Rieke, *The Rhetoric of Black Americans* (Columbus, Ohio: Charles E. Merrill Publishing, 197 (1971), 408–9.
8. Kathleen Cleaver and George Katsiaficas, eds., *Liberation, Imagination and the Black Panther Party: A New Look at the Panthers and Their Legacy* (New York: Routledge, 2000), appendixes: October 1966 Black Panther Party Platform and Program, 285–286.
9. William L. Patterson, ed., *We Charge Genocide: The Historic Petition to the United Nations* (New York: International Publishers, 1971).
10. William A. Darity Jr., "Reparations," in *Encyclopedia of African-American Culture and History*, ed. Jack Salzman, David Lionel Smith, and Cornel West (New York: Simon-Schuster Macmillan, 1996), 4: 2315–2318. The late Queen Mother Moore was a venerated figure in the

nationalist/Pan-Africanist community; she died at the age of 99 in the late 1990s. Always resplendent in African fashions, she earned her honorific through her regal bearing, her travels to Africa where she was so anointed, and her long history of struggle which included phases as a Garveyite—and a communist! Though I have personal recollections of her dating back to 1968, I am indebted to the encyclopedia entry by Darrity for specifics about her reparations activity. See also Veronica D. DiConti, "Reparations," in *Encyclopedia of Minorities in American Politics*, ed. Jeffrey Schultz et al. (Phoenix: Oryx Press, 2000), 1: 146–147.

11. Ibid.

12. Ibid.

13. Chokwe Lumumba, "Notes on Reparations for New Afrikans in America," in *Reparations Yes*, by Chokwe Lumumba, Imari Obadele, and Nkechi Taifa, 3rd ed. (Baton Rouge: House of Songhay, 1993), 15. Lumumba cites as his source Leronne Bennett Jr., *Before the Mayflower* (Chicago: Johnson Publishing, 1969), 189.

14. Darlene Clark Hine et al., *The African American Oddessy* (Upper Saddle River, N.J.: Prentice-Hall, 2000), 171–172. Information about Paul Cuffe and the American Colonization Society appears in several black history texts.

15. Ibid., 259–260.

16. Ibid., p 260.

17. For information on the African Blood Brotherhood and its relation to both the Garvey movement and the Communist Party, see Theodore G. Vincent, *Black Power and the Garvey Movement* (San Francisco: Ramparts Press, 1972); Tony Martin, *Race First: The Ideological and Organizational Struggles of Marcus Garvey and the Universal Negro Improvement Association* (Westport, Conn.: Greenwood Press, 1976); Mark Naison, *Communists in Harlem During the Depression* (New York: Grove Press, 1984); Rupert Lewis and Maurice Warner-Lewis, eds., *Garvey: Africa, Europe, the Americas* (Trenton, N.J.: Africa World Press, 1994); Judith Stein, *The World of Marcus Garvey: Race and Class in Modern Society* (Baton Rouge: Louisiana State University Press, 1996); Winston James, *Holding Aloft the Banner of Ethiopia: Caribbean Radicalism in the Early Twentieth Century* (New York: Verso, 1998); and Rod Bush, *We Are Not What We Seem: Black Nationalism and Class Struggle in the American Century* (New York: New York University Press, 1999).

18. See n. 7 above.

19. John A. Williams, *The Man Who Cried I Am* (Boston: Little, Brown, 1967); Gill Scott-Heron, record album, *Free Will* (Flying Dutchman label, 1972). Black People's Topographical Centers were a national network of political education centers located in the ghettos of major cities in the 1970s. Virtually unknown outside of the inner city, "the Top" had a major impact on the consciousness of all blacks who took the three-hour "tour." Replete with impressive color-coded maps of the "ghetto-reservations" that "confine the captive black American population" and photographs of thirty-foot poison gas canisters located in detention centers, the tour of "the Top" was a chilling, political, paranoia-inducing experience.

20. J. Dollard, L. W. Doob, N. E. Miller, O. H. Mowrer, and R. R. Sears, *Frustration and Aggression* (New Haven: Yale University Press, 1939).

21. Henry George, *Progress and Poverty* (1879; New York: Robert Schalkenbach Foundation, 1992), 340–341.

22. Abdul Alkalimat, *Introduction to Afro-American Studies: A People's College Primer*, 6th ed. (Chicago: Twenty-First Century Books, 1986), 61.

23. First Reparations Education and Mobilization Campaign Conference, 2–4 November 2001, City College of New York, Harlem. Munford's paper was entitled "Forms of Reparations:

Problems of Political Economy." In addition to C. J. Munford's conference paper and his other written works, it may be useful to scan old and current issues of the *Review of Political Economy* for economic assessment and critique of various reparations models. According to William A. Darrity Jr.'s article "Reparations" (see n. 10), "One organization that received its start from funds generated in response to [James Forman's] maifesto was the Black Economic Research Center [which] began publishing the *Review of Black Political Economy* a journal now published under the auspices of the National Economic Association, the professional organization of black economists. In the early issues of the *Review*, Robert S. Browne, director of the research Center advocated substantial reparations to correct disparities in wealth between blacks and whites."

24. Gerorge Breitman, ed., *Malcolm X Speaks* (New York: Grove Press, 1965), 38–39. From the speech entitled "The Ballot or the Bullet" delivered by Malcolm X in Cleveland, Ohio, on 3 April 1964.

25. Robert L. Allen, *Black Awakening in Capitalist America* (1969; Trenton, N.J.: Africa World Press, 1990), 19.

26. Ibid.

27. Bill E. Lawson, *The Underclass Question* (Philadelphia: Temple University Press, 1992), 2.

28. Tom Bottomore's *A Dictionary of Marxist Thought* (Cambridge, Mass.: Harvard University Press, 1983) states that Marx, in the *Eighteenth Brumaire of Loius Bonaparte*, part 5, describes the lumpenproletariat as "'the refuse of all classes,' 'a disintegrated mass,' comprising 'ruined and adventurous offshoots of the bourgeoisie, vagabonds, discharged soldiers, discharged jailbirds, pickpockets, brothel keepers, rag-pickers, beggars' etc." (292).

29. The Black Panther Party adopted, from Frantz Fanon's observations in *The Wretched of the Earth*, the controversial position that the lumpenproletariat were the most oppressed segment of the masses, and that since they had the least to lose and the most to gain, they would be the most revolutionary group in the society, "the vanguard of the revolution." The black revolutionary culture of the late 1960s and early 1970s reflected this belief. On the album *This Is Madness* (Douglas 7 label, 1971) recorded by the legendary Last Poets, Omar ben Hassen's poem "Related to What" contains the lines "An Armageddon jumped off on the corners of 125th Street and 7th Avenue as the junkies, winos, pimps and prostitutes finally reclaimed their rightful name as a vanguard party." This echoes Fanon, in *The Wretched of the Earth* (New York: Grove Press, 1968), who speaks of rural peasants who have migrated to the city and cannot find employment as the lumpenproletariat who will spearhead the urban revolution: "That horde of starving men, uprooted from their tribe and from their clan, constitutes one of the most spontaneous and the most radically revolutionary forces of a colonized people. . . . So the pimps, the hooligans, the unemployed, and the petty criminals . . . throw themselves into the struggle for liberation like stout working men. These classless idlers will by militant and decisive action discover the path that leads to nationhood" (129–130). The Nation of Islam in its heyday was known for reforming lumpen and turning them into nation builders. Malcolm X was, of course, the quintessential "lumpen–turned–nationalist revolutionary."

30. Maulana Karenga, *Kawaida Theory: An Introductory Outline* (Inglewood, Calif.: Kawaida Publications, 1980), 15, 17, 18–20.

31. Na'im Akbar, *Breaking the Chains of Psychological Slavery*, (Tallahasee, Fla.: Mind Productions and Associates, 1996).

32. The struggle to convince black people that a personal reparations check is not the best formulation of reparations will be a difficult uphill battle. There are formidable forces rallying

around the concept of a check, as this message from Dr. Conrad Worrill, chairman of the National Black United Front, indicates:

"The Campaign To Cash The Check," spearheaded by Rev. Al Sharpton of the National Action Network based in New York City, and a host of other activists and organizers from around the country, have emerged as a force willing to take to the streets, in the spirit of Dr. Martin Luther King, to make known to the world the critical issues affecting Black people in this country. "It's obvious today," Dr. King challenged us in 1963, "that America has defaulted on it s promissory note in so far as her citizens of color are concerned. Instead of honoring this sacred obligation. America has given the Negro people a bad check, a check which has come back marked insufficient funds." Dr. King continued: "We refuse to believe that there are insufficient funds in the great vaults of opportunity of this nation. And so we've come to cash this check, a check that will give us upon demand the riches of freedom and the security of justice."

It should be clear to all African people that both the Republican and Democratic Parties, the last several years, have participated in compromising any efforts to "Cash The Check." In fact, both parties have compromised many of the hard fought gains that came out of the Civil Rights and Black Power Movements of the 1960s. Therefore, The Campaign To Cash The Check will focus on one of the most critical issues Black people should demand, and fight for. That is the continued demand for Reparations.

The Check that Dr. King was talking about Cashing in 1963, that has not been cashed, is the Check of Reparations.

33. Nor should reparation checks be sent to the working class or the black middle class to be used as luxury money for vacation trips (not even to Africa). Reparations should not be viewed as extra cash for Christmas presents or for adding a new garage to the house. This would trivialize reparations.

34. Some reparations proposals, such as one presented in Randall Robinson's *The Debt*, argue for tuition exemption for higher education for all African Americans for at least two generations. It is not clear whether the federal or state governments would be responsible for reimbursing the schools or if the schools—given that the original endowments of many elite institutions came from profits earned from the slave—should be responsible for footing the bill themselves. If this burden of footing the bill were placed on all colleges across the board regardless of their complicity in profiting from slavery, the historically black colleges would be adversely affected. If the historically black institutions had to foot the bill for all of their students they would go bankrupt; if they were exempt from footing the bill, students would choose to attend the predominantly white free tuition colleges and universities. Besides tuition exemption, the most widely discussed example of reparations structured as services rendered with cost exemption is income tax exemption. Veronica D. DiConto (see end of n. 10) states that recent attempts to demand reparations "have included claims filed by some African Americans with the Internal Revenue Service (IRS). In 1996, the IRS received and denied thousands of tax claims for slavery reparations.... Variations of the black tax story have been floating around the country since at least 1993, when an article in *Essence* Magazine, a periodical aimed at black women, urged readers to seek reparations from the Internal Revenue Service on their tax forms and gave instruction on how to do so. More than 20,000 people followed *Essence* author L. G. Sherrod's advice" (146–147).

35. A lot of energy has also been spent on deciding who gets paid. Are African Caribbean immigrants eligible for reparations? Or is the U.S. government only legally responsible for paying reparations to the black people whose ancestors were enslaved within the borders of

the United States and/or the thirteen original British colonies which became the United States? On the face of it, it would seem that if repartion is compensation for enslavement alone, then Caribbean immigrants would have to take their legal claims to the governments of Britain, France, Spain, or the Netherlands. If it is compensation for slavery *and continued oppression* then Caribbean immigrants—at least second- or third-generation descendents of Caribbean immigrants—should have a stake in the claim. From another angle, since the reparations movement is one of international solidarity, a Pan-African claim can be made against all of the Western powers involved in slavery or colonialism—and African people wherever they are, or whatever their origin, can collect. The slave trade itself was after all international. During enslavement and after emancipation there was movement of Diaspora blacks back and forth from the Caribbean to the mainland, many of the slaves being "broken" in the Caribbean before being brought to North America. The structuring of reparations as community reconstruction and development programs rather than as cash payments eliminates one set of problems but introduces another. The inner-city communities eligible for reconstruction funds would have to be populated predominantly by African Americans (descendents of those enslaved in the United States). If large numbers of African Caribbean immigrants live in those neighborhoods, they of course would benefit. But can reparation funds be legally invested in areas where the black population consists primarily of immigrants? On the face of it, it would seem like communities which are overwhelmingly composed of African Caribbean immigrants would not be legally entitled to reparations, unless an international indictment against all Western powers were made on behalf of all African peoples.

36. Deadria C. Farmer-Peallmann is one of the leaders in this research. She unearthed the connection between Aetna Insurance Company and slave trade profits. She delivered the results of her ongoing research, linking Aetna and other contemporary corporations to slave-trade profiteering, in a paper entitled "In Her Majesty's Service" at the conference on "Slavery and Reparations" sponsored by the Society for the Study of Africana Philosophy. Philosophy Born of Struggle, seventh annual conference, 20–21 October 2000, New School University, Dr. Everet Green, coordinator.

37. Plenary Session address delivered on 3 November at the First Reparations Education and Mobilization Campaign Conference, 2–4 November 2001, City College of New York, Harlem.

38. A short but excellent introduction would be William L. Van Deburg, *New Day in Babylon: The Black Power Movement and American Culture, 1965–1975* (Chicago: University of Chicago Press, 1992), chapter 4, "The Ideologies of Black Power," 112–191; The late Amos Wilson left a monumental nine-hundred-page posthumously published legacy, *Blueprint for Black Power: A Moral, Political and Economic Imperative for the Twenty-First Century* (New York: Afrikan World InfoSytems, 1998), which also deserves our study.

39. Final speech of Plenary Session delivered on 3 November at the First Reparations Education and Mobilization Campaign Conference, 2–4 November 2001, City College of New York, Harlem.

40. Amy Jacques-Garvey, ed., *Philosophy and Opinions of Marcus Garvey* (New York: Atheneum, 1973).

Repatriation as Reparations for Slavery and Jim Crow

ROBERT JOHNSON JR.

Repatriation represents the oldest form of African American nationalist sentiments, traceable to the fifteenth century when the first Africans were taken from the continent. As Africans were ripped from the continent and their cultural and spiritual way of life, most yearned for a return to the homeland. This yearning for reconnection with Africa has never ended. Rather, it has been nurtured and developed over the past four centuries, gaining critical momentum in the nineteenth century in the form of a variety of different colonization efforts and moving closer to an authentic, mass-based model in the twentieth century.

Recently, many scholars and activists such as Clarence Munford, Ronald Daniels, John Hope Franklin, Ronald Walters, U.S. Rep. John Conyers, James Forman, and Rev. Alfred Sharpton have examined and espoused the concept of reparations. Essentially, they articulate the need for African Americans to receive "restitution," "compensation," "indemnity," or "recompense" for centuries of slavery and decades of judicially sanctioned racial subordination. In addition, some of these activists have demanded that white institutions, such as churches, provide monetary compensation. On April 26, 1969, the National Black Economic Development Conference, convened in Detroit, Michigan, issued a *Black Manifesto* that demanded $500 million from the white religious community[1] (see Documents, section 4).

Although some activists, such as Gaidi Obadele and Imari Obadele of the Republic of New Afrika, have argued that African Americans should be granted land within the United States, few have argued that an essential element of the reparations debate should include repatriation to Africa.[2]

Repatriation must be afforded its rightful place within the discourse on reparation ideologies. Drawing upon different Back-to-Africa movements of the nineteenth and twentieth centuries, this essay argues that it is essential that repatriation take a prominent place in the academic and political discourse on reparations for the twenty-first century.

Repatriation in the Nineteenth Century

Repatriation in the nineteenth century occurred through the American Colonization Society, black nationalist efforts, or black revolutionary efforts. The latter was best represented by those kidnaped Africans who, under the leadership of the legendary Cinque, not only mutinied but also demanded that they be taken back to Africa. The insurrection occurred in 1839, but the legal battle to allow their return to Africa was not settled until 1841, when the U.S. Supreme Court, in *United States v. Amistad*,[3] decided that they were free to return home. Since the *Amistad* has been the subject of much research, as well as a recent film, this essay will not discuss repatriation through black revolutionary efforts.

Black Nationalist Efforts: Paul Cuffe (1759–1817)

Repatriation in the nineteenth century began with the efforts of Paul Cuffe, as part of the African American independence movement. His voyages were African American conceived, financed, and executed. Cuffe was born to free parents in Westport, Massachusetts, on January 17, 1759. Cuffe Slocum, his father, a native of Ghana, had purchased his freedom in 1728.[4] Beginning in 1775, young Cuffe began to work on whaling ships, and by 1881 he had acquired sufficient maritime skills to construct his own ship and set sail for Sierra Leone. His aim was to engage in commerce and investigate the possibility of repatriating African Americans to Africa. He planned to finance his ventures by selling products acquired in Europe and Africa.

When Cuffe and his crew of nine African American men and one Swede arrived in Sierra Leone on March 1, 1811, they were greeted by the governor of the colony. Even though Cuffe was afforded the best treatment by British colonial officials, he did not fail to meet with traditional rulers and people. He understood that in order for his repatriation plans to succeed, he would need the assistance of the indigenous African people.

After sailing from Sierra Leone to England, Cuffe returned to the United States to garner more support for his repatriation plans. He set sail for Sierra Leone on December 4, 1815, with thirty-eight passengers. On February 3, 1816, he and the repatriates arrived on African soil. These pioneers were from New York City, Philadelphia, and Boston and had joined Cuffe's voyage because they believed in the importance of reestablishing their ties with Africa. Each of these free African Americans paid for the cost of their passage, which ranged from $100 to $250 per person.[5]

Although Cuffe was aided by white Quaker friends, both in England and

America, the entire venture was an African American effort. Among the repatriates and their Quaker supporters, resettlement was seen as a means of righting a wrong that had begun two centuries earlier. For them, as it should be for us, the return to Africa was understood to be a specific, narrowly tailored form of restitution for slavery. It was a most dramatic reparation.

American Colonization Society

For most of the nineteenth century, the American Colonization Society controlled resettlement efforts to Africa. These initiatives were carried out by the U.S. government, southern plantation owners, northern industrialists, and African Americans who were willing to compromise their nationalist (black independence, black self-help) views in order to get to Africa. The results from this unusual partnership were tangible: establishment of the colony of Liberia and the repatriation of a substantial number of African Americans, including John Brown Russwurm (1799–1851), the most illustrious of the early repatriates.

The American Colonization Society was formed in Washington, D.C., one year after Paul Cuffe's Sierra Leone voyage. Its first president was Bushrod Washington, nephew of President George Washington. Both Washingtons favored the resettlement of Africans. Henry Clay, the founding secretary of the Society, had this to say about Africans in America: "Can there be a nobler cause than that which, whilst it proposed to rid our country of a useless and pernicious, if not dangerous portion of our population, contemplates the spreading of civilized life, and the possible redemption from ignorance and barbarism of a benighted quarter of the globe."[6]

Clearly the founders of the American Colonization Society did not have the best interests of African Americans at heart. Rather, they saw resettlement as a means of eliminating from the American population free African Americans who could agitate against slavery and for competitive labor. Industrialists and plantation owners, on the other hand, saw the removal of rebellious slaves as a means of securing the plantation system and the southern way of life.

Rarely, if ever, did officials of the American Colonization Society equate colonization with reparations. Nevertheless, they provided substantial financial resources for resettlement. Congress also appropriated a series of large grants (the first being for $100,000) to help fund the Society's resettlement efforts.[7] Although the goals of the Society were designed to advance the interests of whites, several thousand slaves and free blacks were able to utilize its considerable support to realize their dream of repatriation.[8]

Bishop Henry McNeal Turner (1834–1915)

By 1892, after the American Colonization Society ceased its active involvement with Liberia, the outspoken Bishop Henry McNeal Turner of the African Methodist Episcopal Church assumed a leadership role in marshaling support for repatriation. It was Bishop Turner who began, for the first time, to connect the ideas of repatriation and reparations. Bishop Turner was born on February 1, 1834, in Newberry, South Carolina. Like Cuffe, he had been born to free parents. From the end of the Civil War into the twentieth century, Turner was the leading supporter of repatriation.

Despite the promises of a new life after the Civil War, most African Americans found themselves abandoned by the federal government and northern carpetbaggers. As a result, Jim Crow laws restricting the newfound freedom and opportunity of African Americans — enforced by lynching and such hate groups as the Ku Klux Klan — began to emerge. Between 1883 and 1899, 2,500 African Americans were lynched. In the first years of the new century and before the beginning of World War One, 1,100 African Americans met the same fate.[9] It is reported that in 1917, three thousand whites in Tennessee came out to see what was advertised as the burning of a "live Negro."[10]

The deteriorating socioeconomic and political conditions of African Americans caused Bishop Turner to join a chorus of individuals and groups who supported repatriation to Africa as a necessary component of reparations. Some of the organizations that sprang into existence included the Kansas African Emigration Association (1887) and the Liberian Exodus Company, founded by Turner and Martin Delany. The latter organization bought a ship and transported two hundred African Americans to Liberia.[11] Other noteworthy attempts included that of Dr. Alpert Thone, who attempted to transport African Americans to the Belgian Congo in 1915, but failed. From the Gold Coast, Alfred C. Sam raised $100,000 in Kansas and Oklahoma and, in 1915, transported sixty African Americans to Liberia in his ship, *The Liberia*.[12]

In 1891, the Council of Bishops authorized Bishop Turner to take an exploratory trip to Africa. In February 1892, Bishop Turner returned to the United States determined not only to establish missions in Africa, but to repatriate African Americans. His plan was to repatriate 5 million to 10 million African Americans per year. He had hoped that wealthy African Americans would provide support, but few expressed an interest in leaving the United States. Turner believed that the federal government should provide financial assistance as well.[13] The U.S. government, he argued, owed reparations of about $40 billion for the free service African Americans had provided the United States for two hundred years.

In his appeal to the working-class poor, Turner's philosophy foreshadowed that of Marcus Garvey. The genius of Bishop Turner stemmed from his undying love for African people and his firm belief that in order for Africans to be respected, they must become a nation.

Repatriation in the Twentieth Century

For the most part, nineteenth-century black nationalist leaders of the repatriation movement came from privileged backgrounds and appealed to a select group of African Americans. The twentieth-century movement, in contrast, was more of a working-class, mass movement. Under his Universal Negro Improvement Association, incorporated in the United States on July 2, 1918, Marcus Garvey sought as his goal "the establishment of a central nation for black people"[14] (see Documents, section 4). By 1925 he had established 996 branches in the United States and around the world, with a membership of more than 2 million.[15]

Garvey's movement provided a clear articulation of the need for repatriation. Not only would the return home be a means to escape the hardships of America, but it would also lead to the redemption of Africa. He envisioned 400 million black people worldwide uniting in a common effort to rid Africa of European control and exploitation. Hence, for Garvey, repatriation served as reparations not only for African Americans, but for Africa as well.

Repatriation efforts were put forth by others, including W. E. B. Du Bois. Ironically, Du Bois led the opposition to Garvey's movement in the 1920s. Eventually, Du Bois repatriated to Ghana, where he died in 1963. His arrival in Africa was significant because he represented the quintessential self-made African American intellectual who, while adopting a Pan-African viewpoint as early as 1919, fundamentally believed himself to be an American.

Between 1971 and 1998 I conducted several interviews with men and women in Africa (east and west) who had left the United States. Many left out of frustration with the racial situation. One man stated as reasons for leaving:

> My ancestors were taken from another land against their will and none of their descendants were ever given the privilege or opportunity to ascertain as to whether or not they wanted to stay or be taken to the land their ancestors came from. Citizenship was forced on my ancestors and they could only live from hand to mouth and could never have the privilege of traveling.... The only way I have an opportunity to win is to first constitute the majority. Here in this land my Blackness constitutes the majority and that's why I left there.[16]

Like other black professionals who have resettled in Africa during the past three decades, this repatriate saw Africa as a way to escape continued racial injustice in the United States. Repatriation was deemed to be a form of reparations effected through self-help rather than governmental policy.

The Strategy for the Twenty-First Century

What will be the obstacles to raising repatriation as a viable and necessary component of the ongoing reparations debate? Given the history of the past two centuries, factors both within and outside the community will contribute to the creation of obstacles. Internally, most African Americans do not have a realistic understanding of Africa, its people and culture. Scholars can help bridge this educational gap by providing seminars on Africa both on college campuses and in the community.

Another internal hurdle will come from those African Americans who have acquired a "comfortable" place in America (psychologically as well as socioeconomically). They will continue to question the viability and necessity of repatriation as a form of reparations. Even some who view themselves as nationalists (believers in nation building and self-help) will object to the idea of material resources being provided by government or business to facilitate the exodus of large segments of the African American population. This opposition should not be considered unusual. It is an inevitable reflection of the integration/separation dichotomy that has always been part of the black experience in America.[17]

Some African American intellectuals will also raise objections. Though involved in the study of African people from a global perspective, many of these scholars have attained the same financial security as the African American middle class and, therefore, would not be willing to leave or to engage in serious scholarly debate on the merits of repatriation. They are driven in their academic pursuits, not by any love for African people and their need for liberation, but by their individual needs for recognition and validation by the very forces, within and outside the academy, that oppress African people.

Some African American politicians will present even more virulent objections. Many will be unwilling to raise the banner of repatriation because such efforts would run counter to their essentially integrationist understanding of the African American political reality. To them, "community" is merely a specific geographic-political district where a loyal constituency of registered and active voters return them to office, election after election. Consequently, a change in their political agenda would directly undermine their hegemony. These politicians would likely be the most vociferous opponents of any plan that might lead to separation.

What forces and factors will most likely advance repatriation as a necessary component of reparations? A prime factor will be the deteriorating socioeconomic conditions of the African American masses. While a significant number of African Americans have entered the middle class over the past three decades, the lives of the vast majority have deteriorated. The nation's leading sociologists and theorists are clear on this point. In his important work, *When Work Disappears*, William Julius Wilson writes:

> For the first time in the twentieth century most adults in many inner-city ghetto neighborhoods are not working in a typical week. The disappearance of work has adversely affected not only individuals, families, and neighborhoods, but the social life of the city at large as well. Inner-city joblessness is a severe problem that is often overlooked or obscured when the focus is placed mainly on poverty and its consequences. Despite increases in the concentration of poverty since 1970, inner cities have always featured high levels of poverty, but the current levels of joblessness in some neighborhoods are unprecedented.[18]

Overall, the median income for an African American family, compared to a white family, has declined over the past twenty years. But most appalling is the fact that African American family income is only 59.8 percent of white family income.[19]

In addition to declining incomes and loss of jobs in the inner city, the massive influx of drugs has destroyed neighborhoods and caused middle-class African Americans to flee from the cities. Manning Marable, professor of history at Columbia University, sees the federal government as failing to do much to combat the crack cocaine epidemic in the inner cities: "What else intensifies racism and inequality in the 1990's? Drugs. We are witnessing the complete disintegration of America's inner cities, the home of millions of Latinos and blacks. We see the daily destructive impact of gang violence inside our neighborhoods and communities, which is directly attributable to the fact that for 20 years the federal government has done little to address the crisis of drugs inside the ghetto and the inner city."[20]

Conclusion

As socioeconomic conditions continue to deteriorate, African Americans will have more incentive to embrace repatriation as perhaps the only viable and effective form of reparations. But rather than the victims shouldering the burden, repatriation must be implemented like all other forms of reparations. Select African American intellectuals must join with militant community–based leadership to articulate the historical precedent for governmental support for repatriation. They can cite the Marshall Plan and support for Israel, not as paradigms, but as examples for the type of involvement that will be necessary to fully compensate African Americans. Reparations must be seen as a means to make whole a people and their descendants who were stolen from a foreign land and forced to work for centuries without compensation. Scholars must argue that concomitant with the development of America and Europe, there has occurred a corresponding underdevelopment of African Americans and Africans.[21]

In addition, this cadre of enlightened leadership must establish meaningful professional relationships among lawyers, businesspeople, and diplomats to develop a comprehensive plan for locating and procuring a site in Africa for pilot repatriation efforts. The ultimate goal would be to lobby for and obtain congressional commitment to allocate funds for individuals who wish to repatriate. Congress would appear to have this power under both the Thirteenth and Fourteenth Amendments to the Constitution. If not, certainly Congress can draw on the precedent of the financial support it provided to the American Colonization Society in the nineteenth century. Congress has the resources to provide meaningful reparations for racial injustice. The only question is whether it has the will.

Notes

1. On May 4, 1969, James Forman interrupted services at New York's Riverside Church to present their demands. See Lecky and Wright, *The Black Manifesto*, 3.
2. The Republic of New Afrika demanded in March 1968 that the U.S. government pay $400 billion for the establishment of a black republic in five southern states. See Munford, *Race and Reparations*, 418–420.
3. 40 U.S. 518 (1841).
4. Sheldon H. Harris, *Paul Cuffe: Black America and the African Return* (New York: Simon and Schuster, 1972), 15.
5. Ibid., 192.
6. Robert J. Rotberg, *A Political History of Tropical Africa* (New York: Harcourt, Brace and World, 1965), 210.
7. Roy L. Brooks, *Integration or Separation?* (Cambridge, Mass.: Harvard University Press, 1996), 158.
8. Ibid., 159.
9. John Hope Franklin, *From Slavery to Freedom: A History of Negro Americans*, 3d ed. (New York: Knopf, 1967), 439.
10. Ibid., 474.

11. Amy Jacques Garvey, *The Philosophy and Opinions of Marcus Garvey*, 2 vols. (New York: Atheneum Press, 1970).

12. Edwin S. Redkey, *Black Exodus: Black Nationalist and Back to Africa Movements, 1890–1910* (New Haven: Yale University Press, 1969), 292.

13. Ibid., 251.

14. Tony Martin, *Race First* (Dover, Md.: Majority Press, 1976), 6.

15. Ibid., 15.

16. Author interview of Duke Carter, Dar es Salaam, Tanzania, 17 December 1971.

17. W. E. B. Du Bois has written about this "twoness" in his *Souls of Black Folk* (New York: Vintage Books, 1990), 8–9.

18. William Julius Wilson, *When Work Disappears: The World of the New Urban Poor* (New York: Vintage Books, 1996), xiii.

19. James Jennings, *Understanding the Nature of Poverty in Urban America* (Westport, Conn.: Praeger, 1994), 68.

20. Manning Marable, *Speaking Truth to Power: Essays on Race, Resistance, and Radicalism* (Boulder, Colo.: Westview, 1996), 91.

21. This line of argument would advance the ideas that have been ably presented by the late historian Walter Rodney in his seminal work *How Europe Underdeveloped Africa* (Boston: South End Press, 1983) and by Manning Marable in *How Capitalism Underdeveloped Black America* (Washington, D.C.: Howard University Press, 1981).

What's Next?

Japanese American Redress and African American Reparations

ERIC K. YAMAMOTO

In 1991 the Office of Redress Administration presented the first reparations check to the oldest Hawai'i survivor of the Japanese American internment camps. I attended the stately ceremony. The mood, while serious, was decidedly upbeat. Tears of relief mixed with sighs of joy. Freed at last.

Amid the celebration I reflected on the Japanese American redress and wondered about its impacts over time. The process had been arduous, with twists and turns. Many Japanese Americans contributed, and their communities overwhelmingly considered reparations a great victory, as did I (see Documents, section 1).

Other racial groups lent support. Yet some of that support seemed begrudging. What about redress for them? As an African American scholar observed, "The apology [to Japanese Americans] was so appropriate and the payment so justified . . . that the source of my ambivalent reaction was at first difficult to identify. After some introspection, I guiltily discovered that my sentiments were related to a very dark brooding feeling that I had fought long and hard to conquer—inferiority. A feeling that took first root in the soil of 'Why them and not me.'"[1]

These questions led me to ask then about what political role Japanese Americans might play in future struggles for racial justice in America. That question in turn led to a 1992 essay about the social meanings of Japanese American redress.[2] The essay started with recognition that Japanese American beneficiaries of reparations benefited personally, sometimes profoundly. The trauma of racial incarceration without charges or trial and the lingering self-doubt across two generations left scars on the soul. The government's apology and bestowal of symbolic reparations fostered long-overdue healing for many.

But, I wondered, even given personal benefits, what would be the long-term effects of reparations—the social legacy beyond personal benefits? Would societal attitudes toward communities of color generally and Asian Americans particularly change? Would institutions, especially those that curtailed civil liberties in the name of national security, be restructured? Would Japanese American redress serve as a catalyst for redress for others?

I identified and critiqued two emerging and seemingly contradictory views of reparations for Japanese Americans and then offered a third. The first view was that redress shows that America does the right thing, that the Constitution works (if belatedly), and that the United States is far along on its march to inevitable racial justice for all. I criticized that view as unrealistically bright.

The second view was that reparations legislation had the potential of becoming a civil rights law that at best delivers far less than it promises and that at worst creates illusions of progress, functioning as a hegemonic device to perpetuate long-standing systemic inequalities. I criticized that view as overly bleak. As part of this critique, and drawing upon critical race theory insights, I offered a third view.

> Reparations legislation and court rulings in [the *coram nobis*] cases such as *Korematsu* do not . . . inevitably lead to a restructuring of governmental institutions, a changing of societal attitudes or a transformation of social relationships, and the dangers of illusory progress and co-optation are real. At the same time, reparations claims, and the rights discourse they engender in attempts to harness the power of the state, can . . . be appreciated as intensely powerful and calculated political acts that challenge racial assumptions underlying past and present [social inequalities].[3]

In light of this third view, I posited that the legacy of Japanese American redress was yet to be determined. I suggested that the key to the legacy of redress was how Japanese Americans acted when faced with continuing racial subordination of African Americans, Native Americans, Native Hawaiians, Latinas/os, and Asian Americans. Would Japanese Americans draw upon the lessons of the reparations movement and work to end all forms of societal oppression, or would we close up shop because we got ours?

Nearly a decade has passed. In important respects, the United States, indeed the world, has gone apology crazy. Indeed, Japanese American redress has stimulated a spate of race apologies.[4] Some apologies appear to reflect heartfelt recognition of historical and current injustice and are backed by reparations. Other apologies appear empty, as strategic maneuvers to release pent-up social pressure.

Amid this phenomenon African Americans have renewed their call for reparations for the legally sanctioned harms of slavery and Jim Crow oppression. Perhaps more so than at any time since early post–Civil War Reconstruction—when Congress and the president sought to confiscate southern land and provide freed slaves with forty acres and a mule — their claims have gained momentum.[5] The Florida legislature approved reparations for survivors and descendants of the 1923 Rosewood massacre.[6] The African American victims of the Tuskegee syphilis experiment received reparations and a presidential apology. One African American reparations lawsuit was filed on the West Coast and a class action is contemplated on the East Coast. Representative John Conyers's resolution calling for a Congressional Reparations Study Commission, reintroduced every year since 1989, has garnered endorsements from an impressive array of political organizations.[7] (For the above reparations claims, see Documents, sections 1 and 2.)

And in every African American reparations publication, in every legal argument, in almost every discussion, the topic of Japanese American redress surfaces. Sometimes as legal precedent. Sometimes as moral compass. Sometimes as political guide. In similar fashion, Native Hawaiian reparations claims against the United States for the illegal overthrow of the sovereign Hawaiian nation in 1893 and against the State of Hawai'i for mismanagement of Hawaiian trust lands also cite reparations for Japanese Americans.[8]

In light of this recent history, the diverging views of Japanese American redress, and the August 1998 closure of the Office of Redress Administration's doors, the time is ripe to explore in some depth the legacy of Japanese American redress. And in doing so, it is time to assess what redress means not only to Japanese Americans but also to other reparations movements.

With this in mind, I raise in this essay three themes. The first asks about the extent of Japanese American commitment to support other groups currently seeking redress for historic injustice. The second theme is more conceptual. It asks what lessons — both bright and dark — might be drawn from the political and legal processes of Japanese American redress. The third theme offers an expanded vision of reparations not as compensation but as "repair" — the restoration of broken relationships through justice. Each of these themes links Japanese American redress and African American claims.

Japanese Americans and Support for Other Redress Movements

Movements to redress historical racial injustice mark our global landscape. These movements are part of the Japanese American redress legacy. Permit me a brief catalogue. Internationally, the Canadian government just apologized to and promised substantial reparations for Canada's indigenous peoples for destruction of their culture and way of life; the British offered reparations to New Zealand's Maori for British-initiated nineteenth-century bloody race wars; French President Chirac recognized French complicity in the deportation of 76,000 Jews to death camps; the Catholic Church apologized for its assimilationist policy in Australia that contributed to Aborigines' spiritual and cultural destruction. Nationally, President Clinton apologized to indigenous Hawaiians for the illegal U.S.-aided overthrow of the sovereign nation and the near decimation of Hawaiian life that followed; and the Methodist Church apologized to Native Americans in Wyoming for the 1865 post-treaty slaughter at the hands of the U.S. Calvary led by a Methodist minister. And still on the table: the Korean so-called comfort women forced into prostitution by the Japanese government; the Japanese Latin American claimants in the *Mochizuki v. U.S.* lawsuit who are seeking reparations for their kidnapping from Latin American countries and their placement in U.S. internment camps as U.S. hostages during World War Two; Native Hawaiian claims for land and money reparations; and, of course, the African American reparations claims.

So I reraise the question asked in 1991. In what ways have Japanese Americans engaged with these recent and ongoing reparations efforts by others? Have the Japanese Americans — community and legal organizations, media, politicians, educators — lent organizational help and political and legal muscle to the movements of others (have they been asked to do so)? Or have they sat back and said, "You're on your own." Of course, Japanese American activists have supported other groups in their political struggles and have worked hard to forge multiracial alliances. Nevertheless the question persists: Why do some activists in the current reparations movements perceive that Japanese Americans receiving reparations, as a whole, have offered relatively little financial aid and political and spiritual support to others in their justice struggles?

Is this perception completely false? Or partially true? If it is false, why does the perception exist? If true in some part, what are the explanations, and what is the Japanese American response?

These questions engender complicated inquiries well beyond present-day Japanese American political activities. They entail inquiry into historical and contemporary intergroup relations. This may require digging into whether other groups opposed the Japanese American internment and later supported redress. For example, Devon Carbado's research reveals an apparent lack of NAACP opposition to the internment at the time, although black journalists voiced dissent.[9] Has this apparent historical lack of opposition influenced current Japanese American participation in the black reparations movement? Did it create an obligation to assist in Japanese Americans' struggles for redress? Consider the strong support for Japanese American redress in the 1980s by black congressional representatives like Ron Dellums. The inquiry may also require digging beyond the far-reaching effects of white supremacy into the extent to which Japanese Americans (and Asian Americans) were complicit in the subordination of African American communities over the last fifty years. Do Asian Americans have an obligation to aid in the healing of African American communities?

These many questions speak to something larger: Are Japanese American reparations about redress for Japanese Americans, or are they also about ending racial injustice for all?

Lessons from the Redress Movement

The second theme is less an open-ended question and more a conceptual point. What larger lessons might communities of color in the United States draw from Japanese American redress? Most addressing this question talk about how the government rectified a serious violation of constitutional liberties and how a diverse racial community banded together to achieve reparations legislation. These are important salutary lessons. I start with the premise that reparations can be beneficial and at times transformative for recipients.

This essay then takes a different tack. It focuses on the underside of the reparations process—a darker though realistic side often overlooked amid the hot rhetoric justifying reparations for historical injustice. A darker side requiring careful strategic attention by those seeking reparations and requiring forthright acknowledgment by those who have achieved it. To simplify, I separate this underside into three related categories: the distorted legal framing of reparations claims, the dilemma of reparations process, and the ideology of reparations. My thesis is not that this underside diminishes the significance of achieving reparations or forecloses future redress efforts. Rather, it is that the risks caution careful strategic framing of debate and action and thoughtful, anticipatory grappling with a reparations movement's both bright and dark potential.

Legal Framing of Reparations Claims

The first category is the distorted legal framing of reparations claims. Reparations that actually repair are costly. For this reason, those responsible for repairing racial harms always resist. And they employ legalisms in two ways to aid their resistance. First, they cite the sufficiency of existing laws: since existing civil rights laws already afford individuals equal opportunity, there is no need for additional reparations legislation to rectify social inequalities.

Second, those resisting reparations raise objections shaped by narrow legal concerns. They argue the criminal law defense of lack of bad intent on the part of wrongdoers; they assert the procedural bar of lack of standing by claimants (the difficulty of identifying specific perpetrators and victims); they cite the lack of legal causation (specific acts causing specific injuries); and they cite the impossibility of accurately calculating damages (or compensation).

These concerns seem compelling to lawyers and judges because they resonate with what is familiar: the common law paradigm of a lawsuit — where an individual wrongfully harmed by the specific actions of another in the recent past is entitled to recover damages to compensate for actual personal losses. The typical situation is the pedestrian hit by a speeding car. That paradigm works poorly, however, where, over time, members of a group act to preserve the group's system of dominance and privilege by denigrating other groups and excluding those groups' members from housing, businesses, jobs, and political and social opportunities; that is, situations of systemic racial oppression.

Yet, despite the misfit for most reparations claims, the common law paradigm persists — at a cost. For instance, many proponents of black redress cast reparations as claims by slave descendents for compensation for lost wages and property during slavery. This legal framing of the claims assumes individual rights and remedies. It requires each present-day African American claimant to do the practically impossible: prove with specific evidence how she and her ancestors were financially injured by slavery. This legal framing also requires acceptance of the proposition that almost all whites were in some ways perpetrators — indeed, that all white Americans today have benefited over time from the spoils of slave labor. Right or wrong, the courts legally and mainstream America politically have been unwilling to find legal liability under these circumstances. As happened in the recent Ninth Circuit ruling *Cato v. United States*, the courts recognize the horrors of slavery and Jim Crow segregation but find no valid legal claim.[10]

In backward fashion, Japanese American redress underscores this point about the potency of the individual rights and remedies paradigm. The redress movement stalled in the late 1970s. Despite hindsight recognition of historical injustice, government decision makers opposed to reparations cited the Supreme Court's constitutional validation of the internment in *Korematsu*. There is no valid legal claim, the argument went; therefore, we cannot compensate. Indeed, the *Hohri* class action case, filed on behalf of internees in the early 1980s seeking monetary compensation, ran aground on the shoals of legal procedure: the statute of limitations.

The redress movement regained its political momentum in the mid-1980s in part from the court rulings in the *Korematsu* and *Hirabayashi coram nobis* cases. Those cases reopened the original World War Two internment decisions by the Supreme Court on the basis of now declassified government documents. The federal courts found that the Justice and War Departments during the war had destroyed and suppressed key evidence and lied to the Supreme Court about the military necessity basis for the interment. It was these court "findings of fact," in specific cases, involving individual claimants, about particular government officials' illegal attempts to justify the internment, coupled with the Congressional Commission's similar conclusions, that provided the missing traditional legal cornerstone for reparations.

From this, one might argue that Japanese Americans succeeded on their reparations claims not because they transcended the individual rights/remedies paradigm, but because ultimately they were able to fit their claims tightly within it. Consider these facets of the internees' claim: (1) their challenge addressed a specific executive order and ensuing military orders; (2) the challenge was based on recognized constitutional norms (due process and equal protection); (3) both a Congressional Commission and the courts identified specific facts amounting to a violation of those norms; (4) the plaintiffs were easily identifiable as individuals (those who had been interned and were still living); (5) the government defendant's agents were identifiable (military and Justice and War Department officials); (6) the illegal acts resulted directly in imprisonment of innocent people, causing their injuries; (7) the damages, although uncertain, covered a fixed time and were limited to survivors; and (8) payment meant finality. The traditional rights/remedies paradigm, in the end, appears to have bolstered rather than hindered the internees' reparations claim.

Consider also: in 1995, Florida awarded each of the nine Rosewood massacre survivors $150,000 and 145 Rosewood descendants between $375 and $22,535 as compensation for property damage(see Documents, section 4).

By contrast, African American groups seeking broad redress for slavery and Jim Crow segregation have encountered considerable difficulty in framing their reparations claims in terms of individual rights and remedies. Legally framed claims for lost wages, liberty, and property meet the slew of standard legal objections identified earlier. Indeed, the Ninth Circuit in *Cato v. United States* validated many of those objections. This does not mean that the claims lack merit. It means that the legal framing of sweeping reparations claims, based largely on a vast array of historical events, carries heavy baggage.

That baggage does not counsel abandonment of legal claims and court battles. Rather, it counsels a dual strategy. One strategic path focuses on bite-sized legal claims, with limited numbers of claimants, well defined in time and place — like Rosewood and Tuskegee and, to some extent, the internment — framed in terms of individual rights and remedies. The second, and simultaneous, strategic path recognizes the distortions of legal framing. It therefore reconceptualizes law and litigation broadly as key components of larger political strategies. This means treating law and court process — regardless of formal legal outcome — as generators of "cultural performances," as means for providing outsiders an institutional public forum, for communicating counternarratives to dominant stories about the racial order, and for attracting media attention to help organize racial communities politically in support of more sweeping reparations claims.

Dilemma of Reparations

The second category of reparations' darker underside is the dilemma of reparations. Reparations, if thoughtfully conceived, offered, and administered, can change the material conditions of group life and send deep political messages about social justice. But when reparations stimulate change, they generate resistance. Proponents suffer backlash. Thus, when reparations claims are treated seriously, they tend to inflame old wounds and to trigger regressive reactions. This is the dilemma of reparations.

Seeing these dual possibilities in all redress movements, Professor Joe Singer describes the potential for further victimization in two contemporary situations. He describes Jews' publicized demands in 1997 that Swiss banks account for and restore Jewish money held by the banks for Nazis during World War Two. Those demands, however justified and appropriately asserted, also resurrected the harsh historical stereotypes of Jews "as money-grubbing, as having both accumulated secret bank accounts in the past and as caring now about nothing more than money."[11] In addition, other groups (such as Hungarian gypsies who were exterminated by Nazis) expressed resentment because only Jews were getting reparations.[12]

Singer also describes responses to demands for African American reparations. Some understand those demands as a call for redress of past injustice; others see them as a "refusal to grow up." The result, he says, evident in the volatile affirmative action debates, is that "calls to repair the current effects of past injustice are met with derisory denials that continuing injustice exists and that the problems of African Americans are now purely of their own making."[13]

More specifically, each year since 1989 Democratic Congressman John Conyers of Michigan has introduced legislation proposing an African American reparations study commission. The proposed commission, patterned after the Japanese American study commission, however, has received little congressional support. In June 1997, Representative Tony Hall of Ohio introduced a seemingly innocuous resolution calling for a simple apology from the United States to African Americans for slavery.[14] The call met with overwhelming resistance (see Documents, section 1).

The Conyers and Hall legislation and the reparations demands of the National Coalition of Blacks for Reparations in America (N'COBRA) have generated a variety of still-ringing negative reactions. First, much of the swift public opposition to Hall's resolution was steeped in hate and denial. Second, for some, the calls for an apology and reparations reinscribed victim status. They not only reopened old wounds; for some, they also painted blacks as pandering and overreaching.

A third type of negative reaction came from the other direction. It addressed the perceived inadequacy of Conyers's study commission approach — that this approach (a) did not go far enough because it asked only for a study, and (b) even if individual monetary payments resulted, those payments would be mere tokens.

The dilemma of reparations played out — but in a different way — after Japanese American redress. Since past government sin had been absolved, Asians in America were once again permissible targets for the government and mainstream America. What do I mean? The president and Congress criticized Japanese competition in the auto industry and extensive real estate purchases in the United States, fanning the flames of anti-Asians-in-America sentiment. Soon after, Asian immigrants became the target of state initiatives like California's Proposition 187 and federal welfare reforms. The recent congressional investigation into campaign finance tarred with the taint of "yellow peril" not only Asian nationals and immigrants, but also all Asian American citizens. Some believe that although the redress process did educate many about the historical injustice, reparations, combined with a feeling that "now the system works," also let the government off the hook so that it no longer needed to vigorously oppose racism against Asian Americans.

A lesson, then, vivified by the dilemma of reparations, is that reparations, by its very dynamic, even where salutary in many important ways, can generate disappointments and backlash. This means that even where successful, reparations activists and beneficiaries must be constantly vigilant and work ceaselessly both to hold government accountable for its present actions and to support racial justice efforts of others.

Ideology of Reparations

The third category of the darker underside of the reparations process is the ideology of reparations. Ideology is illuminated by Derrick Bell's interest-convergence thesis. That thesis suggests that dominant groups will only concede "rights" to minorities when the exercise of those rights benefits the dominant groups' overall interests. That is, a government is likely to confer reparations only at a time and in a manner that furthers the interests of those in power.

After the Civil War and during Reconstruction, Congress decided to seize 400 million acres of land from the wealthiest southerners and distribute 40 acres to each adult former slave. Support for the redistribution came from those who believed the establishment of an African American economic base was critical to the dissolution of the economic legacy of slavery.[15] After two years of lobbying, Congress created a commission to distribute all "captured and abandoned land." In January 1865, possessory title to 485,000 acres was awarded to 40,000 former slaves, and many immediately began to settle and work the land. Later that same year, however, in the face of rising southern states' opposition to Reconstruction, President Andrew Johnson rescinded the land reparations program, ordered the black settlers to leave the occupied land, and returned the land to former southern slave owners. Land reparations threatened the nation's newfound peace. So the president scrapped the program, assuring peace among the states, but at incalculable long-term cost to former slaves.

Broadly conceived, the interest-convergence thesis underscores reparations ideology in this instance. While no one ideology controls all situations, several related strands of reparations ideology appear to be significant. I will touch upon one. It involves the characterization of group "worthiness" for reparations.

Professor Chris Iijima has traced the congressional debates preceding Japanese American reparations. Politicians, Japanese American lobbyists, and media largely shaped the reparations debates around the cooperativeness of the internees, the heroism of the 442nd Regimental Combat Team, and the "good citizenship" of Japanese Americans during and after the internment.[16] Mike Masaoka's words, for example, were uplifted in the debates. Masaoka, spokesperson for the Japanese American Citizens League, had urged Japanese American acquiescence to the internment.

> Because I believe in America, and I trust she believes in me, and because I have received innumerable benefits from her I pledge myself to do honor to her at all times and in all places, to support her Constitution, to obey her laws, to respect her Flag, to defend her against all enemies, foreign or domestic, to actively assume my duties and obligations as a citizen, cheerfully and without any reservations whatsoever, on the hope that I may become a better American in a greater America.[17]

According to Iijima's research, Congress, at least in part, appeared to award redress for deserving "superpatriots." It thereby refined the image of a "model minority": those who are loyal to and sacrifice for the United States. This point was reinforced at a recent gathering of redress activists: "There could be no question about our patriotism after people [of the 442nd Regimental Combat Team, who were] locked up in camp, went to war for the U.S. I don't think redress would have passed without the 442nd, without those who gave up their lives and gave themselves for the war effort while their families were interned."[18]

The superpatriot/model minority vision was bolstered by Congressmen Shumway (Japanese Americans are "some of the most respectable, hardworking, loyal Americans that we have in this country"), Brown (Japanese Americans are some of Colorado's "finest citizens . . . some of our most honest, hardworking, and productive human beings"), and Lehman (the bill for reparations will show "the respect we all have for the contributions that Japanese-Americans have made to our society"). There is truth to these statements.

Most interesting, though, according to Iijima's research, is the truth that was not highlighted. The mid-1980s congressional reparations debates avoided reference to Japanese American draft resisters — those who refused to fight while their families were wrongfully imprisoned. The debates also failed to address the riots and work and hunger strikes during which internees voiced discontent with internment conditions. Throughout the internment, considerable disagreement existed within the Japanese American community over cooperation with and support for the government — disagreements later ignored by the narrow framing of redress around sacrifice and patriotism.

Framing reparations worthiness in terms of the superpatriot/model minority served several interests. Certainly, and pragmatically, it aided Japanese American internees — they received long-overdue reparations. That framing also served, it appears, practical and policy government interests. Practically, it enabled the government to award reparations to a relatively small number of "highly deserving" Japanese Americans without opening the floodgates to reparations for others. In terms of policy, it enabled the United States unblushingly to tout democracy and human rights in its hard push against communism in the Soviet Union and central Europe.

I support Japanese American redress. Reparations were well deserved, an appropriate response to a horrendous violation of constitutional liberties and to human suffering. I honor the 442nd for its heroic efforts.

Yet, difficult questions about ideology bear asking. In the big picture, were reparations a monetary buy-off of protest, an assuaging of white American guilt without changes in mainstream attitudes and the restructuring of institutions? Were reparations a transactional exchange: "We'll admit you into the club for now if you don't challenge our exclusion of others"? In my view, Japanese American redress will not likely be seen by the mainstream and by other communities of color as a buy-off, as an exclusive transactional exchange. But that danger exists unless Japanese Americans now and tomorrow press for racial, immigrant, gender, class, and sexual orientation justice in the United States. "The 'danger [of reparations] lies in the possibility of enabling people to "feel good" about each other' for the moment, 'while leaving undisturbed the attendant social realities' creating the underlying conflict.... Redress ... could in the long term 'unwittingly be seduced into becoming one more means of social control that attempts to neutralize the need to strive for justice.' "[19]

With the risks of reparations ideology in mind, what the interest-convergence thesis means is not that African Americans must subordinate their interests to those of white Americans. Rather, it means that blacks need to devise a reparations strategy that serves African American interests while furthering, or appearing to further in some important way, mainstream interests. Those interests, as traditionally described, include the United States' international and domestic reputation on human rights issues, peace in American cities, bolstering the American economy.[20]

Japanese American redress lends moral authority to the African American reparations movement: if the United States can attempt to right one serious historic racial injustice, then why not rectify an even more extensive, longer-standing injustice? It is not clear, however, whether much of America is yet willing to see this liberating lesson, if applied to African Americans, as serving its larger interests.

For instance, the Conyers, Hall, and N'COBRA efforts have fared poorly with the conservative mainstream. Although the United States has sought to expand its political influence in China, the Middle East, and central Europe, there is yet no clearly articulated American interest internationally in African

American "liberation" through reparations. (By contrast, at the time Japanese Americans lobbied hard for reparations, the United States was fighting to win the Cold War against the Soviet bloc and needed to be perceived as liberators.) Nor is there yet developed a cogent vision of far-reaching domestic benefits for the American polity from black redress.

In addition, as mentioned, Congress appeared to bestow reparations upon a "worthy," superpatriotic racial minority. Professor Iijima characterizes this reparations narrative as a celebration of "blind obedience to injustice." The narrative, he suggests, sent a pointed ideological message to those subject to racial and other forms of aggression in America: be "patriotic," do not complain, succeed on your own, and you may be rewarded later. Or, conversely, if your group's "character" marks it as "unworthy," do not come seeking reparations.

Thus, although the moral justification for Japanese American redress applies many times over to African American claims, the political strategies and rhetoric of 1980s Japanese American redress do not translate readily into African American reparations in a late-1990s conservative political environment. How African American reparations proponents handle the superpatriot/model minority narrative and its linkage to the social justification for reparations may be key, particularly in light of politicians' casting of African Americans in recent years as undeserving of special government benefits. Will the rise of overt white racism, the abolition of affirmative action, glass ceiling discrimination, high black male incarceration rates, and the cutbacks in social programs and public assistance generate enough black anger and mainstream anxiety to create a national interest in black reparations? Will the "resegregation of America"—President Clinton's words—detract from America's capacity to police global democracy and thereby create impetus for black reparations? Will Japanese American redress beneficiaries disavow the superpatriot/model minority narrative of reparations worthiness and publicly support African American justice claims? The ideology of reparations poses these open questions to Japanese Americans, African Americans, and all groups seeking some form of redress.

In sum, at the turn of the millennium, how might the African American reparations movement wend its way through obstacles generated by the distorted legal framing of reparations claims, the dilemma of reparations, and the ideology of reparations? How might it translate the moral power of its claims into politically viable action? There is, of course, no encompassing answer. No magic bullet.

What I offer are not specific arguments for African American reparations

—which, I believe are not only appropriate but necessary. Rather, I offer a reframing of the concept of reparations itself that may assist in the formulation of those arguments as part of a larger political strategy of "repair." This is my third thematic point.

Reparations as Repair

The many ideas raised thus far point toward a reframing of the prevailing reparations paradigm—a new framing embracing the notion of reparations as "repair" (rather than legal compensation). Indeed, reparation, in singular, means "repair." It encompasses acts of repairing damage to the material conditions of racial group life—disbursing money to those in need and transferring land ownership to those dispossessed, building schools, churches, community centers, and medical clinics, creating tax incentives and loan programs for businesses and scholarships for students. It also encompasses acts of restoring injured human psyches—enabling those harmed to live with, but not in, history. Finally, reparations as repair fosters the restoration of broken relationships, the mending of tears in the social fabric, the repairing of breaches in the polity.

For example, slavery, Jim Crow apartheid, and mainstream resistance to integration inflicted horrendous harms upon African American individuals and their communities, harms now apparently exacerbated by the increasing resegregation of America. Reparations improving the material conditions of life for African Americans and their communities are appropriate and just.

In addition, the racial harms to African Americans also wounded the American polity. They grated on America's sense of morality (do we really believe in freedom, equality, and justice?); they destabilized the American psyche (are we really oppressors?); they generated personal discomfort and fear in daily interactions (will there be retribution?); and they continue to do so. Reparations for African Americans, conceived as repair, can also help mend this larger tear in the social fabric for the benefit of blacks, Latinos, Native Americans, Asian Americans, as well as mainstream white America.

So viewed, reparations are potentially transformative. For both bestower and beneficiary, they "condemn exploitation and adopt a vision of a more just world."

And the only way to realize this brighter side of the reparations process, I submit, is to grapple with its darker potential. How Japanese Americans (and not just Nisei and Sansei but also young Yonsei adults) respond in the new millennium, particularly in the face of African American reparations claims, may well determine the legacy of Japanese Americans redress. What's next?

Notes

This essay is based on a talk given at the UCLA Asian American Studies Center, spring 1998.

1. Verdun, "If the Shoe Fits, Wear It," 597, 647.

2. Eric K. Yamamoto, "Friend, Foe or Something Else: Social Meanings of Redress and Reparations," *Denver Journal of International Law and Politics* 20 (1992): 223. See also Sarah L. Brew, "Making Amends for History: Legislative Reparations for Japanese Americans and Other Minority Groups," *Law and Inequality* 8 (1989): 179; and Tyron J. Sheppard and Richard Nevis, "Constitutional Equality/Reparations at Last," *University of Western Louisiana Law Review* 22 (1991): 105.

3. Yamamoto, "Friend, Foe or Something Else."

4. Eric K. Yamamoto, "Race Apologies," *Iowa Journal of Race, Gender and Justice* 1 (1997).

5. See Salim Muwakkil, "Does America Owe Blacks Reparations?," *In These Times*, 30 June 1997, describing mounting community activism in support of reparations. See also Verdun, describing five African American reparations movements since the Civil War.

6. In 1995, each of the nine survivors was awarded $150,000 in reparations, and the descendants of persons killed in the massacre received between $315 and $22,000 for loss of property. Lori Robinson, "Righting a Wrong among Black Americans: The Debate Is Escalating over Whether an Apology for Slavery Is Enough," *Seattle Post-Intelligencer*, 29 June 1997.

7. See Commission to Study Reparation Proposals for African-Americans Act, HR 40, 105th Congress 1997.

8. Scholars have made compelling moral arguments for African American reparations based on the economic and psychological harms of slavery, of Jim Crow violence and legalized segregation, and of continuing institutional discrimination. See Boris Bittker, *The Case for Black Reparations* (New York: Random House, 1973); and Derrick A. Bell Jr., *Race, Racism and American Law*, 2nd ed. (Boston: Little, Brown, 1980). For Native Hawaiian reparations based on U.S.-aided illegal overthrow of the sovereign Hawaiian government in 1893, see Melody Kapilialoha MacKenzie, *Native Hawaiian Rights Handbook* (Honolulu: Office of Hawaiian Affairs, 1991); and Haunani-Kay Trask, *From a Native Daughter: Colonialism and Sovereignty in Hawaii* (Monroe, Me.: Common Courage Press, 1993).

9. Devon Carbado, unpublished manuscript, on file with author.

10. *Korematsu v. United States*, 323 U.S. 214, 1944.

11. Joseph William Singer, "Reparation" (1997), unpublished manuscript on file with author.

12. Alex Bundy, "Gypsies Demand Compensation for Suffering during Holocaust," *Honolulu Advertiser*, 4 August 1997, A10.

13. Singer.

14. Caitlin Rother, "Should an Apology for Slavery Be Made? African-Americans Have Mixed Opinions," *San Diego Union-Tribune*, 12 August 1997, 1.

15. Rhonda V. Magee, "Note, the Master's Tools, from the Bottom Up: Responses to African-American Reparations Theory in Mainstream and Outsider Remedies Discourse," *Virginia Law Review* 79, no. 863 (1993): 906–907.

16. Chris Iijima, "Reparations and the 'Model Minority' Ideology of Acquiescence: The Necessity to Refuse the Return to Original Humiliation," *Boston College Law Review* 40, no. 385 (1998), and *Boston College Third World Journal* (1998).

17. Mike Masaoka, 134 *Congressional Record* H6308–09 (daily edition, August 4, 1988).

18. Takeshi Nakayama, "Rare Victory of Spirit over Numbers," *Rafu Shimpo*, 16 September 1997, A1.

19. Yamamoto, "Friend, Foe, or Something Else," 232.

20. Ibid., 231.

The Reparations Movement

An Assessment of Recent and Current Activism

SAM ANDERSON, MUNTU MATSIMELA,
AND YUSUF NURUDDIN

Yusuf Nuruddin interviews veteran activist attorney Muntu Matsimela and veteran activist scholar Sam Anderson, organizers of the Reparations Mobilization Coalition, for their analyses and candid impressions of the current status of the reparations movement. This interview was conducted on December 15, 2002, through the courtesy, and via the recording studios, of WBAI Pacifica Radio in New York City.

YUSUF NURUDDIN: In assessing the current status of the reparations movement, we should give a little historical background, beginning with the Durban Conference of August 2001. Muntu, you attended the conference. So, first give us your impressions of Durban and then we'll move forward to where we are today.

MUNTU MATSIMELA: Durban, that is, the World Conference against Racism, Xenophobia, and Other Related Intolerances [WCAR] was essentially a three-year process where people met in large gatherings called prep-cons [preparatory conferences]. These were regional meetings that occurred in the Americas, in Europe, in Africa, in Asia. There were also intersession meetings where everybody — all the various regions — met at the same time. These were held at the United Nations in Geneva. I participated in WCAR activities and speaking in various preparatory conferences starting around December 2000. And then I attended a large gathering, specifically for the African and African Descendant Caucus, which was held in Vienna April 27–29, 2001. Then I was in the second intersession preparatory conference in Geneva, in May 2001. Then, of course, I went to Durban, for the conference itself, which was essentially in two parts. The first part was the Non-Governmental Organization [NGO] conference, from August 27 to September 1; then came the government portion of the WCAR, September 1–8. I participated in the full range of those discussions, both the NGO and the government portions of the conference, and the various committees and activities, largely through the African and African Descendants Caucus, which was a group of Africans throughout Africa and the diaspora who built an alliance through the WCAR process and unified with various other coalitions and groups—indigenous groups, social movements, and regional coalitions and alliances.

The WCAR allowed the critical issues of transatlantic slave trade, systemic slavery, systemic racism, and colonialism to be brought to the world stage by African people and people of African descent. Really, largely for the first time, they were taken seriously, even though it was a major struggle throughout the three-year process for those issues to be discussed qualitatively. Ultimately, we prevailed in having them discussed, and in getting UN memberstates as well as hundreds of NGOs from around the world to participate in this discussion. What was achieved was unprecedented in terms of the level of unity, the level of respect and consideration that was given to issues of transatlantic slave trade, with slavery being declared a crime against humanity. This declaration was one of the primary goals of the African and African Descendant group. The unity that we forged with our brothers and sisters from Africa, from the motherland, on the question of colonialism and then systemic racism brought the diaspora together in a way that was unprecedented. It turned strategically and tactically on building coalitions, on lobbying the other member-states of the UN. Subsequently, after the WCAR was over, a number of the groups, particularly African/African Descendant groups, created a strategy to continue the work. Out of Durban came the African and African Descendant Caucus international steering committee, of which I became a member, as well as a strategy to have a follow-up conference in Barbados in October 2002.

YUSUF: I would like to ask you about the role that the United States played—or failed to play—in the conference. There has been a rapid acceleration in world events since August 2001, and our memories might be cloudy about pre-9/11 events. So first of all, refresh our memories about the composition of the U.S. government's delegation to the Durban conference. Do I remember correctly that President Bush refused to attend, but that he sent Secretary of State Colin Powell, and that Powell basically played a negative role in terms of creating disunity around the question of reparations?

MUNTU: Well, actually, the secretary of state was not sent. The president of the United States never had any intention of going to the World Conference against Racism even though many heads of state did come to it. But in the main, you had heads of state as well as the foreign ministers; the secretary of state would have been a high-level delegation. Up to the last couple of months, the U.S. government tried to make it appear as if it was still unsettled whether or not the secretary of state would attend the Durban conference.

But ultimately they decided against it and sent a delegation of low-level bureaucrats and other individuals, which was really insulting. Some government members — some members of Congress — attended as members of the U.S. delegation, but it was clearly very low-level in comparison to the full delegations that were sent by most of the world. The United States never supported the World Conference against Racism, as we understand.

This was the third UN conference against racism. The first one was in 1978, which the United States boycotted. The second was in 1983, and again the United States boycotted. It threatened to boycott the 2001 conference in Durban, but because of the pressure that was being put on them, they ultimately did send a delegation. But they were clearly opposed philosophically and politically to the issues, particularly to the fact that people of African descent were going to insist that their issue of the transatlantic slave trade and of reparations was going to be raised qualitatively and categorically. The U.S. government continuously opposed having that issue discussed at the World Conference and did everything they possibly could for two years to put pressure on various governments — particularly African governments — not to discuss the issue of reparations, not to discuss the issue of the transatlantic slave trade being a crime against humanity. They put economic and political pressure on these governments and overtly tried to keep the American people from even knowing about the WCAR, which was their real strategy in order to prevent any kind of qualitative discussion in the media and throughout the country on the issues that would be covered at the Durban conference.

YUSUF: One of the charges in the mainstream press was that the Palestinians were "disrupting the conference" because they kept insisting that the conferees and official conference documents adopt the language that "Zionism is racism." Can you comment on that?

MUNTU: First of all, that never happened. But what was clear was that the U.S. government was using that as a red herring. It was using the issue of the so-called link that was being made between Zionism and racism, which they maintained would be raised at the World Conference. It was really just a smoke screen. Their real opposition was to the issue of reparations being discussed fully and completely by member states, by their allies, by their friends, by people who oppose U.S. policies in the world. The Palestinian people came obviously to deal with the issue of their condition in Palestine, their condition with respect to their fifty-year struggle for self-determination, for an independent Palestinian state. They did equate Israeli occupation with the occupation that occurred during apartheid in South Africa, and they talked about the conditions of racist treatment, disparate treatment, human rights violations that occur repeatedly on the West Bank. These were the issues they raised. But they did not come with any strategy to block discussions. They were fully respectful during the entire conference. Yasser Arafat, by the way, spoke at the opening ceremony of the round-table with a number of heads of state.

The Palestinians had issues that they were raising. They were a very public force, a very vibrant force in the NGO conference as well as the government portion of the conference, but at no time was the issue of Zionism as racism raised in any way that elevated it as a central issue. This never occurred. In fact, when it was raised, it was raised by the U.S. government, not at Durban but in the media during the months leading up to Durban, in effect, as a rationale or pretext for them bowing out and not attending, not sending a full delegation. And then ultimately, the U.S. government officially pulled out of the World Conference against Racism. I think it was around September 3 that they pulled their delegation out and left — according to them — based on this issue. And it was an absolute lie, an absolute falsehood. That issue was never raised to any controversial level. In fact, it wasn't raised at all. We never heard about it, we never discussed it during the whole course of the World Conference against Racism in any way, shape, or form. Yes, the Palestinians had their agenda, as they should have had, just as a host of people from all over the world brought their issues, as did various organizations — NGOs, Jewish NGOs, as well as organizations representing the Israeli government — they all came. And so you'd think that this issue had some prominence — some ascendancy — and it was absolutely not true.

YUSUF: Would you care to comment on the group known as the Durban 400 and what impact they had on the conference, if any?

MUNTU: The Durban 400 was the group of Africans and African-descendant people from the United States largely led by the December 12th movement. December 12th was leadership of Africans, African-descendants in general who had been engaged in organizing and mobilizing for the World Conference against Racism since the very beginning, actually since 1997. They were one of the first groups to promote the conference here in the States. Also included in that was the Chicago-based chapter of the National Black United Front and Dr. Conrad Worrill. So you had the two groups, Chicago and New York, that is, the National Black United Front and the December 12th movement, who were the organizers of the Durban 400. Given that D12 had consultative status with the UN and with the Organization of African Unity, and had been going back and forth to Geneva and to Africa for about ten to twelve years and had substantial experience in lobbying and working with the various diplomats and government delegations at the UN, their experience was used and well received. They put together the Durban 400 as their own organizational process and they brought that group of people to the WCAR, largely to lobby the government portion of the conference — not to participate in the NGO portion of the conference, which many people felt was an error on their part. But they participated fully in the government portion, lobbying Africans, lobbying the various countries, the various groupings or alliances of governments around the world. And together with the African and African Descendant Caucus, we represented a formidable force — building alliances, building joint strategies with the various indigenous movements, the various peoples participating in the conference. So I would say that the Durban 400 had a significant role to play in bringing the issue of the transatlantic slave trade, the issue of systemic racism, of slavery and reparations, the rights of the descendants of these atrocities, of these crimes against humanity — they played a major role in bringing those issues formally to the WCAR.

YUSUF: What role, if any, did Silas Muhammed and the Lost/Found Nation of Islam play on an international level in terms of reparations?

MUNTU: Well, Silas's group, the Lost/Found Nation of Islam, of course were at the WCAR, but not visibly. They participated, they supported the work that was done by the African and African Descendant Caucus, and we generally worked together because we all had the same agenda. We all had the strategy to get the transatlantic slave trade, to get slavery, and to get the issue of reparations adopted formally by the WCAR. I don't know the specifics of their participation, but I do know that they were there, and given the fact that they had been involved in the UN process for a number of years prior to the Durban conference, I'm sure they were consistent in their work and efforts.

YUSUF: On this question, I'm going to turn to Sam [Anderson]. I want to know what impact September 11 had on derailing the movement for reparations.

SAM ANDERSON: The September 11 incident had, I sensed, the effect of a temporary setback. We, meaning the Reparations Coalition, had been planning a conference for November 2001. And we felt prior to September 11 that there would be most likely six hundred to eight hundred people that would show, and we had a little over three hundred people that showed. But by December there were a number of things up and running about the issue of reparations in North America, and then by the winter, obviously, with the development of the corporate lawsuits and so forth, reparations in terms of black America was back high on the agenda. A lot of people were fearful of traveling during the few months right after September 11, because of the kind of high-security madness that was occurring on airplanes and so forth. But I think that folks got to realize that the issue of reparations was so important that the need to communicate and travel turned out to be much more urgent than being afraid of what the state was going to do in terms of the clampdown with the security apparatus and the antiterrorist nonsense. To make a long story short, September 11 was, for me, a sixty- to maybe eighty-day slowdown of the reparations momentum. But after that, it really picked up again across the country.

YUSUF: The reason I ask the question is because the sense that I received from a lot of activists was that they were all fired up to make this a major issue . . . make a major activist onslaught and put pressure on the government . . . make reparations the burning issue of 2001. And because of the attacks on the World Trade Center and the Pentagon, the nation's attention was focused elsewhere and reparations just got "lost in the sauce," so to speak.

SAM: Yes, on one level, in terms of the media, yes. In terms of the media, definitely it got "lost in the sauce" for a few months. But in terms of the actual work on the ground by various organizations, on college campuses, within organized labor, within the religious community, the reparations movement has continually grown since September 11.

YUSUF: Now, you were one of the major organizers behind the Reparations Mobilization Coalition, and I wanted you to give us a history of that group, including the November 2001 conference you mentioned.

SAM: Well, the Reparations Mobilization Coalition felt that it was important to come together to deal with the issue of education at the grassroots level around reparations, to begin to create a mobilization effort at the grassroots level nationwide. And we felt that it was very, very important that the basic education — what is reparations, why we should be demanding reparations, how we should go about struggling for it, and what form reparations should take — had to be addressed on the grass-roots level. So we called the conference to bring together as many as possible of the brothers and sisters who were working in and around the issue of reparations, to begin to address those questions. The other factor that we included in the development of the conference was the international character of the reparations movement in the twenty-first century. The reparations movement, as Muntu pointed out in terms of the WCAR, is an international struggle, and we in North America are merely part of that worldwide struggle. So we had black people from other parts of the world who also were able to come and participate in this, particularly from England and out of the Caribbean and South Africa, which was essential to the whole development of our follow-through, what we planned to do afterward.

The other thing we realized was that we also need to begin work on creating a National Reparations Congress, where we would invite all the reparations groups and key individuals to come together, to be able to have a united front strategy and tactic around the struggle for reparations. We realize that when we throw the net out there very wide, there are a number of people, a number of organizations, who would not necessarily come into that fold, but we understand that the majority of our brothers and sisters doing reparations work would come together on that. So that's something that we are currently looking at developing and possibly having a National Reparations Congress in 2004.

YUSUF: How does the work of the Reparations Mobilization Coalition differ from that of N'COBRA [National Coalition of Blacks for Reparations in America]?

SAM: We're focusing on three major things right now. One is grass-roots education and mobilization through developing—in conjunction with the Global African Congress (a post-Durban, post-Barbados formation)—a reparations primer, an inexpensive little book on reparations that would be used throughout North America, primarily at this stage to inform people on the basics. Second is the work of informing organizations and reparations activists on the importance of building the National Reparations Congress, hopefully in 2004, if we can begin to mobilize on a strong level in 2003. Third, since the reparations struggle is a full-time struggle, we realize that if we don't have organizers and an office with all the necessary twenty-first-century equipment and full-time staff, the movement will be stunted at best. So we have to raise the necessary money. We cannot move in 2003 without having a central place, a telephone, staff, travel expenses, material to work out of the office, et cetera, et cetera. The reparations movement would only be rhetorical and symbolic if we don't have that. So those are the three things that we're really concentrating on for the next couple of years.

YUSUF: What about the difference between your work and that of N'COBRA?

SAM: N'COBRA's work is, right now, primarily geared to develop a presence in 2003 within the halls of Congress. In other words, what they're doing at this point—besides some basic grass-roots mobilization and creating chapters throughout the country—is planning a major lobbying effort to be directed at elected officials, with a particular focus on getting the HR 40 bill, the John Conyers bill to study reparations, up and running. I was at a meeting yesterday with N'COBRA people in New Jersey, and this is what they had laid out as one of their primary objectives of work. And I think the other level of work—which is secondary, if not tertiary—is building the Global African Congress in North America, since Sister Dorothy Lewis, who's their national president, is also the U.S. representative to the international steering committee of the Global African Congress that came out of Barbados.

YUSUF: Let me ask a question for Muntu since you brought up the issue of legislation. I also want to bring up the issue of litigation and since Muntu is a lawyer I want to ask him about those two issues. I want to talk about the recent and very prominent lawsuit brought by Deadria Farmer-Paellmann. And I'd like you to make the distinction between the legislative efforts and the litigation efforts and just how you see the direction of either one of those.

MUNTU: Well, the lawsuit initiated by Deadria Farmer-Paellmann as a class-action plaintiff is a lawsuit against corporations, specifically insurance companies like Aetna, and railways like CSX. In the lawsuit, as you know, the charge is—

YUSUF: I think FleetBoston is the third.

MUNTU: FleetBoston is another one—that they benefited from slavery, that is to say, that the corporations that they were, prior to the name change, during the period of slavery, benefited and profited from slavery in various ways. Aetna Life actually wrote insurance policies that protected the slave traders in terms of their property and so on—the slave ships during the Middle Passage. So these corporations are being sued in a class-action lawsuit, the class being all African descendants from slaves. And again, the litigation strategy is part of the panorama, or overview, of the various approaches to the issue of reparations. Lawsuits, by their very nature, give exposure to the issue they indict—the proper targets that they expose—in a way which is formal and official. And it brings attention to the issue in a way that's unique to litigation, in this country and around the world. Indeed, much of the motivation—aside from the broad political implications of having the transatlantic slave trade and slavery being declared crimes against humanity, with reparations being owed to the descendants of these crimes and atrocities—in effect had to do with the legal ramifications, in that for crimes against humanity as declared by international law, there is no statute of limitations. Thus one's standing becomes a proper issue within the context of crimes against humanity.

Other lawsuits are being prepared by N'COBRA—reparations lawsuits, some of which will be against corporations as well as the government. The reparations lawsuits are being filed by the Reparations Coordinating Committee, which is a group of attorneys led by prominent litigators such as

Charles Ogletree Jr., Johnny Cochrane (deceased), and William Gary. Those lawsuits, as I understand, will in fact be against the U.S. government. So again, we see in the Reparations Mobilization Coalition—in issues that Sam and I have been raising, in the course of our speaking around the world and in this country, at various conferences and at all kinds of events and gatherings—that litigation, the legal strategy with respect to reparations, is an important strategy. But it is one that has its limitations as well. And those limitations are largely based—as we understand the way the court system works—on an issue of reparations. Given the nature of the issue, particularly when you're talking about reparations for crimes against humanity, for slavery, for ill-gotten gains from slavery, from the labor of slaves—not to even go into all of the very, very important related issues of dehumanization and degradation, physical harm, mass rape, mass murder, mayhem, mischief, destruction of culture, historical memory—given all these things, we see litigation (legal strategy) as one of several strategies that must be utilized in an overall reparations strategic program. And we see litigation just as we see legislation, both of which have clear limitations.

All litigation is going to wind up in the Supreme Court, if the Supreme Court chooses to hear it. That is to say, it will be taken to the Supreme Court by either side: by the plaintiff, that is to say the class of Africans that the reparations lawsuits—and they all are class-action lawsuits—represent; or by the defendants, whether corporate entities, estates, or state or federal government entities. The legal expertise on both sides will be very high. So the Supreme Court will obviously do one of three things. First, they'll decide either to hear it or not to hear it, in which case they'll send it back to the local court or U.S. Court of Appeals, or the original court where it was heard. If they hear it, they will probably decide against it. If they don't hear it, they may indeed make a decision that they do not have the jurisdiction to hear issues of reparations because it represents largely a political issue and must be resolved not by the judiciary but by the legislative branch of the government, and they will in fact send it to Congress for its ultimate decision.

So, within the context of strategic approaches to the reparations movement, we place political mobilization of the great numbers of our people and allies and supporters in this country as the essential ingredient, the essential factor in achieving reparations. One approach impacts on the others. And so that's the way we see litigation. We think that all litigation has an initial impact, and the nature of litigation is that these things go into virtually a cave for years while they're going through the court system, and reparations lawsuits take many years for resolution one way or the other. But the political mobilization is a day-to-day reality that must go forward to build a political movement, and the movement impacts on how the courts indeed will eventually look at the issue. This is not to say that it may be a determining factor, but clearly it's a factor and ultimately, the legislative branches of government are obviously 100 percent impacted by political mobilization on these issues. So, here it is. And of course, the international is the other area that we see as critical and that we identify within the reparations movement.

YUSUF: Two questions then. First of all, numerous plaintiffs are bringing various test cases to various court jurisdictions and ultimately maybe to the Supreme Court. Isn't there a sort of weakness in this strategy since, on a national movement level, there really isn't a coherent, systematic, or uniform method of filing these litigation cases?

MUNTU: I agree. Clearly, that's the reason why — in the Reparations Mobilization Committee — we raise, as Sam spoke to, the need for a Congress in 2004. I would hope we would have one next year [2003], quite frankly. That's a national congress on reparations where we'll have a democratic assembly. A cross-section of our community in this country will come together and essentially decide what will be the program of the reparations movement and how we would impact all of the various areas of strategy, of mass mobilization, international strategy, litigation, the legal strategy and legislative strategy such as the issue of HR 40, which many of us support. Indeed, we all support HR 40 although we may have different opinions as to its strategic importance at this time. But also, state legislative reparations initiatives will be going on in various state jurisdictions throughout the United States. So a congress would be a way of consolidating this strategy within legal strategy.

Obviously, some people think that having multilitigations or multilitigants on reparations is a positive thing. That's one school. The other school feels that it creates confusion, chaos, division within the overall reparations movement. Obviously a family of African Americans — people of African descent — in the United States may identify, for example, an estate, where they trace their family and determine that it profited by having slaves and being slave owners, and choose to sue that estate. Of course, they have the right to do that. But having this myriad of litigations — with respect to corporations or corporate entities as well as other governmental entities — by various plaintiffs that are not part of a unified cohesive plan that's based on strategic unity and alliance of the reparations movement, I believe is an error and in effect can do more harm than good.

YUSUF: I said I had two questions. The second one is — and I want to ask you first and then Sam — since you talked about the political character of reparations and the political mobilization that's necessary, how do you see reparations in relation to the civil rights struggle that Martin Luther King Jr. led and the human rights struggle that Malcolm X talked about?

MUNTU: First of all, clearly Malcolm supported reparations, so Malcolm was one of the primary and more prominent leaders in our history who raised the issue of human rights. And they even counterposed the human rights issue—the human rights aspect of our movement—to its civil rights aspect. Malcolm saw human rights as a higher level of political mobilization for black people in this country because it took our struggle outside its purely domestic context and put it in an international arena. He saw it as the proper forum when an entire people are opposed by a government and cannot get any redress from the judiciary and criminal justice apparatus of that government. They must go to another forum, and that forum, he believed, was the world forum of the United Nations, the World Court, and the international community. And so, he elevated human rights strategically above civil rights.

But clearly, reparations as a movement, as an issue, has been around—was being raised officially—for at least 140 years in this country, in various ways: in courts, in Congress, in the Senate, in the late nineteenth century and early and mid-twentieth century, by many different people, very prominent people, Queen Mother Moore, Malcolm X, Paul Robeson, a number of people of various organizations and various times. The Black Panther Party, the Nation of Islam, and so on, raised the issue of reparations throughout the 1960s and 1970s and 1980s, and various groups as we know them today are prominent in the reparations movement (see Documents, section 4). Malcolm saw human rights as the most strategic forum for the issue of our movement, and reparations would have clearly fallen into that category. We see reparations as being both a civil rights issue and a human rights issue. When we were in Durban, the national civil rights organizations—for example, the Black Leadership Forum, which encompassed the NAACP, the Urban League, SCLC [Southern Christian Leadership Conference]—all supported the various points that were being put forth by the African/African Descendants Caucus: the transatlantic slave trade being declared a crime against humanity; slavery; systemic racism, colonialism, and the right of its descendants to be compensated for those atrocities. All these organizations saw it as a civil rights issue because it talked about systemic racism—structural racism—as it occurs: the ongoing damages that came out of slavery, that came out of Jim Crow, that came out of U.S. apartheid. And if you fight, if you're a civil rights activist, if you've been involved in the civil rights movement, all those issues are raised within the universe of the reparations issue. So, there's a direct relationship—an inextricable link—between civil rights and human rights; and reparations encompasses both of them.

YUSUF: I want to ask the same question, basically, to Sam. What I want you to comment on is the fact that the civil rights movement sought certain political gains and political rights, but it really didn't do anything in terms of economic justice and how reparations actually fulfills that mission.

SAM: Well, my comment . . . I think you answered it in your question: the civil rights movement really was a limited movement and it didn't address the issues of economic justice nor the issues of — as Brother Muntu pointed out — the past crimes against humanity. The civil rights movement had really reached its point of exhaustion with affirmative action. Affirmative action in practice, when we look at it objectively, impacts white women more than any other sector of the labor force. So for many of the "civil rights organizations," reparations was and is the logical next step for them to take. And I think that's one of the reasons why they were there in Durban supporting the struggle for reparations, and today, many of the organizations do that, either indirectly or directly.

I think another factor, which Muntu has pointed out, in terms of the struggle for human rights that is also very central to our struggle today is the issue — two issues — one around political prisoners and prisoners in general, and the other around education. The United Nations last year — in October through January — had a special researcher on education come to the United States to see whether education in this country had any human rights violations. And this European woman came — right after 9/11 — and the experience in traveling across this country blew her mind. She wrote a very powerful indictment of various human rights violations around education, and the central piece of this was the issue of racism, white supremacy: systematically making sure that people of color — particularly African Americans and Latinos — were undereducated and/or miseducated. In fact, she did two documents: one formally for the United Nations, and the second one informally, on the devastating education disparities she found in New York City. These kinds of documents, in terms of our mobilization/education work, could be used to bring people around to understanding that when we struggle for education we can no longer just be confined to the issue of civil rights, narrow legal issues; there is a serious human rights violation: the miseducation/undereducation of black people is a criminal act. And this miseducation/undereducation is a state-sanctioned process. So I think that the motion now coming in 2003 around certain issues that were at one point looking like civil rights is now going to be a struggle around human rights.

The other thing I wanted to point out around the education issue is the end of affirmative action as we know it, at the university level, and then the systematic reversal — or the attempt to reverse — every single aspect of affirmative action when it comes to people of African or Latino descent. The University of Michigan case, the cases that are developing in Texas and so forth, are cases where the right wing, the rabid racists, are trying to undermine and reverse what little gains happened for black people and Latinos under affirmative action. Similarly, within the job market also, we are beginning to see the reversal. And so, many organizations and individuals who are working around civil rights are beginning to see that it's important to take it beyond that level of civil rights — so confining in the international arena for the human rights struggle.

YUSUF: You had mentioned political prisoners. Do you want to elaborate on that issue?

SAM: Very simply, our political prisoners — black political prisoners in this country — are our freedom fighters; they were fighting for the freedom of our people. Historically, if we didn't have the vestiges of slavery — that is, racism and racial oppression and class oppression in the black community — we would not have the need for freedom fighters. So it's one of those demands that we feel is central to the development and actualization of reparations: the freeing of our freedom fighters, the brothers and sisters who were out there in the forefront, struggling for our freedom, and got swept up by the counterintelligence program and imprisoned on trumped-up charges — most, if not all of them, imprisoned for longer than any Mafia character or corporate crime person that might have been imprisoned at that same time. We say that the time is now that they should be released without any fallback or anything, but with compensation for all the time they have spent in prison. In other words, they'd be released not with just ten dollars in their pocket but with all the compensation that's necessary for them to survive in the future and for the criminal act of criminalizing them and putting them in prison.

YUSUF: Thus far we've been linking reparations to the black liberation movement or the social movement for justice among African Americans. But can we talk about the proletarian character of reparations and why this is really a working-class agenda and why the Left in general — white or black — should support reparations?

SAM: Yes. Historically, the vast majority of black people — 90 percent and at one point 100 percent almost — were in fact the working class in this society during the time of slavery. We were the laborers, and at the same time we were capital. We were the people who were at the primary point of production of almost everything in North American society. So historically, people of African descent have been at the center of the working class in this society. Postslavery, similar things developed in terms of the vast majority of black people being in the working class at various levels. And in the present stage, because of racism—systemic, institutionalized, state-sanctioned racism—we have the vast majority of our people in highly underdeveloped, depressed communities and in extremely low-paying positions within labor, and because of that, we are not able to actualize our potential, our great potential. The issue of class discrimination in this society is exacerbated within the black community because of the issue of racism—systemic, institutionalized racism—that keeps us from advancing in any sectors of the working class or beyond. All skilled labor positions are defined in racial terms, and those of us who are able to get into labor positions, when we do have the skills, are there because of the struggles of our people within organized labor and within the state and federal legal apparatus. That's one thing. The other thing—which is very, very fundamental for us to continually acknowledge—is that 90 to 95 percent of black people in the United States are in the working class, in spite of what they may see on television or in the movies or in magazines. We are in the working class; the vast majority of us who are in that working class are, in fact, working. Even though there is a high unemployment rate, we are working. But we are working, as I stated earlier, in the lowest positions. We are racially discriminated against within the labor force and that is a vestige, a holdover, or an evolution from the days of slavery.

YUSUF: I have basically two more questions and either one of you can handle them. The first one is about the August 17th [2002] "Millions for Reparations" march on Washington, and the second one is about the Barbados Conference. Sam, do you want to handle the march on Washington and maybe Muntu can handle the Barbados Conference?

SAM: Yeah. Very succinctly, the August 17th march on Washington was a good idea that was underdeveloped. And by that I mean the organizers needed to realize that we needed more time to mobilize people. They—meaning the December 12th movement and the Chicago grouping of the National Black United Front—made the call right after returning from Durban in 2001, for the demo to happen in 2002. We needed more time, particularly with the 9/11 event, like I said, setting us back a month or two. And the other factor was that there was really no formal coalition work in organizing for that rally; people and organizations had to go to D12 or to the Black United Front and work within their definitions of things. The reparations movement by its very nature demands coordinated work, cooperative work, coalition work. This was not forthcoming in the development of the August 17th effort, and when it did happen it was at the very last minute, within a month before the development, because then, at that point, people in D12 and in the Black United Front realized that they didn't have the money, the resources, or the human power to pull off a major demonstration in Washington, D.C. We, the Reparations Mobilization Coalition, supported it with great reluctance, but felt that it was important that we try to help out in various ways to get people there. But the main thing was that when you're doing something as large as a march on Washington for reparations, you need to spend the time with all the different constituencies in bringing them together into one united march-organizing or rally-organizing committee. And everybody would have an input into that.

The last thing I want to say is that there was absolutely no mobilization effort in the black community in Washington, D.C. That was an absolute no-no; we never ever should go into Washington, D.C. and try to organize something about black people without spending considerable time mobilizing in the Washington-Baltimore area. It just didn't happen. There were forces there who would be able to bring out probably at a minimum ten thousand black people just in that area, if it was done from the early stages. But it didn't happen. So we learned from that. We learned seriously from that, and we move on from there and understand that any major public outcry or demonstration for reparations we do on a coalition basis and we do it in a systematic way and we take our time to do it. We don't rush into it unless it's an emergency; then there's a whole other level of strategy and tactic that we work on.

YUSUF: Thank you. I want to ask this last question to Muntu. I just want to ask you about the conference in Barbados, unless you had any comments on the march on Washington.

MUNTU: Well, I think Sam said basically everything that I thought was important to say about the mobilization. I just think that reparations is an issue that demands national unity. A cohesive, unified strategy built on a broad consensus draws a full spectrum of our community because it impacts every single individual in our community. Therefore, you don't even make a call until you get that consensus. You have to have a unified strategy to build a movement. That would then allow you to make the kind of accurate evaluation — an assessment of your resources, of your organizational infrastructure capabilities, your mobilization capabilities. And then, when you're able to make that accurate assessment, then you're able to logistically determine dates and times that are consistent with that assessment and don't come out there prematurely, which then is reflected in low turnouts. You cannot have national mobilization on reparations where you're addressing a community of millions and millions of people and have small turnouts. It's just not something that makes political sense.

As for the Barbados Conference, it was an African and African Descendants conference, a follow-up to the World Conference against Racism. It's seen as a conference for reparations, even though myriad issues were incorporated: health care, education, globalization issues, issues of gender, issues of criminal justice, international community justice issues; youth, organizing and mobilizing youth and other key constituencies in our community. The conference took place October 2–6, 2002. Barbados activists, in alignment with elements of the Barbados government, gave full support for the venue. This was the first major global conference of Africans and people of African descent since Durban.

When we're going to talk about something like a world conference, objective and scientific evaluation and assessment is absolutely important. That is to say, you must do feasibility studies; you must do objective assessments of the capacity of organizations, the capacity of venues, the politics of a given country where the conference is being held, the geopolitical issues that may impact the conference at any given time; and then you make a determination about when and where you will try to mobilize and organize a world conference. It was critical that these things be done, and I would just say as a general criticism that that was not done to the extent that was necessary for the mobilization in Barbados. The conference in Barbados occurred; there were a number of key issues of discussion, most of which I listed. All were discussed and there were working groups in each area. Those working groups met throughout the conference and made critical resolutions and reports and drafts on things that were discussed and agreed upon. There were approximately eight hundred people in attendance, with maybe one thousand the first evening.

Again, the weaknesses I think were because of the resources. We needed probably something in the neighborhood of $750,000 to $1 million to have a conference of that nature. We have to bring people from throughout the African diaspora, and as we all know, our people do not have the capacity to participate in a global conference without some financial assistance. That was one of the objectives of the conference, but because a number of things, including reliance on certain funding promises made by the Barbadan government, never reached fruition, it fell through. As a consequence, we weren't able to get participation from African Latin America, Afro-Latin American countries such as Brazil, Venezuela, Uruguay, Colombia, Honduras, Costa Rica. Even countries in the Caribbean were not able to send people. Also unable to go were many Afro-Europeans, with the exception of those from the United Kingdom, who sent a large delegation.

YUSUF: What we heard through the black news media—those of us who were not able to attend—was that the conference fell into chaos over the question of whether whites should be excluded. Was that a major factor?

MUNTU: I don't know if "chaos" is the word I would use. I think "controversy" would be much closer to the actual set of circumstances. Clearly, political decisions were made that did not lend clarity but lent confusion to the process. Indeed, a decision was made at the beginning of the conference that was raised by, in particular, certain delegations to the congress about participation of non-Africans. Clearly, this issue should never even have been discussed because the conference had already invited . . . First of all, it was a conference [not only] for Africans and people of African descent, but also for their friends and supporters, their allies. If you looked at our website on the conference in Barbados, it clearly stated this fact. You cannot invite people to a global conference—have them come hundreds of miles, some even thousands of miles—and then disinvite them after they arrive. So that clearly was a fundamental error, in my opinion, and I am a member of the Global African Congress, the organization that was founded in Barbados. I'm also a member of the international steering committee that was elected there. And so you have an issue that created a lot of controversy and bad feelings, and clearly overshadowed all of the very, very positive, progressive, and, in fact, radical discussions that took place.

I think that this is going to be an ongoing dynamic and discussion that we must see as a protracted issue. Clearly some people have identified it as critical—as pivotal, in fact—to the creation of the Global African Congress. Obviously, it's very important that it get resolved. But the process by which it gets resolved, discussed, dialogued on, I think is as important as the issue itself. My position was that that question should never have been taken to a plenary session, should never have been voted on, that this contradicted earlier decisions made by the leadership. Although I was a prominent member of the International Coordinating Council, I was not at the conference at the time that decision was made. Unfortunately, I came one day late. I clearly would have opposed the decision, and I might have had some impact on its outcome. So, in any event, we have an issue.

First of all, let me say that African people, people of African descent—given our history of repression, exploitation, our history of being kept out, left out by various forms of apartheid, racism, institutional racism, et cetera—have a need for meetings and conferences where we feel free to discuss sensitive issues that reflect the centuries of pain that our people have gone through. And often the only way you can have these discussions is behind closed doors. That's not an issue here. It's not an issue about whether or not we have a right to closed meetings, whether we have a right to call a conference where just people of African descent are participating. We have absolutely that right. The issue here is when you have a global conference—people coming from all over the world—we often will utilize, given our level of resources, venues that belong to governments or entities that have formal rules and regulations that they must adhere to on inclusiveness et cetera. Where the international media, where various prominent international institutions—the United States as well as governments and their delegations are attending—can you make decisions like that on the fly? And the answer to that, in my opinion, is "Absolutely not." And I disagree with the decision 100 percent. There are people who think that this decision represents the historical moment for the dynamic of building a global pan-African organization; I disagree. I think that we will discuss this issue critically, and it must be discussed because I think that ultimately the decision is going to be that all our conferences will be open unless we predetermine them not to be so and give forewarning, promotion, and establish that fact in an open way so that people will know what to expect prior to any decision that they may make to attend.

YUSUF: Thank you very much. Are there any closing comments from either one of you (because I've asked most of my questions)? Any particular directions that you want to see in the reparations movement?

MUNTU: No. I just think that the reparations movement ebbs and flows; that we may be in a period that reflects some degree of stagnation. I think it's critical to understand that the reparations movement, as Sam laid out, must have an official, formal office that addresses the work full time, that employs a professional and efficient staff who are paid at a level where they can really work with commitment and dedication without having to worry about the basic things like benefits, et cetera, et cetera. All these things must be incorporated in an organization that will dedicate itself to building the reparations movement. That organization has to have proper funding. It must be able to employ a sufficient number of staff both domestic, local, and global. Strategies would be entertained by such an office, things that we've talked about over the course of this discussion. If you have that office, then these periods of lull or stagnation will not occur because you'd be building on a grass-roots level the kind of effort—in contacts, information, and educational processes—that must go down. The reparations movement will only mushroom—will only expand exponentially—if you have the proper organizational mechanisms in place.

YUSUF: I just want to ask Sam if he had any closing statements. Thank you, Muntu.

MUNTU: Thank you, brother.

SAM: I concur with Muntu on that, and I think that another factor is, as we said, we see the reparations movement as a political movement, and in that context, we see the impending war in the Middle East as something that, as reparationists, we're in opposition to, with specific reference to U.S. imperialist military bases being placed in Africa and the use of black people from the United States as cannon fodder in this up-and-coming war.

YUSUF: It's interesting, the one word I haven't heard all night is "genocide," a word we used to use a lot, and I was wondering...

SAM: Right, that's right. The old question of genocide. It's still as true in the present as it was in the past—

MUNTU: We think that the United Nations imposed sanctions on Iraq justifiably [at first] for the invasion of Kuwait, but that those sanctions on Iraq are in effect a form of reparations payment by the Iraqis, which have caused the deaths of almost a million people in Iraq since 1990, and that they should cease; that the U.S. government's war against Iraq in 1990 caused the death of 200,000 Iraqis; that the United States and Great Britain—its running dog—have been bombing Iraq, imposing a no-fly zone in violation of international law, and that this should cease; that in fact, they owe the Iraqi people reparations. The U.S. government owes the Iraqi people reparations. And if they invade and attack Iraq, they will be war criminals who should be tried and convicted in international criminal court, and in addition to being held to all criminal sanctions due, should also be forced to pay reparations to the people of Iraq who probably will lose somewhere between a half a million and a million people if this war occurs. The U.S. government is looking for every phony pretext to denounce the UN inspectors because, as we now realize, it never really supported the process of the United Nations utilizing inspectors. This was just a ruse to appear as if they were being reasonable by going through the UN Security Council. So, in effect, they're just waiting for some phony pretext and obviously they're going to create their own to go forward with this invasion. Their refusal to acknowledge their criminal past and history against people of African descent in slavery, systemic racism, ongoing violations of our human rights, and their failure to pay us reparations is in direct contradiction to their phony and hypocritical pronouncements about the alleged human rights violations and indeed even the documented human rights violations of the Iraqi government against its own people.

U.S. imperialist war is an enemy of people of African descent. As Sam laid out, they use the military bases that they have in Africa for their whole strategy of world military domination. We oppose them. We oppose them going into Africa. They owe the whole continent of Africa reparations. We think that this country must give up its warmongering, neofascist policies that are coming out of the White House. The Bush administration should apologize to people around the world that they have consistently oppressed, exploited, and subjected to massive systemic terrorism and human rights violations, and they must apologize to people of African descent in this country.

YUSUF: In that context, can you comment also on the impact of the PATRIOT Act, Homeland Security, and the suspension of civil liberties on the reparations movement, and how this impact should be viewed by black activists in particular and black people in general.

MUNTU: Any reparations movement is a movement that criticizes the history of the U.S. government; it criticizes policies of the last four centuries. It speaks to the issue of civil rights violations, the issue of human rights violations against people of African descent. The Homeland Security Act essentially penalizes those who criticize the U.S. government. It violates our civil liberties, and surely they would see that the reparations movement would be diametrically opposed to the implementation of the Homeland Security Act, the various laws that they've implemented in the INS [Immigration and Naturalization Service] against immigrants, these violations of immigrant rights, these mass deportations, these arrests without charges that have been occurring since 9/11. When we came out of Durban, we were involved in a movement that would expose the history of the United States, the history of its domestic terrorism against people in this country, against African people in this country. So the Homeland Security Act and the various related laws that they have passed since 9/11 we see as a direct attack on people of African descent to, in effect, repress our demand for reparations, to repress our criticism of the U.S. government, and to try to push the movement and the motion on reparations aside.

YUSUF: Thank you.

Reparations

Strategic Considerations for Black Americans

C. J. MUNFORD

Rumblings and ruminations about reparations reverberate throughout the black world. As the second millennium turns to the third millennium—as Western civilization reckons time—strong voices cry out for compensation all across the African continent, from Nigeria to the pan-African movement, headquartered in Kampala, Uganda, to the Organization of African Unity seated in Addis Ababa. In the Caribbean and among Brazil's African millions a black consciousness stirs, focused on the black diaspora's just claims for indemnification and remediation. In the United States the National Coalition of Blacks for Reparations in America (N'COBRA) spearheads the drive.

Supporters of reparations must strive to create an *alternative* discourse within the black community, one that has the potential to become the dominant discourse. By discourse we mean both formal discussion in writing and open public talk of tactics and strategies, appropriate to black emancipation and uplift at millennium's end. This must be our conscious purpose, if "honing the weapon of theory" is not to be an empty slogan. We must craft derivative political projects and maneuvers in such a manner as to win the battle of ideas, not merely in the black academy, but, more important, among our ordinary people, inner city included. Reparations' slogans and buzzwords must become household words across black America. We must put our issues and topics on every African American lip. Thereby we may hope to regenerate the mass black liberation movement that has languished in suspended animation since the 1970s.

We must be careful, however. There is a political Waterloo of monumental proportions lurking in this affair. Acceptance of a small symbolical grant, like that doled out to Japanese Americans recently, would end our historical and moral claim to compensation.

Reparations as an Attack on Capitalism

Black reparations is a claim on the Western capitalist socioeconomic system. It is not a claim on socialism, communism, or any other noncapitalist "mode of production" or society. Our unpaid forced labor laid the foundations of the Western capitalist order, and no other. Our enslavement alone enabled European civilization to snare the Western Hemisphere, appropriate its resources, and anchor white wealth and might in the Americas.[1] It is Western capitalism that owes us the debt. Hence, despite some of the rhetoric we use at times, the lobbyists for black reparations are not social revolutionaries in the traditional Western, left-wing Marxist sense.[2] We can't afford to be. I will explain why.

Inasmuch as we insist upon reparations, that aim cannot logically encompass the overthrow of the socioeconomic order, since the claim for compensation and indemnification is made specifically against Western capitalism — the beneficiary of our ancestors' unpaid labor and the perpetrator of racist atrocities against us. Reparation is addressed precisely to those debts and crimes.

So although many blacks have no use for capitalism — with good reason — the campaign for reparations, both for Africa and the diaspora, requires Western capitalism for the claim to register. Anti-black racism is deeply rooted among ordinary whites.[3] Ostensibly, lower-class whites would provide the main backing for any noncapitalist order — and would be its main beneficiaries. We suspect that under any postcapitalist setup, as under capitalism, the vast majority of whites would continue to look for excuses to deny our just claims. We lay charges against the existing social order. Western capitalism's disappearance *before* the debt is paid is not in the interest of black people.

Reparations as a Race-Specific Matter

Historically, black liberation activism has addressed issues specific to racial discrimination against African Americans. The maximum agenda targeted *white racism* — its theory and practice — and *white supremacy* as a macrosystem. In an otherwise fine book, Charles V. Hamilton has sought to prove the contrary.[4] The black struggle, he asserts, has always given equal time and effort to race-neutral social welfare issues. He is, I think, mistaken. The historical mandate of black liberation has *always* been black-race specific, and not merely from the 1950s to 1964. It remains the same today.

Yet the black agenda is increasingly criticized for failing to widen or shift its focus to "universal" human rights issues, or at least to issues germane to the "mainstream" white, middle-class lobbies. There is pressure on the racial agenda to give way to bones of contention pertinent to ethnic origin, gender, multiculturalism, religion, or sexual preference. From the National Association for the Advancement of Colored People (NAACP) to the Southern Christian Leadership Conference (SCLC), the civil rights establishment is browbeaten to switch chiefly to class, poverty-type problems. Martin Luther King III, newly chosen head of the SCLC, has succumbed to this temptation, for instance. The substitute agenda campaigns for reforms designed to better the lot of poor people per se, the absolute majority of whom in the United States and Canada are still said to be *white*. This is an attack on the classical black rights agenda. The traditional program uttered the demand for freedom, protection, and compensation (the classic "forty acres") on behalf of African-descended persons, enslaved, Jim Crowed, terrorized, and discriminated on the basis of *race*.

The arm twisting comes simultaneously from two opposite political camps — from the right and from the left. Conservatives claim that race-specific advocacy spearheads "racial preferences," quotas, and affirmative action — policies white conservatives hate. The left offers the class analysis that sacrifices black interests on the altar of "broader," "national" working-class issues. Higher or lower in register, this refrain is rung by all of today's radicals, social democrats, socialists, communists, white trade unionists, and sundry other leftists. They reject "narrow" racial discourse in order to vindicate social reform, class, and socialist agendas, and "unite America's multiracial working class." They also complain that tax-funded reparations will make African Americans "winners," casting poor whites and ethnics in the role of "losers."

We must not allow the push for reparations to be diverted into any "universalistic" reforms "good for all Americans." History establishes *priorities*. After all, during the Civil War, thousands of white families lost boys, killed or maimed in the Union army, fighting against the pro-slavery army of the Confederacy. In the eyes of those families, they themselves and their lost kin were the "losers," sacrificed to the freedom needs of blacks, who were despised by many of these northerners for racist reasons. Nevertheless, the historical needs of the republic were served.

Reparations as a Discourse on Race

The best way, to my mind, to seize the political initiative and change the timbre of the national discussion of race is to be aggressive in our demands for reparations. Discourse on race is permanent and unavoidable in the United States of America, a constitutive element of life, dictated by the historical centrality of African Americans. Moreover, there are conjunctural political events, such as President Clinton's Race Commission and "national dialogue" on races, times when a critical state of affairs brings issues to a head. This is one of those times. Targeting the mass media, we must make it our priority in the dialogue to obliterate the currently popular anti-black phraseology, uttered in catchwords such as "racial preferential treatment" and "racial preference." This hateful discourse must be smothered in favor of phrases such as "racist crimes restitution." The nation should be discussing programs of redress. We must get everyone arguing about policies to cancel out the harm done African Americans by slavery, Jim Crow, and current racial discrimination. In other words, we must steer the debate onto favorable grounds. Reframing the race debate must become the historical imperative for the early years of the twenty-first century, just as the abolition of chattel slavery became the historical imperative of the nineteenth century, and just as the removal of Jim Crow laws was the historical imperative of our twentieth century.

We propose this as a frank and militant approach. We advance it in the expectation of long-run political benefits that can never be gained from meekly assuring that African Americans have no wish to "reverse-discriminate" against anyone. Avoiding confrontation on matters of principle, compromising a people's fundamental rights, never brings victory. We must forge strategies that go beyond mere lobbying for leverage in the White House, or chasing down liberal legislators in the hope of coaxing enlightened "color-blind" reforms.

Conclusion

We should voice our demands for compensation and protection in unmistakable terms and get on with the historic labor of forming an uncompromising pro-black coalition with antiracist whites, comparable to the antislavery coalition of blacks and whites. We should do so with the full understanding that such a coalition would be temporary, not permanent, just as the antislavery coalition of the mid-1800s was short-lived — unfortunately.

People do not act *only* according to their own narrow racial, class, religious, or personal interests. At least not everyone, not all the time. A minority of people sometimes take moral stands, a minority of white people included. They stand up for principles they believe will foster the long-range betterment of human society. However, to motivate these sentiments among the minority of whites who are antiracist, we must proclaim the priority of black needs bluntly and unambiguously to provide them the opportunity to make a clear moral choice. Only we, African Americans, can activate the relatively few whites (a silent minority) who are antiracists. Some will accept our leadership and fight unselfishly for black reparations. A coalition between a black America *united* for reparations and an antiracist white minority rallying in support of black reparations can prevail over mass white opposition, just as the coalition between a black community united in opposition to slavery and white abolitionists—a small minority—helped to bring down chattel slavery 135 years ago. Forging the bloc will not be easy. It will take time, collective effort, sensitivity, and personal sacrifice from all involved, black and white. But history is patient and bows to determination.

Notes

1. Clarence J. Munford, *The Black Ordeal of Slavery and Slave Trading in the French West Indies, 1625–1715*, 3 vols. (Lewiston, N.Y.: Edwin Mellen Press, 1991).
2. Robin D. G. Kelley, *Race Rebels, Politics and the Black Working Class* (New York: Free Press, 1994).
3. Jared Taylor, *Paved with Good Intentions: The Failure of Race Relations in Contemporary America* (New York: Carroll and Graf, 1994).
4. Cooper Hamilton, Dona Hamilton, and Charles V. Hamilton, *The Dual Agenda: Race and Social Welfare Policies of Civil Rights Organizations* (New York: Columbia University Press, 1997).

Tulsa Reparations

The Survivors' Story

CHARLES J. OGLETREE JR.

Introduction

Reparations advocacy has dominated the news as of late. While many dismissed reparationists in the past as members of a narrow and ideologically driven fringe movement, reparations today is discussed and debated in the *New York Times*, the *Wall Street Journal*, many news programs, and even in popular culture.[1] The comedian Chris Rock has introduced it as part of his routine, and the recent controversial and commercially successful comedy *Barbershop* included a lengthy dialogue about the movement.[2] Nevertheless, despite the growing interest in reparations by supporters and opponents, it would be a mistake to view reparations advocacy as a popularity contest. Reparations advocates are deeply committed to the goal of reparations for descendants of African slaves and do not believe that popular acceptance of the effort can or should drive the movement.

Indeed, reparationists do not seek the endorsement of the majority of the American population or even the majority of the African American population for what we do. We do not seek your vote, your support, or even your encouragement when engaging in this type of advocacy because the motivations that sustain us come not from public accolades but from empathy with our clients — those who survived the violence of slavery and segregation and those who did not. One of the fundamental goals of reparations for African Americans is to ensure that those who were sacrificed are not forgotten in our rush to move beyond the painful lessons of our past.[3]

But reparations is more than an exercise in education and remembrance. Reparations advocates ultimately seek the redistribution of resources from one group to another. To that extent, reparations is another manifestation of the progressive agenda articulated by President Lyndon B. Johnson and his vision of addressing the needs of the "Great Society."[4] Reparations is, in other words, yet another expression of the demand for political, social, and economic equality that, since the failure of the civil rights movement in the 1970s, has been stifled and suppressed in this country.

Reparations is controversial and distinctive, however, because race is one of the criteria justifying the redistribution: those who are to pay should do so because they injured a racially identifiable group of people. In fact, the link between race and injury is closer than this; those who inflicted the injury did so using race as perhaps one of many justifications.[5] Demanding payment from whites on the basis of their government's or their ancestors' racism results in a relatively predictable and forceful denial of liability for restitution to the victims of those injuries.

This overwhelmingly negative response poses a problem for reparations advocates: while legal battles may be fought and won without widespread social approval of the litigation's goals, the type of social change pursued through reparations advocacy would seem to require sacrifices from, and perhaps the approval of, that segment of the population most adamantly opposed to reparations. Whether or not one believes that the current allocation of resources depends upon the illegitimate exploitation of African Americans,[6] those who have the resources will lose some of them should they be redistributed along the lines suggested by reparations advocates.

The problem faced by reparations advocates is a familiar one for civil rights advocates and has been described under the rubric of "interest convergence" by Professor Derrick Bell.[7] As Bell argues, only when the interests of the majority converge with those of the minority will the minority achieve its goals. Only "when whites perceive that it will be profitable or at least cost-free to serve, hire, admit, or otherwise deal with blacks on a nondiscriminatory basis, [will] they do so. When they fear — accurately or not — that there may be a loss, inconvenience, or upset to themselves or other whites, discriminatory conduct usually follows."[8] In an earlier article on reparations, Bell suggested that the type of interest convergence necessary to support reparations was a long way off.[9] A recent study confirms that this is still the case.[10] What are the prospects for changing these attitudes, and how can it be done?

This symposium [of the *Boston College Third World Law Journal*, 14 March 2003] is one sign of hope. It is wonderful to witness the diverse range of scholars who are here to comment on the reparations movement, if the ad hoc and fragmented set of groups pursuing reparations can be called a movement. But movement there is — through the courts and in the legislatures of various states and cities around the country.[11] The momentous nature of much of the currently filed litigation renders all the more urgent scholarly contributions to the development of reparations doctrine and policy. This forum is timely in that it comes on the heels of an important effort to address reparations in the court system, most recently seen in a lawsuit seeking reparations, *Alexander v. Governor of Oklahoma*,[12] filed in the Northern District of Oklahoma. So it is particularly enjoyable to participate in this symposium having just filed that suit, and to receive predominantly positive feedback from the participants on its merits.

My goal in this essay is to suggest that reparations litigation can provide a means of transforming the debate about race in such a manner that the majority resistance to racial justice can be abated. One way in which to do so is to demonstrate the convergence of interests between the advocates of reparations and the majority population. As Professor Ewart Guinier recognized in another early reparations article, reparation is likely to help whites as well as African Americans because "the cure for difficulties in correcting institutionally-imposed inequity is more correcting of inequity. In short, legislation for reparations could be generalized to erase societal disadvantages suffered by whites as well as blacks."[13] In this way, reparations litigation can provide the kind of interest convergence that is necessary to overcome the challenges facing reparations advocates.

The Reparations Effort in Greenwood, Oklahoma

On the night of May 31 through June 1, 1921, a mob of white rioters, including individuals deputized by the chief of police of the city of Tulsa and properly activated members of the Oklahoma State National Guard, descended upon Greenwood, the African American district of Tulsa popularly known as the "black Wall Street."[14] Within twelve hours, over eight thousand African Americans had been forced to flee their homes.[15] Some kept running, relocating in different towns within Oklahoma.[16] Otis Clark, who was eighteen at the time, fled all the way to California, refusing to return until well into his nineties.

After the mob had done its work, as many as three hundred African Americans had been murdered and over twelve hundred residences had been burned to the ground in a forty-acre stretch of land.[17] The riot caused more than $20 million (in today's dollars) worth of property damage.[18] Those who stayed were rounded up and herded into detention camps, later to spend the winter like refugees in tents provided by the Red Cross.[19] Fifteen days after the riot, Judge Loyal J. Martin, chair of the Emergency Committee appointed to restore order after the riot, acknowledged, "Tulsa can only redeem herself from the country-wide shame and humiliation into which she is today plunged by complete restitution and rehabilitation of the black belt. The rest of the United States must know that the real citizenship of Tulsa . . . will make good the damage, so far as it can be done, to the last penny."[20] Eighty years later, the commission created by the state to determine the causes of the riot and to assess culpability agreed that "reparations are the right thing to do."[21] Yet, as of today, neither the state of Oklahoma nor the city of Tulsa has paid one cent to any of the victims or their descendants.

There are over 120 survivors of the riots still living; for example, Otis Clark, who recently celebrated his one-hundredth birthday, is still alive and seeking justice.[22] These survivors have come together as a group, along with the descendants of those who did not live long enough to see justice done and to have their experiences acknowledged and addressed directly by the municipal, state, and federal government. I am the lead attorney on the Oklahoma lawsuit, and two other contributors to this symposium are participating in the litigation.[23]

The Oklahoma lawsuit is a model of the transformative process of interest convergence between the advocates of reparations and the majority population.[24] The suit is based upon the model of compensatory damages that Professor Keith Hylton endorses in this symposium,[25] and it is intended to serve as a paradigm by creating concrete cases with actual living victims and by identifying the fact of racial repression as a present and continuing injustice.

Professor Hylton's assessment of the validity of the social welfare model of reparations litigation deserves serious analysis.[26] While the discussion of interest convergence may suggest that such cases have been filed prematurely, the "deliberate speed" of racial reform in this country, at least since the second opinion in *Brown v. Board of Education*, has been a disappointment to many of those seeking racial justice.[27] We have hardly begun the task of changing the racial climate in America in the thirty-five years since the end of de jure segregation. We are approaching the 140th anniversary of the end of the Civil War and the passing of the Thirteenth Amendment, yet attitudes to race remain mired in animosity and distrust. If we have learned one thing, it is that this is not a problem that money alone can solve. It involves, as well, the consideration of new directions in our national project of racial reconciliation and a new beginning in the task of founding a new and fairer America.

Interest Convergence and the Eradication of Racism

Professor Bell's discussion of interest convergence can be understood against the background of two different theories of racism in America. A moderately pessimistic theory has been propounded by Professor Roy Brooks, who suggests that it is "naive [to] expect that whites will act more nobly than African

Americans or any other group would act under similar circumstances" by looking beyond their self-interests when confronted with a demand to redistribute social benefits.[28] Professor Brooks's theory contends that, although integration has been a failure, that failure is limited and may be overcome by a strategy of limited separation.[29] The theory contends that integration has failed and continues to fail many African Americans, and that the white community lacks a generalized will to overcome race-based social and economic disparities.[30] Nonetheless, Professor Brooks clearly believes that racism can be overcome by strategies based on African American self-help.[31]

Professor Bell's more pessimistic analysis suggests that racism is not merely an accidental by-product of American society or culture that can be undone by a sustained effort to eradicate it. Rather, Bell sees racism as endemic—a definitive, structural feature of liberal democracy in America.[32] Far from a problematic but essentially transient social or psychological condition, racism is a permanent feature of American society, necessary for its stability and for the well-being of the majority of its citizens.[33] Thus, according to Bell, "Black people will never gain full equality in this country. Even those herculean efforts we hail as successful will produce no more than temporary 'peaks of progress,' short-lived victories that slide into irrelevance as racial patterns adapt in ways that maintain white dominance."[34]

These two theories address the issue of redistributive racial goals (whether expressly or implicitly) from the perspective of interest convergence. Brooks's discussion assumes that whites will not act against their interest, and so African American self-help ought to be a major part of any strategy seeking to overcome racism. Bell's thesis is distinguishable from Brooks's. Interest convergence, he argues, explains how African Americans are able to achieve political gains despite the essentially racist nature of American society. Political and social power is retained by the white majority—in fact, true power is retained by a white *minority* that has power and wishes to conserve it, and the rest of white society is empowered only relative to African Americans.[35] Thus, while not only African Americans, but a large portion of white society, are denied effective political, social, or economic power, the relative position of African Americans to the rest of society serves to mask the disenfranchisement of the majority of whites.[36] Interest convergence suggests that, against this consolidation of power in an elite, redistributive gains are only possible when the interests of the elite and the rest coincide.

Accordingly, interest convergence works as a safety valve, to permit short-term gains for African Americans when doing so furthers the short- or long-term goals of the white elite. As a side effect, it has the important consequence of convincing the minority population (or others that lack power) that social change is possible, rather than ephemeral, and that participation in the social and political system will provide redistributive benefits. This is an important check on widespread disaffection that may end in revolution.

Reparations, understood in this light, can only be politically successful to the extent that it can be presented as providing short- or long-term benefits for the empowered portion of the population. To the extent that reparations is predominantly, or only, a "black thing," it has little chance of succeeding. Thus, even with large-scale social backing, there can be no reparations unless those in power can see their interests converging with those who demand reparations (see Yamamato, part 5).

The potential of the reparations movement to persuade a white power elite that some form of social action is required may not be as fanciful as some have imagined. As respected historian Eric Foner noted recently, the major problem with affirmative action is not the manner in which it is administered, but its separation from the other programs introduced along with it in the 1960s.[37] Public education continues to fail African Americans in significantly greater numbers than whites,[38] and it is this failure that ensures the continuing relevance of affirmative action as a stop-gap measure to help the unfortunate succeed.

As Bell notes, however, the move to integrated education — and indeed the whole civil rights revolution of the 1960s — can be regarded as an effort by white America to head off the real possibility of race-based mass civil disobedience.[39] Since the end of slavery, whites have resisted the challenge of integration and have found more or less sophisticated ways by which to resist the efforts of African Americans to participate on equal terms in American society.[40] As in the 1960s, the frustrations of second-class citizenship have led to the inevitable resurgence of black nationalism, as best demonstrated in the now broadly accepted, although controversial, momentum for reparations. With the failure of a race-neutral liberalism to provide a populist political alternative, reparations is, for many African Americans, the only remaining option to seek the sort of redistribution of resources promised under the "Great Society." White failure to embrace the modest civil rights or integration programs envisaged during the 1970s and into the 1980s has allowed the black underclass to grasp the issue of reparations. As the situation currently stands, it looks like they will not let go until they receive justice.

Slavery Reparations and Redistribution

Reparations is an attempt to obtain restitution for the wrongs inflicted through slavery and segregation and persisting through the current landscape of racial discrimination in America. At bottom, it is premised upon a principle of compensation: those who have inflicted an injury must compensate those who have suffered the injury in an amount appropriate to the wrong inflicted. As is well recognized, the problem with slavery reparations is that all of the victims are dead, as are the individuals who participated in and perpetrated slavery and its related institutions. Nevertheless, some of those institutions survive, among them a range of corporations, other private institutions such as universities and colleges, and state and federal governments.

There are a number of obvious and well-detailed hurdles to seeking reparations through litigation.[41] Two principal barriers are the lack of living plaintiffs and the various statutes of limitations. These impediments militate against the traditional forms of recovery of tort law and quasi-contract. Furthermore, quite apart from the issue of "deep pockets," there are important symbolic factors at stake when selecting defendants in reparations cases. Where the state has condoned the wrong in the very document constituting it as a polity, the state is rightly regarded as the principal target for suit.[42] Thus, plaintiffs have resorted to a variety of constructive legal arguments in reparations claims.

The controlling slavery reparations case is *Cato v. United States*, in which an African American woman brought an action for damages against the U.S. government, alleging the kidnapping, enslavement, and transshipment of her ancestors, as well as continuing discrimination on the part of the government.[43] She also sought a court acknowledgment of the injustice of slavery and Jim Crow oppression, as well as an official apology from the U.S. government.[44] The court dismissed the case, citing the government's failure to consent to suit under the Tucker Act, and the failure of the Thirteenth Amendment to provide a remedy under the Administrative Procedures Act.[45]

More recently, the Court of Federal Claims in *Obadele v. United States* dismissed a slavery reparations claim filed under the Civil Liberties Act, which provides for payments to Japanese American internees detained during World War Two[46] (see Documents, section 1). Plaintiffs argued that the Act rested upon an unconstitutional racial classification, and sought payment to descendants of slaves under the Act.[47] The court upheld the Act's constitutionality while at the same time commenting that "the Plaintiffs have made a powerful case for redress as representatives of a racial group other than Americans of Japanese ancestry."[48] Clearly, *Cato* and *Obadele* present major obstacles for plaintiffs seeking reparations against the federal government.

The currently filed slavery litigation lawsuits are grappling with these precedents.[49] The distinctive feature of several of these suits is their choice of defendants: corporations that participated in slavery in a variety of capacities. The issue is whether such suits present a sufficient basis for the courts to grant relief, or whether they will suffer the fate of *Cato* and *Obadele*. In his contribution to this symposium, Professor Hylton suggests that, in casting around for a basis for suit, the slavery litigation suits have adopted a theory of litigation and of relief that inherently compromises their chance of success. These suits, he argues, "aim for a significant redistribution of wealth," adopting "social welfare" as their underlying policy or goal.[50] These policy considerations are reflected not only in the relief sought and in the class of plaintiffs, but in the claims articulated: conspiracy, demand for accounting, human rights violations, conversion, and unjust enrichment.[51]

And yet, while the problems faced by such lawsuits are well known and are the subject of many differences of opinion, there is merit in the various strategies employed by the wide variety of efforts to secure reparations.[52] In terms of interest convergence, however, many people will view these commendable efforts as too far removed from present injustices to have much of an impact on the national consciousness. Arguably, no one in the white majority, and certainly not anyone in the power elite identified by Bell, feels the immediacy of slavery. Furthermore, the question of the appropriate response toward the bitter history of slavery is a fraught one, even within the African American community. Notably, there has been fairly widespread disagreement over not only the appropriate manner in which to memorialize slavery, but also over whether such a memorial should exist at all.[53] Those who object to a slavery museum claim that such a memorial is either too painful or too stigmatizing for African Americans even today.[54]

Such problems are magnified when the harms inflicted during slavery are used as a justification for redistributions of wealth and power, as efforts to secure legislative reparations indicate. The type of study that could make the case for that justification has been continually resisted at the federal level. In particular, Representative John Conyers's bill, HR 40, entitled "Commission to Study Reparation Proposals for African Americans Act," has been defeated every year since its introduction in 1989[55] (see Documents, section 1). Given this general resistance to reparations, the challenge to look to the past to solve problems related to race remains, and must not be ignored. For interest convergence to succeed, we must make a serious effort to confront past, and not simply present, injustices.

Certainly, were the federal government to sponsor such a study, even if no payment would be included in the report's recommendations, it would provide an indication that the government wishes to take seriously the issue of reparations. The idea that the state should make an effort to investigate and acknowledges its responsibility has resulted in two major reparations successes: the Civil Liberties Act of 1988, by which payments were made to World War Two Japanese American internees; and the Rosewood Act, under which the state of Florida made payments to the survivors and descendants of the Rosewood Massacre of 1923[56] (see Documents, sections 1 and 5). Thus, there is a good chance that a federal commission would provide a legal basis for suit to recover payments should a commission so recommend. That is certainly the basis for suit in two recent holocaust reparations suits, and it is the case we are currently making in Oklahoma.[57]

Nonetheless, while a federal commission would provide a necessary legal basis for reparations lawsuits, it is not clear that the sort of commission proposed under HR 40 can overcome the failure of interest convergence. Even after the Riot Commission's report, the current reparations litigation in Oklahoma has been presented as a white-against-black struggle,[58] with many white citizens opposed to reparations for the survivors of the Tulsa race riot. Private donations to reparations funds have dried up and local citizens have resented the intrusion by "national" lawyers in their local issues.[59]

Jim Crow Litigation as a First Step

Compared to political activism, reparations advocacy through litigation may have greater potential to create interest convergence. As Professor Hylton and others have noted, the chances of successful litigation are greatly increased where the reparations claim can be framed as a traditional civil rights issue, allowing the courts to concentrate on statute of limitations problems rather than on creative theories of litigation.[60] Two recent holocaust litigation cases suggest that, in circumstances similar to those presented in the Oklahoma litigation, there are, at the very least, grounds for tolling the statute of limitations.[61] Given that the Oklahoma litigation does not seek to rely on a novel theory of injury, the statute of limitations issue is essentially the only bar to recovery.[62]

The point of reparations advocacy through litigation, as opposed to reparations political activism, is to create convergence by changing the stakes of the debate. That is certainly what happened during the litigation leading up to the decision in *Brown v. Board of Education*,[63] and litigation success—indeed, perseverance—also changed the stakes in the Japanese American internment debate. Once the Ninth Circuit Court of Appeals found that the federal government had made a material misrepresentation about the military exigency of its curfew and exclusion policies of 1942, which it then hid for almost forty years, the statute of limitations was tolled and a suit was allowed to proceed in the mid-1980s.[64] It was that outcome that prompted the reparations payments under the Civil Liberties Act.

The history of *Brown* demonstrates that incremental successes won on a divergent but related legal theory can result in convergence on the underlying goal of an initially unpopular legal strategy. *Brown* also demonstrates that such a strategy need not appeal to the majority of whites, but only those who have the power to change things. In other words, Bell is perhaps unduly pessimistic to suggest that "the interest of blacks in achieving racial equality will be accommodated only when it converges with the interests of whites. . . . The Fourteenth Amendment, standing alone, will not authorize a judicial remedy providing effective racial equality for blacks where the remedy sought threatens the superior societal status of middle- and upper-class whites."[65]

Thus, at the state level, the convergence of interests in the Oklahoma lawsuit may, in the short term, be limited to persuading the state to make changes to the Oklahoma educational system rather than paying out large sums of money. Nonetheless, such short-term convergence may bear long-term fruit. A well-structured educational package offers an opportunity to teach about the manner in which interests converge, providing a stepping stone to reorient the public's perception about what people's interests are and where they converge.

The benefit of Jim Crow reparations litigation is not simply the relative simplicity, as compared to slavery reparations suits, of stating a claim. The relative immediacy of the injury, symbolized by the presence of living survivors such as Otis Clark, underlines the recency of such acts of discrimination and violent repression, demonstrating the persistent breadth and depth of racism in this country. Racism is broad in the sense that the virulent attacks on African Americans (and other minorities) have not been limited to a particular location. Many of us consider racial repression as a southern phenomenon, forgetting that all our towns, including New York, Boston, Chicago, Detroit, Omaha, Dallas, Los Angeles, and San Francisco, were segregated on the basis of race. All of these towns have suffered race riots. Most of these riots were perpetuated by white mobs attempting to subjugate the black citizenry.[66] In addition, all of these riots happened during this century. People who were there and who suffered are still alive. Some people who inflicted the suffering may still be alive.[67]

Racism is deep because of the extreme measures we take to deny its existence. The shame that frequently — and rightly — accompanies the identification of an individual as a racist does not always result from a disavowal of the underlying beliefs but from a recognition of the social sanctions that follow from such an identification. It is the attitude of white peers to the tag "racist" that is regarded as problematic, not the failure properly to acknowledge the humanity of African Americans (or other minorities). As Bell notes, these attitudes have not disappeared, but resurface in white efforts to avoid integration.[68]

Jim Crow reparations litigation forces the prevalence of segregationist practices upon the American public in all of its recency, its breadth, and its depth. It demands that the institutions that adopted these segregationist policies pay for them directly to identifiable victims or their children. If the reparations movement, at least in its Jim Crow aspect, has one benefit, it will be in giving the lie to the suggestion of *Aderand Contractors, Inc. v. Pena* and *City of Richmond v. J. A. Croson Co.* that discrimination is a thing of the past, and in tracing the identifiable legal and social effects of slavery and segregation in current society.[69] Furthermore, by providing a federal forum for real people to share their experiences in a way that forces the larger public to recognize their humanity, Jim Crow reparations litigation undermines the denial surrounding anti–African American racism. Empathy, which sustains us as reparations advocates, is, on this view, one step toward manifesting interest convergence.[70]

Conclusion

Several signs of interest in Jim Crow reparations, if not in convergence, are forthcoming. The recent academic endorsement of Jim Crow lawsuits is an indication of changing attitudes on the topic in the twenty-first century.[71] This is especially so as the academy is just the type of elite audience that has generally proved resistant to reparations except in limited circumstances. A judicial endorsement of Jim Crow litigation would be even more gratifying, particularly for the victims and descendants of the Tulsa race riot. A legal victory, even if only on the statute of limitations issue, has obvious value as precedent for other cases that could be filed around the country.

Nevertheless, as I have argued elsewhere, the rejection of slavery reparations is a little too convenient.[72] It permits us to forget that many of the founding fathers were slaveholders and racists who, over the objections of their colleagues, ensured that the Constitution reflected the views of slaveholders and not those of abolitionists.[73] Nowadays, Americans prefer to consider the Civil War as fought by the foes of slavery rather than by anti-secessionists, many of whom were pro-slavery (or at least ambivalent about its suppression), and ignore the fact that the Emancipation Proclamation preserved slavery in those states loyal to the North. Perhaps most concerning, the rejection of slavery reparations allows us to forget or deny that slavery imposed a holocaust that resulted in the extermination of millions of Africans through transshipment alone — individuals who were tossed overboard as ballast or spoiled cargo as needs required.

Thus, while Jim Crow lawsuits are a good beginning, reparations lawsuits must not stop at compensation alone. Some more general form of redistributive justice should be contemplated. Professor Hylton is opposed to this type of redistributive lawsuit, arguing that throwing money at the problem has not worked thus far.[74] Nonetheless, Hylton's case against wealth redistribution, while interesting, is unproven because it fails to take into account a variety of factors that might impede wealth distribution as a cure for the ills inflicted by racism and segregation. Wealth redistribution is an important goal for reparations, although (in the manner discussed by Hylton) that may be some way down the road.

In addition to wealth redistribution, the major goal of reparations litigation, one that is generally underemphasized, is knowledge redistribution. Knowledge redistribution engenders the empathy that may foster interest convergence; it also publicizes the voices of the alienated African Americans willing to endorse the likes of such outsiders as Al Sharpton in his run for president of the United States. These outsider voices must not only be represented but also addressed for the sake of whites as well as African Americans. The turn to nationalism and separationism under a politics of confrontation promises to create a racial powder keg of disenfranchised African Americans who have little to lose by engaging in desperate acts of protest.[75] Yet the reparations movement has a long way to go before it persuades white elites that the sort of redistribution contemplated is a good thing. For the sake of all American citizens, let us hope we succeed sooner rather than later.

Notes

1. See Conley, "The Cost of Slavery," A1 (proposing a net-worth-based solution for reparations and generating several subsequent letters to the editor); Allen Guelzo, "Reason in Despair," *Wall Street Journal*, 22 November 2002, available at 2002 WL-WSJ 103126916 (criticizing a conference at Columbia University on reparations and the law); Gary L. Schell, "Slain Union Soldiers Paid 'Blood Costs' for Slavery," letter to the editor, *Wall Street Journal*, 3 December 2002, available at 2002 WL-WSJ 103127610 (responding to "Reason in Disrepair" by suggesting the lives sacrificed by Union soldiers during the Civil War are ignored by reparations advocates); sources cited in n. 2.

2. *ABC News 20/20:* "America's IOU" (ABC television broadcast, 23 March 2001) (including clips of Chris Rock asking strangers on the streets of New York for their opinions on reparations for slavery as part of his show); *Barbershop* (MGM Pictures 2002).

3. See Charles J. Ogletree Jr., "Reparations for the Children of Slaves: Litigating the Issues,"

University of Memphis Law Review 245, 245–247 (2003) (discussing motivation for reparations as representation of those who worked and died as a result of slavery).

4. I have made the connection between President Johnson and reparations in Charles J. Ogletree Jr., "Repairing the Past: New Efforts in the Reparations Debate in America," 38 *Harvard Civil Rights–Civil Liberties Law Review* 279, 317–318 (2003).

5. See, e.g., *Price Waterhouse v. Hopkins* 490 U.S. 228 (1989) (recognizing "mixed motive" discrimination); see also *Desert Palace, Inc. v. Costa*, 123 S. Ct. 2148 (2003) (clarifying the evidentiary standard to be applied in mixed motive cases).

6. And so any redistribution of resources along the lines suggested by reparations advocates is justified, and the continuing failure to redistribute is wrongful.

7. See Derrick A. Bell Jr., "*Brown v. Board of Education* and the Interest Convergence Dilemma," in *Critical Race Theory: The Key Writings That Formed the Movement* 20, 22 (Kimberle Crenshaw et al. eds., 1995).

8. Derrick Bell, *Faces at the Bottom of the Well: The Permanence of Racism* 7 (1992).

9. See Derrick A. Bell Jr., "Dissection of a Dream," 9 *Harvard Civil Rights–Civil Liberties Law Review* 156, 157 (1974) (reviewing Bittker, *The Case for Black Reparations*).

10. See Harbour Fraser Hodder, "Riven by Reparations: The Price of Slavery," *Harvard Magazine*, May/June 2003, at 12, 13.

11. See, e.g., Plaintiff's Complaint and Jury Trial Demand, *Farmer-Paellmann v. FleetBoston Fin. Corp.* (E.D.N.Y. filed Mar. 26, 2002) (No. 02-CV-1862); Slavery Era Insurance Policies Act, Cal. Ins. Code 13810–13813 (West Supp. 2003); Act of May 4, 1994, 1994 Fla. Sess. Law Serv. ch. 94–359 (West) (relating to Rosewood, Florida) (codified in part at Fla. Stat. ch. 1004.60, 1009.55 (2003)); 1921 Tulsa Race Riot Reconciliation Act of 2001, Okla. Sess. Law Serv. ch. 315 (West) (codified at Okla. Stat. Ann. tit. 74, 8000.1(3) (2002)); John M. Broder, "The Business of Slavery and Penitence," *New York Times*, 25 May 2003, section 4, at 4 (discussing Los Angeles City Council's unanimous approval of "an ordinance . . . that would require any company wishing to do business with Los Angeles to investigate and disclose any profits derived from the American slave trade"); Sabrina L. Miller and Gary Washburn, "New Chicago Law Requires Firms to Tell Slavery Links," *Chicago Tribune*, 3 October 2002, section 2, at 1 (discussing Chicago Ordinance).

12. Plaintiffs' First Amended Complaint, *Alexander v. Governor of Oklahoma* (N.D. Okla. filed Feb. 28, 2003) (No. 03-CV-133).

13. Ewart Guinier, book review, 82 *Yale Law Journal* 1719, 1723 (1973) (reviewing Bittker, *The Case for Black Reparations*).

14. See Plaintiffs' First Amended Complaint pp. 2, 17, *Alexander* (No. 03-CV-133); Don Ross, "Prologue," in *Tulsa Race Riot: A Report by the Oklahoma Commission to Study the Tulsa Race Riot of 1921*, at ix, xi (2001), available at www.okhistory.mus.ok.us/trrc/freport.htm (accessed 12 November 2003).

15. See Alfred L. Brophy, *Reconstructing the Dreamland: Contemplating Civil Rights Actions and Reparations for the Tulsa Race Riot of 1921*, at 3 (2000) (preliminary draft of report to Tulsa Race Riot Commission), available at www.law.ua.edu/staff/bio/abrophy/abrophy_links.html (accessed 12 November 2003) [hereinafter Brophy, Preliminary Report].

16. Plaintiffs' First Amended Complaint pp. 5, 9, *Alexander* (No. 03-CV-133).

17. Okla. Stat. Ann. tit. 74, 8000.1(3) (2002); John Hope Franklin and Scott Ellsworth, "History Knows No Fences: An Overview," in *Tulsa Race Riot*, at 21, 22–23.

18. See Okla. Stat. Ann. tit. 74, 8000.1(3).

19. Scott Ellsworth, "The Tulsa Race Riot," in *Tulsa Race Riot*, at 37, 88.

20. "Tulsa," 112 *The Nation* 833, 839 (1921), quoted in Brophy and Kennedy, *Reconstructing the Dreamland*, at 107.

21. *Tulsa Race Riot*, at 20.

22. See Plaintiffs' First Amended Complaint PP66, 557, *Alexander* (No. 03-CV-133).

23. Professor Alfred L. Brophy, who wrote the seminal book on the riot and its legal consequences, has been indefatigable in his efforts to ensure that the plaintiffs had their day in court. It is no understatement to say that this lawsuit could not have been filed without that fantastic resource. See generally Brophy and Kennedy, *Reconstructing the Dreamland*. Professor Brophy also served on the Oklahoma Commission to Study the Race Riot of 1921 and contributed a chapter to its report. See Alfred L. Brophy, "Assessing State and City Culpability: The Riot and the Law," in *Tulsa Race Riot*, at 163, 163–183. He also wrote a more trenchant and as yet unpublished argument for reparations for the riot victims. See generally Brophy, Preliminary Report. Professor Eric J. Miller, Michele A. Roberts, Adjoa A. Aiyetoro, Suzette M. Malveaux, Johnnie Cochran, Denis C. Sweet III, and several local Oklahoma attorneys, including Leslie Mansfield and James O. Goodwin, are among the individuals who assisted me in drafting the complaint in *Alexander*, which is the suit brought on behalf of survivors of the Tulsa race riot of 1921 and descendants of the victims of that riot, suing the governor of the state of Oklahoma, the city of Tulsa, the chief of police of the city of Tulsa, and the Tulsa Police Department for damages and injunctive relief under the Fourteenth Amendment, 42 U.S.C. 1981, 1983, and 1985, and for supplemental state-law claims. See Plaintiffs' First Amended Complaint pp. 38, 489, 518–64, *Alexander* (No. 03-CV-133).

24. See Bell, *Faces at the Bottom of the Well*, at 7; Guinier, book review, at 1719, 1723.

25. See Keith N. Hylton, "A Framework for Reparations Claims," 24 *Boston College Third World Law Journal* 31, 32–33 (2004).

26. Ibid.

27. 349 U.S. 294, 301 (1955) (*Brown II*). The first of the *Brown* opinions outlawed racial discrimination in public education. See *Brown v. Bd. of Educ.*, 347 U.S. 483, 1495 (1954) (*Brown I*).

28. Roy L. Brooks, *Integration or Separation? A Strategy for Racial Equality* 190 (1996).

29. Ibid., 104, 189–213.

30. Ibid., 190, 105. Brooks's analysis replicates that of Professor Bell in his early article on interest convergence. See Bell, *Interest Convergence*, at 23–24.

31. See Brooks, *Integration or Separation?*, at 256, 263–269, 284–285.

32. See Bell, *Faces at the Bottom of the Well*, at 10. Bell considers the relationship between racism and liberal democracy to be "symbiotic," such that " 'liberal democracy and racism in the United States are historically, even inherently, reinforcing; American society as we know it exists only because of its foundation in racially based slavery, and it thrives only because racial discrimination continues' " (quoting Jennifer Hochschild, *The New American Dilemma* 5 (1984)).

33. Bell, *Faces at the Bottom of the Well*, at 3–10. As evidence of the permanence of racism, Bell points to the "unstated understanding by the mass of whites that they will accept large disparities in economic opportunity in respect to other whites as long as they have a priority over blacks and other people of color for access to the few opportunities available" (10).

34. Ibid., 12.

35. Ibid., 8–9.

36. Ibid., 7.

37. See Eric Foner, "Diversity over Justice," *The Nation*, 14 July 2003, at 4, 4.

38. See, e.g., Neil J. Smelser et al., Introduction to *America Becoming: Racial Trends and*

Their Consequences 1, 12–13 (Neil J. Smelser et al. eds., 2001) (stating that research suggests that stereotypes lead teachers to expect less of black students than non-Hispanic whites, and this expectation leads to lower performance on test scores); James P. Smith, "Race and Ethnicity in the Labor Market: Trends over the Short and Long Term," in 2 Smelser et al., *America Becoming*, 52, 56 (stating that on average, blacks complete fewer years of education than whites).

39. See Bell, *Interest Convergence*, at 23–24.

40. See Robinson, *The Debt*, 85–86.

41. See generally Hylton, "A Framework for Reparations Claims," at 36–38 (discussing hurdles such as identifying the victims and defendants, causation, and statutes of limitation); Calvin Massey, "Some Thoughts on the Law and Politics of Reparations for Slavery," 24 *Boston College Third World Law Journal* 157, 161–165 (2004) (discussing hurdles related to the passage of time).

42. See, e.g., U.S. Const. art. I, 2, cl. 3 (three-fifths clause); U.S. Const. art. IV, 2, cl. 3 (fugitive clause); Robinson, *The Debt*, at 204–208.

43. 70 F.3d 1103, 1106, 1111 (9th Cir. 1995).

44. Ibid.

45. Ibid., 1111; see Administrative Procedures Act, 5 U.S.C. 702 (2000); Tucker Act, 28 U.S.C. 1491, 1505 (2000).

46. Civil Liberties Act of 1988, 50 U.S.C. app. 1989–1989d (2000); *Obadele v. United States*, 52 Fed. Cl. 432, 444 (2002).

47. *Obadele*, 52 Fed. Cl. at 436.

48. Ibid., 442.

49. See Plaintiffs' First Amended Complaint, *Alexander* (No. 03-CV-133); Plaintiff's Complaint and Jury Trial Demand, *Farmer-Paellmann* (No. 02-CV-1862); First Amended Complaint, *Hurdle v. FleetBoston Fin. Corp.* (Cal. Super. Ct. filed Sept. 10, 2002) (No. CGC-02-412388); see also Ogletree, "Repairing the Past," at 298–308 (commenting on these suits).

50. Hylton, "A Framework for Reparations Claims," at 33–34.

51. See, e.g., Plaintiff's Complaint and Jury Trial Demand pp. 50–70, *Farmer-Paellmann* (No. 02-CV-1862).

52. See Ogletree, "Repairing the Past," at 281.

53. See, e.g., Jim Auchmutey, "Slave Museums Confront a Painful Past," *Atlanta Journal-Constitution*, 9 March 2003 (describing "the sensitive nature" of the topic of memorializing slavery), available at 2003 WL 13244321; Jacqueline Trescott, "Capitol Site Favored for Black History Museum; Presidential Panel's Report Envisions 2011 Completion," *Washington Post*, 3 April 2003, (discussing "the long and often fractious history of deciding whether a museum dedicated to the African American story should be built on the [National] Mall [in Washington, D.C.]"), available at 2003 WL 17425494.

54. See Auchmutey, "Slave Museums."

55. See, e.g., Commission to Study Reparation Proposals for African Americans Act, H.R. 40, 108th Cong. (2003); H.R. 3745, 101st Cong. (1989); see also Ogletree, "Repairing the Past," at 281, 290 (discussing Representative Conyers's introduction of this bill each year for the last fourteen years).

56. Civil Liberties Act of 1988, 50 U.S.C. app. 1989–1989b-9 (2000); Act of May 4, 1994, 1994 Fla. Sess. Law Serv. ch. 94–359 (West) (relating to Rosewood, Florida) (codified in part at Fla. Stat. ch. 1004.60, 1009.55 [2003]).

57. See *Rosner v. United States*, 231 F. Supp. 2d 1202, 1205 (S.D. Fla. 2002) (discussing Plaintiff's assertion that it was only after the Presidential Advisory Commission on Holocaust

Assets released its report that they had the necessary facts for their complaint); *Bodner v. Banque Paribas*, 114 F. Supp. 2d 117, 123–24 (E.D.N.Y. 2000) (discussing commissions created by the French government to draft proposals for redress of Holocaust-era injuries); Plaintiffs' First Amended Complaint p. 22, *Alexander* (No. 03-CV-133).

58. *Tulsa Race Riot*. See "Double Jeopardy: Suit Cites Statute of No Limitations," editorial, *Daily Oklahoman*, 28 February 2003 (recharacterizing the 1921 riot as a "racial war" that left both blacks and whites dead, and referring to reparationists as "professional race-baiters"), available at 2003 WL 13945084.

59. See Arnold Hamilton, "'21 Tulsa Riot Case Polarizes: Some See Suit Emerging as Bellwether for Black Reparations Movement," *Dallas Morning News*, 23 June 2003, at 1A.

60. See Hylton "A Framework for Reparations Claims," at 36–38; Anthony J. Sebok, *How a New and Potentially Successful Lawsuit Relating to a 1921 Race Riot in Tulsa May Change the Debate over Reparations for African-Americans*, 10 March 2003, pp. 1–4, available at www.writ.news.findlaw.com/sebok/20030310.html.

61. See *Rosner*, 231 F. Supp. 2d at 1204 (tolling statute of limitations for fifty-eight years); *Bodner*, 114 F. Supp. 2d at 121, 134–36 (tolling statute of limitations for over fifty years).

62. See Sebok, *New and Potentially Successful Lawsuit*, 22–27.

63. 347 U.S. 483 (1954); see also Bell, *Interest Convergence*, at 20–24 (suggesting the Court's opinion in *Brown* can best be understood by looking at its value to whites).

64. See *Hirabashi v. United States*, 828 F.2d 591 (9th Cir. 1987). But see *Hohri v. United States*, 586 F. Supp. 769 (D.D.C. 1984) (dismissing reparations claim on statute of limitations grounds).

65. Bell, *Interest Convergence* at 22.

66. See Claudia Kolker, "A Painful Present as Historians Confront a Nation's Bloody Past," *Los Angeles Times*, 22 February 2000, available at 2000 WL 2213090; Nicholas Von Hoffman, "U.S. History, U.S. Riots: A Thread of Mob Violence, Civil Unrest," *Los Angeles Times* 15 May 1992, available at 1992 WL 2914207.

67. Graphic evidence of this history of violence, often sponsored by states and municipalities, has been collected in photographs in *Without Sanctuary* (James Allen ed., 2000), a memorial to the victims of lynching throughout the nation. Many of the photos can be viewed online at the Without Sanctuary Musarium, www.musarium.com/withoutsanctuary/main.html (accessed 12 November 2003). These trophy pictures were circulated as souvenirs of the lynchings they depict. A similar photograph, entitled "Running the Negro out of Tulsa," is depicted in Professor Brophy's excellent book *Reconstructing the Dreamland* and in the Greenwood Cultural Center's Riot Museum in Tulsa, Oklahoma. The Greenwood Center also maintains an online museum of the Tulsa Race Riot at www.greenwoodculturalcenter.com/ (accessed 12 November 2003).

68. Bell, *Interest Convergence*, at 20–24.

69. 515 U.S. 200 (1995); 488 U.S. 469 (1989). See Spencer Overton, "Racial Disparities and the Political Function of Property," 49 UCLA *Law Review* 1553, 1558–1559, 1568–1570 (2002). Professor Overton states that mandatory segregation policies in education, employment, housing, and business increased the inequality in the control of resources between white Americans and black Americans (1558–1559). Furthermore, he asserts that wealth disparities that stem from past segregation reduce the ability of significant numbers of people of color to participate in democracy by making campaign contributions, purchasing airtime and billboards, and retaining lobbying assistance (1568–1570).

70. On empathy or "intimacy" as a goal of the reparations movement, see Eric J. Miller,

"Reconceiving Reparations: Multiple Strategies in the Reparations Debate," 24 *Boston College Third World Law Journal* 45, 78–79 (2004).

71. See, e.g., Sebok, *New and Potentially Successful Lawsuit*.
72. See Ogletree, "Repairing the Past," at 308–319.
73. See Derrick Bell, "*Brown v. Board of Education*: Forty-Five Years after the Fact," 26 *Ohio Northern University Law Review* 171, 175 (2000).
74. See Hylton "A Framework for Reparations Claims," at 34–36.
75. See Miller "Reconceiving Reparations," at 48–56.

Race for Power

The Global Balance of Power and Reparations

GERALD HORNE

According to certain polls, something like 75 percent of people in the United States are opposed to reparations to African Americans. This should not be deemed surprising in a nation with a Euro-American majority that has been birthed and suckled on the notion that blacks receive "preferential treatment" via affirmative action programs that—in truth—mostly benefit Euro-American women.[1]

Yet stating this bald fact presents both a dilemma and a historical perspective for examining this all-important question of reparations. The dilemma is simple: How does one obtain an objective that an overwhelming majority does not support? But the historical perspective provides an answer to this otherwise nettlesome dilemma: consider that if a plebiscite had been held in the Deep South on the Voting Rights Act of 1965, most likely the Euro-American majority would have voted against that too.

The "secret" to whatever African American advance that has occurred in this nation has been support from the international community that has then compelled the majority in the United States to "do the right thing." Historians now acknowledge, for example, that the Cold War had everything to do with the erosion of Jim Crow in the 1950s and the 1960s. How could Washington credibly charge Moscow with human rights violations, pose as a paragon of human rights virtue, and win "hearts and minds" among "colored" peoples globally, as long as peoples of color in this nation were treated so atrociously?[2] Jim Crow had to go and those Euro-Americans who objected to this epochal transition were dragged to an accommodation scratching and flailing all the while by the force of the international community.

Consequently, the proposition that a majority of people in the United States may oppose reparations should not detain or derail us; to the contrary, it should cause us to heighten our lobbying efforts within the constituency that ultimately matters: the international community. It was decades ago that W. E. B. Du Bois reminded us that "the Negro problem in America is but a local phase of a world problem."[3] This remains true but too often of late many African Americans — perhaps intoxicated with their only recently proclaimed citizenship rights — have acted as if this was solely a local problem only worth ventilating in domestic circles. But this approach has not worked for some time now — it has reached a point of virtual exhaustion — and, minimally, should be subjected to severe reconsideration.

Those who may have doubts about this thesis should do no more than examine the movement against the death penalty. Majorities have been registered for years in favor of this draconian measure, though routinely African Americans are the disproportionate victim of this policy, despite the suggestion that those who kill African Americans are less likely to get the death penalty — which means our lives are worth less than those of others. Evidentiary of the bipartisan support for the death penalty is the fact that both parties' presidential standard-bearers in 2000 supported execution as the price for committing certain crimes. Yet as international condemnation of the death penalty mounts — including fervent protests from the likes of Germany and the European Union — it is apparent that second thoughts about this measure are growing. This helps to explain why former Black Panther Mumia Abu-Jamal has yet to be executed and why a death penalty moratorium was called by a Republican governor in Illinois.

In any event, it is well that we begin to look abroad, for just as contradictions between the United States and the U.S.S.R. created an opening for the emergence of a movement against Jim Crow, similar contradictions between the United States and its growing list of opponents worldwide may do the same for the movement in favor of reparations. There is some evidence to suggest that it might be possible to take advantage of the emerging contradictions between the burgeoning European Union and the United States, for example. Some time ago, it was reported that certain E.U. nations — leading members of which were prominent in the slave trade — may be open to heeding a call for reparations from the descendants of enslaved Africans in the United States but were less enthusiastic about reparations to African nations, which would have to come from the coffers of, for example, London, Paris, Lisbon, the Hague, and Brussels in the first place.[4] Of course, it would be unwise for the reparations movement to selfishly and incorrectly opt for reparations in the Western Hemisphere while leaving the African continent to fend for itself. On the other hand, it would be quite appropriate to seek to take advantage of emerging tensions between the two major forces in the global economy — the E.U. and the United States — on behalf of the reparations movement.

Certainly, it appears that the U.S. government is seeking to leverage elements of the international community against the reparations movement. Thus, it has been reported that the U.S. protest about condemning Zionism and/or Israel at the United Nations–sponsored World Conference against Racism (WCAR) in Durban, South Africa, during the summer of 2001 may have had motives that were less than transparent. As one usually well-informed journal put it, "Some believe the U.S. action regarding Israel is a convenient way for Washington to prevent discussion of the slavery issue, which could have deep political and financial implications." A leading "diplomat" affirmed this hypothesis, declaring, "For the U.S. slavery is far more important and Israel is a smoke screen."[5] Thus, although sectors of the reparations movement may have forgotten about the international community, the international community has not forgotten about the reparations movement.

Hence, the question becomes not *whether* the reparations movement should survey the international community for openings and leverage but *how* to go about it.

A useful first step in that regard is to examine what used to be called the "global correlation of forces" or the "balance of power" in order to ascertain what are the pressure points to be probed.

As the comment above suggests, it would be a mistake to assume that there are no differences between and among the member states of the E.U. and the United States. A quick perusal of the twentieth century finds that the United States has waged war on a number of E.U. states more than once, principally Germany — the locomotive of this developing superstate. Though France has been allied with the United States in major wars, it is worth noting that Paris has been a moving force behind the "euro," the common European currency, which hopes to challenge — if not replace — the dollar, with a possibly disastrous impact on the U.S. economy. And raging disputes between Washington and Brussels (capital of the E.U.) continue to boil on matters as disparate as beef, barley, cinema, aerospace, and more. Thus, Airbus, the European plane manufacturer, has been challenging Boeing, particularly in the lucrative realm of constructing jumbo jets, which are worth tens of millions of dollars. France, along with a number of other E.U. member states, is irate about the fact that Hollywood has invaded the French and European market, while successfully throwing up barriers to curb the influx of their films into the United States.[6]

Indeed, in the wake of the tragic events of 11 September 2001, it is evident that in the long term the value of the dollar will fall — as the idea of the United States as a safe haven sinks under the rubble of the World Trade Center — and the value of the "euro" will rise. The increased U.S. reliance on the E.U. —

and, indeed, the international community — to wage war against "terrorism" also suggests that Washington will become more reliant on the world and, thus, will have to heed clarion calls coming from abroad.

The position of Germany in this context is striking. Compared to Britain and France, Germany was not a major colonial power — in Africa or elsewhere; indeed, one of the major causes of the two bloodlettings called World War One and World War Two was Berlin's effort to gain a larger share of the division of the world that would be more in line with what its ruling elite saw as the nation's actual power. The end result was that Germany wound up losing what colonies it had, particularly in Namibia, southwest Africa, which — after Berlin's ignominious defeat in World War One — was handed over to South Africa. Interestingly, though the WCAR was boycotted by most high-level representatives of North America and western Europe, Germany dispatched its foreign minister, who expressed contrition for slavery and colonialism.

Not only is the E.U. embroiled in furious conflicts with the United States over all manner of bread-and-butter issues — issues which have served as a pretext for war in different times — but, as well, there are sharp ideological disputes between the two giants as well. The foreign minister of Germany is a member of the Green Party — a party not unlike the party of the same name represented by the much-reviled Ralph Nader during the 2000 presidential race — and the chancellor, Gerhard Schroeder, is a social democrat. "Socialism" is not a dirty word in the E.U. as social democrats play a leading role in Brussels, the "capital" of the E.U. Many in Europe look askance at the United States and its "cowboy capitalism" that Washington has sought to foist on the rest of the planet by dint of its leading role in multinational institutions, for example, the World Bank (led by the Australian American James Wolfensohn) and the International Monetary Fund. Many Europeans look down their nose at George W. Bush as a Bible-quoting, gun-toting, abortion-obsessed, environment-polluting, toxic Texan. They resent his seeking to gut international treaties on global warming, small arms, the International Criminal Court, and more. Just as there are those in Washington who no doubt find it convenient to have leverage against Germany because of Holocaust lawsuits, there are those in Europe who would like to have leverage against the United States because of reparations claims. Indeed, those seeking to file lawsuits about U.S. reparations would be well advised to look into the possibility of filing such claims in European courts, just as those nongovernmental organizations seeking leverage should also be peering across the Atlantic.

The prime minister of France, Lionel Jospin, is not only a socialist but a former Trotskyite. Interestingly, he recently endorsed the potentially far-reaching "Tobin Tax," named after Yale professor James Tobin, which would place a tax on cross-border capital movements, the funds from which could then be deployed on behalf of the developing world. Thus far, President Fidel Castro of Cuba — another prominent defender of reparations — has been one of the few international leaders bold enough to endorse this measure. That Jospin of France would do so is indicative of how quickly political currents can shift — something reparations advocates should keep in mind. Of course, the "Tobin Tax" has been a nonstarter on this side of the Atlantic, not worthy of mention in polite circles. Yet its redistributive nature is not unlike reparations and is animated by the same spirit.[7] Also worthy of note is that Berlin — at the prompting of Paris — also has taken the "Tobin Tax" under advisement.

Similarly, at the Durban conference, the French minister of cooperation, Charles Josselin, declared, "The French parliament has unanimously adopted a law recognizing that slavery, the trans-Atlantic slave trade, perpetrated from the 15th century against Africans, Amerindians, Malagasies and Indians, constitutes a crime against humanity." One awaits a similar declaration from the U.S. Congress.

In the meantime, it would be quite useful for advocates of reparations to establish firm linkages with the so-called antiglobalization movement, which has shaken the foundations of the leading powers from Seattle to Quebec City to Prague to Genoa. One idea that reparations advocates could usefully bring to antiglobalization circles is the idea that protecting sovereignty — particularly U.S. sovereignty — is not necessarily and always a value worth defending. As noted here, often it has been necessary to override U.S. sovereignty (e.g., to protect the human rights of peoples of color, particularly African Americans). In fact, this notion that antiglobalization means upholding U.S. sovereignty is possibly one reason why participation of peoples of color in the massive antiglobalization marches have been up to par.

In any case, the reparations movement must engage with the European Union in order to advance its worthy goals. Keep in mind that a number of leading members of the E.U. were neither slave-trading nations nor colonizing powers; the Scandinavian nations, whose foreign aid to Africa is proportionally higher than that of the United States, come quickly to mind. Social democrats too play a leading role in this region. And just as the Communist Party USA has special ties to ruling communists in Cuba and Vietnam, the Democratic Socialists of America (DSA) — which has included former Congressman Ronald V. Dellums among its leaders — has special ties to European social democrats that are well worth exploring.

In that regard, reparations advocates should not only pursue such ties but should also move forthwith to dispatch delegations to leading E.U. capitals to engage in intensive discussions with political parties and other organs of civil society. This is nothing new. During the era of slavery, Frederick Douglass spent a considerable amount of time touring Europe drumming up opposition against the lords of the lash — the demon slave owners of the South. That Britain did not intervene on behalf of the South during the Civil War (though breaking up and weakening the United States had been a long-term goal of London, at least since the War of 1812) was not least because of the influence wielded in the U.K. by lobbyists like Douglass. Likewise, the turning point for the crusade against lynching spearheaded by Ida B. Wells-Barnett took place when she toured Europe, bringing to the attention of a larger audience the heinous extrajudicial crimes then being perpetrated against (mostly) African Americans.

Thus, there is ample precedent for such delegations or, alternatively, opening an office in the E.U. capital, Brussels.

Needless to say, reparations advocates should not limit our lobbying to the E.U. alone. As of now, relations between the United States and the world's second leading national economy, Japan, appear to be quite close. Right now, Washington — after sending the Soviet Union into oblivion after the expenditure of trillions of dollars in taxpayers' money — is eyeing hungrily the prospect of destabilizing the Communist Party of China, with the assistance of Tokyo. As will be noted below, the U.S. ruling elite is not united on the question of China, not least because of the massive investment there by such giants as General Motors, Kodak, Motorola, and others. Still, surrounding China by dint of alliances with Australia, India, and — if they will cooperate — Vietnam and South Korea is high on the agenda of the Bush White House and Japan is seen as a keystone in this arch of containment.

Yet, though it is now largely forgotten, Japan was the nation most admired by African Americans in the period leading up to the bombing of Pearl Harbor.[8] It was Booker T. Washington who told his Japanese interlocutors, "Speaking for the masses of my own race in this country, I think I am safe in saying that there is no other race outside of America whose fortunes the Negro peoples of this country have followed with greater interest or admiration . . . in no other part of the world have the Japanese people a larger number of admirers and well-wishers than among the black people of the United States."[9] A few years later, the FBI reported nervously that Marcus Garvey "preached that the next war will be between the Negroes and the Whites unless their demands for justice are recognized and that with the aid of Japan on the side of the Negroes they will be able to win such a war."[10] Black Nationalists generally and the Nation of Islam specifically were in the vanguard of this "Tokyo/Negro" or "Asiatic Black Man" formation.[11] Once again, it was this leverage that African Americans had gained abroad that led to concessions at home, on the grounds that having a disaffected and alienated minority at home was not the surest path to national security.[12]

The bombing of Hiroshima and Nagasaki changed this "Negro-Tokyo" alliance. Yet even today there is a sizable opposition to the U.S. bases sited in Okinawa and elsewhere; a mutually advantageous alliance between those forces and the reparations movement, based on mutual opposition to a common foe, could be easily brokered. Similarly, one of the largest communist parties in the industrialized world is based in Japan; their Sunday newspaper sells more issues than the *New York Times*. This party too is unsympathetic to continued U.S. occupation of their country. Hence, in addition to creating a liaison with such movements across the Pacific, the long-term interests of African Americans also suggest that an office in Tokyo is well advised.

One sure road to Tokyo runs through New Delhi. Though not stressed in this nation, the fact is that Indians may have been more besotted with pre-1945 Japan than African Americans. A leading hero of India today — Subhas Chandra Bose — who ranks with Nehru and Gandhi, fought side by side with forces from Tokyo against the Allies during World War Two. Today Washington hopes to play upon both Tokyo's and New Delhi's long-standing problems with Beijing in pursuit of its anti-China alliance. Unfortunately, one of the many blunders of Beijing in recent times was its 1962 war against India.

India, on the other hand, was a stalwart of the antiapartheid movement, not least because of South Africa's large Indian minority that at one time included Gandhi himself. In order to entice India into an anti-China alliance, the United States probably will push for India to secure a permanent seat on the critically important United Nations Security Council, which can only serve to increase its weight in the international community. Furthermore, there are sizable Indian populations in such critically important nations as Trinidad, Guyana, Kenya, Mauritius, Tanzania, Uganda, South Africa, as well as other nations often thought to be part of a Pan-African bloc. This means that reparations advocates would be well advised to explore extensive and intensive discussions with our Indian counterparts. Of course, this should not exclude alliances with the "Dalits" — or the "untouchables" — whose presence within India is not unlike that of African Americans.

As in New Delhi, so in Beijing. Though there is sizable U.S. investment in China, it is apparent that ever more powerful forces in this nation would like to dislodge the Communist Party from power. Certainly, the Communist Party of China has made more than its share of blunders and errors vis-à-vis peoples of African descent, particularly in Southern Africa in the 1970s. And this is no more than a pale reflection of even larger crimes committed against the Chinese people, the Chinese working class above all.[13] Yet it is equally clear that Washington should spend more time getting its own human rights house in order—for example, by giving serious consideration to the aftermath of the crimes of slavery and Jim Crow—and spend less time seeking to destabilize nations around the world.

Furthermore, it would be inadvisable for African Americans to join what well may be a quixotic crusade against China, just because a sector of the U.S. ruling class has awakened to the sober reality that despite the "death of communism," there remains a Communist Party in power in the largest nation on the planet. Most of all, in international councils, one of the most resolute voices in favor of reparations has been that of China.

Consider Russia as a negative example. During the era of the Soviet Union, Moscow spoke out vigorously against racism in the United States, helping immeasurably to boost the fortunes of African Americans. With the advent of the bumbling administration of Boris Yeltsin, what had once been a booming voice shrank dramatically beyond sotto voce to the inaudible. Another "victory" like that and we will be totally undone.

Moreover, sound diplomatic relations with China will open the door to positive relations with other nations with large Chinese populations, including Singapore, Indonesia (which is also the largest predominantly Islamic nation in the world), Malaysia (a nation which does not mind objecting to U.S. policies, as evidenced by their warm relations with Cuba and their refusal to follow the "Washington consensus" in the wake of the 1997 currency crisis in Asia). And, of course, positive relations with Asian nations should not hurt the reparations movement in forging positive relations with the ever-growing Asian American population.

What holds true for China is even truer for Cuba. Just as Beijing in the 1970s aligned with apartheid South Africa against liberation movements in Angola and elsewhere, it was Havana that fought side by side with the liberation movements to the ultimate victory. It was no accident that the foreign leader receiving the most applause during the inauguration of Nelson Mandela in 1994 was Fidel Castro. It was no accident that one of the few non-African heads of state who found time to trek to Durban for the WCAR was President Fidel Castro; there he declaimed forcefully on the need for reparations.

The reparations movement needs to engage in urgent consultations with our allies in Havana, for no government in the hemisphere is better informed on developments in the Americas. High on the list should be obtaining their reading on developments in Brazil and Venezuela. The Quebec City meeting in April 2001 meant to put forward a so-called Free Trade Agreement of the Americas (FTAA)—otherwise known as NAFTA (North American Free Trade Agreement) on steroids—was slowed down in part by the opposition of Brasilia and Caracas. Brazil, which is larger in territory than the United States, has pretensions of hemispheric domination all of its own. Moreover, unlike the United States, it has strong progressive political parties, including the Workers Party, which rules the sprawling megalopolis of São Paulo—one of the largest cities in the world—and has realistic designs on the presidency. Of course, there are those in Brasilia who may be concerned about what endorsing reparations in the United States may mean for their own country, whose African-derived population may very well be larger than that of Nigeria. At the same time, if reparations for Africa and African Americans is to become reality, it will be difficult to effectuate if Brasilia does not have a prominent seat at the table.

Venezuela also has a large African-derived population, as one glance at the visage of President Hugo Chavez will verify. The charismatic former officer has angered Washington, which is concerned with the growing bonds—trade and otherwise—between Caracas and Havana, not to mention Venezuela's forward-looking foreign policy, which of late has embraced China warmly. As one of the largest oil suppliers to the United States, this nation is not without leverage all its own in the United States.

The same holds true for Mexico, the largest Spanish-speaking nation in the world and the tenth largest economy in the world. The abject importance of Mexico is one reason why the 2001 election in the city of Los Angeles was of such concern to many reparations advocates. There African Americans voted overwhelmingly for a staid Euro-American candidate against a progressive Mexican American candidate, who formerly was a union organizer: the charismatic Antonio Villaraigosa. African Americans were joined in this effort by the most conservative forces in the city, one of the first times such a "black-conservative" alliance has been forged. That the winning campaign also employed offensive white supremacist stereotypes directed at Villaraigosa makes this development even more troubling.

But it is even more troubling from the point of view of the reparations movement. This movement will require allies in the international community, particularly because of the polls showing 75 percent of the population in this nation is opposed to reparations as of now. Mexico, which has maintained sound ties with Cuba since the Revolution and influences profoundly every Latin American nation, cannot be ignored and in fact must be courted assiduously if the reparations movement is to gain friends in the international community.

The case of Mexico also points up an advantage of a global strategy. As the Bush administration—and the center-right consensus that he represents—becomes more and more unpopular in the international community, it becomes even more important for reparations advocates to reach out abroad and distinguish ourselves sharply from the government that purports to represent us. Doing so becomes problematic when African Americans are voting in lockstep with conservatives in Los Angeles.

In fact, the kind of vote that took place in Los Angeles only confirms—incorrectly, I think—in the minds of some that African Americans are just as parochial as their Euro-American counterparts. This cannot help the reparations movement, particularly in an area that will be absolutely essential to ally with: the Caribbean and Africa. The sovereign states there often look to Mexico, rightfully, as an important and influential nation, whose voice it is important to heed, most notably in the higher councils of the Organization of American States and the United Nations. This remains the case despite the often regressive domestic policies of the present Mexican leadership.

Since the days of Marcus Garvey, the voice of Jamaica in particular has been critical in the Pan-African movement; this remains true today as the noted Jamaican diplomat Dudley Thompson played a pivotal role in Durban. But for all of the historic importance of the Caribbean, it is appropriate to conclude with the key region that must be courted if reparations is to become a reality is Africa. Africa's support for reparations should not be taken for granted, as the example of the Senegalese leadership, which has expressed skepticism about reparations, suggests. There are three key nations on the continent and, fortunately, all should be supportive: South Africa, Nigeria, and Egypt. Cairo will be critical in this regard for despite our common stances concerning reparations, this North African nation is justifiably skeptical about the position of African Americans concerning a matter dear to their heart: the question of Israel's illegal occupation and settlements in Palestine. Other than the United States and Israel, the international community is united in opposition to occupation and settlements and if African Americans think they can obtain reparations while remaining silent, or worse, supportive of Israel's illegalities, they are dreaming in never-never land. Joining the international community on settlement and occupations also will garner the reparations movement a friendly audience in the region from Egypt to Iran, and possibly Indonesia and Malaysia as well—the latter two being similarly important, predominantly Islamic nations.

In short, the reparations movement must not stop trying to gain support here at home; to do otherwise would be foolish. Yet it would be equally misguided to think that reparations can be obtained absent massive support from the international community. The domestic struggle is already presumed. It is the global struggle that must be engaged if we are to overcome.

Notes

1. See, e.g., Gerald Horne, *Reversing Discrimination: The Case for Affirmative Action* (New York: International, 1992).
2. See, e.g., Gerald Horne, *Black and Red: W. E. B. Du Bois and the Afro-American Response to the Cold War, 1944–1963* (Albany: State University of New York Press, 1986); Mary Dudziak, *Cold War Civil Rights: Race and the Image of American Democracy* (Princeton, N.J.: Princeton University Press, 2000); Gerald Horne, "Race from Power: U.S. Foreign Policy and the General Crisis of 'White Supremacy,'" in Michael Hogan, ed., *The Ambiguous Legacy: U.S. Foreign Relations in the "American Century"* (New York: Cambridge University Press, 1999), 302–336.
3. W. E. B. Du Bois, "The Color Line Belts the World," in Herbert Aptheker, ed., *Writings by W. E. B. Du Bois in Periodicals Edited by Others* (Millwood, N.Y.: Kraus-Thomason, 1982), 330 (from *Collier's Weekly*, 20 October 1906).
4. See, e.g., *Financial Times*, 26 March 2001.
5. *Financial Times*, 31 August 2001.
6. See, e.g., Gerald Horne, *Class Struggle in Hollywood, 1930–1950: Moguls, Mobsters, Stars, Reds and Trade Unionists* (Austin: University of Texas Press, 2001).
7. *Financial Times*, 30 August 2001.
8. See, e.g., Reginald Kearny, *African-American Views of the Japanese: Solidarity or Sedition?* (Albany: State University of New York Press, 1998).
9. Booker T. Washington to Naoichi Masaoka, 5 December 1912, in Louis Harlan and Raymond W. Smock, eds., *Booker T. Washington Papers*, Vol. 12: *1912–1914* (Urbana: University of Illinois Press, 1982), 84.
10. "Bureau of Investigation Reports," New York City, 5 December 1918, in Robert A. Hill, ed., *The Marcus Garvey and Universal Negro Improvement Association Papers*, Vol. 1: *1826–August 1919* (Berkeley: University of California Press, 1983), 306.
11. See, e.g., Karl Evanzz, *The Messenger: The Rise and Fall of Elijah Muhammad* (New York: Pantheon, 1999); Robert Hill, ed., *The FBI's RACON: Racial Conditions in the United States During World War II* (Boston: Northeastern University Press, 1995).
12. See, e.g., Christopher Thorne, *The Far Eastern War: States and Societies, 1941–1945* (London: Unwin, 1986), 178.
13. See, e.g., Gerald Horne, *From the Barrel of a Gun: The United States and the War against Zimbabwe, 1965–1980* (Chapel Hill: University of North Carolina Press, 2001). See also Gerald Horne, *Race Woman: The Lives of Shirley Graham Du Bois* (New York: New York University Press, 2000).

Documents

Introduction

As noted in the editors' introductory chapter, this part of the book consists of primary and secondary source materials that are referenced by the contributors. Together they constitute useful background information relevant to the issues under study and the historical periods they inform and frame. These source materials are not exhaustive, but rather are intended to exemplify the legal, legislative, and political mobilizing activities in the long history of reparations in the United States.

The documents are organized into six sections.

Section 1 contains federal acts and resolutions that historicize claims for reparations and the federal government's response.

Sections 2 and 3 include legislative enactments by states and municipalities, respectively, in support of various compensatory approaches that redress historical injustices involving African Americans, as well as to support House Resolution 40—first proposed in the United States House of Representatives in 1989 and consistently re-introduced in subsequent Congressional sessions.

Section 4 consists of advocacy and activism for reparations, including statements, petitions, and manifestos representing distinctive but related efforts at redress by the Black Panther Party, the Nation of Islam, N'COBRA, the NAACP, the American Bar Association, and the Episcopal Church, as well as appeals to international bodies to garner support.

Section 5 includes case studies of redress, including President Clinton's apology for the Tuskegee study, the Oklahoma Commission to Study the Tulsa Race Riot of 1921, the Greensboro Truth and Reconciliation Commission that investigated the murder of five labor activists by the Ku Klux Klan, and the state of Florida's investigation of the Rosewood Massacre of 1923.

Section 6 is comprised of a lawsuit filed by black farmers seeking compensation from the U.S. Department of Agriculture and the African American Descendents Litigation, which represents the consolidation of several court cases, charging that contemporary corporations derived substantial profits during the slave trade, and naming several tobacco, banking, insurance, and railway companies. As of September 2006, the plaintiffs were seeking a hearing in a federal appeals court in Illinois, where a decision is pending; the document in this book covers the district court's 2004 ruling to dismiss the case.

Section 1

Federal Acts and Resolutions

The Second Confiscation Act (1862)

CHAP. CXCV.—*An Act to suppress Insurrection, to punish Treason and Rebellion, to seize and confiscate the Property of Rebels, and for other Purposes.*

Be it enacted by the Senate and House of Representatives of the United States of America in Congress assembled, That every person who shall hereafter commit the crime of treason against the United States, and shall be adjudged guilty thereof, shall suffer death, and all his slaves, if any, shall be declared and made free; or, at the discretion of the court, he shall be imprisoned for not less than five years and fined not less than ten thousand dollars, and all his slaves, if any, shall be declared and made free; said fine shall be levied and collected on any or all of the property, real and personal, excluding slaves, of which the said person so convicted was the owner at the time of committing the said crime, any sale or conveyance to the contrary notwithstanding.

SEC. 2. *And be it further enacted,* That if any person shall hereafter incite, set on foot, assist, or engage in any rebellion or insurrection against the authority of the United States, or the laws thereof, or shall give aid or comfort thereto, or shall engage in, or give aid and comfort to, any such existing rebellion or insurrection, and be convicted thereof, such person shall be punished by imprisonment for a period not exceeding ten years, or by a fine not exceeding ten thousand dollars, and by the liberation of all his slaves, if any he have; or by both of said punishments, at the discretion of the court.

SEC. 3. *And be it further enacted,* That every person guilty of either of the offences described in this act shall be forever incapable and disqualified to hold any office under the United States.

SEC. 4. *And be it further enacted,* That this act shall not be construed in any way to affect or alter the prosecution, conviction, or punishment of any person or persons guilty of treason against the United States before the passage of this act, unless such person is convicted under this act.

SEC. 5. *And be it further enacted,* That, to insure the speedy termination of the present rebellion, it shall be the duty of the President of the United States to cause the seizure of all the estate and property, money, stocks, credits, and effects of the persons hereinafter named in this section, and to apply and use the same and the proceeds thereof for the support of the army of the United States, that is to say:

First. Of any person hereafter acting as an officer of the army or navy of the rebels in arms against the government of the United States.

Secondly. Of any person hereafter acting as President, Vice-President, member of Congress, judge of any court, cabinet officer, foreign minister, commissioner or consul of the so-called confederate states of America.

Thirdly. Of any person acting as governor of a state, member of a convention or legislature, or judge of any court of any of the so-called confederate states of America.

Fourthly. Of any person who, having held an office of honor, trust, or profit in the United States, shall hereafter hold an office in the so-called confederate states of America.

Fifthly. Of any person hereafter holding any office or agency under the government of the so-called confederate states of America, or under any of the several states of the said confederacy, or the laws thereof, whether such office or agency be national, state, or municipal in its name or character: *Provided,* That the persons, thirdly, fourthly, and fifthly above described shall have accepted their appointment or election since the date of the pretended ordinance of secession of the state, or shall have taken an oath of allegiance to, or to support the constitution of the so-called confederate states.

Sixthly. Of any person who, owning property in any loyal State or Territory of the United States, or in the District of Columbia, shall hereafter assist and give aid and comfort to such rebellion; and all sales, transfers, or conveyances of any such property shall be null and void; and it shall be a sufficient bar to any suit brought by such person for the possession or the use of such property, or any of it, to allege and prove that he is one of the persons described in this section.

SEC. 6. *And be it further enacted,* That if any person within any State or Territory of the United States, other than those named as aforesaid, after the passage of this act, being engaged in armed rebellion against the government of the United States, or aiding or abetting such rebellion, shall not, within sixty days after public warning and proclamation duly given and made by the President of the United States, cease to aid, countenance, and abet such rebellion, and return to his allegiance to the United States, all the estate and property, moneys, stocks, and credits of such person shall be liable to seizure as aforesaid, and it shall be the duty of the President to seize and use them as aforesaid or the proceeds thereof. And all sales, transfers, or conveyances, of any such property after the expiration of the said sixty days from the date of such warning and proclamation shall be null and void; and it shall be a sufficient bar to any suit brought by such person for the possession or the use of such property, or any of it, to allege and prove that he is one of the persons described in this section.

SEC. 7. *And be it further enacted,* That to secure the condemnation and sale of any of such property, after the same shall have been seized, so that it may be made available for the purpose aforesaid, proceedings in rem shall be instituted in the name of the United States in any district court thereof, or in any territorial court, or in the United States district court for the District of Columbia, within which the property above described, or any part thereof, may be found, or into which the same, if movable, may first be brought, which proceedings shall conform as nearly as may be to proceedings in admiralty or revenue cases, and if said property, whether real or personal, shall be found to have belonged to a person engaged in rebellion, or who has given aid or comfort thereto, the same shall be condemned as enemies' property and become the property of the United States, and may be disposed of as the court shall decree and the proceeds thereof paid into the treasury of the United States for the purposes aforesaid.

SEC. 8. *And be it further enacted,* That the several courts aforesaid shall have power to make such orders, establish such forms of decree and sale, and direct such deeds and conveyances to be executed and delivered by the marshals thereof where real estate shall be the subject of sale, as shall fitly and efficiently effect the purposes of this act, and vest in the purchasers of such property good and valid titles thereto. And the said courts shall have power to allow such fees and charges of their officers as shall be reasonable and proper in the premises.

SEC. 9. *And be it further enacted,* That all slaves of persons who shall hereafter be engaged in rebellion against the government of the United States, or who shall in any way give aid or comfort thereto, escaping from such persons and taking refuge within the lines of the army, and all slaves captured from such persons or deserted by them and coming under the control of the government of the United States; and all slaves of such person found on [or] being within any place occupied by rebel forces and afterwards occupied by the forces of the United States, shall be deemed captives of war, and shall be forever free of their servitude, and not again held as slaves.

SEC. 10. *And be it further enacted,* That no slave escaping into any State,

Territory, or the District of Columbia, from any other State, shall be delivered up, or in any way impeded or hindered of his liberty, except for crime, or some offence against the laws, unless the person claiming said fugitive shall first make oath that the person to whom the labor or service of such fugitive is alleged to be due is his lawful owner, and has not borne arms against the United States in the present rebellion, nor in any way given aid and comfort thereto; and no person engaged in the military or naval service of the United States shall, under any pretence whatever, assume to decide on the validity of the claim of any person to the service or labor of any other person, or surrender up any such person to the claimant, on pain of being dismissed from the service.

SEC. 11. *And be it further enacted,* That the President of the United States is authorized to employ as many persons of African descent as he may deem necessary and proper for the suppression of this rebellion, and for this purpose he may organize and use them in such manner as he may judge best for the public welfare.

SEC. 12. *And be it further enacted,* That the President of the United States is hereby authorized to make provision for the transportation, colonization, and settlement, in some tropical country beyond the limits of the United States, of such persons of the African race, made free by the provisions of this act, as may be willing to emigrate, having first obtained the consent of the government of said country to their protection and settlement within the same, with all the rights and privileges of freemen.

SEC. 13. *And be it further enacted,* That the President is hereby authorized, at any time hereafter, by proclamation, to extend to persons who may have participated in the existing rebellion in any State or part thereof, pardon and amnesty, with such exceptions and at such time and on such conditions as he may deem expedient for the public welfare.

SEC. 14. *And be it further enacted,* That the courts of the United States shall have full power to institute proceedings, make orders and decrees, issue process, and do all other things necessary to carry this act into effect.

APPROVED, July 17, 1862.

Special Field Orders, No. 15 (1865)

I. The islands from Charleston, south, the abandoned rice fields along the rivers for thirty miles back from the sea, and the country bordering the St. Johns River, Florida, are reserved and set apart for the settlement of the negroes now made free by the acts of war and the proclamation of the President of the United States.

II. At Beaufort, Hilton Head, Savannah, Fernandina, St. Augustine and Jacksonville, the blacks may remain in their chosen or accustomed vocations — but on the islands, and in the settlements hereafter to be established, no white person whatever, unless military officers and soldiers detailed for duty, will be permitted to reside; and the sole and exclusive management of affairs will be left to the freed people themselves, subject only to the United States military authority and the acts of Congress. By the laws of war, and orders of the President of the United States, the negro is free and must be dealt with as such. He cannot be subjected to conscription or forced military service, save by the written orders of the highest military authority of the Department, under such regulations as the President or Congress may prescribe. Domestic servants, blacksmiths, carpenters and other mechanics, will be free to select their own work and residence, but the young and able-bodied negroes must be encouraged to enlist as soldiers in the service of the United States, to contribute their share towards maintaining their own freedom, and securing their rights as citizens of the United States.

Negroes so enlisted will be organized into companies, battalions and regiments, under the orders of the United States military authorities, and will be paid, fed and clothed according to law. The bounties paid on enlistment may, with the consent of the recruit, go to assist his family and settlement in procuring agricultural implements, seed, tools, boots, clothing, and other articles necessary for their livelihood.

III. Whenever three respectable negroes, heads of families, shall desire to settle on land, and shall have selected for that purpose an island or a locality clearly defined, within the limits above designated, the Inspector of Settlements and Plantations will himself, or by such subordinate officer as he may appoint, give them a license to settle such island or district, and afford them such assistance as he can to enable them to establish a peaceable agricultural settlement. The three parties named will subdivide the land, under the supervision of the Inspector, among themselves and such others as may choose to settle near them, so that each family shall have a plot of not more than (40) forty acres of tillable ground, and when it borders on some water channel, with not more than 800 feet water front, in the possession of which land the military authorities will afford them protection, until such time as they can protect themselves, or until Congress shall regulate their title. The Quartermaster may, on the requisition of the Inspector of Settlements and Plantations, place at the disposal of the Inspector, one or more of the captured steamers, to ply between the settlements and one or more of the commercial points heretofore named in orders, to afford the settlers the opportunity to supply their necessary wants, and to sell the products of their land and labor.

IV. Whenever a negro has enlisted in the military service of the United States, he may locate his family in any one of the settlements at pleasure, and acquire a homestead, and all other rights and privileges of a settler, as though present in person. In like manner, negroes may settle their families and engage on board the gunboats, or in fishing, or in the navigation of the inland waters, without losing any claim to land or other advantages derived from this system. But no one, unless an actual settler as above defined, or unless absent on Government service, will be entitled to claim any right to land or property in any settlement by virtue of these orders.

V. In order to carry out this system of settlement, a general officer will be detailed as Inspector of Settlements and Plantations, whose duty it shall be to visit the settlements, to regulate their police and general management, and who will furnish personally to each head of a family, subject to the approval of the President of the United States, a possessory title in writing, giving as near as possible the description of boundaries; and who shall adjust all claims or conflicts that may arise under the same, subject to the like approval, treating such titles altogether as possessory. The same general officer will also be charged with the enlistment and organization of the negro recruits, and protecting their interests while absent from their settlements; and will be governed by the rules and regulations prescribed by the War Department for such purposes.

VI. Brigadier General R. SAXTON is hereby appointed Inspector of Settlements and Plantations, and will at once enter on the performance of his duties. No change is intended or desired in the settlement now on Beaufort [Port Royal] Island, nor will any rights to property heretofore acquired be affected thereby.

BY ORDER OF MAJOR GENERAL W. T. SHERMAN:

Special Field Orders, No. 15, Headquarters Military Division of the Mississippi, 16 Jan. 1865, Orders & Circulars, ser. 44, Adjutant General's Office, Record Group 94, National Archives.

Freedmen's Bureau Act (1865)

CHAP. XC.—*An Act to establish a Bureau for the Relief of Freedmen and Refugees.*

Be it enacted by the Senate and House of Representatives of the United States of America in Congress assembled, That there is hereby established in the War Department, to continue during the present war of rebellion, and for one year thereafter, a bureau of refugees, freedmen, and abandoned lands, to which shall be committed, as hereinafter provided, the supervision and management of all abandoned lands, and the control of all subjects relating to refugees and freedmen from rebel states, or from any district of country within the territory embraced in the operations of the army, under such rules and regulations as may be prescribed by the head of the bureau and approved by the President. The said bureau shall be under the management and control of a commissioner to be appointed by the President, by and with the advice and consent of the Senate, whose compensation shall be three thousand dollars per annum, and such number of clerks as may be assigned to him by the Secretary of War, not exceeding one chief clerk, two of the fourth class, two of the third class, and five of the first class. And the commissioner and all persons appointed under this act, shall, before entering upon their duties, take the oath of office prescribed in an act entitled "An act to prescribe an oath of office, and for other purposes," approved July second, eighteen hundred and sixty-two, and the commissioner and the chief clerk shall, before entering upon their duties, give bonds to the treasurer of the United States, the former in the sum of fifty thousand dollars, and the latter in the sum of ten thousand dollars, conditioned for the faithful discharge of their duties respectively, with securities to be approved as sufficient by the Attorney-General, which bonds shall be filed in the office of the first comptroller of the treasury, to be by him put in suit for the benefit of any injured party upon any breach of the conditions thereof.

SEC. 2. *And be it further enacted,* That the Secretary of War may direct such issues of provisions, clothing, and fuel, as he may deem needful for the immediate and temporary shelter and supply of destitute and suffering refugees and freedmen and their wives and children, under such rules and regulations as he may direct.

SEC. 3. *And be it further enacted,* That the President may, by and with the advice and consent of the Senate, appoint an assistant commissioner for each of the states declared to be in insurrection, not exceeding ten in number, who shall, under the direction of the commissioner, aid in the execution of the provisions of this act; and he shall give a bond to the Treasurer of the United States, in the sum of twenty thousand dollars, in the form and manner prescribed in the first section of this act. Each of said commissioners shall receive an annual salary of two thousand five hundred dollars in full compensation for all his services. And any military officer may be detailed and assigned to duty under this act without increase of pay or allowances. The commissioner shall, before the commencement of each regular session of congress, make full report of his proceedings with exhibits of the state of his accounts to the President, who shall communicate the same to congress, and shall also make special reports whenever required to do so by the President or either house of congress; and the assistant commissioners shall make quarterly reports of their proceedings to the commissioner, and also such other special reports as from time to time may be required.

SEC. 4. *And be it further enacted,* That the commissioner, under the direction of the President, shall have authority to set apart, for the use of loyal refugees and freedmen, such tracts of land within the insurrectionary states as shall have been abandoned, or to which the United States shall have acquired title by confiscation or sale, or otherwise, and to every male citizen, whether refugee or freedman, as aforesaid, there shall be assigned not more than forty acres of such land, and the person to whom it was so assigned shall be protected in the use and enjoyment of the land for the term of three years at an annual rent not exceeding six per centum upon the value of such land, as it was appraised by the state authorities in the year eighteen hundred and sixty, for the purpose of taxation, and in case no such appraisal can be found, then the rental shall be based upon the estimated value of the land in said year, to be ascertained in such manner as the commissioner may by regulation prescribe. At the end of said term, or at any time during said term, the occupants of any parcels so assigned may purchase the land and receive such title thereto as the United States can convey, upon paying therefor the value of the land, as ascertained and fixed for the purpose of determining the annual rent aforesaid.

SEC. 5. *And be it further enacted,* That all acts and parts of acts inconsistent with the provisions of this act, are hereby repealed.

APPROVED, March 3, 1865.

Southern Homestead Act (1866)

Thirty-Ninth Congress. Sess. I. Ch. 123, 124, 126, 127. 1866.

June 21, 1866.

CHAP. CXXVII.—*An Act for the Disposal of the Public Lands for Homestead Actual Settlement in the States of Alabama, Mississippi, Louisiana, Arkansas, and Florida.*

All public lands in certain States to be disposed of only according to the provisions of the homestead law, 1862, ch 75 Vol xii. p 392. 1864, ch. 38. Vol. xiii. p 85.

No entry to be for more than 80 acres.

$5 to be paid on issue of patent

No distinction for race or color.

Mineral lands excepted

Be it enacted by the Senate and House of Representatives of the United States of America, in Congress assembled, That from and after the passage of this act all the public lands in the States of Alabama, Mississippi, Louisiana, Arkansas, and Florida shall be disposed of according to the stipulations of the homestead law of twentieth May, eighteen hundred and sixty-two, entitled "An act to secure homesteads to actual settlers on the public domain," and the act supplemental thereto, approved twenty-first of March, eighteen hundred and sixty-four, but with this restriction, that until the expiration of two years from and after the passage of this act, no entry shall be made for more than a half-quarter section, or eighty acres; and in lieu of the sum of ten dollars required to be paid by the second section of said act, there shall be paid the sum of five dollars at the time of the issue of each patent; and that the public lands in said States shall be disposed of in no other manner after the passage of this act: *Provided,* That no distinction or discrimination shall be made in the construction or execution of this act on account of race or color: *And provided further,* That no mineral lands shall be liable to entry and settlement under its provisions.

Mode of procedure in applying for the benefit of this act. 1862, ch. 75, 2. Vol. xii. p. 392.	SEC. 2. *And be it further enacted,* That section second of the above-cited homestead law, entitled "An act to secure homesteads to actual settlers on the public domain," approved May twentieth, eighteen hundred and sixty-two, be so amended as to read as follows: That the person applying for the benefit of this act shall, upon application to the register of the land office in which he or she is about
Affidavit.	to make such entry, make affidavit before the said register or receiver that he or she is the head of a family, or is twenty-one years or more of age, or shall have performed service in the army or navy of the United States, and that such application is made for his or her exclusive use and benefit, and that said entry is made for the purpose of actual settlement and cultivation, and not either directly or indirectly for the use or benefit of any other person or persons whomsoever; and upon filing the said affi-
Payment of $5.	davit with the register or receiver, and on payment of five dollars, when the entry is of not more than eighty acres, he or she shall thereupon be permitted
No certificate to be given nor patent to issue, until after five years from entry.	to enter the amount of land specified: *Provided, however,* That no certificate shall be given, or patent issued therefor, until the expiration of five years from the date of such entry; and if, at the expiration of such time, or at any time within two years thereafter, the person making such entry, or, if he be dead, his widow; or in case of her death, his heirs or
Proof of residence or cultivation, &c.	devisee, or in case of a widow making such entry, her heirs or devisee, in case of her death, shall prove by two credible witnesses that he, she, or they have resided upon or cultivated the same for the term of five years immediately succeeding the time of filing
Affidavit.	the affidavit aforesaid, and shall make affidavit that no part of said land has been alienated, and that he will bear true allegiance to the government of the United States; then, in such case, he, she, or they, if at that time a citizen of the United States, shall be entitled to a patent, as in other cases provided by law: *And provided further,* That in case of the

When rights enure to the benefit of infant children

Executor, &c., may sell.

Title of purchaser.

Additional oath prior to January 1, 1867.

Provisions of homestead law, &c, made applicable hereto.

death of both father and mother, leaving an infant child or children under twenty-one years of age, the right and fee shall enure to the benefit of said infant child or children, and the executor, administrator, or guardian may, at any time within two years after the death of the surviving parent, and in accordance with the laws of the State in which such children, for the time being, have their domicile, sell said land for the benefit of said infants, but for no other purpose; and the purchaser shall acquire the absolute title by the purchase, and be entitled to a patent from the United States on the payment of the office fees and sum of money herein specified *Provided,* That until the first day of January, eighteen hundred and sixty-seven, any person applying for the benefit of this act shall, in addition to the oath, hereinbefore required, also make oath that he has not borne arms against the United States, or given aid and comfort to its enemies.

SEC. 3. *And be it further enacted,* That all the provisions of the said homestead law, and the act amendatory thereof, approved March twenty-first, eighteen hundred and sixty-four, so far as the same may be applicable, except so far as the same are modified by the preceding sections of this act, are applied to and made part of this act as fully as if herein enacted and set forth.

APPROVED, June 21, 1866.

House Resolution 29 (1867)

A Bill Introduced by Thaddeus Stevens of Pennsylvania, H.R. 29 First Session Fortieth Congress, March 11, 1867: A Plan For Confiscation

Whereas it is due to justice, as an example of future times, that some proper punishment should be inflicted on the people who constituted the "confederate States of America," both because they, declaring an unjust war against the United States for the purpose of destroying republican liberty and permanently establishing slavery, as well as for the cruel and barbarous manner in which they conducted said war, in violation of all the laws of civilized warfare, and also to compel them to make some compensation for the damages and expenditures caused by the war: Therefore,

Be it enacted . . . That all the public lands belonging to the ten States that formed the government of the so-called "confederate States of America" shall be forfeited by said States and become forthwith vested in the United States.

Sec. 2. The President shall forthwith proceed to cause the seizure of such of the property belonging to the belligerent enemy as is deemed forfeited by the act of July 17, A.D. 1862, and hold and appropriate the same as enemy's property, and to proceed to condemnation with that already seized.

Sec. 3. In lieu of the proceeding to condemn the property thus seized as enemy's property, as is provided by the act of July 17, A.D. 1862, two commissions or more, as by him may be deemed necessary, shall be appointed by the President for each of the said "confederate States," to consist of three persons each, one of whom shall be an officer of the late or present Army, and two shall be civilians, neither of whom shall be citizens of the State for which he shall be appointed; the said commission shall proceed to adjudicate and condemn the property aforesaid, under such forms and proceedings as shall be prescribed by the Attorney General of the United States, whereupon the title to said property shall become vested in the United States.

Sec. 4. Out of the lands thus seized and confiscated, the slaves who have been liberated by the operations of the war and the amendment of the Constitution or otherwise, who resided in said "confederate States" on the 4th day of March, A.D. 1861, or since, shall have distributed to them as follows, namely: to each male person who is the head of a family, forty acres; to each adult male, whether the head of a family or not, forty acres; to each widow who is the head of a family, forty acres; to be held by them in fee simple, but to be inalienable for the next ten years after they become seized thereof. For the purpose of distributing and allotting said land, the Secretary of War shall appoint in each State as many commissions as he may deem necessary, to consist of three members each, two of whom at least shall not be citizens of the State for which he is appointed. At the end of ten years the absolute title to said homesteads shall be conveyed to said owners or to the heirs of such as are then dead.

Sec. 5. Out of the balance of the property thus seized and confiscated there shall be raised, in the manner hereinafter provided, a sum equal to fifty dollars, for each homestead, to be applied by the trustees hereinafter mentioned toward the erection of buildings on the said homesteads for the use of said slaves; and the further sum of $500,000,000, which shall be appropriated as follows, to wit: $200,000,000 shall be invested in the United States six per cent securities; and the interest thereof shall be semi-annually added to the pensions allowed by law to the pensioners who have become so by reason of the late war; $300,000,000, or so much thereof as may be needed, shall be appropriated to pay damages done to loyal citizens by the civil or military operations of the government lately called the "Confederate States of America."

Sec. 6. In order that just discrimination may be made, the property of no one shall be seized whose whole estate on the fourth day of March, anno Domini eighteen hundred and sixty-five, was not worth more than five thousand dollars, to be valued by the said commission, unless he shall have voluntarily become an officer or employee in the military or civil service of the "Confederate States of America," or in the civil or military service of some one of said States, and in enforcing all confiscations the sum or value of five thousand dollars in real or personal property shall be left or assigned to the delinquent.

Sec. 7. The commission shall put a just and impartial valuation on all the property thus seized and forfeited, and when such valuation shall be completed in the several States, all the said commissioners shall meet in the city of Washington and assess the five hundred millions aforesaid, as well as the allowances for homestead buildings, pro rata, on each of the properties or estates thus seized, and shall give notice of such assessment and apportionment by publication for sixty days in two daily newspapers in the city of Washington, and in two daily newspapers in the capitals of each of the said "Confederate States."

Sec. 8. If the owners of said seized and forfeited estates shall, within ninety days after the first of said publications, pay into the Treasury of the United States the sum assessed on their estates respectively, all of their estates and lands not actually appropriated to the liberated slaves shall be released and restored to their owners.

Sec. 9. All the land, estates and property, of whatever kind, which shall not be redeemed as aforesaid within ninety days, shall be sold and converted into money, in such time and manner as may be deemed by the said commissioners the most advantageous to the United States: *Provided,* That no arable land shall be sold in tracts larger than 500 acres.

U.S. Congress. House. HR 29, 40th Congr., 1st sess., Library of Congress, March 11, 1867 (http:/www.memory.loc.gov; accessed March 10, 2007).

Civil Liberties Act (1988)

Enacted by the United States Congress
August 10, 1988

"The Congress recognizes that, as described in the Commission on Wartime Relocation and Internment of Civilians, a grave injustice was done to both citizens and permanent residents of Japanese ancestry by the evacuation, relocation, and internment of civilians during World War II.

As the Commission documents, these actions were carried out without adequate security reasons and without any acts of espionage or sabotage documented by the Commission, and were motivated largely by racial prejudice, wartime hysteria, and a failure of political leadership.

The excluded individuals of Japanese ancestry suffered enormous damages, both material and intangible, and there were incalculable losses in education and job training, all of which resulted in significant human suffering for which appropriate compensation has not been made.

For these fundamental violations of the basic civil liberties and constitutional rights of these individuals of Japanese ancestry, the Congress apologizes on behalf of the Nation."

Based on the findings of the Commission on Wartime Relocation and Internment of Civilians (CWRIC), the purposes of the Civil Liberties Act of 1988 with respect to persons of Japanese ancestry included the following:

1) To acknowledge the fundamental injustice of the evacuation, relocation and internment of citizens and permanent resident aliens of Japanese ancestry during World War II;
2) To apologize on behalf of the people of the United States for the evacuation, internment, and relocations of such citizens and permanent residing aliens;
3) To provide for a public education fund to finance efforts to inform the public about the internment so as to prevent the recurrence of any similar event;

4) To make restitution to those individuals of Japanese ancestry who were interned;
5) To make more credible and sincere any declaration of concern by the United States over violations of human rights committed by other nations.

Civics Online, http://www.civics-online.org

House Resolution 356 (2000)

HCON 356 IH
106th CONGRESS
2d Session
H. CON. RES. 356
Acknowledging the fundamental injustice, cruelty, brutality, and inhumanity of slavery in the United States and the 13 American colonies, and for other purposes.
IN THE HOUSE OF REPRESENTATIVES
June 19, 2000
Mr. HALL of Ohio (for himself, Mr. BONIOR, Ms. CARSON, Mrs. CLAYTON, Mr. COBURN, Mr. COSTELLO, Mr. JACKSON of Illinois, Ms. JACKSON-LEE of Texas, Mr. JEFFERSON, Mrs. JONES of Ohio, Mr. LEWIS of Georgia, Ms. MCKINNEY, Mr. MCNULTY, Mr. MEEKS of New York, Mr. RUSH, Mr. TRAFICANT, Mr. ENGEL, Ms. LEE, AND Ms. KAPTUR) submitted the following concurrent resolution; which was referred to the Committee on Judiciary

CONCURRENT RESOLUTION

Acknowledging the fundamental injustice, cruelty, brutality, and inhumanity of slavery in the United States and the 13 American colonies, and for other purposes.

Whereas approximately 4,000,000 Africans and their descendants were enslaved in the United States and the 13 American colonies in the period 1619 through 1865;

Whereas slavery was a grave injustice that caused and continues to cause African-Americans to suffer enormous damages and losses, both material and intangible, including the loss of human dignity and liberty, the frustration of careers and professional lives, and the long-term loss of income and opportunity;

Whereas slavery in the United States denied African-Americans the fruits of their own labor and was an immoral and inhumane deprivation of life, liberty, the pursuit of happiness, citizenship rights, and cultural heritage;

Whereas, although the achievements of African-Americans in overcoming the evils of slavery stand as a source of tremendous inspiration, the successes of slaves and their descendants do not overwrite the failure of the Nation to grant all Americans their birthright of equality and the civil rights that safeguard freedom;

Whereas an apology is an important and necessary step in the process of racial reconciliation, because a sincere apology accompanied by an attempt at real restitution is an important healing interaction;

Whereas a genuine apology may restore damaged relationships, whether they are between 2 people or between groups of people;

Whereas African-American art, history, and culture reflects experiences of slavery and freedom, and continued struggles for full recognition of citizenship and treatment with human dignity, and there is inadequate presentation, preservation, and recognition of the contributions of African-Americans within American society;

Whereas there is a great need for building institutions and monuments to promote cultural understanding of African-American heritage and further enhance racial harmony; and

Whereas it is proper and timely for the Congress to recognize June 19, 1865, the historic day when the last group of slaves were informed of their freedom, to acknowledge the historic significance of the abolition of slavery, to express deep regret to African-Americans, and to support reconciliation efforts: Now, therefore, be it

> Resolved by the House of Representatives (the Senate concurring), That—

(1) the Congress—
> (A) acknowledges the fundamental injustice, cruelty, brutality, and inhumanity of slavery in the United States and the 13 American colonies;
> (B) apologizes to African-Americans on behalf of the people of the United States, for the wrongs committed against their ancestors who suffered as slaves;
> (C) expresses condemnation of and repudiates the gross and wanton

excesses perpetrated against African-Americans while the institution of slavery existed;

(D) recognizes the Nation's need to redress these events;

(E) commends efforts of reconciliation initiated by organizations and individuals concerned about civil rights and civil liberties and calls for a national initiative of reconciliation among the races; and

(F) expresses commitment to rectify misdeeds of slavery done in the past and to discourage the occurrence of human rights violations in the future; and

(2) it is the sense of the Congress that —

(A) a commission should be established —

(i) to examine the institution of slavery, subsequent racial and economic discrimination against African-Americans as a matter of law and as a matter of fact, and the impact of slavery and such discrimination on living African-Americans;

(ii) to issue a standardized, historical curriculum for use in public schools on the institution of slavery in the United States; and

(iii) to explore the possibility of establishing a scholarship and research fund; and

(B) a National museum and memorial should be established regarding slavery as it relates to the history of the United States, and other significant African-American history.

House Resolution 40 (2005)

109th CONGRESS
1st Session
H.R. 40
To acknowledge the fundamental injustice, cruelty, brutality, and inhumanity of slavery in the United States and the 13 American colonies between 1619 and 1865 and to establish a commission to examine the institution of slavery, subsequently de jure and de facto racial and economic discrimination against African-Americans, and the impact of these forces on living African-Americans, to make recommendations to the Congress on appropriate remedies, and for other purposes.
IN THE HOUSE OF REPRESENTATIVES
January 4, 2005
Mr. CONYERS (for himself, Ms. CORRINE BROWN of Florida, Mr. CLAY, Mr. DAVIS of Illinois, Ms. JACKSON-LEE of Texas, Ms. LEE, Mr. MEEK of Florida, Mr. NADLER, Mr. OLVER, Mr. PAYNE, Mr. RUSH, Mr. THOMPSON of Mississippi, Ms. WATERS, Mr. WATT, Mr. JACKSON of Illinois, Mr. MCDERMOTT, Mr. MEEKS of New York, Ms. MILLENDER-MCDONALD, Ms. NORTON, Mr. OWENS, Mr. RANGEL, Ms. SCHAKOWSKY, Mr. TOWNS, and Ms. WATSON) introduced the following bill; which was referred to the Committee on the Judiciary

A BILL

To acknowledge the fundamental injustice, cruelty, brutality, and inhumanity of slavery in the United States and the 13 American colonies between 1619 and 1865 and to establish a commission to examine the institution of slavery, subsequently de jure and de facto racial and economic discrimination against African-Americans, and the impact of these forces on living African-

Americans, to make recommendations to the Congress on appropriate remedies, and for other purposes.

Be it enacted by the Senate and House of Representatives of the United States of America in Congress assembled,

SECTION 1. SHORT TITLE.

This Act may be cited as the "Commission to Study Reparation Proposals for African-Americans Act."

SEC. 2. FINDINGS AND PURPOSE.

(a) Findings — The Congress finds that —
    (1) approximately 4,000,000 Africans and their descendants were enslaved in the United States and colonies that became the United States from 1619 to 1865;
    (2) the institution of slavery was constitutionally and statutorily sanctioned by the Government of the United States from 1789 through 1865;
    (3) the slavery that flourished in the United States constituted an immoral and inhumane deprivation of Africans' life, liberty, African citizenship rights, and cultural heritage, and denied them the fruits of their own labor; and
    (4) sufficient inquiry has not been made into the effects of the institution of slavery on living African-Americans and society in the United States.

(b) Purpose — The purpose of this Act is to establish a commission to —
    (1) examine the institution of slavery which existed from 1619 through 1865 within the United States and the colonies that became the United States, including the extent to which the Federal and State Governments constitutionally and statutorily supported the institution of slavery;
    (2) examine de jure and de facto discrimination against freed slaves and their descendants from the end of the Civil War to the present, including economic, political, and social discrimination;
    (3) examine the lingering negative effects of the institution of slavery and the discrimination described in paragraph (2) on living African-Americans and on society in the United States;
    (4) recommend appropriate ways to educate the American public of the Commission's findings;

(5) recommend appropriate remedies in consideration of the Commission's findings on the matters described in paragraphs (1) and (2); and
(6) submit to the Congress the results of such examination, together with such recommendations.

SEC. 3. ESTABLISHMENT AND DUTIES.

(a) Establishment — There is established the Commission to Study Reparation Proposals for African-Americans (hereinafter in this Act referred to as the "Commission").
(b) Duties — The Commission shall perform the following duties:
    (1) Examine the institution of slavery which existed within the United States and the colonies that became the United States from 1619 through 1865. The Commission's examination shall include an examination of —
        (A) the capture and procurement of Africans;
        (B) the transport of Africans to the United States and the colonies that became the United States for the purpose of enslavement, including their treatment during transport;
        (C) the sale and acquisition of Africans as chattel property in interstate and intrastate commerce; and
        (D) the treatment of African slaves in the colonies and the United States, including the deprivation of their freedom, exploitation of their labor, and destruction of their culture, language, religion, and families.
    (2) Examine the extent to which the Federal and State governments of the United States supported the institution of slavery in constitutional and statutory provisions, including the extent to which such governments prevented, opposed, or restricted efforts of freed African slaves to repatriate to their homeland.
    (3) Examine Federal and State laws that discriminated against freed African slaves and their descendants during the period between the end of the Civil War and the present.
    (4) Examine other forms of discrimination in the public and private sectors against freed African slaves and their descendants during the period between the end of the Civil War and the present.
    (5) Examine the lingering negative effects of the institution of slavery and the matters described in paragraphs (1), (2), (3), and (4) on living African-Americans and on society in the United States.

(6) Recommend appropriate ways to educate the American public of the Commission's findings.

(7) Recommend appropriate remedies in consideration of the Commission's findings on the matters described in paragraphs (1), (2), (3), and (8). In making such recommendations, the Commission shall address among other issues, the following questions:

> (A) Whether the Government of the United States should offer a formal apology on behalf of the people of the United States for the perpetration of gross human rights violations on African slaves and their descendants.
>
> (B) Whether African-Americans still suffer from the lingering effects of the matters described in paragraphs (1), (2), (3), and (4).
>
> (C) Whether, in consideration of the Commission's findings, any form of compensation to the descendants of African slaves is warranted.
>
> (D) If the Commission finds that such compensation is warranted, what should be the amount of compensation, what form of compensation should be awarded, and who should be eligible for such compensation.

(c) Report to Congress — The Commission shall submit a written report of its findings and recommendations to the Congress not later than the date which is one year after the date of the first meeting of the Commission held pursuant to section 4(c).

SEC. 4. MEMBERSHIP.

(a) Number and Appointment —

> (1) The Commission shall be composed of 7 members, who shall be appointed, within 90 days after the date of enactment of this Act, as follows:
>
> > (A) Three members shall be appointed by the President.
> >
> > (B) Three members shall be appointed by the Speaker of the House of Representatives.
> >
> > (C) One member shall be appointed by the President pro tempore of the Senate.
>
> (2) All members of the Commission shall be persons who are especially qualified to serve on the Commission by virtue of their education, training, or experience, particularly in the field of African-American studies.

(b) Terms — The term of office for members shall be for the life of the Commission. A vacancy in the Commission shall not affect the powers of the Commission, and shall be filled in the same manner in which the original appointment was made.

(c) First Meeting — The President shall call the first meeting of the Commission within 120 days after the date of the enactment of this Act, or within 30 days after the date on which legislation is enacted making appropriations to carry out this Act, whichever date is later.

(d) Quorum — Four members of the Commission shall constitute a quorum, but a lesser number may hold hearings.

(e) Chair and Vice Chair — The Commission shall elect a Chair and Vice Chair from among its members. The term of office of each shall be for the life of the Commission.

(f) Compensation —

(1) Except as provided in paragraph (2), each member of the Commission shall receive compensation at the daily equivalent of the annual rate of basic pay payable for GS-18 of the General Schedule under section 5332 of title 5, United States Code, for each day, including travel time, during which he or she is engaged in the actual performance of duties vested in the Commission.

(2) A member of the Commission who is a full-time officer or employee of the United States or a Member of Congress shall receive no additional pay, allowances, or benefits by reason of his or her service to the Commission.

(3) All members of the Commission shall be reimbursed for travel, subsistence, and other necessary expenses incurred by them in the performance of their duties to the extent authorized by chapter 57 of title 5, United States Code.

SEC. 5. POWERS OF THE COMMISSION.

(a) Hearings and Sessions — The Commission may, for the purpose of carrying out the provisions of this Act, hold such hearings and sit and act at such times and at such places in the United States, and request the attendance and testimony of such witnesses and the production of such books, records, correspondence, memoranda, papers, and documents, as the Commission considers appropriate. The Commission may request the Attorney General to invoke the aid of an appropriate United States district court to require, by subpoena or otherwise, such attendance, testimony, or production.

(b) Powers of Subcommittees and Members — Any subcommittee or member of the Commission may, if authorized by the Commission, take any action which the Commission is authorized to take by this section.

(c) Obtaining Official Data — The Commission may acquire directly from the head of any department, agency, or instrumentality of the executive branch of the Government, available information which the Commission considers useful in the discharge of its duties. All departments, agencies, and instrumentalities of the executive branch of the Government shall cooperate with the Commission with respect to such information and shall furnish all information requested by the Commission to the extent permitted by law.

SEC. 6. ADMINISTRATIVE PROVISIONS.

(a) Staff — The Commission may, without regard to section 5311(b) of title 5, United States Code, appoint and fix the compensation of such personnel as the Commission considers appropriate.

(b) Applicability of Certain Civil Service Laws — The staff of the Commission may be appointed without regard to the provisions of title 5, United States Code, governing appointments in the competitive service, and without regard to the provisions of chapter 51 and subchapter III of chapter 53 of such title relating to classification and General Schedule pay rates, except that the compensation of any employee of the Commission may not exceed a rate equal to the annual rate of basic pay payable for GS-18 of the General Schedule under section 5332 of title 5, United States Code.

(c) Experts and Consultants — The Commission may procure the services of experts and consultants in accordance with the provisions of section 3109(b) of title 5, United States Code, but at rates for individuals not to exceed the daily equivalent of the highest rate payable under section 5332 of such title.

(d) Administrative Support Services — The Commission may enter into agreements with the Administrator of General Services for procurement of financial and administrative services necessary for the discharge of the duties of the Commission. Payment for such services shall be made by reimbursement from funds of the Commission in such amounts as may be agreed upon by the Chairman of the Commission and the Administrator.

(e) Contracts — The Commission may —
    (1) procure supplies, services, and property by contract in accordance with applicable laws and regulations and to the extent or in such amounts as are provided in appropriations Acts; and
    (2) enter into contract with departments, agencies, and instrumentalities of the Federal Government, State agencies, and private firms, institutions, and agencies, for the conduct of research or surveys, the

preparation of reports, and other activities necessary for the discharge of the duties of the Commission, to the extent or in such amounts as are provided in appropriations Acts.

SEC. 7. TERMINATION

The Commission shall terminate 90 days after the date on which the Commission submits its report to the Congress under section 3(c).

SEC. 8. AUTHORIZATION OF APPROPRIATIONS.

To carry out the provisions of this Act, there are authorized to be appropriated $8,000,000.

Senate Resolution 39 (2005)

109th CONGRESS 1st SESSION
S. RES. 39
Apologizing to the victims of lynching and the descendants of those victims for the failure of the Senate to enact anti-lynching legislation.

IN THE SENATE OF THE UNITED STATES

FEBRUARY 7, 2005
Ms. LANDRIEU (for herself, Mr. ALLEN, Mr. LEVIN, Mr. FRIST, Mr. REID, Mr. ALLARD, Mr. AKAKA, Mr. BROWNBACK, Mr. BAYH, Ms. COLLINS, Mr. BIDEN, Mr. ENSIGN, Mrs. BOXER, Mr. HAGEL, Mr. CORZINE, Mr. LUGAR, Mr. DAYTON, Mr. McCAIN, Mr. DODD, Ms. SNOWE, Mr. DURBIN, Mr. SPECTER, Mr. FEINGOLD, Mr. STEVENS, Mrs. FEINSTEIN, Mr. TALENT, Mr. HARKIN, Mr. JEFFORDS, Mr. JOHNSON, Mr. KENNEDY, Mr. KOHL, Mr. LAUTENBERG, Mr. LEAHY, Mr. LIEBERMAN, Mr. NELSON of Florida, Mr. PRYOR, and Mr. SCHUMER) submitted the following resolution; which was referred to the Committee on the Judiciary

RESOLUTION

Apologizing to the victims of lynching and the descendants of those victims for the failure of the Senate to enact anti-lynching legislation.
   Whereas the crime of lynching succeeded slavery as the ultimate expression of racism in the United States following Reconstruction;
   Whereas lynching was a widely acknowledged practice in the United States until the middle of the 20th century;

Whereas lynching was a crime that occurred throughout the United States, with documented incidents in all but 4 States;

Whereas at least 4,742 people, predominantly African-Americans, were reported lynched in the United States between 1882 and 1968;

Whereas 99 percent of all perpetrators of lynching escaped from punishment by State or local officials;

Whereas lynching prompted African-Americans to form the National Association for the Advancement of Colored People (NAACP) and prompted members of B'nai B'rith to found the Anti-Defamation League;

Whereas nearly 200 anti-lynching bills were introduced in Congress during the first half of the 20th century;

Whereas, between 1890 and 1952, 7 Presidents petitioned Congress to end lynching;

Whereas, between 1920 and 1940, the House of Representatives passed 3 strong anti-lynching measures;

Whereas protection against lynching was the minimum and most basic of Federal responsibilities, and the Senate considered but failed to enact anti-lynching legislation despite repeated requests by civil rights groups, Presidents, and the House of Representatives to do so;

Whereas the recent publication of "Without Sanctuary: Lynching Photography in America" helped bring greater awareness and proper recognition of the victims of lynching;

Whereas only by coming to terms with history can the United States effectively champion human rights abroad; and

Whereas an apology offered in the spirit of true repentance moves the United States toward reconciliation and may become central to a new understanding, on which improved racial relations can be forged: Now, therefore, be it

Resolved, That the Senate—

(1) apologizes to the victims of lynching for the failure of the Senate to enact anti-lynching legislation;

(2) expresses the deepest sympathies and most solemn regrets of the Senate to the descendants of victims of lynching, the ancestors of whom were deprived of life, human dignity, and the constitutional protections accorded all citizens of the United States; and

(3) remembers the history of lynching, to ensure that these tragedies will be neither forgotten nor repeated.

Senate Resolution 44 (2005)

109th CONGRESS
1st SESSION
S. RES. 44
Celebrating Black History Month.

IN THE SENATE OF THE UNITED STATES

FEBRUARY 8, 2005
Mr. ALEXANDER (for himself and Mr. COLEMAN) submitted the following resolution; which was referred to the Committee on the Judiciary

RESOLUTION

Celebrating Black History Month.
 Whereas the first African Americans were brought forcibly to these shores as early as the 17th century;
 Whereas African Americans were enslaved in the United States and subsequently faced the injustices of lynch mobs, segregation, and denial of basic, fundamental rights;
 Whereas in spite of these injustices, African Americans have made significant contributions to the economic, educational, political, artistic, literary, scientific, and technological advancement of the United States;
 Whereas in the face of these injustices Americans of all races distinguished themselves in their commitment to the ideals on which the United States was founded, and fought for the rights of African Americans;
 Whereas the greatness of America is reflected in the contributions of African Americans in all walks of life throughout the history of the United States:

in the writings of W. E. B. Du Bois, James Baldwin, Ralph Ellison, and Alex Haley; in the music of Mahalia Jackson, Billie Holiday, and Duke Ellington; in the resolve of athletes such as Jackie Robinson and Muhammad Ali; in the vision of leaders such as Frederick Douglass, Thurgood Marshall, and Martin Luther King, Jr.; and in the bravery of those who stood on the front lines in the battle against oppression such as Harriet Tubman and Rosa Parks;

Whereas the United States of America was conceived, as stated in the Declaration of Independence, as a new nation dedicated to the proposition that "all Men are created equal, that they are endowed by their Creator with certain inalienable Rights, that among these are Life, Liberty and the Pursuit of Happiness";

Whereas the actions of Americans of all races demonstrate their commitment to that proposition: actions such as those of Allan Pinkerton, Thomas Garrett, and the Rev. John Rankin who served as conductors on the Underground Railroad; actions such as those of Harriet Beecher Stowe, who shined a light on the injustices of slavery; actions such as those of President Abraham Lincoln, who issued the Emancipation Proclamation, and Senator Lyman Trumbull, who introduced the 13th Amendment to the Constitution of the United States; actions such as those of President Lyndon B. Johnson, Chief Justice Earl Warren, Senator Mike Mansfield, and Senator Hubert Humphrey, who fought to end segregation and the denial of civil rights to African Americans; and the thousands of Americans of all races who marched side-by-side with African Americans during the civil rights movement;

Whereas since its founding the United States has been an imperfect work in progress toward these noble goals;

Whereas American History is the story of a people regularly affirming high ideals, striving to reach them but often failing, and then struggling to come to terms with the disappointment of that failure before recommitting themselves to trying again;

Whereas from the beginning of our Nation the most conspicuous and persistent failure of Americans to reach our noble goals has been the enslavement of African Americans and the resulting racism;

Whereas the crime of lynching succeeded slavery as the ultimate expression of racism in the United States following Reconstruction;

Whereas the Federal Government failed to put an end to slavery until the ratification of the 13th Amendment in 1865, repeatedly failed to enact a federal anti-lynching law, and still struggles to deal with the evils of racism; and

Whereas the fact that 61 percent of African American 4th graders read at a below basic level and only 16 percent of native born African Americans have earned a Bachelor's degree; 50 percent of all new HIV cases are reported in African Americans; and the leading cause of death for African American males ages 15 to 34 is homicide demonstrates that the United States continues to struggle to reach the high ideal of equal opportunity for all Americans: Now, therefore, be it

Resolved, That the Senate —

(1) acknowledges the tragedies of slavery, lynching, segregation, and condemns them as an infringement on human liberty and equal opportunity so that they will stand forever as a reminder of what can happen when Americans fail to live up to their noble goals;

(2) honors those Americans who during the time of slavery, lynching, and segregation risked their lives in the underground railway and in other efforts to assist fugitive slaves and other African Americans who might have been targets and victims of lynch mobs and those who have stood beside African Americans in the fight for equal opportunity that continues to this day;

(3) reaffirms its commitment to the founding principles of the United States of America that "all Men are created equal, that they are endowed by their Creator with certain inalienable Rights, that among these are Life, Liberty, and the Pursuit of Happiness"; and

(4) commits itself to addressing those situations in which the African American community struggles with disparities in education, health care, and other areas where the Federal Government can play a role in improving conditions for all Americans.

Section 2

State Legislation

Michigan House Bill No. 5562 (2000)

April 11, 2000, Introduced by Reps. Hale, Thomas, Vaughn, Clark, Kilpatrick, Hardman, Rison, Price, Quarles, Garza, Clarke, Scott, Stallworth, Reeves, Daniels and Lemmons and referred to the Committee on Tax Policy. A bill to amend 1967 PA 281, entitled "Income tax act of 1967" (MCL 206.1 to 206.532) by adding section 267.

THE PEOPLE OF THE STATE OF MICHIGAN ENACT:

SEC. 267. (1) For tax years that begin after December 31, 1999, a qualified taxpayer may claim a credit equal to $16,500.00 against the tax imposed by this act which shall be claimed in 20 consecutive years starting with the taxpayer's tax year that begins in calendar year 2000.

(2) The total amount claimed for all tax years by a taxpayer under this section shall not exceed $330,000.00.

(3) If the amount of the credit allowed under this section exceeds the tax liability of the taxpayer for the tax year, that portion of the credit that exceeds the taxpayer's tax liability shall be refunded.

(4) As used in this section, "qualified taxpayer" means an individual who meets either of the following criteria:

(A) He or she was born in this state, his or her birth certificate states that he or she is of African-American descent, and he or she has resided in this state for the 10 years immediately preceding the tax year in which the credit under this section is first claimed.

(B) He or she has resided in this state for the 10 years immediately preceding the tax year in which the credit under this section is first claimed and can prove that he or she is of African-American descent.

California Senate Bill No. 2199 (2000)

CHAPTER 934

An act to add Chapter 5 (commencing with Section 13310) to Division 3 of the Insurance Code, relating to insurance.
[Approved by Governor September 29, 2000. Filed with Secretary of State September 30, 2000.]

LEGISLATIVE COUNSEL'S DIGEST

SB 2199, Hayden. Slavery era insurance policies.
Existing law requires an insurer doing business in this state that sold certain policies of insurance directly or through a related company to persons in Europe between 1920 and 1945 to provide certain information to the Insurance Commissioner for entry into the Holocaust Era Insurance Registry, as specified.

This bill would require the commissioner to request and obtain information from insurers doing business in this state regarding any records of slaveholder insurance policies issued by any predecessor corporation during the slavery era, which policies provided coverage to slaveholders for damage to or death of their slaves. This bill would require insurers to research and report on these policies, and would require the commissioner to make this information available to the public and the Legislature. This bill would state that descendants of slaves are entitled to full disclosure.

The people of the State of California do enact as follows:

SECTION 1. The Legislature finds and declares all of the following:
(a) Insurance policies from the slavery era have been discovered in the archives of several insurance companies, documenting insurance coverage for slaveholders for damage to or death of their slaves, issued by a pre-

decessor insurance firm. These documents provide the first evidence of ill-gotten profits from slavery, which profits in part capitalized insurers whose successors remain in existence today.

(b) Legislation has been introduced in Congress for the past 10 years demanding an inquiry into slavery and its continuing legacies.

(c) The Insurance Commissioner and the Department of Insurance are entitled to seek information from the files of insurers licensed and doing business in this state, including licensed California subsidiaries of international insurance corporations, regarding insurance policies issued to slaveholders by predecessor corporations. The people of California are entitled to significant historical information of this nature.

SEC. 2. Chapter 5 (commencing with Section 13810) is added to Division 3 of the Insurance Code, to read:

CHAPTER 5. SLAVERY ERA INSURANCE POLICIES

13810. The commissioner shall request and obtain information from insurers licensed and doing business in this state regarding any records of slaveholder insurance policies issued by any predecessor corporation during the slavery era.

13811. The commissioner shall obtain the names of any slaveholders or slaves described in those insurance records, and shall make the information available to the public and the Legislature.

13812. Each insurer licensed and doing business in this state shall research and report to the commissioner with respect to any records within the insurer's possession or knowledge relating to insurance policies issued to slaveholders that provided coverage for damage to or death of their slaves.

13813. Descendants of slaves, whose ancestors were defined as private property, dehumanized, divided from their families, forced to perform labor without appropriate compensation or benefits, and whose ancestors' owners were compensated for damages by insurers, are entitled to full disclosure.

California Senate Joint Resolution No. 1 (2001)

RESOLUTION CHAPTER 86

Senate Joint Resolution No. 1 — Relative to slavery.
[Filed with Secretary of State July 19, 2001.]

LEGISLATIVE COUNSEL'S DIGEST

SJR 1, Murray. Slavery.
This measure would memorialize Congress to enact legislation similar to House Concurrent Resolution 356, which, among other things, would acknowledge the fundamental injustice, cruelty, brutality, and inhumanity of slavery in the United States and the 13 American colonies, apologize to African-Americans on behalf of the people of the United States for the wrongs committed against their ancestors who suffered as slaves, and urge the establishment of a national museum and memorial regarding slavery as it relates to the history of the United States, and other significant African-American history. The measure would also memorialize Congress to enact legislation similar to House Resolution 40, which would establish the Commission to Study Reparation Proposals for African-Americans.

WHEREAS, Approximately 4,000,000 Africans and their descendants were enslaved in the United States and the 13 American colonies in the period 1619 through 1865; and
WHEREAS, Slavery was a grave injustice that caused and continues to cause African-Americans to suffer enormous damages and losses, both material and intangible, including the loss of human dignity and liberty, the frustration of careers and professional lives, and the long-term loss of income and opportunity; and
WHEREAS, Slavery in the United States denied African-Americans the fruits

of their own labor and was an immoral and inhumane deprivation of life, liberty, the pursuit of happiness, citizenship rights, and cultural heritage; and

WHEREAS, Although the achievements of African-Americans in overcoming the evils of slavery stand as a source of tremendous inspiration, the successes of slaves and their descendants do not overwrite the failure of the nation to grant all Americans their birthright of equality and the civil rights that safeguard freedom; and

WHEREAS, An apology is an important and necessary step in the process of racial reconciliation, because a sincere apology accompanied by an attempt at real restitution is an important healing interaction; and

WHEREAS, A genuine apology may restore damaged relationships, whether they are between two people or between groups of people; and

WHEREAS, African-American art, history, and culture reflect experiences of slavery and freedom, and continued struggles for full recognition of citizenship and treatment with human dignity, and there is inadequate presentation, preservation, and recognition of the contributions of African-Americans within American society; and

WHEREAS, There is a great need for building institutions and monuments to promote cultural understanding of African-American heritage and further enhance racial harmony; and

WHEREAS, A commission to study reparation proposals for African-Americans should be established; now, therefore, be it

Resolved by the Senate and Assembly of the State of California, jointly, That the Legislature respectfully memorializes the United States Congress to enact legislation similar to House Concurrent Resolution 356, which was introduced on June 19, 2000, and House Resolution 40, which was introduced on January 6, 1989; and be it further

Resolved, That the Secretary of the Senate transmit copies of this resolution to the Speaker of the House of Representatives, the Chairpersons of the House and Senate Judiciary Committees, and to each Senator and Representative from California in the Congress of the United States.

New Jersey African-American Reconciliation Study Commission Act (2003)

An Act establishing the New Jersey African-American Reconciliation Study Commission and making an appropriation.
Be It Enacted by the Senate and General Assembly of the State of New Jersey:

1. The Legislature finds and declares that:

a. The institution of slavery in America dates back to the beginning of the colonial period. Slavery was constitutionally and statutorily sanctioned by the United States government from 1789 through 1865. During that period, millions of persons of African origin were brought to this country against their will, deprived of their liberty, their property, their children and often their lives. Slavery assaulted the dignity and humanity of the persons who were enslaved, treating them as property and forced them to work under brutal physical and psychological conditions.

b. The presence of slavery in New Jersey can be dated from the beginnings of Dutch settlement, between 1625 and 1626.

c. The growing influence of the abolitionist movement in this State led to the outlawing of the importation of slaves in 1786, the progressive manumission of slaves in 1794, and legislation enacted in 1804 to abolish slavery gradually.

d. Slavery continued in New Jersey despite these laws. The State Legislature passed "Peace Resolutions" denying President Lincoln's power to emancipate slaves and later voted against the 13th Amendment to the United States Constitution. Slavery was not abolished in this State until the 1865 enactment of the 13th Amendment.

e. Emancipation was followed by over one hundred years of legal segregation and widespread discrimination against African-Americans. Core elements of our democracy were affected, including voting and other political and constitutional rights and our system of civil and criminal justice. These legacies of slavery impeded African-American efforts to protect themselves and their communities through political action.

f. Slaves and their descendants were deprived of access to real property, public accommodations, public benefits and other resources that have enabled voluntary immigrant groups to advance economically in America.

g. The legacy of slavery survives in New Jersey to this day, in the form of racial discrimination, racial profiling and social and economic segregation. These legacies affect all areas of individual and community life, including housing, education, employment, health care, spiritual life, political rights, law enforcement and justice.

h. The full effects of the institution and legacies of slavery on African-Americans living in New Jersey and their communities have never been sufficiently examined, nor has there been formal acknowledgment of such effects, remedies for past injustice and present harm, or sufficient efforts at reconciliation.

i. Reconciliation between the African-American community and other communities in New Jersey would benefit all persons in this State.

j. Precedents in our country for reconciliation and remedies for past injustice have involved Native Americans, Japanese Americans, Jews, Filipino veterans and African-Americans victimized by the 1930s' syphilis experiments, and the Rosewood riots.

k. The Legislature declares that it is in the interest of the State and of the people of New Jersey for government to initiate and foster methods of improving knowledge and understanding between African-Americans and other peoples in New Jersey and adopting and initiating tested methods to foster communication and dialogue, for the purpose of achieving reconciliation and peace.

2. There is established in the Executive Branch of the State Government a commission to be known as the New Jersey African-American Reconciliation Study Commission. For the purpose of complying with the provisions of Article V, Section IV, paragraph 1 of the New Jersey Constitution, the commission is allocated within the Department of State.

3.a. The commission shall consist of 39 members, chosen to ensure ethnic diversity and broad geographic representation within New Jersey. Commission members shall be persons who are leaders in African-American organizations or communities, or have training or a verifiable interest in the history of slavery in America, New Jersey history and political science, African-American history, African-Caribbean history, labor history, penal history and law enforcement, economics, education, health, housing, human services, law, psychology, religion or sociology.

b. The Secretary of State shall be a member of the commission. The Governor shall appoint 31 public members, three shall be historians, two shall be students or members of youth organizations that support the work of the commission, two shall be members of the public, one person shall have expertise in public health administration and policies affecting the African-American community, one shall be recommended by the Director of the Division on Civil Rights in the Department of Law and Public Safety, one shall be recommended by the Director of the Office of Bias Crimes and Community Relations in the Division of Criminal Justice in the Department of Law and Public safety, one shall be recommended by Amnesty International-USA, one shall be recommended by the American Civil Liberties Union of New Jersey, one shall be recommended by the National Association for the Advancement of Colored People, one shall be recommended by the New Jersey Human and Civil Rights Association, one shall be recommended by the New Jersey Black Issues Convention, one shall be recommended by the National Coalition of Blacks for Reparations in America, one shall be recommended by the New Jersey Coalition for Reparations, one shall be recommended by the Coalition for Justice, one shall be recommended by the Urban League, one shall be recommended by the New Jersey Chapter of the Association of Black Psychologists; one attorney shall be recommended by the Association of Black Women Lawyers of New Jersey and one attorney shall be recommended by the New Jersey Bar Association, each of which shall have experience in reparations, the representation of African-Americans or advocacy on behalf of the interests of African-Americans; one shall be recommended by the Black Cops Against Police Brutality, one shall be recommended by the Black Ministers Council, one shall be recommended by the Black Psychiatrists of America, one shall be recommended by the Black Trade Unionists, one shall be recommended by the Education Law Center, one shall be recommended by the Fair Share Housing Center, one shall be recommended by the New Jersey Chapter of the National Economic Association, one shall be recommended by the New Jersey Association of Black Sociologists, and one shall be recommended by the New Jersey Association on Correction. No more than 16 members appointed by the Governor shall be members of the same political party.

c. Each Senate President shall appoint one member of the Senate, each of whom shall be a member of a different political party. The Speaker of the General Assembly and the Majority Leader and the Minority Leader of the General Assembly shall each appoint one member of the General Assembly, no more than two of which shall be members of the same political party. The

Senate Presidents, together with the Speaker of the General Assembly and the Minority leader thereof shall jointly appoint two additional members, each shall be recommended by the Black and Latino Caucus and each shall be members of different political parties.

d. Vacancies in the membership of the commission shall be filled in the same manner as the original appointments were made.

4. The members of the commission shall be appointed and shall hold their initial organizational meeting within 60 days after the effective date of this act. The members shall elect one of the members to serve as chair and the chair may appoint a secretary, who need not be a member of the commission. The members of the commission shall serve without compensation, but shall be eligible for reimbursement for necessary and reasonable expenses incurred in the performance of their official duties within the limits of funds appropriated or otherwise made available to the commission for its purposes. In addition, the commission shall solicit, receive and accept appropriations, gifts and donations. Legislative members shall serve during the term for which they were elected or selected.

5. The commission shall meet at least monthly and at the call of the chair. A meeting of the commission shall be called upon the request of 20 of the commission's members and 20 members of the commission shall constitute a quorum at any meeting thereof.

6.a. The commission shall hold at least five public hearings in different parts of the State, including Newark, Paterson, New Brunswick, Trenton and Camden at such times and places as the commission shall determine. The mayor of the city or municipality in which the hearing is held, the members of the board of chosen freeholds and the members of the Human Relations Committee of the county in which the city or municipality is located shall be invited to testify before the commission. All issues raised by those testifying at the hearings shall be recorded and included, together with the commission's responses if any, in the commission's report to the Governor and Legislature.

b. The commission shall publicize its mission and procedures throughout the State, through county human rights committees, the organizations recommending members of the commission and other ways. The commission shall invite public comment on the issues raised by the commission as part of its responsibilities.

7. The commission shall have the following responsibilities:

a. examine the institution of slavery and its legacies in the colony and the State between 1625 and the present;

b. examine the extent to which the State supported the institution of slavery in its Constitutional and statutory law and in its regulations, policies, practices and judicial decisions;

c identify the State-created or supported entities that profited or attempted to profit from commercial involvement with the international and domestic trade of African slaves or from the forced labor of African slaves and their descendants;

d. examine the extent to which State laws that discriminated against freed African slaves, their decedents and other African-Americans residing in New Jersey, and to identify policies and practices, including economic, political and social discrimination by the State and State-created or supported entities, between 1865 and the present;

e. examine the extent to which the State and State-created and supported entities benefited from the institution and legacies of slavery;

f. examine the effects of the institution and legacies of slavery on African-Americans and their communities in New Jersey;

g. quantify the debt owed by the State of New Jersey, local governments and State-created and supported entities to African-Americans residing in New Jersey for wages, benefits, interest and compensation for the de jure and de facto support and protection of the institution of slavery and its legacies;

h. recommend specific remedies be offered to African-Americans residing in New Jersey and their communities for violations of the human and civil rights of African-Americans during two centuries of slavery, and the continuing suffering and harm caused by segregation, discrimination and other social, economic and political effects of slavery and its legacies;

i. determine eligibility requirements for individuals and communities to be offered such remedies;

j. research methods and materials for facilitating education, community dialogue, symbolic acknowledgment and other formal actions leading to reconciliation and a sense of justice among the peoples of this State;

k. make recommendations for local, county and Statewide actions to follow up the commission's recommendations;

l. estimate the intended benefits and costs of the commission's recommendations; and

m. consider such other matters relating to the institution and legacies of slavery in New Jersey as the members of the commission may deem appropriate.

8.a. The commission is authorized to call upon any department, office, division or agency of the State, or of any county, municipality or school district of the State, to supply such data, program reports and other information, personnel and assistance as it deems necessary to discharge its responsibilities under this act.

b. These departments, offices, divisions and agencies shall, to the extent possible and not inconsistent with any other law of this State, cooperate with the commission and shall furnish it with such information, personnel and assistance as may be necessary or helpful to accomplish the purposes of this act.

c. The commission is authorized to procure the services of such experts and consultants to assist with its work as it deems necessary.

9. The commission shall report its initial findings and recommendations to the Governor, the Legislature and the public within 16 months of its initial organizational meeting. The initial report shall be disseminated widely throughout the State, with notice given that additional comments received by the commission within 60 days after the release of the initial report shall be forwarded to the Governor and the Legislature. After the initial report is released, the commission shall provide quarterly reports of its activities and findings to the Governor and the Legislature for the duration of its existence.

10. There shall be appropriated from the General Fund to the commission the sum of $75,000 to effectuate its provisions.

11. This act shall take effect immediately and shall expire on the day exactly five years after the commission submits its findings and recommendations to the Governor and Legislature.

Texas House Joint Resolution 25 (2003)

78R2164 MTB-F
TEXAS HOUSE (H.J.R. No. 25)

JOINT RESOLUTION NO. 25

proposing a constitutional amendment prohibiting discrimination against or preferential treatment of a person in public employment, public education, or public contracting after the economic effects of past discrimination have been offset through the payment of *reparations*.

BE IT RESOLVED BY THE LEGISLATURE OF
THE STATE OF TEXAS:

SECTION 1. Article I, Texas Constitution, is amended by adding Sections 3b and 3c to read as follows:

Sec. 3b. (a) To the extent that African Americans, Native Americans, Hispanic Americans, and women in Texas were victims of past discrimination sanctioned by the state and political subdivisions of the state, African Americans, Native Americans, Hispanic Americans, and women who are Texas residents are entitled to reparations to compensate for the economic effects of that discrimination.

(b) A reparations commission composed of nine members shall be appointed. Four members shall be appointed by the lieutenant governor, four members shall be appointed by the speaker of the house of representatives, and one member shall be appointed by the governor. The member appointed by the governor and a majority of the members of the commission appointed by the lieutenant governor and the speaker must be members of a group

entitled to reparations under Subsection (a) of this section. Members serve until the commission is abolished. In the event of a vacancy, the appointing authority shall appoint a replacement. Notwithstanding other law, a person who holds other public office may serve as a member of the commission. A member of the commission serves without compensation but is entitled to reimbursement in the manner provided by law for actual expenses incurred in the performance of official commission duties.

(c) The commission shall study past de jure and de facto racial and economic discrimination against members of the groups described by Subsection (a) of this section and the impact of that discrimination on living persons who are members of those groups. The amount of reparations to which a person is entitled shall be established by the reparations commission. The commission shall complete its study no later than December 31, 2004.

(d) Not later than the convening of the 79th Legislature in 2005, the commission shall adopt a schedule of reparations payments for persons who are members of groups entitled to reparations. Each member of a group is entitled to an equal dollar amount of the reparations, but the commission may establish different dollar amounts among groups.

(e) Reparations are payable from funds appropriated for that purpose. Payment shall be made in the manner provided by law under the general supervision of the reparations commission. The legislature shall determine by general law an individual's entitlement to reparations. All reparations must be paid not later than December 31, 2010.

(f) On December 31, 2010, the governor shall issue a proclamation that the economic effects of past discrimination against members of the groups entitled to reparations have been offset.

Sec. 3c. The state and its political subdivisions may not discriminate against or grant preferential treatment to a person because of the person's race, sex, sexual orientation, color, ethnicity, or national origin in matters of public employment, public education, or public contracting.

SECTION 2. The following temporary provision is added to the Texas Constitution:

TEMPORARY PROVISION. (a) This temporary provision applies to the constitutional amendment proposed by the 78th Legislature, Regular Session, 2003, that creates a reparations commission and prohibits certain discrimination or preferential treatment after the payment of reparations. This temporary provision expires January 2, 2011.

(b) On January 1, 2011:
(1) the reparations commission is abolished;
(2) Section 3b, Article I, of this constitution expires; and
(3) Section 3c, Article I, of this constitution first takes effect.

SECTION 3. This proposed constitutional amendment shall be submitted to the voters at an election to be held November 4, 20c3. The ballot shall be printed to permit voting for or against the proposition: "The constitutional amendment to prohibit discrimination against or preferential treatment of persons in public employment, public education, or public contracting after the economic effects of past discrimination have been offset through the payment of *reparations*."

Maryland House Joint Resolution 4 (2004)

2004 Regular Session
4lr2170
CF 4lr2684
By: Delegates Marriott, Benson, Branch, Cane, Carter, Conroy, Gaines, Goodwin, Griffith, Haynes, Howard, Kirk, McIntosh, Oaks, Paige, Patterson, Proctor, Taylor, V. Turner, and Vaughn
Introduced and read first time: February 9, 2004
Assigned to: Rules and Executive Nominations

HOUSE JOINT RESOLUTION

A House Joint Resolution concerning

    Reparations for the Enslavement of African Americans

  FOR the purpose of supporting the national request for congressional hearings and a federal commission to study and consider reparations for African Americans; and educating Americans about the history of slavery and its current repercussions.
  WHEREAS, The dehumanization and atrocities of slavery in the United States were mandated by formal laws that were codified and enshrined within the United States Constitution; and
  WHEREAS, The United States government has never acknowledged, apologized, or otherwise taken responsibility for its role in slavery or segregation, de jure and de facto, and has never made reparations to African Americans for the generations of labor expropriated from them, deprivation of their freedom and rights, and terrorism against them resulting in widespread injury and death; and

WHEREAS, The 2001 United Nations World Conference Against Racism held in Durban, South Africa, acknowledged that the transatlantic slave trade and slavery were crimes against humanity; and

WHEREAS, H.R. 40, pending before the United States House of Representatives, acknowledges the fundamental injustice and inhumanity of slavery; establishes a commission to study slavery, its subsequent racial and economic discrimination against freed slaves and the impact of those forces on living African Americans today; and makes recommendations to Congress on appropriate remedies; and

WHEREAS, H.R. 40 and the concept of reparations have been supported by state and local resolutions across the country, including legislation passed in the states of Louisiana and California and the city councils of Detroit, Michigan; Cleveland, Ohio; Chicago, Illinois; Evanston, Illinois; Atlanta, Georgia; Washington, D.C.; Baltimore, Maryland; Inglewood, California; Dallas, Texas; Philadelphia, Pennsylvania; Paterson, New Jersey; and Burlington, Vermont; and

WHEREAS, Numerous national, state, and local organizations, as well as religious institutions, legal organizations, and labor unions have officially endorsed the concept of reparations and H.R. 40; and

WHEREAS, The United States government has acknowledged and taken responsibility for its role in the unjust internment of Japanese Americans during the second World War and has undertaken to pay reparations to the internees and their descendants and to apologize for the unjust abrogation of their rights; and

WHEREAS, The United States has lent its support to other reparations claims even where such claims did not take place on United States soil; now, therefore, be it

RESOLVED BY THE GENERAL ASSEMBLY OF MARYLAND, That we hereby express our support for H.R. 40 and call upon the State congressional delegation to endorse the bill and advocate for its passage in Congress; and be it further

RESOLVED, That we engage in supportive activities to publicize the concept of reparations and the passage of H.R. 40; and be it further

RESOLVED, That a copy of this Resolution be forwarded by the Department of Legislative Services to the Honorable Robert L. Ehrlich, Jr., Governor of Maryland; the Honorable Thomas V. Mike Miller, Jr., President of the Senate of Maryland; and the Honorable Michael E. Busch, Speaker of the House of Delegates; and be it further

RESOLVED, That a copy of this Resolution be forwarded by the Department of Legislative Services to the Honorable John Conyers, Jr., United

States Representative of Michigan, author and primary sponsor of H.R. 40, 2426 Rayburn Building, Washington, D.C. 20515; and the Maryland Congressional Delegation: Senators Paul S. Sarbanes and Barbara A. Mikulski, Senate Office Building, Washington, D.C. 20510; and Representatives Wayne T. Gilchrest, C. A. Dutch Ruppersberger III, Benjamin L. Cardin, Albert R. Wynn, Steny Hamilton Hoyer, Roscoe G. Bartlett, Elijah E. Cummings, and Christopher Van Hollen, Jr., House Office Building, Washington, D.C. 20515.

Section 3

Municipal Resolutions

City of Detroit (1989)

Resolution Taken from the Journal of the Detroit City Council

APPROVED
REGULAR SESSION
WEDNESDAY, APRIL 19, 1989

RESOLUTION

By COUNCIL MEMBER CLEVELAND:
Joined By ALL COUNCIL MEMBERS:
WHEREAS, The United States Government and various States therein, have seen fit to provide some balm to the wounds that they have caused by their previous bigoted actions toward Original Americans and Americans of Japanese heritage, and

WHEREAS, This balm can be cited as a payment to the Ottawa and Chippewa Indians of Michigan in the amount of $32 million which represents money plus interest on the money promised them by the United States Government by a treaty signed in 1836, and to the Klamath Indians of Oregon who were awarded $81 million, and the Chippewa of Wisconsin who were awarded $30 million, and Seminoles of Florida who were awarded $12 million plus, and the Sioux Indians of South Dakota who were awarded $105 million plus one million acres of land, and,

WHEREAS, The United States Government has acknowledged the cruelty, the prejudice and arrogance, and racism, assuredly the superciliousness of their acts to confine Japanese-Americans to concentration camps during World War II. Said acknowledgement resulted in an agreement to compensate survivors with the sum of $20,000 each, and

WHEREAS, We applaud these token compensatory expressions of conscience on the part of the United States Government; and

WHEREAS, African-Americans suffered too, as did Native Americans and Japanese Americans, from broken promises, broken contracts, abandonment of moral justice and were deprived of land, cf life, of freedom, of property. Further African-Americans labored in the chains of slavery on the farmlands, highways and byways of this country and thus contributed fruitfully toward the growth and development of this nation, NOW, THEREFORE, BE IT

RESOLVED, That the Detroit City Council commend to the attention of the United States Congress, its obligation to acknowledge its debt to the descendants of African-American slaves, and award them just compensation in the amount of $40 billion placed into a National Education Fund by the U.S. Government to be used to give free scholarships to any African-American who desires to attend and is accepted by any college, university, trade or vocational school, for the deprivation, indignities, cruelty, imposed upon them, and BE IT FURTHER

RESOLVED, That a copy of this resolution be forwarded to the Mayor of the City of Detroit, the Governor of the State of Michigan, and the City of Detroit delegations in Lansing and Washington, D.C.

Adopted as follows

Yeas — Council Members Cleveland, Collins, Eberhard, Hood, Kelley, Mahaffey, Peoples, Ravitz and President Henderson — 9.

Nays — None.

City of Chicago (2000)

Resolution

Whereas, More than 30 million Black African Americans are direct descendants of slaves brought to the shores of America almost 400 years ago; and

Whereas, It is estimated that 80 to 100 million Africans died from starvation, disease, execution or other brutal treatment while being transported to the Americas and other regions of the globe during centuries of a horrible Black holocaust; and

Whereas, Slave labor was the primary source for clearing, cultivating, planting and harvesting the land, processing the products, and all other duties necessary for the economic enrichment of slave owners and their families; and

Whereas, The use of free slave labor is the major cause for the rise of the United States as the strongest, wealthiest nation in the world, and

Whereas, Free slave labor, championed by the United States Government, allowed slave owners and their families to accumulate great wealth that was bequeathed to their descendants, while the slaves and their families had only the products of poverty to consign to their descendants; and

Whereas, Slaves were considered only three-fifths of a person in the United States constitution and were deprived of pursuing any of the basic rights and privileges afforded other citizens; and

Whereas, Emancipation, followed by 100 years of legal segregation supported by laws that continued to deny freed slaves and their families the same basic rights as former slave holders, and

Whereas, The cruel and inhuman treatment and the denial of opportunity to Black people caused extreme, lasting social and psychological damage to the descendants of slaves that continue to impede their social, economic and educational progress; and

Whereas, The brutality and trauma suffered by prisoners of World War

Two described as the Helsinki Syndrome was a microcosm of the post slavery trauma suffered by descendants of American slaves, passed on by culture, language and emotions; and

Whereas, The inhumanity of slavery followed by 100 years of government sponsored discrimination against Black people also resulted in extreme psychological damage to the descendants of slave owners that continue to fuel racial division and hostilities; and

Whereas, There will never be racial healing until America decides to face the criminal debauchery that people enriched themselves by committing wrongful acts against African American slaves; and

Whereas, The original Freedmen's Bureau Act of 1865 did propose assigning 40 acres of abandoned and confiscated land to freed slaves as reparation, but under President Andrew Johnson the terms of the act that became law in July 1866 actually restored the land to former white owners, many of them formerly accused of treason to the union; and

Whereas, At least eight bills were introduced in the United States Congress, including S.1978, introduced February 6, 1896 and S.1176, introduced December 11, 1899 to compensate freed slaves, but all failed to pass out of committee; and

Whereas, The freed slaves and their descendants have never received any compensation of the generations of free labor, oppression and degradation, while making great contributions to economic strength, safety and security of this nation; and

Whereas, The United States government has actively supported other initiatives to indemnify people wronged or forced to labor for others without compensation, including native Americans, Japanese, Jews and others; and

Whereas, The Trans-Atlantic slave trade has been deemed a crime against humanity, we support reparations for African Nations from all western countries that participated in the capture, transporting, merchandising and holding of African Slaves; and

Whereas, We recognize and support the emergence of other initiatives advocating reparations for descendants of American slaves, including Race Riot Commissioners in Tulsa, Oklahoma and Rosewood, Florida; resolutions passed in cities in the states of California, Michigan, Ohio, Texas, Louisiana; and

Whereas, We support the joint Illinois Senate/House Resolution to form the Illinois Riot and Reparations Commission to study violent historic events that resulted in the loss of African American lives and property; and

Whereas, We join other organizations (NAACP, National Conference of Black Lawyers, National Bar Association, Council of Independent Black

Institutions, International Association of Black Professional Firefighters, Association of Black Psychologists, National Conference of Black Political Scientists, National Coalition of Blacks for Reparations) in supporting Congressman John Conyers HR-40 to form the Commission to Study Reparation Proposals for African Americans; now therefore,

BE IT RESOLVED, that the Chicago City Council Finance and Human Relations Committees will initiate and schedule a series of hearings to discuss the issue of reparations for the descendants of American slaves as a remedy to the continuing economic imbalance and injurious racial attitudes between Black and white Americans.

BE IT FURTHER RESOLVED, that the Chicago City Council calls on members of the State of Illinois House and Senate; the United States House and Senate to schedule and conduct hearings to examine equitable methods to finally award reparations to descendants of African American slaves who were forced to supply their labor under extreme conditions of tyranny and injustice to build this nation.

BE IT FURTHER RESOLVED, that the hearings should be scheduled in each Senate and House District with the objective to formulate reparation instruments and channels to positively impact on the health, education, welfare and economic opportunities of descendants of African American slaves.

BE IT FURTHER RESOLVED, that a copy of this resolution be forwarded to the Mayor of the City of Chicago, the Governor of Illinois and the President of the United States.

City of San Francisco (2001)

Reparations Resolution from San Francisco

[Endorsing H.R. 40]
Resolution endorsing House of Representative Resolution 40 (H.R.), Congressman John Conyers's African-American Reparations Act.

WHEREAS, House Resolution 40 (H.R.) introduced by Congressman John Conyers (Dem.-MI) calls for the establishment of a federal commission to study the impact of slavery and discrimination against African-Americans and to make recommendations to Congress for repairs; and

WHEREAS, H.R. 40 is complementary to the findings of the 2001 World Conference Against Racism that concluded the Atlantic slave trade was a crime against humanity; and,

WHEREAS, 4 million Africans and their descendants were enslaved in the United States from 1619 to 1865 and the institution of slavery was constitutionally and statutorily sanctioned by the government of the United States 1789 through 1865; and,

WHEREAS, the United States Congress amended the Freedmen's Bureau Act of 1865 to eliminate the requirement that freed slaves receive 40 acres of land as compensation for slavery; and,

WHEREAS, since the end of the period of the Civil War known as Reconstruction, when the Federal Government briefly attempted to compensate the former slave community for hundreds of years of bondage, African-Americans have been widely prevented through legal and extralegal measures from obtaining equal education, employment, housing and health care; in short prevented from joining the American middle class in substantial numbers; and,

WHEREAS, slavery in America constituted an immoral and inhumane deprivation of life, liberty, citizenship rights and cultural heritage for African slaves and denied them the fruits of their own labor while building a great and wealthy nation; and,

WHEREAS, the United States has a long history of supporting reparations and reconciliation including a formal apology and reparations to Japanese Americans interned during World War II and reparations to various Indian nations; and,

WHEREAS, Michigan Congressman John Conyers, with the full support of California Barbara Lee, Maxine Waters, Diane Watson and Juanita Milender-McDonald, has introduced H.R. 40 and it has the endorsement of cities such as Oakland and Berkeley, CA, Chicago, IL, Detroit, MI, Richmond, VA, Baltimore, MD, and others; now, therefore, be it

RESOLVED, That the City and County of San Francisco Board of Supervisors hereby fully endorses H.R. 40; and be it,

FURTHER RESOLVED, that the City and County of San Francisco Board of Supervisors direct the Clerk of the Board to forward copies of this resolution to the Speaker of the House of Representatives, the Chairpersons of the House and Senate Judiciary Committees, and to each member of the California congressional delegations.

City of New York Resolution 41 (2002)

Res. No. 41

Resolution urging the establishment of a Commission on Queen Mother Moore Reparations for Descendants of Africans of New York City.
By Council Members Barron, Perkins, Liu, Foster, Sanders Jr., Seabrook, Martinez, Jackson, Rivera and Serrano; also Council Members Quinn and Vann

Whereas, In 1625 the Dutch established the village of New Amsterdam on Manhattan Island and began the wholesale kidnapping and enslavement of African people from the Caribbean and Africa; and

Whereas, African laborers in 1639 worked daily in Manhattan Islands' Northern Forest (Upper East Side and Harlem) clearing timber and cutting lumber at the Colony's Sawmill (74th Street and Second Avenue); and

Whereas, These Africans also built farms beyond New Amsterdam, i.e. (Staten Island, Brooklyn and Queens); and

Whereas, In 1664 the English won control of New Amsterdam and renamed it New York after the Duke of York, and continued the wholesale thievery of African people from the Caribbean and Africa; and

Whereas, These Africans were forced to provide "Free Labor" to New York City under British rule that was even more aggressive and cruel in its participation in the so-called Transatlantic slave trade; the greatest crime committed against humanity; and

Whereas, These Africans during New York City's colonial period of enslavement, cleared land, built houses, paved roads, built forts and bridges, planted and harvested crops; and

Whereas, The enslavement of Africans continued in New York City after the colonial period when the United States ratified its constitution in 1789 and became the United States of America, until New York City abolished slavery in the 1840's; and

Whereas, In short, Africans built New York City's infrastructure and economy and were never paid; and

Whereas, Not only were these Africans never paid, they were subjected to the worse kind of rape, torture, brutality and murder the human mind can conjure up; and

Whereas, Evidence of this cruelty can be validated by the over 20,000 African ancestral remains located in downtown Manhattan, particularly 427 of those African ancestral remains that have been excavated from the African Burial Ground located on Duane and Reade Streets; and

Whereas, These Africans are now represented by over 2.1 million people of African ancestry in New York City; and

Whereas, Queen Mother Moore, born Audley F. Moore on July 27th, 1898, and passed on to be with the ancestors on May 2nd, 1997, spent seventy-seven years of her life fighting for Human Rights, Civil Rights, Liberation, Black Nationalism and Reparations for African People; and

Whereas, Queen Mother Moore spent decades of her struggle fighting in Harlem, New York City; and

Whereas, In the early 1960's, Queen Mother Moore formed "The Reparations Committee of Descendants of United States Slaves" to demand Reparations for Africans in America from the U.S. Government. She canvassed the country to get over a million signatures to petition the government and was successful in presenting the signatures to President John F. Kennedy; and

Whereas, Queen Mother Moore continued the struggle of I. H. Dickerson and Callie House, who engaged in one of the earliest calls for Reparations when they established the "Ex-Slaves Pension Movement" from 1890 to 1920; and

Whereas, Queen Mother Moore joined many other Africans in America in the fight for Reparations, such as; Marcus Mosiah Garvey, Malcolm X., Martin Luther King Jr., The Republic of New Africa, The National Coalition of Blacks for Reparations in America (N'COBRA), The December 12th Movement, The Black Radical Congress, The Patrice Lumumba Coalition, United African Movement, National Action Network, The Black United Front, The Unity Party and countless others; now, therefore, be it

Resolved, That a "Queen Mother Moore" Reparations for Descendants of Africans of New York City Commission be established; and further

Resolved, That this Queen Mother Moore Reparations Commission be created by individuals and organizations of the New African Community of New York City in conjunction with the Black and Latino Caucus of the City Council; and further

Resolved, That the Queen Mother Moore Reparations Commission be funded by the City of New York for the duration of time deemed necessary by the Commission to hold hearings, conduct research and recommend compensation to the New African Descendant Community of New York City for the debt owed for the enslavement of their African Ancestors during the colonial and post-colonial periods in New York City.

City of New York Resolution 219 (2002)

Res. No. 219

Resolution calling upon the Congress of the United States to hold fact-finding hearings to establish and define the bases and justifications for the government of the United States to pay reparations to African-American descendants of African ancestors who were held in slavery in this country, and its original colonies, between 1619 and 1865.
By Council Members Foster, Barron, Comrie, Perkins, Sanders, Seabrook, Serrano, Stewart and Vann; also Council Member Clarke

Whereas, The United States government has never acknowledged or taken responsibility for its role in the enslavement of Africans and the promotion of white supremacy; and

Whereas, The experience of enslavement, segregation, and discrimination continues to limit the life choices and opportunities of African-Americans; and

Whereas, African-Americans have sought repeatedly to improve their educational status, economic condition, and living situation and have been held back by prejudice, lawless white violence and official indifference thereto; and

Whereas, African-Americans have sought repeatedly to obtain reparations in the courts of the United States and through appeals to its government ever since the de jure end of slavery and have been unjustly denied relief; and

Whereas, All Americans and the United States government have benefited enormously, and continue to benefit, from the unjust expropriation of uncompensated labor by enslaved Africans, the subordination and segregation of the descendants of the enslaved, as well as from discrimination against African-Americans; and

Whereas, The United States government has acknowledged and taken responsibility for its role in the unjust internment of Japanese-Americans during the second World War and has undertaken to pay reparations to the internees and their successors and to apologize for the unjust abrogation of their rights; and

Whereas, The principle that reparations is the appropriate remedy whenever a government unjustly abrogates the rights of a domestic group or foreign people whose rights such government is obligated to protect or uphold has been internationally recognized; and

Whereas, The United States government has acceded to and approved the above stated reparations principle on the basis of treaty obligations and through its numerous actions in support of reparations on behalf of Jewish survivors of the Holocaust and their successors; and

Whereas, Individual states of the United States have undertaken to pay reparations to portions of the African-American community within their jurisdictions who have suffered specific harm due to white violence and official inaction to prevent or correct such harm in a timely fashion or to punish the perpetrators; and

Whereas, The harms inflicted on the African-American community as a whole and the debt owed to African-Americans is subject to exact proof and quantification; now, therefore, be it

Resolved, That Council of the City of New York calls upon the Congress of the United States to hold fact-finding hearings to establish and define the bases and justifications for the government of the United States to pay reparations to African-American descendants of African Ancestors who were held in slavery in this country, and its original colonies, between 1619 and 1865.

District of Columbia (2003)

An Act

In the Council of the District of Columbia

To establish, on a temporary basis, the Emancipation Day Fund to accept and use gifts for the purpose of funding the Emancipation Day Parade and related activities to commemorate the celebration of the private legal holiday, the District of Columbia Emancipation Day.

BE IT ENACTED BY THE COUNCIL OF THE DISTRICT OF COLUMBIA, That this act may be cited as the "Emancipation Day Fund Temporary Act of 2003."

Sec. 2. Definitions.

For the purposes of this act, the term:

(1) "Emancipation Day Fund" means the fund established in section 4.
(2) "Emancipation Day Parade" means the parade to celebrate and commemorate the District of Columbia Emancipation Day.

Sec. 3. Authority.

Pursuant to the District of Columbia Emancipation Day Amendment Act of 2000, effective April 3, 2001 (D.C. Law 13-237; 48 DCR 597), April 16th was established as the date for a private legal holiday, District of Columbia Emancipation Day, to commemorate and celebrate the day President Abraham Lincoln signed the District of Columbia Emancipation Act ending slavery in the District of Columbia. Pursuant to section 115 of the District of

Columbia Appropriations Act, 2002, approved December 21, 2001 (Pub. L. No. 107-96; 115 Stat. 949), the Council may accept and use gifts without prior approval by the Mayor.

Sec. 4. Emancipation Day Fund.

(a) There is established the Emancipation Day Fund ("Fund") to receive monies for the purposes of funding the Emancipation Day Parade and activities associated with the celebration and commemoration of Emancipation Day.

(b) The monies in the Fund shall not be a part of, nor lapse into, the General Fund of the District or any other fund of the District.

(c) By August 1st of each year, a report shall be submitted to the Council which will include a specific accounting of how monies in the Fund were expended and the amount of any remaining balance. The accounting shall include the following:

(1) The name of any donors or anonymous contributions;

(2) The amounts of each contribution;

(3) A description of any donated property;

(4) The identification of the use of funds for purposes of presenting the parade in recognition of the private legal holiday, known as Emancipation Day; and

(5) The support for those parade-related programs, activities, and functions for which the funds have been expended.

(d) Monies may only be expended from the Fund for the administration of the Emancipation Day Parade and activities associated with the parade.

Sec. 5. Establishment of Emancipation Day Parade.

There shall be a parade and activities associated with the District of Columbia Emancipation Day each year in commemoration and celebration of this private legal holiday.

Sec. 6. Fiscal impact statement.

The monies in the Fund shall not be included in the District's revenues nor will the obligations generated by payment for the celebration be part of the District's obligations, therefore the Emancipation Day Fund will have no fiscal impact on the District. The Council adopts the attached fiscal impact statement as the fiscal impact statement required by section 602(c)(3) of the District of Columbia Home Rule Act, approved December 24, 1973 (87 Stat. 813; D.C. Official Code 1-206.02(c)(3)).

Sec. 7. Effective date.

(a) This act shall take effect upon its approval by the Mayor (or in the event of veto by the Mayor, action by the Council to override the veto), a 30-day period of Congressional review as provided in section 602(c)(1) of the District of Columbia Home Rule Act, approved December 24, 1973 (87 Stat. 813; D.C. Official Code 1-206.02(c)(1)) and publication in the District of Columbia Register.

(b) This act shall expire after 225 days of its having taken effect.

City of New York Resolution 57 (2004)

Res. No. 57

Resolution calling upon the State Legislature to enact Assembly Bill A5357, establishing a New York State commission to quantify the debt owed to people of African descent and permitting certain claims and making an appropriation therefor.

By Council Members Perkins, Barron, Sanders, Stewart, Clarke and Reed

Whereas, Slavery was practiced in New York State for nearly two centuries; and

Whereas, The government of New York State not only legalized the enslavement of Africans and their descendants, but also enacted "slave codes," taxes on the sale of enslaved persons and fines payable to the local government or poor house administrators for violations of the "slave codes"; and

Whereas, New York's colonial and subsequent State and local governments and businesses sanctioned and profited from the inhumane and immoral trade in men, women, and children of African ancestry; and

Whereas, Tremendous profits were made from the wages, unjust enrichment, forced labor, and second class citizenship of enslaved Africans; and

Whereas, Slavery's legacy of poverty, illiteracy, segregation and discrimination has never been adequately addressed; and

Whereas, Financial reparations for crimes against humanity and for State sponsored discrimination have become a remedy for victims of such crimes — Native Americans, Jewish holocaust victims, Japanese Americans interned during World War II, and victims and their descendants of the Rosewood riots in Florida are all recent examples of this standard; and

Whereas, This bill, sponsored by Assembly Member Roger L. Green of Brooklyn, will provide a mechanism for research and deliberations on how to compensate communities, especially children and families of African descent for the collective wrongs suffered as a result of state sanctioned slavery and discrimination; now, therefore, be it

Resolved, That the Council calls upon the State Legislature to enact Assembly Bill A5357, establishing a New York State commission to quantify the debt owed to people of African descent and permitting certain claims and making an appropriation therefor.

City of New York Resolution 195 (2004)

Res. No. 195

Resolution declaring March 21, 2004 as "Reparation Awareness Day" and to recognize the Trans-Atlantic Slave Trade and Slavery as crimes against humanity.
By Council Members Barron, Perkins, Comrie, Boyland, Foster, Rivera, Sanders, Liu, Seabrook, Vann, Baez, Clarke, Gerson, Gonzalez, Jackson, Martinez, Monserrate and Reed

Whereas, In South Africa, on March 21st, 1960, 15,000 black protesters gathered at the Sharpville Township to protest against the pass laws, which required Africans to carry identity cards at all times; and

Whereas, Police opened fire on the unarmed protesters and within minutes, 56 people were killed and nearly 200 were injured; and

Whereas, More Africans were killed in a similar protest at Langa Township near Capetown; and

Whereas, The Sharpville Massacre is commemorated annually by people around the world who struggle against racism and racial discrimination; and

Whereas, The United Nations now observes March 21 as the International Day for the Elimination of Racial Discrimination; and

Whereas, Last year, the United Nations held its historic World Conference Against Racism, Racial Discrimination, Xenophobia and Related Intolerance in Durban, South Africa, resulting in The Durban Declaration and Program of Action, which recognizes that the Trans-Atlantic Slave Trade and Slavery were crimes against humanity; and

Whereas, In recognition of the long-suppressed history of slavery and racism that are part of New York City's past and the damage they have wrought, reparations are consequently due the descendants of the victims of the Trans-Atlantic Slave Trade, Slavery and Racism; and

Whereas, In recognition of the 42nd anniversary of the Sharpville Massacre, in recognition of the United Nations International Day for the Elimination of Racial Discrimination, in recognition of the achievements of the United Nations World Conference against Racism, Racial Discrimination, Xenophobia and Related Intolerance in Durban, South Africa, and particularly in its acknowledgment that the Trans-Atlantic Slave Trade and Slavery were crimes against humanity; now, therefore, be it

Resolved, That March 21, 2004, be declared "Reparation Awareness Day" and the Trans-Atlantic Slave Trade and Slavery recognized as crimes against humanity.

City of Philadelphia (2004)

City Council
2/19/2004
Bill No. 040133
Introduced February 19, 2004
Councilmembers Reynolds Brown and Goode
Referred to the Committee on Finance

WARNING:

This bill is shown in the form in which it was first introduced in Council. It may have since been amended by Council, and the bill as shown here DOES NOT INCLUDE ANY SUCH AMENDMENTS.
To determine whether this bill has been amended, and to obtain a current version of this bill that includes any amendments, contact the Office of the Chief Clerk, Room 402 City Hall, Philadelphia, PA 19107 (Telephone: 215-686-3410).

BILL NO. 040133

Introduced February 19, 2004
Councilmembers Reynolds Brown and Goode
Referred to the Committee on Finance

AN ORDINANCE

Amending Section 17-104 entitled "Prerequisites to the Execution of City Contracts" by adding a new subsection (2) entitled "Slavery Era Business/

Corporate Insurance Disclosure" to promote full and accurate disclosure to the public about any slavery policies sold by any companies or profits from slavery by other industries (or their predecessors) who are doing business with the City of Philadelphia and recodifying Section 17-104 by incorporating various technical changes; all under certain terms and conditions.

THE COUNCIL OF THE CITY OF PHILADELPHIA
HEREBY ORDAINS:

SECTION 1. Section 17-104 of The Philadelphia Code is hereby amended to read as follows:

17-104. Prerequisites to the Execution and Validity of City Contracts. [(2) Prohibited Contracts]

[(a)](1) Definitions. For the purpose of this subsection, the following definitions shall apply.

([.1]a) Business Entity Any individual, domestic corporation, foreign corporation, association, syndicate, joint stock company, partnership, joint venture, or unincorporated association, including any parent company, subsidiary, exclusive distributor or company affiliated therewith, engaged in a business or commercial enterprise;

([.2]b) City. The City of Philadelphia;

([.3]c) City Agency. The City of Philadelphia, its departments, boards and commissions;

([.4]d) City-related Agency. All authorities and quasi-public corporations which either:

([i].1) receive appropriations from the City; or

([ii].2) have entered into continuing contractual or cooperative relationships with the City; or

([iii].3) operate under legal authority granted to them by City ordinance.

([.5]e) Department. The Procurement Department.

(2) Slavery Era Business/Corporate Insurance Disclosure.

(a) Business, Corporate and Slavery Era Insurance Ordinance. This subsection shall be known and cited as the "Business, Corporate and Slavery Era Insurance Ordinance." The purpose of this subsection is to promote full and accurate disclosure to the public about any slavery policies sold by any companies, or profits from slavery by other industries (or their predecessors) who are doing business with any City Agency or City-related Agency.

(b) Each contractor with whom a City Agency enters into a contract, whether subject to competitive bid or not, within the first 90 days after the contract's execution, shall complete an affidavit verifying that the contractor has searched any and all records of the company or any predecessor company regarding records of investments or profits from slavery or slaveholder insurance policies during the slavery era. The names of any slaves or slaveholders described in those records must be disclosed in the affidavit.

(c) The Department shall make the information contained in the affidavit available to the public, including but not limited to making the information accessible on the City's internet accessible world wide web home page and provide an annual report to the City Council.

(d) Any contract between a City Agency and a contractor which fails to provide the requisite affidavit within ninety (90) days of the contract's execution or which includes material false information on such affidavit shall be rendered null and void.

(e) City Related Agencies. Any contract, lease, grant condition or other agreement entered into by the City with any City-related Agency shall contain a provision requiring the City-related Agency, in the procurement of goods and services purchased pursuant to such contract, lease, grant condition or other agreement with the City, to abide by the provisions of subsection 17-104(2).

Section 4

Advocacy and Activism

United Negro Improvement Association (1920)

"Declaration of the Rights of the Negro Peoples of the World":
The Principles of the Universal Negro Improvement Association

PREAMBLE

Be It Resolved, That the Negro people of the world, through their chosen representatives in convention assembled in Liberty Hall, in the City of New York and United States of America, from August 1 to August 31, in the year of Our Lord one thousand nine hundred and twenty, protest against the wrongs and injustices they are suffering at the hands of their white brethren, and state what they deem their fair and just rights, as well as the treatment they propose to demand of all men in the future.

We complain:

1. That nowhere in the world, with few exceptions, are black men accorded equal treatment with white men, although in the same situation and circumstances, but, on the contrary, are discriminated against and denied the common rights due to human beings for no other reason than their race and color.

We are not willingly accepted as guests in the public hotels and inns of the world for no other reason than our race and color.

2. In certain parts of the United States of America our race is denied the right of public trial accorded to other races when accused of crime, but are lynched and burned by mobs, and such brutal and inhuman treatment is even practiced upon our women.

3. That European nations have parcelled out among them and taken possession of nearly all of the continent of Africa, and the natives are compelled to surrender their lands to aliens and are treated in most instances like slaves.

4. In the southern portion of the United States of America, although citizens under the Federal Constitution, and in some States almost equal to the whites in population and are qualified land owners and taxpayers, we are,

nevertheless, denied all voice in the making and administration of the laws and are taxed without representation by the State governments, and at the same time compelled to do military service in defense of the country.

5. On the public conveyances and common carriers in the southern portion of the United States we are jim-crowed and compelled to accept separate and inferior accommodations and made to pay the same fare charged for first-class accommodations, and our families are often humiliated and insulted by drunken white men who habitually pass through the jim-crow cars going to the smoking car.

6. The physicians of our race are denied the right to attend their patients while in the public hospitals of the cities and States where they reside in certain parts of the United States.

Our children are forced to attend inferior separate schools for shorter terms than white children, and the public school funds are unequally divided between the white and colored schools.

7. We are discriminated against and denied an equal chance to earn wages for the support of our families, and in many instances are refused admission into labor unions and nearly everywhere are paid smaller wages than white men.

8. In the Civil Service and departmental offices we are everywhere discriminated against and made to feel that to be a black man in Europe, America and the West Indies is equivalent to being an outcast and a leper among the races of men, no matter what the character attainments of the black men may be.

9. In the British and other West Indian islands and colonies Negroes are secretly and cunningly discriminated against and denied those fuller rights of government to which white citizens are appointed, nominated and elected.

10. That our people in those parts are forced to work for lower wages than the average standard of white men and are kept in conditions repugnant to good civilized tastes and customs.

11. That the many acts of injustices against members of our race before the courts of law in the respective islands and colonies are of such nature as to create disgust and disrespect for the white man's sense of justice.

12. Against all such inhuman, unchristian and uncivilized treatment we here and now emphatically protest, and invoke the condemnation of all mankind.

In order to encourage our race all over the world and to stimulate it to overcome the handicaps and difficulties surrounding it, and to push forward to a higher and grander destiny, we demand and insist on the following Declaration of Rights:

1. Be it known to all men that whereas all men are created equal and entitled to the rights of life, liberty and the pursuit of happiness, and because of this we, the duly elected representatives of the Negro peoples of the world, invoking the aid of the just and Almighty God, do declare all men, women and children of our blood throughout the world free denizens, and do claim them as free citizens of Africa, the Motherland of all Negroes.

2. That we believe in the supreme authority of our race in all things racial; that all things are created and given to man as a common possession; that there should be an equitable distribution and apportionment of all such things, and in consideration of the fact that as a race we are now deprived of those things that are morally and legally ours, we believed it right that all such things should be acquired and held by whatsoever means possible.

3. That we believe the Negro, like any other race, should be governed by the ethics of civilization, and therefore should not be deprived of any of those rights or privileges common to other human beings.

4. We declare that Negroes, wheresoever they form a community among themselves should be given the right to elect their own representatives to represent them in Legislatures, courts of law, or such institutions as may exercise control over that particular community.

5. We assert that the Negro is entitled to even-handed justice before all courts of law and equity in whatever country he may be found, and when this is denied him on account of his race or color such denial is an insult to the race as a whole and should be resented by the entire body of Negroes.

6. We declare it unfair and prejudicial to the rights of Negroes in communities where they exist in considerable numbers to be tried by a judge and jury composed entirely of an alien race, but in all such cases members of our race are entitled to representation on the jury.

7. We believe that any law or practice that tends to deprive any African of his land or the privileges of free citizenship within his country is unjust and immoral, and no native should respect any such law or practice.

8. We declare taxation without representation unjust and tyran[n]ous, and there should be no obligation on the part of the Negro to obey the levy of a tax by any law-making body from which he is excluded and denied representation on account of his race and color.

9. We believe that any law especially directed against the Negro to his detriment and singling him out because of his race or color is unfair and immoral, and should not be respected.

10. We believe all men are entitled to common human respect and that our race should in no way tolerate any insults that may be interpreted to mean disrespect to our race or color.

11. We deprecate the use of the term "nigger" as applied to Negroes, and demand that the word "Negro" be written with a capital "N."

12. We believe that the Negro should adopt every means to protect himself against barbarous practices inflicted upon him because of color.

13. We believe in the freedom of Africa for the Negro people of the world, and by the principle of Europe for the Europeans and Asia for the Asiatics, we also demand Africa for the Africans at home and abroad.

14. We believe in the inherent right of the Negro to possess himself of Africa and that his possession of same shall not be regarded as an infringement of any claim or purchase made by any race or nation.

15. We strongly condemn the cupidity of those nations of the world who, by open aggression or secret schemes, have seized the territories and inexhaustible natural wealth of Africa, and we place on record our most solemn determination to reclaim the treasures and possession of the vast continent of our forefathers.

16. We believe all men should live in peace one with the other, but when races and nations provoke the ire of other races and nations by attempting to infringe upon their rights[,] war becomes inevitable, and the attempt in any way to free one's self or protect one's rights or heritage becomes justifiable.

17. Whereas the lynching, by burning, hanging or any other means, of human beings is a barbarous practice and a shame and disgrace to civilization, we therefore declare any country guilty of such atrocities outside the pale of civilization.

18. We protest against the atrocious crime of whipping, flogging and overworking of the native tribes of Africa and Negroes everywhere. These are methods that should be abolished and all means should be taken to prevent a continuance of such brutal practices.

19. We protest against the atrocious practice of shaving the heads of Africans, especially of African women or individuals of Negro blood, when placed in prison as a punishment for crime by an alien race.

20. We protest against segregated districts, separate public conveyances, industrial discrimination, lynchings and limitations of political privileges of any Negro citizen in any part of the world on account of race, color or creed, and will exert our full influence and power against all such.

21. We protest against any punishment inflicted upon a Negro with severity, as against lighter punishment inflicted upon another of an alien race for like offense, as an act of prejudice and injustice, and should be resented by the entire race.

22. We protest against the system of education in any country where Negroes are denied the same privileges and advantages as other races.

23. We declare it inhuman and unfair to boycott Negroes from industries and labor in any part of the world.

24. We believe in the doctrine of the freedom of the press, and we therefore emphatically protest against the suppression of Negro newspapers and periodicals in various parts of the world, and call upon Negroes everywhere to employ all available means to prevent such suppression.

25. We further demand free speech universally for all men.

26. We hereby protest against the publication of scandalous and inflammatory articles by an alien press tending to create racial strife and the exhibition of picture films showing the Negro as a cannibal.

27. We believe in the self-determination of all peoples.

28. We declare for the freedom of religious worship.

29. With the help of Almighty God we declare ourselves the sworn protectors of the honor and virtue of our women and children, and pledge our lives for their protection and defense everywhere and under all circumstances from wrongs and outrages.

30. We demand the right of an unlimited and unprejudiced education for ourselves and our posterity forever[.]

31. We declare that the teaching in any school by alien teachers to our boys and girls, that the alien race is superior to the Negro race, is an insult to the Negro people of the world.

32. Where Negroes form a part of the citizenry of any country, and pass the civil service examination of such country, we declare them entitled to the same consideration as other citizens as to appointments in such civil service.

33. We vigorously protest against the increasingly unfair and unjust treatment accorded Negro travelers on land and sea by the agents and employees of railroad and steamship companies, and insist that for equal fare we receive equal privileges with travelers of other races.

34. We declare it unjust for any country, State or nation to enact laws tending to hinder and obstruct the free immigration of Negroes on account of their race and color.

35. That the right of the Negro to travel unmolested throughout the world be not abridged by any person or persons, and all Negroes are called upon to give aid to a fellow Negro when thus molested.

36. We declare that all Negroes are entitled to the same right to travel over the world as other men.

37. We hereby demand that the governments of the world recognize our leader and his representatives chosen by the race to look after the welfare of our people under such governments.

38. We demand complete control of our social institutions without interference by an alien race or races.

39. That the colors, Red, Black and Green, be the colors of the Negro race.

40. Resolved, That the anthem "Ethiopia, Thou Land of Our Fathers etc.," shall be the anthem of the Negro race....

41. We believe that any limited liberty which deprives one of the complete rights and prerogatives of full citizenship is but a modified form of slavery.

42. We declare it an injustice to our people and a serious Impediment to the health of the race to deny to competent licensed Negro physicians the right to practice in the public hospitals of the communities in which they reside, for no other reason than their race and color.

43. We call upon the various government[s] of the world to accept and acknowledge Negro representatives who shall be sent to the said governments to represent the general welfare of the Negro peoples of the world.

44. We deplore and protest against the practice of confining juvenile prisoners in prisons with adults, and we recommend that such youthful prisoners be taught gainful trades under human[e] supervision.

45. Be it further resolved, That we as a race of people declare the League of Nations null and void as far as the Negro is concerned, in that it seeks to deprive Negroes of their liberty.

46. We demand of all men to do unto us as we would do unto them, in the name of justice; and we cheerfully accord to all men all the rights we claim herein for ourselves.

47. We declare that no Negro shall engage himself in battle for an alien race without first obtaining the consent of the leader of the Negro people of the world, except in a matter of national self-defense.

48. We protest against the practice of drafting Negroes and sending them to war with alien forces without proper training, and demand in all cases that Negro soldiers be given the same training as the aliens.

49. We demand that instructions given Negro children in schools include the subject of "Negro History," to their benefit.

50. We demand a free and unfettered commercial intercourse with all the Negro people of the world.

51. We declare for the absolute freedom of the seas for all peoples.

52. We demand that our duly accredited representatives be given proper recognition in all leagues, conferences, conventions or courts of international arbitration wherever human rights are discussed.

53. We proclaim the 31st day of August of each year to be an international holiday to be observed by all Negroes.

54. We want all men to know that we shall maintain and contend for the freedom and equality of every man, woman and child of our race, with our lives, our fortunes and our sacred honor.

These rights we believe to be justly ours and proper for the protection of the Negro race at large, and because of this belief we, on behalf of the four hundred million Negroes of the world, do pledge herein the sacred blood of the race in defense, and we hereby subscribe our names as a guarantee of the truthfulness and faithfulness hereof, in the presence of Almighty God, on this 13th day of August, in the year of our Lord one thousand nine hundred and twenty.

Civil Rights Congress (1951)

"We Charge Genocide"

We Charge Genocide, The Historic Petition to the United Nations for Relief from A Crime of the United States Government against the Negro People

Introduction

Out of the inhuman black ghettos of American cities, out of the cotton plantations of the South, comes this record of mass slayings on the basis of race, of lives deliberately warped and distorted by the willful creation of conditions making for premature death, poverty and disease. It is a record that calls aloud for condemnation, for an end to these terrible injustices that constitute a daily and ever-increasing violation of the United Nations Convention on the Prevention and Punishment of the Crime of Genocide.

It is sometimes incorrectly thought that genocide means the complete and definitive destruction of a race or people. The Genocide Convention, however, adopted by the General Assembly of the United Nations on December 9, 1948, defines genocide as any killings on the basis of race, or, in its specific words, as "killing members of the group." Any intent to destroy, *in whole or in part,* a national, racial, ethnic or religious group is genocide, according to the Convention. Thus, the Convention states, "causing serious bodily or mental harm to members of the group" is genocide as well as "killing members of the group."

We maintain, therefore, that the oppressed Negro citizens of the United States, segregated, discriminated against and long the target of violence, suffer from genocide as the result of the consistent, conscious, unified policies of every branch of government.

The Civil Rights Congress has prepared and submits this petition to the General Assembly of the United Nations on behalf of the Negro people in the interest of peace and democracy, charging the Government of the United

States of America with violation of the Charter of the United Nations and the Convention on the Prevention and Punishment of the Crime of Genocide.

We believe that in issuing this document we are discharging an historic responsibility to the American people, as well as rendering a service of inestimable value to progressive mankind. We speak of the American people because millions of white Americans in the ranks of labor and the middle class, and particularly those who live in the southern states and are often contemptuously called poor whites, are themselves suffering to an ever-greater degree from the consequences of the Jim Crow segregation policy of government in its relations with Negro citizens. We speak of progressive mankind because a policy of discrimination at home must inevitably create racist commodities for export abroad — must inevitably tend toward war.

We have not dealt here with the cruel and inhuman policy of this government toward the people of Puerto Rico. Impoverished and reduced to a semi-literate state through the wanton exploitation and oppression by gigantic American concerns, through the merciless frame-up and imprisonment of hundreds of its sons and daughter, this colony of the rulers of the United States reveals in all its stark nakedness the moral bankruptcy of this government and those who control its home and foreign policies.

History has shown that the racist theory of government of the U.S.A. is not the private affair of Americans, but the concern of mankind everywhere.

It is our hope, and we fervently believe that it was the hope and aspiration of every black American whose voice was silenced forever through premature death at the hands of racist-minded hooligans or Klan terrorists, that the truth recorded here will be made known to the world; that it will speak with a tongue of fire loosing an unquenchable moral crusade, the universal response to which will sound the death knell of all racist theories.

We have scrupulously kept within the purview of the Convention on the Prevention and Punishment of the Crime of Genocide which is held to embrace those "acts committed with intent to destroy in whole or in part a national, ethnical, racial or religious group as such."

We particularly pray for the most careful reading of this material by those who have always regarded genocide as a term to be used only where the acts of terror evinced an intent to destroy a whole nation. We further submit that this Convention on Genocide is, by virtue of our avowed acceptance of the Covenant of the United Nations, an inseparable part of the law of the United States of America.

According to international law, and according to our own law, the Genocide Convention, as well as the provisions of the United Nations Charter, supersedes, negates and displaces all discriminatory racist law on the books of the United States and the several states.

The Hitler crimes, of awful magnitude, beginning as they did against the heroic Jewish people, finally drenched the world in blood, and left a record of maimed and tortured bodies and devastated areas such as mankind had never seen before. Justice Robert H. Jackson, who now sits upon the United States Supreme Court bench, described this holocaust to the world in the powerful language with which he opened the Nuremberg trials of the Nazi leaders. Every word he voiced against the monstrous Nazi beast applies with equal weight, we believe, to those who are guilty of the crimes herein set forth.

Here we present the documented crimes of federal, state and municipal governments in the United States of America, the dominant nation in the United Nations, against 15,000,000 of its own nationals — the Negro people of the United States. These crimes are of the gravest concern to mankind. The General Assembly of the United Nations, by reason of the United Nations Charter and the Genocide Convention, itself is invested with power to receive this indictment and act on it.

The proof of this fact is its action upon the similar complaint of the Government of India against South Africa.

We call upon the United Nations to act and to call the Government of the United States to account.

We believe that the test of the basic goals of a foreign policy is inherent in the manner in which a government treats its own nationals and is not to be found in the lofty platitudes that pervade so many treaties or constitutions. The essence lies not in the form, but rather, in the substance.

The Civil Rights Congress is a defender of constitutional liberties, human rights, and of peace. It is the implacable enemy of every creed, philosophy, social system or way or life that denies democratic rights or one iota of human dignity to any human being because of color, creed, nationality or political belief.

We ask all men and women of good will to unite to realize the objectives set forth in the summary and prayer concluding this petition. We believe that this program can go far toward ending the threat of a third world war. We believe it can contribute to the establishment of a people's democracy on a universal scale.

But may we add as a final note that the Negro people desire equality of opportunity in this land where their contributions to the economic, political and social developments have been of splendid proportions, and in quality second to none. They will accept nothing less, and continued efforts to force them into the category of second-class citizens through force and violence, through segregation, racist law and an institutionalized oppression, can only end in disaster for those responsible.

Respectfully submitted by the Civil Rights Congress as a service to the peoples of the world, and particularly to the lovers of peace and democracy in the United States of America.

—WILLIAM L. PATTERSON
National Executive Secretary
Civil Rights Congress . . .

The Petitioners

Alzira Albaugh, *New Mexico*
Mike Babinchok, *Ohio*
Charlotta A. Bass, *California*
Isadore Begun, *New York*
Richard O. Boyer, *New York*
Maurice Braverman, *Maryland*
Louis E. Burnham, *New York*
Harold Christoffel, *Wisconsin*
Charles Collins, *New York*
Ralph Cooper, *New Jersey*
Dr. Matthew Crawford, *California*
George Crockett Jr., *Michigan*
Wendell Phillips Dabney, *Ohio*
John Daschbach, *Washington*
Benjamin J. Davis Jr., *New York*
Carmen Davis, *Tennessee*
Lester Davis, *Illinois*
Angie Dickerson, *South Carolina*
Dr. W. E. B. Du Bois, *New York*
Roscoe Dunjee, *Oklahoma*
Jack Dyhr, *Oregon*
Collis English, *New Jersey*
Howard Fast, *New York*
Winifred Feise, *Louisiana*
James Ford, *New York*
Josephine Grayson, *Virginia*

Abner Green, *New York*
Yvonne Gregory, *New York*
Aubrey Grossman, *New York*
William Harrison, *Massachusetts*
Harry Haywood, *New York*
James R. Herman, *Louisiana*
Rev. Charles A. Hill, *Michigan*
William Hood, *Michigan*
W. Alphaeus Hunton, *New York*
Dorothy Hunton, *New York*
Arnold Johnson, *Pennsylvania*
Dr. Oakley C. Johnson, *Louisiana*
Claudia Jones, *New York*
John Hudson Jones, *New York*
Rev. Obadiah Jones, *Missouri*
Leon Josephson, *New York*
Albert Kahn, *New York*
Mary Kalb, *Virginia*
Maude White Katz, *New York*
Stetson Kennedy, *Florida*
Kay Kerby, *Florida*
Elizabeth Keyser, *California*
Yetta Land, *Arizona*
Elizabeth Lawson, *New York*
Amy Mallard, *Georgia*
Doris Mallard, *Georgia*

James Malloy, *New York*
Larkin Marshall, *Georgia*
Rosalee McGee, *Mississippi*
Arthur McPhaul, *Michigan*
Bessie Mitchell, *New York*
Russell Meek, *New York*
Thelma Meites, *Connecticut*
Anna H. Morgan, *Ohio*
Lewis Moroze, *New Jersey*
George Murphy Jr., *New York*
Andrew Nelson, *Louisiana*
Jerry Newson, *California*
Josephine Nordstrand, *Wisconsin*
Louise Thompson Patterson, *New York*
William L. Patterson, *New York*
Sally Peek, *District of Columbia*
Pettis Perry, *New York*
John Pittman, *New York*
Eslanda Goode Robeson, *Connecticut*
Paul Robeson, *Connecticut*
Paul Robeson Jr., *New York*
Margarite Robinson, *California*
Elaine Ross, *New York*
Nat Ross, *New York*
Ida Rothstein, *California*
Geneva Rushin, *Georgia*
Millie Salwen, *New Jersey*
Anne Shore, *Michigan*
Ferdinand Smith, *New York*
Leon Straus, *New York*
Lumir J. Subrt, *Wisconsin*
Mary Church Terrell, *Dist. of Colum.*
James Thorpe, *New Jersey*
Decca Treuhaft, *California*
Robert Treuhaft, *California*
Paul Washington, *Louisiana*
Abe Weisburd, *New York*
Wesley Robert Wells, *California*
Claude White, *Hawaii*
Rev. Eliot White, *New York*
Horace Wilson, *New Jersey*
Elsie Zazrivy, *Ohio* . . .

Part 1. The Opening Statement

A Review of the Case and an Offer of Proof, giving something of the scope and historical background of the genocide being committed against the Negro people of the United States.

To the General Assembly of the United Nations:

The responsibility of being the first in history to charge the government of the United States of America with the crime of genocide is not one your petitioners take lightly. The responsibility is particularly grave when citizens must charge their own government with mass murder of its own nationals, with institutionalized oppression and persistent slaughter of the Negro people in the United States on a basis of "race," a crime abhorred by mankind and prohibited by the conscience of the world as expressed in the Convention on the Prevention and Punishment of the Crime of Genocide adopted by the General Assembly of the United Nations on December 9, 1948.

Genocide Leads to Fascism and to War

If our duty is unpleasant it is historically necessary both for the welfare of the American people and for the peace of the world. We petition as American patriots, sufficiently anxious to save our countrymen and all mankind from the horrors of war to shoulder a task as painful as it is important. We cannot forget Hitler's demonstration that genocide at home can become wider massacre abroad, that domestic genocide develops into the larger genocide that is predatory war. The wrongs of which we complain are so much the expression of predatory American reaction and its government that civilization cannot ignore them nor risk their continuance without courting its own destruction. We agree with those members of the General Assembly who declared that genocide is a matter of world concern because its practice imperils world safety.

But if the responsibility of your petitioners is great, it is dwarfed by the responsibility of those guilty of the crime we charge. Seldom in human annals has so iniquitous a conspiracy been so gilded with the trappings of respectability. Seldom has mass murder on the score of "race" been so sanctified by law, so justified by those who demand free elections abroad even as they kill their fellow citizens who demand free elections at home. Never have so many individuals been so ruthlessly destroyed amid so many tributes to the sacredness of the individual. The distinctive trait of this genocide is a cant that mouths aphorisms of Anglo-Saxon jurisprudence even as it kills.

The genocide of which we complain is as much a fact as gravity. The whole world knows of it. The proof is in every day's newspapers, in every one's sight and hearing in these United States. In one form or another it has been practiced for more than three hundred years although never with such sinister implications for the welfare and peace of the world as at present. Its very familiarity disguises its horror. It is a crime so embedded in law, so explained away by specious rationale, so hidden by talk of liberty, that even the conscience of the tender minded is sometimes dulled. Yet the conscience of mankind cannot be beguiled from its duty by the pious phrases and the deadly legal euphemisms with which its perpetrators seek to transform their guilt into high moral purpose.

Killing Members of the Group

Your petitioners will prove that the crime of which we complain is in fact genocide within the terms and meaning of the United Nations Convention providing for the prevention and punishment of this crime. We shall submit evidence, tragically voluminous, of "acts committed with intent to destroy, in whole or in part, a national, ethnical, racial or religious group as such," — in this case the 15,000,000 Negro people of the United States.

We shall submit evidence proving "killing members of the group," in violation of Article II of the Convention. We cite killings by police, killings by incited gangs, killings at night by masked men, killings always on the basis of "race," killings by the Ku Klux Klan, that organization which is chartered by the several states as a semi-official arm of government and even granted the tax exemptions of a benevolent society.

Our evidence concerns the thousands of Negroes who over the years have been beaten to death on chain gangs and in the back rooms of sheriff's offices, in the cells of county jails, in precinct police stations and on city streets, who have been framed and murdered by sham legal forms and by a legal bureaucracy. It concerns those Negroes who have been killed, allegedly for failure to say "sir" or tip their hats or move aside quickly enough, or, more often, on trumped up charges of "rape," but in reality for trying to vote or otherwise demanding the legal and inalienable rights and privileges of United States citizenship formally guaranteed them by the Constitution of the United States, rights denied them on the basis of "race," in violation of the Constitution of the United States, the United Nations Charter and the Genocide Convention.

Economic Genocide

We shall offer proof of economic genocide, or in the words of the Convention, proof of "deliberately inflicting on the group conditions of life calculated to bring about its destruction in whole or in part." We shall prove that such conditions so swell the infant and maternal death rate and the death rate from disease, that the American Negro is deprived, when compared with the remainder of the population of the United States, of eight years of life on the average.

Further we shall show a deliberate national oppression of these 15,000,000 Negro Americans on the basis of "race" to perpetuate these "conditions of life." Negroes are the last hired and the first fired. They are forced into city ghettos or their rural equivalents. They are segregated legally or through sanctioned violence into filthy, disease-bearing housing, and deprived by law of adequate medical care and education. From birth to death, Negro Americans are humiliated and persecuted, in violation of the Charter and the Convention. They are forced by threat of violence and imprisonment into inferior, segregated accommodations, into jim crow busses, jim crow trains, jim crow hospitals, jim crow schools, jim crow theaters, jim crow restaurants, jim crow housing, and finally into jim crow cemeteries.

We shall prove that the object of this genocide, as of all genocide, is the perpetuation of economic and political power by the few through the destruction of political protest by the many. Its method is to demoralize and divide an entire nation; its end is to increase the profits and unchallenged control by a reactionary clique. We shall show that those responsible for this crime are not the humble but the so-called great, not the American people but their misleaders, not the convict but the robed judge, not the criminal but the police, not the spontaneous mob but organized terrorists licensed and approved by the state to incite to a Roman holiday.

We shall offer evidence that this genocide is not plotted in the dark but incited over the radio into the ears of millions, urged in the glare of public forums by Senators and Governors. It is offered as an article of faith by powerful political organizations, such as the Dixiecrats, and defended by influential newspapers, all in violation of the United Nations charter and the Convention forbidding genocide.

This proof does not come from the enemies of the white supremacists but from their own mouths, their own writings, their political resolutions, their racist laws, and from photographs of their handiwork. Neither Hitler nor Goebbels wrote obscurantist racial incitements more voluminously or viciously than do their American counterparts, nor did such incitements circulate in Nazi mails any more freely than they do in the mails of the United States.

Conspiracy to Genocide

Through this and other evidence we shall prove this crime of genocide is the result of a massive conspiracy, more deadly in that it is sometimes "understood" rather than expressed, a part of the mores of the ruling class often concealed by euphemisms, but always directed to oppressing the Negro people. Its members are so well-drilled, so rehearsed over the generations, that they can carry out their parts automatically and with a minimum of spoken direction. They have inherited their plot and their business is but to implement it daily so that it works daily. This implementation is sufficiently expressed in decision and statute, in depressed wages, in robbing millions of the vote and millions more of the land, and in countless other political and economic facts, as to reveal definitively the existence of a conspiracy backed by reactionary interests in which are meshed all the organs of the Executive,

Legislative and Judicial branches of government. It is manifest that a people cannot be consistently killed over the years on the basis of "race" — and more than 10,000 Negroes have so suffered death — cannot be uniformly segregated, despoiled, impoverished and denied equal protection before the law, unless it is the result of the deliberate, all-pervasive policy of government and those who control it.

Emasculation of Democracy

We shall show, more particularly, how terror, how "killing members of the group," in violation of Article II of the Genocide Convention, has been used to prevent the Negro people from voting in huge and decisive areas of the United States in which they are the preponderant population, thus dividing the whole American people, emasculating mass movements for democracy and securing the grip of predatory reaction on the federal, state, county and city governments. We shall prove that the crimes of genocide offered for your action and the world's attention have in fact been incited, a punishable crime under Article III of the Convention, often by such officials as Governors, Senators, Judges and peace officers whose phrases about white supremacy and the necessity of maintaining inviolate a white electorate resulted in bloodshed as surely as more direct incitement.

We shall submit evidence showing the existence of a mass of American law, written as was Hitler's law solely on the basis of "race," providing for segregation and otherwise penalizing the Negro people, in violation not only of Articles II and III of the Convention but also in violation of the Charter of the United Nations. Finally we shall offer proof that a conspiracy exists in which the Government of the United States, its Supreme Court, its Congress, its Executive branch, as well as the various state, county and municipal governments, consciously effectuate policies which result in the crime of genocide being consistently and constantly practiced against the Negro people of the United States.

The Negro Petitioners

Many of your petitioners are Negro citizens to whom the charges herein described are not mere words. They are facts felt on our bodies, crimes inflicted on our dignity. We struggle for deliverance, not without pride in our valor, but we warn mankind that our fate is theirs. We solemnly declare that continuance of this American crime against the Negro people of the United

States will strengthen those reactionary American forces driving towards World War III as certainly as the unrebuked Nazi genocide against the Jewish people strengthened Hitler in his successful drive to World War II.

We, Negro petitioners whose communities have been laid waste, whose homes have been burned and looted, whose children have been killed, whose women have been raped, have noted with peculiar horror that the genocidal doctrines and actions of the American white supremacists have already been exported to the colored peoples of Asia. We solemnly warn that a nation which practices genocide against its own nationals may not be long deterred, if it has the power, from genocide elsewhere. White supremacy at home makes for colored massacres abroad. Both reveal contempt for human life in a colored skin. Jellied gasoline in Korea and the lynchers' faggot at home are connected in more ways than that both result in death by fire. The lyncher and the atom bomber are related. The first cannot murder unpunished and unrebuked without so encouraging the latter that the peace of the world and the lives of millions are endangered. Nor is this metaphysics. The tie binding both is economic profit and political control. It was not without significance that it was President Truman who spoke of the possibility of using the atom bomb on the colored peoples of Asia, that it is American statesmen who prate constantly of "Asiatic hordes."

"Our Humanity Denied and Mocked"

We Negro petitioners protest this genocide as Negroes and we protest it as Americans, as patriots. We know that no American can be truly free while 15,000,000 other Americans are persecuted on the grounds of "race," that few Americans can be prosperous while 15,000,000 are deliberately pauperized. Our country can never know true democracy while millions of its citizens are denied the vote on the basis of their color.

But above all we protest this genocide as human beings whose very humanity is denied and mocked. We cannot forget that after Congressman Henderson Lovelace Lanham, of Rome, Georgia, speaking in the halls of Congress, called William L. Patterson, one of the leaders of the Negro people, "a God-damned black son-of-bitch," he added, "We gotta keep the black apes down." We cannot forget it because this is the animating sentiment of the white supremacists, of a powerful segment of American life. We cannot forget that in many American states it is a crime for a white person to marry a Negro on the racist theory that Negroes are "inherently inferior as an immutable fact of Nature." The whole institution of segregation, which is training for killing, education for genocide, is based on the Hitler-like theory of the "inherent inferiority of the Negro." The tragic fact of segregation is the basis for the statement, too often heard after murder, particularly in the South, "Why I think no more of killing a n— —r, than of killing a dog."

We petition in the first instance because we are compelled to speak by the unending slaughter of Negroes. The fact of our ethnic origin, or which we are proud—our ancestors were building the world's first civilizations 3,000 years before our oppressors emerged from barbarism in the forests of western Europe—is daily made the signal for segregation and murder. There is infinite variety in the cruelty we will catalogue, but each case has the common denominator of racism. This opening statement is not the place to present our evidence in detail. Still, in this summary of what is to be proved, we believe it necessary to show something of the crux of our case, something of the pattern of genocidal murder, the technique of incitement to genocide, and the methods of mass terror.

Our evidence begins with 1945 and continues to the present. It gains in deadliness and in number of cases almost in direct ratio to the surge towards war. We are compelled to hold to this six years span if this document is to be brought into manageable proportions. . . .

Summary and Prayer

There may be debate as to the expediency of condemning the Government of the United States for the genocide it practices and permits against the 15,000,000 of its citizens who are Negroes. There can be none about the existence of the crime. It is an undeniable fact. The United States Government itself, through the Report of the President's Committee on Civil Rights quoted earlier, admits the institutionalized Negro oppression, written into the law, and carried out by police and courts. It describes it, examines it, surveys it, writes about it, talks about it, and does everything but change it. It both admits it and protects it.

Thus it was easy for your petitioners to offer abundant proof of the crime. It is everywhere in American life. And yet words and statistics are but poor things to convey the long agony of the Negro people. We have proved "killing members of the group"—but the case after case after case cited does nothing to assuage the helplessness of the innocent Negro trapped at this instant by police in a cell which will be the scene of his death. We have shown "mental and bodily harm" in violation of Article II of the Genocide Convention but this proof can barely indicate the life-long terror of thousands on thousands of Negroes forced to live under the menace of official violence, mob law and the Ku Klux Klan. We have tried to reveal something of the deliberate infliction "on the group of conditions which bring about its physical destruction in whole or in part"—but this cannot convey the hopeless despair of those forced by law to live in conditions of disease and poverty because of race, of birth, of color. We have shown incitements to commit genocide, shown that a conspiracy exists to commit it, and now we can only add that an entire people, not only unprotected by their government but the object of government-inspired violence, reach forth their hands to the General Assembly in appeal. Three hundred years is a long time to wait. And now we ask that world opinion, that the conscience of mankind as symbolized by the General Assembly of the United Nations turn not a deaf ear to our entreaty.

We plead as patriotic Americans, knowing that any act that can aid in removing the incubus of United States oppression of the American Negro people from our country is the highest patriotism. The American Dream was for justice, justice for all men, regardless of race, creed, or color. He who betrays it, betrays our country, betrays the world itself since the United States is a power in it for good or for evil.

We speak, too, as world citizens, certain that if the forces of predatory reaction are allowed to continue their present policies, are allowed to continue a profitable genocide against Americans, the time will not be long removed, the world being what it is, that the same forces will practice genocide on a wider scale against the nationals of other nations. So we plead not for ourselves alone but for all mankind. We plead not only for an end of the crime of genocide against the Negro people of the United States but we plead, too, for peace.

If the General Assembly acts as the conscience of mankind and therefore acts favorably on our petition, it will have served the cause of peace, the protection of which is the fundamental reason for its being. We recall the words of Mr. Justice Jackson at the Nuremberg trial of the Nazi war criminals when he declared that silence in the face of such crimes would make us a partner of them. We cannot believe that the General Assembly will not condemn the crimes complained of in this petition.

We ask that the General Assembly of the United Nations find and declare by resolution that the Government of the United States is guilty of the crime of Genocide against the Negro people of the United States and that it further demand that the government of the United States stop and prevent the crime of genocide.

We further ask that the General Assembly by resolution condemn the Government of the United States for failing to implement and observe its solemn international obligations under the Charter of the United Nations and the Genocide Convention and that the General Assembly also demand that the United States immediately take effective steps to carry out and fulfill its international obligations under the Charter and the Genocide Convention.

In Part II of this petition we asked, and now ask again, for action under Article VIII of the Genocide Convention which provides that a contracting party can "call upon the competent organs of the United Nations to take action under the Charter for the prevention and suppression of acts of Genocide."

May we express the urgent hope that for the sake of justice and world peace, for the integrity of the United Nations Charter and the good faith of the Genocide Convention, that a contracting party now make our case its own and "call upon the competent organs of the United Nations to take action...."

In addition we asked in Part II of this petition, and now ask again, that any dispute as to the applicability of the Genocide Convention to the crime here alleged be submitted to the International Court of Justice in accordance with Article IX of the Genocide Convention.

From the first it has been emphasized, to use the words of the Secretariat of the United Nations in a note to the Ad Hoc Committee which drafted the Genocide Convention, that "The Convention will be concerned not only with punishment of genocide but also with its prevention."

We ask now, therefore, that the General Assembly take steps to assure that prevention. And we ask, finally, for whatever other measures shall be deemed proper by the General Assembly, under the Charter of the United Nations and the Genocide Convention, to assure the safety of the Negro people of the United States. In doing so it will contribute to the peace of the world.

Malcolm X (1964)

Appeal to African Heads of State

Your Excellencies:

The Organization of Afro-American Unity has sent me to attend this historic African summit conference as an observer to represent the interests of 22 million African-Americans whose *human rights* are being violated daily by the racism of American imperialists.

The Organization of Afro-American Unity (OAAU) has been formed by a cross-section of America's African-American community, and is patterned after the letter and spirit of the Organization of African Unity (OAU).

Just as the Organization of African Unity has called upon all African leaders to submerge their differences and unite on common objectives for the common good of all Africans — in America the Organization of Afro-American Unity has called upon Afro-American leaders to submerge their differences and find areas of agreement wherein we can work in unity for the good of the entire 22 million African-Americans.

Since the 22 million of us were originally Africans, who are now in America not by choice but only by a cruel accident in our history, we strongly believe that African problems are our problems and our problems are African problems.

Your Excellencies:

We also believe that as heads of the Independent African states you are the shepherd of *all* African peoples everywhere, whether they are still at home on the mother continent or have been scattered abroad.

Some African leaders at this conference have implied that they have enough problems here on the mother continent without adding the Afro-American problem.

With all due respect to your esteemed positions, I must remind all of you that the good shepherd will leave ninety-nine sheep, who are safe at home, to go to the aid of the one who is lost and has fallen into the clutches of the imperialist wolf.

We, in America, are your long-lost brothers and sisters, and I am here only to remind you that our problems are your problems. As the African-Americans "awaken" today, we find ourselves in a strange land that has rejected us, and, like the prodigal son, we are turning to our elder brothers for help. We pray our pleas will not fall upon deaf ears.

We were taken forcibly in chains from this mother continent and have now spent over 300 years in America, suffering the most inhuman forms of physical and psychological tortures imaginable.

During the past ten years the entire world has witnessed our men, women and children being attacked and bitten by vicious police dogs, brutally beaten by police clubs, and washed down the sewers by high-pressure water hoses that would rip the clothes from our bodies and the flesh from our limbs.

And all of these inhuman atrocities have been inflicted upon us by the American governmental authorities, the police themselves, for no reason other than we seek the recognition and respect granted other human beings in America.

Your Excellencies:

The American government is either unable or unwilling to protect the lives and property of your 22 million African-American brothers and sisters. We stand defenseless, at the mercy of American racists who murder us at will for no reason other than we are black and of African descent.

Two black bodies were found in the Mississippi River this week; last week an unarmed African-American educator was murdered in cold blood in Georgia; a few days before that three civil-rights workers disappeared completely, perhaps murdered also, only because they were teaching our people in Mississippi how to vote and how to secure their political rights.

Our problems are your problems. We have lived for over 300 years in that American den of racist wolves in constant fear of losing life and limb. Recently, three students from Kenya were mistaken for American Negroes and were brutally beaten by New York police. Shortly after that, two diplomats from Uganda were also beaten by the New York City police, who mistook them for American Negroes.

If Africans are brutally beaten while only visiting in America, imagine the physical and psychological suffering received by your brothers and sisters who have lived there for over 300 years.

Our problem is your problem. No matter how much independence Africans get here on the mother continent, unless you wear your national dress at all times, when you visit America, you may be mistaken for one of us and suffer the same psychological humiliation and physical mutilation that is an everyday occurrence in our lives.

Your problems will never be fully solved until and unless ours are solved. You will never be fully respected until and unless we are also respected. You will never be recognized as free human beings until and unless we are also recognized and treated as human beings.

Our problem is your problem. It is not a Negro problem, nor an American problem. This is a world problem; a problem for humanity. *It is not a problem of civil rights but a problem of human rights.*

If the United States Supreme Court justice, Arthur Goldberg, a few weeks ago, could find legal grounds to threaten to bring Russia before the United Nations and charge her with violating the human rights of less than three million Russian Jews, what makes our African brothers hesitate to bring the United States government before the United Nations and charge her with violating the human rights of 22 million African-Americans?

We pray that our African brothers have not freed themselves of European colonialism only to be overcome and held in check now by American *dollarism*. Don't let American racism be "legalized" by American dollarism.

America is worse than South Africa, because not only is America racist, but she also is deceitful and hypocritical. South Africa preaches segregation and practices segregation. She, at least, practices what she preaches. America preaches integration and practices segregation. She preaches one thing while deceitfully practicing another.

South Africa is like a vicious wolf, openly hostile towards black humanity. But America is cunning like a fox, friendly and smiling, but even more vicious and deadly than the wolf.

The wolf and the fox are both enemies of humanity; both are canine; both humiliate and mutilate their victims. Both have the same objectives, but differ only in methods.

If South Africa is guilty of violating the human rights of Africans here on the mother continent, then America is guilty of worse violations of the 22 million Africans on the American continent. And if South African racism is not a domestic issue, then American racism also is not a *domestic* issue.

Many of you have been led to believe that the much publicized, recently passed civil-rights bill is a sign that America is making a sincere effort to correct the injustices we have suffered there. This propaganda maneuver is part of her deceit and trickery to keep the African nations from condemning her racist practices before the United Nations, as you are now doing as regards the same practices of South Africa.

The United States Supreme Court passed a law ten years ago making America's segregated school system illegal. But the federal government has yet to enforce this law even in the North. If the federal government cannot enforce the law of the highest court in the land when it comes to nothing but equal rights to education for African-Americans, how can anyone be so naive as to think all the additional laws brought into being by the civil-rights bill will be enforced?

These are nothing but tricks of the century's leading neo-colonialist power. Surely, our intellectually mature African brothers will not fall for this trickery.

The Organization of Afro-American Unity, in cooperation with a coalition of other Negro leaders and organizations, has decided to elevate our freedom struggle above the domestic level of civil rights. We intend to "internationalize" it by placing it at the level of human rights. Our freedom struggle for human dignity is no longer confined to the domestic jurisdiction of the United States government.

We beseech the independent African states to help us bring our problem before the United Nations, on the grounds that the United States government is morally incapable of protecting the lives and the property of 22 million African-Americans. And on the grounds that our deteriorating plight is definitely becoming a threat to world peace.

Out of frustration and hopelessness our young people have reached the point of no return. We no longer endorse patience and turning-the-other-cheek. We assert the right of self-defense by whatever means necessary, and reserve the right of maximum retaliation against our racist oppressors, no matter what the odds against us are.

From here on in, if we must die anyway, we will die fighting back and we will not die alone. We intend to see that our racist oppressors also get a taste of death.

We are well aware that our future efforts to defend ourselves by retaliating — by meeting violence with violence, eye for eye and tooth for tooth — could create the type of racial conflict in America that could easily escalate into a violent, world-wide, bloody race war.

In the interests of world peace and security, we beseech the heads of the independent African states to recommend an immediate investigation into our problem by the United Nations Commission on Human Rights.

If this humble plea that I am voicing at this conference is not properly worded, then let our elder brothers, who know the legal language, come to our aid and word our plea in the proper language necessary for it to be heard.

One last word, my beloved brothers at this African summit:

"No one knows the master better than his servant." We have been servants in America for over 300 years. We have a thorough, inside knowledge of this man who calls himself "Uncle Sam." Therefore, you must heed our warning: Don't escape from European colonialism only to become even more enslaved by deceitful, "friendly" American dollarism.

May Allah's blessings of good health and wisdom be upon you all. Salaam Alaikum.

Malcolm X, Chairman
Organization of Afro-American Unity

Black Panther Party for Self Defense (1967)

What We Want; What We Believe

WHAT WE WANT WHAT WE BELIEVE

What we want now!:

1. We want freedom. We want power to determine the destiny of our black community.
2. We want full employment for our people.
3. We want an end to the robbery by the white man of our black community.
4. We want decent housing fit for shelter of human beings.
5. We want education for our people that exposes the true nature of this decadent American society. We want education that teaches us our true history and our role in the present day society.
6. We want all black men to be exempt from military service.
7. We want an immediate end to *police brutality* and *murder* of black people.
8. We want freedom for all black men and women held in federal, state, county, and city prisons and jails.
9. We want all black people when brought to trial, to be tried in court by a jury of their peer group or people from their black communities, as defined by the Constitution of the United States.
10. We want land, bread, housing, education, clothing, justice and peace.

What we believe:

1. We believe that black people will not be free until we are able to determine our destiny.
2. We believe that the federal government is responsible and obligated to give every man employment or a guaranteed income.

We believe that if the white American business men will not give full employment, then the means of production should be taken from the business men and placed in the community so that the people of the community can organize and employ all of its people and give a high standard of living.

3. We believe that this racist government has robbed us and now we are demanding the overdue debt of forty acres and two mules. Forty acres and two mules was promised 100 years ago as retribution for slave labor and mass murder of black people. We will accept the payment in currency which will be distributed to our many communities. The Germans are now aiding the Jews in Israel for the genocide of the Jewish people. The Germans murdered 6,000,000 Jews. The American racist has taken part in the slaughter of over 50,000,000 black people; therefore, we feel that this is a modest demand that we make.

4. We believe that if the white landlords will not give decent housing to our black community then the housing and the land should be made into cooperatives so that our community, with government aide, can build and make decent housing for its people.

5. We believe in an educational system that will give to our people a knowledge of self. If a man does not have knowledge of himself and his position in society and the world, then he has little chance to relate to anything else.

6. We believe that black people should not be forced to fight in the military service to defend a racist government that does not protect us. We will not fight and kill other people of color in the world who, like black people, are being victimized by the white racist government of America. We will protect ourselves from the force and violence of the racist police and the racist military, by whatever means necessary.

7. We believe we can end police brutality in our black community by organizing black *self defense* groups that are dedicated to defending our black community from racist police oppression and brutality. The Second Amendment of the Constitution of the United States gives us a right to bear arms. We therefore believe that all black people should arm themselves for *self defense*.

8. We believe that all black people should be released from the many jails and prisons because they have not received a fair and impartial trial.

9. We believe that the courts should follow the United States Constitution so that black people will receive fair trials. The 14th Amendment of the U.S. Constitution gives a man a right to be tried by his peer group. A peer is a person from a similar economical, social, religious, geographical, environmental, historical and racial background. To do this the court will be forced

to select a jury from the black community from which the black defendant came. We have been, and are being tried by all white juries that have no understanding of the "average reasoning man" of the black community.

10. When in the course of human events, it becomes necessary for one people to dissolve the political bonds which have connected them with another, and to assume among the powers of the earth, the separate and equal station to which the laws of nature and nature's God entitle them, a decent respect to the opinions of mankind requires that they should declare the causes which impel them to the separation.

We hold these truths to be self-evident, that all men are created equal, that they are endowed by their Creator with certain unalienable rights, that among these are life, liberty and the pursuit of happiness. That to secure these rights, governments are instituted among men, deriving their just powers from the consent of the governed, — *that whenever any form of government becomes destructive of these ends, it is the right of people to alter or to abolish it, and to institute new government, laying its foundation on such principles and organizing its powers in such form, as to them shall seem most likely to effect their safety and happiness.*

Prudence, indeed, will dictate that governments long established should not be changed for light and transient causes; and accordingly all experience hath shewn, that mankind are more disposed to suffer, while evils are sufferable, than to right themselves by abolishing the forms to which they are accustomed. *But when a long train of abuses and usurpations, pursuing invariably the same object, evinces a design to reduce them under absolute despotism, it is their right, it is their duty, to throw off such government, and to provide new guards for their future security.*

Republic of New Africa (1968)

Declaration of Independence

What Is the Republic of New Africa?

The Republic of New Africa is the organized black nation in America.
A nation must have three things:

1. People with the same culture (that means, *the same way of living*), the same history, and (usually) the same language;
2. People living together on the same land, and
3. People accepting the same government, their own government.

WE HAVE ALL THREE
WHERE IS OUR LAND?
The land of our nation is all the land in America where black people have lived a long time, and that we have built on or farmed or improved in any way, and that we have fought to stay on. This is international law. It means that most of the South and parts of many cities really belong to us.

But this land is all under a government that is run by white people, *for* white people, the United States government. For the sake of peace, *our* black government, the *Republic of New Africa,* is willing to make a just settlement. We will settle for five states. (That is only ten per cent of the United States and we are ten per cent of the people in the United States.) The states are *Louisiana, Mississippi, Alabama, Georgia,* and *South Carolina.*

The United States government must also pay black people *something* for all the labor which they stole from us during slavery and for cheating us out of a chance for a better life, by discriminating against us, *after* slavery. This is called *reparations.* Although the United States government owes us more than this, right now we would settle for $10,000 for every black person. Out of this $4,000 would go to the person; $6,000 would go to our government, the REPUBLIC OF NEW AFRICA. Our government would use reparations money to build the nation for all our people.

Declaration of Independence

We, the Black People in America, in consequence of arriving at a knowledge of ourselves as a people with dignity, long deprived of that knowledge, as a consequence of revolting with every decimal of our collective and individual beings against the oppression that for three hundred years has destroyed and broken and warped the bodies and minds and spirits of our people in America, in consequence of our raging desire to be free of this oppression, to destroy this oppression wherever it assaults mankind in the world, and in consequence of our inextinguishable determination to go a different way, to build a new and better world do hereby declare ourselves free and independent of the jurisdiction of the United States of America and the obligations which that country's unilateral decision to make our ancestors and ourselves paper citizens placed on us.

We claim no rights from the United States of America other than those rights belonging to human beings anywhere in the world, and these include the right to damages, reparations, due us for the grievous injuries sustained by our ancestors and ourselves by reason of United States' lawlessness.

Ours is a revolution against oppression — our own oppression and that of all people in the world. And it is a revolution for a better life, a better station for mankind, a surer harmony with the forces of life in the universe. We therefore, see these as the aims of our revolution:

— To free black people in America from oppression;
— To support and wage the world revolution until all people everywhere are so free;
— To build a new Society that is better than what we now know and as perfect as man can make it;
— To assure all people in the New Society maximum opportunity and equal access to that maximum;
— To promote industriousness, responsibility, scholarship, and service;
— To create conditions in which freedom of religion abounds and man's pursuit of God and/or the destiny, peace, and purpose of man in the Universe will be without hindrance;
— To build a black independent nation where no sect or religious creed subverts or impedes the building of the New Society, The New State Gov-

ernment, or the achievement of the aims of the Revolution as set forth in this Declaration;
— To end exploitation of many by man or his environment;
— To assure equality of rights for the sexes;
— To end color and class discrimination, while not abolishing salubrious diversity, and to promote self-respect and mutual respect among all people in the Society;
— To protect and promote the personal dignity and integrity of the individual, and his natural rights;
— To assure justice for all;
— To place the major means of production and trade in the trust of the state to assure the benefits of this earth and man's genius and labor to society and all its members, and
— To encourage and reward the individual for hard work and initiative and insight and devotion to the Revolution.

In mutual trust and great expectation, we the undersigned, for ourselves and for those who look to us but who are unable personally to fix their signatures hereto, do join in this solemn Declaration of Independence, and to support this Declaration and to assure the success of our Revolution, we pledge without reservation ourselves, our talents, and all our worldly goods.

THE NEW AFRICAN CREED

1. I believe in the spirituality, humanity and genius of black people, and in our new pursuit of these values.
2. I believe in the family and the community, and in the community as a family, and I will work to make this concept live.
3. I believe in the community as more important than the individual.
4. I believe in constant struggle for freedom, to end oppression and build a better world. I believe in collective struggle: in fashioning victory in concert with my brothers and sisters.
5. I believe that the fundamental reason our oppression continues is that we, as a people, lack the power to control our lives.
6. I believe that the fundamental way to gain that power, and end oppression, is to build a sovereign black nation.
7. I believe that all the land in America, upon which we have lived for a long time, which we have worked and built upon, and which we have fought to stay on, is land that belongs to us as a people.

8. I believe in the Malcolm X Doctrine: that we must organize upon this land, and hold a plebiscite to tell the world by a vote that we are free and our land independent and that after the vote, we must wage war to defend ourselves, establishing the nation beyond contradiction.

9. Therefore, I pledge to struggle without cease, until we have won sovereignty. I pledge to struggle without fail until we have built a better condition than man has yet known.

10. I will give my life, if that is necessary. I will give my time, my mind, my strength and my wealth because this IS necessary.

11. I will follow my chosen leaders and help them.

12. I will love my brothers and sisters as myself.

13. I will steal nothing from a brother or sister, cheat no brother or sister, misuse no brother or sister, inform on no brother or sister, and spread no gossip.

14. I will keep myself clean in body, dress and speech, knowing that I am a light set on a hill, a true representative of what we are building.

15. I will be patient and uplifting with the deaf, dumb and blind, and I will seek by word and deed to heal the black family, to bring into the Movement and into the Community mothers and fathers, brothers and sisters left by the wayside.

Now, freely and of my own will, I pledge this creed, for the sake of freedom for my people and a better world, on pain of disgrace and banishment if I prove false. For I am no longer deaf, dumb or blind. I am — by grace of Malcolm — a New African.

Black Panther Party (1969)

Reparations for Vietnam

AT LEAST A million Vietnamese people have been killed by the Americans or by puppet forces armed and directed by the U.S. Precious human lives can never be replaced with money or goods. Yet material compensation must be granted to the survivors. Using the racist standards of imperialism, the U.S. government has paid $34 per person to relatives of persons killed by its armed forces "by accident" in so-called "friendly areas." Such token payments measure nothing but the depravity of the U.S. military rules.

Here is a suggested standard. The U.S. grants each serviceman a $10,000 life insurance policy, for a token premium of $2 yearly. This may be taken as the minimum value of a human life. Applied to the million plus killed by U.S. imperialism in Vietnam, it comes to a total of more than $10 billion.

National Black Economic Development Conference (1969)

The Black Manifesto

[This document was presented by James Forman to the National Black Economic Development Conference in Detroit, Michigan, and adopted on April 26, 1969.]

We the black people assembled in Detroit, Michigan, for the National Black Economic Development Conference are fully aware that we have been forced to come together because racist white America has exploited our resources, our minds, our bodies, our labor. For centuries we have been forced to live as colonized people inside the United States, victimized by the most vicious, racist system in the world. We have helped to build the most industrialized country in the world.

We are therefore demanding of the white Christian churches and Jewish synagogues, which are part and parcel of the system of capitalism, that they begin to pay reparations to black people in this country. We are demanding $500,000,000 from the Christian white churches and the Jewish synagogues. This total comes to fifteen dollars per nigger. This is a low estimate, for we maintain there are probably more than 30,000,000 black people in this country. Fifteen dollars a nigger is not a large sum of money, and we know that the churches and synagogues have a tremendous wealth and its membership, white America, has profited and still exploits black people. We are also not unaware that the exploitation of colored peoples around the world is aided and abetted by the white Christian churches and synagogues. This demand for $500,000,000 is not an idle resolution or empty words. Fifteen dollars for every black brother and sister in the United States is only a beginning of the reparations due us as people who have been exploited and degraded, brutalized, killed and persecuted. Underneath all of this exploitation, the racism of this country has produced a psychological effect upon us that we are beginning to shake off. We are no longer afraid to demand our full rights as a people in this decadent society.

We are demanding $500,000,000 to be spent in the following way:

(1) We call for the establishment of a southern land bank to help our brothers and sisters who have to leave their land because of racist pressure, and for people who want to establish cooperative farms but who have no funds. We have seen too many farmers evicted from their homes because they have dared to defy the white racism of this country. We need money for land. We must fight for massive sums of money for this southern land bank. We call for $200,000,000 to implement this program.

(2) We call for the establishment of four major publishing and printing industries in the United States to be funded with ten million dollars each. These publishing houses are to be located in Detroit, Atlanta, Los Angeles, and New York. They will help to generate capital for further cooperative investments in the black community, provide jobs and an alternative to the white-dominated and controlled printing field.

(3) We call for the establishment of four of the most advanced scientific and futuristic audio-visual networks to be located in Detroit, Chicago, Cleveland and Washington, D.C. These TV networks will provide an alternative to the racist propaganda that fills the current television networks. Each of these TV networks will be funded by ten million dollars each.

(4) We call for a research skills center which will provide research on the problems of black people. This center must be funded with no less than thirty million dollars.

(5) We call for the establishment of a training center for the teaching of skills in community organization, photography, moving making, television making and repair, radio building and repair and all other skills needed in communication. This training center shall be funded with no less than ten million dollars.

(6) We recognize the role of the National Welfare Rights Organization, and we intend to work with them. We call for ten million dollars to assist in the organization of welfare recipients. We want to organize welfare workers in this country so that they may demand more money from the government and better administration of the welfare system of this country.

(7) We call for $20,000,000 to establish a National Black Labor Strike and Defense Fund. This is necessary for the protection of black workers and their families who are fighting racist working conditions in this country.

(8) We call for the establishment of the International Black Appeal (IBA). This International Black Appeal will be funded with no less than $20,000,000. The IBA is charged with producing more capital for the establishment of cooperative businesses in the United States and in Africa, our Motherland. The International Black Appeal is one of the most important demands that

we are making, for we know that it can generate and raise funds throughout the United States and help our African brothers. The IBA is charged with three functions and shall be headed by James Forman:

(a) Raising money for the program of the National Black Economic Development Conference.
(b) The development of cooperatives in African countries and support of African liberation movements.
(c) Establishment of a Black Anti-Defamation League which will protect our African image.

(9) We call for the establishment of a black university to be founded with $130,000,000, to be located in the South. Negotiations are presently under way with a southern university.
(10) We demand the IFCO [Interreligious Foundation for Community Organizing] allocate all unused funds in the planning budget to implement the demands of this conference.

In order to win our demands, we are aware that we will have to have massive support, therefore:

(1) We call upon all black people throughout the United States to consider themselves as members of the National Black Economic Development Conference and to act in unity to help force the racist white Christian churches and Jewish synagogues to implement these demands.
(2) We call upon all the concerned black people across the country to contact black workers, black women, black students and the black unemployed, community groups, welfare organizations, teachers' organizations, church leaders and organizations, explaining how these demands are vital to the black community of the United States. Pressure by whatever means necessary should be applied to the white power structure. All black people should act boldly in confronting our white oppressors and demanding this modest reparation of fifteen dollars per black man.
(3) Delegates and members of the National Black Economic Development Conference are urged to call press conferences in the cities and to attempt to get as many black organizations as possible to support the demands of the conference. The quick use of the press in the local areas will heighten the tension, and these demands must be attempted to be won in a short period of time, although we are prepared for protracted and long-range struggle.
(4) We call for the total disruption of selected church-sponsored agencies operating anywhere in the United States and the world. Black workers, black

women, black students and the black unemployed are encouraged to seize the offices, telephones, and printing apparatus of all church-sponsored agencies and to hold these in trusteeship until our demands are met.

(5) We call upon all delegates and members of the National Black Economic Development Conference to stage sit-in demonstrations at selected black and white churches. This is not to be interpreted as a continuation of the sit-in movement of the early sixties, but we know that active confrontation inside white churches is possible and will strengthen the possibility of meeting our demands. Such confrontation can take the form of reading the Black Manifesto instead of a sermon, or passing it out to church members. The principle of self-defense should be applied if attacked.

(6) On May 4, 1969, or a date thereafter, depending upon local conditions, we call upon black people to commence the disruption of the racist churches and synagogues throughout the United States.

(7) We call upon IFCO to serve as a central staff to coordinate the mandate of the conference and to reproduce and distribute en masse literature, leaflets, news items, press releases and other material.

(8) We call upon all delegates to find within the white community those forces which will work under the leadership of blacks to implement these demands by whatever means necessary. By taking such actions, white Americans will demonstrate concretely that they are willing to fight the white skin privilege and the white supremacy and racism which has forced us as black people to make these demands.

(9) We call upon all white Christians and Jews to practice patience, tolerance, understanding and nonviolence as they have been encouraged, advised and demanded that we as black people should do throughout our entire enforced slavery in the United States. The true test of their faith and belief in the Cross and the words of the prophets will certainly be put to a test as we seek legitimate and extremely modest reparations for our role in developing the industrial base of the western world through our slave labor. But we are no longer slaves, we are men and women, proud of our African heritage, determined to have our dignity.

(10) We are so proud of our African heritage and realize concretely that our struggle is not only to make revolution in the United States but to protect our brothers and sisters in Africa and to help them rid themselves of racism, capitalism and imperialism by whatever means necessary, including armed struggle. We are and must be willing to fight the defamation of our African image wherever it rears its ugly head. We are therefore charging the steering committee to create a black Anti-Defamation League to be founded by money raised from the International Black Appeal.

(11) We fully recognize that revolution in the United States and Africa, our Motherland, is more than a one dimensional operation. It will require the total integration of the political, economic and military components, and therefore we call upon all our brothers and sisters who have acquired training and expertise in the fields of engineering, electronics, research, community organization, physics, biology, chemistry, mathematics, medicine, military science and warfare to assist the National Black Economic Development Conference in the implementation of its program.

(12) To implement these demands we must have a fearless leadership. We must have a leadership which is willing to battle the church establishment to implement these demands. To win our demands we will have to declare war on the white Christian churches and synagogues, and this means we may have to fight the total government structure of this country. Let no one here think that these demands will be met by our mere stating them. For the sake of the churches and synagogues, we hope that they have the wisdom to understand that these demands are modest and reasonable. But if the white Christians and Jews are not willing to meet our demands through peace and goodwill, then we declare war, and we are prepared to fight by whatever means necessary. We are, therefore, proposing the election of the following steering committee:

Lucius Walker
Renny Freeman
Luke Tripp
Howard Fuller
Mark Comfort
Earl Allen
Robert Browne
Vincent Harding
James Forman
John Watson
Dan Aldridge
John Williams

Ken Cockrel
Chuck Wooten
Fannie Lou Hamer
Julian Bond
Mike Hamlin
Len Holt
Peter Bernard
Michael Wright
Muhammed Kenyatta
Mel Jackson
Howard Moore
Harold Homes

[This list was later revised, more Church representatives were added — eds.]

Brothers and sisters, we are no longer shuffling our feet and scratching our heads. We are tall, black and proud.

And we say to the white Christian churches and Jewish synagogues, to the government of this country and to all the white racist imperialists who compose it, there is only one thing left you can do to further degrade black people and that is to kill us. But we have been dying too long for this country. We have died in every war. We are dying in Vietnam today fighting the wrong enemy.

The new black man wants to live, and to live means that we must not become static or merely believe in self-defense. We must boldly go out and attack the white Western world at its power centers. The white Christian churches are another form of government in this country, and they are used by the government of this country to exploit the people of Latin America, Asia and Africa, but the day is soon coming to an end. Therefore, brothers and sisters, the demands we make upon the white Christian churches and the Jewish synagogues are small demands. They represent fifteen dollars per black person in these United States. We can legitimately demand this from the church power structure. We must demand more from the United States Government.

But to win our demands from the church, which is linked up with the United States Government, we must not forget that it will ultimately be by force and power that we will win.

We are not threatening the churches. We are saying that we know the churches came with the military might of the colonizers and have been sustained by the military might of the colonizers. Hence, if the churches in colonial territories were established by military might, we know deep within our hearts that we must be prepared to use force to get our demands. We are not saying that this is the road we want to take. It is not, but let us be very clear that we are not opposed to force and we are not opposed to violence. We were captured in Africa by violence. We were kept in bondage and political servitude and forced to work as slaves by the military machinery and the Christian Church working hand in hand.

We recognize that in issuing this Manifesto we must prepare for a long-range educational campaign in all communities of this country, but we know that the Christian churches have contributed to our oppression in white America. We do not intend to abuse our black brothers and sisters in black churches who have uncritically accepted Christianity. We want them to understand how the racist white Christian church with its hypocritical declarations and doctrines of brotherhood has abused our trust and faith. An attack on the religious beliefs of black people is not our major objective, even though we know that we were not Christians when we were brought to this country, but that Christianity was used to help enslave us. Our objective in issuing this Manifesto is to force the racist white Christian church to begin the payment of reparations which are due to all black people, not only by the church but also by private business and the United States government. We see this focus on the Christian church as an effort around which all black people can unite.

Our demands are negotiable, but they cannot be minimized, they can only be increased, and the church is asked to come up with larger sums of money than we are asking. Our slogans are:

All Roads Must Lead to Revolution
Unite with Whomever You Can Unite
Neutralize Wherever Possible
Fight Our Enemies Relentlessly
Victory to the People
Life and Good Health to Mankind
Resistance to Domination by the White Christian Churches and the Jewish Synagogues
Revolutionary Black Power
We Shall Win Without a Doubt

National Black Political Agenda (1972)

The Gary Declaration

Presented to The National Black Political Convention
Gary, Indiana
March 11, 1972

Introduction

The Black Agenda is addressed primarily to Black people in America. It is our attempt to define some of the essential changes which must take place in this land as we and our children move to self-determination and true independence. It assumes that no truly basic change for our benefit takes place in Black or white America unless we Black people organize to initiate that change. It assumes that we must have some essential agreement on overall goals, even though we may differ on many specific strategies. Therefore, this is our initial statement of goals and directions, our first definition of some crucial issues around which Black people must organize and move in 1972 and beyond. Anyone who claims to be serious about the survival and liberation of Black People must be serious about the implementation of the Black Agenda.

What Time Is It?

We come to Gary in an hour of great crisis and tremendous promise for Black America. While the white nation hovers on the brink of chaos, while its politicians offer no hope of real change, we stand on the edge of history and are faced with an amazing and frightening choice: We may choose in 1972 to slip back into the decadent white politics of American life, or we may press forward, moving relentlessly from Gary to the creation of our own Black life. The choice is large, but the time is very short.

Let there be no mistake. We come to Gary in a time of unrelieved crisis for our people. From every rural community in Alabama to the high-rise compounds of Chicago, we bring to this Convention the agonies of the masses of our people. From the sprawling Black cities of Watts and Nairobi in the West to the decay of Harlem and Roxbury in the East, the testimony we bear is the same. We are the witnesses to social disaster.

Our cities are crime-haunted dying grounds. Huge sectors of our youth—and countless others—face permanent unemployment. Those of us who work find our paychecks able to purchase less and less. Neither the courts nor the prisons contribute to anything resembling justice or reformation. The schools are unable—or unwilling—to educate our children for the real world of our struggles. Meanwhile, the officially approved epidemic of drugs threatens to wipe out the minds and strength of our best young warriors.

Economic, cultural, and spiritual depression stalk Black America, and the price for survival often appears to be more than we are able to pay. On every side, in every area of our lives, the American institutions in which we have placed our trust are unable to cope with the crimes they have created by their single-minded dedication to profits for some and white supremacy above all.

Beyond These Shores

And beyond these shores there is more of the same. For while we are pressed down under all the dying weight of a bloated, inwardly decaying white civilization, many of our brothers in Africa and the rest of the Third World have fallen prey to the same powers of exploitation and deceit. Wherever America faces the unorganized, politically powerless forces of the non-white world, its goal is domination by any means necessary—as if to hide from itself the crumbling of its own systems of life and work.

But Americans cannot hide. They can run to China and the moon and to the edges of consciousness, but they cannot hide. The crises we face as Black people are the crises of the entire society. They go deep, to the very bones and marrow, to the essential nature of America's economic, political, and cultural systems. They are the natural end-product of a society built on the twin foundations of white racism and white capitalism.

So, let it be clear to us now: The desperation of our people, the agonies of our cities, the desolation of our countryside, the pollution of the air and the water—these things will not be significantly affected by new faces in the old places in Washington, D.C. This is the truth we must face here in Gary if we are to join our people everywhere in the movement forward toward liberation.

White Realities, Black Choice

A Black political convention, indeed all truly Black politics must begin from this truth: The American System does not work for the masses of our people, and it cannot be made to work without radical fundamental change (indeed, this system does not really work in favor of the humanity of anyone in America.)

In light of such realities, we come to Gary and are confronted with a choice. Will we believe the truth that history presses into our face — or will we, too, try to hide? Will the small favors some of us have received blind us to the larger sufferings of our people, or open our eyes to the testimony of our history in America?

For more than a century we have followed the path of political dependence on white men and their systems. From the Liberty Party in the decades before the Civil War to the Republican Party of Abraham Lincoln, we trusted in white men and white politics as our deliverers. Sixty years ago, W. E. B. Du Bois said he would give the Democrats their "last chance" to prove their sincere commitment to equality for Black people — and he was given white riots and official segregation in peace and in war.

Nevertheless, some twenty years later we became Democrats in the name of Franklin Roosevelt, then supported his successor Harry Truman, and even tried a "non-partisan" Republican General of the Army named Eisenhower. We were wooed like many others by the superficial liberalism of John F. Kennedy and the make-believe populism of Lyndon Johnson. Let there be no more of that.

Both Parties Have Betrayed Us

Here at Gary, let us never forget that while the times and the names and the parties have continually changed, one truth has faced us insistently, never changing: Both parties have betrayed us whenever their interests conflicted with ours (which was most of the time), and whenever our forces were unorganized and dependent, quiescent and compliant. Nor should this be surprising, for by now we must know that the American political system, like all other white institutions in America, was designed to operate for the benefit of the white race: It was never meant to do anything else.

That is the truth that we must face at Gary. If white "liberalism" could have solved our problems, then Lincoln and Roosevelt and Kennedy would have done so. But they did not solve ours nor the rest of the nation's. If America's problems could have been solved by forceful, politically skilled and aggressive individuals, then Lyndon Johnson would have retained the presidency. If the true "American Way" of unbridled monopoly capitalism, combined with a ruthless military imperialism could do it, then Nixon would not be running around the world, or making speeches comparing his nation's decadence to that of Greece and Rome.

If we have never faced it before, let us face it at Gary: The profound crisis of Black people and the disaster of America are not simply caused by men nor will they be solved by men alone. These crises are the crises of basically flawed economics and politics, and of cultural degradation. None of the Democratic candidates and none of the Republican candidates—regardless of their vague promises to us or to their white constituencies—can solve our problems or the problems of this country without radically changing the systems by which it operates.

The Politics of Social Transformation

So we come to Gary confronted with a choice. But it is not the old convention question of which candidate shall we support, the pointless question of who is to preside over a decaying and unsalvageable system. No, if we come to Gary out of the realities of the Black communities of this land, then the only real choice for us is whether or not we will live by the truth we know, whether we will move to organize independently, move to struggle for fundamental transformation, for the creation of new directions, towards a concern for the life and the meaning of Man. Social transformation or social destruction, those are our only real choices.

If we have come to Gary on behalf of our people in America, in the rest of this hemisphere, and in the Homeland—if we have come for our own best ambitions—then a new Black Politics must come to birth. If we are serious, the Black Politics of Gary must accept major responsibility for creating both the atmosphere and the program for fundamental, far-ranging change in America. Such responsibility is ours because it is our people who are most deeply hurt and ravaged by the present systems of society. That responsibility for leading the change is ours because we live in a society where few other men really believe in the responsibility of a truly humane society for anyone anywhere.

We Are The Vanguard

The challenge is thrown to us here in Gary. It is the challenge to consolidate and organize our own Black role as the vanguard in the struggle for a new society. To accept that challenge is to move independent Black politics. There can be no equivocation on that issue. History leaves us no other choice. White politics has not and cannot bring the changes we need.

We come to Gary and are faced with a challenge. The challenge is to transform ourselves from favor-seeking vassals and loud-talking, "militant" pawns, and to take up the role that the organized masses of our people have attempted to play ever since we came to these shores: That of harbingers of true justice and humanity, leaders in the struggle for liberation.

A major part of the challenge we must accept is that of redefining the functions and operations of all levels of American government, for the existing governing structures — from Washington to the smallest county — are obsolescent. That is part of the reason why nothing works and why corruption rages throughout public life. For white politics seeks not to serve but to dominate and manipulate.

We will have joined the true movement of history if at Gary we grasp the opportunity to press Man forward as the first consideration of politics. Here at Gary we are faithful to the best hopes of our fathers and our people if we move for nothing less than a politics which places community before individualism, love before sexual exploitation, a living environment before profits, peace before war, justice before unjust "order," and morality before expediency.

This is the society we need, but we delude ourselves here at Gary if we think that change can be achieved without organizing the power, the determined national Black power, which is necessary to insist upon such change, to create such change, to seize change.

Towards A Black Agenda

So when we turn to a Black Agenda for the seventies, we move in the truth of history, in the reality of the moment. We move recognizing that no one else is going to represent our interests but ourselves. The society we seek cannot come unless Black people organize to advance its coming. We lift up a Black Agenda recognizing that white America moves towards the abyss created by its own racist arrogance, misplaced priorities, rampant materialism, and ethical bankruptcy. Therefore, we are certain that the Agenda we now press for in Gary is not only for the future of Black humanity, but is probably the only way the rest of America can save itself from the harvest of its criminal past.

So, Brothers and Sisters of our developing Black nation, we now stand at Gary as a people whose time has come. From every corner of Black America, from all liberation movements of the Third World, from the graves of our fathers and the coming world of our children, we are faced with a challenge and a call: Though the moment is perilous we must not despair. We must seize the time, for the time is ours.

We begin here and now in Gary. We begin with an independent Black political movement, an independent Black Political Agenda, an independent Black spirit. Nothing less will do. We must build for our people. We must build for our world. We stand on the edge of history. We cannot turn back.

Black Panther Party (1973)

Petition to the United Nations

We, the undersigned citizens of the United States, gravely concerned with the continued racist persecution, conscious and unconscious, and centuries-old denial of Constitutional rights and respect for human dignity to men, women and children of red, brown, yellow and particularly black Americans, assert that:

The savage police activities, based upon official policies of Federal, State and City governments, has resulted in innumerable beatings, frameups, arrests and murders of black Americans, the classical example of which is the Black Panther Party. The murderous attacks on black youth in Chicago, Illinois, Orangeburg, South Carolina, Augusta, Georgia, Jackson, Mississippi, and the innumerable beatings, legal frameups of brown, red, yellow and black youths are not only in violation of their legal rights, but as well of this government's commitment under the Charter of the United Nations.

The Genocide Convention adopted by the General Assembly of the United Nations on December 9, 1948, defines as genocide "killing members of the group and any intent to destroy in whole or in part a national racial or ethnic or religious group." And further, according to the Convention, "Causing serious bodily or mental harm to members of the group" is Genocide.

We assert that the Genocide Convention has been flagrantly violated by the Government of the United States. We further assert that the United Nations has jurisdiction in this matter, to hold otherwise is to repudiate its position regarding apartheid in South Africa and as well its universal Declaration of Human Rights, and its Convention for the Prevention and Punishment of Genocide.

The racist planned and unplanned terror suffered by more than 40 million of black, brown, red and yellow citizens of the United States cannot be regarded solely as a domestic issue. The continuance of these practices threatens the struggle of mankind throughout the world to achieve peace, security and dignity.

On the basis of simple justice, it is time for the Human Rights Commission of the United Nations to call for universal action, including political and economic sanctions against the United States. We further demand that the United States government make reparations to those who have suffered the damages of racist and genocidal practices.
NAME
Huey P. Newton
Bobby Seale
   UNDER THE AUSPICES OF: *The Committee to Petition The United Nations,* of the Conference Committee, 33 Union Square W., New York, N.Y., 10003, Room 907

Nation of Islam (1990)

A Case for Reparations

"Add It Up"

By Minister Louis Farrakhan

[Editor's Note: The following text is part of a transcript from the "Stop the Killing" speech delivered by Minister Louis Farrakhan at the Omni Center in Atlanta on 28th April 1990.]

America, you owe us something. We don't want you to dole it out in welfare checks. If you give us what you owe us, we'll take it from there. But will America do that? We don't know.

However, America did detain thousands of Japanese-Americans in concentration camps (during World War II) and confiscated their property. Now Congress says America treated the Japanese-Americans wrongly and have okayed several billions of dollars to be paid to the Japanese in reparations.

The Germans recognize the evil that they did to the Jews, and right now they are paying reparations to Israel. East Germany wanted to unite with West Germany and in order to do so, they repented and stated their intentions to pay Israel reparations.

"We ask the Jews of the world to forgive us," the East German parliament said in a formal statement. "We ask the people of Israel to forgive us for the hypocrisy and hostility of official East German policy toward Israel, and for the persecution and the degradation of Jewish citizens, also after 1945, in our country.

"We declare our willingness to contribute as much as possible to the healing of mental and physical sufferings of survivors and to provide just compensation for material losses."

That's a wonderful thing done by the East Germans. Now let's rewrite this a little bit and let's put it in the hands of America. Wouldn't it be wonderful if America said, "We ask the blacks of the world to forgive us. We ask the black people of America to forgive us for our hypocrisy and the hostility of official

United States policy toward black people, and for the persecution and degradation of black people, even after 1863 when we called them citizens and said they were free.

"And we (the government of America) declare our willingness to contribute as much as possible to the healing of mental and physical suffering of any survivors and to provide just compensation for material losses."

Now, let's add up what they owe us. Do you have your computers? Let's start in Africa. According to the late, great scholar W. E. B. Du Bois, a conservative estimate of black lives lost in the Middle Passage was from 50 to 100 million black lives. We don't need to minimize the Jewish Holocaust. Six million lives is a lot of lives, but are you telling me that six million white lives are more valuable than 100 million black lives? You can't be saying that. For the Bible says "a life for a life."

Well, if 100 million of us lost our lives in the Middle Passage, add it up. What is one black life worth? Three hundred years working from "can't see morning to can't see night," for no pay. Three hundred years working millions of slaves for nothing. Add it up! Add it up! Add it up!

The killing of our fathers and mothers after mating them like animals, then taking the children and naming us after the slave master, stripping us of our language, our God, our religion, our minds. Add it up! Add it up. Think about it. The destruction of our families.

Black folk fought in the Revolutionary War that made America free from England, yet, we're not free. Add it up. We fought in the War of 1812. Add it up. We fought in the Civil War — 400,000 blacks on the side of the North and the South, some fighting to preserve the old South, others fighting to preserve the Union. After the Union was preserved, we had no Union, but thousands of black lives were lost in that war. Add it up!

You brought us into religion, not to make us closer to Jesus, but to turn us inside out in Jesus' name. You know Jesus was no white man. Look at him. The Bible says he had hair like lamb's wool, and feet like brass burnt in an oven. But you made us white-minded and destroyed our love for ourselves. Add it up!

We fought in the Spanish-American War. We helped America steal Texas, New Mexico, Arizona and California from the Mexicans. Add it up. World War I came. You got in trouble. Black soldiers went, you got a victory over Germany. We got nothing but more hell. Add it up. World War II came along. Hitler got started. We joined the Army. You say, "Well, if you joined, you joined on your own." No, no, baby . . . when you joined the Army and signed your name "Willis Jackson," "Henry Morgan," "Larry Higginbotham," you signed the wrong name. You were out of your mind — didn't know who you were. Somebody took advantage of you and sent you to fight for your enemy. Add it up!

We left our fathers on Normandy Beach, in Palermo, in Rome, in Naples, in Sicily. We left our bodies on the streets of Paris, in Belgium. Add it up. We joined the war. They used us in Hawaii, in Bataan, in Corregidor, in the Solomon Islands, in Iwo Jima. We lost our lives fighting for America. And after the war was over, America rebuilt Germany. Now the West German economy is the strongest in all of Europe. We rebuilt Japan. Now the Japanese are world leaders, but black people who helped you win the war, they are homeless in Atlanta, homeless in Chicago, homeless in Detroit, homeless in Boston, in the streets looking for a job, looking for a handout. We helped you to win, but you offered us nothing. I say, add it up. Add it up. Add it up!

We developed leaders to help us. Marcus Garvey came and talked to us, but here in Georgia you trumped up charges against him and you brought him into court and you lied on him and you sent him to prison unjustly. Then you deported him and broke his movement. Only later did we learn that Garvey was a good man, he had a good movement, he had a good program, but you destroyed it all. Add it up. Add it up. Add it up.

In the 1960s, when black folk began to move, we had CORE, SNCC, the NAACP, the Southern Christian Leadership Conference, the Black Panthers, the Nation of Islam. All of these brothers and sisters were fighting for the liberation of black people, but there in Washington, D.C., the government of America started plotting against our leaders, and we lost Whitney Young off the coast of Africa under suspicious circumstances. We lost Medgar Evers. They broke up CORE. They broke up SNCC. They broke up the organization called US (under Ron Karenga). They jailed the leaders of the Republic of New Africa. They murdered Rev. Dr. Martin Luther King Jr. They weakened the NAACP and the Urban League. Everything that fought for justice for us, they tore it up and tore it down. I say, add it up. America owes the black man. Add it up.

What is the life of Martin Luther King worth? What is the life of Malcolm X worth? What is the life of our leaders worth? What is the life of Louis Farrakhan worth? You want me dead, but I say you don't want that. You don't really want that. If you know what I know, you don't want that. No, you don't want that.

The way God looks at this thing, the present generation of whites, they didn't do this to us. The present generation of whites are innocent of what their grandfathers did, but they are in a privileged position because of what their fathers did; and we're in a hell of a condition because of what their fathers did. So if the present generation of whites wants to escape what is justly due, then they've got to do the right thing. They've got to do justice by the black man.

What is the right thing? You (this generation of whites) have got to apologize for what you did. You've got to repent for what you did. You've got to say, "we've been wrong. Now, we know we don't want you, we don't like you, but we'll give you justice."

Now what does justice look like? If you add it up, white folks, you are going to have to give us the whole country. Add it up, white man. The whole thing belongs to the oppressed, if you add it up. We're not asking for the whole thing, but we do deserve the whole thing. Just give us some of it and let us go, to build a nation for ourselves. Since you don't want us, don't keep us here and kill us. Let us go and let us build a new reality in the name of God. Let us build for God.

"And what if we don't do that?" It's your thing; do what you wanna do. You don't have to give us anything, but God said He's the Power today, and He'll take the Kingdom from whom He pleases, and He will give it to whom He pleases. When I ask for reparations, I'm asking you to save your life. But if you don't want to save your life, then leave it to God. He'll settle it.

Let me tell you how He'll settle it: An eye for an eye, a tooth for a tooth and a life for a life. Add it up. Add it up. Add it up.

One hundred million in the Middle Passage and you have 150 million white people in America today. Add it up. If it's a life for a life, then God is justified in killing everything that refuses to submit, as He killed Pharaoh and his people, as He destroyed Babylon, and Sodom and Gomorrah. And He warned you that it was water the first time, but it will be fire next time. You'd better add it up.

Black Radical Congress (1999)

The Freedom Agenda

The Freedom Agenda (FA) of the Black Radical Congress (BRC). Ratified by the BRC National Council (NC), April 17, 1999, Baltimore, Maryland.

PREAMBLE

During the last 500 years, humanity has displayed on a colossal scale its capacity for creative genius and ruthless destruction, for brutal oppression and indomitable survival, for rigid tradition and rapid change. The Americas evolved to their present state of development at great cost to their original, indigenous peoples, and at great cost to those whose labor enabled modernization under the yoke of that protracted crime against humanity, slavery. Even so, a good idea is implicit in the Declaration of Independence of the United States: that all people are "endowed with certain inalienable rights, and among these are life, liberty and the pursuit of happiness." That the idea of a just society, contained in those words, remains unrealized is what compels this declaration.

Not only has the idea not been realized, but we are moving further away from its realization by the hour. Global capitalism, both the cause and effect of neo-liberal and Reaganist policies, has facilitated the transfer of enormous wealth from the bottom to the top of society in recent years, concentrating the control of abundant resources in ever fewer hands. As a result, the working people who constitute the vast majority of people have confronted a steady decline in their prospects for earning a decent living and controlling their lives. In the U.S., the threat of sudden unemployment hangs over most households. We pay unfair taxes and receive fewer services, while multi-billion-dollar fortunes accumulate in the private sector. Prisons proliferate as budgets are slashed for public schools, day care, healthcare and welfare. The grip of big money on the two-party electoral process has robbed us of control over the political institutions that are mandated to serve us. We are losing ground, and democracy is more and more elusive.

As for people of African descent, most of whose ancestors were among the shackled millions who helped build the edifices and culture of the Americas, we carry an enormously disproportionate burden. In the U.S., the living legacy of slavery, and the pervasiveness of institutional white supremacy, have placed us on all-too-familiar terms with poverty, urban and rural; exploitative conditions of employment; disproportionately high rates of unemployment and underemployment; inferior health care; substandard education; the corrosive drug trade, with its accompanying gun violence; police brutality and its partner, excessive incarceration; hate-inspired terrorism; a biased legal system, and discrimination of every kind—persistent even after the end of legal segregation.

Resistance is in our marrow as black people, given our history in this place. From the Haitian revolution, to the U.S. abolitionist movement against slavery, to the 20th Century movement for civil rights and empowerment, we have struggled and died for justice. We believe that struggle must continue, and with renewed vigor. Our historical experiences suggest to us, by negative example, what a truly just and democratic society should look like: It should be democratic, not just in myth but in practice, a society in which all people—regardless of color, ethnicity, religion, nationality, national origin, sex, sexual orientation, age, family structure, or mental or physical capability—enjoy full human rights, the fruits of their labor, and the freedom to realize their full human potential. If you agree, and if you are committed to helping achieve justice and democracy in the 21st Century, please sign your name and/or the name of your organization to this 15-point Freedom Agenda.

THE FREEDOM AGENDA

I. We will fight for the human rights of black people and all people.

We will struggle for a society and world in which every individual enjoys full human rights, full protection of the United Nations Declaration of Human Rights, and in the United States equal protection of the Constitution and of all the laws. We seek a society in which every individual—regardless of color, nationality, national origin, ethnicity, religion, sex, sexual orientation, age, family structure, or mental or physical capability—is free to experience "life, liberty and the pursuit of happiness." We affirm that all people are entitled to:

a. a safe and secure home;
b. employment at a living wage — that is, compensation for the full value of their labor;
c. free, quality health care, including full reproductive freedom with the right to choose when or whether to bear children, and free, quality child care;
d. free, quality public education.

We oppose the Human Genome Project in its current form and with its current leadership, and we oppose all sociobiological or genetic experiments that are spurred by, and help perpetuate, scientific racism.

We will fight for a society and world in which every individual and all social groups can live secure, dignified lives.

II. We will fight for political democracy.

We will struggle to expand political democracy to ensure the people's greater participation in decision-making. In the U.S., we will work to replace the current two-party, winner-take-all electoral system with a more democratic multiparty system based on proportional representation, and we will fight to abolish all registration procedures that restrict the number of eligible voters. We oppose private financing of electoral campaigns, especially corporate contributions; we will work to replace the present corrupt system with public financing.

III. We will fight to advance beyond capitalism, which has demonstrated its structural incapacity to address basic human needs worldwide and, in particular, the needs of black people.

Guided by our belief that people should come before profits, we will fight to maximize economic democracy and economic justice:

a. We seek full employment at livable wages, public control of private sector financial operations, worker control of production decisions, and a guaranteed annual income for the needy;
b. we will fight to end racial discrimination by capitalist enterprises, especially banks, insurance companies and other financial institutions;
c. we seek a society in which working people enjoy safe working conditions and flexible hours to accommodate family responsibilities, leisure and vacations;

d. we seek laws mandating public ownership of utilities, and mandating federal and local budgetary emphases on programs for the general welfare — health care, education, public transportation, recreation and infrastructure;
e. we will struggle for laws that regulate private sector business practices, especially regarding prices, fees, plant shutdowns and job relocations — where shutdowns are permitted, adequate compensation to workers shall be required;
f. we support the historical mission of trade unions to represent workers' interest and to negotiate on their behalf;
g. we seek a fair, equitable, highly progressive tax system that places the heaviest taxes on the wealthiest sector, and we seek expansion of the earned income tax credit.

IV. We will fight to end the super-exploitation of Southern workers.

More than 50 percent of people of African descent residing in the U.S. live in the South, where workers' earnings and general welfare are besieged by corporate practices, and where "right to work" laws undermine union organizing. Thus, we seek relief for Southern workers from corporate oppression, and we will struggle to repeal anti-union laws. We will also fight for aid to black farmers, and for the restoration of farm land seized from them by agribusiness, speculators and real estate developers.

V. We will struggle to ensure that all people in society receive free public education.

We affirm that all are entitled to free, quality public education throughout their lifetime. Free education should include adult education and retraining for occupational and career changes. We will fight to ensure that curricula in U.S. schools, colleges and universities are anti-racist, anti-sexist and anti-homophobic, and for curricula that adequately accommodate students' needs to express and develop their artistic, musical or other creative potential.

VI. We will struggle against state terrorism.

We will fight for a society in which every person and every community is free from state repression, including freedom from state-sponsored surveillance. We seek amnesty for, and the release of, all political prisoners. We will struggle to repeal all legislation that expands the police power of the state and undermines the U.S. Constitution's First and Fourth Amendments. We will fight to eliminate the deliberate trafficking in drugs and weapons in our communities by organized crime, and by institutions of the state such as the Central Intelligence Agency.

VII. We will struggle for a clean and healthy environment.

We will fight for a society in which the welfare of people and the natural environment takes precedence over commercial profits and political expediency. We will work to protect, preserve and enhance society's and the planet's natural heritage — forests, lakes, rivers, oceans, mountain ranges, animal life, flora and fauna. In the U.S., we will struggle against environmental racism by fighting for laws that strictly regulate the disposal of hazardous industrial waste, and that forbid both the discriminatory targeting of poor and non-white communities for dumping and despoilment of the natural environment.

VIII. We will fight to abolish police brutality, unwarranted incarceration and the death penalty.

We are determined to end police brutality and murder:

a. We will fight for strong civilian oversight of police work by elected civilian review boards that are empowered to discipline police misconduct and enforce residency requirements for police officers;
b. we seek fundamental changes in police training and education to emphasize public service over social control as the context in which law enforcement occurs, and to stress respect for the histories and cultures of the U.S.-born and immigrant communities served;
c. we seek to limit incarceration to the most violent criminals, only those who have clearly demonstrated their danger to the lives and limbs of others;
d. regarding non-violent offenders, we demand that they be released and provided with appropriate medical, rehabilitative and educative assistance without incarceration;
e. we will struggle for abolition of the death penalty, which has been abolished in the majority of developed nations. In the U.S., the history of the death penalty's application is inextricable from the nation's origins as a slave state. Since Emancipation, it has been a white supremacist tool intended to maintain control over a population perceived as an alien, on-

going threat to the social order. Application of the death penalty, which is highly discriminatory on the basis of color and class, violates international human rights law and must be eliminated.

IX. *We will fight for gender equality, for women's liberation, and for women's rights to be recognized as human rights in all areas of personal, social, economic and political life.*

We will work to create a society and world in which women of African descent, along with their sisters of other colors, nationalities and backgrounds, shall enjoy non-discriminatory access to the education, training and occupations of their choice. We will struggle to ensure that all women enjoy equal access to quality health care and full reproductive rights, including the right to determine when or whether they will bear children and the right to a safe, legal abortion. We will fight to end domestic abuse and sexual harassment in the workplace.

X. *We recognize lesbian, gay, bisexual and transgender people as full and equal members of society, and of our communities.*

We affirm the right of all people to love whom they choose, to openly express their sexuality, and to live in the family units that meet their needs. We will fight against homophobia, and we support anti-homophobic instruction in public schools. We will fight for effective legal protections for the civil rights and civil liberties of lesbian, gay, bisexual and transgender people, and we demand that violence and murder committed against such people be prosecuted as hate crimes. We will also fight to end discrimination against this sector in employment, health care, social welfare and other areas.

XI. *We support affirmative action.*

We will fight to retain and expand affirmative action policies in education, employment, the awarding of government contracts and all other areas affected by historical and contemporary injustices. Affirmative action, with goals and timetables, is indispensable for achieving equal opportunity, justice and fairness for the members of all historically oppressed groups.

XII. *We will fight for reparations.*

Reparations is a well-established principle of international law that should be applied in the U.S. Historically, the U.S. has been both the recipient and disburser of reparations. As the descendants of enslaved Africans, we have the legal and moral right to receive just compensation for the oppression, systematic brutality and economic exploitation Black people have suffered historically and continue to experience today. Thus, we seek reparations from the U.S. for

a. its illegal assault on African peoples during the slave trade;
b. its exploitation of black labor during slavery, and
c. its systematic and totalitarian physical, economic and cultural violence against people of African descent over the last four centuries.

XIII. *We will struggle to build multicultural solidarity and alliances among all people of color.*

We will fight against white supremacist tactics aimed at dividing people of color. We seek alliances with other people to develop unified strategies for achieving multicultural democracy, and for overcoming the divisions that exist around such issues as immigration, bilingual education, political representation and allocation of resources.

XIV. *We will uphold the right of the African American people to self-determination.*

The formation of the Black Radical Congress in June 1998 was an act of African American self-determination, a principle which is codified in the United Nations Declaration of Human Rights. The African American people are entitled to define the direction, priorities, allies and goals of our struggle against national and racial oppression. Building the power to exercise these prerogatives is central to our struggle against all the systems of oppression confronting our people. Therefore, we will fight for both a national program of liberation and for a mass base of power in the social sectors, institutions, all levels of government, communities and territories of society that affect the lives of our people.

XV. *We support the liberation struggles of all oppressed people.*

We affirm our solidarity with peoples of African descent throughout the African diaspora. We support their struggles against imperialism and neo-colonialism from without, as well as against governmental corruption, exploitation and human rights abuses from within. We especially support struggles against transnational corporations, whose global market practices gravely exploit all workers, abuse workers' rights and threaten all workers' welfare. We affirm our solidarity with all oppressed people around the world, whatever their color, nation or religion—none of us is free unless all are free. We believe that all people everywhere should enjoy the right to self-determination and the right to pursue their dreams, unfettered by exploitation and discrimination.

[End of Freedom Agenda – Ratified April 17, 1999]

Reparations Support Committee (1999/2000)

"To the President of the United States of America"

To the President of the United States of America

Whereas we, United States of America citizens of European descent, are in support of the just demands of African Americans for fair, long-overdue reparations for the crimes of slavery endured in the United States of America,

Whereas we, United States of America citizens of European descent, have the political and economic power to end racism, and ensure social and economic justice for the descendants of the people who suffered and survived the crimes and legacy of slavery endured in the United States of America,

Whereas the government of the United States of America has been instrumental in having pressured the German and Japanese governments into the payment of reparations to the people who suffered and survived the crimes and legacy of slavery endured during World War II,

Whereas the government of the United States of America has also already paid reparations to the Japanese-Americans who were detained in concentration camps during World War II,

Whereas, upon the ending of slavery in the United States of America, the government of the United States of America promised the former slaves forty acres and a mule as compensation, and then broke its promise,

Whereas, the payment of fair, long-overdue reparations are an investment in the future of America, a future where America has a place in the family of nations as a fair, civilized country which respects civil and human rights, encourages opportunity for and the well-being of all her people, and can be trusted by other nations as a nation who honors her word,

We, United States of America citizens of European descent, in support of the just demands of African Americans for fair, long-overdue reparations for the crimes and legacy of slavery endured in the United States of America, do enjoin and direct you to use all the powers of your good offices to implement fair reparations as previously promised by the government of the United States of America to the descendants of slaves in the United States of America without delay.

Randall Robinson, TransAfrica Forum (2000)

Restatement of the Black Manifesto

I. Statement of Facts

1. Whereas the United States government has never acknowledged or taken responsibility for its role in the enslavement of Africans and the promotion of white supremacy;

2. Whereas the experience of enslavement, segregation, and discrimination continues to limit the life chances and opportunities of African Americans;

3. Whereas African Americans have sought repeatedly to improve their educational attainment, economic condition, and living situation and have been held back by lawless white violence and official indifference thereto;

4. Whereas African Americans have sought repeatedly to obtain reparations in the courts of the United States and through appeals to its government ever since the de jure end of slavery and have been unjustly denied relief;

5. Whereas all Americans and the United States government have benefitted enormously and continue to benefit from the unjust expropriation of uncompensated labor by enslaved Africans, the subordination and segregation of the descendants of the enslaved, as well as from discrimination against African Americans;

6. Whereas the United States government has acknowledged and taken responsibility for its role in the unjust internment of Japanese Americans during the second World War and has undertaken to pay reparations to the internees and their successors and to apologize for the unjust abrogation of their rights;

7. Whereas the principle that reparations is the appropriate remedy whenever a government unjustly abrogates the rights of a domestic group or foreign people whose rights such government is obligated to protect or uphold has been internationally recognized;

8. Whereas the United States government has acceded to and approved the above stated reparations principle on the basis of treaty obligations and

through its numerous actions in support of reparations on behalf of Jewish survivors of the Holocaust and their successors;

9. Whereas individual states of the United States have undertaken to pay reparations to portions of the African American community within their jurisdictions who have suffered specific harm due to white violence and official inaction to prevent or correct such harm in a timely fashion or to punish the perpetrators;

10. Whereas the harms inflicted on the African American community as a whole and the debt owed to African Americans is susceptible to exact proof; let it be hereinafter resolved:

II. Statement of Positions

First, it's not too late. It is neither too late in the sense that the claim of reparations for African Americans is stale, nor is it too late in the sense that there is no one or nothing left to compensate. It is never too late to seek justice. Reparations for African Americans are justified by the legal doctrine of unjust enrichment: unjust enrichment of a person occurs when he has and retains money or benefits which in justice and equity belong to another. A person or group should not be permitted unjustly to enrich himself or themselves at the expense of another, but is required to make restitution for property or benefits received, retained or appropriated, where it is just and equitable that such restitution be made. Slavery, the expropriation of the labor of another without compensation, is a paradigm instance of unjust enrichment. Through intergenerational transfers (inheritance) the ill-gotten gains continue to accumulate to the greater impoverishment of African Americans and their descendants and the greater support of white supremacy. The denial of a fair forum in which to seek redress cannot evaporate the legitimacy of African American claims on their ancestors' stolen legacy.

Second, the government bears responsibility. The denial of a fair forum in which to see redress is part of the burden that American civilization must carry along with its responsibility for creating the context in which slave trading could be carried on as ordinary commerce, slave ownership could be protected by the fundamental law of the land, segregation could be enforced, and white supremacy could thrive. *However, because any beneficial program of reparations for African Americans should occur with the aim of positive improvement and healing of and for every member of American society, private individuals and groups shall not be held responsible for any returns constituting reparations. In this sense, built into the fabric of the reparations process is an intercommunity absolution that resolves the hopeless and divisive arguments over blame, guilt and responsibility. With these contemporary roadblocks removed, the reparations process can occur in a guilt-free environment of earnest interest in the further repair and just inclusion of African Americans in American society.* The United States government is the party that must make restitution to African Americans for abrogation of their human rights. Regardless of what private parties may have chosen to do in the exploitative, white supremacist context created by the government, *it was the force and application of the law that fundamentally enabled their ability to exercise their choices.* It is true that most Americans did not own slaves or engage in slave trading. However, the claim of reparations for African Americans is not directed at those who bear no guilt, but to the party who does, the United States government. The United States government sanctioned violations of the human rights of African Americans with the imprimatur of law. In order to redress the injury, the United States government must provide a fair forum for redress, and pay the debt it owes to African Americans.

Third, the injury survives the death of victims. Among the many injuries inflicted by the enslavement of African Americans, poverty ranks as fundamental to the system and enduring in its consequences. The stolen legacy of African Americans' ancestors ensured that each succeeding generation would have that much less in wealth and resources with which to compete in a fiercely competitive world. Although all those who were enslaved are dead, their posterity lives on to combat daily the disabilities caused by the theft over many generations of a birthright. *Furthermore, the shift from slavery to freedom was more partial than whole as the ensuing 75 years witnessed the governmentally supported exclusion or systematic segregation of African Americans from virtually every quarter of American society. Deprivations within the sphere of labor, finance, housing, education, social and cultural institutions bear a direct and formative relationship to the economically, socially, and educationally sub-qualitative facts of African American life today. Thus the existing generations of African Americans are far from lost from the experience of slavery, but remain captured within its chaotic and deprivation-sustaining aftermath.* It must be understood that [t]he injury to the African American community survives the death of individual victims. The injury survives in the overrepresentation of poverty, and all the pathologies it spawns, within the African American community. Not least of such pathologies is self-hate, lack of confidence, and lack of self-understanding. Thus, many African Americans must be educated to understand the justification and legitimacy of their own claim to reparations.

III. Conclusion

Therefore, hearings should be held in the Congress of the United States to establish the basis for reparations to African Americans, and to determine the amount of such reparations; whereinafter, a private trust should be established for the benefit of all African Americans. . . .

National Coalition of Blacks for Reparations in America (2000)

The Reparations Campaign

The Reparations Campaign, for Black people in the United States, emerged more than one hundred years ago as the U.S. Federal Government was trying to survive the ravages of warfare among its citizen. In the wake of the bitter hostilities from the Civil War a decision was made to release from bondage millions of then enslaved Africans.

As U.S. political, civil and business leaders grappled with the pressing question of "what to do with the Negroes?" the newly freed Africans cried out immediately for restitution — payback for centuries of stolen labor, cultural degradation and dehumanizations. Indeed, Africans held as slaves have been struggling for a restored sense of wholeness since being brought to this country as chattel.

Other organizations and individuals have carried the demand for reparations farther into the twentieth century. Many of them have become a part of today's Reparations Campaign which is being spearheaded by N'COBRA.

What do we want?

We want our just inheritance: the trillions of dollars due us for the labor of our ancestors who worked for hundreds of years without pay. We demand the resources required removing all badges and indicia of slavery.

Why do we want it?

We must prepare African people and communities for the demands of the new millennium. Reparations are needed to repair the wrongs, injury, and damage done to us by the U.S. federal and State governments, their agents, and representatives. These have proved that their vision for African people in America is joblessness, more prisons (more killer kkkops), more black women and men in private prisons, AIDS and violence.

The U.S. Eurocentric educational system has failed to prepare African children for liberation, nation-building, and self-determination. This educational system produces people who are anti-black, including many blacks who are self-alienated and anti-black. We want our resources, our inheritance, to do for ourselves without U.S. Federal and State involvement.

When do we want it?

We want it NOW! We know that preparatory steps must be taken before we can receive reparations even when the U.S. Government agrees to pay us everything we demand. But NOW is the time to prepare for reparations.

How do we prepare for reparations? In order for reparations to make us whole, it must remove blacks from dependence on others (the government, and the descendants of slave owners and colonizers), to create our jobs, manufacture the goods we consume, feed, clothe, and shelter us, build our institutions, and oversee our money. There are many things we must do to prepare; only a few will be discussed here. We must determine what is required to enable us as a people, as a community, and as individuals to be self-determining. We need to learn the difference between wealth and money, and more about making money than spending it. And, have that we spend [sic], we need to learn how to keep it in our communities. There are too many of our entertainers, recording artists, athletes, lottery winners, etc., who earn millions of dollars and have nothing to show for it after a few years, but a memory of good times past.

We must study how reparations can be used for our liberation for seven generations to come, and not for a one time shopping spree. We must use this time to develop ways to keep the billions of dollars, which we now earn, in the black community.

How much is owed?

Once we know how much damage has been done to us, and what is required to repair the damage, we will know how much is owed. We cannot allow anyone to offer, or accept on our behalf, some arbitrary figure based on some other peoples' reparations settlement. For example, the four year internment of Japanese in America, or the five year holocaust of Jewish people in Europe may require a different set of remedies than the 500 years holocaust of Africans in America. The nature and extent of the damage and the number of people impacted will dictate the type, duration, and amount of reparations owed. Some estimate eight trillion dollars.

How would reparations be paid?

Payment may include all of the following: land, equipment, factories, licenses, banks, ships, airplanes, various forms of tax relief, education and training, to name a few. A good academic exercise would be to develop a plan for how reparations could be used collectively to enable the African community to become independent from racist institutions and economically self-sufficient for at least seven generations.

Who would pay reparations?

The U.S. Government would pay reparations in the same manner as they voted for and paid billions to Europe through the Marshall Plan after WWII, or billions to Israel every year since WWII, or to Russia, or Eastern Europe, or to prop up some puppet African Government. Just as Americans did not, as individuals, pay for aid to those countries, they will not pay for the debt owed to Africans in America. Nor are we blaming individual Americans, we are simply holding the U.S. Government accountable for its wrongs.

Who would receive reparations?

People identified as Negro, Colored, black, African American, New Afrikan, black American who are the descendants of persons enslaved in the United States. Of course, those who feel that they are not due reparations, or do not need reparations will not be forced to accept it. What about Africans enslaved in other countries? Black reparations is an international movement. The descendants of Africans in Canada, Barbados, Haiti, Jamaica, and Brazil, West Indies, Caribbean, etc., are due reparations, but from their particular European colonizer. Colonized African countries too are due reparations. We recognize that although we were colonized and enslaved by different European colonizers and slavers, we are one people with many family members dispersed to different countries.

What can we do to help?

Make black reparations a household word. Learn to spell, define, and defend it. If we learn how to spell reparations, we will easily say it. Once we learn how to defend it we will raise the issue every time someone talks about affirmative action, welfare reform, jobs, education, housing, health care, prison, building, police brutality, and so on. N'COBRA members have developed books and other informational resources to enable each of us to become able defenders of black reparations. When people talk about building more prisons to deal with the crimes of today, we need to talk about reparations to deal with the effects of 500 years of crimes against the African community that led to the crimes today. We need reparations to keep our people out of prison. When people talk about how criminals must pay for their wrongdoing we must talk about how the U.S. Government must pay reparations for its wrongs.

Second: Support HR 40. This bill has been reintroduced in Congress by Congressman John Conyers of Michigan. It is a first formal step toward reparations in studying the impact of slavery and proposals for remedies. Work with organizations, churches, local governments, and State legislatures to pass a resolution in support of HR 40. Send a copy of each resolution to Mr. Conyers' office and to N'COBRA's National Office.

Third: Join a reparations organization. Have that organization or any organization to which you belong, become a member of N'COBRA. Or, you may join N'COBRA directly.

Fourth: Attend the local, regional, and national meetings on reparations to learn more about what you can do to help. How can I join? Attend an N'COBRA meeting and submit a membership application form, or request an application from the *National office*. Membership is open to organizations and individuals of good moral character who believe that black people in the USA, the descendants of enslaved Africans, are due reparations from the U.S. Government and various State governments.

The NDABA Movement (2004)

National Reparations Petition

The NDABA Movement National Reparations Petition Campaign: A Petition in Support of Black People's Demand for Reparations from the United States Government and Other Private and Public Institutions in America
To: Congress of the United States
THE NDABA MOVEMENT
NATIONAL REPARATIONS PETITION CAMPAIGN
A PETITION IN SUPPORT OF BLACK PEOPLE'S DEMAND FOR REPARATIONS FROM THE UNITED STATES GOVERNMENT AND OTHER PRIVATE AND PUBLIC INSTITUTIONS IN AMERICA
Whereas, we the undersigned people of African ancestry understand that various oppressed peoples have been paid reparations. Indigenous groups such as the Choctaw, Lakota, and Lambuth people have received reparations (and rightly so) for treaty violations that occurred before the emancipation of African Americans. Japanese Americans have received reparations for their inhumane incarceration in internment camps during WWII, as well as the Jews who received reparations after the Nuremberg trials.

Whereas, slavery and the slave trade are recognized by international human rights organizations, e.g., the United Nations, as "crimes against humanity" and as such there are no statutes of limitations against nations who are to pay for these crimes.

Whereas, we the undersigned understand that the demand for reparations for black people in America is a demand for justice for years of injustice and inhumane treatment and not a request for a handout. Elected leaders and those seeking public office must recognize the elementary truth that slavery and historical patterns of discrimination, based on race, are the direct cause of continued increases in unemployment, substandard education, higher mortality, higher rates of incarceration, etc. for African Americans. Similarly rooted in slavery is the engrained psychosis of racism among white Americans.

We, above all others in America, have sacrificed the most for this country. It is clear at this hour in history that the major issue for black people in the upcoming presidential election is restitution for a long-standing debt of the United States Government owed to black people in America since the end of the Civil War.

In 1898, one of the many petitions to Congress in support of slave pension (reparations) legislation stated,

"Whereas, It is a precedent established by patriots of this country to relieve its distressed citizens, both on land and sea, and millions of our deceased people, besides those who still survive, worked as slaves for the development of this country, and Whereas, We believe it is just and right to grant the ex-slaves a pension"

It is in this spirit, as descendants of slavery in America, that we sign this petition in support of our just demand for reparations.
Sincerely,
The Undersigned

NAACP (2005)

NAACP Supports Reintroduction of Reparations Study Legislation

BILL SEEKS TO CREATE FEDERAL AGENCY TO STUDY EFFECTS OF SLAVERY ON AFRICAN AMERICANS AND TO APOLOGIZE FOR THE INJUSTICE, CRUELTY, BRUTALITY AND INHUMAINTY OF SLAVERY

THE ISSUE:

Congressman John Conyers (D-MI) has re-introduced H.R. 40; the formal title of this bill is to establish a *"Commission to Study the Reparation Proposals for African-Americans Act."* Specifically, this legislation, also known as the *"Reparations Act,"* would establish a federal commission to review the institution of slavery, the resulting racial and economic discrimination against African Americans, and the impact of these forces on African Americans who are living today. The bill would also acknowledge the fundamental injustice, cruelty, brutality and inhumanity of slavery in the United States and the 13 colonies between 1619 and 1865 and make recommendations to help correct the residual effects of these acts.

While this legislation has consistently been a priority of the NAACP, it has, unfortunately, been shunned by Congressional leadership and no action was taken on the proposal in the 108th Congress (which ended in December, 2004). Not to be deterred, however, Congressman Conyers reintroduced H.R. 40 (he asks for, and is given, the same number every Congress) on January 4, 2005, the first day of the 109th Congress. Congressman Conyers was joined by 23 original co-sponsors.

In our continuing effort to advocate for this legislation, the NAACP Washington Bureau is currently working with a few key members of the United States Senate to see a companion bill introduced in the Senate. If we are successful, this would be the first time reparations legislation has been introduced in the Senate and would represent a major step forward in our struggle to help pass this important legislation and for recognition and equality.

THE ACTION WE NEED YOU TO TAKE:

Contact your Representative and both your Senators and URGE THEM TO SUPPORT REPARATIONS LEGISLATION. To contact your Senators and Representative, you may:

Make a Phone Call:

Call your Senators and your Representative in Washington by dialing the Capitol Switchboard and asking to be transferred to your Senators'/Congressman's offices. The switchboard phone number is (202) 224-3121 (see message section, below).

Write a Letter

To write letters to your Senators, send them to:
   The Honorable (*name of Senator*)
   U.S. Senate
   Washington, D.C. 20510
To write a letter to your Representative, send it to:
   The Honorable (*name of Representative*)
   U.S. House of Representatives
   Washington, D.C. 20515

Send a Fax

If you would like to send a fax, call your Senators' or Representative's offices (through the Capitol switchboard) and ask for their fax numbers (you can use either the attached sample letter or the message box, below).

Send an E-Mail

To send an e-mail to your Senators, simply go to www.senate.gov, and click on "*Contacting the Senate*"; you can look your Senators up either alphabetically or by state. To send an e-mail to your Representative, go to www

.house.gov, and click on "*Write Your Representative.*" This will help you identify who your congressman is and how to contact him/her.

THE MESSAGE:

The "Commission to Study Reparation Proposals for African Americans Act" would simply authorize a commission to explore the institution of slavery in America, its impact on current society, and to make recommendations to Congress for appropriate remedies.

Passage of the bill would be an important first step in acknowledging the fundamental cruelty, brutality, and inhumanity of slavery in the United States, and help millions of Americans begin to heal emotional wounds that have festered for centuries.

It is past time to acknowledge—and correct—the greatest injustice perpetuated by this nation in its history.

Only by facing up to our past can we as a nation hope to fulfill our potential for the future.

American Bar Association Recommendation (2006)

ADOPTED BY THE HOUSE OF DELEGATES
February 13, 2006

RECOMMENDATION

RESOLVED, That the American Bar Association urges the United States Congress to 1) create and appropriate funds for a Commission to study and make findings relating to the present day social, political, and economic consequences of both slavery and the denial thereafter of equal justice under law for persons of African descent living in the United States; and 2) authorize the Commission to propose public policies or governmental actions, if any, that may be appropriate to address such consequences.

Episcopal Church (2006)

Call for the Episcopal Church to Study Responsibility for Reparations

Resolution 2006-12
Submitted by:
Diocesan Task Force on Reparations for Slavery:

Ms. Nancy Barrick, The Rev. Ronald H. Miller
Deacon Jane O'Leary, The Rev. Kirk Kubicek,
Ms. Anne Bricker, The Rev. David N. Clark,
Mr. Russell Costley, The Rev. Mary Glasspool,
The Rev. Jane O'Leary, Mr. John James,
Ms. Catherine Morell, Mr. Harold Ramsey,
Mr. Jim Simpson, The Rev. Marshall Thompso[sic]

RESOLVED, that the 22nd Convention of the Diocese of Maryland, meeting May 5–6, 2006, calls upon the 75th General Convention to establish a Task Force to study, document, and report on the enslavement of Africans and their descendants, the legacy of slavery, and the establishment of systematic and institutional racism within the United States of America; and

BE IF FURTHER RESOLVED, that the Task Force specifically research and report on the historical role of the Episcopal Church in these systems of slavery and racism, so that we as a people of God can come to make a full, faithful and informed accounting of the legacy we inherit and better understand how we can work, both individually and collectively, to "repair the breach"; and

BE IT FURTHER RESOLVED, that the Episcopal Church support the passage of legislation to establish a commission to study reparations proposals as affirmation of our commitments to become a transformed, antiracist church and to work toward healing, reconciliation and a restoration of wholeness to the family of God; and

BE IT FURTHER RESOLVED, that the Secretary of Convention is instructed to forward, in a timely manner, this resolution to the Secretary of the General Convention of the Episcopal Church.

Explanation

In 2004 the Convention of the Diocese of Maryland established a Task Force to study the question of reparations for slavery. As a result of its work the Task Force has learned that there is a vast ignorance and misunderstanding of this part of our history and, when the subject is opened for discussion, a great willingness to learn. Resolution 2006-11 is intended to build on this discovery as a way to help address the on-going racism which marks our life.

However, we have seen that the issue is wider than just Maryland, and therefore, Resolution 2006-12 addresses the issue in the wider church and in society at large.

Section 5

Case Studies of Redress

The White House (1997)

Apology for Study Done in Tuskegee

Remarks by the President in Apology for Study Done in Tuskegee
The East Room
May 16, 1997
2:26 P.M. EDT

THE PRESIDENT: Ladies and gentlemen, on Sunday, Mr. Shaw will celebrate his 95th birthday. (Applause.) I would like to recognize the other survivors who are here today and their families: Mr. Charlie Pollard is here. (Applause.) Mr. Carter Howard. (Applause.) Mr. Fred Simmons. (Applause.) Mr. Simmons just took his first airplane ride, and he reckons he's about 110 years old, so I think it's time for him to take a chance or two. (Laughter.) I'm glad he did. And Mr. Frederick Moss, thank you, sir. (Applause.)

I would also like to ask three family representatives who are here — Sam Doner is represented by his daughter, Gwendolyn Cox. Thank you, Gwendolyn. (Applause.) Ernest Hendon, who is watching in Tuskegee, is represented by his brother, North Hendon. Thank you, sir, for being here. (Applause.) And George Key is represented by his grandson, Christopher Monroe. Thank you, Chris. (Applause.)

I also acknowledge the families, community leaders, teachers and students watching today by satellite from Tuskegee. The White House is the people's house; we are glad to have all of you here today. I thank Dr. David Satcher for his role in this. I thank Congresswoman Waters and Congressman Hilliard, Congressman Stokes, the entire Congressional Black Caucus. Dr. Satcher, members of the Cabinet who are here, Secretary Herman, Secretary Slater. A great friend of freedom, Fred Gray, thank you for fighting this long battle all these long years.

The eight men who are survivors of the syphilis study at Tuskegee are a living link to a time not so very long ago that many Americans would prefer not to remember, but we dare not forget. It was a time when our nation failed to live up to its ideals, when our nation broke the trust with our people that is the very foundation of our democracy. It is not only in remembering that shameful past that we can make amends and repair our nation, but it is in remembering that past that we can build a better present and a better future. And without remembering it, we cannot make amends and we cannot go forward.

So today America does remember the hundreds of men used in research without their knowledge and consent. We remember them and their family members. Men who were poor and African American, without resources and with few alternatives, they believed they had found hope when they were offered free medical care by the United States Public Health Service. They were betrayed.

Medical people are supposed to help when we need care, but even once a cure was discovered, they were denied help, and they were lied to by their government. Our government is supposed to protect the rights of its citizens; their rights were trampled upon. Forty years, hundreds of men betrayed, along with their wives and children, along with the community in Macon County, Alabama, the City of Tuskegee, the fine university there, and the larger African American community.

The United States government did something that was wrong—deeply, profoundly, morally wrong. It was an outrage to our commitment to integrity and equality for all our citizens.

To the survivors, to the wives and family members, the children and the grandchildren, I say what you know: No power on Earth can give you back the lives lost, the pain suffered, the years of internal torment and anguish. What was done cannot be undone. But we can end the silence. We can stop turning our heads away. We can look at you in the eye and finally say on behalf of the American people, what the United States government did was shameful, and I am sorry. (Applause.)

The American people are sorry—for the loss, for the years of hurt. You did nothing wrong, but you were grievously wronged. I apologize and I am sorry that this apology has been so long in coming. (Applause.)

To Macon County, to Tuskegee, to the doctors who have been wrongly associated with the events there, you have our apology, as well. To our African American citizens, I am sorry that your federal government orchestrated a study so clearly racist. That can never be allowed to happen again. It is against everything our country stands for and what we must stand against is what it was.

So let us resolve to hold forever in our hearts and minds the memory of a time not long ago in Macon County, Alabama, so that we can always see how adrift we can become when the rights of any citizens are neglected, ignored and betrayed. And let us resolve here and now to move forward together.

The legacy of the study at Tuskegee has reached far and deep, in ways that hurt our progress and divide our nation. We cannot be one America when a whole segment of our nation has no trust in America. An apology is the first step, and we take it with a commitment to rebuild that broken trust. We can begin by making sure there is never again another episode like this one. We need to do more to ensure that medical research practices are sound and ethical, and that researchers work more closely with communities.

Today I would like to announce several steps to help us achieve these goals. First, we will help to build that lasting memorial at Tuskegee. (Applause.) The school founded by Booker T. Washington, distinguished by the renowned scientist George Washington Carver and so many others who advanced the health and well-being of African Americans and all Americans, is a fitting site. The Department of Health and Human Services will award a planning grant so the school can pursue establishing a center for bioethics in research and health care. The center will serve as a museum of the study and support efforts to address its legacy and strengthen bioethics training.

Second, we commit to increase our community involvement so that we may begin restoring lost trust. The study at Tuskegee served to sow distrust of our medical institutions, especially where research is involved. Since the study was halted, abuses have been checked by making informed consent and local review mandatory in federally funded and mandated research.

Still, 25 years later, many medical studies have little African American participation and African American organ donors are few. This impedes efforts to conduct promising research and to provide the best health care to all our people, including African Americans. So today, I'm directing the Secretary of Health and Human Services, Donna Shalala, to issue a report in 180 days about how we can best involve communities, especially minority communities, in research and health care. You must—every American group must be involved in medical research in ways that are positive. We have put the curse behind us; now we must bring the benefits to all Americans. (Applause.)

Third, we commit to strengthen researchers' training in bioethics. We are constantly working on making breakthroughs in protecting the health of our people and in vanquishing diseases. But all our people must be assured that their rights and dignity will be respected as new drugs, treatments and therapies are tested and used. So I am directing Secretary Shalala to work in partnership with higher education to prepare training materials for medical researchers. They will be available in a year. They will help researchers build on core ethical principles of respect for individuals, justice and informed consent, and advise them on how to use these principles effectively in diverse populations.

Fourth, to increase and broaden our understanding of ethical issues and clinical research, we commit to providing postgraduate fellowships to train bioethicists especially among African Americans and other minority groups. HHS will offer these fellowships beginning in September of 1998 to promising students enrolled in bioethics graduate programs.

And, finally, by executive order I am also today extending the charter of the National Bioethics Advisory Commission to October of 1999. The need for this commission is clear. We must be able to call on the thoughtful, collective wisdom of experts and community representatives to find ways to further strengthen our protections for subjects in human research.

We face a challenge in our time. Science and technology are rapidly changing our lives with the promise of making us much healthier, much more productive and more prosperous. But with these changes we must work harder to see that as we advance we don't leave behind our conscience. No ground is gained and, indeed, much is lost if we lose our moral bearings in the name of progress.

The people who ran the study at Tuskegee diminished the stature of man by abandoning the most basic ethical precepts. They forgot their pledge to heal and repair. They had the power to heal the survivors and all the others and they did not. Today, all we can do is apologize. But you have the power, for only you — Mr. Shaw, the others who are here, the family members who are with us in Tuskegee — only you have the power to forgive. Your presence here shows us that you have chosen a better path than your government did so long ago. You have not withheld the power to forgive. I hope today and tomorrow every American will remember your lesson and live by it.

Thank you, and God bless you. (Applause.)

Oklahoma Commission to Study the Tulsa Race Riot of 1921 (2000)

COMMISSIONERS:
Currie Ballard, Coyle
Dr. Bob Blackburn, Oklahoma City
Joel Burns, Tulsa
Vivian Clark, Tulsa
Rep. Abe Deutschendorf, Lawton
Eddie Faye Gates, Tulsa
Jim Lloyd, Tulsa
Sen. Robert Milacek, Wauikomis
Jimmie L. White, Jr., Checotah
CHAIRMAN:
T. D. "Pete" Chruchwell, Tulsa
SPONSORS:
Sen. Maxine Horner, Tulsa
Rep. Donn Ross, Tulsa
ADVISORS:
Dr. John Hope Franklin, Durham NC
Dr. Scott Ellsworth, Portland OR

The Honorable Frank Keating
Governor of the State of Oklahoma
State Capitol building Oklahoma City, OK 73105

Dear Governor Keating:
The Tulsa Race Riot Commission, established by House Joint Resolution No. 1035, is pleased to submit the following preliminary report.
    The primary goal of collecting historical documentation on the Tulsa Race Riot of 1921 has been achieved. Attachment A is a summary listing of the

record groups that have been gathered and stored at the Oklahoma Historical Society. Also included are summaries of some reports and the full text of selected documents to illustrate the breadth and scope of the collecting process. However, the Commission has not yet voted on historical findings, so these materials do not necessarily represent conclusions of the Commission.

At the last meeting, held February 4, 2000, the Commission voted on three actions. They are:

1) The Issue of Restitution

Whereas, the process of historical analysis by this Commission is not yet complete,

And Whereas, the archeological investigation into casualties and mass burials is not yet complete,

And Whereas, we have seen a continuous pattern of historical evidence that the Tulsa Race Riot of 1921 was the violent consequence of racial hatred institutionalized and tolerated by official federal, state, county, and city policy.

And Whereas, government at all levels has the moral and ethical responsibility of fostering a sense of community that bridges divides of ethnicity and race,

And Whereas, by statute we are to make recommendations regarding whether or not reparations can or should be made to the Oklahoma Legislature, the Governor of the State of Oklahoma, and the Mayor and City Council of Tulsa.

That, we, the 1921 Tulsa Race Riot Commission, recommend that restitution to the historic Greenwood Community, in real and tangible form, would be good public policy and do much to repair the emotional as well as physical scars of this most terrible incident in our shared past.

2) The Issue of Suggested Forms of Restitution in Priority Order
The Commission recommends

    1) Direct payment of reparations to survivors of the Tulsa Race Riot.

    2) Direct payment of reparations to descendants of the survivors of the Tulsa Race Riot.

    3) A scholarship fund available to students affected by the Tulsa Race Riot.

    4) Establishment of an economic development enterprise zone in the historic area of the Greenwood District.

    5) A memorial for the reburial of any human remains found in the search for unmarked graves of riot victims.

3) The Issue of an Extension of the Tulsa Race Riot Commission

The Commission hereby endorses and supports House Bill 2468, which extends the life of the Commission in order to finish the historical report on the Tulsa Race Riot of 1921.

We, the members of the Tulsa Race Riot Commission, respectfully submit these findings for your consideration.

Mandate for the Greensboro Truth and Reconciliation Commission (2004)

There comes a time in the life of every community when it must look humbly and seriously into its past in order to provide the best possible foundation for moving into a future based on healing and hope. Many residents of Greensboro believe that for this city, the time is now.

In light of the shooting death of 5 people and the wounding of 10 others in Greensboro, North Carolina on November 3, 1979, and

In light of the subsequent acquittal of defendants in both state and federal criminal trials, despite the fact that the shootings were videotaped and widely viewed, and

In light of the further investigations, passage of time and other factors which allowed a jury in a later civil trial to find certain parties liable for damages in the death of one of the victims, and

In light of the confusion, pain, and fear experienced by residents of the city and the damage to the fabric of relationships in the community caused by these incidents and their aftermath,

The Greensboro Truth and Community Reconciliation Project, including the signers of its Declaration, calls for the examination of the context, causes, sequence and consequence of the events of November 3, 1979.

We affirm that the intention of this examination shall be:

> a.) Healing and reconciliation of the community through discovering and disseminating the truth of what happened and its consequences in the lives of individuals and institutions, both locally and beyond Greensboro.
> b.) Clarifying the confusion and reconciling the fragmentation that has been caused by these events and their aftermath, in part by educating the public through its findings.
> c.) Acknowledging and recognizing people's feelings, including feelings of loss, guilt, shame, anger and fear.

d.) Helping facilitate changes in social consciousness and in the institutions that were consciously or unconsciously complicit in these events, thus aiding in the prevention of similar events in the future.

This examination is not for the purpose of exacting revenge or recrimination. Indeed, the Commission will have no such power. Rather, the Commission will attempt to learn how persons and groups came to be directly or indirectly involved in these events; it will assess the impact of these events on the life and development of this community. It will seek all possibilities for healing transformation.

In addition to exploring questions of institutional and individual responsibility for what happened, as a necessary part of the truth-seeking process we urge the Commission to look deeply into the root causes and historical context of the events of November 3, 1979.

Members of this community, young and old, still find the events of November 3, 1979 nearly incomprehensible. We owe it to ourselves and to future generations to explain what happened and why. Many citizens and institutions of this city have acknowledged the wisdom of, and necessity for, such a process.

It is in this spirit that we affirm the South African Truth and Reconciliation Commission's motto: "Without Truth, no Healing; without Forgiveness, no Future."

Therefore, toward these ends,

1. The Greensboro Truth and Community Reconciliation Project (referred to here as "the Project") hereby establishes a Greensboro Truth and Reconciliation Commission (GTRC), charged with the examination of the context, causes, sequence and consequence of the events of November 3, 1979.

2. The GTRC will consist of seven (7) Commissioners who shall be persons of recognized integrity and principle, with a demonstrated commitment to the values of truth, reconciliation, equity and justice.

The majority of the commissioners will be current residents of the Greensboro area; at least two commissioners will be from outside the Greensboro area. All will be selected in accordance with "The Selection Process for the Greensboro Truth and Reconciliation Commission" document, which is attached. The Commission will designate its chair(s).

Commissioners will serve on an honorary basis and in their personal capacity, but may be reimbursed for expenses incurred in the discharge of their responsibilities.

3. The Commissioners will carry out their mandate by reviewing docu-

ments, inviting people to come forward with information, consulting with experts and by any other means, public or private, they consider appropriate.

4. The Commission may decide to carry out some activities in private in order to protect, to the extent possible, the security and privacy of individuals and the integrity of its ongoing truth-seeking, but in general the Commission's activities will be carried out in a manner that is as public and transparent as possible.

5. The Commission will issue a report to the residents of Greensboro, to the City, to the Project, and to other public bodies, encompassing the items outlined in paragraph 1 and in keeping with the intentions and spirit of the mandate. The Commission will ensure that its findings are fair, based on the information compiled and reviewed, and adequately documented in its report. The Commission may take steps to protect the identity of individual sources, if requested. The Commission will also make specific, constructive recommendations to the City, to the residents of Greensboro, and to other entities as it deems appropriate, particularly to further the intentions set forth in the mandate.

6. The Commission will have no authority either to pursue criminal or civil claims or to grant immunity from such claims. Its focus is reconciliation through seeking, understanding and reporting the truth.

7. The Commission will convene a first meeting, as determined by the Commissioners, no later than 60 days from the date on which the Selection Panel confirms and announces the selection and acceptance of its members. From its first meeting, the Commission will have a period of 15 months to fulfill the terms of its mandate. This period includes initial planning and set-up, the determination of its internal procedures and selection and appointment of its key staff. The Commission may call upon the Project staff and other resources for administrative support during its initial planning and set-up phase. If absolutely necessary, the period of the Commission's mandate may be extended for up to 6 more months, with the permission of the Project.

8. The Commission will carry out its mandate while operating independently from any external influence, including the Project. It may reach cooperative agreements with organizations, institutions and individuals in order to strengthen its capacity and resources, in so far as such agreements do not compromise the Commission's independence. The Commission will have full authority to make decisions on its spending, within the limits of available funds, and may elect to have a fiscal sponsor through another institution so long as that relationship is consistent with the spirit of the mandate and the Commission's substantive independence.

9. At the completion of its work, all documents of the Commission, its

notes, findings, exhibits and other collected materials, shall be permanently archived in Greensboro in an institution whose purpose and tradition is in keeping with the objectives and spirit of the Commission mandate. The identity of this institution and the structure of the archive will be determined by agreement between the Commission and the Project. If deemed appropriate, multiple institutions and locations may be used for archival purposes. Such an archive shall, to the extent feasible and respectful of any recommendations by the Commission with regard to the continued confidentiality of records, be accessible to the public.

The passage of time alone cannot bring closure, not resolve feelings of guilt and lingering trauma, for those impacted by the events of November 3, 1979. Nor can there be any genuine healing for the city of Greensboro unless the truth surrounding these events is honestly confronted, the suffering fully acknowledged, accountability established, and forgiveness and reconciliation facilitated.

Rosewood Victims v. State of Florida (2004)

Special Master's Final Report

March 24, 1994

SPECIAL MASTER'S FINAL REPORT

The Honorable Bo Johnson
Speaker of the House of Representatives
Suite 420, The Capitol
Tallahassee, Florida 32399-1300
RE: HB 591 by Representatives De Grandy and Lawson
Claim of Arnett Goins, Minnie Lee Langley, et al. v. State of Florida

> FINDINGS OF FACT: THIS IS AN EQUITABLE CLAIM SEEKING $7.2 MILLION FOR DAMAGES RESULTING FROM THE 1923 DESTRUCTION OF ROSEWOOD, FLORIDA.

This report is based upon the record presented to House and Senate special masters in the course of legislative hearings conducted pursuant to Rule 6.63, Rules of the Florida House of Representatives. The hearings began on March 4, 1994 and continued on a weekly basis, concluding on March 18, 1994.

    The claimants in this matter are former residents, and descendants of former residents of Rosewood, Florida, who contend that certain acts or omissions of law enforcement and other officials of Levy County and the State of Florida, resulted in the destruction of their community, the deaths of their relatives, and the loss of their property, and inflicted on them both physical and emotional harm for which they should be compensated by the State of Florida. The claimants are represented by the law firm of Holland and Knight.

    The State takes the position that the claims presented in this matter are without legal basis, that the evidence now available does not support a finding that acts or omissions of law enforcement officials caused the damages to the claimants, and that the claims should be barred by the statute of limitations. The State further contends that bringing these claims at this time prohibits the reasonable defense of the allegations since the officials charged are now deceased and cannot be called to testify as to these events. The State of Florida is represented by the Office of the Attorney General.

Because the events relating to this claim occurred more than 71 years ago, the record presented in the legislative hearings is comprised of media accounts of the events, incomplete public records, stories related by former residents and repeated to descendants, and the distant recollections of elderly witnesses not readily subject to corroboration and cross-examination. As will be discussed below, if these proceedings were conducted in a judicial forum, the principles of law dictated by the rules of evidentiary hearsay and the statute of limitations would preclude consideration of these claims. In an equitable claim bill proceeding, however, these principles do not, as a matter of law, restrict the legislature's consideration of these claims. Accordingly, this report is intended to provide the legislature with a description of the events that occurred in and around Rosewood, Florida in 1923, from the available remaining sources of evidence as presented at the legislative hearings, with the understanding that at this time conclusive findings of fact as to all relevant issues do not appear possible.

The events which occurred at Rosewood in 1923 were widely reported at that time not only by the Florida press, but also by the national media. In February of 1923, a month after the violence subsided, a special grand jury was convened in Levy County to investigate these matters. The grand jury returned no indictments, and except for newspaper accounts, no records of the grand jury proceedings remain. It does not appear that any other official investigation of Rosewood was undertaken. Over the years following these events, brief references to the events of Rosewood were made in a few historical studies of racial violence; however, no researched report of these matters was published until July 25, 1982, when a comprehensive article by an investigative journalist, Gary Moore, appeared in *The Floridian* magazine, a Sunday supplement to the *St. Petersburg Times*. Mr. Moore's article prompted a December 13, 1983 CBS 60 Minutes report; however, no other official investigation was conducted at that time.

In 1993 this matter was brought before the Florida Legislature when HB 813 by Representatives DeGrandy and Lawson, and SB 1452 by Senator Jones were filed seeking compensation for persons injured by the violence at Rosewood. In response to the issues raised by HB 813, the Speaker determined that a thorough study of the events surrounding the destruction of Rosewood should be conducted in an objective scholarly manner, and accordingly, after the 1993 Session, an academic research team, which included distinguished professors from Florida State University, Florida A&M University, and the University of Florida was commissioned to research the Rosewood incident and report its findings to the Legislature. The academic research team was chaired by Dr. Maxine Jones of the Florida State Department of History.

The academic research team conducted research during the legislative interim, and on December 22, 1993 issued its report entitled A Documented History of the Incident Which Occurred at Rosewood, Florida in January 1923. Exceptions to the accuracy, findings, methodology, and thoroughness of the report were expressed by investigative journalist, Gary Moore, and in response to Mr. Moore's concerns, an extensive review of the academic study team's report was conducted under the authority of Dr. Richard Greaves, Chairman of the Florida State University Department of History. With minor reservations, the Review of the Rosewood Project endorsed the findings and methodology of the report of the academic study team. In response to the review, Mr. Moore submitted his detailed analysis of the review to the Legislature. All of the academic research studies, reports, reviews, and appendices, as well as Mr. Moore's responses, were received and have been made part of the record in the legislative proceedings....

CONCLUSIONS OF LAW: The initial question of law is the applicability of section 11.065(1), Florida Statutes, which provides:

> No claims against the state shall be presented to the Legislature more than 4 years after the cause for relief accrued. Any claim presented after this time of limitation shall be void and unenforceable.

It is a long-established rule of law that the act of one legislature cannot bind a future legislature. Kirklands v. Town of Bradley, 104 Fla. 390, 139 So. 144 (1932); Tamiami Trail Tours v. Lee, 142 Fla. 68, 194 So. 305 (1940). This principle has been specifically applied to the statute of limitations for legislative claim bills. Attorney General's Opinion 55-82. As stated by the Attorney General, the statute of limitations is an expression of legislative policy, and not a prohibition against the consideration of claims against the state. Accordingly, as a matter of law, should the legislature determine that an equitable basis exists for the consideration of these claims, then there is no legal restriction on the power of the legislature to enact a claim bill under these circumstances.

In this matter, the primary claimants are now elderly former residents of

Rosewood who as children were displaced from their homes due to the destruction of their community. They have a very limited education. Their testimony reflects a profound fear of reprisal and a distrust of state officials. In light of their personal experiences and the racial attitudes at the time, their testimony is substantiated. There is a question as to whether the fears of the claimants of coming forward are justified especially after the 1983 national broadcast of the Rosewood events. The State contends that at least since 1983 there was no justifiable impediment to the bringing of these claims to the legislature. Moreover, the State contends that under the principles of laches, Cone Brothers Construction v. Moore, 193 So. 288 (Fla. 1940), the claimants have delayed too long, that the matters asserted are not subject to a safe conclusion as to the truth thereof, and the State at this time is unable to defend against these allegations.

In balancing the equities of whether to proceed to consider the claims of these claimants, against the obvious difficulties of the State to completely respond to these claims after so many years have passed, it is important to distinguish these proceedings from proceedings at law. As a matter of law, the record does not demonstrate that the claimants could overcome the State's objections if these proceedings were judicial in nature. Claim bill proceedings, however, address the "moral obligations of the state" and are matters purely within the prerogative of the legislature. Gamble v. Wells, 450 So.2d 850 (Fla. 1984); Dickinson v. Board of Public Instruction, 217 So.2d 553, 560 (Fla. 1968). Under these circumstances, neither the provisions of section 11.065(1), Florida Statutes, nor the principles of laches should be construed to preclude the legislature's consideration of these claims to determine whether there is a moral obligation on the part of the State of Florida which should be addressed.

Claimants seek compensation for damages resulting from property loss and for emotional trauma. As to property loss, Florida law in 1923, as well as today, recognizes that compensation is required when state action affects a taking of property which was set forth in Article XVI, section 29 of the Florida Constitution of 1885 and is now incorporated in Article X, section 6 of the Florida Constitution as revised in 1968. While the State of Florida did not affirmatively take title to property in Rosewood, the displacement of the Rosewood population was done with the knowledge and assistance of law enforcement officers. In a case involving the claims of Japanese-Americans who were displaced from their homes and property during World War II, the court held that the claimants were entitled to compensation for their property loss. Hohri v. United States, 768 F.2d 227 (D.C. Cir. 1986). The court stated:

> Given the alleged damage to the appellant's real and personal property directly caused by the evacuation program, there is no question that appellants have stated a claim cognizable under the Takings Clause.

Id. at 242. The court went on to hold that this claim was compensable regardless of whether the government took title to the property. See also United States v. General Motors Corp., 323 U.S. 373 (1945).

Although there are obvious distinctions between the federal evacuation program of Japanese-Americans and the displacement of the residents of Rosewood, in both instances the evacuees were forced to leave their homes and were unable to attend to their property. The residents of Rosewood did not return due to fear, and it appears that many simply abandoned their property because the area was not secured for their safety.

In this respect the State cites the case of Monarch Insurance Company of Ohio v. District of Columbia, 353 F. Supp. 1249 (D.C. D.C. 1973), affirmed, 497 F.2d 684 (D.C. Cir. 1974), cert. denied, 419 U.S. 1021 (1974), where the court dismissed constitutional and statutory claims brought against the United States, the District of Columbia and local law enforcement officials for property damages resulting from riots which occurred after the assassination of Dr. Martin Luther King. The court in Monarch held that the decisions regarding the deployment of law enforcement in riot control situations was a discretionary function that did not subject the government to liability under the federal Tort Claims Act. Similarly, Florida law provides that discretionary governmental functions are not subject to liability. Commercial Carrier Corp. v. Indian River County, 371 So.2d 1010 (Fla. 1979). As recognized by the Monarch court, however, if the claim arises for property, then there is a cognizable cause of action. 353 F. Supp. at 1252.

Moreover, the United States Supreme Court in the case of National Board of Young Men's Christian Assn's v. United States, 395 U.S. 1511 (1969) held that persons whose property was damaged as a result of rioting after occupation of the buildings by federal troops had no Fifth Amendment claim for compensation. However, as Justice Harlan stated:

> ... it is for Congress, not this Court, to decide the extent to which those injured in the riot should be compensated, regardless of the extent to which the police or military attempted to protect the particular property which each individual owns.

395 U.S. at 96. Similarly, while it may be argued that there would not exist a judicially cognizable claim under the takings provisions of the federal and state constitutions, it is nonetheless clear that the legislature has the authority to determine the extent of compensation in this matter.

In relevant circumstances, Congress enacted the Civil Liberties Act to compensate Japanese-Americans for property damages resulting from the federal evacuation policy during World War II. 50 App. U.S.C. s. 1989a(a). The federal law enacted in 1988 recognized that "a grave injustice was done both to citizens and permanent resident aliens of Japanese ancestry by their forced relocation and internment during World War II," and attempted to make amends by issuing a formal apology and $20,000 to each Japanese intern. Jacobs v. Barr, 959 F.2d 313, 314 (D.C. Cir. 1992). The federal law sets forth eligibility standards and provides for time limitations in which eligible individuals must present their claims to the Attorney General.

Under these circumstances, it is appropriate to compensate the claimants in this matter for the property losses sustained by the destruction of Rosewood. While there is not a showing of participation on the part of governmental agents in the destruction of the property, there is no question that governmental officers were aware of the violent situation that existed during the entire week of January 1, 1923, that government officers assisted in the evacuation of the Rosewood residents, that after the destruction the government did not secure the area, that the residents of Rosewood sustained property damage, and that the justice system did not redress the injuries sustained. This is particularly evident when the legislative hearings 71 years later are uncovering evidence identifying the perpetrators of the criminal acts that occurred in Rosewood. In light of these circumstances, and the authorities cited above, the Rosewood families sustaining property damage should be compensated.

As to the emotional and mental anguish damages sought by the claimants, there is no clear remedy. In 1923 the State had not waived sovereign immunity; accordingly, a state cause of action based upon principles of tort law does not arise. See Article III section 22 of the 1885 Constitution which is presently set forth in Article X section 13 of the Florida Constitution. Under section 870.04, Florida Statutes, which also was in force at the time, a sheriff has the duty to order rioters to disperse, but it does not appear that the statute gives rise to a civil cause of action. Cleveland v. City of Miami, 263 So.2d 573 (Fla. 1972).

The federal civil rights acts, section 42 U.S.C. s. 1983 et seq., were in existence, and require a showing that the acts which resulted in personal injury to the claimants were under color of law and done with the intent to deprive the claimants of their constitutional rights. Washington v. Davis, 426 U.S. 229 (1976).

As indicated above, there is evidence that governmental officials knew of the potentially violent situation at Rosewood, but there is no indication of direct participation of governmental officers in the events leading up to the destruction of Rosewood. The most persuasive evidence of governmental responsibility is the failure of any showing that the criminal acts committed at Rosewood were reasonably investigated and redressed by the State of Florida. The record reflects that the death of Sam Carter, who was killed in front of many residents of Sumner, clearly was not properly investigated, and even today there is at least one witness available to testify to the circumstances of that crime. Any records of the investigation conducted by the special grand jury were lost, but it is difficult to understand the grand jury's determination that there was insufficient evidence to proceed on any of the criminal acts when witnesses describing the events and identifying the perpetrators are appearing at legislative hearings.

While this evidence may not be sufficient to sustain a cause of action at law, it does compel the conclusion that a moral obligation exists on the part of the State of Florida to remedy this matter. This conclusion appears to be in keeping with the equitable claim bills redressing "moral obligations" that the legislature has previously enacted. Gamble v. Wells, supra. In Gamble the legislature awarded $150,000 to a child who was physically and emotionally damaged due to the failure of the State to provide adequate foster care. In upholding the constitutionality of Chapter 80-448, Laws of Florida, the Florida Supreme Court in Gamble stated:

> This voluntary recognition of its moral obligation by the legislature in this instance was based on its view of justice and fair treatment of one who had suffered at the hands of the state but was legally remediless to seek damages.

450 So.2d at 853.

This principle is equally applicable here. In the Rosewood claim, although the claimants are now elderly, the damage they sustained was as children, and while ascertaining an amount of damage for emotional harm is subjective, the Gamble case provides guidance as to prior legislative enactments in this regard. Accordingly, it appears that those Rosewood claimants who as children were subjected to the violence and forced to leave their homes should each be awarded compensation in the amount of $150,000.

In the final analysis, the legal authorities cited above support the conclusion that this is an equitable matter that is addressed to the sound discretion of the Florida Legislature. The federal and state cases demonstrate that the legislature's responsibility is to determine whether there is a moral obligation on the part of the State of Florida to compensate the claimants. Although the evidence presented may not be sufficient to establish an action at law, it nonetheless is clear that government officials were responsible for some of the damages sustained by the claimants, if not by the failure to provide reasonable law enforcement prior to the destruction of Rosewood, then surely in the failure to reasonably investigate this matter, to bring the perpetrators to justice and to thereafter secure the area for the safe return of the displaced residents. Under these circumstances, the claimants have met the test for an equitable claim bill by showing that a moral obligation exists to redress their injuries.

COLLATERAL SOURCES: Claimant Minnie Lee Langley received $1,000 for the motion picture rights to her story.

ATTORNEYS FEES: The law firm of Holland & Knight is representing the claimants on a pro bono basis.

RECOMMENDATION: For the above reasons, I recommend that HB 591 be amended as follows:

1. The bill should direct the Florida Department of Law Enforcement, or other appropriate law enforcement officials, to conduct a complete investigation of this matter including interviewing the available witnesses to determine if any criminal proceedings may still be pursued.

2. A fund should be established to compensate the Rosewood families who can demonstrate a property loss as a result of the displacement of the Rosewood residents.

3. The elderly claimants who sustained emotional trauma as a result of the destruction of Rosewood and the evacuation of the residents should each be compensated in the amount of $150,000.

4. A state university scholarship fund should be established for the families and the descendants of the Rosewood residents.

As AMENDED, I recommend HB 591 be reported FAVORABLY.
Respectfully submitted,
Richard Hixson
Special Master

Florida Statute 1004.60 (2004)

Title XLVIII. K-20 Education Code. Chapter 1004
PUBLIC POSTSECONDARY EDUCATION

1004.60 Research of Rosewood incident.
State universities shall continue the research of the Rosewood incident and the history of race relations in Florida and develop materials for the educational instruction of these events.

Florida Statute 1009.55 (2004)

Title XLVIII. K-20 Education Code. Chapter 1009
EDUCATIONAL SCHOLARSHIPS, FEES, AND FINANCIAL ASSISTANCE
1009.55 Rosewood Family Scholarship Program.

(1) There is created a Rosewood Family Scholarship Program for minority persons with preference given to the direct descendants of the Rosewood families, not to exceed 25 scholarships per year. Funds appropriated by the Legislature for the program shall be deposited in the State Student Financial Assistance Trust Fund.

(2) The Rosewood Family Scholarship Program shall be administered by the Department of Education. The State Board of Education shall adopt rules for administering this program which shall at a minimum provide for the following:

    (a) The annual award to a student shall be up to $4,000 but should not exceed an amount in excess of tuition and registration fees.

    (b) If funds are insufficient to provide a full scholarship to each eligible applicant, the department may prorate available funds and make a partial award to each eligible applicant.

    (c) The department shall rank eligible initial applicants for the purposes of awarding scholarships with preference being given to the direct descendants of the Rosewood families. The remaining applicants shall be ranked based on need as determined by the Department of Education.

    (d) Payment of an award shall be transmitted in advance of the registration period each semester on behalf of the student to the president of the university or community college, or his or her representative, or to the director of the career center which the recipient is attending.

(3) Beginning with the 1994–1995 academic year, the department is authorized to make awards for undergraduate study to students who:

(a) Meet the general requirements for student eligibility as provided in s. 1009.40, except as otherwise provided in this section.
(b) File an application for the scholarship within the established time limits.
(c) Enroll as certificate-seeking or degree-seeking students at a state university, community college, or career center authorized by law.

History. s. 433, ch. 2002-387; s. 123, ch. 2004-357.

Section 6

Lawsuits

Timothy Pigford, et al., Plaintiffs, v. Dan Glickman, Secretary, United States Department of Agriculture, Defendant (1998)

Opinion

Civil Action No. 97-1978 (PLF)
UNITED STATES DISTRICT COURT FOR THE DISTRICT OF COLUMBIA
182 F.R.D. 341; 1998 U.S. Dist. LEXIS 16299; 41 Fed. R. Serv. 3d (Callaghan) 1310
October 9, 1998, Decided
October 9, 1998, Filed
DISPOSITION: [**1] Plaintiffs' motion for class certification GRANTED; class CERTIFIED for purposes of determining liability.
COUNSEL: For Plaintiffs: Alexander J. Pires, Jr., Conlon, Frantz, Phelan & Pires, Washington, DC.
 For Defendant: Susan Hall Lennon/Terry Henry, U.S. Dept. Of Justice, Washington, DC.
JUDGES: PAUL L. FRIEDMAN, United States District Judge.
OPINION BY: PAUL L. FRIEDMAN
OPINION: [*342] OPINION
This case is before the Court on plaintiffs' motion for class certification. Upon consideration of plaintiffs' motion, the opposition filed by the government, plaintiffs' reply and the arguments presented by counsel at oral argument, the Court concludes that the class action vehicle is the most appropriate mechanism for resolving the issue of liability in this case. The Court therefore will certify a class for the purpose of determining liability.

I. BACKGROUND

Plaintiffs, four hundred and one African American farmers from Alabama, Arkansas, California, Florida, Georgia, Illinois, Kansas, [*343] Missouri, Mississippi, North Carolina, Oklahoma, South Carolina, Tennessee, Texas and Virginia, allege (1) that the United States Department of Agriculture ("USDA") willfully discriminated against them when they applied for [**2] various farm programs, and (2) that when they filed complaints of discrimination with the USDA, the USDA failed properly to investigate those complaints. Fifth Amended Complaint at 53.n1.

[n1. Between the time the original complaint was filed and the time of oral argument on the motion for class certification, plaintiffs filed five separate motions for leave to file amended complaints. On May 22, 1998, the government indicated that it did not oppose the five motions for leave to amend, and on June 3, 1998, the Court granted plaintiffs' five motions for leave to file amended complaints. While the filing of the amended complaints had not been authorized at the time of argument on the motion for class certification, the issue since has been resolved and the Court therefore will treat the Fifth Amended Complaint as the relevant complaint for purposes of this Opinion.

On October 2, 1998, plaintiffs filed a motion for leave to file a Sixth Amended Complaint. Plaintiffs have stated that the government does not oppose the motion.]

Plaintiffs challenge the USDA's administration of several different farm loan and subsidy programs and/or agencies. Until 1994, the USDA operated two separate programs that provided, *inter alia,* price support loans, disaster payments, "farm ownership" loans and operating loans: the Agricultural Stabilization and Conservation Service ("ASCS") and the Farmers Home Administration ("FmHA"). In 1994, the functions of the ASCS and the FmHA were consolidated into one newly created entity, the Farm Service Agency ("FSA").

A farmer seeking a loan or subsidy from the FSA must submit an application to a county committee, comprised of producers from that county who are elected by other producers in that county. If the county committee approves the application, the farmer receives the subsidy or loan. If the application is denied, the farmer may appeal to a state committee and then to a federal review board. Under the ASCS and the FmHa, the procedure for applying for a loan or subsidy essentially was the same as the current FSA procedure, with several slight variations. If a farmer applied for an ASCS benefit, a County Executive Director was supposed to work with that farmer to help him complete [**4] his application, and the County Executive Director also was supposed to do an initial review of the application. If a farmer applied for a loan from FMHA, the review mechanisms available if the loan was denied differed slightly.

Under the FSA and previously under the ASCS and the FMHA, a farmer who believes that his application was denied on the basis of his race or for other discriminatory reasons has the option of filing a civil rights complaint either with the Secretary of the USDA or with the Office of Civil Rights Enforcement and Adjudication ("OCREA"). In the case of a farmer whose FMHA application was denied, the farmer also had the option of filing a complaint with the FMHA Equal Opportunity Office. A program discrimination complaint filed with USDA is supposed to be forwarded to OCREA, and after reviewing the complaint, OCREA is supposed to return it to the FSA for conciliation and/or preliminary investigation. The FSA then is required to forward the complaint to the Civil Rights and Small Business Utilization Staff ("CR&SBUS"), the division of FSA responsible for investigating complaints alleging discrimination within FSA's programs. CR&SBUS is required to forward the complaint [**5] to the State Civil Rights Coordinator who is supposed to attempt to conciliate the complaint and/or conduct a preliminary investigation and then report back to CR&SBUS. Ultimately, any conciliation agreement or investigatory findings are to be reported to OCREA for a final determination.

Plaintiffs allege a complete failure by the USDA to process discrimination complaints. Plaintiffs allege that in 1983, OCREA essentially was dismantled and that complaints that were filed were never processed, investigated or forwarded to the appropriate agencies for conciliation. As a result, farmers who filed complaints of discrimination never received a response, or if they did receive a response, it was a cursory denial of relief. In some cases, plaintiffs allege that OCREA [*344] simply threw discrimination complaints in the trash without ever responding to or investigating them.

In response to the numerous complaints of minority farmers, Secretary of Agriculture Dan Glickman appointed a Civil Rights Action Team ("CRAT") to "take a hard look at the issues and make strong recommendations for change." See Pls' Motion for Class Certification, Exh. B (Report of the Civil Rights Action Team) at 3. In [**6] February of 1997, the CRAT issued a report which concluded that "minority farmers have lost significant amounts of land and potential farm income as a result of discrimination by FSA programs and the programs of its predecessor agencies, ASCS and FMHA. . . . The process for resolving complaints has failed. Minority and limited-resource customers believe USDA has not acted in good faith on the complaints. Appeals are too often delayed and for too long. Favorable decisions are too often reversed." Id. at 30–31.

Also in February of 1997, the Office of the Inspector General of the USDA issued a report to the Secretary of the USDA indicating that the USDA had a backlog of complaints of discrimination that had not been processed, investigated or resolved. See Pls' Motion for Class Certification, Exh. A (Evaluation Report for the Secretary on Civil Rights Issues). The Report found that immediate action was needed to clear the backlog of complaints, that the "program discrimination complaint process at [the Farm Services Agency] lacks integrity, direction, and accountability," id. at 6, and that "staffing problems, obsolete procedures, and little direction from management have [**7] resulted in a climate of disorder within the civil rights staff at FSA." Id. at 1.

The CRAT Report and the Report of the Inspector General clearly contributed to plaintiffs' decision to file this class action. Even before the reports were issued, however, minority farmers had alleged that the USDA discriminated on the basis of race in the administration of its farm programs. In late 1995, five farmers filed a lawsuit in this Court captioned Williams v. Glickman, Civil Action No. 95-1149 (now captioned Herrera v. Glickman). Williams originally was filed as a class action alleging that the USDA discriminated against minority farmers in the operation of its farm programs. The proposed Williams class was defined as

> All African American or Hispanic American persons who, between 1981 and the present, have suffered from racial or national origin discrimination in the application for or the servicing of loans or credit from the FmHA (now Farm Services Agency) of the USDA, which has caused them to sustain economic loss and/or mental anguish/emotion [sic] distress damages.

See Williams v. Glickman, 1997 U.S. Dist. LEXIS 1683, Civil Action No. 95-1149, Memorandum Opinion of February [**8] 14, 1997 at 7. On February 14, 1997, Judge Thomas A. Flannery denied plaintiffs' motion for class certification. Judge Flannery essentially found that plaintiffs' proposed class definition was too amorphous and overly broad and that the claims of the named plaintiffs were not typical or representative of the claims of potential class members. Judge Flannery also found that even if plaintiffs could meet the requirements of Rule 23(a) of the Federal Rules of Civil Procedure governing class actions, plaintiffs had failed to establish any of the Rule 23(b) requirements. On April 15, 1997, Judge Flannery denied plaintiffs' motion for reconsideration. n2.

[n2. Most of the original Williams plaintiffs settled their claims against the USDA. The two remaining plaintiffs, both of whom are Hispanic, had pending administrative complaints with the USDA, and the court therefore stayed the lawsuit pending an administrative determination by the USDA on the merits of the administrative complaints.]

Civil Actions Nos. 97-1978, 98-1693 (1999)

Opinion

Civil Action No. 97-1978 (PLF), Civil Action No. 98-1693 (PLF)
UNITED STATES DISTRICT COURT FOR THE DISTRICT
OF COLUMBIA
185 F.R.D. 82; 1999 U.S. Dist. LEXIS 5220
April 14, 1999, Decided
April 14, 1999, Filed
DISPOSITION: [**1] Consent Decree approved and entered.
COUNSEL: For Plaintiffs: Alexander J. Pires, Jr., Conlon Frantz Phelan & Pires, Washington, DC.
  For Plaintiffs: Philip L. Fraas, Washington, DC.
  For Defendant: Michael Sitcov, Philip Bartz, U.S. Dept. of Justice, Washington, DC.
JUDGES: PAUL L. FRIEDMAN, United States District Judge.
OPINION BY: PAUL L. FRIEDMAN

OPINION: [*85] OPINION

Forty acres and a mule. As the Civil War drew to a close, the United States government created the Freedmen's Bureau to provide assistance to former slaves. The government promised to sell or lease to farmers parcels of unoccupied land and land that had been confiscated by the Union during the war, and it promised the loan of a federal government mule to plow that land. Some African Americans took advantage of these programs and either bought or leased parcels of land. During Reconstruction, however, President Andrew Johnson vetoed a bill to enlarge the powers and activities of the Freedmen's Bureau, and he reversed many of the policies of the Bureau. Much of the promised land that had been leased to African American farmers was taken away and returned to Confederate loyalists. For most African

Americans, the promise of forty [**2] acres and a mule was never kept. Despite the government's failure to live up to its promise, African American farmers persevered. By 1910, they had acquired approximately 16 million acres of farmland. By 1920, there were 925,000 African American farms in the United States.

On May 15, 1862, as Congress was debating the issue of providing land for freed former slaves, the United States Department of Agriculture was created. The statute creating the Department charged it with acquiring and preserving "all information concerning agriculture" and collecting "new and valuable seeds and plants; to test, by cultivation, the value of such of them as may require such tests; to propagate such as may be worthy of propagation, and to distribute them among agriculturists." An Act to establish a Department of Agriculture, ch. 71, 12 Stat. 387 (1862). In 1889, the Department of Agriculture achieved full cabinet department status. Today, it has an annual budget of $67.5 billion and administers farm loans and guarantees worth $2.8 billion.

As the Department of Agriculture has grown, the number of African American farmers has declined dramatically. Today, there are fewer than 18,000 African American [**3] farms in the United States, and African American farmers now own less than 3 million acres of land. The United States Department of Agriculture and the county commissioners to whom it has delegated so much power bear much of the responsibility for this dramatic decline. The Department itself has recognized that there has always been a disconnect between what President Lincoln envisioned as "the people's department," serving all of the people, and the widespread belief that the Department is "the last plantation," a department "perceived as playing a key role in what some see as a conspiracy to force minority and disadvantaged farmers off their land through discriminatory loan practices." See Pls' Motion for Class Certification, Exh. B, Civil Rights at the United States Department of Agriculture: A Report by the Civil Rights Action Team (Feb. 1997) ("CRAT Report") at 2.

For decades, despite its promise that "no person in the United States shall, on the ground of race, color, or national origin, be excluded from participation in, be denied the benefits of, or be otherwise subjected to discrimination under any program or activity of an applicant or recipient receiving Federal financial [**4] assistance from the Department of Agriculture," 7 C.F.R. 15.1, the Department of Agriculture and the county commissioners discriminated against African American farmers when they denied, delayed or otherwise frustrated the applications of those farmers for farm loans and other credit and benefit programs. Further compounding the problem, in 1983 the

Department of Agriculture disbanded its Office of Civil Rights and stopped responding to claims of discrimination. These events were the culmination of a string of broken promises that had been made to African American farmers for well over a century.

It is difficult to resist the impulse to try to undo all the broken promises and years of discrimination that have led to the precipitous decline in the number of African American farmers in the United States. The Court has before it a proposed settlement of a class action lawsuit that will not undo all that has been done. Despite that fact, however, the Court finds that the settlement is a fair resolution of the claims brought in this case [*86] and a good first step towards assuring that the kind of discrimination that has been visited on African American farmers since Reconstruction will [**5] not continue into the next century. The Court therefore will approve the settlement.

In re African-American Slave Descendants Litigation (2004)

Opinion

MDL No. 1491, Lead Case No. 02 C 7764
UNITED STATES DISTRICT COURT FOR THE NORTHERN DISTRICT OF ILLINOIS, EASTERN DIVISION
2004 U.S. Dist. LEXIS 872
January 26, 2004, Decided
January 26, 2004, Docketed
PRIOR HISTORY: *In re* African-American Slave Descendants Litig., 2004 U.S. Dist. LEXIS 864 (N.D. Ill., Jan. 26, 2004).
DISPOSITION: [*1] Defendants' Joint Motion to Dismiss brought pursuant to Federal Rules of Civil Procedure 12(b)(1) and (6) granted without prejudice.
COUNSEL: For DEADRIA PAELLMANN-FARMER, MARY LACEY MADISON, ANDRE CARRINGTON, JOHN BANKHEAD, RICHARD E BARBER, SR, HANNAN JANE HURDLE-TOOMEY, MARCELLE PORTER, BILLY GENE MCGEE, EMMA MARIE CLARK, INA HURDLE MCGEE, C DOE, M DOE, C W DOE, M L DOE, E H DOE, A L DOE, A D DOE, I DOE, C W DOE, ANTOINETTE MILLER, plaintiffs: Lionel Jean-Baptiste, Jean-Baptiste and Raoul, Evanston, IL. Benjamin Obi Nwoye, Mendoza & Nwoye, P.C., Chicago, IL. Roger S Wareham, Thomas Wareham & Richards, Brooklyn, NY. Bryan R Williams, New York, NY. Morse Geller, Forest Hills, NY. Diana E Sammons, Nagel, Rice, Dreifuss & Mazie, Livingston, NJ. Pius Akamdi Obioha, Law Offices of Pius A. Obioha, New Orleans, LA. Gary L Bledsoe, Law Offices of Gary L. Bledsoe, Austin, TX. Harry E Cantrell, Jr, Cantrell Law Firm, New Orleans, LA. Dumisa Buhle Ntsebeza, Cape Town, South Africa.

For BROWN & WILLIAMSON TOBACCO COMPANY, defendant: Andrew R. McGaan, Douglas Geoffrey Smith, Kirkland & Ellis LLP, Chicago, IL.

For R.J. REYNOLDS TOBACCO Co., defendant: [*2] Thomas F. Gardner, Susan Lynn Winders, Jones Day, Chicago, IL.

For CSX, defendant: David Michael Kroeger, Jenner & Block, LLC, Chicago, IL. Heidi K Hubbard, Andrew W Rudge, Williams & Connolly, Washington, DC.

For FLEETBOSTON FINANCIAL CORPORATION, defendant: Christina M. Tchen, Ryan James Rohlfsen, Skadden Arps Slate Meagher & Flom, LLP, Chicago, IL. Gary DiBianco, Andrew L Sandler, Skadden, Arps, Slate, Meagher & Flom LLP, Washington, DC.

For NORFOLK SOUTHERN RAILWAY COMPANY, defendant: Jack E. McClard, Maya M Eckstein, Hunton & Williams, Richmond, VA. Frank E Emory, Jr., Hunton & Williams, Charlotte, NC.

For CANADIAN NATIONAL RAILWAY CO, defendant: James A. Fletcher, Fletcher & Sippel, LLC, Chicago, IL. Michael J. Barron, Canadian National Railway Company, Chicago, IL.

For THE SOCIETY OF LLOYD'S, defendant: Debra Torres, Fried, Frank, Harris, Shriver & Jacobson LLP, Jacobson, New York, NY.

For AETNA, INC., defendant: John Niblock, O'Melveny & Myers, Washington, DC.

JUDGES: CHARLES RONALD NORGLE, Judge, United States District Judge.

OPINION BY: CHARLES RONALD NORGLE

OPINION: OPINION AND ORDER

CHARLES R. NORGLE, District Judge:
Before the court is Defendants' [*3] Joint Motion to Dismiss. For the following reasons, the motion is granted.

I. INTRODUCTION

This case arises out of the institution of human chattel slavery as it existed in the North American colonies and the latter-formed United States of America. The allegations in Plaintiffs' First Amended and Consolidated Complaint ("FACC" or "Complaint") retell the generally acknowledged horrors of the institution of slavery, and the malignant actions of the sovereigns, entities and individuals that supported that institution. Plaintiffs' Complaint asks the courts to reexamine a tragic period in our Nation's history and to hold various corporate defendants liable for the commercial activities of their alleged predecessors before, during and after the Civil War in America. Defendants acknowledge that slavery marked a deplorable period in our Nation's history. However, they assert that Plaintiffs' claims, which arise from that period, cannot be heard in 2004 in a court of law. . . .

(d). *Conclusion*

In response to all these deficiencies, Plaintiffs argue that "'standing can be supported by a very slender reed of injury.'" Pls.' Resp. to Defs.' Mot. to Dismiss, at 4 (citing 13 Charles Allen Wright, Arthur R. Miller & Edward H. Cooper, Federal Practice and Procedure 3531.4 (2d ed. 1984)). Plaintiffs are correct that standing can be supported by a very slender reed of injury, as the cases which they cite provide. Yet, this "slender [*61] reed" must still have its roots in the soil of an injury personal to the Plaintiffs, not a "derivative harm" uprooted from the soil of another's injury.

Plaintiffs wish to litigate the issue of slavery without establishing that they have suffered some concrete and particularized injury as a result of the putatively illegal conduct of the Defendants. See Valley Forge, 454 U.S. at 472; Lujan 504 U.S. at 560. However, "the fundamental aspect of standing is that it focuses on the party seeking to get his complaint before a federal court and not on the issues he wishes to have adjudicated." Flast, 392 U.S. at 99. "In other words, when standing is placed in issue in a case, the question is whether the person whose standing is challenged is a proper party to request an adjudication of a particular issue and not whether the issue itself is justiciable." Id. at 99–100. Plaintiffs cannot satisfy the first and most basic requirement of constitutional standing—a concrete and particularized personal injury. See Lujan, 504 U.S. at 560. Plaintiffs cannot establish a personal injury sufficient to confer standing [*62] by merely alleging some genealogical relationship to African-Americans held in slavery over one-hundred, two-hundred, or three-hundred years ago. In attempting to litigate the unopposed issue of slavery rather than their personal injuries, Plaintiffs also cannot satisfy the second requirement of constitutional standing—injury that is fairly traceable to the conduct of the defendants. See id. Plaintiffs do not allege that they had any present property interest that was injured as a result of the Defendants' actions, nor that any action of the Defendants wronged them in any way that would be cognizable under tort theory. Plaintiffs fail to allege any conduct by the eighteen specifically named Defendants that individually affected any of the Plaintiffs.

In sum, the allegations of Plaintiffs' Complaint fail to support their standing to maintain this suit, as required by Article III of the United States Constitution.

(2). *Prudential Limitations on the Standing Doctrine*
Beyond the constitutional limitations on the standing doctrine, there are prudential limitations on the exercise of federal court jurisdiction. See, e.g., Warth, 422 U.S. at 498. These [*63] additional prudential limitations on standing may exist even though the Article III requirements are met because "the judiciary seeks to avoid deciding questions of broad social import where no individual rights would be vindicated and to limit access to the federal courts to those litigants best suited to assert a particular claim." Gladstone, Realtors, 441 U.S. at 99–100. Like the constitutional limitations on the standing doctrine, these prudential limitations ensure that federal courts adhere to the separation of powers concept and are "founded in concern about the proper, and properly limited, role of the courts in a democratic society." Warth, 422 U.S. at 498. However, "unlike their constitutional counterparts, they can be modified or abrogated by Congress." Bennett v. Spear, 520 U.S. 154, 162, 137 L. Ed. 2d 281, 117 S. Ct. 1154 (1997).

One of these prudential limits on standing is that a litigant must normally assert his own legal interests rather than those of third parties. See Singleton v. Wulff, 428 U.S. 106, 113–14, 49 L. Ed. 2d 826, 96 S. Ct. 2868 (1976); Warth, 422 U.S. at 499. Another is that the federal courts should [*64] "refrain[] from adjudicating 'abstract questions of wide public significance' which amount to 'generalized grievances,' pervasively shared and most appropriately addressed in the representative branches." Valley Forge, 454 U.S. at 475 (citing Warth, 422 U.S. at 499–500).

(a). *Plaintiffs Impermissibly Attempt to Assert the Legal Rights of Absent Third Parties*
As a general rule, a litigant must assert his own legal rights and cannot assert the legal rights of a third-party. See, e.g., Powers v. Ohio, 449 U.S. 400, 410, 113 L. Ed. 2d 411, 111 S. Ct. 1364 (1991); Singleton, 428 U.S. at 113–14. However, a litigant may assert the rights of absent third-parties in certain limited situations. In determining whether a litigant who seeks standing to assert the legal rights of a third-party may do so, a two-part inquiry is involved. See Caplin & Drysdale, Chartered v. United States, 491 U.S. 617, 623 n.3, 105 L. Ed. 2d 528, 109 S. Ct. 2646, 109 S. Ct. 2667 (1989). First, the litigant must have personally suffered some injury-in-fact adequate to satisfy Article III's case or controversy requirement. See id.; see also Singleton, 428 U.S. at 112. [*65] Second, certain prudential considerations must point in favor of permitting the litigant to assert the third-party's legal rights. See id. Among the prudential considerations to consider are the requirements that the litigant must have a legally sufficient relation to the third-party, see Powers, 499 U.S. at 411; see also Craig v. Boren, 429 U.S. 190, 196,

50 L. Ed. 2d 397, 97 S. Ct. 451 (1976), and there must exist some hindrance to the third-party's ability to protect his or her own rights, see Powers, 499 U.S. at 411; see also Singleton, 428 U.S. at 115–116.

To the extent that Plaintiffs are attempting to assert the legal rights of their ancestors, Plaintiffs cannot do so because they themselves have failed to establish that they have personally suffered some injury-in-fact adequate to satisfy Article III's case-or-controversy requirement. See Singleton, 428 U.S. at 112. In addition, prudential considerations militate against allowing such claims. First, Plaintiffs have not alleged a legally sufficient relation to their ancestors. All that Plaintiffs allege is a genealogical relationship, and more is required [*66] under the law in order to confer third-party standing. Cf. Gilmore v. Utah, 429 U.S. 1012, 1016–17, 50 L. Ed. 2d 632, 97 S. Ct. 436 (1976) (indicating that a mother had no standing to contest her son's execution). Plaintiffs make no allegations of any relationship sufficient, whether by common law or statute, to confer them standing to pursue the claims of their deceased ancestors. Cf. Whitmore v. Arkansas, 495 U.S. 149, 163, 109 L. Ed. 2d 135, 110 S. Ct. 1717 (1990) (recognizing a next-friend's standing to sue in certain situations); United Food & Comm. Workers Union Local 751 v. Brown Group, 517 U.S. 544, 558, 134 L. Ed. 2d 758, 116 S. Ct. 1529 (1996) (recognizing that the Worker Adjustment and Retraining Notification Act, 29 U.S.C. 2101 *et seq.*, grants unions standing to sue on behalf of its members). Furthermore, Plaintiffs do not allege that they are assignees of a legally cognizable claim against the named Defendants. Second, Plaintiffs have not alleged that any hindrance existed to their ancestors' ability to have protected their own rights over the last century. Cf. Johnson v. McAdoo, 45 App. D.C. 440, 441 (D.C. 1916), aff'd, [*67] 244 U.S. 643, 61 L. Ed. 1367, 37 S. Ct. 649 (1917) (evidencing a claim for slavery-based reparations nearly a century ago).

In sum, Plaintiffs have not established third-party standing to assert the legal rights of their ancestors.

Selected Bibliography

Publications

Allen, Robert L. "Past Due: The African American Quest for Reparations." *The Black Scholar* 28, no. 2 (1998): 2–17.
America, Richard F. "Reparations and Public Policy." *Review of Black Political Economy* 26, no. 3 (1999): 77–83.
———, ed. *The Wealth of Races*. Westport, Conn.: Greenwood Press, 1990.
"And Justice for All? The Claims of Human Rights." *SAQ* 103, nos. 2–3 (2004).
Arnesen, Eric. "Like Banquo's Ghost, It Will Not Down: The Race Question and the American Railroad Brotherhoods, 1880–1920." *American Historical Review* 99 (1994): 1601–1633.
Ashmore, Harry S. *Hearts and Minds: The Anatomy of Racism from Roosevelt to Reagan*. New York: McGraw-Hill, 1982.
Baier, Annette. "The Rights of Past and Future Generations." In *Responsibilities to Future Generations*, ed. Ernest Partridge, 171–186. Buffalo, N.Y.: Prometheus Books, 1980.
Baker, Lillian. *The Japanning of America: Redress and Reparations Demands by Japanese-Americans*. Central Point, Oreg.: Webb Research Group Publishers, 1991.
Bales, Kevin. *Disposable People: New Slavery in the Global Economy*. Berkeley: University of California Press, 1999.
———, ed. *Understanding Global Slavery*. Berkeley: University of California Press, 2005.
Ball, Edward. *Slaves in the Family*. New York: Farrar, Straus & Giroux, 1998.
Baraka, Amiri. "The Case for Reparations." *Black Collegian* 29, no. 1 (1998): 26–27.
———. *The Essence of Reparations*. Philipsburg, St. Martin: House of Nehesi Publishers, 2003.
Barkan, Elazar. *The Guilt of Nations: Restitution and Negotiating Historical Injustices*. New York: Norton, 2000.
Bedau, Hugo. "Compensatory Justice and the Black Manifesto." *Monist* 56 (1972): 20–42.
Benveniste Luis, Martin Carnoy, and Richard Rothstein. *All Else Equal*. New York: Routledge, 2002.
Berlin, Ira. *Generations of Captivity: A History of African-American Slaves*. Cambridge, Mass.: Belknap Press of Harvard University Press, 2003.
Berry, Mary Francis. *Black Resistance, White Law*. New York: Penguin Books, 1995.
Bittker, Boris I. *The Case for Black Reparations*. Boston: Beacon Press, 2003.
Blackburn, Robin. *The Making of New World Slavery*. New York: Verso, 1997.
Blank, Rebecca, and David Card. *Poverty, Income Distribution and Growth: Are They Still*

Connected? Evanston, Ill.: Center for Urban Affairs and Policy Research, Northwestern University, 1993.
Bloche, M. Gregg. "Race and Discretion in American Medicine." *Yale Journal of Health Policy, Law, and Ethics* (2001): 95–121.
Blumstein, Alfred. "On the Racial Disproportionality of United States Prison Populations." *Journal of Criminal Law and Criminology* 73 (1982): 1259–1281.
Boudette, Neal E. "Seeking Reparation: A Holocaust Claim Cuts to the Heart of the New Germany." *Wall Street Journal*, 29 March 2002.
Boxill, Bernard. "The Morality of Reparations." *Social Theory and Practice* 2, no. 1 (1972): 113–123.
———. "The Morality of Reparations II." In Tommy Lott, ed., *A Companion to African American Philosophy*, 134–147. Malden, Mass.: Blackwell Publishing, 2003.
Boyd, Herb, ed. *Race and Racism*. Boston: South End Press, 2002.
Branch, Watson. "Reparations for Slavery: A Dream Deferred." *San Diego International Law Journal* 3 (2002): 177–206.
"Bridging the Color Line: The Power of African-American Reparations to Redirect America's Future." *Harvard Law Review* 115, no. 6 (2002): 1689–1712.
Brooks, Roy L. *Atonement and Forgiveness: A New Model for Black Reparations*. Berkeley: University of California Press, 2004.
———, ed. *When Sorry Isn't Enough: The Controversy over Apologies and Reparations for Human Injustice*. New York: New York University Press, 1999.
Brophy, Alfred, and Randall Kennedy. *Reconstructing the Dreamland: The Tulsa Riot of 1921, Race, Reparations, and Reconciliation*. New York: Oxford University Press, 2002.
Brown, Michael K. *Race, Money, and the American Welfare State*. Ithaca: Cornell University Press, 1999.
Brown, Michael K., and Steven P. Erie. "Blacks and the Legacy of the Great Society: The Economic and Political Impact of Federal Social Policy." *Public Policy* 29, no. 3 (1981): 299–330.
Brysk, Alison. *Globalization and Human Rights*. Berkeley: University of California Press, 2002.
Byrd, W. Michael, and Linda A. Clayton. *An American Health Dilemma*. Vol. 1, *A Medical History of African Americans and the Problem of Race: Beginnings to 1900*. New York: Routledge, 2000.
Campbell, Tom. "Tax Preparer Can Keep Working, but Judge Says Foster Must No Longer Claim 'Slavery Reparations.'" *Richmond Times-Dispatch*, 26 October 2002.
Carnoy, Martin, *Faded Dreams: The Politics and Economics of Race in America*. New York: Cambridge University Press, 1994.
Cha-Jua, Sundiata Keita. "Slavery, Racist Violence, American Apartheid: The Case for Reparations." *New Politics* 8, no. 3 (2001): 46–64.
Cole, David. *Equal Justice: Race and Class in the American Criminal Justice System*. New York: New Press, 1999.
Conley, Dalton. *Being Black, Living in the Red: Race, Wealth, and Social Policy in America*. Berkeley: University of California Press, 1999.
———. "The Cost of Slavery." *New York Times*, 15 February 2003.
Corlett, J. Angelo. *Race, Racism, and Reparations*. Ithaca: Cornell University Press, 2003.
Crocker, David. "Retribution and Reconciliation." *Institute for Philosophy and Public Policy* 20, no. 1 (2003), www.publicpolicy.umd.edu/IPPP/Winter-Springoo/retribution_and_reconciliation.htm (accessed 30 April 2006).

Danziger, Sheldon, and Peter Gottschalk. *America Unequal*. New York: Russell Sage Foundation, 1995.
Darity, William, Jr. "What's Left of the Economic Theory of Discrimination?" In Steven Shulman and William Darity Jr., eds., *The Question of Discrimination*. Middletown, Conn.: Wesleyan University Press, 1989.
Darity, William, Jr., and Dania Frank. "The Economics of Reparations," *American Economic Review* 93, no. 2 (2003): 326–329.
Darity, William A., Jr., and Patrick L. Mason. "Evidence on Discrimination in Employment: Codes of Color, Codes of Gender." *Journal of Economic Perspectives* 12, no. 2 (1998): 63–90.
Darity, William, Jr., and Samuel L. Myers Jr. *Persistent Disparity: Race and Economic Inequality in the United States since 1945*. Northampton, Mass.: Edward Elgar Publishing, 1998.
Davis, David Brion. *Challenging the Boundaries of Slavery*. Cambridge, Mass.: Harvard University Press, 2003.
———. *In the Image of God: Religion, Moral Values, and Our Heritage of Slavery*. New Haven: Yale University Press, 2001.
Digeser, Peter. "Forgiveness and Politics: Dirty Hands and Imperfect Procedures." *Political Theory* 26, no. 5 (1998): 700–724.
Downie, R. S. "Forgiveness." *Philosophical Quarterly* 15 (April 1965): 128–134.
Dwyer, Susan. "Reconciliation for Realists." *Ethics and International Affairs* 13 (1999): 81–98.
Ellinikos, Maria. "American MNCs Continue to Profit from the Use of Forced and Slave Labor—Begging the Question: Should America Take a Cue from Germany?" *Columbia Journal of Law and Social Problems* 35, no. 1 (2001): 1–33.
Evans, Malcolm D., and Rachel Murray, eds. *The African Charter on Human and Peoples' Rights*. New York: Cambridge University Press, 2002.
Feagin, Joe R. *Racist America: Roots, Current Realities, and Future Reparations*. New York: Routledge, 2000.
Feagin, Joe R., and Melvin P. Sikes. *Living with Racism: The Black Middle-Class Experience*. Boston: Beacon Press, 1994.
Fehrenbacher, Don E. *The Slaveholding Republic: An Account of the United States Government's Relations to Slavery*. Completed and edited by Ward M. McAfee. New York: Oxford University Press, 2001.
Feinberg, Joel. "Collective Responsibility." *Journal of Philosophy* 65 (1968): 674–688.
Ferencz, Benjamin B. *Less Than Slaves*. Cambridge, Mass.: Harvard University Press, 1979.
Ferguson, Ronald F. "Shifting Challenges: Fifty Years of Economic Change toward Black–White Earnings Equality." In Obie Clayton Jr., ed., *An American Dilemma Revisited*. New York: Russell Sage Foundation, 1996.
Finkelman, Paul. *Slavery and the Founders: Race and Liberty in the Age of Jefferson*. Armonk, N.Y.: M. E. Sharpe, 1996.
Fletcher, Bill, and Adolph Reed. *Reparations? Yes/No*. New York: New Press, 2003.
Fullinwider, Robert. "Slavery, Reparations and Moral Clarity." Paper presented at the conference Moral Legacy of Slavery, Bowling Green State University, Bowling Green, Ohio, 18–19 October 2002.
Gates, Henry Louis, Jr. "The Future of Slavery's Past." *New York Times*, 29 July 2001.
Ghannam, Jeffrey. "Repairing the Past." *American Bar Association Journal* (November 2000): 39–43.
Gibney, Mark, and Erik Roxstrom. "The Status of State Apologies." *Human Rights Quarterly* 23, no. 4 (2001): 911–939.

Goldman, Alan H. "Reparations to Individuals or Groups?" *Analysis* 35 (April 1975): 168–179.
Grahame, James. *Who Is to Blame? Or, Cursory Review of "American Apology for American Accession to Negro Slavery."* London: Smith, Elder, 1842.
Greer, Edward. *Black Liberation Politics: A Reader.* Boston: Allyn and Bacon, 1971.
Haley, James, ed. *Reparations for American Slavery.* San Diego: Greenhaven Press, 2003.
Harris, Bonnie. "Making a Case for Reparations." *Indianapolis Star*, 17 October 2002.
Harris, Lee A. "Political Autonomy as a Form of Reparations to African-Americans." *Southern University Law Review* 29 (2001): 25.
Hayner, Priscilla B. *Unspeakable Truths: Facing the Challenge of Truth Commissions.* New York: Routledge, 2002.
Heckman, James J. "The Central Role of the South in Accounting for the Economic Progress of Black Americans." *American Economic Review* 80, no. 2 (1990): 242–246.
Henderson, Michael. *Forgiveness: Breaking the Chain of Hate.* Portland, Ore.: Arnica Publishing, 2003.
Higginbotham, A. Leon, Jr. *In the Matter of Color: The Colonial Period.* New York: Oxford University Press, 1978.
Hirsch, James S. *Riot and Remembrance: The Tulsa Race War and Its Legacy.* Boston: Houghton Mifflin, 2002.
Hitchens, Christopher. "Who's Sorry Now?" *Nation*, 29 May 2000.
Hopkins, Kevin. "Forgive U.S. Our Debts? Righting the Wrongs of Slavery." *Georgetown Law Review* 89 (2001): 2531–2356.
Ishay, Micheline R. *The History of Human Rights.* Berkeley: University of California Press, 2004.
Johnson, Walter, ed. *The Chattel Principle: Internal Slave Trades in the Americas.* New Haven: Yale University Press, 2005.
Katz, Michael B., ed. *The "Underclass" Debate: Views from History.* Princeton: Princeton University Press, 1993.
Kluegel, James R., and Eliot R. Smith. "Whites' Beliefs about Blacks' Opportunity." *American Sociological Review* 47 (1982): 518–532.
Kluger, Richard. *Simple Justice: The History of* Brown v. Board of Education *and Black America's Struggle for Equality.* New York: Knopf, 1976.
Kousser, J. Morgan. *Colorblind Injustice: Minority Voting Rights and the Undoing of the Second Reconstruction.* Chapel Hill: University of North Carolina Press, 1999.
Kramer, Lance. "Study: Slavery's Effects Lasted Just 2 Generations." *The Dartmouth*, 6 November 2002, www.thedartmouth.com/article.php?aid=2002110601O3 (accessed 30 April 2006).
Krauthammer, Charles. "Reparations for Black Americans." *Time*, 31 December 1990, 18.
Ladd, Helen F. "Evidence on Discrimination in Mortgage Lending." *Journal of Economic Perspectives* 12, no. 2 (1998): 41–62.
Lazare, Aaron. *On Apology.* New York: Oxford University Press, 2004.
Lecky, Robert S., and H. Elliott Wright, eds. *Black Manifesto: Religion, Racism, and Reparations.* New York: Sheed and Ward, 1969.
Leo, John. "Enslaved to the Past." *U.S. News and World Report*, 15 April 2002, 39.
Lewan, Todd, and Dolores Barclay. "'When They Steal Your Land, They Steal Your Future.' History: Study Details Black Landowners' Losses, Now Worth Millions." *Los Angeles Times*, 2 December 2001, 1.

Lewin, Tamar. "Calls for Slavery Restitution Getting Louder." *New York Times*, 4 June 2001.
———. "Slave Reparation Movement Begins Gaining Momentum." *San Diego Union-Tribune*, 8 June 2001.
Lieberman, Robert. *Shifting the Color Line: Race and the American Welfare State*. Cambridge, Mass.: Harvard University Press, 1998.
Lipsitz, George. *The Possessive Investment in Whiteness: How White People Profit from Identity Politics*. Philadelphia: Temple University Press, 1998.
Lott, Tommy, ed. *Subjugation and Bondage: Critical Essays on Slavery and Social Philosophy*. Lanham, Md.: Rowman and Littlefield, 1998.
Loury, Glenn C. *The Anatomy of Racial Inequality*. Cambridge, Mass.: Harvard University Press, 2001.
———. "It's Futile to Put a Price on Slavery." *New York Times*, 29 May 2000.
Madigan, Tim. *The Burning: Massacre, Destruction, and the Tulsa Race Riot of 1921*. New York: St. Martin's Press, 2001.
Maki, Mitchell T., Harry H. L. Kitano, and S. Megan Berthold. *Achieving the Impossible Dream: How Japanese Americans Obtained Redress*. Urbana: University of Illinois Press, 1999.
"Making the Case for Racial Reparations: Does America Owe a Debt to the Descendants of Its Slaves? A Forum." *Harper's* (November 2000): 37–41.
Maloney, Thomas N. "Wage Compression and Wage Inequality between Black and White Males in the United States, 1940–1960." *Journal of Economic History* 54 (1994): 358–381.
Maltz, Earl. "Slavery, Federalism, and the Structure of the Constitution." *American Journal of Legal History* 36 (1992): 468.
Mangum, Charles S., Jr. *The Legal Status of the Negro*. Chapel Hill: University of North Carolina Press, 1940.
Marable, Manning. "In Defense of Black Reparations." *Along the Color Line*, October 2002.
———. "Reparations, Black Consciousness, and the Black Freedom Struggle." *Along the Color Line*, September 2002.
———. "Reparations: The New Civil Rights Agenda." *Along the Color Line*, April 2003.
Martin, Michael T., and Marilyn Yaquinto, eds. *America's Unpaid Debt: Slavery and Racial Justice*. Working Papers Series on Historical Systems, Peoples, and Cultures, nos. 13–15, Department of Ethnic Studies, Bowling Green State University, Bowling Green, Ohio, 2003.
———. "Reparations for 'America's Holocaust': Activism for Global Justice." *Race and Class* 45, no. 4 (April–June 2004): 1–25.
Martin, Vivian B. "Everyone Stands to Gain from Reparations Debate." *Hartford Courant*, 7 November 2002.
Massey, Douglas, and Nancy Denton. *American Apartheid: Segregation and the Making of the Underclass*. Cambridge, Mass.: Harvard University Press, 1993.
Mazrui, Ali A. *Black Reparations in the Era of Globalization*. Binghamton, N.Y.: Institute of Global Cultural Studies, 2002.
McGary, Howard, Jr. "Justice and Reparations." *Philosophical Forum* 9, nos. 2–3 (1977–78): 256–263.
———. "'Reparations' and 'Inverse Discrimination.'" *Dialogue* (Journal of Phi Sigma Tau) 17, no. 1 (1974): 8–10.
McLemee, Scott. "The Slave History You Don't Know: A Scholar's Startling Study of the Southwest Wins Unprecedented Acclaim." *Chronicle of Higher Education*, 16 May 2003.

McWhorter, John H. "The Reparations Racket: America Has Already Made Amends for Slavery." *City Journal* 14, no. 2 (2004).
Meier, August, and John H. Bracey Jr. "The NAACP as a Reform Movement, 1909–1965: They Reach the Conscience of America." *Journal of Southern History* 59 (1993): 3–30.
Meillassoux, Claude. *The Anthropology of Slavery: The Womb of Iron and Gold*. Translated by Alide Dasnois. Chicago: University of Chicago Press, 1991.
Mills, Charles. W. *The Racial Contract*. Ithaca: Cornell University Press, 1997.
Milovanovic, Dragan, and Katheryn K. Russell, eds. *Petit Apartheid in the U.S. Criminal Justice System: The Dark Figure of Racism*. Durham: Carolina Academic Press, 2001.
Minow, Martha. *Between Vengeance and Forgiveness: Facing History after Genocide and Mass Violence*. Boston: Beacon Press, 1998.
Munford, Clarence J. *Race and Reparations: A Black Perspective for the Twenty-First Century*. Trenton, N.J.: Africa World Press, 1996.
Murray, Charles. *Losing Ground: American Social Policy, 1950–1980*. New York: Basic Books, 1984.
Myrdal, Gunnar. *An American Dilemma: The Negro Problem and Modern Democracy*. New York: Harper and Bros., 1944.
National Urban League. *The State of Black America 2005*. Executive summary. National Urban League.
Neubeck, Kenneth J., and Noel A. Czenave. *Welfare Racism: Playing the Race Card against America's Poor*. New York: Routledge, 2001.
Nickel, James W. "Should Reparations Be to Individuals or to Groups?" *Analysis* 34 (April 1974): 154–160.
Ogletree, Charles J. "The Case of Reparations," *U.S.A. Weekend Magazine*, 18 August 2002.
———. "Repairing the Past: New Efforts in the Reparations Debate in America." *Harvard Civil Rights–Civil Liberties Law Review* 38, no. 2 (2003): 279–320.
Oliver, Melvin L., and Thomas M. Shapiro. *Black Wealth/White Wealth: A New Perspective on Racial Inequality*. New York: Routledge, 1995.
O'Neill, Onora. "Rights to Compensation." *Social Philosophy and Policy* 5 (1987): 72–87.
Orfield, Gary, and Carole Ashkinaze. *The Closing Door: Conservative Policy and Black Opportunity*. Chicago: University of Chicago Press, 1991.
Orfield, Gary, and Susan E. Eaton. *Dismantling Desegregation: The Quiet Reversal of Brown v. Board of Education*. New York: New Press, 1996.
Page, Clarence. "African-Americans Still Haven't Escaped Shackles of Slavery." *St. Paul Pioneer Press*, 5 July 2000.
Painter, Nell Irwin. "Soul Murder and Slavery: Toward a Fully Loaded Cost Accounting." In Alice Kessler-Harris, Linda K. Kerber, and Kathryn Kish Sklar, eds., *U.S. History as Women's History*, 125–146. Chapel Hill: University of North Carolina Press, 1995.
Patterson, Orlando. *Slavery and Social Death: A Comparative Study*. Cambridge, Mass.: Harvard University Press, 1982.
Pettigrew, Thomas, ed. *Racial Discrimination in the United States*. New York: Harper and Row, 1975.
Posner, Eric A., and Adrian Vermeule. "Reparations for Slavery and Other Historical Injustices." *Columbia Law Review* 103 (2003): 689–747.
Poussaint, Alvin E., and Amy Alexander. *Lay My Burden Down: Suicide and the Mental Health Crisis among African-Americans*. Boston: Beacon Press, 2000.

"A Price for Pain? Economic Analysis of Proposed Reparations for Descendants of Slaves." *The Economist*, 13 April 2002.

Quadagno, Jill. *The Color of Welfare: How Racism Undermined the War on Poverty*. New York: Oxford University Press, 1994.

Redkey, Edwin S. *Black Exodus*. New Haven: Yale University Press, 1969.

Reed, Adolph, Jr., ed. *Without Justice for All: The New Liberalism and Our Retreat from Racial Equality*. Boulder: Westview Press, 1999.

"Reparations Movement." *Congressional Quarterly Researcher* 11, no. 24 (2001): 529–552.

Rescher, Nicholas. "Collective Responsibility." *Journal of Social Philosophy* 29 (1998): 46–58.

Reskin, Barbara F. *The Realities of Affirmative Action in Employment*. Washington, D.C.: American Sociological Association, 1998.

Review of Black Political Economy. Special Issue on Reparations, vol. 32, nos. 3–4 (2005).

"Rice against Reparations for Slavery." *San Diego Union-Tribune*, 10 September 2001.

Richards, Norvin. "Forgiveness." *Ethics* 99 (October 1988): 77–97.

Robinson, Randall. "America's Debt to Blacks." *The Nation*, 13 March 2000.

——. *The Debt: What America Owes to Blacks*. New York: Dutton, 2000.

Roediger, David. *Colored White: Transcending the Racial Past*. Berkeley: University of California Press, 2002.

——. *The Wages of Whiteness*. New York: Verso, 1991.

Rohatyn, Dennis A. "Black Reparations: A Black and White Issue?" *Personalist* 60 (1979): 433–437.

Roosevelt, Margot. "A New War over Slavery." *Time*, 9 June 2003, 20.

Sacerdote, Bruce. "Slavery and the Intergenerational Transmission of Human Capital." 10 September 2002, www.dartmouth.edu/bsacerdo/wpapers/Slavery3.pdf (accessed 1 May 2006).

Salzberger, Ronald P., and Mary C. Turck. *Reparations for Slavery: A Reader*. Lanham, Md.: Rowman and Littlefield, 2004.

San Juan, E., Jr. "Preparing for the Time of Reparation: Speculative Cues from W. E. B. Du Bois, George Jackson, and Mumia Abu-Jamal. *Souls* 7, no. 2 (2005): 63–74.

——. *Racism and Cultural Studies: Critiques of Multiculturalist Ideology and the Politics of Difference*. Durham: Duke University Press, 2002.

Schedler, George. "Principles for Measuring the Damages of American Slavery." *Public Affairs Quarterly* 16, no. 4 (2002): 377–404.

Scheffler, Samuel. "Relationships and Responsibilities." *Philosophy and Public Affairs* 26, no. 3 (1998): 189–209.

Schuchter, Arnold, ed. *Reparations: The Black Manifesto and Its Challenge to White America*. Philadelphia: Lippincott, 1970.

Sears, David O., Jim Sidanius, and Lawrence Bobo, eds. *Racialized Politics: The Debate about Racism in America*. Chicago: University of Chicago Press, 2000.

Sebok, Anthony J. "The Brooklyn Slavery Class Action: More Than Just a Political Gambit." FindLaw, 9 April 2002, www.writ.news.findlaw.com/sebok/20020409.html (accessed 30 April 2006).

Sher, George. "Ancient Wrongs and Modern Rights." *Philosophy and Public Affairs* 10 (1980): 3–17.

Shriver, Donald W., Jr. *An Ethic for Enemies: Forgiveness in Politics*. New York: Oxford University Press, 1995.

Soyinka, Wole. *The Burden of Memory, the Muse of Forgiveness*. New York: Oxford University Press, 1999.

Spivak, Gayatri Chakravorty. "Righting Wrongs." *South Atlantic Quarterly* 103, nos. 2–3 (2004): 523–581.

Spriggs, William E., and Rhonda M. Williams. "What Do We Need to Explain about African American Unemployment?" In Robert Cherry and Williams Rodgers III, eds., *Prosperity for All? The Economic Boom and African Americans*. New York: Russell Sage Foundation, 2000.

Sterba, James. "Understanding Evil: American Slavery, the Holocaust, and the Conquest of the American Indians." *Ethics* 106, no. 2 (1996): 424–448.

Thernstrom, Stephan, and Abigail Thernstrom. *America in Black and White: One Nation, Indivisible*. New York: Simon and Schuster, 1997.

Thomas, Laurence. "American Slavery and the Holocaust: Their Ideologies Compared." *Public Affairs Quarterly* 5 (1991): 191–210.

Thompson, Jana. *Taking Responsibility for the Past: Reparation and Historical Injustice*. Boston: Polity Press, 2002.

Torpey, John. *Making Whole What Has Been Smashed: On Reparations Politics*. Cambridge, Mass.: Harvard University Press, 2006.

———, ed. *Politics and the Past: On Repairing Historical Injustices*. Lanham, Md.: Rowman and Littlefield, 2003.

Tucker, Neely. "A Long Road of Broken Promises for Black Farmers: USDA Fights Claims after Landmark Deal." *Washington Post*, 13 August 2002.

Tutu, Desmond. *No Future without Forgiveness*. New York: Doubleday, 1999.

United Nations. "Report of the World Conference against Racism, Racial Discrimination, Xenophobia, and Related Intolerance, Durban, South Africa, August 8–September 7, 2001." www.un.org/WCAR/ (accessed 30 April 2006).

"Vatican Recommends Reparations to Atone for Slavery." *San Diego Union-Tribune*, 30 August 2001.

Verdun, Vincene. "If the Shoe Fits, Wear It: An Analysis of Reparations to African Americans." *Tulane Law Review* 67 (1993): 597–668.

"Vision Statement Synopsis." National Black Agenda Convention, 5 February 2004. Schomburg Center for Research in Black Culture at the New York Public Library, Collections.

Waldron, Jeremy. "Superseding Historical Injustice." *Ethics* 103 (1992): 4–28.

We Charge Genocide. New York: International Publishers, 1951.

Westley, Robert. "Many Billions Gone: Is It Time to Reconsider the Case for Black Reparations?" *Boston College Law Review* 40 (1998): 429–478.

Wheeler, Samuel C., II. "Reparations Reconstructed." *American Philosophical Quarterly* 34, no. 3 (1997): 301–318.

Wildman, Stephanie M. *Privilege Revealed: How Invisible Preference Undermines America*. New York: New York University Press, 1996.

Williams, Bernard. *Shame and Necessity*. Berkeley: University of California Press, 1993.

Williams, Juan. "Slavery Isn't the Issue." *Wall Street Journal*, 9 April 2002, 26.

Wilson, William Julius. *The Bridge over the Racial Divide: Rising Inequality and Coalition Politics*. Berkeley: University of California Press, 1999.

———. *The Truly Disadvantaged*. Chicago: University of Chicago Press, 1987.

———. *When Work Disappears: The World of the New Urban Poor*. New York: Random House, 1996.

Winbush, Raymond A. ed. *Should America Pay? Slavery and the Raging Debate on Reparations*. New York: Amistad, 2003.

Yamamoto, Eric Y. *Interracial Justice*. New York: New York University Press, 1999.

Selected Websites

African American History, University of Washington Library, www.lib.washington.edu/subject/History/tm/black.html
African American History and Culture, www.loc.gov/rr/mss/guide/african.html
African American History Digital Library, www.academicinfo.net/africanamlibrary.html
African American Newswire Service, www.blackpr.com/
AOL Black Voices, www.africana.com
Gilder Lehrman Center for the Study of Slavery, Resistance, and Abolition, www.yale.edu/glc/index.html
Global Black News Communications, www.globalblacknews.com
Library of Congress, African American Odyssey, www.memory.loc.gov/ammem/aaohtml/exhibit/aointro.html
Reparations Central, www.reparationscentral.com
Schomburg Center for Research in Black Culture, www.nypl.org/research/sc/sc.html
Schomburg Collection, Images of African Americans in the 19th Century, www.digital.nypl.org/schomburg/images_aa19/
Schomburg Collection, Images of Harlem, www.si.umich.edu/CHICO/Harlem/

Contributors

Richard America is professor of the practice at the School of Business, Georgetown University, and the author of *Paying the Social Debt: What White America Owes Black America*.

Sam Anderson is education director of the Center for Law and Social Justice, Medgar Evers College, The City University of New York.

Martha Biondi is associate professor of African American studies at Northwestern University and the author of *To Stand and Fight: the Struggle for Civil Rights in Postwar New York City*.

Boris L. Bittker (deceased) was professor of law at Yale Law School, Yale University and the author of *The Case for Black Reparations*.

James Bolner is professor emeritus of political science at Louisiana State University and the author of "Toward a Theory of Racial Reparations" in *Phylon*.

Roy L. Brooks is professor of law at the University of San Diego School of Law and the author of *Atonement and Forgiveness: A New Model for Black Reparations*.

Michael K. Brown is professor of politics at the University of California at Santa Cruz and the author of *Race, Money, and the American Welfare State*.

Robert S. Browne (deceased) was economist and founder of the Black Economic Research Center and the author of *Lagos Plan of Action vs. the Berg Report (Monographs in African Studies)*.

Martin Carnoy is professor of education and economics at Stanford University and the author of *Faded Dreams: The Economics and Politics of Race in America*.

Chiquita Collins is assistant professor of sociology and African and African American studies at the University of Texas at Austin and the coauthor of "Reparations—a Viable Strategy to Address the Enigma of African American Health," in *American Behavioral Scientist*.

J. Angelo Corlett is professor of philosophy and ethics at San Diego State University and the author of *Race, Racism, and Reparations*.

Contributors

Elliott Currie is lecturer in the Legal Studies Program at the University of California at Berkeley and the author of *Reckoning: Drugs, the Cities, and the American Future*.

William Darity Jr. is professor of economics and director of the Institute of African American Research at the University of North Carolina at Chapel Hill and the coauthor of *Persistent Disparity: Race and Economic Inequality in the U. S. Since 1945*.

Adrienne D. Davis is professor of law at the University of North Carolina School of Law and the author of "The Case for United States Reparations to African Americans."

Troy Duster is professor of sociology and senior fellow at the Institute for the History of the Production of Knowledge at New York University and the author of *The Legislation of Morality*.

Dania Frank is a former researcher at Harvard University and the coauthor of "The Economics of Reparations" in *The American Economic Review*.

Robert Fullinwider is senior research scholar at the Institute for Philosophy and Public Policy at the University of Maryland and the author of *Civil Society, Democracy, and Civic Renewal*.

Charles P. Henry is professor of African American studies at the University of California at Berkeley and the editor of *Foreign Policy and the Black (Inter)national Interest*.

Gerald Horne is professor of history, African and Afro-American studies, and communication studies at the University of North Carolina at Chapel Hill and the author of *From the Barrel of a Gun: The U. S. and the War against Zimbabwe 1965–1980*.

Robert Johnson Jr. is professor of Africana studies at the University of Massachusetts at Boston and the author of *Race, Law and Public Policy: Cases and Materials on Law and Public Policy of Race*.

Robin D. G. Kelley is professor of history and American studies and ethnicity at the University of Southern California. His publications include *Race Rebels: Culture, Politics, and the Black Working Class*.

Jeffrey R. Kerr-Ritchie is visiting associate professor of U.S. history at the University of North Carolina at Greensboro and the author of *Freedpeople in the Tobacco South: Virginia, 1860 to 1900*.

Theodore Kornweibel Jr. is professor of African American history at San Diego State University and the author of *Seeing Red: Federal Campaigns against Black Militancy, 1919–1925*.

David Lyons is professor of philosophy and law at Boston University and the author of *Rights, Welfare and Mill's Moral Theory*.

Contributors

Michael T. Martin is professor of African American and African diaspora studies and the director of Black Film Center/Archives at Indiana University. He is the coauthor of "Reparations for 'America's Holocaust': Activism for Global Justice" in *Race and Class*.

Douglas S. Massey is professor of sociology at Princeton University and the coauthor of *Smoke and Mirrors: U.S. Immigration Policy in the Age of Globalization*.

Muntu Matsimela is adjunct professor at John Jay College of Criminal Justice and the producer-coordinator of Special Broadcasts and Events at WBAI-Pacifica, New York.

C. J. Munford (deceased) was professor of history at the University of Guelph and the author of *Race and Reparations: A Black Perspective for the 21st Century*.

Yusuf Nuruddin is adjunct professor of African American studies and social science at New School University. His publications include "The Sambo Thesis Revisited: Slavery's Impact upon the African American Personality" in *Socialism and Democracy*.

Charles J. Ogletree Jr. is professor of law and the vice dean for Clinical Programs at Harvard Law School. Among his publications is *All Deliberate Speed: Reflections on the First Half-Century of* Brown v. Board of Education.

Melvin L. Oliver is professor of sociology and policy studies at the University of California at Santa Barbara and the coauthor of *Black Wealth/White Wealth: A New Perspective on Racial Inequality*.

David B. Oppenheimer is professor of law at Golden Gate University School of Law and a frequent contributor to law journals on discrimination law and affirmative action.

Thomas M. Shapiro is professor at the Heller School for Social Policy and Management at Brandeis University. He is the author of *Population Control Politics: Women, Sterilization, and Reproductive Choice*.

Marjorie M. Shultz is professor of law at the School of Law, University of California at Berkeley, and a frequent contributor to law journals on race, gender, family issues, and health care.

Alan Singer is associate professor and the graduate coordinator for social studies at the Department of Curriculum and Teaching at Hofstra University. He is the author of "Nineteenth Century New York City's Complicity with Slavery: Documenting the Case for Reparations" in *The Negro Educational Review*.

David Wellman is professor of community studies and research sociologist at the Institute for the Study of Social Change, University of California at Berkeley, and the author of *Portraits of White Racism*.

David R. Williams is professor of sociology and epidemiology at the Population Studies Center at the University of Michigan and author of the forthcoming "The Health of U.S. Racial and Ethnic Populations" in the *Journal of Gerontology: Social Sciences*.

Eric K. Yamamoto is professor of law at the William S. Richardson School of Law, University of Hawai'i at Manoa, and the coauthor of *Race, Rights, and Reparation: Law of the Japanese American Internment*.

Marilyn Yaquinto is assistant professor of communication in the Department of Communication at Truman State University. She is a former journalist for the *Los Angeles Times* and the coauthor of "Reparations for 'America's Holocaust': Activism for Global Justice" in *Race and Class*.

Acknowledgment of Copyrights

The editors gratefully acknowledge the following contributors, their works, and their publishers with the following copyright notices.

Richard America. "The Theory of Restitution: The African American Case," from *In a Different Vision: Recent Public Policy* (Vol. 2), edited by Thomas D. Boston, © 1997. Reprinted by permission of the author.

Sam Anderson and Muntu Matsimela. "The Reparations Movement: An Assessment of Recent and Current Activism," from *Socialism and Democracy*, Issue 33, Vol. 17, No. 1, 2003. © 2003. Reprinted by permission of the publisher.

Martha Biondi. "The Rise of the Reparations Movement," from *Radical History Review*, Issue 87, 2003. © 2003. Reprinted by permission of the publisher and author.

Boris L. Bittker and Roy L. Brooks. "The Constitutionality of Black Reparations," from *When Sorry Isn't Enough: The Controversy over Apologies and Reparations for Human Justice (Critical American Series)*, edited by Roy L. Brooks. © 1999. Reprinted by permission of New York University Press.

James Bolner. "Toward a Theory of Racial Reparations," from *Phylon*, Vol. 29, No. 1, 1968. © 1968. Reprinted by permission of the publisher.

Michael K. Brown, Martin Carnoy, Elliott Currie, Troy Duster, David B. Oppenheimer, Marjorie M. Shultz, and David Wellman. "Race Preferences and Race Privilege," from *Whitewashing Race: The Myth of a Color-Blind Society*. © 2003. Reprinted by permission of University of California Press.

Robert S. Browne. "The Economic Basis for Reparations to Black America," from *The Review of Black Political Economy*, Vol. 21, 1993. © 1993. Reprinted by permission of the publisher.

J. Angelo Corlett. *Race, Racism, and Reparations*. © 2003. Reprinted by permission of Cornell University Press.

William Darity Jr. and Dania Frank. "The Economics of Reparations," from *The American Economic Review*, Vol. 93, No. 2, 2003. © 2003. Reprinted by permission of the publisher and authors.

Adrienne Davis. "The Case for United States Reparations to African Americans," from *Human Rights Brief*, Vol. 3, Issue 3, 2003. © 2003. Reprinted by permission of the publisher and author.

Robert Fullinwider. "The Case for Reparations," from *The Institute for Philosophy and Public Policy*, Vol. 20, Nos. 2–3, 2000. © 2000. Reprinted by permission of the author.

Charles P. Henry. "The Politics of Racial Reparations," from *Journal of Black Studies*, Vol. 34, No. 2, 2003. © 2003. Reprinted by permission of the publisher and author.

Robert Johnson Jr. "Repatriation as Reparations for Slavery and Jim Crowism," from *When Sorry Isn't Enough: The Controversy over Apologies and Reparations for Human Justice (Critical American Series)*, edited by Roy L. Brooks. © 1999. Reprinted by permission of New York University Press.

Robin D. G. Kelley. "A Day of Reckoning: Dreams of Reparations," from *Freedom Dreams: The Black Radical Imagination*. © 2003. Reprinted by permission of Beacon Press and the author.

Jeffrey R. Kerr-Ritchie. "Forty Acres, or, An Act of Bad Faith," from *Souls: A Critical Journal of Black Politics, Culture and Society*, Vol. 5, No. 3, 2003. © 2003. Reprinted by permission of the publisher.

Theodore Kornweibel Jr. "Railroads, Race, and Reparations," from *Souls: A Critical Journal of Black Politics, Culture and Society*, Vol. 5, No. 3, 2003. © 2003. Reprinted by permission of the publisher.

Douglas S. Massey. "American Apartheid: Residential Segregation and Persistent Urban Poverty," from *Social Service Review*, Vol. 68, 1994. © 1994. Reprinted by permission of University of Chicago Press.

C. J. Munford. "Reparations: Strategic Considerations for Black Americans," from *When Sorry Isn't Enough: The Controversy over Apologies and Reparations for Human Justice (Critical American Series)*, edited by Roy L. Brooks. © 1999. Reprinted by permission of New York University Press.

Yusuf Nuruddin. "Promises and Pitfalls of Reparations," from *Socialism and Democracy*, Issue 31, Vol. 16, No. 1, 2002. © 2002. Reprinted by permission of the publisher and author.

Charles J. Ogletree Jr. "Tusla Reparations: The Survivors' Story," from *Boston College Third World Law Journal*, Vol. 24, No. 1, 2004. © 2004. Reprinted by permission of the publisher.

Melvin L. Oliver and Thomas M. Shapiro. "A Sociology of Wealth and Racial Inequality," from *Black Wealth/White Wealth: A New Perspective on Racial Inequality*. © 1997. Reprinted by permission of Routledge, New York.

Alan Singer. "19th Century New York City's Complicity with Slavery: Documenting the Case for Reparations," from *The Negro Educational Review*, Vol. 54, Nos. 1–2, 2003. © 2003. Reprinted by permission of the publisher.

David R. Williams and Chiquita Collins. "Reparations: A Viable Strategy to Address the Enigma of African American Health," from *American Behavioral Scientist*, Vol. 47, No. 7, 2004. © 2004. Reprinted by permission of the publisher and authors.

Eric K. Yamamoto. "What's Next? Japanese American Redress and African American Reparations," from *Amerasia Journal*, Vol. 25, No. 2, 1999. © 1999. Reprinted by permission of the publisher.

Index

Abolitionism, 226
Abu-Jamal, Mumia, 470
Abuja Proclamation, 266, 358–59
A. Philip Randolph Institute, 257
Adarand Contractors, Inc. v. Peña, 150, 151, 152, 153, 354, 462
Address of the Colored Convention to the People of Alabama, 230
Administrative Procedures Act, 458
Aetna Life Insurance Company, 15, 170, 182, 256, 263, 273, 360, 434
Affirmative action, 55, 58, 60, 63, 65, 78, 84, 85, 86 n. 21, 119–20, 155–56, 418, 449, 457, 469; as "earned" wage, 191; as remedy for existing racism, 373; as reparations, 3, 10, 31, 167, 194; Supreme Court opposition to, 354
Africa Action and Human Rights Watch, 262, 266
African American Party of National Liberation, 210
African and African Descendants Caucus, 18, 264, 437; at WCAR, 427–28, 430, 431
African and African Descendants NGO Follow-Up Conference, 266
African Free School, 279
African Methodist Episcopal Church, 405
African Nationalist Independence-Partition Party of North America, 209
African National Reparations Organization, 362
African People's Socialist Party, 362
African Wesleyan Methodist Episcopal Church, 281

Africa Reparations Movement (ARM), 217
Afrocentrism, 381
Aid to Families with Dependent Children (AFDC), 82, 96, 98–99
Aiyetoro, Adjoa A., 13, 257, 362, 372
Akbar, Na'im, 393
Alaska Claims Settlement of 1971, 205
Alaskan natives, 249
Aleutian Islanders, 357
Alexander v. State of Oklahoma, 454
Alger, Horatio, 260
Allen, Robert, 206, 390, 391
All for Reparations and Emancipation, 264
America, Richard, 5, 6, 120, 165, 193, 253
American Anti-Slavery Society, 280
American apartheid, 91, 345, 437
American Bar Association, 483, 634
American Colonization Society, 384, 403–5, 409. *See also* Repatriation
American Enterprise Institute, 165
American Federation of Labor, 83
American Railroad Journal, 295
Americans for Historical Accuracy, 357
American Telephone & Telegraph (AT&T), 289, 291, 368
Amistad, 280
Anderson, Arthur, 384
Anderson, Jourdon, 203–4, 205
Anderson, P. H., 203
Anderson, Sam, 19, 21, 22, 351, 352
Anti-Depression Program of the Republic of New Africa, 214, 215, 216. *See also* Republic of New Africa

Anti-slavery amendment. *See* Thirteenth Amendment
Apology, 154, 249, 259, 353, 360, 367, 414, 484, 638–41; Senate Resolution 39 as, 513–14
Appeal to African Heads of State (Malcolm X), 580–84
Ashley, James M., 230
Asiatic Black Man, 475
Atlantic slave trade, 275–79, 281–90; New York's opposition to, 279–81

Babangia, Ibrahim, 358
Back to Africa Movements, 402. *See also* Repatriation
Bacon's Rebellion, 36
Bailey, Frederick Washington (Frederick Douglass), 281, 474
Baker, Lillian, 357
Baraka, Amiri, 396
Barbershop, 452
Bartlett, Donald, 100
Becker, Gary S., 245
Beecher, Henry Ward, 279, 281
Bell, Derrick, 131, 420, 453, 455–56, 459, 462, 465 n. 33
Bethune, Mary McLeod, 255
Bickel, Alexander, 145
Bill of Rights, 181, 182, 184
Biondi, Martha, 14, 202
Bittker, Boris L., 5, 6, 12, 120, 131, 145, 146, 150, 162–63, 213
Black agenda, 362
Black Anti-Defamation League, 212
Black codes, 40
Black Economic Development Conference (BEDC), 211, 212, 213, 214, 382
Black Manifesto, 4, 121, 211–13, 214, 238, 257, 402, 593–99; demands in, 382–83
Black middle class, 363
Black neoconservatism, 78, 364, 381
Black Panther Party for Self Defense, 8, 211, 257, 392, 437, 483; reparations for Vietnam sought by, 592; ten-point program of, 383, 585–87; UN petitioned by, 606–7

Black People's Topographical Research Centers, 386
Black Power Movement, 382
Black Radical Congress (BRC), 17, 206, 264; freedom agenda of, 17, 612–19
Black Reparations Commission, 362
Black Star Publications, 213
Black United Front, 362
Black Workers Congress, 213
Board of Commissioners for the Emancipation in the District of Columbia, 207
Bobo, Lawrence, 66, 91
Boggs, Grace Lee, 221
Bolling v. Sharpe, 137, 148
Bolner, James, 5–6, 119, 120, 201
Bonacich, Edna, 103
Boxill, Bernard, 113, 175–77, 179, 180
Braceros, 22
Bradley, Aaron A., 228
Brennan, William, 153
Bridgetown Protocols, 266
Brookings Institution, 165
Brooks, Roy L., 5, 6, 12, 120, 151, 213, 359–60, 455–56
Brown, John, 280
Brown, Michael, 3, 31, 119, 215
Brown, Oscar, Jr., 256
Brown and Williamson, 263
Brown Brothers Harriman, 263
Brown University, 16
Browne, Robert S., 201–2, 352; minimal reparations claim of, 8–9
Brown v. Board of Education, 6, 45, 57, 119, 128, 137, 139, 145, 146, 148, 151, 291, 314, 455, 460–61
Bryant, William Cullen, 280
Bureau of Labor Statistics, 165
Bureau of Negro Affairs, 227
Bureau of Refugees, Freedmen and Abandoned Land, 7, 41, 42, 207, 222–23, 305, 385
Burlington Northern Santa Fe Railway (BNSF), 302
Burr, Aaron, 279–80
Bush, George W., 354, 356, 361, 428, 445, 472
Butler, Benjamin F., 225

Butler, Gabe, 234
Butler, John, 102–3

California Senate Bill No. 2199, 520–21
California Senate Joint Resolution No. 1, 522–23
Canadian National Railway Company, 263, 302
Carbado, Devon, 414
Cardozo, Benjamin, 137
Carnoy, Martin, 55, 114
Carpetbaggers, 232
"Case for Reparations, A," 608–11
Castro, Fidel, 473, 476
Cato v. United States, 416, 417–18, 458, 459
Center for Budget and Policy Priorities, 166
Chachere, Bernadette, 253
Chachere, Gerald, 253
Chattel slavery, 33–41
Chavez, Hugo, 477
Child, Lydia Maria, 203
Chirac, Jacques, 414
"Cinquez," 403
Circular Order No. 13, 224, 385. *See also* Freedmen's Bureau
Citibank, 289–91
City of Chicago resolution, 539–41
City of Detroit resolution, 537–38
City of New York resolution 41, 44–46
City of New York resolution 57, 552–53
City of New York resolution 195, 554–55
City of New York resolution 219, 547–48
City of Philadelphia resolution, 556–58
City of Richmond v. J. A. Croson Company, 153, 354, 462
City of San Francisco resolution, 542–43
Civil Actions Nos. 97-1978, 98-1693, 665–67
Civil Liberties Act of 1988, 11, 121, 123, 127, 153–54, 155, 205, 356, 358, 361, 365, 458, 460, 461, 501–2
Civil Rights Act of 1866, 374
Civil Rights Act of 1964, 45, 63, 119, 138, 155, 183
Civil Rights Act of 1966, 138

Civil Rights Act of 1968, 67, 312
Civil Rights Bill of 1990, 354
Civil Rights Congress, 567–79
Clark, Kenneth, 311
Clark, Otis, 454, 455, 461
Clay, Henry, 404
Clinton, Bill, 10, 11, 323, 353, 354, 360, 363, 414, 423, 450, 483–84; apology of for Tuskegee study, 638–41
Cochran, Johnnie, 435
Cockrel, Kenneth, 211
Coker, Daniel, 384
Colbert, Douglas, 375, 376
Cold War, 2, 19, 44, 423, 469
Collective moral liability, 6–7
Collins, Chiquita, 16, 68, 273
Colored People's Convention of South Carolina, 230
Committee on Economic Development, 166
Communist Party of United States of America (CPUSA), 210, 473. *See also* Moore, Audley
Community Reinvestment Act of 1977, 48
Comprehensive Employment and Training Act (CETA), 48
Con Edison, 289, 291
Conference on Jewish Material Claims against Germany, 249. *See also* Holocaust
Confiscation Act of 1861, 201
Congressional Budget Office, 165
Congressional Confiscation Acts, 225
Conley, Dalton, 74, 130
Connell, W. J., 208
Conrad, Alfred H., 244
Constitution, U.S., 3, 37, 38, 40, 123, 135, 146, 150, 153, 181–82, 184, 229, 276, 279, 288, 354, 365, 409, 412, 462; amendments of, as compensation, 9; Fifth Amendment to, 143, 144, 145, 153; three-fifths clause of, 37, 38
Conway, Thomas, 224
Conyers, John, 12, 112, 121, 205, 259, 358, 372, 402, 413, 419, 422, 433, 459. *See also* House Resolution 40
Corlett, J. Angelo, 5, 6, 9, 120, 201

Covington and Ohio Railroad, 300
Cox, Wanda, 224, 231
Crenshaw, Kimberle, 206
CSX, 15, 170, 256, 263, 273, 302, 360, 434
Cuba, 473, 476, 477
Cuffe, Paul, 384, 403, 404, 405

Daniels, Ronald, 358, 362, 402
DARAS, 16
Darity, William, Jr., 9, 72, 201, 202, 206, 251
Davis, Adrienne, 21, 260–61, 351–52
Davis, Jefferson, 226
Davis, Joseph, 226
Dawson, Michael, 364
December 12th Movement, 22, 264, 265, 385, 440; at WCAR, 430
"Declaration of Self-Determination of the African-American Captive Nation," 209. *See also* Nationalist discourse
Delany, Martin, 405
Dellums, Ron, 415, 473
Democratic Socialists of America (DSA), 473
Denton, Nancy, 16, 91, 273–74, 310, 311, 312, 313, 314, 324, 325, 355
Department of Agriculture, 13, 211–12, 258, 262, 484, 661–64
Department of Defense, 417
Department of Housing and Urban Development, 274, 336–37, 339, 342–44
Department of Justice, 274, 342, 417
Dickerson, Isaiah H., 208, 209
Direct Tax Act of 1862, 225
District of Columbia Resolution, 549–51
Dixan, Sally, 222, 234
Dixiecrat Party 356
Dorn, Edwin, 111
Douglass, Frederick, 281, 474
Downey, Samuel Smith, 296, 297
Dred Scott v. Sandford, 38, 79, 128, 232, 374
D'Souza, Dinesh, 59, 60, 62, 205
Du Bois, W. E. B., 55, 56, 84, 107, 255, 258, 291, 379, 406, 469–70
Dukakis, Michael, 354

Duke, David, 51
Durban Declaration and Program of Action, 265
Durban 400, 265, 430–31
Dworkin, Ronald, 181

Economic development commissioners (EDCs), 217. *See also* National Coalition of Blacks for Reparations in America
Economic Policy Institute, 166
Edsall, Mary, 114
Edsall, Thomas, 114
Eisenhower, Dwight D., 366
Eizenstat, Stuart E., 10
Ellsworth, Olver, 38
Emancipation Proclamation, 210, 223, 229, 241, 462
Employment Act of 1946, 79
Episcopal Church, 483, 635–36
Epstein, Richard, 64, 65
Equal Employment Act of 1972, 45
European Union (EU), 22, 470, 471, 473, 474
Ex-Slave Mutual Relief, Bounty and Pension Association, 208, 209
Ex-Slave Pension Club, 208

Fagan, Edward, 267, 360
Fair Housing Act of 1968, 45, 47–48, 109, 335
Fair Labor Standards Act, 81
Fanon, Frantz, 395, 399 n. 29
Farmer-Paellman, Deadria, 15, 256, 262, 360, 401 n. 36, 401 n. 43, 668–72
Federal Housing Act, 80
Federal Housing Administration, 215, 338
Federal Housing Authority (FHA), 96–98, 108, 109
Federal Reserve Board, 165
Feinberg, Joel, 183, 184, 188, 189
Fifteenth Amendment, 41, 84, 260, 374
Fifth Amendment, 143, 144, 145, 153
First Pan-African Conference on Reparations, 218
FleetBoston Financial Corporation, 15, 170, 256, 263, 273, 360, 434
Fleming, Walter, 234

Fletcher, Bill, 17
Foner, Eric, 277–78, 281
Ford, Gerald, 344
Forman, James, 211–12, 214, 238, 257, 382, 387–88, 402. See also *Black Manifesto*
"Forty acres and a mule," 7, 190, 201, 203, 206, 209, 222–23, 225, 227, 229, 230, 233, 235, 256
Forty-ninth State Movement, 209
Fourteenth Amendment, 41, 84, 145, 146, 153, 213, 374–75, 409, 461
Frank, Barney, 357
Frank, Dania, 9, 72, 201, 202, 206, 251
Franklin, John Hope, 402
Franklin, Raymond, 92, 98, 111
Frazier, Garrison, 223, 227
Free black convict labor, 300–301
Freedmen's Bureau, 7, 41, 42, 207, 222–23, 305, 385
Freedmen's Bureau Act, 231, 493–94
Freedmen's Home Colonies, 226
Freedom Agenda, 17, 612–19
Freedom Budget, 257
Fugitive slave laws, 37, 38, 185
Fullinwider, Robert, 5–6, 119, 120, 201, 206

Gaita, Raimond, 196
Galster, George, 336, 337–38
Garnet, Henry Highland, 280
Garrison, William Lloyd, 278–79, 280
Garvey, Marcus, 121, 255, 380, 397, 406, 474, 478
Garvey movement, 209, 210, 362
Gary, Williams, 435
Gary Declaration, 600–605
Gates, Henry Louis, 5, 291
General Accounting Office, 165
George, Henry, 387
Georgia Sea Islands, 7, 41, 231. See also Atlantic slave trade; Special Field Order No. 15
G.I. Bill, 377–78
Global African Congress, 19, 433, 434, 443
Global Afrikan Congress, 266

Global apartheid, 1, 23 n. 3
Glover, Danny, 17
Gordon, Nathaniel, 283–84
Gore, Al, 360
Grant, Ulysses S., 42, 226
Great Society, 55, 63, 80, 391, 452, 457
Greeley, Horace, 281
Greensboro Truth and Reconciliation Commission, 484, 645–48
Gresson, David, 367
Gross, Andrew, 16, 91, 273–74, 310, 311, 312, 313, 314, 324, 325, 355
Grossman, James, 250
Group of Eminent Persons, 358–59. See also Mazrui, Ali A.
Guinier, Ewart, 454

Hacker, Andrew, 59, 84, 354
Haiti, 256
Hall, Tony, 353, 360, 419
Hamilton, Alexander, 279
Hamilton, Charles V., 448
Hamlin, Mike, 211
Harlan, John Marshall, 128, 135, 144, 148
Harris, Abram, 104
Harvard Law School, 16
Hayden, Tom, 371
Hayes-Tilden agreement, 41
Healthy People 2010, 323
Henderson, Wade, 4–5, 18
Henry, Charles P., 21, 351
Henry, Milton, 214, 403
Henry, Richard, 214, 216, 255, 257, 362, 402
Hershberg, Theodore, 164
Hicks, Joseph T., 296–97
Hill, Walter B., 208
Hirabayashi v. United States, 357, 417
Hochschild, Jennifer, 363
Hohri v. United States, 357, 416
Holocaust, 33; reparations for, 9, 10, 11, 25 n. 28, 129, 177, 186–87, 194, 195, 205, 209, 211, 240, 249, 250, 259, 263, 267, 275, 366, 371, 379, 383, 418; slavery's, 463
Homeland Security Act, 446

Home Mortgage Disclosure Act of 1975, 48
Homestead Act, 232
Horne, Gerald, 22, 352
Horton, Willie, 354
House, Callie D., 208, 209
House and Senate Budget Committees, 165
House Resolution 29, 498–500
House Resolution 40, 12, 14, 17, 112, 259, 262, 263, 358, 359–60, 372, 379, 413, 433, 459, 460, 483, 506–12
House Resolution 356, 503–5
House Resolution 8965, 247. See also Repatriation
House Ways and Means Committee, 165
Housing Act of 1937, 82
Housing and Community Development Act of 1974, 48, 343
Housing Discrimination Study (HDS), 337
Houston, Charles, 81, 82
Howard, Oliver, 224, 385
Howard University, 277
Human rights, 379
Human Rights Commission (UN), 264
Hyde, Henry, 122, 124
Hylton, Keith, 455, 460, 463

Indian Claims Commission, 240
Industrial Revolution, 388. See also Slave labor
Inouye, Daniel, 357
In re African American Slave Descendants Litigation, 668–72
Institute of the Black World, 362
Internal colony thesis, 8
International Conference on Reparations (Lagos), 358
International Coordinating Council, 443
International Criminal Court of Justice (ICC), 23, 175, 437, 472
International Human Rights Association for American Minorities, 362
Inter-religious Foundation for Community Organization (IFCO), 211, 213
Israeli occupation, 429–30

Jacobs, Turner, 234
Jacobs v. Barr, 153–54
J. A. Croson v. City of Richmond, 153, 354, 462
Jacoby, Tamar, 56, 59, 60, 61
Jamaica Reparations Movement, 18
Japanese American Citizens League (JACL), 357, 421
Japanese American redress, 112, 174, 177, 186–88, 194, 249, 250, 258–59, 352, 356–58, 359, 360, 364–66, 384, 411, 412, 413–15, 419, 420–22, 424–25, 458; lessons from, 415–18. See also Civil Liberties Act of 1988; Yamamoto, Eric K.
Japanese exclusion cases, 6. See also Civil Liberties Act of 1988
Japanese Latinos, 22, 353
Jay, Hohn, 279, 280
Jim Crow, 1, 2, 5, 7, 9, 16, 31, 33, 44, 45, 65, 73, 128, 148, 208, 215, 219, 261, 263, 405, 412, 416, 417, 424, 437, 449, 450, 458, 461–62, 463, 469, 470, 476; legacy of, 46–48, 55, 56, 61, 63, 64, 75, 102, 109, 123, 149, 175, 274; reparations for, 120, 124, 127, 154, 172–73, 178, 180, 181, 182, 192, 193, 201, 202, 210, 213, 246; U.S. government complicity in, 172–73, 176, 184–85, 250, 253, 352
Johnson, Andrew, 40–41, 43, 207, 227, 228, 305, 420
Johnson, Harry G., 252
Johnson, Lyndon Baines, 63, 391, 452
Johnson, Robert, Jr., 8, 202, 215, 352
Joint Center for Political and Economic Studies, 165
Joint Economic Committee, 165
Jones v. Alfrea H. Mayer Company, 375
Jospin, Lionel, 472
Josselin, Charles, 473
Julian, George W., 225, 232

Kansas African Emigration Association, 405
Kansas City Southern Railway (KCS), 302
Karenga, Maulana, 392–93, 396, 397

Katz, Michael, 98, 99
Katz, William, 278
Kelley, Robin D. G., 8, 201, 202
Kennedy, John F., 78, 79, 210
Kerner Commission, 59, 311, 331
Kerr-Ritchie, Jeffrey R., 7, 201
Keynes, John Maynard, 252
King, Martin Luther, Jr., 7–8, 56, 57, 61, 238, 257, 368, 380, 437, 449
King, Rodney, 55
Kly, Yussef Naim, 362
Korematsu v. United States, 357, 416, 417
Kornweibel, Theodore, Jr., 15, 263, 273
Ku Klux Klan, 234, 405, 484

Lafayette Avenue Presbyterian Church, 281
Laissez-faire racism, 66, 91
Lara, Oruno D., 23
Laremont, Ricardo Rene, 23
Lawson, William, 391
Leadership Conference for Civil Rights (LCCR), 4, 262
League of Revolutionary Black Workers, 211
Leahy, Patrick, 360
Lewis, Dorothy, 362, 434
Liberator, 278
Liberia, 405
Liberian Exodus Company, 405
Liggett Group, 263
Lincoln, Abraham, 40, 223, 229, 234, 277, 281, 284
Lipsitz, George, 97
Lloyd's of London, 263
Loews Corporation, 263
Lost/Found Nation of Islam, 264, 363, 431
Lott, Trent, 356
Louisiana Purchase, 163
Loury, Glenn, 10–11
Lumpenbourgeoisie, 382
Lumpenproletariat, 391–92, 399 n. 29
Lumumba, Patrice, 267
Lyons, David, 3, 31, 119

Macdonald, Dwight, 183
Maduna, Penuell, 267

Magee, Rhonda, 124, 126, 127
Magna Carta, 82–83
Maintenance of way, 299–300
Malcolm X, 255, 258, 386, 389–90, 437; appeal of, to African heads of state, 580–84
Malcolm X Grassroots Coalition, 385–86
Malcolm X Society, 8
Mandela, Nelson, 476
Mandingos, 280
Maori, 413
Marable, Manning, 408
Marketti, James, 243, 244, 253
Marshall Plan, 166, 238, 325–26, 389, 409
Marshall Plan for Black America, 257
Martin, Loyal J., 454
Maryland House Joint Resolution 4, 533–35
Mason Bill, 208
Massey, Douglas S., 16, 91, 273–74, 310, 311, 312, 313, 314, 324, 325, 355
Matsimela, Muntu, 19, 20, 21, 351, 352
Matsuda, Mari, 124, 126, 129, 366
Matsui, Robert, 357
Matsunaga, Spark, 357
May, Samuel, J., 278
Mazrui, Ali A., 5, 19
McGary, Howard, 175, 177, 178
McWhorter, John, 10, 364, 366
Means, Marianne, 78
Methodist Church, 353, 414
Methodist Encyclopedia, 210
Metro Broadcasting, Inc. v. FCC, 153
Meyer, John R., 244
Michigan House Bill No. 5562, 519
Middle Passage, 434
Millions for Reparations March, 17, 22, 267, 440–41
Mineta, Norm, 357
Mink, Gwendolyn, 95
Mississippi and Pearl River Railroad, 296
Mobile and Great Northern Railroad, 297–98
Mochizuki v. United States, 414
Modell, John, 103

Montgomery and West Point Railroad, 297, 301
Moore, Audley ("Queen Mother"), 210, 255, 257, 361–62, 384, 397 n. 10, 437
Moss, Francis, 230
Muhammad, Elijah, 383
Muhammad, Khalid, 389
Muhammad, Silas, 362, 431
Muhammad Speaks, 383
Munford, Clarence J., 20, 206, 351, 362, 389, 390, 394, 402
Myers, Samuel, Jr., 9, 72, 201, 202, 206, 251
Myrdal, Gunnar, 241, 311

National Advisory Commission on Civil Disorders, 311
National Association for the Advancement of Colored People (NAACP), 83, 165, 262, 364, 366, 414, 449, 483; HR 40 backed by, 631–33
National Association of Realtors, 343–44
National Black Economic Development Conference, 402. See also *Black Manifesto*
National Black Labor Strike Fund, 212
National Black Political Agenda, 600–605
National Black Political Assembly (NBPA), 362
National Black United Front (NBUF), 22, 264, 430, 440
National Bureau of Economic Research, 165
National Coalition of Blacks for Reparations in America (N'COBRA), 13, 14, 17, 22, 206, 216, 217, 256, 257, 259, 263, 264, 358, 360, 362, 372, 379, 386, 419, 422, 433, 434, 447, 483; reparations campaign waged by, 625–28
National Commission for Reparations, 362
National Conference of Black Lawyers, 362
National Council for Japanese American Redress (NCJAR), 357, 358
Nationalist discourse, 257, 258, 392–93; on Afro-Asian solidarity, 474–75; internal colonialism and, 8, 24 n. 19, 384; on land question 8, 195, 202; Malcolm X's position and, 389–90; on repatriation, 402–7; on self-determination, 396; on territorial grant, 247
National Movement for a 49th State, 384
National Reparations Congress, 433
National Urban League, 165, 257, 364, 366, 437
National Welfare Rights Organization, 212
Nation of Islam, 8, 211, 257, 383, 437, 474, 483; reparations backed by, 608–11
Native American claims, 36, 37, 38, 191, 196; African American claims vs., 6–7, 170–75, 180, 198 n. 29, 232, 241, 353, 412, 424, 424
Native Hawaiians, 412, 413, 414; apology to, 353
Native nations, 371
NDABA movement, 629–30
Neal, Larry, 253
Negro burial ground, 277
New African Liberation Front (NALF), 385
New African People's Organization (NAPO), 385–86
New Afrikan Movement, 216, 217
New Deal, 31, 79, 80, 83, 95, 261
New Jersey African-American Reconciliation Study Commission Act, 524–29
Newton, Huey, 255
New York Life Insurance Company, 15, 263
New York Manumission Society, 279
"New York's Freedom Trail," 273, 275
Nix, Robert N., 247
Norfolk Southern Corporation, 263, 302
North American Free Trade Agreement (NAFTA), 477
North Carolina Mutual Insurance Company, 105
Northern Pacific, 15, 170, 256, 263, 273, 302, 360, 434
North–South polarity, 2, 19
Northwest Territory, 40
Nuruddin, Yusuf, 8, 19, 20, 202, 352

Obadele, Imari, 214, 216, 255, 257, 362, 402
Obadele v. United States, 458, 459
Obadelo, Gaida, 214, 402
O'Connor, Sandra Day, 153
Office of Management and Budget, 165
Office of Redress Administration, 411, 413
Ogletree, Charles J., 13, 14, 16, 18, 20, 21, 257, 351, 360, 366, 380, 435
Oklahoma Commission to Study the Tulsa Race Riot of 1921, 13, 642-44
Oliver, Melvin L., 3, 31, 75, 160, 206, 215, 262, 310, 318. *See also* Racial reparations movement
Olusegun, Kalonji T., 362
Opportunity hoarding, 71
Organization of African Unity, 5, 266, 358, 430, 447
Ottawa tribe, 249

Palestine, 429-30, 478
Pan-Africanism, 380
PATRIOT Act, 446
Patterson, William, 255, 383. *See also* Civil Rights Congress
Pension Bureau, 208
People's Party, 44
Petition to the United Nations, 606-7
Philbrick, Edward, 231
Phillips, Wendell, 225
Pierce, Edward, 231
Pierce, Joseph A., 105
Pigford v. Glickman, 661-64
Plessy v. Ferguson 41, 64, 84, 128, 144, 148, 149
Plymouth Church of the Pilgrims, 281
"Possessive investment in whiteness," 83-85, 97
Powell, Colin, 428
Powell, Lawrence N., 232
Prather, Leon, 106
Progressive Policy Institute, 165
Proposition 187 (California), 419
Proposition 209 (California), 146, 149, 157 n. 14
Providence Bank, 15, 170, 256, 263, 273, 360, 434

Quadagno, Jill, 80, 96

Racial hierarchy. *See* Racial inequality
Racial inequality, 31-32, 91-94, 130, 189; black self-employment and, 102-7; creation of, 72-74; durability of, 66-68, 75-83; in health, 273, 305-30; during Jim Crow, 251; persistence of, 108-10, 164-65, 354-55; in residential segregation, 47-48, 273-74, 355; state's role in, 95-101, 107-8; trade theory analogy to, 252
Racial realists, 59, 62
Racial reparations movement, 4, 112-14. *See also* Oliver, Melvin L.
Rainbow PUSH Coalition, 262
Ransom, Roger, 253
Rawls, John, 188
Reagan, Ronald, 354, 361
Reconstruction, 7, 40-44, 45, 51 n. 53, 84, 104, 181, 184, 201, 207, 213, 218-19, 222, 227, 229-33, 250, 260, 412, 420
Redress: for colonization, 1-2, 5, 174, 358-59; constitutionality of, 143-56; for Jim Crow, 1, 2, 5, 9, 127, 190, 218-19, 246, 460-62; liability and, 112-27, 175-90; meaning of, 3; as racial justice and human rights, 2, 16, 19-20, 263, 379, 448-49; for slavery, 1-2, 3, 5, 14, 15, 25 n. 61, 127-28, 163-64, 172, 246, 302, 358-59, 457-60
Regents of the University of California v. Bakke, 151, 158 n. 32
Rehnquist, William, 153
Reparations, 625-28; antitrust policy and, 367; apologies and, 154, 249, 259, 353, 360, 367, 414, 484, 638-41; assessment for, 5; cash payments as, 393-96; coalitions among activists for, 447-51; eligibility for, 128-31, 400 n. 35; estimates of, 211-12, 243, 248, 248 n. 10, 253, 382, 395, 402; ideological factors and, 381; international struggles for, 1-2, 5, 10-11, 17-19, 20, 22-23, 264-68, 353, 362-63, 432-33, 469-79; legal claims and, 415-18; legislation and, 12, 21,

Reparations (*continued*)
419; litigation and, 13–16, 20–21, 202, 260–61, 274, 351–52, 377–78, 434–36, 454–63, 668–72; opposition to, 9–11, 122, 190–94, 204–5, 324–25, 360–61, 363, 469; outcomes of, 252; parameters of, 246; political mobilization and, 16–22, 352, 361–63, 435–36; as socialist project, 20, 388–89; tax policy and, 114, 138, 161, 195, 252; territorial grants as, 8, 213–17, 247, 386–87; types of, 5, 8–9, 168, 198 n. 29, 247–48, 305–6, 381, 396; trust and, 5, 9, 15–16, 202; tuition exemptions as, 400 n. 34; in United States, 16–17, 262–65, 361–68. *See also* D'Souza, Dinesh; McWhorter, John

Reparations Committee for Descendants of U.S. Slaves, 210, 257, 384

Reparations Coordinating Committee (RCC), 13, 14, 17, 255, 257, 263, 360, 434–35

Reparations for Vietnam, 592

Reparations Litigation Committee, 372

Reparations Mobilization Coalition, 17, 22, 431, 433, 436, 441

Reparations Support Committee, 620

Repatriation, 3, 8–9, 24 n. 18, 202, 247–48, 402–9

Republic of New Africa (RNA), 214–17, 257, 362, 385–86, 402; indemnification claim of, 242, 248 n. 10; independence declared by, 588–91

Residential segregation, 46–48, 92, 273–74, 305, 310–22; causes of, 333–39; health affected by, 322–23; public policy considerations and, 342–45; urban schools and, 355. *See also* Oliver, Melvin L.

Restatement of the Black Manifesto, 4–5, 9, 15, 23, 202, 621–24

Restitution, 6, 160–69

Revolutionary Action Movement (RAM), 210

Revolutionary War, 279

R. J. Reynolds, 263

Robeson, Paul, 255, 383, 437

Robinson, Randall, 13, 14, 119, 121, 126–27, 131–32, 206, 257, 362, 364, 366, 379–80. *See* also *Restatement of the Black Manifesto*

Rock, Chris, 452

Roosevelt, Franklin D., 79, 81

Rosewood Act, 460

Rosewood race riot, 11, 250, 205–6, 259, 413, 417, 460, 284, 649–59

Rosewood Victims v. State of Florida, 649–56

Rush, Bobby, 361

Russwurm, John Brown, 404

Rustin, Bayard, 57

Sam, Alfred C., 405

Santorum, Rick, 360–61

Satel, Sally, 69–70

Saxton, Rufus, 224, 492

Scalia, Antonin, 145

Schakowsy, Jan, 262

Schultz, Theodore, 245

Scott-Heron, Gil, 386

Second Confiscation Act, 486–89

Second Reconstruction, 44–48, 354

Sedler, Robert, 15

Senate Resolution 39, 513–14

Senate Resolution 44, 515–17

Servicemen's Readjustment Act of 1944 (G.I. Bill), 377–78

Sharpton, Al, 61, 402, 463

Sherman, William Tecumseh, 7, 8, 42, 207, 222–23, 224, 227, 228, 233, 234, 256, 384. *See also* Special Field Order No. 15

Sherraden, Michael, 99

Shipp, E. R., 10

Singer, Alan, 16, 273

Singer, Joe, 418

Slave codes, 37–41

Slave labor, 15, 95, 120, 163–64, 175, 180, 227, 263, 273, 303 n. 4, 371; of black women, 297, 300–302, 304 n. 13; City Bank and, 290; industrialization and, 242–43, 295–96, 388; in railroading, 294–302; sexual slavery and, 202, 256, 268, 371–72

Slave Reparation Act, 359

Slave trade provisions, 37
Slavocracy, 276
Sleeper, Jim, 56, 59, 60
Slocum, Cuffe, 403
Smith, David Barton, 68, 73
Snowe, Olympia, 361
Social Security Act of 1935, 79, 80, 81, 95
Social Security Administration, 81
Southern Baptist Convention, 353
Southern Christian Leadership Conference (SCLC), 262, 437, 449
Southern Claims Commission, 208
Southern Homestead Act, 7, 43, 232, 495–97
Southern Land Bank, 211
Southern Pacific Railroad, 242
Special Field Order No. 15, 7, 207, 222–23, 228, 256, 384–85, 490–92
Spivak, Chakravorty, 2
Stanton, Edwin, 228
Staples, Brent, 277, 278
Starobin, Robert S., 242
Steele, James, 100
Steele, Shelby, 59, 150
Stevens, Thaddeus, 42–43, 207, 224, 225
Stowe, Harriet Beecher, 281
Strict scrutiny test, 6, 120
Stuart, Merah, 103
Student Nonviolent Coordinating Committee (SNCC), 257
Sumner, Charles, 225
Supplementary Social Security Act, 96
Sutch, Richard, 253
Swinton, David, 206, 253

Taney, Roger, 38, 79, 128, 232, 374
Tappan, Lewis, 280
Taylor, Moses, 289–90
Texas House Joint Resolution 25, 530–32
Thernstrom, Abigail, 59, 60, 61, 62, 63, 65, 69, 70, 71, 74, 75, 86–87 n. 22
Thernstrom, Stephen, 59, 60, 61, 62, 63, 65, 69, 70, 71, 74, 75, 86–87 n. 22
Thirteenth Amendment, 21, 37, 84, 204, 351–52, 409, 455, 458; as confiscation, 229; opposition to, 276; as reparations strategy, 260–61, 374–78

Thomas, Clarence, 150
Thompson, Dudley, 358, 478
Thompson v. Metropolitan Life Insurance Company, 263
Thone, Alpert, 405
Thurmond, Strom, 356
Thurow, Lester, 165
Tilly, Charles, 71
Tobin Tax, 473
Tocqueville, Alexis de, 84
"Tokyo/Negro," 475
Townsley, Eleanor, 70
TransAfrica Forum, 13, 16, 17, 22, 362–63, 379
Trinity Church, 277
Trotter, Monroe, 255
Truth, Sojourner, 205
Truth and Reconciliation Commission (South Africa), 10–11, 267, 367
Tucker Act, 458
Tulsa race riot, 13–14, 17, 21, 105–7, 250, 359, 454–55, 484; commission on, 642–44; lawsuit over, 455, 460
Turner, Henry McNeal, 205, 257, 405–6
Tuskegee study, 413, 484, 638–41

Ujamaa, 214
Underground railroad, 273, 275
Union Pacific Corporation, 263, 302
United Black Appeal, 212
United Nations, 44, 216, 383, 428, 437, 438, 445, 478; Security Council, 5. *See also* World Conference against Racism, Racial Discrimination, Xenophobia and Related Intolerance
United States Colored Troops (USCT), 226, 228
United States v. Amistad, 403
Universal Association of Ethiopian Women, 210, 361–62
Universal Declaration of Human Rights. *See* United Nations
Universal Negro Improvement Association (UNIA), 560–66. *See also* Garvey movement; Nationalist discourse
University of California v. Bakke, 151, 158 n. 32

Upjohn Institute, 165
Urban Institute, 166

Van Wyck, Cornelius, 276
Vatican, 11
Vaughan, William R., 208
Vedder, Richard, 253
Verdun, Vincente, 125–26, 127, 131
Voluntary Affirmative Market Agreement, 343
Voting Rights Act of 1965, 45, 63, 119, 138, 260, 469

Wagner Act, 79, 80, 81, 82, 83
Walters, Ronald, 363, 402
Wannsee Conference, 33
Wards Cove Packing Co., Inc. v. Antonio, 354
War on Poverty, 210, 391
Warren, Earl, 374–75
Washington, Booker T., 474
Washington, Bushrod, 404
Washington, George, 404
Watson, John, 211
Weber, Max, 102
We Charge Genocide, 567–79
Week, James, 281
Weeksville, 281
Wells, Ida B., 255
Westley, Robert, 220, 250
White, Byron, 153
Wilder, C. B., 227
Wilkins, Roy, 83

Williams, David R., 16, 68, 273
Williams, John A., 386
Williams, Juan, 364
Williams, Walter E., 10
Wilmington, N.C., 250
Wilson, William Julius, 91, 92, 408
Winbush, Raymond, 250, 251
Wolfe, Alan, 59, 61
Wolfensohn, James, 472
Wood, Fernando, 276, 287–88
Woodward, C. Vann, 105
Working Group of Experts on People of African Descent Living in the Diaspora, 266
Works Progress Administration, 234
World Bank, 5, 472
World Conference against Racism, Racial Discrimination, Xenophobia and Related Intolerance (WCAR), 17–18, 204, 249, 255, 264, 265–66, 431, 476; criticism of, 26 n. 54; preparations for, 427–28; U.S. delegation to, 26 n. 51, 265, 428–29, 471–72
Worrill, Conrad, 362, 430
Wyat, Bayley, 227

Yale University, 16, 77, 261
Yamamoto, Eric K., 21, 22, 352, 365–66
Yardley, Jonathan, 130
Young, Whitney, 238

Zenger, John Peter, 276
Zionism, 429–30, 471

Michael T. Martin is professor of African American and African diaspora studies and the director of Black Film Center/Archives at Indiana University. He is the editor of *New Latin American Cinema* (1997) and *Cinemas of the Black Diaspora: Diversity, Dependence, and Oppositionality* (1995) and coeditor with Terry R. Kandal of *Studies of Development and Change in the Modern World* (1989).

Marilyn Yaquinto is a former journalist with the *Los Angeles Times* and currently is assistant professor of communication in the Department of Communication at Truman State University. She is the author of *Pump 'Em Full of Lead: A Look at Hollywood Gangsters* (1998) and coauthor of *Sastun: My Apprenticeship with a Maya Healer* (1994); "Reparations for 'America's Holocaust': Activism for Global Justice" in *Race and Class* (2004); and "Diasporic Cinema" for *Schirmer Encyclopedia of Film* (2006).

Library of Congress Cataloging-in-Publication Data

Redress for historical injustices in the United States : on reparations for slavery, Jim Crow, and their legacies / edited by Michael T. Martin and Marilyn Yaquinto.
p. cm.
Includes bibliographical references and index.
ISBN 978-0-8223-4005-8 (cloth : alk. paper)
ISBN 978-0-8223-4024-9 (pbk. : alk. paper)
1. African Americans — Reparations. 2. African Americans — Reparations — History — Sources. 3. African Americans — Legal status, laws, etc. — History — Sources. 4. African diaspora. 5. Reparations for historical injustices. 6. Social movements. I. Martin, Michael T. II. Yaquinto, Marilyn.
E185.89.R45R43 2007
362.84′96073 — dc22   2006102943